"There has never been a more crucial time for us to teach at the apex of our expertise. *The Craft of Teaching in Public Affairs* delivers tangible, thought-provoking pedagogical insights for any good public affairs instructor who wants to be great. This is a must read for the modern classroom."

Hillary J. Knepper, *Professor/Associate Provost for Student Success, Pace University, USA*

"This is an excellent resource for faculty interested in honing the craft of teaching Public Affairs. While there are journals that cover the topic, this outstanding book from respected public administration faculty across the globe condenses years of research knowledge about teaching public affairs into an easily accessibl e guide for faculty and graduate students. This is a must for PA faculty and Ph.D. programs in Public Affairs/Administration."

Doug Goodman, *Professor & Director, School of Public Administration, the University of Central Florida, USA*

"*The Craft of Teaching in Public Affairs* fills a major gap in our knowledge about teaching in public affairs, an applied field that influences outcomes significant to societies worldwide. As I read the book, I warmed quickly to three features – its comprehensiveness, reliance on evidence, and inclusion of sage advice from award-winning public-affairs teachers. I am grateful to have this book in my collection. It is a great tool for learning about my most important role, teacher."

James L. Perry, *Distinguished Professor Emeritus, Paul H. O'Neill School of Public and Environmental Affairs, Indiana University, Bloomington, USA*

THE CRAFT OF TEACHING IN PUBLIC AFFAIRS

This book explores the art and science of teaching in public affairs programs by asking top instructors to discuss their tools and tips for the trade.

Public affairs is a discipline that builds scholarly knowledge but also trains and educates public administrators to improve their careers, organizations, and communities. Instructors in public affairs programs at the university level therefore play a vital role in safeguarding the governing capacity of public bureaucracies and nonprofits, and it is crucial that their teaching is effective. Containing chapters written by award-winning teachers, grounded in first-hand experience and supplemented with education research, this book offers guidance to new and veteran instructors alike on what works (and doesn't) in public affairs classrooms. Topics covered include teaching at the undergraduate and graduate levels, teaching nontraditional students, promoting inclusivity in the classroom, managing classrooms, teaching effectively online, and defining student success in the classroom, among other themes.

This book will be of keen interest to instructors currently teaching courses on public administration, public policy, and nonprofit management, as well as PhD students looking to enhance their teaching skills.

William Hatcher is a professor of political science and public administration and chair of the Department of Social Sciences at Augusta University, USA. He serves as a co-editor of the Routledge series on Public Affairs Education. His research has appeared in journals such as the *Journal of Public Affairs Education, Public Administration Review,* the *American Journal of Public Health*, and the *American Review of Public Administration*. He is the author of *The Curious Public Administrator* (Routledge, 2022).

Beth M. Rauhaus is a professor and department head of Political Science at the University of Louisiana at Lafayette, USA. She recently served as the MPA Program Coordinator at Texas A&M University, Corpus Christi. Much of her research explores gender representation, equity, and diversity in the public sector. She currently serves on the editorial board for the *American Review of Public Administration*, the *Journal of Public Affairs Education, Administrative Theory & Praxis*, and *Public Personnel Management*.

Bruce D. McDonald III is a professor of public budgeting and finance and director of the School of Public Service at Old Dominion University, USA. He also serves as an editor-in-chief of *Public Administration*, a co-editor-in-chief of the *Public Finance Journal*, and an editor of both Routledge's Public Affairs Education Book Series and Routledge's Public Budgeting and Finance Book Series. His research focuses on public budgeting and finance in the context of social equity budgeting and the fiscal health of local governments. His research has appeared in journals such as the *Journal of Public Administration Research and Theory, Public Administration Review*, and the *American Review of Public Administration*.

Routledge Public Affairs Education

Editors
Bruce D. McDonald III
Professor of Public Budgeting and Finance
Old Dominion University, Norfolk VA
William Hatcher
Professor of Public Administration
Augusta University, Augusta GA

The Routledge Public Affairs Education series, edited by William Hatcher and Bruce D. McDonald III, publishes books designed to assist faculty in the classroom and in the management of public administration, public affairs, and public policy programs. To accomplish this, the book series explores evidence-based practices, commentary about the state of public administration education, and pedagogical perspectives. The Routledge Public Affairs Education series examines the future of public administration education, teaching practices, international public administration education, undergraduate public administration programming, and other relevant topics to advance the field's knowledge. For more information about the series, or to submit a book proposal, please contact series editors William Hatcher at wihatcher@augusta.edu and Bruce D. McDonald, III at bmcdona@ncsu.edu.

RECENTLY PUBLISHED BOOKS

Managing Gender Inequity in Academia
A Guide for Faculty and Administrators in Public Affairs Programs
Gina Scutelnicu Todoran

The Craft of Teaching in Public Affairs
Instructors Reflecting on the Tools and Tips of Their Trade
Edited by William Hatcher, Beth M. Rauhaus,
and Bruce D. McDonald III

For more information about this series, please visit: www.routledge.com/

THE CRAFT OF TEACHING IN PUBLIC AFFAIRS

Instructors Reflecting on the Tools and Tips of Their Trade

Edited by William Hatcher,
Beth M. Rauhaus, and Bruce D. McDonald III

Routledge
Taylor & Francis Group

NEW YORK AND LONDON

Designed cover image: © Getty Images – g-stockstudio

First published 2025
by Routledge
605 Third Avenue, New York, NY 10158

and by Routledge
4 Park Square, Milton Park, Abingdon, Oxon, OX14 4RN

Routledge is an imprint of the Taylor & Francis Group, an informa business

© 2025 selection and editorial matter, William Hatcher, Beth M. Rauhaus and Bruce D. McDonald III; individual chapters, the contributors

The right of William Hatcher, Beth M. Rauhaus and Bruce D. McDonald III to be identified as the authors of the editorial material, and of the authors for their individual chapters, has been asserted in accordance with sections 77 and 78 of the Copyright, Designs and Patents Act 1988.

All rights reserved. No part of this book may be reprinted or reproduced or utilised in any form or by any electronic, mechanical, or other means, now known or hereafter invented, including photocopying and recording, or in any information storage or retrieval system, without permission in writing from the publishers.

Trademark notice: Product or corporate names may be trademarks or registered trademarks, and are used only for identification and explanation without intent to infringe.

ISBN: 978-1-032-67128-4 (hbk)
ISBN: 978-1-032-67127-7 (pbk)
ISBN: 978-1-032-67129-1 (ebk)

DOI: 10.4324/9781032671291

Typeset in Sabon
by Apex CoVantage, LLC

*This book is for my professors at Georgia College
and Mississippi State University, who practiced a
little curiosity about me and, through their craft
of teaching, helped me find my way to a career in
academia.*
−WH

*For my students and colleagues, who have taught
me so much over the years and have made my
career an enjoyable adventure.*
−BMR

*4: 46492 1144 12157 2617 44117 1247+(259−2)
29096 3967*
−BM

CONTENTS

Contributors	*xii*
Abbreviations	*xvii*

1 Introduction and Setting of the Stage   1
   William Hatcher, Beth M. Rauhaus,
   and Bruce D. McDonald III

SECTION I
Developing Skills for the Craft   **9**

2 Surveying the Literature on Being a Successful
   Teacher in Public Affairs   11
   William Hatcher, Beth M. Rauhaus,
   and Rhucha Samudra

3 Teaching Undergraduate Public Affairs Students   28
   Madinah F. Hamidullah

4 Teaching Public Affairs Students at the MPA Level   43
   Sara R. Rinfret and Michelle C. Pautz

5 Mentorship and Inclusive Teaching in Public
   Administration   56
   Meghna Sabharwal

x Contents

6 Teaching Effectively Online   74
   Saman Afshan, Honey Minkowitz, and
   Bruce D. McDonald III

7 How to Teach Diversity, Equity, Inclusion, and
   Accessibility   89
   Sean A. McCandless and Mary E. Guy

8 Third Culture Professors   108
   Kim Moloney, Mehmet Akif Demircioglu, and
   Kohei Suzuki

SECTION II
Becoming Experts in the Craft   **131**

9 Becoming an Expert in the Craft   133
   Norma M. Riccucci

10 Becoming an Expert Teacher: Turn It Inside Out   143
    Rosemary O'Leary

11 Teaching With an Informed Mind and Relentless
    Curiosity   148
    Stephen Page

12 Learning How to Teach, Teaching How to Learn   156
    Camilla Stivers

13 Practicing Curiosity as an Instructor, a Scholar, and
    an Individual   164
    William Hatcher

14 Becoming an Engaged Instructor in the MPA
    Classroom   175
    Beth M. Rauhaus

15 Learning to Be a Teacher 184
 Bruce D. McDonald III

16 Concluding Thoughts on the Craft of Teaching 195
 William Hatcher, Beth M. Rauhaus, and
 Bruce D. McDonald III

Index *201*

CONTRIBUTORS

Saman Afshan is a doctoral student of public administration at North Carolina State University, USA, and a doctoral fellow in the Municipal Research Lab. She also serves as an editorial assistant for *Public Finance Journal*. She received her BA in Economics from the University of Delhi, India, MA in Economics from Jamia Millia Islamia, India, and MPA from North Carolina State University.

Mehmet Akif Demircioglu is a faculty member at the School of Public Policy and Administration at Carleton University in Ottawa, Canada. He is also affiliated with the Smart Government Lab at the University of St. Gallen, the Lee Kuan Yew School of Public Policy's Executive Education, the Institute for Future Government at Yonsei University, the Institute for Development Strategies at Indiana University, and the Center for Organization Research and Design at Arizona State University. His research focuses on public sector innovation, good governance, effective leadership, and entrepreneurship. His co-authored book, *Public Sector Innovation*, is forthcoming.

Mary E. Guy is University of Colorado Distinguished Professor in the School of Public Affairs at the University of Colorado Denver, USA. Her teaching and research focus on the humanity of public service work. She pays special attention to social equity and emotionally intense work demands. She is a co-editor-in-chief of the *Journal of Social Equity and Public Administration,* fellow of the National Academy of Public Administration, and the past president of the American Society for Public Administration. She is the recipient of numerous awards for her research, leadership, and mentoring, including the Provan Award, Nesta Gallas Award, Van Riper Award, and Waldo Award.

Madinah F. Hamidullah is a professor and director of the Master of Public Administration program at Kennesaw State University. Her major research areas are public and nonprofit administration leadership and management, specifically how it applies to human resource management practices and policies. She is developing a research focus on women's organizations and their collective impact in philanthropy, service, and professional development. Diversity, equity, inclusion, and accessibility are critical aspects of her research, teaching, and overall life focus.

William Hatcher is a professor of political science and public administration and chair of the Department of Social Sciences at Augusta University, USA. He serves as a co-editor of the Routledge series on Public Affairs Education. He received both his BS in political science and MPA from Georgia College and State University and PhD in public policy and administration from Mississippi State University. His research has appeared in journals such as the *Journal of Public Affairs Education, Public Administration Review,* the *American Journal of Public Health*, and the *American Review of Public Administration*. He is the author of *The Curious Public Administrator* (Routledge, 2024).

Sean A. McCandless serves as an associate professor of public and nonprofit management at the University of Texas at Dallas, USA. With Susan T. Gooden and Richard Greggory Johnson III, he co-founded the *Journal of Social Equity and Public Administration*. With S. Nicole Diggs, he co-chairs the Diversity and Social Equity committee of the Network of Schools of Public Policy, Affairs, and Administration. In 2021, he was named a University Scholar of the University of Illinois System and as a Public Voices fellow.

Bruce D. McDonald III is a professor of public budgeting and finance and director of the School of Public Service at Old Dominion University, USA. He also serves as an editor-in-chief of *Public Administration,* a co-editor-in-chief of *Public Finance Journal,* and an editor of both Routledge's Public Affairs Education Book Series and Routledge's Public Budgeting and Finance Book Series. He received his BA in communications from Mercer University, MA in international peace and conflict resolution from American Military University, MSc in economic history from the London School of Economics, MEd in training and instructional design from NC

xiv Contributors

State University, and PhD in public administration and policy from Florida State University. His research focuses on public budgeting and finance in the context of social equity budgeting and the fiscal health of local governments. His research has appeared in journals such as the *Journal of Public Administration Research and Theory, Public Administration Review*, and the *American Review of Public Administration*.

Honey Minkowitz is an assistant professor at the University of Nebraska Omaha, USA. She is also a senior fellow in the Workforce Leadership Institute and a research fellow in the Municipal Research Lab at North Carolina State University. She received both her BA in English and her MA in higher adult and lifelong education from Michigan State University, an MPA from the State University of New York at Albany, and a PhD in public administration from North Carolina State University.

Kim Moloney is an assistant professor at Hamad Bin Khalifa University, Qatar. Her research focuses on intersections of public administration with international organizations and transnational administration and, separately, with small states. She has also published on social equity and, separately, intellectual histories in public administration. Her 25+ articles have appeared in journals like *Public Administration Review, Policy and Society*, the *American Review of Public Administration, Perspectives on Public Management and Governance, Review of Public Personnel Administration, Global Policy*, and *International Review of Administrative Sciences*, among others. Her book, *Who Matters at the World Bank*, was published in 2022.

Rosemary O'Leary is Distinguished Professor Emerita both at the Maxwell School of Syracuse University and at the School of Public Affairs at the University of Kansas, USA. Working with students was the most fun and rewarding part of her career, and she was rewarded with 11 teaching awards – two of them national. Her students at KU, Syracuse, and Indiana remember her pacing around the classroom, pounding on desks, urging them to "buck up buckeroos!" always with a smile and a laugh. She was the co-creator of E-PARCC at Syracuse University, a collection of free, online teaching materials on civic engagement, collaboration, and conflict resolution, still used today by hundreds of thousands of students and trainers around the world.

Stephen Page is an associate professor at the Daniel J. Evans School of Public Policy and Governance at the University of Washington, USA. His research and teaching interests include leadership, management, collaboration, and strategy. His publications explore these issues in the areas of education, health and human services, housing, and transportation. He consults regularly with local governments and nonprofit organizations.

Michelle C. Pautz is a professor of Political Science and Associate Dean for Curriculum and Student Academic Success at the University of Dayton, USA. She holds a PhD in public administration and an MPA from Virginia Tech and a BA in economics, political science, and public administration from Elon University. Her research largely focuses on two areas: the implementation of environmental regulation, particularly at the state level, and the portrayal of bureaucracy and bureaucrats in contemporary American cinema and its effects on audiences.

Beth M. Rauhaus is a professor and department head of Political Science at the University of Louisiana at Lafayette, USA. She recently served as the MPA Program Coordinator at Texas A&M University, Corpus Christi. She holds a PhD in public policy and administration from Mississippi State University. Much of her research explores gender representation, equity, and diversity in the public sector. She currently serves on the editorial board for the *American Review of Public Administration*, the *Journal of Public Affairs Education, Administrative Theory & Praxis*, and *Public Personnel Management*. Her research can be found in the *Journal of Public Affairs Education, Public Administration Review*, the *American Review of Public Administration*, and *Administrative Theory & Praxis*, among others.

Norma M. Riccucci is the Board of Governors Distinguished Professor at Rutgers University, Newark, USA. She received her BPA from Florida International University, her MPA from the University of Southern California, and her PhD in public administration from Syracuse University. She is the author of numerous publications and books, most recently *Policy Drift: Shared Powers and the Making of U.S. Law and Policy* (2018). Riccucci's research interests lie in the broad area of public management, with specific interests in social equity policies and representative bureaucracy.

Sara R. Rinfret is Associate Vice Provost for Faculty Affairs and a professor of Public Administration at Northern Arizona University, USA. She has more than a decade of higher education leadership experience, serving in roles such as acting dean, associate dean, chair, and Master of Public Administration director. Her scholarship is globally recognized in the areas of regulatory policy, environmental policy, and women, and government, public administration, and the scholarship of teaching and learning.

xvi Contributors

Meghna Sabharwal is a professor in the Public and Nonprofit Management Program at the University of Texas at Dallas (UTD), USA, and a National Academy of Public Administration (NAPA) fellow. She also serves as the Associate Provost of Faculty Success at UTD. Her research focus lies in public human resources management, particularly addressing issues such as workforce diversity, equity, and inclusion, high-skilled immigration, and comparative public human resources. Meghna has authored five books and over 70 peer-reviewed journal articles and book chapters, earning six best paper awards. She is the editor-in-chief of the *Review of Public Personnel Administration* (ROPPA).

Rhucha Samudra is an assistant professor of Public Administration at Augusta University, USA. Her research focuses on U.S. Social Safety Net programs and their effect on income, employment, and health outcomes for low-income populations. She has also worked for local governments in Michigan, Arizona, and Washington, DC. Dr. Samudra received her PhD in Public Administration from American University.

Camilla Stivers taught at Evergreen State College in Washington State and the Levin College of Urban Affairs at Cleveland State University, USA. Prior to becoming an academic, she spent 20 years in the nonprofit sector, mostly in community-based organizations. Her published work centers on the normative aspects of administration, including the significance of gender and race for how we understand and practice in public agencies.

Kohei Suzuki is an assistant professor at Leiden University's Institute of Public Administration in the Netherlands. He holds a PhD in Public Policy from Indiana University, Bloomington. His research focuses on bureaucratic structures, meritocracy, and quality of government from a broad comparative perspective. He also examines municipal government reform and performance, particularly in Japanese local governments. His research has been published in academic journals such as *Governance, Public Administration Review*, and *Public Management Review*, among others. He received the 2024 MPSA Kenneth J. Meier Award for his co-authored research on politicization and turnover intention.

ABBREVIATIONS

ABD	All But Dissertation
APA	American Psychological Association
ARNOVA	Association for Research on Nonprofit Organizations and Voluntary Action
BLDM	Blended Learning Distance Mediation
BLM	Black Lives Matter
CRT	Critical Race Theory
CV	Curriculum Vitae
DEIA	Diversity, Equity, Inclusion, and Accessibility
EA	Expatriate Academic
ESL	English as a Second Language
FWCI	Field-Weighted Citation Index
GCSU	Georgia College and State University
HR	Human Resources
HRM	Human Resource Management
JPAE	*Journal of Public Affairs Education*
MOOC	Massive Open Online Course
MPA	Master of Public Administration
NAPA	National Academy of Public Administration
NASPAA	Network of Schools of Public Policy, Affairs, and Administration
NPA	New Public Administration
PA	Public Administration
Q1	Top Quarter
R1	Carnegie Research 1 University

xviii Abbreviations

RTD	Regional Transportation District
SET	Student Evaluation of Teaching
SoTL	Scholarship of Teaching and Learning
SUNY	State University of New York
TA	Teaching Assistant
TCK	Third Culture Kid
TCP	Third Culture Professor
TESC	The Evergreen State College
TPA	*Teaching Public Administration*

1

INTRODUCTION AND SETTING OF THE STAGE

William Hatcher[1], Beth M. Rauhaus[2], and Bruce D. McDonald III[3]

[1]*Augusta University, Augusta, GA,* [2]*University of Louisiana at Lafayette, Lafayette, LA, and* [3]*Old Dominion University, Norfolk, VA*

As a practice- oriented discipline, public affairs is responsible for building scholarly knowledge and educating public administrators to improve their careers, organizations, and communities (Hatcher & Ginn, 2020; McDonald et al., 2024). Given this multiple focus of the field, there is a need to connect theory and practice in academic programs and the classroom – in other words, through the craft of teaching (Hall & McDonald, 2023; Hatcher et al., 2023). Teaching public affairs often occurs in graduate programs focused on public affairs, policy, and administration. Many universities offer Master of Public Administration (MPA) and other public affairs degrees, with hundreds of instructors training and educating public administrators in the classroom. These instructors play such an incredible role in ensuring the governing capacity of public bureaucracies and nonprofits that they must be effective, or better yet, excellent at teaching.

In the United States, there are more than 89,000 governmental units and over 1.8 million nonprofits. MPA faculty are responsible for preparing their students to excel in public sector and nonprofit organizations and become leaders of these organizations. This is an important calling, but it comes with the need to be vigilant about the quality of teaching in the field. However, the PhD programs in public affairs often do not help guide their students toward becoming excellent educators. This is a disservice to our students, the people we serve, and the overall capacity of government because, as we stress again, MPA instructors need to be excellent in the classroom. In this book, we seek to contribute to the state of teaching in public affairs. The text focuses on the craft of teaching in public affairs

DOI: 10.4324/9781032671291-1

2 William Hatcher, Beth M. Rauhaus, and Bruce D. McDonald III

programs by asking the leading instructors of the field to discuss their tools and tips for the trade.

The chapters included in this book are grounded in the experience of the authors and supplemented with research on teaching and learning. Each chapter is written by an instructor who has been recognized for their teaching in public affairs classrooms. We include two types of essays in the book. In the first group of essays, we asked a group of instructors to write about specific topics regarding teaching public affairs. The topics include teaching undergraduate students, teaching MPA students, teaching PhD students, teaching nontraditional students, promoting inclusivity in the classroom, managing classrooms, teaching effectively online, defining student success in their classrooms, etc. For the second group of essays, we gave authors the instructions to write about their experiences in the classroom. What has worked for them? What is their teaching philosophy? What have they learned over the years about their students, the field, and teaching? These essays will focus on how each award-winning instructor approaches the job of teaching. Some authors may write about their teaching philosophies and pedagogy and how they approach their jobs of educating public servants. In requesting these chapters, we gave the authors few instructions beyond discussing the tools and philosophies that guide them in the public affairs classroom.

Thus, the goals of the book for the reader are threefold:

1. Surveying the state of teaching in the field's scholarship of teaching and learning (SoTL);
2. Providing a book of essays from impactful educators discussing what the craft of teaching means to them; and
3. Considering possible research questions to improve instruction in the future.

Before we go forward with presenting this content in the chapters, we would like to make a few notes to help guide the reader. First, public affairs can be a confusing and multifaceted description of the field. We use the phrase "public affairs" as a catchall to include our discipline's focus on public policy, public administration, nonprofit management, and governance in general. Throughout the book, we and our contributors often use the phrase public affairs interchangeably with public administration, public policy, and nonprofit management. Additionally, we acknowledge that other public affairs-related degrees exist, such as the Master of Public Policy, Master of Public Management, and Master of Nonprofit Management. As with public affairs, we use MPA as a catchall term since they are the most numerous academic programs in our field, training public

Introduction and Setting of the Stage **3**

administrators, and because the MPA degree is the primary graduate credential for public service management.

Second, we would like to explain the book's focus on the "craft" of teaching. As the three of us, to varying degrees, discuss in our essays on teaching, we view instruction as a skill that can be learned, not an outdated view of it as a trait. Moreover, we have learned a lot over the years about teaching. We hope this book helps others learn, improve their skills or craft of teaching in public affairs, and develop tools helpful in crafting an excellent pedagogical approach.

What Do We Know About Quality Teaching?

As Chapter 2 of this book details, we know surprisingly little about quality teaching in public affairs. Even within the field's SoTL, sparse attention is paid to the features of quality instruction and teaching, with most studies focusing on broader curriculum issues, diversity, and the overall state of the discipline (Raadschelders et al., 2019). Again, this may be due to our field's lack of focus on teaching and instruction in our PhD programs. Moreover, the field historically has not valued SoTL as much as research in other areas of public affairs (McDonald, 2023; McDonald & Hatcher, 2020), contributing to the lack of literature on quality teaching. Thus, we argue that this book fills an important gap in the literature by guiding emerging teachers and seasoned faculty on teaching.

However, there is a wealth of research and knowledge in other fields on the features of quality instruction in college classrooms. Effective instruction often includes teachers practicing flexibility in designing courses, seeking mentorship and coaching from experienced instructors, and conducting a variety of assessments of student learning (Morrison et al., 2019). Still, many of these tactics are not rooted in solid empirical evidence. For instance, research has demonstrated that instructional coaching as professional development does not positively affect teacher quality (Desimone & Pak, 2017). Again, this highlights the importance of our field developing scholarship on what makes for effective instruction.

Chapter 2 and the remainder of the book present themes of effective teaching, which include the need to connect theory and practice, the importance of active learning instead of passive instruction, the need for experience-based learning, and the importance of program flexibility in delivery. Given the lack of clear empirical answers to effective, there is a need for us to build guidance based on what has worked in the classroom for other instructors. A large portion of this book seeks to achieve this goal. As noted, the book includes several chapters from leading scholars on how they approach teaching. We hope readers will appreciate the wealth of

4 William Hatcher, Beth M. Rauhaus, and Bruce D. McDonald III

expertise in these pages, and the guidance offered will help them improve how they teach and train public managers.

While our field has not developed robust literature on teaching quality, it has a long history of concern with training public managers, especially in MPA programs (Farrell et al., 2022; McDonald et al., 2022). The emergence of the field's primary SoTL outlet, the *Journal of Public Affairs Education,* is a key moment in this history. The scholars behind the journal's creation were concerned with teaching effectiveness and social equity in public administration (Frederickson, 2004). This focus aligns with some of the other scholarship on teaching in public administration, which has been concerned with broad factors such as teaching ethics and values in the field (Bowman & Menzel, 1998). Other reflections on teaching in public administration have considered the overall nature of the field, which is mostly influenced by factors outside of how teachers approach their courses (Ventriss, 1991). Cunningham and Weschler (2002) have called for the use of postmodernism in instruction, an even more philosophical approach to how our field teaches public administration, which may not provide the need for guidance on quality teaching in public affairs.

The recently released *Handbook of Teaching Public Administration* by Bottom et al. (2022) is a volume that further contributes to our scholarship of teaching and learning in our discipline. In this book, there is an excellent application section on the use of case studies in the public administration classroom, which is especially beneficial to instructors in the field (see also Hatcher et al., 2018; Jordan & McDonald, 2021; Rauhaus, 2024). Still, as with other reflections, the book focuses mostly on discipline-wide issues, not the nuts and bolts of quality teaching in the field. Given the lack of reflective texts on teaching in our field, we are confident of the need for this book.

Concluding Thoughts and Outline of the Book

Public trust in democracy is wavering. At the risk of moving focus broadly away from the nuts and bolts of teaching, there is a vital need in our field to educate public managers who can help reverse the erosion of democracy throughout the world. The best way for us to do this is to ensure that we train effective public managers who will improve the capacity of governments. We fight against the erosion of democracy through teaching. Accordingly, ensuring we have quality teachers in public affairs classrooms is vital not just to our field but to the state of bureaucracy and democracy throughout the world.

As noted, the book is divided into two overall sections. Chapters 2 through 8 present research-based discussions on key issues of teaching in

Introduction and Setting of the Stage   **5**

public affairs, such as teaching at the MPA level, doctoral instruction, and promoting diversity and a global context in the classroom. In Chapter 2, William Hatcher, Beth Rauhaus, and Rhucha Samudra survey the surprisingly limited research on teaching quality in the field's SoTL. The authors develop a framework describing the scholarship on the craft of teaching and develop tips for faculty in the public administration classroom.

The next few chapters focus on teaching public affairs at the various levels of instruction: undergraduate, MPA, and doctoral. In Chapter 3, Madinah Hamidullah builds on her research into undergraduate instruction in public affairs. In recent years, there has been a resurgence of undergraduate public affairs and nonprofit degrees. These programs have special needs that differ from graduate-level instruction in the field. In Chapter 4, Sara Rinfret and Michelle Pautz examine instruction at the MPA level. In the field of public affairs, the MPA degree is the oldest and most prominent graduate credential. Most faculty in the field will teach in MPA programs, especially in the U.S. context. In their chapter on instruction at this level, the authors discuss "contemporary challenges faced by public sector employees, including bureaucrat bashing, pandemic-induced burnout, and political complexities." They call for a caring approach to instruction that promotes diversity and public service. In Chapter 5, Meghna Sabharwal reflects on PhD instruction by discussing the importance of mentorship to her education and academic career. The author incorporates the research on PhD instruction and mentorship in this reflection.

The next few chapters focus on what we view as vital issues to the future of instruction in our field. In Chapter 6, Saman Afshan, Honey Minkowitz, and Bruce McDonald sketch the growth of online education in the field and how to teach public affairs, an inherently applied profession, to current and future public managers through online instruction. In Chapter 7, Sean McCandless and Mary Guy provide a framework for new faculty on incorporating diversity, equity, and inclusion into the MPA classroom. In Chapter 8, Kim Moloney, Mehmet Demircioglu, and Kohei Suzuki cover the crucial topic of teaching public administration in a global context. The field can often be too focused on public administration in the U.S. context, which does a disservice to our students and the quality of public administration in the United States and throughout the world.

In Chapters 9 through 15, the book transitions into reflective essays from expert teachers in the field of public affairs. These experts are from various stages in the academic career, highlighting faculty's continual growth and development. Some of these experts hold decades of experience teaching in the field, while others are scholars in the middle part of their careers. Some hold significant experience in practice, while others have been solely in academia for their careers and learned their craft of teaching. Across their

6 William Hatcher, Beth M. Rauhaus, and Bruce D. McDonald III

essays, there is the commonality of the importance of constant improvement in building one's craft of teaching public administration. We hope you enjoy the journey through these reflective essays and learn how to improve your craft of teaching.

References

Bottom, K. A., Diamond, J., Dunning, P. T., & Elliott, I. C. (Eds.). (2022). *Handbook of teaching public administration*. Edward Elgar Publishing.

Bowman, J. S., & Menzel, D. C. (Eds.). (1998). *Teaching ethics and values in public administration programs: Innovations, strategies, and issues*. SUNY Press.

Cunningham, R., & Weschler, L. (2002). Theory and the public administration student/practitioner. *Public Administration Review, 62*(1), 104–111. https://doi.org/10.1111/1540-6210.00159

Desimone, L. M., & Pak, K. (2017). Instructional coaching as high-quality professional development. *Theory into Practice, 56*(1), 3–12. https://doi.org/10.1080/00405841.2016.1241947

Farrell, C., Hatcher, W., & Diamond, J. (2022). Reflecting on over 100 years of public administration education. *Public Administration, 100*(1), 116–128. https://doi.org/10.1111/padm.12808

Frederickson, H. G. (2004). The Journal of Public Affairs Education at age ten: History, content, and prospects. *Journal of Public Affairs Education, 10*(2), 83–89. https://doi.org/10.1080/15236803.2004.12001349

Hall, J. L., & McDonald, B. D. (2023). Scholarly hypocrisy or apostasy in public administration: Preaching to the choir, or to an empty room? *Public Administration Review, 83*(4), 725–733. https://doi.org/10.1111/puar.13686

Hatcher, W., & Ginn, M. H. (2020). Recruiting and retaining a diverse student body. In B. D. McDonald & W. Hatcher (Eds.), *The public affairs faculty manual: A guide to the effective management of public affairs programs* (pp. 203–222). Routledge.

Hatcher, W., McDonald, B. D., & Brainard, L. A. (2018). How to write a case study for public affairs. *Journal of Public Affairs Education, 24*(2), 274–285. https://doi.org/10.1080/15236803.2018.1444902

Hatcher, W., Raushaus, B., & Meares, W. L. (2023). The career paths of the chief administrative officers of US cities: A survey of city managers and content analysis of how they discuss their careers. *Local Government Studies, 49*(6), 1312–1332. https://doi.org/10.1080/03003930.2022.2132386

Jordan, M., & McDonald, B. D. (2021). Using case studies in public budgeting and finance. In B. D. McDonald & M. Jordan (Eds.), *Teaching public budgeting and finance: A guide for teaching professional competencies* (pp. 257–276). Routledge.

McDonald, B. D. (2023). The dark horse of public administration: The challenge of pedagogical research. *Teaching Public Administration, 41*(1), 3–10. https://doi.org/10.1177/01447394231159983

McDonald, B. D., & Hatcher, W. (Eds.). (2020). *The public affairs faculty manual: A guide to the effective management of public affairs programs*. Routledge.

McDonald, B. D., Hatcher, W., & Abbott, M. E. (2022). History of public administration education in the United States. In K. A. Bottom, P. Dunning, I. Elliot, & J. Diamond (Eds.), *Handbook on the teaching of public administration* (pp. 57–64). Edward Elgar Publishing.

McDonald, B. D., Hatcher, W., Bacot, H., Evans, M. D., McCandless, S. A., McDougle, L. M., Young, S. L., Elliott, I. C., Emas, R., Lu, E. Y., Abbott, M. E., Bearfield, D. A., Berry-James, R. M., Blessett, B., Borry, E. L., Diamond, J., Franklin, A. L., Gaynor, T. S., Gong, T., . . . Zhang, Y. (2024). The scholarship of teaching and learning in public administration: An agenda for future research. *Journal of Public Affairs Education*, *30*(1), 11–27. https://doi.org/10.1 080/15236803.2023.2294654

Morrison, G. R., Ross, S. J., Morrison, J. R., & Kalman, H. K. (2019). *Designing effective instruction*. John Wiley & Sons.

Raadschelders, J., Whetsell, T., Dimand, A. M., & Kieninger, K. (2019). Journal of Public Affairs Education at 25: Topics, trends, and authors. *Journal of Public Affairs Education*, *25*(1), 51–72. https://doi.org/10.1080/15236803.2018. 1546506

Rauhaus, B. M. (2024). "How may I help?": Using New Amsterdam as a case study to link theory to practice. *Teaching Public Administration*, *42*(1), 60–72. https://doi.org/10.1177/01447394231159984

Ventriss, C. (1991). Contemporary issues in American public administration education: The search for an educational focus. *Public Administration Review*, *51*(1), 4–14. https://doi.org/10.2307/976631

SECTION I

Developing Skills for the Craft

2

SURVEYING THE LITERATURE ON BEING A SUCCESSFUL TEACHER IN PUBLIC AFFAIRS

William Hatcher[1], Beth M. Rauhaus[2], and Rhucha Samudra[1]

[1]*Augusta University, Augusta, GA, and [2]University of Louisiana at Lafayette, Lafayette, LA*

Reflecting on the tenth anniversary of the *Journal of Public Affairs Education* (JPAE) (originally the *Journal of Public Administration Education*), Founding Editor H. George Frederickson (2004) asked the question, "How could it be that an academic field as big and well established as public administration took so long to develop a journal specializing in education?" (p. 283). He goes on to trace the scholarly events leading up to the creation of the journal. However, the question can be broadened to apply to public affairs teaching overall and is still relevant today. Why is a field so concerned with educating effective public managers through connecting theory with practice but not supporting research into the features of an effective instructor?

Public administrator academics often become professors without being taught how to teach during their PhD programs. Moreover, the scholarship of teaching and learning (SoTL) is frequently undervalued on the pages of the promotion and tenure portfolios of emerging scholars in the field. Even the two top journals focusing on education in the field (the *Journal of Public Affairs Education* and *Teaching Public Administration* [TPA]) dedicate a surprisingly small number of pages in their issues to evidence-based papers on what makes a successful teacher. As a professional field, we talk about the need for quality teaching. Still, we need to do more to apply our research skills to identify these techniques in public administration classrooms. We are not practicing what we preach – that is, the need to use our methodological skills to question how we develop evidence-based teaching tools for our public administration classrooms and overall programs.

DOI: 10.4324/9781032671291-3

12   William Hatcher, Beth M. Rauhaus, and Rhucha Samudra

Since the creation of JPAE, as Frederickson noted, there has been a movement to expand our focus on research that informs teaching in our field. However, this research is often not considered rigorous, and many academic programs do not consider SoTL publications as research that counts toward tenure and promotion. This is a mistake. How can we improve public administration if we are not doing our best to advance how we teach current and future public managers? Moreover, SoTL research in public administration, as McDonald (2023) has found, is often cited more than scholarship in other areas that historically have been viewed as more critical. With the emergence of JPAE and TPA as prominent journals in the field, what makes for an effective public administration instructor has been revisited. This chapter details the research that we have accumulated in this area.

Since the research is primarily found on the pages of JPAE and TPA, the chapter relies mainly on the articles in these two journals. Over the years, these journals have focused on many areas of SoTL research, including teaching and classroom topics, course development, curriculum development, accreditation issues, online learning, etc. Articles focusing solely on successful teaching are shockingly less numerous than we thought. For example, over its 28-year history, JPAE has published around 55 papers explicitly focused on teaching. Upon the journal's 25th anniversary, Raadschelders and colleagues (2019) analyzed the content of papers in JPAE. They found "teaching methodology" to be the primary focus in 49 papers, which at the time was 7.57% of published research in the journal. Curriculum issues, diversity, and inclusion were the top focus areas for papers in the journal. Thus, even in the field's top SoTL journals, there tend to be few articles dedicated solely to teaching. We hope this book will encourage a scholarly discussion on the need for more research to describe and explain the features of successful teaching. The future of public administration practice depends on us having outstanding teachers who practice evidence-based pedagogy.

In the following sections, we review the literature on the craft of teaching public administration. We develop a thematic framework for this scholarship, explaining what we know about teaching practices in public administration. From this framework, we develop lessons or tips for instructors seeking to improve their craft of teaching.

A Review of the Teaching Literature in JPAE

JPAE scholarship over the years can be divided into two major themes: the first theme deals with the overall understanding of public administration pedagogy and the second theme deals with a specific focus on elements of

Surveying the Literature on Being a Successful Teacher in Public Affairs **13**

public administration pedagogy. Scholars have focused on quality teaching, teaching modalities, and particular assignments public administration teachers can use.

Developing an overarching pedagogical perspective in the field of public administration has remained an important conversation among scholars over the years. Abel (2009) asserts that given the uncertain nature of practice in the field of public administration, public administration students must learn how to thrive under such uncertainty, make decisions based on incomplete and biased information, and develop political astuteness. Frederickson (1999) emphasizes the value of political astuteness echoing Dwight Waldo "public administration is politics" (p. 10). To ensure that students learn public values as professionals, courses should be developed on the basis of the principles of transparency, participation, accountability, and responsiveness (Balint, 2007). Whittington (2001) says pedagogy is excellent teaching and details effective teaching practices. Holzer (1999) takes these ideas further and asserts that good teaching involves not just classroom instruction but also good mentoring, especially for graduate students. He provides perspectives on mentoring from faculty and students and describes how to maneuver this process in the age of electronic classrooms. These teaching practices become even more critical in the field because MPA classrooms usually have a mix of in-service and pre-service students with different engagement needs. White (2000) suggests using an interactive approach and various instructional methods such as collaboration, experiential learning, and case studies to support the needs of both pre-service and in-service students.

Developing holistic assessment methods for both course- and program-level learning outcomes is necessary to ensure that various teaching and learning activities have helped students achieve stated learning outcomes (Powell, 2009). Managing diversity in public-sector organizations is an important part of the public manager's job, and managing diversity within a classroom community is essential for public administration faculty. While faculty do not have to be experts in diversity issues, they can use a thoughtful course organization to teach any public administration course. Tschirhart and Wise (2002) discuss a model where the faculty treats the course as an organization and designs and delivers the course by carefully using course goals and technology, being mindful of the social structure of the course and external influences on diversity perceptions, and engaging with students as course facilitators. Such course design could be used in public administration classrooms.

Scholars also discuss collaborative learning as essential to public administration pedagogy since public administration practice is inherently collaborative. Administrators collaborate consistently with peers, legislators, nonprofit agencies, and businesses in their work lives. Hence, the public administration faculty must engage students in a collaborative classroom. One of the ways to engage in collaborative classrooms is through the development of team-based learning. While no magic wands exist to create effective project teams, Dickson (1997) provides a step-by-step guide that faculty may find helpful when designing student teams for class projects. It is essential to explain to students the reasoning behind team-based learning activities (Saldivar, 2015) since many of them may have negative experiences with group projects. Once students are bought into the idea of this helpful tool, developing effective teams and managing them becomes an important task. Factors such as how the conflict will be managed and how grades will be distributed as a team and individually are essential points to consider while developing, managing, and assessing teams (Dickson, 1997).

While team-based learning is one way to train students to work in teams in practice, classroom activities, other than team-based learning, can facilitate collaborative learning by enhancing peer interaction in the classroom (Kapucu, 2012). Various graded and ungraded activities such as lectures, case presentations, guest speakers from the field, and group discussions can involve students actively in the classroom. Active engagement from the faculty member as a facilitator is necessary to avoid group cliques. Such deliberate use of the collaborative process is also reiterated by Saldivar (2015).

Classroom engagement continues to remain an essential conversation in the field. Along with hybrid and online classrooms, traditional in-person instruction can also utilize nontraditional pedagogy that is not solely lecture-based (Hansen & Rubin, 1997) to engage students meaningfully. Another way to engage students in coursework is by making them more responsible for learning by creating assignments in various courses that will encourage them to connect concepts from public administration literature and different courses. Instead of instructors showing the roadmap, students should select relevant concepts from courses and apply them in other courses. This type of assessment creates a higher level of learning and empowers students to be in charge of their own learning (Peters, 2014).

Scholars have also focused on specific activities regarding course content and delivery. For example, some scholars focus on how to teach analytical methods to MPA students. There are two prominent ways of teaching analytical methods in public administration classrooms, the traditional research method approach (Fitzpatrick, 2000) or the management science approach (Caulkins, 1999). However, Aristigueta and Raffel (2001) suggest a third approach focusing on management decision-making. Thus, training should focus on developing managers who will become consumers rather than producers of research. Within such analytical methods course use of carefully designed rubrics can improve student performance (Peat, 2006). Another important conversation is about experiential learning. Jelier and Clarke (1999) discuss their experiences with using community analysis as a teaching tool for students, where students got involved in three different communities as a part of the class. While such an approach provides meaningful learning opportunities, it takes a lot of planning and preparation. However, public administration faculty can apply this approach partially in various courses to provide exposure to real-life community issues.

Another vital course content discussion focuses on the use of the case method. The case method helps students to understand deeper issues at hand, appreciate different viewpoints, and reflect on nuances of the problems presented (Massie, 1995). Thus, case studies help students understand how to make administrative decisions (Hatcher et al., 2018). However, good case studies are not easy to write. A good case study puts a student in the shoes of the administrator in the case and imposes decision-making on them (Hatcher et al., 2018). Hatcher et al. (2018) provide a step-by-step guide for public administration scholars to write an effective case study. Careaga et al. (2017) take the case study method further and involve students in writing a case study. They illustrate this experience by discussing how students in three graduate programs in Colombia developed their context-specific case studies with the help of instructors. These students' case studies contributed to developing Colombia-specific cases and increased student engagement in the course. They concluded that such a pedagogical approach is important for developing case studies for countries where case studies may be needed and for helping students enhance their teamwork, research, and reflection skills.

MPA programs train students to become public and nonprofit sector managers. Hence, including professional development activities as a part of the curriculum is essential. While many programs utilize internships as one of the professional development activities for many pre-service students, creative use of portfolio courses can be helpful for professional development, enhance students' learning experience, and be helpful for curriculum assessment and program needs (Williams et al., 1998). Portfolios can help students' self-assessment, integrate multiple courses, and provide professional development (p. 284).

Online education is not a new phenomenon in higher education. According to the National Center for Education Statistics, in 2021, 21% of students at private nonprofit institutions and 28% of students at public institutions were enrolled in distance education courses. Public service courses and programs are not an exception, as more and more courses and programs are participating in distance education or hybrid education.

In 2022–2023, among 200 NASPAA-accredited programs, various modalities were offered, including fully and partially online. Within one program, various modalities can be offered (email communication with Stacy Drudy). Fifty-six programs () were fully online. Fifteen programs () were partially online where students had to visit the campus once. Moreover, programs () offered online coursework. Scholars of public administration teaching have focused on this important development in teaching and learning. Bryan et al. (2018) find that when students interact frequently with their peers using online platforms, they engage in online classes more intensively. Such use on online platforms is discussed by Shea et al. (2016), who focus on hybrid course design and test how Blended Learning Distance Mediation Framework (BLDM) can be used to assess student satisfaction and performance. They conclude that in a hybrid environment, along with teaching presence (e.g., active discussion forums), the social presence of faculty affects student satisfaction. Such a BLDM framework can encourage faculty discussion around hybrid learning. A similar conclusion is drawn by Shea et al. (2015). Both articles emphasize the importance of social presence in a hybrid environment to ensure that some students do not get alienated due to the hybrid nature of the course.

Collaboration and student engagement remain a consistent focus for JPAE scholars. Since public administrators collaborate within and between sectors, effectively engaging students in collaborative exercises in the classroom helps them train for future work. For example, Emerson and Gerlak (2016) discuss their experiences teaching collaborative governance in online classrooms. They find that instructors in online classrooms play three critical roles (as role models of online learning, as learning consultants by facilitating learning, and as connectors who connect online learning content to professional development). Faculty can improve collaborative learning by deliberately developing collaborative spaces in online platforms. Online learning can be challenging, especially in critical courses such as research methods. However, Ya Ni (2013) finds no difference in grades received by online versus in-person students in research methods classes. But Ya Ni also warns that student persistence in an online environment could be challenging. However, student engagement may be higher in online environments, especially for more reserved students. To be effective in such a setting, the author points toward using consulting, advising, and tutoring in person as a supplement to the course delivery. To ensure that online students succeed, programs can use data analytics to catch poor performers early and provide them with appropriate support to successfully complete the course and the program (Bainbridge et al., 2015).

Higher education has a long history of using student evaluation of teaching (SET) to improve teaching quality at a program, department, and college level (Otani et al., 2012). Two articles in JPAE specifically focus on the SETs and discuss what specific variables influence higher SETs and how to use them systematically for course and program improvement. Campbell et al. (2005) found that the more the students feel that they have learned in the course, the higher the SET score. Similarly, academic rigor is associated with higher SETs. Similar results were found by Otani et al. (2012). Teaching effectiveness (such as clear explanations, effective use of class time, and stimulating course materials) improves SETs. Both articles suggest that instructors can use feedback to improve course design. Otani et al. (2012) also suggest that such feedback should be used to continue discussion among instructors for overall program improvement. However, Campbell et al. (2005) suggest that given the presence of bias in SETs, which can systematically disadvantage women and older faculty members, SETs should be used with other measures to address the overall teaching effectiveness.

A Review of the Teaching Literature in TPA

Teaching Public Administration (TPA) offers insight into the diverse approaches to teaching and learning in public sector management and organizations. It serves as an instrument for learning more about effective teaching and learning public administration from an international perspective. The global approach of the journal provides examples of how educators can prepare public servants for the many challenges they will face in leadership roles and beyond in various governmental settings. There are articles published in this journal that can be used to prepare individuals for public service in a comparative context. To further highlight the unique comparative lens of the journal, Fenwick (2018) identifies the key themes of TPA from 1996 to 2016. He notes that much of the scholarship has expanded beyond the original focus on British public administration to include an international scope and an analysis of the future of the discipline of public administration.

This global trend has continued as published works explore best practices for teaching public administration in Ethiopia, Mexico, Britain, Bangladesh, Australia, Kazakhstan, South Africa, and beyond. The body of literature certainly emphasizes the importance of public affairs education, preparation for the future, and the adaptability of the core curriculum in the discipline. The scholarship in this journal offers educators' insight into best-governing practices that work in various forms of government and moves beyond examining bureaucracies in democracies. The scholarship in the journal also emphasizes the environment of the public sector globally, as these external conditions will impact how to best prepare future public managers. An awareness of structures of government, centralization of power, and how politics impact what public managers do is certainly a significant theme throughout TPA. On the other hand, there are several contributions to the discussion of teaching and learning in public administration education; as the world continues to change, problems become more complex, which in turn mandates more rigorous and comprehensive training of future public managers.

The works featured in TPA include case studies, pedagogical reflection, and models for curriculum design in public administration education. The articles focused on curriculum design, explored challenges in the field, and offered perspectives on better preparing public servants to govern in turbulent times with a wide array of skills that transcend place and form of government. One overarching aim of the journal is to address contemporary issues that impact public administration education from a global perspective. Rosenbaum (2014) comprehensively examines critical issues in public administration education globally while including a discussion of states with varying degrees of capacity, democratic traits, and cultural diversity, and most of these critical issues remain pertinent today. For example, in this particular work, Rosenbaum (2014) examines the emergence of public-sector disillusionment and suggests that public managers worldwide have become the targets of attacks from politicians throughout the last two decades of the twentieth century. This challenge is increasingly becoming more prevalent worldwide.

Scholars have continued to contribute to the discussion of the ever-changing environment of government and how public administration education can adapt. Exploring and understanding how the external environment impacts the future of public administration are must for public administration educators and aspiring public managers. McDonald (2021, 2023) explores how the COVID-19 pandemic impacted public administration education and online pedagogy while pondering what it means for the future of training public managers. In his work, he highlights the importance of recognizing the ever-changing environment and how contemporary issues will impact pedagogical approaches to public affairs and administration. His research recognizes that educators and students in public administration have "been faced with multiple 'once in a lifetime' economic events," and the environment of the public sector is filled with increasing uncertainty, as global warming, global security and terrorism, and political uncertainty (McDonald, 2021, p. 5).

Offering innovative pedagogical approaches and teaching tactics is an essential objective of *Teaching Public Administration,* and scholars have consistently contributed to the discussion. Advances in technology will undoubtedly impact public managers, and public administration educators seem to recognize this. A recently published study has explored how social media impacts the public-sector workplace. The authors share how faculty can use this case study in their teaching to examine relevant, contemporary issues that arise from integrating social media into public affairs (McBeth et al., 2020). Public administration educators also recognize the need for more online pedagogical offerings to meet student needs. With this, the latest publications in TPA have showcased the importance of teaching with technology. For instance, ChatGPT can assist ESL learners' speaking skills in a flipped classroom, allowing for an engaged learning environment (Muniandy & Selvanathan, 2024).

Toward an Evidence-Based Framework of Effective Teaching in Public Affairs

As stressed throughout this chapter, many faculty members in public affairs need to receive training in their doctoral programs on the vital topics of education, pedagogy, and general instructional tools. This is a disservice to our field, as many new instructors need an evidence-based understanding of how to teach their subjects. They often learn by trial and error, which hinders the academic growth and future success of current and future public managers. Instruction must be effective in our classes because there is a vital need to connect theory with practice to improve public administration. In the hopes of helping strengthen our field's advice on teaching, we develop a framework describing the research on teaching reviewed in this chapter.

Such a framework needs to include the major themes covered in the scholarly literature on teaching in public affairs. These themes and topics focus on delivery modalities, active learning exercises, and classroom issues, making sense of evaluations, ethics, and the importance of diversity, equity, inclusion, and accessibility. These topics can be classified into the following areas: classroom management, program management, and ethics and democratic teaching.

Classroom Management

The issues facing the instructor in the classroom range from developing effective learning exercises to motivating students. These factors are often ones that instructors have some influence, albeit very limited at times. Based on the review of the literature in this chapter, the following are key classroom management factors:

- Teaching includes effective mentoring of students (Holzer, 1999). Public administration students are diverse and have multiple needs. Teachers in our field have a role to play in helping mentor the field's diverse collection of students and develop processes that best serve a mixture of in-service and pre-service students.

- Effective goal-based designs of courses (Tschirhar & Wise, 2002). Teachers need to be strategic in how they design their courses, using the field's understanding of developing goals, attaching student learning outcomes, and assessing success.
- Team-based learning and collaboration among students (Dickson, 1997; Saldivar, 2015). Public administrators work in teams, and teachers in our field have a strong need to reinforce the importance of groups through team-based learning in their classes.
- The designing of online, hybrid, and/or face-to-face instruction (Bryan et al., 2018). Individual instructors often do not determine the delivery modality of their courses. Many programs in the field may request that their faculty members teach a combination on on-campus, hybrid, and/or online courses. Teachers need to be aware of the differences among these modalities and strive to build community in any type of course.
- The need for active learning, even though online courses (Shea et al., 2016). Often online courses are viewed as passive in how learning assignments are structured. This does not have to be the case. Instructors need to develop a variety of online learning assessments and try to build some assignments that require students to actively engage with their classmates and the material.
- The efficacy of flipped classrooms in public affairs (Muniandy & Selvanathan, 2024). Technology can be used in courses to make them more engaging, for instance, using ChatGPT to help ESL learners strengthen their speaking skills.

At the instructor level, the literature's findings primarily focus on the need for collaborative learning that links theory with practice and connects pre-service students with in-service ones. Additionally, the importance of active learning and team-based tools is stressed throughout the literature. Lastly, faculty in public affairs need to approach teaching not just as classroom lecturing but as a holistic process involving team-building, active learning, and mentoring.

Program Management

As units of analysis are shifted from the instructor to the program, some of the same factors and findings remain but others become more prominent in the literature. At the program level, the literature's findings emphasize that

Surveying the Literature on Being a Successful Teacher in Public Affairs **21**

program, department, school, and leaders need to focus on the following factors:

- Designing and implementing learning outcomes (Powell, 2009). Programs need to have clear plans for how they design and implement their learning outcomes. For MPA programs, this often means having an assessment plan that is linked to the program's mission and overall evaluation plans.
- Program assessment and the use of student evaluations of teaching (Otani et al., 2012). Student evaluations of teaching are often flawed instruments that are biased against people of color, women, and LGBTQ communities. Programs need to take this into account when designing assessments of student evaluations.
- Program-wide case study analysis (Careaga et al., 2017). Programs can integrate particular case studies across multiple courses and learning points for the students.
- The efficacy of internships and/or capstone learning experiences (Williams et al., 1998). Programs need to promote experiential learning opportunities, such as internships, especially for pre-service MPA students. Capstone or culminating learning experiences are also vital parts of MPA programs.
- Program-wide modality delivery – online, hybrid, and/or face-to-face (Bryan et al., 2018). Programs need to consider the efficacy of delivery modality in serving their program missions, students, alumni, and other stakeholders.

At the program level, the literature focuses on programmatic review issues, teaching methods throughout classes, internship and capstone experiences, and program delivery.

Ethics and Democratic Teaching

Within the teaching literature and the broader SoTL work is a focus on the importance of ethics and democracy in the classroom, our programs, and the overall field. At this environmental level, the literature's findings on teaching emphasize the following:

- The need for democratic governance (Rosenbaum, 2014). Public administrators have been attacked by politicians. Democratic governance is an important feature of our classrooms. Students need to be taught how to handle attacks by the public and politicians against their profession.

They also need to know how to make the case for the administrative state as a vital component of functioning democracies.

• Managing diversity in public organizations (Tschirhart & Wise, 2002). Students need to have learning opportunities focusing on how they manage diverse organizations.

• Promoting diversity, equity, and inclusion (Raadschelders et al., 2019). The field has developed a wealth of knowledge on how to promote diversity, equity, and inclusion, but these efforts have come under attack by politicians and the public. Students need to know this context, examine the research on DEI, and how to promote diversity in organizations.

However, it is striking that, from reviewing the literature focused solely on teaching, many articles do not address the need for diversity and promoting democratic values in the classroom. We are surprised by this finding because these vital topics comprise a large part of the overall research in SoTL and the papers in JPAE (Raadschelders et al., 2019). This leads us to think that the lack of focus in the teaching-related articles is due to these topics needing a broader focus outside of what makes an effective teacher. Nevertheless, it is important to stress that the need for a global perspective, democratic values, and managing diversity are key features focusing on how you teach public affairs.

Lessons for the Public Affairs Teacher

From this chapter's reviewed literature and framework to make sense of that literature, we can derive lessons for the instructor, programs, and the field. These lessons are also rooted in our over 30 combined years of experience teaching in the field and managing academic programs.

First, instructors, programs, and our field must encourage effective teaching to ensure our graduates connect theory to practice. The field needs to do this to train quality public administrators who promote efficiency, effectiveness, and equity. We need to help train future professors to teach the virtues of diversity, equity, and inclusion. Importantly, we need teachers who can help public managers understand that they will need to lead diverse organizations and need the tools to do it successfully.

Second, active learning in our field is crucial. Being a field of practice, the public affairs classroom needs students to learn in an active manner instead of traditional, top-down lectures. Surprisingly, there are a small number of papers on active learning in public affairs reviewed in this chapter. The papers reviewed focused on active learning methods and how to do it via online learning (Shea et al., 2016). Active learning in the classroom may include discussions, group and team-based learning, enhanced discussion boards for online courses, and other methods that empower students as active learners instead of passive ones.

Third, experiential learning in our field is crucial. This is even more important for our students who need to gain significant work experience. Being a professional field, our students need to be given the opportunity to learn by doing. The internship experience is a critical tool for this goal. However, faculty and program leaders can also offer job shadowing on a more limited basis than full internships or integrate practitioners into classes through methods ranging from guest lectures to integrated projects.

Fourth, community-engaged learning is crucial. Such learning expands experiential opportunities, such as internships. Programs can have capstone courses where students work in teams to assist actual public organizations and nonprofits with their work, such as planning, program evaluation, budgeting, applied research, and other areas. Faculty and program leaders can integrate by having a clear mission statement for public affairs programs and using community-engaging learning projects as capstone learning experiences (Hatcher et al., 2024).

Fifth, instructors, programs, and our field must be as flexible as possible regarding the course and program modality. While it is less widespread than in the past, there has been opposition to online learning in our field. However, over the past 15 years and, accelerated during COVID-19, there has been a greater appreciation for the benefits of online learning. The students in our field are professionals and need the flexibility of different modalities. Traditional on-campus learning works for some programs, but completely asynchronous online programs work for others. Faculty and leaders need to look to their mission statements and the needs of their students in designing modalities. One thing that is for sure, though, is that they need to be open to new technologies and modalities in delivery.

Sixth, our field needs to teach the limitations and the virtues of democratic governance. We need to make a standard on how public administration in a democracy should be our normative goals as a field, scholars, and public servants. Efficiency may work in a non-democratic government, but that should not be the only goal. Democratic governance and strengthening should be the normative goal of our teaching.

Lastly, instructors need to constantly teach themselves and their students. They need to focus on their craft of teaching, seeking to improve their skills and looking to others for insights. Often, these insights and improvements come from our students. Instructors need to remain curious and open to learning from our students, who often have significant experience serving as public administrators.

Thus, on the basis of our framework and literature review, we offer the following tips for teachers in public affairs:

1. Connect theory with practice through mentoring and focusing on managing diversity.
2. Use active learning instead of passive learning exercises.
3. Offer experiential learning opportunities.
4. Build community-engaged learning projects.
5. Practice flexibility about program delivery modality.
6. Respect and teach the importance of democracy and a professional bureaucracy's role in maintaining it.
7. Remain a student and practice curiosity when teaching.

Concluding Thoughts

In 2023, the then leadership and editorial board of JPAE wrote an essay on the future of SoTL research in our field (McDonald et al., 2024). These leading scholars stressed the importance of researching topics related to what we teach and how we teach our students. However, historically, SoTL research has not been as valued as other areas of public administration. This is changing with the emergence of respect for SoTL research and a movement in public administration to advance our knowledge of teaching. However, even with these trends, few SoTL articles deal solely with the factors affecting teaching, seeking to answer the simple question, "What makes an effective teacher?" Overall, this book attempts to answer this question by surveying the relevant literature. In this chapter, we reviewed the literature that focuses solely on teaching in hopes of providing the context for this overall book and developing a framework for evidence-based teaching in public affairs.

We identified the important findings in the literature regarding classroom management, program management, and broader questions on democratic values. Through using this framework to help us understand the literature, we identified tips or suggestions for faculty members, along with program leaders, looking to refine their teaching skills. These tips focus on mentoring students from diverse backgrounds, promoting active learning in all forms of courses, being open to flexibility in the delivery of courses, respecting and promoting democracy, and being curious about what can be learned from students.

References

Abel, C. F. (2009). Toward a signature pedagogy for public administration. *Journal of Public Affairs Education, 15*(2), 145–160. https://doi.org/10.1080/1523680 3.2009.12001550

Aristigueta, M. P., & Raffel, J. A. (2001). Teaching techniques of analysis in the MPA curriculum: Research methods, management science, and "the third path". *Journal of Public Affairs Education, 7*(3), 161–169. https://doi.org/10.1080/152 36803.2001.12023511

Bainbridge, J., Melitski, J., Zahradnik, A., Lauría, E. J., Jayaprakash, S., & Baron, J. (2015). Using learning analytics to predict at-risk students in online graduate public affairs and administration education. *Journal of Public Affairs Education, 21*(2), 247–262.

Balint, P. J. (2007). Practicing what we preach: Approaching praxis through classroom governance. *Journal of Public Affairs Education, 13*(3–4), 509–518. https://doi.org/10.1080/15236803.2007.12001495

Bryan, T. K., Lutte, R., Lee, J., O'Neil, P., Maher, C. S., & Hoflund, A. B. (2018). When do online education technologies enhance student engagement? A case of distance education at University of Nebraska at Omaha. *Journal of Public Affairs Education, 24*(2), 255–273. https://doi.org/10.1080/15236803.2018. 1429817

Campbell, H. E., Steiner, S., & Gerdes, K. (2005). Student evaluations of teaching: How you teach and who you are. *Journal of Public Affairs Education, 11*(3), 211–231. https://doi.org/10.1080/15236803.2005.12001395

Careaga, M., Rubaii, N., & Leyva, S. (2017). Beyond the case method in public affairs education: Unexpected benefits of student-written cases. *Journal of Public Affairs Education, 23*(1), 571–590. https://doi.org/10.1080/15236803.2017. 12002270

Caulkins, J. P. (1999). The revolution in management science instruction: Implications for teaching public affairs students. *Journal of Public Affairs Education, 5*(2), 107–117.

Dickson, E. L. (1997). Structuring effective student teams. *Journal of Public Administration Education, 3*(2), 191–202. https://doi.org/10.1080/10877789. 1997.12023428

Emerson, K., & Gerlak, A. K. (2016). Teaching collaborative governance online: Aligning collaborative instruction with online learning platforms. *Journal of Public Affairs Education, 22*(3), 327–344. https://doi.org/10.1080/15236803. 2016.12002251

Fenwick, J. (2018). Teaching public administration: Key themes 1996–2016. *Teaching Public Administration, 36*(1), 6–13. https://doi.org/10.1177/0144739417740180

Fitzpatrick, J. (2000). What are our goals in teaching research methods to public administrators? *Journal of Public Affairs Education, 6*(3), 173–181.

Frederickson, H. G. (1999). Dwight Waldo and education for public administration. *Journal of Public Affairs Education, 5*(1), 5–11. https://doi.org/10.1080/1 5236803.1999.12022048

Frederickson, H. G. (2004). The journal of public affairs education at age ten: History, content, and prospects. *Journal of Public Affairs Education, 10*(2), 83–89. https://doi.org/10.1080/15236803.2004.12001349

Hansen, E. J., & Rubin, R. S. (1997). Strategies for teaching a student-centered large lecture course in public affairs. *Journal of Public Administration Education, 3*(3), 329–344. https://doi.org/10.1080/10877789.1997.12023448

Hatcher, W., Ginn, M. H., & Meares, W. L. (2024). Using engaged projects to assess Master of Public Administration (MPA) programs. In J. Schafer & B. D. McDonald (Eds.), *Engaged learning in the public service classroom.* Routledge.

Hatcher, W., McDonald, B. D., & Brainard, L. A. (2018). How to write a case study for public affairs. *Journal of Public Affairs Education, 24*(2), 274–285. https://doi.org/10.1080/15236803.2018.1444902

Holzer, M. (1999). Mentoring as a commitment to teaching. *Journal of Public Affairs Education, 5*(1), 1–4. https://doi.org/10.1080/15236803.1999.12022047

Jelier, R. W., & Clarke, R. J. (1999). The community as a laboratory of study: Getting out of the ivory tower. *Journal of Public Affairs Education, 5*(2), 167–180. https://doi.org/10.1080/15236803.1999.12022066

Kapucu, N. (2012). Classrooms as communities of practice: Designing and facilitating learning in a networked environment. *Journal of Public Affairs Education, 18*(3), 585–610. https://doi.org/10.1080/15236803.2012.12001701

Massie, C. Z. (1995). Teaching introduction to public administration via the case method. *Journal of Public Administration Education, 1*(2), 102–115. https://doi.org/10.1080/10877789.1995.12023370

McBeth, M. K., Brewer, A. M., & Smith, M. N. (2020). Teaching social media and public administration: Applying four approaches to an emerging issue. *Teaching Public Administration, 38*(2), 168–186. https://doi.org/10.1177/0144739419886630

McDonald, B. D. (2021). Teaching in uncertain times: The future of public administration education. *Teaching Public Administration, 39*(1), 3–8. https://doi.org/10.1177/0144739420963154

McDonald, B. D. (2023). The dark horse of public administration: The challenge of pedagogical research. *Teaching Public Administration, 41*(1), 3–10. https://doi.org/10.1177/01447394231159983

McDonald, B. D., Hatcher, W., Bacot, H., Evans, M. D., McCandless, S. A., McDougle, L. M., Young, S. L., Elliott, I. C. Emas, R., Lu, E. Y., Abbott, M. E., Bearfield, D. A., Berry-James, R. M., Blessett, B., Borry, E. L., Diamond, J., Franklin, A. L., Gaynor, T. S., Gong, T., . . . Zhang, Y. (2024). The scholarship of teaching and learning in public administration: An agenda for future research. *Journal of Public Affairs Education, 30*(1), 11–27. https://doi.org/10.1080/15236803.2023.2294654

Muniandy, J., & Selvanathan, M. (2024). ChatGPT, a partnering tool to improve ESL learners' speaking skills: Case study in a public university, Malaysia. *Teaching Public Administration.* https://doi.org/10.1177/01447394241230152

Ni, A. Y. (2013). Comparing the effectiveness of classroom and online learning: Teaching research methods. *Journal of Public Affairs Education, 19*(2), 199–215. https://doi.org/10.1080/15236803.2013.12001730

Otani, K., Kim, B. J., & Cho, J. I. (2012). Student evaluation of teaching (SET) in higher education: How to use SET more effectively and efficiently in public affairs education. *Journal of Public Affairs Education, 18*(3), 531–544. https://doi.org/10.1080/15236803.2012.12001698

Peat, B. (2006). Integrating writing and research skills: Development and testing of a rubric to measure student outcomes. *Journal of Public Affairs Education, 12*(3), 295–311. https://doi.org/10.1080/15236803.2006.12001437

Peters, R. A. (2014). Motivating MPA students to independently develop linkages among multiple courses. *Journal of Public Affairs Education, 20*(2), 163–180. https://doi.org/10.1080/15236803.2014.12001780

Powell, D. C. (2009). How do we know what they know? Evaluating student-learning outcomes in an MPA program. *Journal of Public Affairs Education, 15*(3), 269–287. https://doi.org/10.1080/15236803.2009.12001561

Raadschelders, J., Whetsell, T., Dimand, A. M., & Kieninger, K. (2019). Journal of Public Affairs Education at 25: Topics, trends, and authors. *Journal of Public Affairs Education, 25*(1), 51–72. https://doi.org/10.1080/15236803.2018.1546506

Rosenbaum, A. (2014). Putting first things first: Critical issues for public administration education. *Teaching Public Administration, 32*(1), 80–94. https://doi.org/10.1177/0144739414523286

Saldivar, K. M. (2015). Team-based learning: A model for democratic and culturally competent 21st century public administrators. *Journal of Public Affairs Education, 21*(2), 143–164. https://doi.org/10.1080/15236803.2015.12001825

Shea, J., Joaquin, M. E., & Gorzycki, M. (2015). Hybrid course design: Promoting student engagement and success. *Journal of Public Affairs Education, 21*(4), 539–556. https://doi.org/10.1080/15236803.2015.12002219

Shea, J., Joaquin, M. E., & Wang, J. Q. (2016). Pedagogical design factors that enhance learning in hybrid courses: A contribution to design-based instructional theory. *Journal of Public Affairs Education, 22*(3), 381–397 https://doi.org/10.1080/15236803.2016.12002254

Tschirhart, M., & Wise, L. R. (2002). Responding to a diverse class: Insights from seeing a course as an organization. *Journal of Public Affairs Education, 8*(3), 165–177. https://doi.org/10.1080/15236803.2002.12023548

White Jr, R. D. (2000). On pedagogy and andragogy: Balancing the learning needs of pre-service and in-service MPA students. *Journal of Public Affairs Education, 6*(2), 69–78. https://doi.org/10.1080/15236803.2000.12023460

Whittington, L. A. (2001). Detecting good teaching. *Journal of Public Affairs Education, 7*(1), 5–8. https://doi.org/10.1080/15236803.2001.12023490

Williams, D. G., Plein, L. C., & Lilly, R. (1998). Professional and career development: The MPA portfolio approach. *Journal of Public Affairs Education, 4*(4), 277–285. https://doi.org/10.1080/15236803.1998.12022040

3

TEACHING UNDERGRADUATE PUBLIC AFFAIRS STUDENTS

Madinah F. Hamidullah

Kennesaw State University, Kennesaw, GA

Teaching has been an area of great interest to me. I think back to my first interactions with instruction (outside of my family), and it is probably because I had some amazing and influential dance and cheerleading instructors. I think about the skills I learned and how those interactions have influenced me to this day. My time as a dance student and instructor has truly shaped my approach and outlook on my teaching style. I originally went to college to study dance education. However, I became a double major in dance and political science after taking a class in the American presidency. I know one class can change the direction of someone's life. Besides my unexpected interest in political science, I also decided to drop the dance education major because I was told I would have to stay in school for five years to do both the dance and education classes. As a junior in college, I calculated that five years in college was too long, and I ultimately stayed in college for seven more years!

Most of my decision to continue my educational journey was because of the influence of advisors, professors, and family. I also know that having dedicated and committed educators can make a difference in the success of a program. With all of that in mind, I approach teaching with compassion, collaboration, and accessibility at the top of my mind. My goal is to create a safe learning environment for all students to exchange diverse ideas and thoughts. Also, pulling from my dance and cheer experience, I create an environment where it is ok to fail. To take big leaps and jumps, even if that leaves you on the ground.

Community engagement and service-learning projects with my students are a significant focus in my teaching. These projects are the connection

DOI: 10.4324/9781032671291-4

between theory and practice, and they are often the projects that I enjoyed most and the projects that students frequently state as their most impactful experiences. When I was in my MPA program at the University of North Carolina Charlotte, we did an experiential capstone, and it has always stuck with me as one of my most memorable experiences. In addition to engaged teaching and learning experiences, one thing that I found most eye-opening in my first teaching experience was the variety of experiences of the undergraduate students. It is important to recognize the variety of undergraduate student experiences. In some areas, undergraduate students are likely to have significant life and professional experiences. You will never know what you can achieve if you don't try. When reflecting on my teaching journey for this essay, I really gained more of an appreciation for the classroom environment and its ability to influence people beyond what they read. In doing so, I hope to encourage students to look broadly and creatively at the issues that they will face in serving the public. This essay will discuss some of my history teaching undergraduate programs. It will also provide information on the administration areas that are crucial to having a thriving undergraduate public affairs program.

Administrative Lessons

General Education Students Versus Public Affairs Majors

Students come to public affairs education with a variety of backgrounds. It may be the case that some of our public affairs courses are also counted in our universities as general education requirements. These classes are an excellent exposure point for our public affairs programs. Many general education courses are requirements for students from all backgrounds and all majors. Being able to get public affairs courses on the general education credit list is one way that programs can make sure that they provide more exposure to students who may not have thought initially about public affairs as their education destination to begin with. These public affairs courses can be the catalyst that changes their mind and the activity that opens their eyes to how a degree in public and nonprofit administration is better suited to them than maybe another degree that they were thinking about. This doesn't leave out how vital our majors are to our program and how important they are often to telling others about the programs. Students are often the best walking advertisement for our degrees. Overall, making sure that we have the most exposure we can across our universities and that we schedule public affairs courses in the broadest way possible are great ways to make sure that we are doing the best we can for our undergraduate students.

30   Madinah F. Hamidullah

At times, the inclusion of programs into the general education require-ments can be a little bit daunting and overwhelming, but I believe it's worth it. I encourage those who are interested in developing broader outreach of their public affairs undergraduate courses to explore what the general edu-cation requirements might be and what sort of classes they have that might satisfy a particular need. Being creative and making sure that a class has broad appeal will be important in this process, but what better program is suited for that than public affairs, which deals with issues of public govern-ance involvement by all sectors in our lives?

Transfer Students

The diversity of undergraduate students is something to consider as well. It is often the case that students come to the classroom with a variety of lived experiences. Age is not always an indication of experience, so even tradi-tional undergraduate students (ages 18–22) may have a wealth of work and life experience. This is especially relevant when teaching public affairs classes, as the inclusion of real-world examples can help bring theory to life. We never want to discount students because we never know what experiences they have had. We never know what they're coming to the classroom to contribute, and I think sometimes our undergraduate stu-dents will surprise us. An undergraduate classroom can have just as fruitful a discussion as a graduate classroom.

Some programs actively recruit from two-year colleges, high schools, or even other programs on campus. One of the common themes that I experi-enced in my time as an undergraduate program director was that students do not necessarily select public administration (public affairs) as their first choice. It often takes some time and exposure to the program for them to see what public administration means. Many students don't come to school thinking, "Oh, I want to work in government." This creates an exciting opportunity for public affairs programs to make sure that they are letting students know early and often that public affairs education is for them. Some students may be interested in nonprofit organizations, and some students may be interested in government services. Having variety in the curriculum is something that we cannot underestimate when it comes to providing public affairs education to undergraduate students.

The creation of accelerated degree programs and the inclusion of public affairs courses in general education courses might be again one of the ways in which we can truly make the best impact on our universities broadly. One way that we can serve transfer students is to offer timely pathways not just to graduation for their four-year degree but also to graduate education. Transfer students may come in with their full list of general education credits completed. And we need to make sure our curriculums supplement those foundation classes and still provide them with timely pathways to graduation. This can take the form of 2 + 1 programs. This would be an example of somebody coming into an undergraduate program with an associate degree from a two-year college and having to take the final two years of their undergraduate degree. Because of how the accelerated master's program is modeled, they would only have one more year of coursework to complete a graduate MPA program. This would place them right on track with a traditional four-year student. In five years, our transfer students could still complete their master's degree.

Undergraduate students come in various forms, and they come to undergraduate education with various experiences and backgrounds. Students also transfer for a variety of reasons. Whether students are transferring from other majors on campus, other four-year universities, or two-year colleges, all students should have the same opportunities to receive a stellar public affairs education and continue to graduate school should that be something that they decide.

Recruitment

I'm going to speak from my own experience with regard to recruiting undergraduate students to public affairs education for several years. For several years, I served as the undergraduate committee chair for the Network of Schools of Public Policy, Affairs, and Administration (NASPPA). Through this capacity, I hosted a session at the organization's annual conference. One of the interesting things that often came up is that many programs found challenges in recruiting students directly into public affairs programs. One thing that wasn't necessarily an issue was encouraging students to transfer from other programs after taking public affairs classes. What many of us observed was that while students didn't select public affairs education as their first choice (for whatever reason), often, when they were exposed to the classes, the professors, and the course content, they became very interested and ultimately would become public affairs majors or minors. In this instance, students not knowing what the public affairs major or minor might be means they may not feel connected to the program until they experience its classes. This is an interesting opportunity when asking how we recruit better students to come directly into public affairs education. We want students to decide that public affairs education is their first stop, not their last choice, after they've been burnt out or kicked out of another discipline.

One of the ways we do that is through promotion to ensure students at all levels are aware of the value of public affairs education. This might

32 Madinah F. Hamidullah

include engaging alumni or other public officials to come and speak to students. This can take place before students are even accepted. The goal is to increase awareness and exposure to the program. Programs could host panels or other events as a way to profile alumni and/or highlight careers in public service. Students don't always know what they will do with their degree once they are finished.

The name of the program may also help a program recruit students for a public affairs degree. This means that you might have to change your degree name. And I'm speaking on this once again from my own experience. When I first began my first teaching job, our program major was public service. This was a great title to reflect the intention of the program and the ideals and values that we were trying to instill in graduates. However, one of the challenges we found was that public service did not connect to the job readiness aspect that many students and their parents expect to receive out of their four-year education. One student even went as far as to say they were afraid public service meant they were getting a degree in volunteering. I still laugh and think fondly of that student because it was important to hear that perspective. Hearing that the name of the degree that our faculty and university felt so strongly about, felt so drawn to, did not connect to our desired target audience was a learning experience.

After a few years, we rebranded the degree, and it became a degree in public and nonprofit administration. We almost found an immediate uptick in applications. I would venture to say that because of the inclusion of the nonprofit administration. Many students in the area were interested in either starting a nonprofit organization or learning more about nonprofits broadly. It can't be underestimated that naming matters. We've seen this even in the naming of course classes and trying to make class names more engaging and fun. Of course, sometimes this is the challenge because, let's face it, what are we really going to call public budgeting other than public budgeting?

Just as we try to train our students to be creative and come up with interesting solutions to the problems and the challenges in their communities, I would say we have that same responsibility when it comes to naming and developing our degree programs. We must be creative, and we have to meet students where they are. We must show students the value of the education that they're going to receive and the prospect of jobs that they're going to have after they graduate. Any attempt made to collect that information, to collect where your graduates gain employment, whether that be graduate school straight to industry. Whatever they might decide, being able to show students that there's a pipeline and pathway to a future with this degree is always a great recruitment tool.

One of the most exciting things is to make sure you have a rich alumni network. And I don't mean rich in the financial sense (even though that doesn't hurt); I mean rich as in they are engaged, they're willing to come back to talk to students, and they're eager to share their stories. Sharing stories is often one of the best ways to make the connection of what our degrees mean. It's not every day that our students see what they can be with a degree that they just might have read about online. Being able to capture those stories and initiatives is always a positive thing. With regard to recruitment, keep in touch with your alumni. Make sure that they know about your students and that your students know about them. Let them know if they have jobs in their organizations to make sure that they reach back and pull up the next generation of those coming out of their program with them.

Overall, when it comes to recruitment, getting out might be your best recruitment tool. Talking to students, talking to potential employers, and engaging with alumni are all the ways that you can make sure that your undergraduate program is attractive to students. Inviting those alumni to come back as guest speakers or inviting industry leaders to your program to talk about how the program connects with jobs and careers is a great way to make sure that students remain engaged and encouraged about public affairs education. One thing that stays on the top of mind not just for the students but also for many in administration is whether we are preparing students for jobs and the workforce. You can even engage alumni in class-room job readiness exercises. Benefits such as improved interview skills, career exposure, and a better understanding of the connection between theory and practice were found in a class exercise connecting students and alumni (Larsson et al., 2021). I believe that public administration programs do a great job of preparing students for careers broadly, regardless of the sector. But often, it's about being willing to share our story with others to make sure they know about the great work and the great education that lies within public affairs programs.

Recruitment in Action – Student Ambassador

Programs like student ambassadors, "lunch and learns," and tabling at different college fairs at high schools are all great ways to get the word out about your public affairs program. It's important to know that a bit of work might be required because, once again, most people don't neces-sarily think about public administration or even nonprofit administration directly when it comes to their educational pursuits. Planting the seed early is helpful whether that's going to high school or college fairs, making sure

34 Madinah F. Hamidullah

you participate in any bridge programs that might happen between high schools and your university, and presenting at those types of summer programs is an excellent opportunity to get the word out about your public affairs degree. Using current students with this population might be helpful. Adopting a student ambassador can help with promotion and student engagement at the university. It has also been found that participation in such programs have positive impacts on the participants as well (Gannon et al., 2018). The students may not always come directly to you, but when they know about you and the great work being done in the public affairs program, they will engage more. Promoting the connection that public affairs education allows them to have between their passions and having a solid profession that they value and want is important. Often, we don't know what we don't know, and it is our job to make sure that people know about the great things that they can do with public affairs education and the amazing career paths that they can have with it. Current student ambassadors are a great way to build that connection.

Online Education

Public affairs programs can come in many different modalities. Although our undergraduate programs are not NASPAA-accredited, many of them are housed in NASPAA-accredited programs (McDonald et al., 2021). As a result, they may reflect some of those same ideals and modalities. More and more, we are finding that students want flexibility, convenience, and accessibility. Often, this can come in the form of online education. Even if your undergraduate degree cannot be offered entirely online, you may find that offering some classes online may help meet students where they are. Just as our graduate students may need a particular level of flexibility, our undergraduate students may often need those same accommodations. Experimenting with different course delivery models, like the inclusion of telepresence robots, could have a significant impact on engaging online learners (Rinfret, 2020). As I mentioned, many of our undergraduate students may not be as traditional as they may have been in the past. You might find that more of the students are working full-time jobs or in jobs with different types of shifts, and some online education might be helpful for them.

Testing out different class times and different modalities is something that can be very helpful when planning undergraduate public affairs programs. It may be the case that students need more night classes or more daytime classes. Or they might need online courses. Some of the modality issues will be unique to your institution and what you are able to do.

Knowing your student body and your student profile is very important, and this may not always be the entire university's profile. Sometimes, our degrees may have different overall profiles, so making sure that we know the uniqueness of our students is going to be very helpful in creating our undergraduate programs.

Pipeline Development

Undergraduate education is a place that starts or continues the foundation of interest in professions in public and nonprofit organizations. One of the reasons why this might be so helpful is that not only does it help us develop our undergraduate programs, but it also lays the foundation for those who might be interested in master's level work. Making sure that we value our undergraduate programs as a recruitment tool or a pathway tool to graduate education is something that should be at the top of mind for our undergraduate program developers. Many institutions allow things like accelerated BA or BS/MPA degrees. That's something that we should make sure that our undergraduate students know about. It always hurts my heart just a little when I meet a student who just graduated from our university and is joining our master's program but didn't take advantage of or didn't know about some of our pathway and pipeline programs that might have been available to them. These programs are helpful because they often allow undergraduate students to take graduate coursework at the undergraduate cost level. At some universities, students are able to even complete up to one whole year of their master's program as an undergraduate student. Making sure our students are aware and knowledgeable of these types of programs should be one of the main things that we think about developing future public leaders. Kohler and Cropf (2007) document several factors that aid in the success of accelerated BA-MPA programs. This article has a unique focus on nontraditional students, who could be the student profile in many public administration programs.

We have a responsibility to make sure that our students are able to make a timely progression toward their degree. However, if they desire to continue to graduate coursework, those options should be available. We want to make sure that we have those pathways available for them. We shouldn't look at our undergraduate students as the solution to enrollment issues at the master's level, but we shouldn't discount them either. Often, once we get to master-level programs, we have students from a variety of professions and from a variety of measures that come to the MPA programs. However, we have a great opportunity to have students who have undergraduate degrees available to them and have taken advantage of pathway

36 Madinah F. Hamidullah

programs that help them with the affordability of higher education. This helps give them the richest degree that they can have to connect whatever they're passionate about to whatever profession they desire.

Diversity of Students

I know there's been a little discussion about transfer students and major-changing students, but the diversity of student profiles at the undergraduate level is something that we can't ignore, especially the diversity of our students. I've had the pleasure of teaching at one of the most diverse campuses in the country. While this may bring about some very interesting and challenging classroom discussions, I will say that the makeup and the composition of students' life experiences, background profiles, and languages have only made my teaching experiences better. My students have made my teaching experiences better, and they often challenge me to be better.

Often, I tell students I learn just as much from them as I hope they learn from me. This could be something as simple as them keeping me up to date on what's most recent in social media news or what's most exciting in the things that they care about. I really have considered my classrooms to be a two-way learning environment. I still remember when I had a student telling me that she was doing research on Instagram. I remember laughing as this was in the early days (over 10 years ago) before Instagram really became a thing, and now you can directly cite social media. There's an APA citation style for social media content. If you can name any online media, you can cite it. Often, it is a place where people share their research and their information; I was just not used to it, and it was new. Like I said, I've learned so much from my students.

Considering the makeup of what our students look like and the makeup of what our community looks like is something that we must keep in mind when it comes to public affairs education. One thing that I like about some accreditation requirements is the profile, not just of the student body but also of the community in which you serve. Sometimes, recruitment of faculty can be challenging, but programs can engage speakers and community leaders to participate in our programs. Community engagement has been one way that some programs have found that nice balance. And that's the balance needed if faculty/staff are not ingrained in the community. As faculty, we must make sure that we're in touch with the students and the individuals with whom they will interact. Just as much as I think it's important to have appropriate pathways to graduate education, it is also of the utmost importance that we have appropriate career pathways laid out for students. If our programs in public affairs can approach higher education with a "both-and" mentality, our programs will be better off, and our students will have better outcomes because we have directly matched the needs of the community with the needs of the students.

Creating Engaging Public Affairs Education Experiences

Experiential Philanthropy in Courses

One of the exciting programs that I was able to bring to the classroom was experiential philanthropy. Through this program, two of my classes and the Cooperman College Scholars program were awarded over to distribute to local nonprofits in the Greater Newark Community. We were able to combine classroom knowledge with researching how local organizations put the theory into practice. "A Philanthropist is . . . You" (McDougle & Patton, 2019) documents the experiential philanthropy learning of the Cooperman College Scholars, which I had the pleasure of leading.

Curriculum and Program Development

As the director of the undergraduate program, we developed partnerships with local county colleges. We developed programs where students entering community colleges would be able to transition to Rutgers Newark seamlessly. We felt this process would serve as an effective recruitment tool and aid in the retention of students while in their two-year associate degree program. During my time as program director, we developed three enrollment pathway programs with county colleges. Some of our most promising undergraduate and graduate students at our school have come from county colleges, and I aspire to continue developing programs to keep enrollment pathways and pipelines open.

During my time as the undergraduate director, I worked closely with the administration of the MPA program. We formalized our accelerated BA/MPA degree program and developed several partnerships with local and international universities. In addition to serving as the undergraduate program director, I have served on both the PhD and MPA committees. This has allowed me to be on the other side of graduate education and influence the decision-making process on the admittance of our students.

Professional Organizations

Professionally, I have served as the Undergraduate Committee chair for NASPAA. In this capacity, I served on the conference committee and chaired the undergraduate program track that was featured at the 2020 annual conference. During my time as committee chair, we were also able to establish the first Undergraduate Education section for NASPPA. This will be a wonderful way to get more support for the exciting work that is taking place at the undergraduate level in public affairs education. I also served as the Undergraduate Diversity Scholars program chair for the Association for Research on Nonprofit Organizations and Voluntary Action (ARNOVA). Through ARNOVA, I lead the implementation of the Undergraduate Diversity Scholars Program, which helps give students exposure to graduate education opportunities and research areas in nonprofit education.

With both appointments, I work directly with administrative staff and executive directors at top international organizations. While this work is focused at the undergraduate program level, the networks and connections would translate well and benefit graduate programs as well. My professional service continues to show that I contribute to the field of public and nonprofit administration locally and nationally. Leading both of the undergraduate education committees at major professional associations has been an honor, and I know I will continue to work with both organizations in various ways. I encourage undergraduate program directors to get involved in professional organizations and committees. Conferences and committee participation allow us to share our challenges and our wins.

Reflections on Community Engagement and Service

As the director of the undergraduate program (Fall 2012–Spring 2018), I lead the transition for the undergraduate program from Public Service to Public and Nonprofit Administration during my first year in the position. During my time as the second director of the undergraduate program, the major became one of the fastest-growing majors on the campus. Each course description was updated or developed to reflect this new direction. Promotional information and the website description of the program were updated as well. With the support of the undergraduate executive committee, we developed the direction for the undergraduate major. We continued to improve our delivery of a well-rounded education that prepares our students for work in public and nonprofit institutions.

One way we do this is by enhancing our internship program and expanding community engagement opportunities. Our internship opportunities were a major attraction for students looking to explore public or nonprofit organizations. One of the benefits of being directly involved in community service is meeting people who have placements for our students. Placements that I have facilitated included hospitals and various positions in local government. The president of the hospital was so impressed with our first intern placement that he welcomed the opportunity to enter a formal arrangement with our program. This was a great opportunity for our students as many of them are interested in healthcare administration. When keeping student diversity in mind, programs should be attentive to the need for both paid and unpaid internship opportunities, as this could create an equity imbalance (Baker & Johnson, 2021).

Conclusion

Undergraduate and Graduate Program Instruction

Many of the students in undergraduate programs are looking for instruction that they can directly apply to their future or current places of employment. As a result of teaching the Leadership course, I have developed new initiatives for this course. In the past, this course has dealt with leadership techniques, characteristics, and traits. Moving forward, the course will also have students look internally at their personal leadership philosophy and encourage them to explore nontraditional paths to being successful leaders. Many of the readings will be from journals and not a formal textbook. In the last two years, I have worked to make sure the voices that students heard were more representative of the society that they are a part of. Pulling in different approaches to leadership and service from people of color and women has been a focus in my teaching. I often offer the students the chance to read historical theories and then contrast them with examples of the theories in practice in our local community. This has been a very rewarding experience for students and has been a constant learning experience for me.

Service learning is a very interactive class where students are constantly encouraged to find ways to link their passion with the service they do and are ultimately challenged to see how that can lead to a profession. Many innovative *TED* talks as well as contemporary knowledge about how to attain success in life are incorporated into this class. With virtual teaching, I was able to invite former students back to speak with them during prerecorded interviews. This was a great chance for students to see the possibilities that can be gained firsthand from their peers during a service-learning experience.

In the MPA program, I taught Introduction to Public Administration, Managing Public Organizations, and Human Resource Management. These classes are directly related to my main research areas but are often linked to courses offered in our undergraduate program. One method I employ to keep these courses exciting is to incorporate popular public administration cultural references as a teaching tool. In many classes, I show episodes of Parks and Recreation or The Office, popular network television programs. These programs bring class lectures to life, and students often tell me how this additional dimension of instruction has positively impacted them. I've also had the pleasure of teaching Leadership, Equity, and Diversity. This was a great experience for expanding my teaching and service to the school. Teaching at all programs and now directing an MPA program, undergraduate public affairs education has always been special to me. I think it is because I have seen the "spark" happen many times in my undergraduate class.

Students must be offered the opportunity and pathway at both the graduate and undergraduate levels to see the relevance of classroom learning in real-world applications. Teaching in different environments has given me exposure to varying campus experiences that have greatly enriched my research interests and teaching ability.

Being My Authentic Self

One thing that I learned a little later than I wish I would have is why being my authentic self was so important in my teaching journey. It's especially important when it comes to teaching undergraduate students because they will humble you. I only say that because they are not afraid to speak up on certain things, they're not scared to give unsolicited feedback, and they're not afraid to say things about what is going on or any recent current events. Because of some of those reasons, I wish I had just been comfortable with being myself a little earlier on my journey. This is not because I didn't think people would like me. I was modeling my teaching behavior after how other people taught. In certain ways, as a newly minted PhD, I mirrored others. Looking back, I was an image or the compilation of a lot of different faculty that I had had throughout my life. This never really worked because I wasn't necessarily me. Maybe I should say I wasn't being the best me I could be, for lack of better words.

With that being said, it was clear that I wasn't being myself, and I think that that was reflected in my evaluations, even in my interactions with students. It was clear that they enjoyed the class, but something just always seemed to be missing. It took a while for me to realize that what was missing was me. What was missing was my own me bringing myself to the classroom. I was missing bringing my own experiences, my background, and my types of thoughts and views to public affairs education. Once I started doing that, I felt better. In return, I feel like the students felt better. I think everybody was just better all the way around when I got a little more comfortable in the classroom! I realize now that everything comes with time. Being fresh out of graduate school, I didn't think I had a choice but to use other professors as my example, so it took me a few semesters to develop my style.

When I graduated from my PhD program, I had been in college for the last 10 years, and sometimes, I wasn't much older than many of my students. Understanding how to strike that balance just took a little bit of time. When I felt like 'I got it,' I realized I actually pulled more on some of that early educational journey that I had when I went to college as a dance education major. I realized that many of the things that I learned in my teaching young dancers classical ballet (that was an actual course name) and in my other classes that worked on merging dance and education were skills that I could apply to any classroom. How to structure a class, how to provide feedback, and how to make sure you have appropriate test measures were all things I pulled from my experience in dance. I didn't realize how much I learned in my dance degree, and my leaning into my past was a big part of being authentic in myself. Once I settled into being me, the whole teaching environment became much clearer and much more engaging for everybody.

It's not always easy to say, I'll just be myself because sometimes you don't always know how that's going to be received. Students at any level seem to appreciate it a little more when they think you're being genuine with them and genuine about how you feel about the class. I think if I could stress one thing when it comes to teaching undergraduate public affairs classes, it would be to make sure that you are yourself and that you are trying to be comfortable even when having difficult conversations. Some of the topics that we must cover in public affairs courses are not easy, and depending on where you live, some of those topics could get you into trouble with your human resource systems, governing bodies, board of regents, and even the community. We must protect our classroom environment, so I would encourage people to look for ways to strike those balances and explore different types of programs for education preparation, classroom management, and things of that nature. We don't have to do these things alone, and often, our universities have programs and resources to help with this. Programs like those offered by the Association of College and University Educators or the National Council for Faculty Diversity might be good programs to see if your university already has a membership.

Additionally, there may be training opportunities in your public affairs associations that you can participate in. Many organizations have webinars that you could join in when you have a chance to. Sometimes, I may put a webinar on and listen to it even though I may not be able to commit fully to sitting there and being on camera. I'm still benefiting from hearing the presentation, and I'm still supporting my fellow speakers. Part of being your authentic self is knowing where you may need opportunities for growth and where you may need opportunities to learn more about what is going on.

References

Baker, D. L., & Johnson, M. (2021). Social inequity on the Network of Schools of Public Policy, Affairs, and administration's doorsteps: Unpaid governmental internships. *Journal of Public Management & Social Policy, 28*(1), 5.

Gannon, S., Tracey, D., & Ullman, J. (2018). Bolstering graduates' success through working as student ambassadors in university widening participation programs. *Higher Education Research & Development, 37*(4), 715–729. https://doi.org/10.1080/07294360.2018.1455643

Kohler, J. M., & Cropf, R. A. (2007). Creating an accelerated joint BA-MPA degree program for adult learners. *Journal of Public Affairs Education, 13*(2), 383–401. https://doi.org/10.1080/15236803.2007.12001486

Larsson, C. F., Marshall, B., & Ritchie, B. (2022). The alumni project: Fostering student-alumni engagement in the curriculum. *Journal of Education for Business, 97*(4), 253–260. https://doi.org/10.1080/08832323.2021.1932704

McDonald, B. D., Decker, J. W., Leight, M. D., & Abbott, M. (2021). To accredit or not to accredit. In M. Hamidullah (Ed.), *Undergraduate public affair education: Building the next generation of public and nonprofit administrators* (pp. 103–118). Routledge.

McDougle, L., & Patton, R. (2019, April). *A philanthropist is . . . you.* https://youtu.be/dEPWXICODh8

Rinfret, S. R. (2020). Telepresence robots: A new model for public administration course delivery. *Journal of Public Affairs Education, 26*(3), 380–390. https://doi.org/10.1080/15236803.2020.1744798

4

TEACHING PUBLIC AFFAIRS STUDENTS AT THE MPA LEVEL

Sara R. Rinfret[1] and Michelle C. Pautz[2]

[1]*Northern Arizona University, Flagstaff, AZ, and* [2]*University of Dayton, Dayton, OH*

Governments are one of the largest employers in the United States with individuals working in state, local, federal, and tribal organizations (Oliveira et al., 2023). Historically, public service careers were touted as one of the most admirable professions, with an ability to give back to a person's community. However, in 2024, public sector employees confront myriad issues from bureaucrat bashing, burnout due to a global pandemic, and navigating difficult political environments (McCandless et al., 2023). Amidst these circumstances, higher education plays an instrumental role in shaping the government workforce and demonstrating the importance of public service education.

Across the globe, public and private higher education institutions offer a terminal, graduate degree – Master of Public Administration (MPA). These programs offer a core curriculum (e.g., human resource management, budgeting, policy analysis, public administration, organization behavior, and ethics), often including regionally focused electives for degree completion. Individuals who enroll in these programs include current working professionals (in-career) as well as pre-career students (those individuals who have recently completed undergraduate degrees with little to no professional work experience). The central focus of an MPA program is simple: to provide the necessary skills for students to excel in public sector careers.

This chapter is rooted in our perspectives as faculty members who have taught in and directed MPA programs for almost two decades, and we argue we must help our students recognize the value and importance of bureaucracy. Our experiences and stories inform how we approach teaching at the MPA level. Specifically, our chapter is organized by focusing on

DOI: 10.4324/9781032671291-5

44 Sara R. Rinfret and Michelle C. Pautz

why we teach; the tools we adopt to understand our students to inform our approaches to curriculum; and be adept to the changing nature of a diverse and changing workforce. The chapter begins with an overview, defining why we teach, and understanding the students who enroll in our programs. Due to the day-to-day nuances that our students must navigate, we argue for a student-centered learning approach to teaching. We conclude with a call to action, so we do not succumb to cynical detachment, but a radical act of hope (Gannon, 2020).

Why We Teach

A story or a person's experience makes meaning of how and why they do something (see Lewicki et al., 2003; Nisbet, 2010; Rinfret, 2021). Together, we have served in a variety of roles in higher education both in direct ways with MPA programs (e.g., public administration professor, chair, and director), and in university-level capacities (e.g., associate dean, acting dean, assistant provost, and associate vice provost). Regardless of our position, we are grounded in our commitment to public service. We believe it is important to begin this chapter with our own stories because it informs our approach to teaching and serving public servants.

Professor Rinfret's trajectory as an educator is informed by her familiarity with public service. Growing up, her parents, and several members on her maternal and paternal side of her family were employed as public servants. For the first 18 years of her life, her family exposed her to a variety of public service professions – public school teacher, county attorney, public defender, bus driver, domestic violence liaison, social worker, and public health official. Because of her family, a strong public service ethos was instilled at a young age; however, it was not until Professor Rinfret completed a bachelor's degree in political science and history that she understood the significant impact of an MPA degree.

In the early 2000s, Professor Rinfret worked as a government affairs liaison for a nonprofit organization, focusing on access to Medicare and Medicaid. She attended a local career fair and came across a table promoting an MPA degree from a large public institution. In speaking with the campus' representative, she realized that she could obtain a degree in the evening, as she worked during the day. Still lacking an understanding of an MPA degree, the program offered her the ability to take a few classes as a non-degree student. In her first few classes, Professor Rinfret was intrigued by her peers, because much like her family, they came from a range of careers, at different levels – top of the organization to entry-level. Additionally, many of her faculty had decorated careers in public service, leading strategic planning efforts for large state agencies to managing human resources, to name a few. If it was not for the MPA degree, Professor Rinfret would not be in higher education today. Given her ability to connect her professional experience, with the classroom, a faculty member encouraged her to go into higher education, another venue to serve the public. Because of her MPA, Rinfret remembers the importance of connecting theory to practice and that a degree affords multiple public service pathways.

Professor Pautz has a similar story. She always loved social studies and striving to understand the machinations of government. When she began her college career, studying economics and political science was a logical outgrowth of those interests. She was fortunate to attend an undergraduate institution that had a rare curricular offering, a program in public administration. Although Pautz added this major later and perhaps less intentionally at the time, it became clear in hindsight that public administration was the natural progression of her interests and her desire to understand why the government was the way it was. Through internships in state government and connecting with pivotal mentors, she found her way to graduate studies in public administration. Deepening her understanding of government in the public sector enabled her to delve into the complexities of government and help work toward public policy goals, especially in the context of environmental policy, as a way to give back. During her MPA, her passion for understanding the "doing" of government only intensified and her love of both theory and praxis deepened, leading to her doctoral studies in the same field. In retrospect, this path seemed destined as it was the perfect amalgamation of social studies and tackling public problems, and her lifelong desire to be a teacher.

We recognize as white women that we have been afforded opportunities that might not have been available to marginalized communities. Our positionalities within our institutions serve as two key reminders: (1) we are here to serve our students and (2) provide opportunities to individuals who have different or unique stories from our own. Our own stories serve as a reminder that our public administration students come from a variety of disciplines and it is our job to ensure their success.

Understanding Our Students

As we think about our work in the academy and our teaching, it is easy for us to focus on the research questions we are trying to answer, the knowledge we are trying to ascertain, and the pursuits of the mind. When it comes to the courses we teach, it can similarly be easy for us to focus on the content we want and feel compelled to cover, and the learning we want for our students. However, before we even consider things such as learning objectives and textbook selection, we have to start with our students. Understandably, our eagerness for a new course and a new semester leaves us pondering readings and assignments, but without thinking first and foremost about who students are, we are not going to foster the learning that we desire. The consideration of who students are is much deeper than whether they are mid-career or pre-career MPA students.

In approaching any course – even if it is a course you teach with regularity – the starting point, every semester, should be: who are my students? More specifically, we should be interested in who they are as humans, as individuals. What are their backgrounds? What generations do they represent? What seminal events have defined their lives to date? These events could be significant, societal ones, such as September 11 or the fall of the Berlin Wall, and they could also be far more personal and specific. At what point in their lives did the onset of the COVID-19 pandemic affect them? Were they working in high school when the pandemic upended lives and sent them home to learn and to engage with others only through screens? Were they working in the public sector and having to endure the challenges of serving citizens when a public health emergency erupted? Were they trying to navigate their professional lives while fretting over the health and well-being of family members particularly at risk to COVID? Although we are still grappling with the impacts the pandemic will have on us as individuals and as a broader society, these are key aspects in the lives of the students in our classrooms.

Furthermore, beyond whether our MPA students are just beginning their careers or have been serving the public for decades and returning to the classroom, we have to think about what kind of careers they have and the kind of careers that they want. Are they focused at the local or regional level? Or are they working at the federal level? Or is the nonprofit community their focus? Or, perhaps, are they not particularly interested in the public sector at all? Although the Network of Schools of Public Policy, Affairs, and Administration (NASPAA) reports that more than students are enrolled in graduate programs they accredit, a sizable portion of the graduates do not work in the public sector (NASPAA, 2023).

Based on data from the academic year 2021 to 2022, 18% of graduates went on to work in the private sector. In light of the diversity of paths for our students, we have to think about the goals our students bring with them to the program and to the individual course and acknowledge that those goals may very well change over time. Even in our own experience as students, we recognize that our own goals may have changed over time and we certainly remember that our goals with a particular class varied. Indeed, lofty goals of pursuing a life of the mind may have been crowded out with practical considerations of employment. And on a more micro level, we all know students often approach research methods and statistics courses, for instance, with different goals and expectations. A fuller understanding of our students, who they are and what they are bringing to a program and to a course, is important, but the question invariably arises: how do we do this?

There are many ways to get to know our students, the experiences they bring to their learning, and what they hope to gain from that learning. A simple online survey could be created to anonymously collect information from students at the beginning of a program or at the beginning of a course. The survey could pose questions about educational goals, employment interests, background or preparedness for a particular subject, and so forth. It is critical, however, in the creation of such a survey to be clear with students about why the information is useful and how the information is going to be used. Faculty should convey that this information helps them design a course, for example, as it considers the level of interest in local versus federal government service. In every way possible, the survey should remind students completing it that their willingness to disclose honest information is intended to help their learning environment and will not be held against them.

The survey design should offer options for students not to respond to particular questions. After gathering this information, a discussion of what you as the faculty member learned and how the students' willingness to share information informed the course design, for example, is very important. Not only does this provide another venue for increasing your understanding of the students, but it also demonstrates to the students that you took seriously the information they were willing to share and how you were able to use it to help foster the learning environment you want for them. A survey could easily be designed and administered in the weeks leading up to the start of a term electronically.

Another way to advance our understanding of who our students are is to engage them in conversation. In addition to a survey – or even instead of a survey – a discussion early in the semester with the students would also enrich our understanding of them. And it would have the benefit of helping students understand one another as well. It is important to set the parameters for such a conversation so that students do not feel compelled to share or disclose information that they may not wish to in a larger group setting. Taking time to develop surveys and conversation prompts may seem challenging given the content concerns we often bring to our courses, but developing this deeper understanding of our students and doing it sooner rather than later can help not only in course and program design and assignment construction but also more profoundly in fostering a learning environment in which deep learning thrives.

We know from the teaching and learning scholarship that building community and connections is critical to learning (Felten & Lambert, 2020), and this is one key reason taking the time to understand more deeply our

48   Sara R. Rinfret and Michelle C. Pautz

students is important. Demonstrating our interest as educators in our students and their interests helps create this environment. Furthermore, we understand from the science of learning that emotional connection is paramount to facilitating learning (Cavanagh, 2016). In building such an environment that is hospitable for learning, we are also able to help our students examine their motivations for learning and surface them. Understanding motivation for learning also helps students and educators alike foster learning (Ambrose et al., 2010).

A second reason to learn about our students is that it helps us abandon the instructor-centric model of teaching and course design and embrace a learner-centric model (Gannon, 2020). Finding out about our students and creating an environment in which they believe their learning is supported and cared about is essential. "Our students cannot succeed in a learning environment in which they think they are devalued or seen as less-than. . . . To be an advocate for student learning . . . we have to be advocates for both students *and* learning" (Gannon, 2020, p. 36; emphasis original).

Our Approaches to Curriculum

As faculty, we have a good deal of discretion over the design of our courses and building curricula (though we acknowledge that there are institutional processes and constraints that can and do limit that control). For us, curriculum design is a rigorous process of active reflection and productive struggle (Trinter & Hughes, 2021). This design process is incredibly important as external pressures, including efforts by states and the increasing distrust of higher education, are increasing and trying to mold what does and does not happen in university classrooms. As stated previously, before a semester begins, we need to understand who our students are, what they need to learn, and how it can inform public-sector practices. In this section of the chapter, we use the context above to inform how we approach curriculum development at the MPA level. Specifically, we conscientiously design our MPA-level courses with an iterative approach, trying not to succumb the temptation to teach the same course content repeatedly. We apply Blessett et al.'s (2016) call to action, rethinking how we can design a public administration course for MPA students.

According to Blessett et al. (2016), "experiences outside of the dominant hegemonic discourse can serve as an opportunity to rethink unquestioned assumptions about people, place, worth, and deservingness" (p. 268). And, if we do not broaden our conversations, we will remain developmentally immature as a discipline (Gooden, 2015), continuing to advantage whites, penalizing non-whites (Alexander & Stivers, 2020; Epp et al., 2014; Fording et al., 2011), and perpetuating structures that are insidiously dominated by whiteness and masculinity (Pandey et al., 2022). We use this call to action to offer sample ideas about how we design our curriculum at a macro level.

We argue that curriculum design should consider a culture of care for student learning and the value of public service. A pedagogy of care for student learning affords faculty in MPA programs the space to consider how we can most effectively advance learning so our students can work in a diverse and changing workforce. According to Miller and Mills (2019), "[A]s institutions of higher education wrestle with greater pressure to retain students and recognize the myriad of ways that faculty contribute to student success, the research on caring as an important factor in student engagement and persistence becomes increasingly relevant" (p. 81). Many of our MPA programs contain a classroom of multigenerational students. For example, the average age in Professor Rinfret's MPA classes is 25–65 years of age. Therefore, we can use the multigenerational classroom to consider how to design our curriculum from the pedagogical viewpoint of caring about what our students learn. Additionally, approaching our courses with care for our students allows us to try and mitigate burnout that is increasingly pervasive in higher education (Malesic, 2022; Pope-Ruark, 2022). This emphasis on care for students helps ensure that we keep what motivates us as educators at the center of our work which is vital in contending with burnout (Dewey et al., 2023).

We know that the public administration classroom has changed dramatically since its inception and often use the pre-course survey to aggregate, across responses, how their students like to approach learning, their background, and what their concerns are for the semester. Then, on the first day of class, the aggregate information is shared with the class, without identifiers on how we will approach learning together. During one semester, for example, several students wanted to connect course content with what was occurring in their work or how they could receive a job. Therefore, at the end of each class session, we spent the last 10 minutes of the class or so discussing how the content was relevant to their current work. If students were not employed, current events were offered for additional points of reference. Taking this approach to student learning is an evolution, changing with each semester and modality. Students tell us they appreciate that their approaches to learning are considered at the beginning of each semester. We also are explicit in connecting how students' input has a through line to particular dimensions of the course syllabi and approach. One of the best pieces of advice Professor Pautz ever received about teaching is always to tell students why, whether that is why a reading is included, a topic is not included, and the like. In her experience, this is sage advice and she goes so far as to tell students that they should always be free to ask her why about anything in the course and she should have an answer.

Goodsell (2014) reminds us that the U.S. bureaucracy is effective, innovative, and one of the best in the world. However, if you turn on the news and scan through one of the many social media outlets, public servants are vilified. Consider the global pandemic where public health officials were threatened for implementing mask mandates or in recent elections where poll workers were threatened due to the outcome of the 2020 presidential election. Nevertheless, another important aspect of our approach to designing a curriculum is the value and importance of the public sector. We offer a few examples for consideration.

For example, how we approach learning about public service education is essential. In conducting a cursory review of more than 10 MPA programs nationally, their foundation courses, adopt a white-centric lens, using readings that do not recognize the representative nature of our student bodies, bureaucracies, the public we serve, or its value pairing. Pairing some of the traditional public administration canon (e.g., Wilson, 1887) that are inherently racist (Starke et al., 2018), with contemporary readings such as Peggy McIntosh's (1989) *White Privilege: Unpacking the Invisible Knapsack,* Guy et al.'s (2015) *Emotional Labor: Putting Service in Public Service*, or short videos about why people choose public service, we present myriad perspectives of how and who defines public administration. Therefore, as faculty, we can set the tone for a learning space that invites learning through a diversity of perspectives.

Another aspect of placing value on the importance of public service is what we do in practice in the classroom. Grading is yet another example of our pedagogical practices as faculty, and more fundamentally, a manifestation of our approach to facilitating learning. We have been normalized by our institutions to use a traditional grading system, which can perpetuate marginalization. If we want to mirror the public sector, we have made a concerted effort to reconsider how we evaluate our students through the lens of what happens in public-sector organizations by adopting ungrading. "Ungrading requires leaving grades out of the student evaluation process. Students do not receive grades for assignments or other assessments, rather, they receive helpful, qualitative feedback that spurs further learning instead of halting it" (Baylor University, 2023). According to Gibbs (2020), "when teachers give feedback together with a grade, the students see the feedback as justification for the grade, but if there is feedback without a grade, then students can see the feedback for its own sake and act on it" (p. 96). In other words, removing a numerical score or letter grade helps students learn and improve by focusing on feedback rather than a summative evaluation.

Table 4.1 illustrates an example of how a class could incorporate competency-based evaluation, modeling the workplace (e.g., performance evaluation). During the semester, for example, the instructor would not

Teaching Public Affairs Students at the MPA Level **51**

TABLE 4.1 Sample Performance-Based Grading

Evaluative Criteria	Description	Letter Grade
Below Expectations (BE)	1. Does not meet assignment expectations or work is not commensurate with graduate-level work (e.g., writing is rushed)	C
Met Expectations (M)	1. Meets the stated criteria for all assignments; 2. Meets due dates for all assignments; 3. Actively participates in *all* class discussions; 4. Asks thoughtful questions during discussions and conversations with the professor, guest speakers, and classmates; 5. Edits all assignments, using course writing guidelines (listed at the top of this page in the syllabus); 6. Uses evidence (refer to readings, link to real-world experiences) in semester discussions and participates clearly and concisely, staying within assignment expectations; 7. Completes mid-semester and end-of-semester learning evaluations; and 8. Checks email and Canvas class site regularly and is responsive to class inquiries.	B
Exceed Expectations (E)	Do everything that you must do to earn an M in addition to: 1. Receive critiques during discussions and written work in a professional and nondefensive manner; 2. Demonstrates a strong commitment and willingness to learn and grow from class assignments; 3. Utilizes the campus writing center to complete quality, written work; 4. Turns in assignments that are concise, carefully edited, and easy to read; and 5. Produces creative, unique assignments (e.g., doing outside research, beyond what is already expected; during discussions make connections across content about why something is essential or challenging, encouraging classmates to work through materials together).	A

Source: Created by the authors.

assign quantitative scores to individual assignments; instead, they would provide written feedback a specified timeline. In the feedback on each assignment, students will know if they exceeded (E), met expectations (M), or are below expectations (BE). In adopting this approach to grading, students begin to focus on the quality of their work, realizing that it is like what occurs in their current or future careers.

This chapter has covered a lot of ground, but as administrators and faculty, we are focused on student success. Over the decades of our professional lives to date, we have pushed ourselves to find new ways to teach at the MPA level and our samples come from our lived experiences. In a recent *Seattle Times* op-ed, Kiran Ahuja (2023), director of the U.S. Office of Personnel Management, noted that we need to do a better job of telling our story about the importance of public service. He eloquently stated as follows:

> For me, working as a public servant is more than the pay and benefits. I started my career as an attorney in the Department of Justice before spending six years supporting underserved communities and leading the White House Initiative on Asian Americans and Pacific Islanders. Through my years of experience in public service, I have seen firsthand the value of investing in our people and bringing in new leaders. That's the power of public service. We are hopeful that our chapter encourages us to continue to tell our story, but that this story is iterative and adaptive.

We have approached writing this chapter by using our own stories to illustrate why we must understand our students by adopting a pedagogy of care to continue to reinforce that public service does matter.

Hope for the Future of Public Service

MPA programs serve as an essential path for career development for current and future working professionals in a variety of positions in local, state, federal, tribal, and nonprofit organizations. In 2024, higher education is at the crossroads, navigating enrollment declines, budget shortfalls, and steep declines in public trust and perceived value. Undoubtedly, the budget cuts at West Virginia University resulted in the elimination of their MPA program (Weaver, 2023). The outcome of this decision is frustrating for public administration faculty but serves as an important reminder for us to tell our story, by partnering with our students to demonstrate the value of a public service education. We posit a few final takeaways to summarize how and why we teach at the MPA level, the focus of this chapter.

Borrowing from Kevin Gannon's *Radical Hope: A Teaching Manifesto*, we suggest that our approach to teaching in MPA programs and further developing this and future generations of public servants, we can chip away at the ails of the public sector. Our approach in the classroom is a representation of who we are and what we value, which is why starting from a foundation of serving our students and understanding who they are is critical. Both the public sector and higher education are under attack from a variety of sources and for a variety of reasons, but this should not come as a surprise to those of us in public administration as it has arguably long been our context. We need to use the context of our field to inform our practices as educators.

Perhaps we are best served by revisiting our motivation as educators, just as we encourage our students to do so. Pautz and Vogel (2020) utilized widely used indicators of public service motivation to look at the motivations of faculty in political science and public administration programs and Dewey et al. (2023) and McCandless et al. (2023) built on this (and other work) to argue that as faculty across higher education are feeling burned out, that we must return to our underlying motivations to rekindle our passion for our professional work. In revisiting our own origin stories for this chapter, we are reminded of why we do what we do. We were reminded of why we are passionate about the public sector and about helping others learn. And we realize that "[t]eaching is a radical act of hope. It is an assertion of faith in a better future in an increasingly uncertain and fraught system" (Gannon, 2020, p. 5). Our goal in writing this chapter is to engender careful reflection of why we all do what we do and how we endeavor to shape current and future public servants.

References

Ahuja, K. (2023, December 8). Next-gen tech leaders, ask what you can do for your country. *Seattle Times*. https://www.seattletimes.com/opinion/next-gen-tech-leaders-ask-what-you-can-do-for-your-country/

Alexander, J., & Stivers, C. (2020). Racial bias: A buried cornerstone of the administrative state. *Administration & Society*, 52(10), 1470–1490. https://doi.org/10.1177/0095399720921508

Ambrose, S. A., Bridges, M. W., DiPietro, M., Lovett, M. C., & Norman, M. K. (2010). *How learning works: Seven research-based principles for smart teaching*. Jossey-Bass.

Baylor University. (2023). *Ungrading*. https://atl.web.baylor.edu/guides/assessing-student-learning-and-teaching/ungrading

Blessett, B., Gaynor, T. S., Witt, M., & Alkadry, M. G. (2016). Counternarratives as critical perspectives in public administration curricula. *Administrative Theory & Praxis*, 38(4), 267–284. https://doi.org/10.1080/10841806.2016.1239397

Cavanagh, S. R. (2016). *The spark of learning: Energizing the college classroom with the science of emotion.* West Virginia University Press.

Dewey, J. L., Pautz, M. C., & Diede, M. K. (2023). How do we address faculty burnout? Start by exploring their motivation. *Innovative Higher Education, 49,* 521–539. https://doi.org/10.1007/s10755-023-09685-2

Epp, C. R., Maynard-Moody, S., & Haider-Markel, D. P. (2014). *Pulled over: How police stops define race and citizenship.* University of Chicago Press.

Felten, P., & Lambert, L. M. (2020). *Relationship-rich education: How human connections drive success in college.* Johns Hopkins University Press.

Fording, R. C., Soss, J., & Schram, S. F. (2011). Race and the local politics of punishment in the new world of welfare. *American Journal of Sociology, 116*(5), 1610–1657. https://doi.org/10.1086/657525

Gannon, K. M. (2020). *Radical hope: A teaching manifesto.* West Virginia University Press.

Gibbs, L. (2020). Let's talk about grading. In S. D. Blum (Ed.), *Ungrading: Why rating students undermines learning (and what to do instead)* (pp. 91–104). West Virginia University Press.

Gooden, S. T. (2015). PAR's social equity footprint. *Public Administration Review, 75*(3), 372–381. https://doi.org/10.1111/puar.12346

Goodsell, C. T. (2014). *The new case for the bureaucracy.* CQ Press.

Guy, M., Newman, M., & Mastracci, S. (2015). *Emotional labor: Putting service in public service.* Routledge.

Lewicki, R., Gray, B., & Elliott, M. (2003). *Making sense of environmental conflicts: Concepts and cases.* Island Press.

Malesic, J. (2022). *The end of burnout: Why work drains us and how to build better lives.* University of California Press.

McCandless, S., McDonald, B., & Rinfret, S. (2023). Walking faculty back from the cliff. *Inside Higher Education.* https://www.insidehighered.com/opinion/views/2023/08/21/institutions-must-take-faculty-burnout-seriously-opinion

McIntosh, P. (1989). White privilege: Unpacking the invisible knapsack. *Peace and Freedom, 40*(3), 10–12.

Miller, A. C., & Mills, B. (2019). If they don't care, I don't care: Millennial and generation z student impact on faculty caring. *Journal of Scholarship of Teaching and Learning. 19*(4), 78–89. https://doi.org/10.14434/josotl.v19i4.24167

Network of Schools of Public Policy, Affairs, and Administration (2023). *Impact, growth, & value: Conveying the importance of public service education.* Network of Schools of Public Policy, Affairs, and Administration.

Nisbet, M. C. (2010). Knowledge into action: Framing the debates over climate change and poverty. In P. D'Angelo, & J. A. Kuypers (Eds.), *Doing news framing analysis: Empirical and theoretical perspectives* (pp. 43–83). Routledge.

Oliveira, E., Abner, G., Lee, S., Suzuki, K., Hur, H., & Perry, P. L. (2023). What does the evidence tell us about merit principles and government performance? *Public Administration, 102*(2), 668–690. https://doi.org/10.1111/padm.12945

Pandey, S. K., Newcomer, K., DeHart-Davis, L., McGinnis Johnson, J., & Riccucci, N. M. (2022). Reckoning with race and gender in public administration and policy: A substantive social equity turn. *Public Administration Review, 82*(3), 386–395. https://doi.org/10.1111/puar.13501

Pautz, M. C., & Vogel, M. D. (2020). Investigating faculty motivation and its connection to faculty work-life balance: Engaging public service motivation to explore faculty motivation. *Journal of Public Affairs Education, 26*(4), 437–457. https://doi.org/10.1080/15236803.2020.1776076

Pope-Ruark, R. (2022). *Unraveling faculty burnout: Pathways to reckoning and renewal*. Johns Hopkins University Press.

Rinfret, S. R. (2021). The untold stories: Women on the front-lines of environmental regulation. *Public Integrity, 25*(1), 65–76. https://doi.org/10.1080/1099992 2.2021.1994708

Starke, A. M., Heckler, N., & Mackey, J. (2018). Administrative racism: Public administration education and race. *Journal of Public Affairs Education, 24*(4), 469–489. https://doi.org/10.1080/15236803.2018.1426428

Trinter, C., & Hughes, H. E. (2021). Teachers as curriculum designers: Inviting teachers into the productive struggle. *Research in Middle Level Education, 44*(3), 1–16. https://doi.org/10.1080/19404476.2021.1878417

Weaver, A. (2023, September, 15). WVU board of governors accept most budget cuts. *WBOY*. https://www.wboy.com/news/monongalia/west-virginia-university/wvu-board-of-governors-accepts-most-proposed-cuts

Wilson, W. (1887). The study of administration. *Political Science Quarterly, 2*(2), 197–222. https://doi.org/10.12307/2139277

5

MENTORSHIP AND INCLUSIVE TEACHING IN PUBLIC ADMINISTRATION

Meghna Sabharwal

University of Texas at Dallas, Dallas, TX

My journey as an international student from India pursuing a Master's in Agribusiness Management in 2000, followed by a shift to Public Administration for my PhD in 2003, provides a unique perspective on the challenges faced by underrepresented individuals in academia. Having been the only non-white PhD student in a cohort of 13 members at the time, I encountered the need to continually prove my worth in a predominantly white, male-dominant discipline. This experience resonates with research indicating that mentoring relationships are pivotal for students from historically oppressed and diverse groups, aiding them in navigating the complexities of graduate school and beyond. At the outset, I must mention that I am encouraged by the growing diversity within our field over the past two decades. This progression highlights the importance of adapting our mentoring practices to suit the individual needs and circumstances of each student. As our field continues to evolve and embrace a broader range of perspectives and backgrounds, it becomes increasingly crucial to recognize and celebrate the unique qualities and challenges that each student brings to the table.

From the time I stood in a long line for an entire night to obtain a student visa to come to the United States more than two decades ago, I always had to prove that I am worthy of being where I am. As an immigrant and a woman of color in a very white, male-dominant discipline of public administration, I had to work harder than my colleagues to succeed. A few exceptionally well-published and well-known faculty in the field whose areas of research aligned well with my interests declined to work with me. These experiences have shaped my identity as a scholar and influenced my

DOI: 10.4324/9781032671291-6

mentoring philosophy. As a mentor, I approach students without doubting their capabilities, recognizing that their presence in a graduate program is a testament to their passion and potential. I strive to create an inclusive and supportive environment, ensuring that every student can achieve their goals by emphasizing their unique strengths. My journey underscores the importance of mentorship in fostering diversity and inclusion in academia, motivating me to empower students and bring out their best.

Mentoring, defined as a nurturing process where a more skilled person guides the professional and personal development of a less experienced individual, has garnered scholarly attention, particularly in academic settings. Formally defined, mentoring is "a dynamic, reciprocal relationship in a work environment between an advanced career incumbent (mentor) and a beginner (protégé) aimed at promoting the career development of both" (Healy & Welchert, 1990, p. 17). Research has explored the evolution of the mentor–protégé relationship (Baker et al., 2014; Bozeman & Feeney, 2009), distinctions between formal and informal mentorships (Fountain & Newcomer, 2016), importance of multiple mentoring relationships (Higgins & Kram, 2001), and the impact of psychological support and identity-similar mentors for the success of women and marginalized groups in academia (Portillo, 2007; Torres et al., 2023). Mentoring doctoral students yields positive outcomes, including reduced dropout rates in academia and enhanced collaboration between doctoral advisors and students in research and publication. Graduate students acknowledge the vital role mentors play in their training, emphasizing benefits such as role modeling, guidance, support, enhanced self-confidence, and career advice. Research suggests that faculty mentoring contributes to career development, research productivity, and publication success for PhD students (Erdem & Aytemur, 2008).

The significance of mentorship became evident to me when I had the privilege of working with my mentor, Dr Elizabeth Corley, at Arizona State University (ASU). She played a pivotal role in shaping my academic journey. As I reflect on my experiences, I realize that the excellent relationship we cultivated during my time as a doctoral student has been instrumental in my present achievements. At the outset of my doctoral program, Dr. Corley, a newly appointed assistant professor, was in search of a graduate research assistant for an NSF grant. I applied for the position and was fortunate to be selected. Working closely with Dr. Corley, I not only gained valuable insights into research methodologies but also acquired essential skills for effective mentorship. The experience went beyond the confines of research tasks; it provided me with a firsthand understanding of what it means to be a supportive and nurturing mentor. This mentor–mentee dynamic significantly influenced my approach to mentoring.

What Should One Look For in a Mentor?

A mentor should embody qualities such as expertise in the field, a genuine commitment to the mentee's growth, effective communication skills, and a willingness to share knowledge and experiences. Additionally, a mentor should inspire and empower the mentee, fostering an environment conducive to learning and personal development. My journey with my mentor highlights the transformative impact of mentorship, emphasizing the reciprocal nature of the mentor–mentee relationship and the invaluable role it plays in academic and professional success.

Mentorship, as suggested by Allen et al. (2011), focuses on nurturing the growth and development of the less-experienced party, emphasizing a dynamic relationship where processes evolve. Their research asserts that supervisors should prioritize guiding students' growth and providing necessary support, motivation, and knowledge-sharing. As students progress through their programs, supervisors must adapt their involvement to align with changing needs and competencies.

The positive impact of mentoring extends beyond the program, influencing doctoral students' research self-efficacy and predicting research productivity in subsequent years (Paglis et al., 2006). Mentorship proves crucial for professional growth, contributing to an improved working environment that influences well-being and performance (Godden et al., 2014). The establishment of a positive work environment largely relies on the mentorship quality offered by supervisors. When searching for a mentor as a doctoral student, consider asking yourself these important questions.

Is Your Mentor Committed to Your Growth?

One crucial aspect to consider in a mentor is their genuine commitment to your growth and success. A reliable mentor will advocate for you, providing opportunities for networking, co-authorship, and collaborative learning. They won't exploit your efforts but will guide you through the intricate process of publishing, ensuring you understand every step. Effective mentors set clear expectations for both themselves and you, recognizing that writing is a fundamental skill in the PhD journey. They exercise patience, allowing room for mistakes as valuable learning experiences, fostering your development in research and writing. Essentially, good mentors show you how the "samosa" is made (for my vegan and vegetarian colleagues who don't eat sausage) without expecting you to perfect making one on your first attempt.

A good mentor always prioritizes your success and places your needs ahead of their own. I once collaborated with a highly esteemed senior scholar who did not want to let go of their first authorship despite my substantial contributions as an early-career researcher. Clearly, that paper's publication meant a lot to me compared to the senior scholar who had countless publications. My advice to early-career doctoral students and assistant professors is to initiate discussions about authorship order early in the collaboration process. While it may feel gratifying to be part of a publication, it's essential not to undervalue your contributions, particularly if you've invested significant effort.

Students highly value faculty members committed to their advising and mentoring roles (Bair et al., 2004). This recognition stems from the understanding that graduate students encounter various stages and challenges, and dependable mentors can assist them in overcoming obstacles, particularly during times when progress stalls (Ahern & Manathunga, 2004). Acknowledging the potential misuse of power in the authoritative context of doctoral supervision, Lee (2008) emphasizes the importance of avoiding toxic mentorship, highlighting that supervisors' styles are shaped by their own experiences as PhD students (Delamont et al., 2000; Lee, 2008).

In a study of mentorship relationships with doctoral students in Canada, the authors interviewed 19 students representing various disciplines across three Canadian provinces in 2018. The study emphasizes the integral role of mentorship within the doctoral supervisor's responsibilities, acknowledging the potential for both positive and toxic mentorship experiences in authoritative contexts like doctoral supervision. Three mentorship quality levels were identified: authentic mentorship, average mentorship, and below-average/toxic mentorship. Authentic mentors, characterized by supportive, engaged, and mindful behaviors, positively impacted students' motivation, satisfaction, and well-being. Conversely, toxic mentors display negative attitudes, such as carelessness, impatience, disrespect, uncontrolled ego, absenteeism, and authoritarianism, which lead to stressed and depressed students, hindering progress and fostering a negative departmental culture. The study highlights the importance of understanding and addressing mentorship dynamics to promote students' well-being and successful program completion (Al Makhamreh & Stockley, 2019).

Is Your Mentor Humble?

While some may perceive humility as a weakness within this cultural context, I hold a different perspective. Humility, often overlooked in mentorship research, is gaining recognition as a crucial trait among successful leaders (Nielsen et al., 2013). As we aspire to nurture the next generation of academics, it becomes imperative for us to exemplify humility ourselves. As noted by Meier (2023, p. 316), "Humility enables one to acknowledge mistakes and actively seek corrective measures." In essence, embracing

60 Meghna Sabharwal

humility not only fosters personal growth but also cultivates an environment conducive to learning and development.

Many of us, including myself, have encountered faculty or administrators who exhibit big egos and rude behavior. In my earlier years, I often excused their behavior, attributing it to their achievements. However, as I've grown academically, I've come to reject this flawed mindset entirely. I no longer tolerate such behavior. Reflecting on why I once accepted it, I realize my socialization and cultural background may have influenced it. Perhaps it was what I considered normal or what I was regularly exposed to.

I advise doctoral students not to perceive rudeness as indicative of achievement or success. And please do not normalize such behaviors. In my view, arrogance reflects weaknesses and low self-esteem rather than prowess. A better approach is to seek mentors who exhibit humility, empathy, and respect. Look for mentors who prioritize your well-being, offer constructive feedback, and foster a supportive and inclusive environment. Consider mentors who actively listen to your concerns, acknowledge your strengths, and guide you with patience and understanding. Additionally, choose mentors who lead by example, demonstrating integrity, professionalism, and a genuine commitment to your academic and personal growth. Ultimately, selecting a mentor who aligns with your values and aspirations will contribute to a more enriching and fulfilling doctoral journey.

Does Your Mentor Care About Your Well-Being?

As a mentor, I strive to reach out to my students on a personal level, especially when I know they are navigating challenging life situations. However, I acknowledge the inherent difficulties faculty members face in providing individualized support due to personal time constraints. This is why building a community of mentors within the academic setting is crucial. I am personally familiar with the struggles of balancing time and demands, but my commitment to fostering a welcoming environment and prioritizing the well-being of my students remains unwavering.

While mentoring forms the basis of a mentor–mentee relationship, there is no denying that mentors wear various hats, serving in roles of counselor, consultant, parent, cheerleader, friend, and more. Students often will approach me to discuss not just research/teaching-related career advice but also several other concerns that are often personal in nature. They are looking for someone to hear them out, lend a listening and empathetic ear, and sometimes seek counsel. While I am not trained as a counselor, I always will refer them to experts, but at the same time, taking the time to listen and offer an empathetic ear might be all they need at that time. As mentors, we also come across students who need mental health support. This is becoming an area that faculty and mentors are increasingly exposed to. We must always refer our students to mental health experts since increasing research is exploring the prevalence of depression and anxiety among doctoral students. A cross-sectional study of 325 doctoral students in a medical university, utilizing scales to measure depression, anxiety, research self-efficacy, and mentoring relationships, found that approximately 23.7% showed signs of depression and one in five exhibited signs of anxiety (Liu et al., 2019). Factors such as grades, frequency of mentor meetings, challenges in article publication, and balancing work-family-doctoral program all correlated with depression and anxiety levels. Research self-efficacy and mentoring relationships demonstrated negative associations with mental health issues. Importantly, mentoring relationships were identified as mediators in the link between research self-efficacy and depression/anxiety. The study highlights the need for educational experts to prioritize the mental health of doctoral students, suggesting that interventions fostering research self-efficacy and supportive mentoring relationships could be effective in preventing or alleviating depression and anxiety (Liu et al., 2019).

The research findings shed light on the intricate relationship between the mental well-being of doctoral students and the pivotal role of mentoring. Recognizing the prevalence of depression and anxiety among these students, the study emphasizes the need for comprehensive support systems, particularly through mentoring relationships. Mentoring is found to be a key factor in mediating the association between research self-efficacy and mental health outcomes.

Incorporating these findings into discussions on mentoring serves to emphasize the vital connection between mental well-being and effective mentorship. Acknowledging and addressing the mental health challenges faced by doctoral students, educators, and mentors can enhance the overall doctoral experience. This understanding reinforces the significance of mentoring not only in academic and research contexts but also in promoting the holistic well-being of doctoral candidates. I hope PA/Policy programs strive to create inclusive spaces where mentors and mentees can engage in open discussions about mental health struggles without fearing repercussions. This is especially important given the increasing diversity of students in our doctoral programs, especially the growing numbers of international students.

Mentoring International Students

Each year, approximately of students enrolled in graduate public affairs programs in the United States are international (NASPAA, 2023). Embarking on a doctoral journey is complex for any student. Yet, international students encounter distinct challenges (Ku et al., 2008), such as linguistic disparities, diverse learning styles, and cultural nuances compared to their U.S. counterparts (Watkins, 1998). The concept of cultural novelty, signifying differences between host and home cultures, adds an extra layer of complexity (Mendenhall & Wiley, 1994). Common obstacles include language barriers, family separation, social adaptation, and academic role conflicts faced by foreign-born students (Zhai, 2004).

Being an international student, I empathize with the difficulties that arise from being far from family and operating within constrained resources. Frequently, I would conceal my challenges from my family to spare them the stress from miles away. This is a shared experience among international graduate students (Murguía Burton & Cao, 2022), and the question arises: to whom can they confide? Ideally, they should be able to share their concerns, anxieties, and tribulations with their mentors. The presence of role models and mentors accessible to international students is crucial. Programs should prioritize the well-being of international students, especially considering their significant representation in the job market, shaping the future of academia.

Despite these challenges, the recruitment and retention of high-quality international students in U.S. postsecondary institutions yield numerous benefits. Positive experiences can transform them into effective ambassadors, fostering favorable attitudes toward the United States upon their return (Ebersole, 1999). Enduring connections formed with institutions and alumni facilitate collaborations and relationships with international organizations (Trice, 2003). International students seeking faculty positions contribute essential global perspectives, enriching the academic landscape and preparing domestic graduates for a worldwide community (Trice, 2003). Nevertheless, despite the rising number of international students pursuing employment in academia, research on academic support mechanisms, especially for those aspiring to become university faculty, remains scarce.

Amid the evolving landscape of diverse PhD programs in public administration and policy in the U.S., there is a noticeable rise in the presence of international scholars in classrooms, conferences, and journal publications. As their numbers increase, it becomes imperative to engage in discussions about the challenges faced by international students. I resonate with these narratives, having been an international student and the sole non-white student in my cohort. Navigating the academic landscape as an international student as well as dealing with language barriers, unfamiliar administrative issues, cultural nuances, and a sense of isolation are formidable. Addressing these challenges is crucial for ensuring a more inclusive and supportive academic environment.

Mentorship and Inclusive Teaching in Public Administration **63**

Mentors are indispensable to international students for their pivotal role in easing the transition to a new academic and cultural environment. These mentors provide invaluable support by offering guidance on academic expectations, helping navigate language barriers, and assisting with cultural adjustments. Beyond academics, mentors serve as advocates, aiding international students in understanding job markets, fostering social integration, and providing a supportive space for emotional discussions. The mentor—mentee relationship becomes a conduit for cultural exchange, enriching both parties with diverse perspectives. Overall, mentors play a vital role in the holistic development and success of international students, offering a blend of academic, social, and emotional support throughout their educational journey in a foreign setting.

Thus, mentoring international students extends beyond conventional career and psychosocial support (Curtin et al., 2016; Kram, 1985) to incorporate crucial dimensions of cultural and social assistance. In addition to guiding these students through career development and offering emotional support, mentors play a pivotal role in helping them navigate cultural nuances. By emphasizing cultural and social support alongside traditional mentoring functions, mentors contribute significantly to the holistic success and well-being of international students throughout their academic and professional endeavors. I expand on the conventional model to add two other important components of mentoring international students, as shown in Figure 5.1. These are cultural and social.

In this process, mentors must exercise caution to avoid imposing their personal cultural and social beliefs on students. Instead, mentors should aim to expose students to diverse contexts distinct from their own, fostering an environment that encourages cross-cultural understanding and appreciation. By refraining from imposing a singular perspective, mentors create space for open dialogue, mutual learning, and the cultivation of a rich cultural exchange. This approach not only broadens the students' worldview but also promotes a more inclusive and respectful mentoring dynamic. The caveat here is that "mentorship needs to come from culturally competent faculty who will affirm REM (racial and ethnic minority) students' identities, validate their experiences, and assist them in navigating through the cultural incongruence between their identities and the academic environment" (Malone & Harper, 2022, p. 4).

To me, mentoring represents a dynamic exchange, a reciprocal journey where I gain valuable insights from my students. Beyond the traditional roles, mentoring becomes a mutual exploration, a shared experience of continuous learning, and the broadening of my cultural and contextual horizons. Each interaction with my students offers not only an opportunity to impart knowledge but also a chance to immerse myself in diverse

64 Meghna Sabharwal

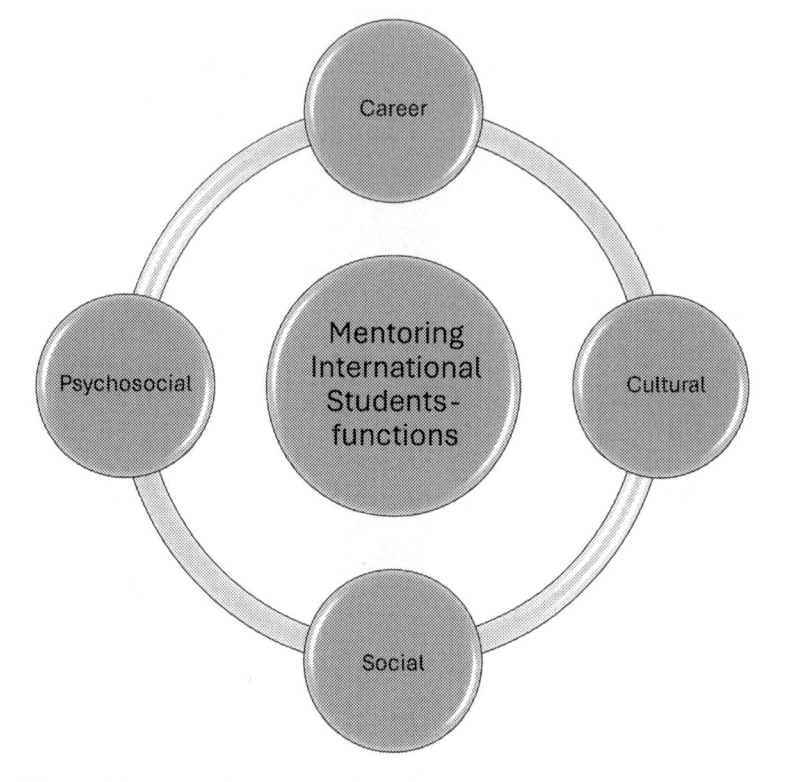

FIGURE 5.1 Mentoring International Students

Source: Created by the author building on Kram (1985)

perspectives and unique cultural backgrounds. In this dynamic process, the flow of learning extends in both directions, fostering a rich and collaborative environment where mentor and mentee contribute to each other's growth and understanding.

Mentoring Is the Key to Inclusion

Mentorship serves as a crucial path to inclusion in academic environments, fostering a sense of belonging and support for individuals from diverse backgrounds (Hall & Liva, 2021; Risner et al., 2020). Through mentorship, individuals can navigate the intricacies of academic culture, overcome barriers, and receive guidance tailored to their unique needs. Mentors play a pivotal role in creating inclusive spaces by advocating for mentees, offering insights into institutional structures, and promoting a culture of openness and diversity. By facilitating meaning-ful connections and providing a platform for shared experiences, mentor-ship contributes significantly to the promotion of inclusivity, ensuring that individuals feel valued, supported, and empowered within their academic communities.

Examples of inclusive mentoring include, but are not limited to, intro-ducing graduate students to valuable networks, accommodating diverse learning styles, being culturally sensitive to their backgrounds, and being mindful of potential stereotypes in evaluating students based on their achievements and potential. This approach fosters a supportive academic community, celebrating diversity and providing personalized guidance for PhD students.

In a study that used 12 focus groups of graduate students, with five stu-dents on average in each focus group, the major theme that emerged was the transformative nature of mentoring. Importantly, mentoring is recog-nized as a path to inclusion, facilitating students' integration into academic culture and overcoming barriers to initiating contact with supervisors. The study advocates for continued efforts to support scholarly communities, ultimately fostering an environment of inclusion, enthusiasm, and inspira-tion for graduate students (Hall & Liva, 2021).

NASPAA Study on Inclusion

In 2018, NASPAA conducted a survey targeting doctoral students in public affairs with the goal of enhancing resources and information for prospec-tive and current PhD candidates. The objective was to gain insights into the existing state of the field, identifying strengths, weaknesses, and neces-sary resources to address any gaps. To achieve this, NASPAA devised two surveys aimed at comprehensively understanding the landscape of doctoral education within the public affairs domain and its programs. The surveys aimed to gather valuable information that would enable the improvement of resources and support mechanisms for individuals pursuing a PhD in public affairs (NASPAA, 2019).

The NASPAA PhD Pathways Initiative uncovered significant themes reflecting the experiences of PhD students regarding inclusiveness. One student expressed the discouragement felt, stating, "It is discouraging . . . told to change my dissertation topic because as a Black person it would not be well received by the popular white audience." Some students of color expressed feeling less supported within their departments, as high-lighted by one respondent: "There is a diverse group of students; how-ever, those of color seem to be struggling more than others due to a lack

66 Meghna Sabharwal

of culturally responsive support." Another noted, "The administrators in my department do not show enough respect for the diversity of ethnicity. Some even showed bold discriminations to African-American Ph.D. students and Asians." These quotes underscore the significance of acknowledging individual identities. For instance, one respondent remarked, "As a white male, I am over-represented," drawing attention to concerns regarding over-representation and the influence of personal backgrounds on openness.

Furthermore, the study revealed apprehensions about faculty diversity and outdated department culture, with a student noting, "Many faculty are older, well-meaning white men. . . ." The theme of mentorship and recruitment also emerged, further shedding light on the challenges of recruiting diverse faculty candidates and mentorship patterns influenced by race and gender. The interviews also brought out concerns about institutional racism, discriminatory practices, and concerns about fairness within the academic environment. As voiced by a student who stated, "The program has an MPA director that openly makes racist comments." These thematic insights, accompanied by poignant quotes, offer a comprehensive understanding of the multifaceted challenges faced by PhD students in their pursuit of inclusiveness.

It is evident from these findings reported by NASPAA that mentoring is clearly important. However, it is most important for our BIPOC (Black, Indigenous, and People of Color), international students, and students of all genders. The importance of mentorship for women and minority students was highlighted by Portillo (2007). The author advocates for a sustained focus on mentoring minority and female students, recognizing their distinct challenges, and fostering the career aspects of mentoring relationships. Furthermore, the study promotes the idea of encouraging peer mentoring among these students, providing psychological support without overwhelming minority and female professors. It emphasizes the potential advantages of initiatives like the Diversity in Academia Initiative, stressing the importance of establishing a robust network and support systems for minority and female scholars to enhance their success in academia.

Students keenly observe both verbal and nonverbal cues, and when incongruence arises between spoken words and body language, it can evoke a sense of dissonance. As a doctoral student, I encountered instances where such dissonance made me feel excluded and unwanted, creating a disconnect between the faculty's expressed values and their actions. For example, during a feedback session with a faculty member, I noticed subtle signs of impatience, such as checking the time repeatedly despite having a scheduled 30-minute appointment. While I now understand the demands on faculty time, these instances weren't isolated, making it challenging to establish genuine connections. This experience highlights the importance of authenticity in interactions with students, emphasizing the need to align actions with professed values, especially given the diverse backgrounds and experiences that students bring to the academic environment. In my 15 years of mentoring over 50 doctoral students, I am keenly aware of the need for authentic mentoring.

Monitoring Mentoring

Monitoring mentoring relationships is important. If problematic mentor–mentee relationships are identified, flexible approaches should be adopted, such as allowing students to change mentors or providing additional research support from alternative faculty members. Creating an open and inclusive environment in the department/program is key to making students feel safe to report problematic mentors. This is not always a possibility, especially in programs with a high power distance between faculty and students. In public administration/affairs programs, international doctoral students are often singled out as the primary targets, given their heightened vulnerability (Young & Wiley, 2021).

The power dynamics existing between professors and students are characterized by an "inherent imbalance, asymmetry, and institutionalization" (Young & Wiley, 2021, p. 280). This imbalance imposes burdens that discourage students from raising their voices, fearing potential repercussions on both personal and professional fronts. Consequently, this discouragement not only deters the reporting of faculty misconduct but also raises apprehensions about possible consequences for those who decide to speak out. Although students may aspire to hold individuals accountable, the prevailing sentiment is that speaking up in such situations feels like a losing proposition, risking the jeopardy of their hard-earned achievements (Young & Wiley, 2021). The authors provide an action-oriented checklist for addressing sexual misconduct at various levels, including individual faculty members, departmental, university, associations, national, state, and federal policy, and societal levels (see Table 5.1). I recommend that each program utilize this checklist as a foundation for discussions among doctoral-level students and faculty. Hosting roundtable discussions with representatives from faculty, administration, and Title IX experts at each level would not only be beneficial but also signal the program's commitment to upholding the highest ethical standards. Alternatively, going through this exercise will also aid in pinpointing any current gaps in departmental and university-level policies as they relate to sexual misconduct.

68 Meghna Sabharwal

TABLE 5.1 Social-Ecological Framework for Confronting Sexual Misconduct in the Discipline of Public Affairs: Checklist for Action

Individual Faculty Members

- Have you expanded and strengthened mentoring relationships as a protective factor?
- Do faculty know and practice effective bystander intervention techniques?

Public Affairs Departments

- Do you have a no tolerance policy? Have you defined the nonnegotiables? Have you communicated the program's no tolerance stance?
- Is your leadership accessible to students, physically and emotionally?
- Do you have checks and balances and connection points in place throughout your program?

Universities

- Do you provide meaningful faculty oversight through annual evaluations and committee reviews?
- Have you formalized the back channels?
- Have you banned predatory NDAs as a settlement agreement term?
- Are your retirement procedures amended to prohibit faculty from filing early retirement paperwork during an active Title IX investigation?
- Are your processes and policies on sanctions for faculty sexual misconduct findings up to date?

Academic Associations for Public Affairs

- Have you taken a no tolerance stance?
- Do you bar individuals with substantiated Title IX findings?
- What protections have you developed for policing against predators at your conferences?

State and Federal Policy

- Have you advocated for a publicly available, searchable database of all substantiated Title IX reports?
- Does your state require sanction decisions be made independent of anyone with a conflict of interest?
- Do your state statutes support faculty termination for sexual misconduct?

Academia as Society

- Have you acknowledged academia's responsibility for its sexual misconduct footprint? Do you actively normalize conversations about ending sexual misconduct?

Source: Young and Wiley (2021, p. 284) (used with permission).

Teaching PhD Students

While mentorship plays a pivotal role in the success of doctoral students, the classroom elements of teaching at this level are equally vital. They are instrumental in imparting foundational knowledge, critical research and analytical skills, fostering teamwork and collaboration, honing presentation abilities, mastering the craft of teaching, and more. Teaching is not only a privilege but also a profound responsibility that I cherish every day. However, teaching doctoral students goes beyond just imparting knowledge; it involves shaping the future of academia, research, and nurturing the next generation of scholars who will lead in their respective fields. It is an opportunity to inspire and empower these students to make significant contributions to their disciplines and society. As educators, we play a pivotal role in nurturing their intellectual curiosity, critical thinking skills, and passion for discovery, ultimately preparing them to become leaders and innovators in academia and beyond.

Utecht and Tullous (2009) outline five critical drivers (CDs) for effective teaching: Connect, Concern, Competence, Clarity of Impact, and Conducting the Class Fairly. These components emphasize the importance of fostering rapport with students, demonstrating genuine care, possessing deep subject knowledge, structuring courses for clarity, and ensuring fair assessment practices. These are important skills that we must model to our doctoral students. In this section, I outline my personal teaching philosophy and highlight a few pedagogical methods I use in my graduate classes.

In my experience, teaching and learning are mutual processes, and both teacher and student play critical roles. Good teaching requires the teacher to grasp the subject deeply and present it in an interesting and accessible manner. Meanwhile, learning is an individual journey requiring active involvement and effort from the student. I aim to create a positive and inclusive learning environment by fostering respect, curiosity, and open communication, as well as by providing hands-on learning opportunities. Recognizing each student's unique background and experiences, I work to create an inclusive curriculum that meets the needs of all students.

The flipped classroom technique has emerged as particularly effective for doctoral students in my teaching experience. This innovative method revolves around assigning pre-class readings and activities, thereby optimizing in-class time for interactive discussions and deeper learning engagements. Through this approach, I've witnessed heightened student engagement, fostering a deeper grasp of course content and encouraging students to assume greater responsibility for their learning journey. By adopting the flipped classroom model, I strive to cultivate a dynamic and student-centered learning environment, in line with my overarching teaching philosophy aimed at empowering learners to participate in their educational experience actively.

In my teaching, I prioritize inclusivity and diversity by implementing a range of strategies to support the success of all students. This includes integrating readings authored by BIPOC (Black, Indigenous, and People of Color) and women faculty members, ensuring their full names are prominently featured in the syllabus. Moreover, I actively incorporate literature from diverse countries to provide students with a global perspective and enrich their learning experience.

By curating a curriculum that reflects diverse voices and perspectives, I aim to foster an inclusive learning environment where every student feels valued and represented. Additionally, I offer flexible learning activities to accommodate various learning styles and preferences, promoting group work to encourage collaboration and peer learning. Open discussions are facilitated to allow students to share their perspectives and engage in meaningful dialogue. Furthermore, I provide opportunities for personalization, allowing students to connect with the material on a deeper level and tailor their learning experience to their interests and goals. Multi-modal instruction is utilized to cater to different learning preferences, while cultural sensitivity is practiced, ensuring that all students feel respected and understood. Using inclusive language is crucial in creating a welcoming and affirming classroom atmosphere where all students feel seen and heard. I offer flexibility with deadlines, acknowledging that life can present unexpected challenges. Several of my doctoral students have families, work full-time, and have high demands on their time. As long as students submit their assignments within a given timeframe, I consider it acceptable. My teaching philosophy emphasizes reintroducing compassion and understanding into the learning process.

Continuous feedback in teaching is paramount for instructional improvement and student success. For instance, I implement exit tickets from time to time to gather ongoing feedback from my students, allowing me to refine my teaching methods continuously. Additionally, I conduct midterm evaluations to gauge the overall effectiveness and student progress. These strategies have proven successful in providing valuable insights into student learning and enabling me to adapt my teaching style accordingly. From a pedagogical perspective, continuous feedback ensures the efficacy of my teaching methods and promotes student engagement and motivation. By receiving regular feedback, we as instructors can make necessary adjustments, ensuring that our students are engaged and motivated to learn, which is a key component of successful pedagogy.

We are not just educators, but we also serve as role models for the next generation. It is incumbent upon us as instructors to train and inspire future public affairs/administration scholars. Therefore, it is upon us to devote time to introspection, reflecting on our teaching methodologies, the content we deliver, and the underlying reasons for our teaching practices (the what, why, and how of teaching). This reflective process allows us to continually refine our approach, ensuring that we are equipping our students with the necessary skills and knowledge to navigate the complexities of the world beyond academia.

Conclusion

This chapter has provided a reflective exploration of my experiences as an international student and scholar, navigating challenges in what was a new academic discipline. Despite encountering numerous obstacles, the journey has been deeply fulfilling, largely due to the invaluable relationships formed with mentors and students. I am profoundly grateful for the support and guidance of my mentors, whose wisdom has greatly influenced my pedagogy and mentoring approach. Similarly, interactions with students have enriched my teaching practice, offering diverse perspectives that broaden my understanding.

Moving forward, my commitment remains steadfast in fostering inclusive and supportive learning environments where every student feels valued and empowered. I look forward to continued growth as an educator and mentor, eagerly sharing my experiences and insights within the academic community. I am optimistic about the direction public administration is taking in fostering inclusive teaching and learning environments. Interacting with students who exhibit thoughtfulness and a strong commitment to issues of equity and justice is truly encouraging. Their dedication not only inspires hope but also indicates positive changes occurring within our field.

Furthermore, I extend my heartfelt gratitude to the editors of this book for providing this opportunity for self-reflection and granting me the freedom to write a chapter that incorporates my own experiences. Their support has been instrumental in shaping the narrative of this chapter, and I am thankful for the chance to contribute to the dialogue on mentorship and teaching in academia.

References

Ahern, K., & Manathunga, C. (2004). Clutch-starting stalled research students. *Innovative Higher Education, 28*(4), 237–254. https://doi.org/10.1023/B:IHIE.0000018908.36113.a5

Al Makhamreh, M., & Stockley, D. (2020). Mentorship and well-being: Examining doctoral students' lived experiences in doctoral supervision context. *International Journal of Mentoring and Coaching in Education, 9*(1), 1–20. https://doi.org/10.1108/IJMCE-02-2019-0013

Allen, T. D., Finkelstein, L. M., & Poteet, M. L. (2011). *Designing workplace mentoring programs: An evidence-based approach.* John Wiley & Sons.

Bair, C. R., Haworth, J. G., & Sandford, M. (2004). Doctoral student learning and development: A shared responsibility. *Journal of Student Affairs Research and Practice, 41*(4), 1277–1295. https://doi.org/10.2202/1949-6605.1395

Baker, V. L., Pifer, M. J., & Griffin, K. A. (2014). Mentor-protégé fit: Identifying and developing effective mentorship across identities in doctoral education.

International Journal for Researcher Development, 5(2), 83–98. https://doi.org/10.1108/IJRD-04-2014-0003

Bozeman, B., & Feeney, M. K. (2009). Public management mentoring: What affects outcomes? *Journal of Public Administration Research and Theory*, 19(2), 427–452. https://doi.org/10.1093/jopart/mun007

Curtin, N., Malley, J., & Stewart, A. J. (2016). Mentoring the next generation of faculty: Supporting academic career aspirations among doctoral students. *Research in Higher Education*, 57(6), 714–738. https://doi.org/10.1007/s11162-015-9403-x

Delamont, S., Atkinson, P., & Parry, O. (2000). *The doctoral experience*. Falmer Press.

Ebersole, J. F. (1999). The challenge and the promise of international education. *Continuing Higher Education Review*, 63(1), 98–106.

Erdem, F., & Aytemur, J. Ö. (2008). Mentoring – A relationship based on trust: Qualitative research. *Public Personnel Management*, 37(1), 55–65. https://doi.org/10.1177/009102600803700104

Fountain, J., & Newcomer, K. E. (2016). Developing and sustaining effective faculty mentoring programs. *Journal of Public Affairs Education*, 22(4), 483–506. https://doi.org/10.1080/15236803.2016.12002262

Godden, L., Tregunna, L., & Kutsyuruba, B. (2014). Collaborative application of the Adaptive Mentorship© model: The professional and personal growth within a research triad. *International Journal of Mentoring and Coaching in Education*, 3(2), 125–140. https://doi.org/10.1108/IJMCE-09-2013-0054

Hall, W. A., & Liva, S. (2021). Mentoring as a transformative experience. *Mentoring & Tutoring: Partnership in Learning*, 29(1), 6–22. https://doi.org/10.1080/13611267.2021.1899583

Healy, C. C., & Welchert, A. J. (1990). Mentoring relations: A definition to advance research and practice. *Educational Researcher*, 19(9), 17–21. https://doi.org/10.3102/0013189X019009017

Higgins, M. C., & Kram, K. E. (2001). Reconceptualizing mentoring at work: A developmental network perspective. *Academy of Management Review*, 26(2), 264–288. https://doi.org/10.5465/amr.2001.4378023

Kram, K. E. (1985). *Mentoring at work: Developmental relationships in organizational life*. Scott, Foresman & Company.

Ku, H. Y., Lahman, M. K., Yeh, H. T., & Cheng, Y. C. (2008). Into the academy: Preparing and mentoring international doctoral students. *Educational Technology Research and Development*, 56(3), 365–377. https://doi.org/10.1007/s11423-007-9083-0

Lee, A. (2008). How are doctoral students supervised? Concepts of doctoral research supervision. *Studies in Higher Education*, 33(3), 267–281. https://doi.org/10.1080/03075070802049202

Liu, C., Wang, L., Qi, R., Wang, W., Jia, S., Shang, D., Shao, Y., Yu, M., Zhu, X., Yan, S., Chang, Q., & Zhao, Y. (2019). Prevalence and associated factors of depression and anxiety among doctoral students: The mediating effect of mentoring relationships on the association between research self-efficacy and depression/anxiety. *Psychology Research and Behavior Management*, 12, 195–208. https://doi.org/10.2147/PRMB.S195131

Malone, C. M., & Harper, E. A. (2022). Liberatory mentoring as an inclusion strategy for racial and ethnic minoritized students. *School Psychology Training and Pedagogy*, 39(2), 1–13

Meier, K. J. (2023). It all depends: Reflections on the art of mentoring PhD students in public affairs. *Journal of Public Affairs Education*, 29(3), 313–326.

Mendenhall, M. E., & Wiley, C. (1994). Strangers in a strange land: The relationship between expatriate adjustment and impression management. *American Behavioral Scientist, 37*(5), 605–620. https://doi.org/10.1177/0002764294037005003

Murguía Burton, Z. F., & Cao, X. E. (2022). Navigating mental health challenges in graduate school. *Nature Reviews Materials, 7*(6), 421–423. https://doi.org/10.1038/s41578-022-00444-x

Network of Schools of Public Policy, Affairs, and Administration. (2019). *NASPAA PhD pathways initiative.* https://www.naspaa.org/data-center/download-naspaa-data/archived-data

Network of Schools of Public Policy, Affairs, and Administration. (2023). *2021–2022 NASPAA annual data report.* https://www.naspaa.org/accreditation/data-accredited-programs

Nielsen, R., Marrone, J. A., & Ferraro, H. S. (2013). *Leading with humility.* Routledge.

Paglis, L. L., Green, S. G., & Bauer, T. N. (2006). Does adviser mentoring add value? A longitudinal study of mentoring and doctoral student outcomes. *Research in Higher Education, 47*(4), 451–476. https://doi.org/10.1007/s11162-005-9003-2

Portillo, S. (2007). Mentoring minority and female students: Recommendations for improving mentoring in public administration and public affairs programs. *Journal of Public Affairs Education, 13*(1), 103–113. https://doi.org/10.1080/15236803.2007.12001470

Risner, L. E., Morin, X. K., Erenrich, E. S., Clifford, P. S., Franke, J., Hurley, I., & Schwartz, N. B. (2020). Leveraging a collaborative consortium model of mentee/mentor training to foster career progression of underrepresented postdoctoral researchers and promote institutional diversity and inclusion. *PloS One, 15*(9), e0238518. https://doi.org/10.1371/journal.pone.0238518

Torres Acosta, M. A., Chandra, S., Li, S., Yoon, E., Selgrade, D., Quinn, J., & Ardehali, H. (2023). The impact of underrepresented minority or marginalized identity status on training outcomes of MD-PhD students. *BMC Medical Education, 23*(1), 428. https://doi.org/10.1186/s12909-023-04399-7

Trice, A. G. (2003). Faculty perceptions of graduate international students: The benefits and challenges. *Journal of Studies in International Education, 7*(4), 379–403. https://doi.org/10.1177/1028315303257571

Utecht, R. L., & Tullous, R. (2009). Are we preparing doctoral students in the art of teaching? *Research in Higher Education Journal, 4,* 1.

Watkins, D. (1998). Assessing approaches to learning: A cross-cultural perspective on the Study Process Questionnaire. In B. Dart & G. Boulton-Lewis (Eds.), *Teaching and learning in higher education* (pp. 124–144). Australian Council for Educational Research.

Young, S. L., & Wiley, K. K. (2021). Erased: Why faculty sexual misconduct is prevalent and how we could prevent it. *Journal of Public Affairs Education, 27*(3), 276–300. https://doi.org/10.1080/15236803.2021.1877983

Zhai, L. (2004). Studying international students: Adjustment issues and social support. *Journal of International Agricultural and Extension Education, 11*(1), 97–104. https://doi.org/10.5191/jiaee.2004.11111

6

TEACHING EFFECTIVELY ONLINE

Saman Afshan[1], Honey Minkowitz[2], and Bruce D. McDonald III[3]

[1]*North Carolina State University, Raleigh, NC,* [2]*University of Nebraska Omaha, Omaha, NE, and* [3]*Old Dominion University, Norfolk, VA*

With the introduction of online learning, the education landscape has shifted dramatically, and public administration is no exception. Our history of online education has been tumultuous (McDonald, 2021), and there is much that we do not know about effective online programming (see McDonald et al., 2024). While some faculty have encouraged the use of online courses and programs as a way to increase the reach and accessibility of MPA programs (Yan et al., 2022), others have noted that offering online courses can provide challenges in terms of both program management and effectiveness (see Hummer & Hersey, 2023; Wukich, 2023). Public administration has not been alone in this debate. Looking across higher education, supporters of online education have pointed to the internet as a tool for providing equal access to education and affordable educational opportunities for learners across the lifespan (Bowen, 2013; Starr & Milheim, 1996). Alternatively, opponents have argued that online education is a watered-down teaching modality that offers little substantive knowledge and active experience for students (Brown & Liedholm, 2002).

While the literature has wavered on the utility of online education, using the modality during the COVID-19 pandemic suggests that online education is likely to be a central modality going forward. Consequently, researchers have been exploring the use of the internet in the classroom over the past couple of years, working to establish whether an online course can be effective and what it takes to teach effectively using the modality (Russell, 1999). This chapter will explore the deep nuances of the online learning environment in public administration education. We examine the differences among modalities of online learning in regard to effective teaching

DOI: 10.4324/9781032671291-7

and engagement. Specifically, we look at research on established pedagogical practices that improve the effectiveness of online teaching, such as active learning and collaborative projects. We begin by investigating the background of online learning in public affairs. We connect this to educational research from the fields of education and public administration that have been conducted as to the effectiveness of online learning. The chapter concludes with considerations for faculty as they engage in teaching in an online environment. In combination, this chapter intends to provide faculty, particularly early-career faculty, with an understanding of online education and guidance on how to be an effective teacher.

Online Learning in Public Affairs Education

Online learning has become increasingly common in public affairs education, providing students with flexible and accessible ways to pursue their academic and professional goals. This overview looks at the evolution of online learning in public affairs education, including its benefits, limitations, and essential concerns for both instructors and learners.

Evolution of Online Learning in Public Affairs Education

The incorporation of online learning in public affairs education has changed dramatically over time, owing to technological improvements, shifting educational paradigms, and a growing need for flexible learning alternatives (Ginn & Hammond, 2012; Naidu, 2019). Meine and Dunn (2017) trace the growth of online education to the influx of funding from the U.S. military as a mechanism for recruitment and retention. MPA programs benefitted from the fund infusion, resulting in an initial expansion of online MPA programs. However, online public affairs courses were initially limited in scope and availability, focusing on extra materials or professional development possibilities (Tallent-Runnels et al., 2006). However, as technology evolved and universities embraced digital transformation, online public affairs programs grew to include entire degree programs, certificate programs, and specialty courses targeted to the needs of a varied range of learners (Kentnor, 2015). Accordingly, the Network of Schools of Public Policy, Affairs, and Administration (NASPAA) lists 32 schools accredited to provide online education of 42 member schools that offer full or partial MPA and related programs online (Meine & Dunn, 2017).

In public affairs education, incorporating online learning presents a multidimensional setting rich with challenges and prospects (Yan et al., 2022). One of the key advantages is the flexibility provided to students, which allows them to pursue academic targets while juggling work responsibilities and personal commitments (Kazmer & Haythornthwaite, 2001; Peat, 2000). This flexibility not only simplifies access to education but also encourages a diverse student population, increasing the learning experience by exchanging ideas and insights (Gillett-Swan, 2017). However, this flexibility brings the problem of ensuring fair access to technology and support services, especially for students from underprivileged regions or with limited access to digital resources (Gulati, 2008; Stone and Springer, 2019). Bridging the digital divide and offering robust technical help is crucial in reducing inequities and fostering inclusivity in online teaching (Laufer, 2021; Warschauer, 2009).

Challenges and Opportunities in Online Education

The internet and the advent of web-based tools, like Zoom and Teams, to teach courses and take classes have revolutionized education. Nguyen (2015) noted that as online learning lost its novelty, brick-and-mortar classrooms, which held a monopoly on education, declined. Indeed, the number of students attending in-person classes declined between 2012 and 2018 from 74% to 65%, while the number of students enrolled in online courses increased from 26% to 35% during the same time period (Sublett, 2020). Barriers to traditional college and university settings, such as rigid class schedules and rising education costs, often make attendance cost-prohibitive and challenging for untraditional and working students, who usually hold one or more jobs while attending school full-time (Bartley & Golek, 2004).

The proliferation of online learning programs has expanded opportunities for higher education, albeit with associated challenges. Specifically, online courses have increased in prevalence in recent years due to the multitude of course options and the availability of online education programs, bringing more flexibility and affordability for students (Bartley & Golek, 2004; Nguyen, 2015), but the quality of the educational experience and equity of opportunity may be compromised.

Undeniably, online education is cost-effective for universities and students. State cuts in funding to colleges and universities have raised tuition rates, shifting more costs to students and their families and deterring low-income students from enrolling (Mitchell et al., 2019). In response to state funding changes, universities have increasingly relied on online education as a revenue diversification mechanism (Ortagus & Yang, 2018).

Despite these benefits and arguments supporting online education, there is little evidence that online education expands access to higher education. Studies have found that online programs primarily serve current students seeking increased flexibility or attracting mid-career professionals rather than bringing in new students, especially from traditionally marginalized populations (Sublett, 2020). Recent research has also uncovered that Black and Asian students are less likely to enroll in online courses than white students (Sublett, 2020). Furthermore, students only attending online classes are generally underserved than students in traditional or hybrid classrooms (Sublett, 2020; Tate & Warschauer, 2022). This disparity is most severe among students of color (Sublett, 2020; Tate & Warschauer, 2022).

From a student perspective, online education provides flexibility to accommodate work schedules and family routines. It also saves students time and money on transportation costs to campus, such as parking fees and commuting time. Students can also learn at their own pace in asynchronous formats. Additionally, many online programs are less expensive than traditional courses because students are not required to pay student fees at many universities, which are charged for using campus resources such as health services and recreational facilities. However, there are doubts about the quality of online education programs. For example, online program management companies (OPMs), which are for-profit companies hired by universities to create and maintain degree programs, may jeopardize program quality due to their profit motive (Wukich, 2023).

A further challenge for online education programs is ensuring academic integrity. In a recent survey, faculty expressed that online education has a higher workload than traditional classes (Yan et al., 2022). Ensuring students meet academic standards and abide by academic honesty codes in online courses can be complex. There have been mixed findings on whether more cheating occurs online than in traditional courses. Still, many novel ways to cheat in online environments exist, especially considering AI, including using AI tools to generate course products (Cotton et al., 2024; Holden et al., 2021). Holden et al. (2021) equivocate that cheating occurs at an individual level when students have opportunity, incentive, or pressure and are consistent with personal values or believe their behavior is aligned with the majority. They suggest implementing honor codes in courses, using online proctoring or by adding challenge questions to examinations.

Effectiveness of Online Programs

Consequently, the findings noted earlier present a quandary when considering the effectiveness of online education. Many studies have explored the effectiveness of online courses compared to the traditional in-person format. For example, studies on the effectiveness of hybrid courses, in which learning activities were presented in-person and fully online, found that fully online students achieved equivalent outcomes to in-person students

(Alpert et al., 2016; Bowen et al., 2014; Joyce et al., 2015; Riffell & Sibley, 2005). Riffell and Sibley (2005) attributed the result to an increased ability of students to reflect on the course material in an online format compared to that they would have in the time-limited classroom. They also found that the interactions between students and instructors were more positive and led to a deeper understanding of the material than traditional courses due to the opportunity to think and reflect, thus allowing more pointed questions. Other studies on the effectiveness of online courses, compared to traditional in-person courses, found similar results of a positive effect (see Harmon & Lambrinos, 2006; Harris & Nikitenko, 2014; Navarro & Shoemaker, 2000).

Despite there are studies pointing to online education as an effective substitute for the traditional education, some studies have found that there are either null or negative effects and performance disparities among students of color compared to white students. Russell's (1999) meta-analysis compiled the findings of studies on distance education. Based on the evidence provided by the studies, he concluded that there is no significant difference in the learning outcomes of distance-based courses, such as online classes, from those offered in a traditional modality. Still others such as Brown and Liedholm (2002) found that students in online classroom settings performed significantly worse on tests than those in traditional classes, even after controlling for GPA and ACT scores. They argued that one reason for the finding was that students in online courses tend to spend less time studying course material than their traditional counterparts, leading to lower levels of familiarity with the material when it came time for the test. These findings are similar to those found in other studies on the effectiveness of online education, with the amount of time dedicated to studying always being a contributing factor (see Hiltz et al., 2000).

Furthermore, scholars have reported performance disparities among students of color in online settings (Tate & Warschauer, 2022). Research has generally discovered that achievement gaps uncovered in traditional classrooms are exacerbated in online environments (Tate & Warschauer, 2022). For example, Figlio et al. (2013) ascertained that Latinx, low-achieving, and males performed better in in-person classes than in online classes. Similarly, Hart et al. (2018) determined that, on average, students in online classes performed worse than those in traditional classrooms. Still, Black and Latinx students had worse outcomes than white and Asian students (Hart et al., 2018).

Effectiveness of Synchronous and Asynchronous Modalities

When it comes to online learning, not all types of online classes result in equivalent outcomes. The online learning landscape can be thought of as a scale measuring the amount of in-person time within the course, including asynchronous, hybrid, and synchronous options. In a synchronous class, faculty engage with students during a scheduled time using Zoom or another video conferencing software, helping to create the feel of a traditional in-person class, albeit one conducted over the internet. Hybrid or blended courses may take different forms, combining in-person and asynchronous opportunities or synchronous and asynchronous activities. In an asynchronous class, students can engage the course material independently within a scheduled time frame. Instructors may open new modules regularly throughout the course so that there is collective student engagement on assignments, like discussion boards. Alternatively, course modules may open as students complete prerequisite assignments to move forward in the course. While both modalities are online, they offer very different approaches to the learning process.

One way to consider the differences among these modalities is how student engagement differs across the approaches. In a novel approach, HyFlex combines hybrid and flexible learning elements. This modality incorporates face-to-face (synchronous) and asynchronous experiences (Beatty, 2019). As noted previously, students in hybrid courses engage in the same combination of synchronous and asynchronous activities. In a "flexible" course, students can participate and engage in activities based on what works best for them (Beatty, 2019). Students can attend class in person, face-to-face synchronously via video conferencing, or watch recorded lectures. All course materials and classes are available in every format without compromising learning objectives.

In a study of student course performance and engagement in the HyFlex modality, Bohórquez et al. (2023) found that a majority of students (60%) reported that asynchronous options and flexibility were significant contributors to their learning. Furthermore, students relied on and preferred to use asynchronous options more than synchronous options, while in-person meetings were utilized the least (Bohórquez et al., 2023). However, students who took advantage of real-time learning through in-person or synchronous meetings had higher performance-related engagement and earned higher grades in the course than students who solely participated asynchronously (Bohórquez et al., 2023). Nollenberger (2017) also revealed in a study about a hybrid MPA course that students wanted the flexibility that online provides but also desired on-campus experiences to connect with faculty and peers.

Considering asynchronous and synchronous modalities, in their study about using tools in online courses, Oztok et al. (2013) conducted an experiment to understand better the engagement of students in these two types of online courses. The experiment consisted of students from nine online graduate education courses at a large university in Canada. Each course incorporated synchronous and asynchronous tools, which students were required to engage with over various assignments. The researchers found that engagement rates were relatively consistent across the two modes. Students who most frequently engaged with synchronous tools also tended to be those who most frequently engaged with asynchronous tools. While engagement might have been relatively consistent, Oztok et al. (2013) found that the depth of the engagement varied across the modalities, with asynchronous tools being associated with more depth. In many ways, this finding gives an interesting perspective to the work of Brown and Liedholm (2002). As noted previously, Brown and Liedholm (2002) uncovered that the depth of engagement in online courses differed from traditional in-person courses, with online students typically not having the level of engagement of traditional students. In the context of the synchronous versus asynchronous debate, the findings of Oztok et al. (2013) suggest that the reason behind Brown and Liedholm's findings is related to how the course was taught and the opportunity for thought that synchronicity provides. Relatedly, Bryan et al. (2018) determined that more intense student engagement occurs when they use online tools, such as discussion forums, to interact with peers. These findings are consistent with other research that has attributed this outcome to having more time for students to consider the course content, whereas, in an in-person classroom, students are expected to respond more quickly (Tallent-Runnels et al., 2006).

Tabak and Rampal's (2014) study about the design consideration of synchronous online learning provides additional context. Using a mixed-methods approach to understanding the effect of synchronous learning materials, Tabak and Rampal found that the opportunity to engage in course material is just as present in an online course as in a traditional one. The risk to learning is a reflection of what has already been mentioned. Synchronous learning may allow for an equal opportunity for student engagement in the course, but the depth of that engagement is reduced. Unlike the previous literature, however, Tabak and Rampal (2014) suggest why the reduction occurs. When using synchronous tools, the window of opportunity to correct a problem is much smaller. Accordingly, students depend more on the university's infrastructure to help walk the students through problems. Comparatively speaking, when using an asynchronous tool, students have more time to work with the tool and figure out the problem when issues arise.

The issue of differences in engagement depth and learning opportunities between synchronous and asynchronous learning leads to the consideration of how learning style influences student outcomes. To explore this question, Shahabadi and Uplane (2015) hypothesized that preference for modality and success in the modality may be tied to the individual student's learning style. This was tested by surveying a sample of students from six virtual universities. Respondents were given a learning style inventory test, with students being categorized as being low, mediocre, or high in academic performance. The data were then tested to see how learning style and academic performance varied across students preferring synchronous classes and students preferring asynchronous classes. They found that students who preferred asynchronous learning also preferred an assimilating and converging learning style.

In contrast, they found that students who preferred synchronous classes had a preference for assimilating and diverging styles of learning. The study also found that a key difference in a student's preference for learning style was tied to their academic performance. Low-performing students in synchronous courses have significantly different learning style preferences from those with higher performance levels. They also found that students tended to self-select into synchronous and asynchronous courses based on their preferred learning style. These findings suggest that any difference in learning outcomes between synchronous and asynchronous learning may be associated with the learning preferences of the student rather than the faculty that teaches the course.

A final consideration of the effectiveness of synchronous online courses compared to asynchronous online courses is whether student responsiveness or preference to the modality reflects how well students do in the course. Khalil et al. (2020) clearly note that students are likely to choose online courses in the future once they have had a positive experience.

The literature discussed earlier shows a difference in the level of engagement and preference based on learning styles. Consequently, there are also differences in learning outcomes. Two studies, in particular, have explored this issue. In the first, Roblyer et al. (2007) take a strict view of course effectiveness in their comparison of 43 online courses. Data on retention, achievement, and student attitudes were collected to compare synchronous and asynchronous courses. Interviews were then conducted with students, teachers, and administrators to clarify perceptions and experiences with the course modalities. While previous research indicated that asynchronous learning would achieve higher outcomes, the researchers found minimal outcome variation. For instance, students reported higher satisfaction with course content and curriculum for synchronous classes, but the score of was only marginally different from 3.58 reported for asynchronous courses.

Interestingly, students reported slightly higher scores for their satisfaction with interactions for asynchronous classes (3.35 compared to 3.32). When asked if the course met their needs, asynchronous students were more likely to report that it did, with saying the course met their needs compared to of synchronous students reporting the same outcome. Asynchronous students were also more likely to sign up for another virtual course, but the difference was minimal. Ultimately, the study was unable to find statistically significant differences in the outcomes and perceptions of synchronous and asynchronous courses.

In the second study, Dahlstrom-Hakki et al. (2020) connect the effectiveness of the course modality with the learning styles to compare the efficacy of synchronous and asynchronous classes for students with disabilities. Using a computer-mediated, blended classroom, they studied students with high-incidence disabilities. Disabilities of the students included learning disabilities, attention-deficit/hyperactivity disorder (ADHD), autism, or some combination of the three. Students were divided into either a synchronous learning module or an asynchronous module. Interestingly, the type of disability was found to have no statistically significant impact on engagement. The results point to a slight but statistically significant decline in student outcomes for those who participated in the synchronous discussion format. The findings of Dahlstrom-Hakki et al. (2020) align with the previous research on student preferences in that more participants reported that they preferred the synchronous format over the asynchronous discussions. This preference was related to the ability to ask the instructor clarifying questions and directly interact with the instructor and classmates. For those who preferred asynchronous discussions, a key reason for the preference was the lack of distractions in the format. The authors argued that asynchronous learning allows students prone to distractions or social anxiety to learn without the stress of their issues.

Fostering Online Engagement and Interaction

One of the primary concerns of faculty members when designing an online class is how to design the course to maximize student learning (Stavredes & Herder, 2014). Russell (1999) noted that online courses can be just as effective as their in-person counterparts. Unlike their traditional courses, however, online courses lack mid-course flexibility. When an in-person class is being taught, and the instructor recognizes that the approach is not working for the students, the instructor can rework portions of the course to improve the outcome. In an online course, this flexibility is not always possible. As such, the initial design of an online course is remarkably important, especially for achieving equitable outcomes for all students. This is particularly true when considering student engagement and interactions within the course.

While many educators traditionally prioritize teacher-driven engagement, a prevalent teaching method that educators and learners are accustomed to, emerging research suggests that empowering students with control may be more effective for the future of learning (see Beatty, 2019). What distinguishes student-driven engagement from its teacher-driven counterpart?

Teaching Effectively Online **83**

While the latter emphasizes building a connection between students and educators through dynamic lectures, the former strives to create collaborative environments, assign roles and responsibilities to students, and aid in their development through progressively challenging tasks. While there are many excellent examples of course and class design for public affairs courses (see Emerson & Gerlak, 2016; Stephens & Morse, 2023), we offer suggestions for effective online course design in this section.

Utilize Discussion Boards

Online discussion boards serve as a pathway to fostering connection and active participation within the online learning environment. The asynchronous nature of these boards provides students with advantages, allowing them additional time to gather and structure their thoughts. Moreover, it reduces the pressure of competing for space when expressing reactions and comments on their peers' posts. To fully leverage the potential of discussion boards, instructors need to exemplify that these platforms are meant for engagement, emphasizing their role beyond just being a repository for ideas that are abandoned after completing assignments.

Encourage Group Activities

During group activities, students can shift away from the conventional classroom interactions confined to the teacher-learner dynamic. Instead, they engage in collaborative efforts with their peers, operating in an environment requiring minimal teacher intervention. The educator's role involves dividing the class into small groups, offering brief guidance, and allowing learners to make academic discoveries through creativity and teamwork. Fostering autonomy in students can be enhanced by assigning them specific roles and responsibilities. For instance, rather than relying on the teacher to check their work and provide answers, students can be empowered to review each other's work, promote equal participation, and seek answers from their peers for their questions.

Set Clear Goals and Expectations

While student-driven engagement encourages teachers to adopt a more passive role, it doesn't diminish the significance of their contribution. For students to effectively take charge, they need a clear understanding of their objectives. Hence, teachers must establish explicit learning goals that outline the skills students are expected to acquire by the end of the lesson. For younger students, breaking down the ultimate goal into smaller

84 Saman Afshan, Honey Minkowitz, and Bruce D. McDonald III

achievements can serve as helpful guidelines. The next steps can be undertaken once a clear and understandable framework is in place.

Promote Student Accountability

With well-defined objectives, students can work together to reach each intermediate milestone by combining their skills and existing knowledge. The freedom to learn through personal discovery rather than passive listening motivates students and enhances their understanding of concepts. As learners become more familiar with the goal-setting process, they may construct a goal structure independently, thereby assuming genuine ownership of their learning progress. In this way, their development becomes a personal endeavor they genuinely care about, transcending the mere completion of tasks without a clear purpose.

Utilize Productive Struggle

Boredom can significantly impact learner engagement and subsequent progress. An often-cited cause is the use of uninspiring learning content that fails to challenge students and encourage them to expand their academic boundaries. Therefore, educators aiming to promote student-driven engagement often embrace the concept of productive struggle. Essentially, they assign learners tasks that progressively increase in difficulty, extending beyond their current capabilities. This approach requires students to explore new thinking avenues and leverage their collective skills to arrive at solutions. Despite the challenges, refraining from immediate intervention fosters increased self-confidence in students and enhances their creativity for future endeavors.

Monitor Progress and Make Adjustments

While your students may appear engaged in the learning process, evaluating whether this engagement translates into improved performance is crucial. Monitor your students' self-tracking data and compare that to their actual work. Assess whether they align, the pace at which they achieve their goals, and which activities yield the best results. Regularly review this data to ensure that your students are enjoying themselves and making significant learning strides. A robust assessment plan facilitates a clearer understanding of what is effective and allows adjustments when needed.

Create a Simple Design Within the Course Management System

An easily navigable course design increases students' likelihood of not missing assignments or course activities and appeals to different learning styles. Some educators advocate for using Universal Design for Learning (UDL), initially developed by the Center for Applied Special Technology, to meet the needs of students with disabilities (CAST, 2018). However, UDL has branched out into a framework for accommodating many different types of learning needs and removes the need for students to disclose their disabilities (Cumming & Rose, 2022). UDL focuses on three-course design principles: provide multiple means of engagement, provide multiple means of representation, and provide multiple means of action and expression (CAST, 2018).

Conclusion

Our aim in this chapter was to provide guidance about some considerations when designing your course for effectiveness. Amidst the COVID-19 pandemic, numerous educators were compelled to transition to online teaching. This shift sparked interest in online education and presented a host of new challenges. The literature demonstrates that online courses are as effective and engaging as traditional courses, but the type of modality is a primary consideration. Research indicates that variations of hybridization, which combine synchronous and asynchronous elements, may be most effective for student achievement and satisfaction. Yet, challenges such as increased faculty workload, course quality considerations, and academic integrity can impede course design. Notably, there are many opportunities for public affairs research to address these challenges in online teaching and equip educators with knowledge that can help them teach the next generation of public servants.

References

Alpert, W. T., Couch, K. A., & Harmon, O. R. (2016). A randomized assessment of online learning. *American Economic Review, 106*(5), 378–382. https://doi.org/10.1257/aer.p20161057

Bartley, S. J., & Golek, J. H. (2004). Evaluating the cost effectiveness of online and face-to-face instruction. *Educational Technology and Society, 7*(4), 167–175. https://doi.org/10.2307/jeductechsoci.7.4.167

Beatty, B. (2019). *Hybrid-flexible Course Design implementing student-directed hybrid classes* (1st ed.). EdTech Books.

Bohórquez, E. B., Khan, S., Battestilli, L., & Fogelman, A. (2023). Measuring student engagement in a HyFlex environment. *E-Journal of Higher Education Research, 6*(3), 1–9.

Bowen, W. G. (2013). *Higher education in the digital age*. Princeton University Press.

Bowen, W. G., Chingos, M. M., Lack, K. A., & Nygren, T. I. (2014). Interactive learning online at public universities: Evidence from a six-campus randomized trial. *Journal of Policy Analysis and Management, 33*(1), 94–111. https://doi.org/10.1002/pam.21728

Brown, B. W., & Liedholm, C. E. (2002). Can web courses replace the classroom in principles of microeconomics? *American Economic Review, 92*(2), 444–448. https://doi.org/10.1257/00028280320191778

Bryan, T. K., Lutte, R., Lee, J., O'Neil, P., Maher, C. S., & Hoflund, A. B. (2018). When do online education technologies enhance student engagement? A case of distance education at University of Nebraska at Omaha. *Journal of Public Affairs Education, 24*(2), 255–273. https://doi.org/10.1080/15236803.2018.1429817

CAST. (2018). *Universal design for learning guidelines, version 2.2.* http://udlguidelines.cast.org

Cotton, D. R., Cotton, P. A., & Shipway, J. R. (2024). Chatting and cheating: Ensuring academic integrity in the era of ChatGPT. *Innovations in Education and Teaching International, 61*(2), 228–239. https://doi.org/10.1080/14703297.2023.2190148

Cumming, T. M., & Rose, M. C. (2022). Exploring universal design for learning as an accessibility tool in higher education: A review of the current literature. *The Australian Educational Researcher, 49*(5), 1025–1043. https://doi.org/10.1007/s13384-021-00471-7

Dahlstrom-Hakki, I., Alstad, Z., & Banerjee, M. (2020). Comparing synchronous and asynchronous online discussions for students with disabilities: The impact of social presence. *Computers & Education, 150,* 103842. https://doi.org/10.1016/j.compedu.2020.103842

Emerson, K., & Gerlak, A. K. (2016). Teaching collaborative governance online: Aligning collaborative instruction with online learning platforms. *Journal of Public Affairs Education, 22*(3), 327–344. https://doi.org/10.1080/15236803.2016.12002251

Figlio, D., Rush, M., & Yin, L. (2013). Is it live or is it internet? Experimental estimates of the effects of online instruction on student learning. *Journal of Labor Economics, 31*(4), 763–784. https://doi.org/10.1086/669930

Gillett-Swan, J. (2017). The challenges of online learning: Supporting and engaging the isolated learner. *Journal of Learning Design, 10*(1), 20–30.

Ginn, M. H., & Hammond, A. (2012). Online education in public affairs: Current state and emerging issues. *Journal of Public Affairs Education, 18*(2), 247–270.

Gulati, S. (2008). Technology-enhanced learning in developing nations: A review. *The International Review of Research in Open and Distributed Learning, 9*(1).

Harmon, O. R., & Lambrinos, J. (2006). *Online format vs. live mode of instruction: Do human capital differences or differences in returns to human capital explain the differences in outcomes?* https://digitalcommons.lib.uconn.edu/econ_wpapers/200607/

Harris, R. A., & Nikitenko, G. O. (2014). Comparing online with brick and mortar course learning outcomes: An analysis of quantitative methods curriculum in public administration. *Teaching Public Administration, 32*(1), 95–107. https://doi.org/10.1177/0144739414523284

Hart, C. M., Friedmann, E., & Hill, M. (2018). Online course-taking and student outcomes in California community colleges. *Education Finance and Policy, 13*(1), 42–71. https://doi.org/10.1162/edfp_a_00218

Hiltz, S. R., Coppola, N., Rotter, N., Toroff, M., & Benhunan-Fich, R. (2000). Measuring the importance of collaborative learning for the effectiveness of ALN: A multi-measure. In *Learning effectiveness and faculty satisfaction: Proceedings of the 1999 Sloan Summer Workshop on asynchronous learning networks.* Olin College.

Holden O. L., Norris, M. E., & Kuhlmeier, V. A. (2021). Academic integrity in online assessment: A research review. *Frontiers in Education, 6,* 639814. https://doi.org/10.3389/feduc.2021.639814

Hummer, D., & Hersey, L. (2023). Mentoring online MPA students: Assessing mentorship qualities and aligning program goals. *Journal of Public Affairs Education, 29*(4), 522–542. https://doi.org/10.1080/15236803.2023.2247471

Joyce, T., Crockett, S., Jaeger, D. A., Altindag, O., & O'Connell, S. D. (2015). Does classroom time matter? *Economics of Education Review, 46*, 64–77. https://doi.org/10.1016/j.econedurev.2015.02.007

Kazmer, M. M., & Haythornthwaite, C. (2001). Juggling multiple social worlds: Distance students online and offline. *American Behavioral Scientist, 45*(3), 510–529.

Kentnor, H. E. (2015). *Investigating and understanding student learning outcomes in an online and face-to-face graduate-level legal administration course: An embedded mixed methods design* (Doctoral dissertation, University of Denver).

Khalil, R., Mansour, A. E., Fadda, W. A., Almisnid, K., Aldamegh, M., Al-Nafeesah, A., Alkhalifah, A., & Al-Wutayd, O. (2020). The sudden transition to synchronized online learning during the COVID-19 pandemic in Saudi Arabia: A qualitative study exploring medical students' perspectives. *BMC Medical Education, 20*, 285. https://doi.org/10.1186/s12909-020-02208-z

Laufer, M. E. (2021). Redefining training for faculty tutors. In *Redefining roles: The professional, faculty, and graduate consultant's guide to writing centers* (vol. 17, pp. 17–30). Louisville, Colorado: University Press of Colorado.

McDonald, B. D. (2021). Teaching in uncertain times: The future of public administration education. *Teaching Public Administration, 39*(1), 3–8. https://doi.org/10.1177/0144739420963154

McDonald, B. D., Hatcher, W., Bacot, H., Evans, M. D., McCandless, S. A., McDougle, L. M., Young, S. L., Elliott, I. C. Emas, R., Lu, E. Y., Abbott, M. E., Bearfield, D. A., Berry-James, R. M., Blessett, B., Borry, E. L., Diamond, J., Franklin, A. L., Gaynor, T. S., Gong, . . . Zhang, Y. (2024). The scholarship of teaching and learning in public administration: An agenda for future research. *Journal of Public Affairs Education, 30*(1), 11–27. https://doi.org/10.1080/15236803.2023.2294654

Meine, M. F., & Dunn, T. P. (2017). MPA programs and internet education: Validation of quality and acceptance despite challenges surrounding online delivery. *Journal of Public Affairs Education, 23*(2), 665–676. https://doi.org/10.1080/15236803.2017.12002277

Mitchell, M., Leachman, M., & Saenz, M. (2019). State higher education funding cuts have pushed costs to students, worsened inequality. *Center on Budget and Policy Priorities, 24*, 9–15.

Naidu, S. (2019). The idea of open education. *Distance Education, 40*(1), 1–4.

Navarro, P., & Shoemaker, J. (2000). Performance and perceptions of distance learners in cyberspace. *American Journal of Distance Education, 14*(2), 15–35. https://doi.org/10.1080/08923640009527052

Nguyen, T. (2015). The effectiveness of online learning: Beyond no significant difference and future horizons. *MERLOT Journal of Online Learning and Teaching, 11*(2), 309–319.

Nollenberger, K. (2017). On-campus versus hybrid courses in a Master of Public Administration program. *Journal of Public Affairs Education, 23*(1), 625–636. https://doi.org/10.1080/15236803.2017.12002273

Ortagus, J. C., & Yang, L. (2018). An examination of the influence of decreases in state appropriations on online enrollment at public universities. *Research in Higher Education, 59*(7), 847–865. https://doi.org/10.1007/s11162-017-9490-y

Oztok, M., Zingaro, D., Brett, C., & Hewitt, J. (2013). Exploring asynchronous and synchronous tool use in online courses. *Computers & Education, 60*(1), 87–94. https://doi.org/10.1016/j.compedu.2012.08.007

Peat, M. (2000). Online self-assessment materials: Do these make a difference to student learning? *ALT-J, 8*(2), 51–57.

Riffell, S., & Sibley, D. (2005). Using web-based instruction to improve large undergraduate biology courses: An evaluation of a hybrid course format. *Computers and Education, 44*(3), 217–235. https://doi.org/10.1016/j.compedu.2004.01.005

Roblyer, M. D., Freeman, J., Donaldson, M. B., & Maddox, M. (2007). A comparison of outcomes of virtual school courses in synchronous and asynchronous formats. *The Internet and Higher Education, 10*(4), 261–268. https://doi.org/10.1016/j.iheduc.2007.08.003

Russell, T. L. (1999). *The no significant difference phenomenon: A comparative research annotated bibliography on technology for distance education: As reported in 355 research reports, summaries and papers.* North Carolina State University.

Shahabadi, M. M., & Uplane, M. (2015). Synchronous and asynchronous e-learning styles and academic performance of e-learners. *Procedia – Social and Behavioral Sciences, 176*, 129–138. https://doi.org/10.1016/j.sbspro.2015.01.453

Starr, R. M., & Milheim, W. D. (1996). Educational uses of the internet: An exploratory survey. *Educational Technology, 36*(5), 19–28.

Stavredes, T., & Herder, T. (2014). *A guide to online course design: Strategies for student success.* John Wiley & Sons.

Stephens, J. B., & Morse, R. S. (2023). Enhancing sense of belonging and satisfaction among online students in multi-track public affairs programs: A case analysis of immersion courses. *Teaching Public Administration, 41*(2), 266–283. https://doi.org/10.1177/01447394221076344

Stone, C., & Springer, M. (2019). Interactivity, connectedness and 'teacher-presence': Engaging and retaining students online. *Australian Journal of Adult Learning, 59*(2), 146–169.

Sublett, C. (2020). *Distant equity: The promise and pitfalls of online learning for students of color in higher education.* American Council on Education.

Tabak, F., & Rampal, R. (2014). Synchronous e-learning: Reflections and design considerations. *International Journal of Education and Development, 10*(4), 80–92.

Tallent-Runnels, M. K., Thomas, J. A., Lan, W. Y., Cooper, S., Ahern, T. C., Shaw, S. M., & Liu, X. (2006). Teaching courses online: A review of the research. *Review of Educational Research, 76*(1), 93–135. https://doi.org/10.3102/00346543076001093

Tate, T., & Warschauer, M. (2022). Equity in online learning. *Educational Psychologist, 57*(3), 192–206. https://doi.org/10.1080/00461520.2022.2062597

Warschauer, M. (2009). Digital literacy studies: Progress and prospects. In M. Baynham & M. Prinsloo (Eds.), *The future of literacy studies* (pp. 123–140). Palgrave Macmillan.

Wukich, C. (2023). Online program management and potential principal-agent problems. *Journal of Public Affairs Education, 29*(1), 72–91. https://doi.org/10.1080/15236803.2022.2105089

Yan, Y., Vyas, L., Wu, A. M., & Rawat, S. (2022). Effective online education under COVID-19: Perspectives from teachers and students. *Journal of Public Affairs Education, 28*(4), 422–439. https://doi.org/10.1080/15236803.2022.2110749

7

HOW TO TEACH DIVERSITY, EQUITY, INCLUSION, AND ACCESSIBILITY

Sean A. McCandless[1] and Mary E. Guy[2]

[1]*University of Texas at Dallas, Dallas, TX, and* [2]*University of Colorado Denver, Denver, CO*

Whether teaching budgeting or program evaluation, human resource management or finance, organization design, or public policy, the subjects of diversity, equity, inclusion, and accessibility need to be laced throughout the course. Our graduates must know how to apply an equity lens to policies, programs, and outcomes. This chapter offers techniques for incorporating the subject in the classroom, whether as a stand-alone course or as a subject integrated into other courses.

First, we make the point that diversity, equity, inclusion, and accessibility (DEIA) is a way of thinking about everything in the public sphere. The Constitution's tenets give rise to the expectation that all residents are entitled to equitable treatment. Second, we focus on how to load these expectations into students' intellectual backpacks. We do this by sharing teaching techniques we have found to be successful. Readers will learn how to infuse their courses with awareness of diversity, equity, inclusion, and accessibility. And readers will learn how to teach skills that will push the equity needle forward for policies, programs, and operations.

Diversity, Equity, Inclusion, and Accessibility as a State of Mind

Ideally, we would like to equip our graduates with the skills to dance around the room backward in high heels. By that, we mean public administrators must do a lot of things well simultaneously. They must be proficient in the tasks they perform, they must work well with others, and in the broader context, they must be attuned to organizational dynamics, agency mission, political pressures, laws, and community expectations. In

DOI: 10.4324/9781032671291-8

this broader context, the four normative "pillars" of public administration reside.

Public service agencies should use their resources efficiently, be effective in achieving their goals, be an economic bargain, and ensure equity in access, process, quality, and outcomes (Norman-Major, 2011; Svara & Brunet, 2004; Svara & Brunet, 2005). It is incumbent on public affairs education programs to teach the skills necessary to actualize these values. While volumes have been written on methods to measure and achieve efficiency, economy, and effectiveness, less has been written about equity. Happily, recent years have brought rising interest in DEIA pedagogy (see, for instance, Gooden & Myers, 2004b; Rivera & Ward, 2008). This increasing interest does not come a minute too soon. Most public service careers require DEIA competencies. Practice skills are necessary across the gamut of administrative work, from participative decision-making to representative staffing patterns to inclusive workplaces accessible to everyone. Graduates must be prepared to work with varied constituencies and be so comfortable with DEIA expectations that the work is second nature (McCandless & Gooden, 2024).

Social equity is a normative and ethical priority for the field and is embodied in codes of ethics like those of the American Society for Public Administration (Svara, 2014). But, codes do not tell how to teach it or how to inspire students to look for inequities and correct them. How can we prepare students to be meaningful participants in identifying inequities, developing solutions, and implementing remedies? Moreover, amidst the pockets of resistance against DEIA, the challenge is to employ teaching techniques that have the durability, resilience, and broad appeal to teach DEIA to those who think they are opposed to it.

Finding Goldilocks

The challenge is finding the right exercises that bring awareness and sensitivity to how the effects of lived experience change people's realities. Goldilocks solutions require Goldilocks teaching techniques. We recommend pitching instruction at an optimal balance that acknowledges each person's differences, whether of race, gender identity, ethnicity, age, ableism, religion, or any other characteristics that constitute the person's uniqueness. The goal is not to erase race or to dismiss class or caste. The goal is to embrace differences and to sensitize students to how differences affect perceptions, understandings, and expectations. Frameworks pave the way.

Frameworks are helpful as a means for focusing students' attention on the big picture of what DEIA is about while extracting detailed information unique to a particular problem, policy, program, or neighborhood. To explain this, we draw on the literature and our classroom experiences. We share strategies and end with reflections.

Context Is Key: The Importance of Levels and Usability

First, we emphasize two key dimensions that impact *all* public affairs classrooms. These are the audience and the usability of what is taught. In other words, class level matters and practical applicability matters.

Level Matters: Teach to the Audience

At this point, it is helpful to reflect on a teaching experience that both of us as authors share. As a senior doctoral student, Sean was getting ready to teach "Introduction to Public Administration" in the Master of Public Administration (MPA) program for the first time. While already experienced with teaching undergraduate classes in political science, English writing, and conversational French, the prospect of teaching graduate students was terrifying. Mary, who was Sean's advisor, gave advice that echoes and inspires to this day: "Don't make the class a mini-PhD seminar." This powerful advice was couched in the reality that a mistake newly minted PhD instructors make is to teach all courses as an abstract, theory-laden promenade with little attention to practical application. Public administration is an applied field, so what we teach should be practically useful. And we must teach to the audience.

How we teach must be tailored to the level – bachelor's, master's, or doctoral.

For instance, bachelor's programs center on teaching students about the "warp and woof" of the field while also imparting important skills (Mitchell, 2018; Weber & Brunt, 2020). Undergraduates are more likely to enter the classroom as "blank slates," needing refreshers in basic government and even crash courses in it. At the same time, they may already be a practitioner yet simply have no formal education in public service.

Master's programs advance this "warp and woof" by teaching advanced skills. Some students are already administrators and are seeking advanced education for promotion opportunities and pay raises. Others are "fresh out of" undergraduate and have no public service experience.

At the doctoral level, the focus is on learning advanced research and analytical skills (Brewer et al., 1999; Meek & Johnson, 1998). We can assume that students (hopefully) understand the basics of the field, such as big themes in the interbranch, intergovernmental, and intersectoral nature of governance. At the same time, these students are still constructing their scholarly identities (Smith & Hatmaker, 2014). Even after their program concludes, a doctoral graduate is both a master and an apprentice of the material (Raadschelders & Douglas, 2003).

In brief, at the bachelor's level, most students are getting ready for public service careers. At the master's, they are likely already in the field, so classes mirror the work of agencies and teach new, advanced skills. At the doctoral level, students enter a different type of public service participation, learning to teach others and learning to conduct research into public programs.

Make It Usable

Another lesson from Sean's story is that the classroom needs to be a practical space. In other words, research should inform practice. Still, there is often an academic-practitioner divide that instructors must navigate (Ancira et al., 2022). Classes need to be practically useful and emphasize skills that can be figuratively and literally used on the job tomorrow. These skills range from the abstract, such as advanced analytic skills, to leadership and management strategies, to technical "nuts and bolts" skills.

Students need to walk away from the public affairs classroom with skills. And as faculty, we need to be able to document how effective our teaching is, not only for improving student success but also for being accountable for our performance and our students' job readiness. So, what does "success" look like, especially in regard to DEIA? To us, it is the documentation, often articulated in student comments like, "I learned something new," "I didn't realize how different my experience is from that of others," or our personal favorite, "I can use what I learned in my job."

Understanding Historical Patterns and Doing the Work

DEIA is important for the public affairs classroom in at least four ways. First, DEIA within the classroom embodies respect for each student's uniqueness. Second, DEIA is a key public service dimension and must be taught. The subject is a "comes with" because it is an imperative in the pursuit of public purposes. Third, today's policies and programs are rooted in history and shaped by often arbitrary forces that cause correctible problems. For students to understand why things are the way they are, they must understand what factors and forces shaped them as such. Fourth, as instructors, we must "do the work." In the process, we take inspiration from Gooden's (2008) encouragement to "add fire" to efforts that foster social equity. By putting energy into the subject matter, each instructor can lean into DEIA and make students aware of the potential they can unleash by raising awareness, correcting inequities, and remaining vigilant for ways to enhance fairness and opportunity.

How to Teach Diversity, Equity, Inclusion, and Accessibility   **93**

Embodying Respect and the Need for DEIA Competency

Public affairs classrooms should embody the same public service values expected of all public administrators. While public administration spaces in the United States are often majority white, this is changing. Our students are more diverse than ever and deserve to be respected and represented in the selection of readings, assignments, and topics. Feeling included is as important for the Black student, the Hispanic student, the Asian student, and the Native American student as it is for the white student (Appe et al., 2016; Blessett, 2018a; Sabharwal, 2014). Having said this, it is essential to note that DEIA concerns extend far beyond race and ethnicity. Students in our classes are not one-dimensional. Each brings a number of characteristics that blend in an intersectional way.

The Guise of Neutrality

The point is that teaching DEIA means having purposeful conversations about what equity means and drawing attention to inequities and narratives that perpetuate inequity (e.g., see Starke et al., 2018). The most powerful biases are those hidden under the guise of neutrality (Portillo et al., 2019, 2023). In fact, there is no such thing as race neutrality, gender neutrality, or administrative neutrality.

Teaching is about correcting narratives that perpetuate inequity. What instructors read heading into the classroom shapes the narratives they tell in the classroom (Evans, 2018). Here is a list of citations that enrich knowledge about DEIA and illuminate the issues instructors should be aware of: Blessett et al. (2016), Cooper and McCandless (2024), Love et al. (2016), Menifield et al. (2024), Portillo (2007), and Williams and Conyers (2016). We encourage readers to examine these sources in detail because they light the way for helping students see what otherwise remains unchallenged.

The Role of Law

The law reflects cultural values and majority opinion. Law encases norms in concrete and forms "lines on the road" that define what is acceptable and what is not. The administrators of today and tomorrow need to understand the legal and constitutional requirements regarding DEIA. This is not a matter of political suasion; it is a matter of doing governance right. The rule of law guides appropriate action. And when laws are inequitable, students must know how to effect change.

In terms of administrative processes, students must be taught about the management and leadership techniques that can foster DEIA. This includes everyday "nuts-and-bolts" of DEIA actions concerning job design, promotion opportunities, team formation, due process rights, constructive rather than destructive organizational cultures, performance measures that prioritize equity, and public service fairly.

Questions That Illuminate the Past

Instructors new to teaching do not need to reinvent the wheel. We recommend dissecting social equity's historical heritage by coming to grips with answers to questions posed by Susan Gooden (2015). First, to Gooden, from the U.S. context, understanding social equity begins by answering questions pertaining to diversity and inclusion, namely "Who is 'We,'" in the phrase "We the People" that appears in the preamble to the U.S. Constitution. The answer reveals the irony that, as notions of freedom and equality were embedded in founding documents, "we" excludes everyone except white male property owners.

The second question concerns how definitions of "We" have expanded. By pointing to constitutional amendments (the 13th, 14th, 15th, 19th, 24th, and 26th amendments), statutory law (such as the 1964 Civil Rights Act), and case law (such as *Brown v. Board of Education* or *Bostock v. Clayton County*), "we" has gradually expanded to embrace many more than the founders originally intended. In other words, the words of the Constitution are catching up with its spirit.

Questions That Illuminate the Present

The third and fourth questions shift into the extent of inequity and why inequities persist. Some of this shift was already presaged by (largely) women authors writing on equity, such as Progressive authors like Mary Parker Follett and Jane Addams and unsung Black social equity heroes like Harriett Frances Williams (Gooden, 2017; Williams, 1947). From the late 1960s onward, the field's discussion of social equity is shaped by the legacy of the 1968 Minnowbrook Conference. The passionate debates on the subject of social equity that occurred there were subsequently popularized by figures like H. George Frederickson and Philip Rutledge. Like a tag team match, Frederickson focused on advancing social equity as a topic for research and Rutledge championed social equity as a cornerstone of practice (Gooden et al., 2023; Yu et al., 2023).

The questions about inequity and its persistence lead to the fifth question, which asks how accountability for social equity will be achieved (Gooden, 2015). Answering this question requires understanding the extent to which public service agencies take responsibility for admitting that inequities exist, prioritizing equity, measuring fairness, reaching out to marginalized

How to Teach Diversity, Equity, Inclusion, and Accessibility **95**

populations, providing meaningful seats at the table, and actively working to remedy inequities.

The third, fourth, and fifth questions coincide with the postmodern deconstruction of systems and processes. This way of thinking led to more scholars asking pointed questions and challenging the status quo. Their challenges engaged both narratives and counter-narratives and ranged from the "official" versions of history to awareness of whose voices were systematically included and whose voices were systematically excluded from the literature (Blessett et al., 2016). Answering the questions also meant borrowing narratives from other fields, and this is where the adaptation of critical inquiry to the subject of social equity has been useful. Critical inquiry causes investigators to look behind the curtain rather than only in front of it. Critically assessing the difference that race makes in terms of lived experience and opportunities enjoyed versus forgone has led to a more accurate understanding of why inequities persist and what they feel like to those who suffer their consequences.

As critical inquiry raised the veil from the nation's eyes, frameworks have proven effective for holding a gaze on matters of equity. For one, within the Code of Ethics of the American Society for Public Administration (ASPA), social equity has become a key ethical principle alongside serving the public interest and enhancing democracy (Svara, 2014, 2015; Svara et al., 2015). Scholars also began using critical race theory and whiteness studies to examine why inequities persist (Gaynor & Lopez-Littleton, 2022; Heckler, 2017), queer theory to understand issues impacting sexuality and gender identity (Larson, 2022), and intersectionality (Blessett, 2018b). Works on the meaning of DEIA and techniques to foster it became available (see Riccucci, 2021) at the same time that local governments, such as King County in Washington and others, began working on ways to define, measure, and advance social equity through all aspects of governance (Gooden, 2014).

Do the Work: Claiming and Owning One's Positionality

While questions such as the five above guide inquiry into the persistence of inequities, owning one's positionality provides an avenue for self-awareness and reflection. Instructors need to "do the work" (Gaynor, 2014; Gaynor & Lopez-Littleton, 2022). What does this mean? It means understanding one's own positionalities (intersectionalities), privileges, and marginalizations and how they impact who we are and how we behave.

"Doing the work" means identifying and owning our own beliefs and experiences regarding bias, prejudice, and discrimination. It also means examining our own beliefs, priorities, and actions regarding who and what we value and why. Do we promote fairness? What values do we embody?

96 Sean A. McCandless and Mary E. Guy

Insights come as these questions are thoughtfully considered (Fountain & Newcomer, 2016; Lopez-Littleton, 2016; Lopez-Littleton et al., 2018).

Using Frameworks to Teach Solutions-Based DEIA

Public administration is an action field and DEIA is a solutions-oriented topic. Rather than admiring the problem, teaching DEIA requires that students become aware of the problems and think their way to a resolution. A solutions-based approach to DEIA means understanding the causes and effects of inequities and translating understanding into action.

Using a framework is helpful for moving from problem identification to generation of solutions to selecting, implementing, and evaluating the remedy. Frameworks make it possible to organize and deepen understanding of a topic because they serve as a scaffold by providing for different levels of understanding that build on each other (Van de Ven, 2007). One framework, namely that enabled by Gooden's five questions, has already been detailed. We discuss four more here.

Framework #1: Law, Politics, and Management

First, Rosenbloom's conception of public administration as an enterprise consisting of law, politics, and management is like a three-dimensional scaffold that can be adapted for social equity discussions (Rosenbloom et al., 2008). His model employs three perspectives: what administrators are and are not required and empowered to do (law), who gets what (politics), and the ins and outs of how agencies run (management). In terms of law, statutory mandates – such as the 1963 Equal Pay Act and the 1964 Civil Rights Act – establish legal regimes outlawing many types of societal and employment discrimination.

In the legal dimension, case law – such as *Bostock v. Clayton County* – stipulates how the law is to be followed. In the case of Bostock, it clarifies that workplaces cannot discriminate based on factors like sexual orientation and gender identity.

In the political dimension, the discussion of politics can use policy tools like the social construction framework to reveal how political power and dominant social constructions converge to impugn racial and gender minorities and those at the intersections (Ingram et al., 2007).

In the management dimension, human resource processes, organizational dynamics, or budgeting priorities are particularly amenable to discussions of DEIA (see Gooden & Myers, 2004a; Gooden & Wooldridge, 2007). In human resource management courses (HR), a focus on DEIA invites discussions of bias across all HR functions, from job analysis to job postings to compensation to interviewing, selecting, developing, promoting, disciplining, and much more (Guy & Sowa, 2022). In budgeting classes, drawing students' attention to whom is advantaged by a given set of budget priorities, and who is disadvantaged by those priorities, reveals the subtleties of how advantage is perpetuated by seemingly "rational" processes (Rubin & Bartle, 2023).

The law/politics/management framework has broad applicability to coursework and invites deliberation about the equity implications of laws, policy debates, political rhetoric, and management. The three dimensions of law, policy/politics, and management are applicable to many different courses and provide a lever for introducing discussions pertaining to diversity, equity, inclusion, and/or accessibility.

Framework #2: Access, Process, Quality, and Outcomes

A second framework is provided by Johnson and Svara's (2015) conceptualization of four dimensions to social equity from an administrative point of view. These include *access* issues, namely the barriers (or lack thereof) different groups face when accessing public services. Second is *procedural fairness*, sometimes shorthanded as "processes," which concerns the degree of fairness in public service processes, such as the fairness in police traffic stops or who gets heard in public hearings. Third are *quality* issues or differences in terms of standards, caliber, condition, and make-up of public resources. And fourth are *outcome* issues, or the consequences of any dimension of the policy, program, or processes.

Instructors can use these four considerations to engage students in an evaluation of any policy or program. This framework also works well with students who conduct an equity audit of a program. As they evaluate the program in terms of each of these dimensions, students find it easy to identify where problems exist and where corrections can be implemented.

Framework #3: Name It; Identify Causation; Assign Accountability

An alternative approach that works to identify inequities and pinpoint causation is the process of naming, identifying causation, and accountability. This is the process of naming, blaming, and claiming, as Gooden (2014) refers to it. To name an inequity is precisely that; it is the admission that an inequity is present. It must be named before attention can be focused on it, so naming is the first step toward remediation. Blaming an inequity can refer to assigning blame to someone or something, but more broadly, it concerns understanding how and why it came about. The third step is to claim the inequity, which means to take meaningful steps to address that inequity.

98   Sean A. McCandless and Mary E. Guy

Framework #4: Pursuing Accountability

A fourth alternative is a framework that blends the approaches of Johnson and Svara (2015) and Gooden (2015). Pursuing accountability puts the emphasis on which actors and actions will be responsible for remedying inequities and how social equity will be achieved. This frame of reference concerns understanding the extent and impacts of what governments do to promote fairness for all, principally admitting issues, centering fairness and measuring progress, engaging in outreach, and providing meaningful participation for those affected by the inequity while resolutions are determined and implemented.

Applying Frameworks

An example of how these frameworks operate in reality will be helpful here. While still a doctoral student at the University of Colorado, Sean co-developed a social equity class with a colleague, Samantha Larson (McCandless & Larson, 2018). McCandless and Larson used a case study to bring to life the frameworks. In Denver, there had been a decades-long discussion of expanding the I-70 corridor in tandem with expanding bus and light rail options with the Regional Transportation District (RTD). At first glance, expanding the highway and transportation lines appeared like a win-win proposition for everyone involved. However, the frameworks above invite a deeper analysis, and each one emphasizes and reveals different components of the debated plan.

A guest lecturer who worked for RTD on equity matters pointed out how expanding the highway would displace low-income communities. Furthermore, expanding transportation options, while it appeared equitable, was hindered by the fact that those who would benefit the most from expanded transportation options were not the ones who had the time or capacity to attend public meetings to provide their input. Using frameworks as guides, many issues became apparent. Access was an issue because of which communities had access to transportation and which had access to the venues where decisions were made. Procedural fairness raised issues because of which communities were consulted and which were not able to voice their concerns as plans evolved. Quality issues, especially in regard to disruptions to quality of life and even displacements, were likely. And outcomes would be in play because of the many long-term consequences stemming from all of these complexities.

Diagnosing these issues led to a discussion of the "solutions" side. The guest lecturer noted how RTD faced issues with where, how, and when to expand ridership options. In typical infrastructure development plans, the

How to Teach Diversity, Equity, Inclusion, and Accessibility **99**

approach for inviting community feedback is to hold public meetings, but timing and lack of transportation made attending prohibitive. One solution, albeit not perfect, was to lower barriers to participation by stationing personnel at key bus stops, speaking with people on their way to work, and asking them to fill out surveys. While not perfect, this strategy showed how administrators had to be concerned with all four pillars of public administration: efficiency, effectiveness, economy, and equity. At the same time, there were actionable ways of thinking about equity in regard to politics, management, and law. Moreover, parsing understanding into issues of access, processes, quality, and outcomes helped administrators take meaningful steps to foster fairness. Beyond applying frameworks in classroom discussions, we move now to descriptions of written assignments.

Crafting Meaningful Assignments

Whether teaching bachelor's, master's, or doctoral courses, a public affairs class will probably incorporate a major written assignment. Analytical writing assignments focused on DEIA are fruitful gateways through which students take stock of DEIA issues, grapple with the consequences of inequity, and generate possible solutions. In this section, we discuss assignment strategies and then provide an example of these strategies in action.

Analytical Assignments That Teach DEIA

The most effective assignments are those that are usable – they apply to practice – while they build the student's skill set. Beyond teaching best practices in regard to planning, organizing, staffing, directing, coordinating, reporting, and budgeting, public affairs education has to teach analytical and writing skills. DEIA discussions are filled with concepts and theories. While classes would be bare without these ideas, they can be hard to translate into practice and it is up to instructors to design lessons that teach students how to make the translation and communicate clearly.

One author (Sean), inspired by his dissertation chair's (Mary) entreaty not to fall into the trap of teaching an MPA course as a mini-doctoral seminar, asked himself, "How can I make theory useful to students?" The trick is not to teach theory as theory but, rather, to teach students what they can *do better* through understanding theory. By focusing course work not just on what theory says but on more fundamental questions – "What can I do with a concept? How can it help administrators understand what is going on around them? How can theory inform solutions that are likely to work?" – theory becomes more useful.

In response to the question "What can I do with a concept" and inspired by books on traditions and techniques of inquiry (see Riccucci, 2010; Van de Ven, 2007), students can do at least four things with everything they learn in an MPA program: describe, explain, predict, and prescribe. First, students can use concepts to *describe*, or understand and articulate, how something is put together or how processes are involved in the production of some public service. For instance, understanding the concept of democracy makes it possible to explain why constituents are entitled to access, fair processes, quality services, and equitable outcomes.

Second, theories provide a starting point for students to extend description into *explanation*. This leads to a deeper understanding of why something works the way it does. Sources of these explanations come from many places, such as decision-making models, motivation, group processes, and more.

Third, students can use concepts to *predict*, or make intelligent guesses, about what might happen in the future. In DEIA terms, this leads to questions like, "What could happen if the status quo remains the same" or "What could happen if the status quo changes in some way?" At more advanced levels, prediction works with abductive reasoning in creating propositions and hypotheses.

Fourth, students can use material learned in classes to *prescribe*, or propose actionable solutions. This application comes in the form of recommending an action that would address an inequity.

These capacities – describe, explain, predict, and prescribe – are advanced by providing four questions that operationalize the concepts. The broad goal is for students to understand how problems arise and what the potential solutions are. The first two questions are from the "problem side" of the issue. These questions are: How did the presence, or absence, of some DEIA-related principles contribute to a problem? How did the principle's use, or misuse, impact DEIA? The "presence" dimension of the first question refers to how something was present that should not have been, whereas the "absence" dimension meant *something* should have been present yet was not. The "use" dimension of the second question refers to how *something* should have been used but was not, and how this led to the problem. The "misuse" dimension refers to how *something* was misused and how this contributed to the problem.

The next two questions are from the "solutions side," and they are the flip of the problems side. These questions ask, "How can correcting the presence or absence, or use or misuse, of some principles impacting DEIA help to address an issue?" By extension, if something was present but should not have been, then the need to remove it becomes obvious. If something was not present but should have been, then the need to add it becomes obvious. If something was used but should not have been, then it should be changed. And if something was misused, then its use should be corrected.

Coupling Description, Explanation, Prediction, and Prescription With Problems and Solutions

Here is an example of how Sean couples the four capacities of theory with the problems and solutions questions. Sean often uses two textbooks to teach DEIA courses with an organizational dynamics twist. The first is Guy and McCandless's (2025) *Achieving Social Equity*. The second is Bolman and Deal's (2017) textbook *Reframing Organizations*, which uses four frames to parse organizational dynamics: structural, human resource, political, and symbolic. Across a semester, students take a deep dive into a DEIA issue that is embedded in organizational dynamics. Topics have been wide-ranging, such as representativeness in police departments, pay equity issues in health and human services agencies, anti-LGBTQ+ discrimination in nonprofit organizational cultures, and more.

The main assignment is oriented around an analysis memo in which students act as if they work as administrators within the public service organization experiencing the problem under investigation. Similar to policy analysis memos (see Weimer & Vining, 2017), the first major section is an "Extended Problem Statement," which defines the problem in high-level terms, charts the history of the issue, and presents the effects of the problem.

The act of defining a problem is a major skill for administrators to develop (Stone, 2011). Students have argued how a particular police department has disproportionate racial representation, which contributes to issues of community mistrust. Or, that gender-based pay inequities are leading women to feel exploited within a health and human services agency. Or, that a culture hostile to LGBTQ+ employees and volunteers in a nonprofit impacts the safety of the work environment. The assignment requires that students go beyond merely defining the problem. They must build a case with data and key events to develop and justify the problem definition.

To thoroughly explicate the DEIA issue, the frameworks discussed earlier are invaluable. For instance, students have used Gooden's five questions (Who is "we"? How has the meaning of "we" expanded? What is the extent of the inequity? Why does the inequity persist? How will accountability be achieved?) to organize their problem statements in terms of historical conditions, extent of and persistence of inequities, and what agencies have (or have not) done to foster accountability for social equity. Students have used Johnson's and Svara's four-part framework – access, processes, quality, and outcomes – to parse the impacts of organizational politics on DEIA. Other students have used Rosenbloom's law, politics, and management framework to separate and examine the multiple stressors concerning a DEIA issue. Put simply, the frameworks (1) trigger how students approach the issue, (2) help students structure their knowledge and their arguments, and (3) lead them to actionable conclusions. The frameworks also remove the issue from hyper-partisan rhetoric and keep students focused on the facts of the inequity.

Next, after the extended problem statement, students provide a more formal analysis. This is where description and explanation couple with the four questions of presence, absence, use, and misuse, and become relevant. Students are required to use concepts from the readings and lectures not only to *describe* what happened but also to *explain* how a problem came about.

To take one example, a student used Heifetz's theory of adaptive leadership to diagnose how the *absence* of a key leadership action – protecting voices from below, particularly among minority front-line workers – contributed to dysfunctional dynamics, which, in turn, negatively impacted agency performance. While there may be a certain amount of "playing with reality" in this exercise, in that students do not always have access to all of the data and information they would need for more extended analyses, students get practice in *using* these concepts to examine how the presence, absence, use, or misuse of administrative principles can and do impact how organizations function.

After the analysis, students must develop at least four recommendations matching to Bolman and Deal's (2017) frames. This section moves from description and explanation to prediction and prescription. In other words, if the analysis identified a structural issue, then the student needs to predict what *could* happen if an agency does not address it. This must be accompanied by a *prescription* for a structural solution, which loops to prediction, namely that better results *could* occur if an agency adopted a particular solution. In other words, problems are balanced out by solutions that are specific enough to be actionable, to the level of detail almost of a recipe in a cookbook.

To return to the example above, the same student who identified a DEIA leadership failing by using Heifetz's theory of adaptive leadership, made several recommendations. These included specific trainings on cultural competency for administrators and redesigning the administrator's job to accentuate the need for DEIA competency. The recommendations were replete with performance metrics to measure progress.

The results of these strategies have been positive. Beyond favorable student evaluations, students frequently report that the analytic exercise and the use of frameworks make the material understandable to them. In fact,

How to Teach Diversity, Equity, Inclusion, and Accessibility **103**

many former students write to note how they applied some of the techniques in their jobs, making the exercise useful to them. This usefulness is all the more important, considering the need to train students to develop actionable solutions and to improve DEIA in their organizations.

Reflections and Conclusions

We hope readers will take away three lessons from this chapter. First, any meaningful discussion of DEIA in the classroom must account for history. Second, we must equip students with the practical skills to diagnose DEIA issues. Frameworks allow students to break a problem into its component parts and translate concepts and theories into practice. Third, we must teach students to adopt a solutions-based approach. Teaching DEIA will necessarily be focused on problems, for if everything were perfect in terms of representativeness, fairness, belonging, and more, we would not need solutions. Using advanced knowledge, to paraphrase Gooden (2008), our classrooms can become incubators that add "fire" to efforts to enhance social equity. This is as it should be, for social equity is an imperative of public administration.

This chapter offers only a sampling of the tools available that make it possible to weave DEIA into public affairs classrooms. Admittedly, we focused primarily on frameworks and writing. Other sources have developed tips on classroom management, which we do not recreate here. Rather, our contribution to this discussion of DEIA pedagogy is to emphasize a practice-based, solutions-based focus. These are tips we have found helpful and for which we have obtained positive results, measured in terms of students saying, "I *will* use this" or, even more rewardingly, "I *have used* this, and it worked well."

Like arrows in a quiver, these strategies should be part of a wide range of pedagogical techniques. If, at the end of the day, we want our graduates to be active participants in promoting social equity, then they must be skilled in diagnosing issues, understanding effects, defining problems, and forwarding solutions. The use of frameworks and analytical writing strategies are effective at accomplishing these goals.

References

Ancira, J., Rangarajan, N., & Shields, P. (2022). Bridging the academic-practitioner divide: Findings from a survey of public administration faculty and practitioners. *Journal of Public Affairs Education, 28*(1), 35–55. https://doi.org/10.1080/15236803.2021.1891396

Appe, S., Rubaii, N., & Stamp, K. (2016). Advancing global cultural competencies: International service learning within NASPAA member programs. *Journal of Public Affairs Education, 22*(1), 67–90. https://doi.org/10.1080/15236803.2016.12002229

Blessett, B. (2018a). Embedding cultural competence and racial justice in public administration programs. *Journal of Public Affairs Education*, *24*(4), 425–429. https://doi.org/10.1080/15236803.2018.1520383

Blessett, B. (2018b). Rethinking the administrative state through an intersectional framework. *Administrative Theory & Praxis*, *41*(1), 1–5. https://doi.org/10.10 80/10841806.2018.1517526

Blessett, B., Gaynor, T. S., Witt, M., & Alkadry, M. G. (2016). Counter-narratives as critical perspectives in public administration curricula. *Administrative Theory & Praxis*, *38*(4), 267–284. https://doi.org/10.1080/10841806.2016.1239397

Bolman, L. G., & Deal, T. E. (2017). *Reframing organizations: Artistry, choice, and leadership* (6th ed.). John Wiley & Sons.

Bostock_v. Clayton County, 590 U.S. ___ (2020).

Brewer, G. A., Facer, R. L., O'Toole, L. J., & Douglas, J. W. (1999) What's in a name? Comparing DPA and Ph.D. programs. *Journal of Public Affairs Education*, *5*(4), 309–317. https://doi.org/10.1080/15236803.1999.12022083

Brown_v. Board of Education of Topeka, 347 U.S. 483 (1954).

Civil_Rights Act of 1964, 78 Stat. 241.

Cooper, T., & McCandless, S. A. (2024). Introduction to public administration. In S. A. McCandless & S. T. Gooden (Eds.), *Teaching social equity in public administration: A cross-curricular guide for faculty and programs* (pp. 17–41). Routledge.

Equal_Pay Act of 1963, 77 Stat. 56.

Evans, M. D. (2018). Gender representation in MPA ethics courses. *Journal of Public Affairs Education*, *24*(3), 342–360. https://doi.org/10.1080/15236803. 2018.1426427

Fountain, J., & Newcomer, K. E. (2016). Developing and sustaining effective faculty mentoring programs. *Journal of Public Affairs Education*, *22*(4), 483–506. https://doi.org/10.1080/15236803.2016.12002262

Gaynor, T. S. (2014). Through *The Wire*: Training culturally competent leaders for a new era. *Journal of Public Affairs Education*, *20*(3), 369–392. https://doi.org/ 10.1080/15236803.2014.12001794

Gaynor, T. S., & Lopez-Littleton, V. (2022) Coming to terms: Teaching systemic racism and (the myth of) white supremacy. *Journal of Public Affairs Education*, *28*(2), 211–225. https://doi.org/10.1080/15236803.2021.1994326

Gooden, S. T. (2008). The politics of ready, aim . . . study more: Implementing the "fire" in race and public policy research. *The Journal of Race & Policy*, *4*(1), 7–21.

Gooden, S. T. (2014). *Race and social equity: A nervous area of government*. M.E. Sharpe.

Gooden, S. T. (2015). From equality to social equity. In M. E. Guy & M. M. Rubin (Eds.), *Public administration evolving: From foundations to the future* (pp. 209–229). Routledge.

Gooden, S. T. (2017). Frances Harriet Williams: Unsung social equity pioneer. *Public Administration Review*, *77*(5), 777–783. https://doi.org/10.1111/puar. 12788

Gooden, S. T., Johnson, R. G., McCandless, S. A., & Berry-James, R. (2023). The *Journal of Social Equity and Public Administration*: From vision to victory. *Journal of Social Equity and Public Administration*, *1*(1), 1–12. https://doi. org/10.24926/jsepa.v1i1.4770

Gooden, S. T., & Myers, S. (2004a). Social equity in public affairs education. *Journal of Public Affairs Education*, *10*(2), 91–97. https://doi.org/10.1080/15236803. 2004.12001350

Gooden, S. T., & Myers, S. (2004b). Teaching social equity in the MPA: Reflections from the Social Equity Symposium. *Journal of Public Affairs Education*, *10*(2), 155–175, https://doi.org/10.1080/15236803.2004.12001355

Gooden, S. T., & Wooldridge, B. (2007). Integrating social equity into the core human resource management course. *Journal of Public Affairs Education, 13*(1), 59–77. https://doi.org/10.1080/15236803.2007.12001467

Guy, M. E., & McCandless, S. A. (2025). *Achieving social equity: From problems to solutions* (2nd ed.). Melvin & Leigh.

Guy, M. E., & Sowa, J. E. (2022). *Human resource essentials for public service: People, process, performance.* Melvin & Leigh.

Heckler, N. (2017). Publicly desired color-blindness: Whiteness as a realized public value. *Administrative Theory & Praxis, 39*(3), 175–192. https://doi.org/10.108 0/10841806.2017.1345510

Ingram, H., Schneider, A. L., & DeLeon, P. (2007). Social construction and policy design. In P. Sabatier (Ed.), *Theories of the policy process* (2nd ed., pp. 93–126). Westview Press.

Johnson, N. J., & Svara, J. H. (2015). Toward a more perfect union: Moving forward with social equity. In N. J. Johnson & J. H. Svara (Eds.), *Justice for all: Promoting social equity in public administration* (pp. 265–290). Routledge.

Larson, S. J. (2022). Actions for queering American public administration. *Administration & Society, 54*(1), 145–163. https://doi.org/10.1177/00953997211011937

Lopez-Littleton, V. (2016). Critical dialogue and discussions of race in the public administration classroom. *Administrative Theory & Praxis, 38*(4), 285–295. https://doi.org/10.1080/10841806.2016.1242354

Lopez-Littleton, V., Blessett, B., & Barr, J. (2018). Advancing social justice and racial equity in the public sector. *Journal of Public Affairs Education, 24*(4), 449–468. https://doi.org/10.1080/15236803.2018.1490546

Love, J. M., Gaynor, T. S., & Blessett, B. (2016). Facilitating difficult dialogues in the classroom: A pedagogical imperative. *Administrative Theory & Praxis, 38*(4), 227–233. https://doi.org/10.1080/10841806.2016.1237839

McCandless, S. A., & Gooden, S. T. (2024). Teaching social equity: Tips from across the chapters, literature, and experience. In S. A. McCandless & S. T. Gooden (Eds.), *Teaching social equity in public administration: A cross-curricular guide for faculty and programs* (pp. 329–349). Routledge.

McCandless, S. A., & Larson, S. J. (2018). Prioritizing social equity in MPA curricula: A cross-program analysis and a case study. *Journal of Public Affairs Education, 24*(3), 361–379. https://doi.org/10.1080/15236803.2018.1426429

Meek, J. W., & Johnson, E. E. (1998) Curriculum, pedagogy, innovation: The professional doctorate in public administration. *Journal of Public Affairs Education, 4*(1)1, 57–63. https://doi.org/10.1080/15236803.1998.12022011

Menifield, C., Estorcien, V., Ndongo, J-C., Quispe, M-P., & McDonald, B. D. (2024). Retention and recruitment of minority students and faculty in public affairs and administration programs. *Journal of Public Affairs Education, 30*(1), 97–117. https://doi.org/10.1080/15236803.2023.2251338

Mitchell, J. (2018). The identity of undergraduate public affairs education: Opportunities and challenges. *Journal of Public Affairs Education, 2*(1), 80–96, https://doi.org/10.1080/15236803.2018.1429811

Norman-Major, K. (2011). Balancing the four Es: Or can we achieve equity for social equity in public administration? *Journal of Public Affairs Education, 17*(2), 233–252. https://doi.org/10.1080/15236803.2011.12001640

Portillo, S. (2007). Mentoring minority and female students: Recommendations for improving mentoring in public administration and public affairs programs. *Journal of Public Affairs Education, 13*(1), 103–111. https://doi.org10.1080/15 236803.2007.12001470

Portillo, S., Bearfield, D., & Humphrey, N. (2019). The myth of bureaucratic neutrality: Institutionalized inequity in local government hiring. *Review of Public Personnel Administration, 40*(3), 516–531. https://doi.org/10.1177/0734371X19828431

Portillo, S. K., Humphrey, N., & Bearfield, D. A. (2023). *The myth of bureaucratic neutrality: An examination of merit and representation*. Routledge.

Raadschelders, J. C. N., & Douglas, J. W. (2003) The Doctoral graduate in public administration: Apprentice or master? *Journal of Public Affairs Education, 9*(4), 229–243. https://doi.org/10.1080/15236803.2003.12023596

Riccucci, N. (2010). *Public administration: Traditions of inquiry and philosophies of knowledge*. Georgetown University Press.

Riccucci, N. (2021). *Managing diversity in public sector workforces* (2nd ed.). Routledge.

Rivera, M. A., & Ward, J. D. (2008). Social equity, diversity, and identity: Challenges for public affairs education and the public service. *Journal of Public Affairs Education, 14*(1), ii–viii. https://doi.org/10.1080/15236803.2008.12001504

Rosenbloom, D., Kravchuk, R., & Clerkin, R. (2008). *Public administration: Understanding management, politics, and law in the public sector*. McGraw-Hill.

Rubin, M. M., & Bartle, J. R. (2023). Equity in public budgeting: Lessons for the United States. *Journal of Social Equity and Public Administration, 1*(2), 11–25. https://doi.org/10.24926/jsepa.v1i2.4995

Sabharwal, M. (2014). Is diversity management sufficient? Organizational inclusion to further performance. *Public Personnel Management, 43*(2), 197–217. https://doi.org/10.1177/009102601452220

Smith, A. E., & Hatmaker, D. M. (2014). Knowing, doing, and becoming: Professional identity construction among public affairs doctoral students. *Journal of Public Affairs Education, 20*(4), 545–564. https://10.1080/15236803.2014.12001807

Starke, A. M., Heckler, N., & Mackey, J. (2018). Administrative racism: Public administration education and race. *Journal of Public Affairs Education, 24*(4), 469–489. https://doi.org/10.1080/15236803.2018.1426428

Stone, D. (2011). *Policy paradox: The art of political decision making*. W.W. Norton and Company.

Svara, J. H. (2014). Who are the keepers of the code? Articulating and upholding ethical standards in the field of public administration. *Public Administration Review, 74*(5), 561–569. https://doi.org/10.1111/puar.12230

Svara, J. H. (2015). From ethical expectations to professional standards. In M. E. Guy & M. M. Rubin (Eds.), *Public administration evolving: From foundations to the future* (pp. 254–273). Routledge.

Svara, J. H., Braga, A., de Lancer Julnes, P., Massiah, M., Gilman, S. Ward, J., & Shields, W. (2015). *Implementing the ASPA code of ethics: Workbook and assessment guide*. https://www.aspanet.org/ASPADocs/Resources/Ethics_Assessment_Guide.pdf

Svara, J. H., & Brunet, J. R. (2004). Filling the skeletal pillar: Addressing social equity in introductory courses in public administration. *Journal of Public Affairs Education, 10*(2), 99–109. https://doi.org/10.1080/15236803.2004.12001351

Svara, J. H., & Brunet, J. R. (2005). Social equity is a pillar of public administration. *Journal of Public Affairs Education, 11*(3), 253–258. https://doi.org/10.1080/15236803.2005.12001398

Van de Ven, A. H. (2007). *Engaged scholarship: A guide for organizational and social research*. Oxford University Press.

Weber, P. C., & Brunt, C. (2020). Continuing to build knowledge: Undergraduate nonprofit programs in institutions of higher learning. *Journal of Public Affairs Education, 26*(3), 336–357. https://doi.org/10.1080/15236803.2019.1607804

Weimer, D., & Vining, A. (2017). *Policy analysis: Concepts and practice* (6th ed.). Routledge.

Williams, F. H. (1947). Minority groups and the OPA. *Public Administration Review, 7*(2), 123–128. https://doi.org/10.2307/972754

Williams, S. A. S., & Conyers, A. (2016). Race pedagogy: Faculty preparation matters. *Administrative Theory & Praxis, 38*(4), 234–250. https://doi.org/10.1080/10841806.2016.1239396

Yu, H., McCandless, S. A., & Rauhaus, B. (2023). Social equity in public administration: Past, present, and the future. *Journal of Public and Nonprofit Affairs, 9*(3), 437–452. https://doi.org/10.20899/jpna.9.3.437-452

8

THIRD CULTURE PROFESSORS

Kim Moloney[1], Mehmet Akif Demircioglu[2], and Kohei Suzuki[3]

[1]*Hamad Bin Khalifa University, Education City, Doha, Qatar,*
[2]*Carleton University, Ottawa, ON, Canada, and* [3]*Leiden University, Leiden, the Netherlands*

Since 2009, there has been an uptick in "expatriate academics" (EA) or "expatriate professors" scholarship. In a recent systematic conceptual review, scholars found research that analyzed the motives behind expatriate academic moves, adjustment observations, job and work outcomes, the mission of the academic work, and career/gender expectations (Przytula, 2023). There are country-specific studies on China, Malaysia, Qatar, Saudi Arabia, South Korea, the United Arab Emirates, and the United States (Asif et al., 2020; Austin et al., 2014; Cai & Hall, 2016; Richardson & Wong, 2018; Romanowski & Nasser, 2015; Sabharwal & Varma, 2015; Shin & Gress, 2018).

An EA is "a member of the higher education sector who has moved their dominant place of residence across national borders to take up legal, long-term, yet time-bound, employment in a teaching or research-related role within a university environment" (Trembath, 2016, p. 116). It is as important to understand who is an EA as it is to understand who is *not* an EA. EAs are not travelers (e.g., for conferences, sabbaticals, and field research), not university employees without teaching or research roles, and not educators or trainers employed outside universities (Trembath, 2016). We suggest the EA definition is important but does not go far enough.

Before introducing the third culture professor (TCP) concept, we must briefly discuss scholarship with several decades of research: third culture kids (TCK). A TCK is a "person who spends a significant part of his or her first 18 years of life accompanying parent(s) into a country that is different from at least one of the parent's passport country(ies) due to a parent's choice of work or advanced training" (Pollock et al., 2017, p. 27; Van

DOI: 10.4324/9781032671291-9

Renken, 2009). TCKs are interculturally mobile children who "are seen by their families, host country nationals and thus themselves, as belonging to their passport countries even though they may not feel a belonging there, as they may not have been born or lived there long" (Tan et al., 2021, p. 82). Compared to their home peers, TCKs often have enhanced sociolinguistic skills, intercultural competencies and adaptabilities, an ability to understand the world from non-home perspectives, and enhanced creativity, interpersonal sensitivity, and problem-solving skills (Tan et al., 2021). TCKs are the cornerstone of teacher-student-family interactions (curriculum, school support, and non-curriculum activities) at the international schools where children of expats and diplomats attend. Teachers are cognizant of the multinational experiences of students, encourage global conversations, and create unique insights into global citizenship education (e.g., Cockburn, 2002; Kwon, 2019).

We draw on the TCK concept to define third culture professor (TCP) as someone who spends a significant portion of his or her academic career working at universities in two or more countries different from their home citizenship(s).[1] TCK is a new concept. In our view, the TCP is a subcategory of EAs. One can be an EA without being a TCP. An EA becomes a TCP once they have spent a significant portion of their post-PhD academic career at more than one university across at least two countries that are not their home country. Each chapter co-author is an EA and a TCP.

EAs and TCPs offer at least three public administration and public policy insights. The first is research-specific. It is one thing to travel to another country for research and quite another to travel to a country, become a professor at a local university, and conduct research. Being local provides advantages. This includes the potential for increased trust between researchers and subjects (aka you are not a "fly-in, fly-out" researcher), your lived presence in a society indicates your interest in specific policy concerns, and your gained "sociopolitical short-hand" clarifies local nuance. Benefits are enhanced once an EA becomes a TCP and gains comparative experience.

For students, EAs and TCPs may offer policy and administrative insights with greater depth and accuracy than a well-traveled but non-TCP. Certainly, short-term travel is important for gaining "snapshot" insights. However, only by living in a location for several years can deeper insights, histories, and reasons for its policy or administrative actions become clear. This is enhanced once an EA becomes a TCP. Our third insight is that TCPs offer comparative experiences of university management. Just as domestic mobile professors gain domestic higher education insights via careers at two or more domestic universities, TCPs gain similar insights on a global scale. TCPs have networks in various countries, learn multiple higher education landscapes, and can become disciplinary "translators" among home and away academic populations.

As TCP co-authors, our chapter shares multiple insights. The chapter proceeds as follows: The next section details our methods and related cautions. This is followed by discussions of how, where, and why context matters in relation to three topics: the initial move (context by adjustment), research (context by university and country environments), and teaching (context in how faculty are addressed, teaching load, pedagogy, lecture style, and grading expectations). We conclude with reflections on TCPs, their disciplinary relevance, and future research.

Methods

The chapter is the collective output of the three TCP co-authors with a combined 33.5 years of work experience as full-time academics working in nine countries outside *their home countries* for two or more years per university. This includes (1) Kim Moloney (KM), an American citizen who has worked as an academic in four countries (Australia, Jamaica, Qatar, and South Korea); (2) Mehmet Demircioglu (MD), a Türkiye citizen, who has worked in three countries (Canada, Singapore, and the United States); and (3) Kohei Suzuki (KS), a Japan citizen, who has worked in three countries (the Netherlands, Sweden, and the United States).

KM's education was exclusive to the United States, and MD's undergraduate was in Türkiye with his MPA and PhD in the United States. MD was also trained in France, Germany, and Italy. KS's education was mainly in Japan before moving to earn his doctorate in the United States. Each co-author earned a PhD (in related fields) in the United States: a PhD in Public Administration from American University (KM), a PhD in Public Affairs from Indiana University (MD), and a PhD in Public Policy from Indiana University (KS). As a consequence, our shared vignettes are neither random nor a sample of TCP countries. We draw from the population of countries where we have worked as academics. Given our co-authorship, our vignettes are first-person experiences written in the third person.

Our chapter reflects a story-telling spirit. Story-telling is a powerful yet underutilized tool in public administration and public policy (Bevir, 2011; Manoharan & Rangarajan, 2023; Rhodes, 2019). It is a narrative method linked to interpretive social science. By reflecting upon our "storied lives" (Clandinin, 2006, p. 45), we "engage an audience in the experience of the narrator. Narratives invite us as listeners, readers, and viewers to enter the perspective of the narrator" (Riessman, 2008, p. 9).[2] As Rhodes (2019) observed, stories help us learn from experiences and help us understand organizations, organizational processes, and cultures. When our stories are shared as vignettes, we create the possibility of an "innovative interlinking with decolonizing and decentering critiques and transgressions" (Langer, 2016, p. 736). We share vignettes to help readers understand the TCP world.

Stories can be relayed as non-fictional metaphors to study "perceptions, beliefs, and attitudes" (Langer, 2016, p. 736). They are self-reflexive as our acts of vignette-telling require us to retell our experiences. We are also self-reflective. Borrowing from one part of the teaching effectiveness scholarship, we engage in two types of self-reflection: content reflection and premise reflection.[3] Content reflection "focuses on the problem itself, e.g., the accurate description of the problem" or, in our case, a discussion of our TCP circumstances (Kirpalani, 2017, p. 74). Premise reflection requires academics to understand "the relevance of the question" being asked, including its importance (Kirpalani, 2017, p. 74). We use premise reflection to question our TCP experiences, to illustrate their comparative relevance, and to consider their disciplinary value.

We offer five cautions related to our methodological choices. The first is that our shared stories are our own. Second, our experiences may not be the experiences of TCPs located in our home countries or of TCPs in countries where we do (have) work(ed). Third, our reflections may be time-sensitive. Circumstances may have shifted since our referenced period. Fourth, our reflections are unlikely to mirror the experiences, requirements, and perspectives of all universities, students, faculties, and researchers. Fifth, our experiences are often university-specific and may not always be generalizable to the country. Just as we should limit nonempirical and atheoretical claims about American universities and American faculty, readers should read our chapter for what it is: an output of our joint conversations as TCPs.

Context Matters: Visas, Documents, and Non-Work Experiences

This section is focused on our observations as we adjust to our new locations. Specifically, we will focus on moving logistics and, separately, non-work TCP benefits. For both, there are two overriding lessons: one should expect the unexpected and be open to differences. While renting an apartment, opening a bank account, obtaining a phone number, buying a car, getting a driver's license, figuring out health care, and learning public transport are common to domestic moves, contextual differences are amplified in global moves. Surprises are inevitable. They can also be challenging, given sociocultural or linguistic differences. If there was one lesson that we wish to "put on repeat" or "shout from the rooftops" throughout the chapter, it is the following: Active listening, patience, limited mountain-making when the issue is a molehill, and a deep well of curiosity-laced resilience are minimum requirements for being a successful TCP.

Visas and Paperwork

To be an EA or TCP, a job offer must be accepted, and a work visa must be obtained. The work visa often requires PhD diploma verification, police background checks, and medical paperwork. This "paperwork portfolio" increases as family size increases. For example, once MD received a job offer from Canada, he applied for a work visa, which took longer than normal. Each step had waiting periods, resulting in multiple government office visits with still more visits to do. For KM, her Australian work visa required a police certificate from each country where she had worked in the prior 10 years. It is not the simplest task to complete, given that KM had been a TCP in Jamaica and South Korea before working in Australia.

We have experienced a range of workplace understanding about international move transitions from limited-to-no assistance on how to operate in a new country to significant assistance on how to open a bank account, rent an apartment, and establish essentials. This included, for KM in Korea, the provision of a furnished apartment, and thus, it was airport-to-apartment in one day. In some countries, we are expected to teach and engage in university service immediately, while in others, we were given a semester-long adjustment.

In building lives from scratch in a foreign country, we have firsthand experience of administrative burdens (Herd & Moynihan, 2019) and societal challenges that may go unnoticed by researchers born in the local context. KS initially believed that living in Sweden and the Netherlands would be a natural extension of his PhD experiences in Bloomington, Indiana. This was not the case. Administrative and personal burdens include unexpected challenges in renting accommodation and limited assistance for new expats to make local connections. During KS's time in Sweden, a renowned welfare state, he had frequent contact with municipal offices and government agencies, whereas in the United States, this was less common. Similarly, in KS's home country of Japan, administrative procedures necessitated frequent in-person visits to government offices, given limited e-services. At the same time, digital services are standard in Sweden and the Netherlands.

Burden variance extends to driving licenses. KM had to take written and road tests in Korea and Qatar, but in Australia, she could transfer her U.S. license to an Australian license without a test. In Jamaica, KM drove with a combination of her U.S. license and a generic international license. This can be partnered with moments of surprise *non*-burden in administration. In

Korea, KM faced no administrative burden to buy a car. She bought her car from the ATM. This is how it worked: she found a model online, test-drove it at a dealership, and then was directed by the dealer to the ATM. At the ATM, she logged into her new Korean bank account, clicked on a screen for the bank name of the car dealership, tapped in the car dealership's bank account number, electronically transferred the money, walked back down the street, and within 20 minutes, had title, insurance, and was driving home. On the other end, burdens may appear in unexpected locations. For example, it only took one month of using very limited A/C in KM's rental home in Australia to learn that she would never do it again. That one month in Western Australia was equivalent to three months of nearly full-time A/C in Miami, Florida.

Non-Work Observations

Adjustment is not exclusive to work. The non-working hours of TCPs often add life experiences that may be unreachable to non-TCPs. MD and his wife appreciated the dynamism and diversity of the United States. It is a feeling replicated in Canada but with an important difference. Contrary to the United States' competitive and individualistic society, the Canadian culture is collaborative and cooperative. MD and his family observed that Canada welcomes everyone and respects cultures, languages, religions, and lifestyles without discrimination. During his stay in the United States, KS went on road trips with friends (including with MD), which allowed them to experience different regions directly.

After moving to Singapore, MD was impressed by the convenience of the bureaucratic infrastructure. This included a university in which staff handled almost every process, from getting the initial work permit to extending his stay. There was an ethic and motivation of public service and a sincere desire to help that is not always explicit elsewhere. In Sweden, KS enjoyed biannual research trips, biweekly Monday breakfasts at work, and collaborative research environments. Some joys also transferred, for example, KS started learning the Cuban salsa in the United States and then found a new Cuban salsa teacher in Sweden.

Joy in our personal lives positively translates to our academic lives. In Jamaica, KM's children learned the national anthem and had their first years filled with the radio tuned to reggae and dancehall. In Australia, a country where her kids hold a passport, they had conversations about the politics of Australia Day, why "fair go" may be an Australian myth, and a debate on whether ANZAC biscuits – a biscuit with national identity importance – taste good. In Qatar, KM and her teenagers attended the World Cup and the Asian Football Cup, F1, and Moto GP, world championships

114 Kim Moloney, Mehmet Akif Demircioglu, and Kohei Suzuki

in swimming, water polo, and diving along world tour stops for track and field and tennis. Such events are impossible without expensive domestic travel in her home country.

In general, around six months after arrival we find our patterns once again. Paths to work are memorized. Teaching is understood. University requirements have been incorporated. Household bills are regularized. Kids are settled into school. Hobbies are arranged. New friends are made. Plans are made to discover the city and country. While our view outside the window may vary from home, we find peace in our new routines. This does not mean that challenges do not arise. They do. In some instances, some of us did not adjust within six months, and instead, for one of us, it took comparatively longer than prior locations. Nonetheless, we do adapt, and eventually, we thrive.

Context Matters: In Research

In the prior section, we shared vignettes of the administrative burdens of becoming a TCP and, separately, brief insights into our non-work lives. This section shares stories about the university environment and, separately, the act of conducting research in our new locations.

Context in University Environments

We have worked in universities with varying levels of research support. This includes countries on the wealthier side, in which most faculty had competitively awarded university-level and/or national-level research grants and where dean-provided annual grants to faculty exceeded per year. But there is variance. We also have worked in high-income countries where if faculty wanted to attend an international conference, the answer was dependent on budgets, prior research outputs, favoritism, and/or a combination. Or, where conference funding was enough to attend a domestic conference, but other conferences required external grants.

For MD, his start-up grant in Singapore was $135,000, while his start-up grant in Canada was $7,500, demonstrating considerable variation in support. With $135,000, MD's research agenda could accelerate via multiple research assistants, conference travel, and fieldwork. While only one of us had worked in a non-wealthy country (KM in Jamaica), the university still offered opportunities for one annual conference abroad and, separately, a very generous book allowance.

Promotion practices also vary. In some universities, the hierarchy is an upside-down pyramid with more assistant professors than full professors. In others, there is a balance among the ranks. In parts of Europe, one can only be promoted to Associate Professor. To become a professor is a far more difficult task. It is equivalent to becoming a titled professor in the United States. Or, how in Australia, one becomes "permanent" (not tenured) after three years regardless of one's rank as lecturer, senior lecturer, reader/associate, or full. Since tenure largely does not exist in Australia, most faculty contracts are unionized. The contracts allow the university to cut faculty during a crisis. The easiest targets are the opposite of the United States: casualized and low-pay graduate assistants (called "tutors" in Australia) and, separately, full professors in the social sciences or humanities (STEM is often untouched) whose salaries, if cut, allow the university to hire two or three new lecturers.[4]

In some countries, research outputs are 50% of one's annual evaluation with an expectation of top Q1 journals, while in another country, publications in the top 10% of Scopus rankings were expected. On the other end, we have experienced universities where research outputs were as low as one journal article per year, where authoring a book was disfavored, or where authoring a book was marked as equivalent to writing a chapter in an edited volume. Finally, unlike parts of Australia, Asia, the Middle East, and the United States, where author order in the social sciences indicates each author's contribution (with the first author contributing the most), in parts of Europe, the expectation is that each co-author has coequally contributed and thus, author order is alphabetical by surname.

Context in Country Research Environment

The last two decades have witnessed a growing discussion about research positionality when non-nationals engage in fieldwork in a country that is not their own. Such fieldwork is typically short term; researchers return to their home university upon completion. Scholars have highlighted the importance of ethics, participatory engagements, and collaboration in such research (Cronin-Furman & Lake, 2018; Sultana, 2007). This includes short-term research abroad via the Fulbright program (Demir et al., 2000; Kahn & MacGarvie, 2016) and the Erasmus program (Yildiz et al., 2011, 2016).

Unlike short-term visitors, TCPs have extended opportunities to learn nuances often unreachable to "fly-in, fly-out" researchers and co-authors, from a place of understanding, with researchers who are either from the country or from the region, and/or who are fluent in a local language. For example, one of us is working with two scholars on a long-term project in which language fluency is necessary for interviews and focus groups.

TCPs can directly observe public-sector commentaries in the classroom that may or may not match theoretical or empirical expectations from the dominant literature and, as a result, can more quickly create a research design to test their observations. Similarly, one can increase the credibility of their potential empirical work via immediate review by local colleagues. For each of us, certain scholarly outputs would not have arisen if we had not been a TCP:

- For KM, she observed that her Jamaican students (many of whom were current civil servants) felt public service motivation (as predicted by the concept) but could not actualize it (as overlooked by the concept). The output was an article in the *American Review of Public Administration* (Moloney & Chu, 2016).
- MD's Singaporean colleagues (practitioners, former Ministers, and top bureaucrats) and his students openly shared knowledge. Thanks to a grant from the National University of Singapore, MD and Zeger van der Wal (an EA from the Netherlands working in Singapore) organized a workshop that led to a special issue in the *Australian Journal of Public Administration* in 2020 (volume 79, issue 3). In addition to their introductory essay (van der Wal & Demircioglu, 2020), there were six articles on public-sector innovation in the Asia-Pacific. Later, with UK-based colleagues, MD co-authored an article (Cinar et al., 2024) on how a city-state (Singapore) articulated administrative innovation.
- Based on KS's experience in Sweden, KS and MD co-authored a paper in *Governance*. While prior studies had highlighted the importance of impartiality in bureaucratic decision-making (Nistotskaya, 2020; Rothstein & Teorell, 2008), they questioned whether impartiality is universally desirable and whether it overlooks varying administrative burdens. KS's perspective as TCP in a country prioritizing impartiality but where he lacked the same local knowledge and social networks as citizens raised such questions. They found that citizen satisfaction with administrative impartiality depended on individual characteristics, with socially disadvantaged individuals favoring customized administrative responses (Suzuki & Demircioglu, 2021).
- Living abroad made KS realize that the problems of declining birthrates and shrinking populations faced by his home country, Japan, are not yet apparent in other countries. This comparative insight led to several publications focused on such challenges for Japan's local governments (Suzuki & Sakuwa, 2016; Suzuki, 2017; Suzuki et al., 2021).

Context Matters: Teaching

Local contexts have teaching, pedagogy, and curriculum implications. This section engages such contexts via subsections on how students, teaching loads, pedagogical choices, lecture styles, and grading expectations address faculty. This section benefitted from an abundance of academic literature on international education (e.g., Akanwa, 2015; Marlina, 2009), multicultural education (e.g., Banks, 1993, 2015), and multiculturalism within the classroom (Llera et al., 2009). This included early work on the risks of a multicultural classroom with "monocultural teachers" (Dean, 1989). Such research is also found, although with far more limited coverage, in the two teaching journals of our field: *Teaching Public Administration* and the *Journal of Public Affairs Education* (e.g., Baracskay, 2021; Devereux & Durning, 2001; Jennings & White, 2005; Straussman & Guinn, 2023). Given that there are no discipline-specific discussions about TCP teaching, our vignettes are a small step toward addressing this gap.

Context by Addressing Faculty

The adaptable TCP allows students to address them as per local expectations. For example, we have worked in locations where "professor" was only given to academics who had earned that rank (and not to assistant or associate or lecturer) (KM in Jamaica), where professor is how all faculty were addressed regardless of rank (KM in Korea; MD in Singapore and Canada), where Dr is followed by first name without the surname (e.g., KM in Qatar), and where professor followed by first name without the surname (MD in Singapore).

This varies from the United States, where faculty are interchangeably addressed as Dr with surname or professor with surname regardless of rank. Each example also differs in Australia, where students culturally expect to address their professors exclusively by their first name, without Dr or professor. This is due to Australia's "tall poppy syndrome" and a presumption, at least rhetorically, of an egalitarian Australian culture (Peeters, 2004).

Context by Teaching Load

There is variance among non-U.S. universities on their teaching, research, and service expectations. We have worked in countries where, given the university's explicit research university emphasis (like an R1 in the United States), the teaching load was "one and two": one course[5] in one semester and two in the next semester with no course enrolling more than 20 students. In other countries, the teaching load is a U.S.-familiar two-and-two, sometimes with 50-plus students per course. We have also worked in universities with higher teaching loads. Our only example arises from the United States, where KM once had a three-and-three teaching load.

In other locations, the teaching load arises from different calculations. In the Netherlands, the research-to-teaching/service allocation is "3:7," with administrative tasks comprising most of the latter. For KS in Sweden and

118 Kim Moloney, Mehmet Akif Demircioglu, and Kohei Suzuki

the Netherlands and KM in Australia, one could increase research time via research grants and opting for a course buyout. In other countries, research grants may not have course buyout options. One of us worked at a university (KM in Australia) where teaching loads were partially dependent on research outputs via weighted publication formulas, for example, weight of a book versus a journal article in a Q1 journal versus a non-Q1 article versus a chapter. Research allocations could be further altered if faculty had a field-weighted citation index (FWCI) >1.5. On a university-specific 1000-point scale of work, a FWCI >1.5 led to a reduction in teaching hours, while a FWCI >2 led to a reduction.

In Sweden and the Netherlands, multiple instructors of the KS team taught the same course but with different topics, many courses end in less than eight weeks, and there are fewer classes conducted throughout the semester. In Australia, KM could teach one course over a semester and, with approval, teach a separate semester-long course in a condensed form of meeting every few weeks at six or eight hours per day. In some countries, all graduate students in public policy or public administration must write a master's thesis or capstone (Jamaica, Netherlands, Sweden, and Qatar), while in others, they do not.

Context by Pedagogical Choice

We are not the first to acknowledge that the public administration and public policy disciplines are overly American (Haque, 2013; Stillman, 1990). This is problematic for teaching not only in the United States but also outside the United States. As noted by Baulderstone and O'Toole (2005), a student's factual observation that "it's different in my country" when faced with a Western canon has added importance for multicultural classrooms in the West but also in TCP classrooms.

For KM in Australia, her graduate-level public sector management courses were split nearly 50/50 between Australian students and students from Africa and Asia. The non-Australian students were often mid-ranked civil servants in their home country studying in Australia via Australian government scholarships. In Qatar, KM's classes had approximately 40% Qatari, with the remaining being citizens of, or having family origins in, the Middle East, North Africa, West Africa, Southeastern Europe, South Asia, and/or Central Asia. In MD's experience in Singapore, about 20% of students were Singaporean, while 80% were international (primarily Asian, predominantly from China and India) from 30+ countries. For KS in the Netherlands, approximately 10% of students are non-European, 30–40% come from European countries other than the Netherlands, and the remaining students are Dutch nationals. In contrast, nearly 100% of

KM's students were Jamaican in Jamaica or Korean in South Korea. This is similar for MD in Canada, where almost all students are Canadian, but many have immigrant backgrounds.

Despite an American-centered discipline, TCPs cannot simply regurgitate the American canon. The American context cannot, and should not, in many cases, apply elsewhere. In general, all three of us avoid restrictive pedagogies. A "restrictive pedagogy" or "traditional pedagogy" will "define parameters for critical discussions and is unlikely to turn inward and interrogate academic institutions" (Hendrix et al., 2003, p. 182). In Australia, Canada, the Netherlands, Singapore, and Sweden, our syllabi have national examples, critical analysis, and comparative sharing.

Each of us also engages in "critical localism," and in some countries, KM has used "counter-hegemonic pedagogy, epistemology, and methodology" (Chan-Tiberghien, 2004, p. 194). In non-Western countries (e.g., for KM in Jamaica and Qatar) where there is limited country-specific scholarship in public administration or public policy, KM emphasizes critical pedagogies. The "principle distinguishing characteristic" of critical (or transformative pedagogy) "is its immediate emphasis on dominant versus nondominant academic practices" (Hendrix et al., 2003, p. 182). In KM's view, it is a disservice to her students if we did not challenge the discipline's methodological Americanism, its methodological whiteness, and if we overlooked the global dynamics of where policy and administrative power and influence are located (Moloney et al., 2023). Local socioeconomic, geographic, and religious contexts alter what is taught.

Incrementally, non-West scholars have begun to share critical pedagogy techniques and the limits of the Western canon (Makiva et al., 2022; Matsiliza, 2020; van Jaarsveldt et al., 2019). While the three of us disagree on the degree of criticality required in our syllabi, we agree that there are far too few articles on when, where, and how to balance traditional versus critical pedagogical needs, degree requirements, personal professorial styles, and student backgrounds.

Since none of us are encouraged to replicate an American canon via restrictive pedagogies, we will share four examples of how we separate from an American-dominant canon:

- *Critical Engagement*: For KM's public management course in Qatar, she starts with readings on the perils of methodological Americanism, requires students to critically query West-focused articles for their (ir) relevance to their home countries, and not only ensures assignments test concept knowledge but requires students to explain when, where, and why a concept does (not) or should (not) apply to their home country. Student defense of their arguments strongly influences their grade.

- *Topic Context*: In her digital governance course in Qatar, KM spends only one week on e-government and e-service delivery. This is despite the subject often filling most weeks of similar syllabi in the West. Given its achievements in both areas, neither topic is where Qatar needs help. Given Qatar's 2030 strategy, the semester is spent learning more important topics (artificial intelligence, blockchain, internet of things, digital currencies, cybersecurity, cyberwarfare, and quantum computing) and discussing their policy implications via policy design, accountability, and trust/privacy debates.
- *Topic Context*: MD taught an elective on public-sector innovation in Singapore, Kazakhstan, and soon, Canada. Many examples come from non-Western settings, particularly Singapore. This included cases related to market and government failures, ethics, government roles in innovation, and sources of innovation. Several cases appear in a forthcoming book co-authored by MD and Audretsch (2024).
- *Comparative Context*: In KS's comparative public management courses in Europe, he suggests that country context, macro-level institutions, and bureaucratic characteristics influence public management effectiveness. His students analyze the differences in bureaucratic structures across countries and discuss how variations affect government performance and societal-economic indicators in each country. The latest empirical research guides the discussions.

Context by Lecture Style

We have taught in countries where the expected lecture style was that the professor teaches, the students listen, and the class ends. Deviation was not the expectation. When hired as a TCP, it is because of our research and teaching competency but also our explicit and hard-learned cultural competency.[6] In short, no one (and with limited exaggeration on the "no one") wants to know how America does it, if America does it better, and whether our new employer and country are "wrong." If the national culture expects strict lectures, it is not a TCP's place to suggest their culture is "wrong." If such a conversation were to occur (and it may never happen, which must be understood by our non-TCP readers as acceptable), the conversation is not for the moment of syllabus design. It can arise, as it does in many countries, during teaching retreats or at university teaching centers.

For MD, no specific lecture format was expected by Singapore and Canada, so faculty are free to develop a course if they cover expected topics. However, there is a difference between Singapore and Canada on power and authority dynamics among faculty, teaching assistants, and students. In

Canada, like the United States, faculty members have significant autonomy to deliver lectures. For example, a faculty member may go to a conference without informing the school if the conference overlaps with a course session. In such an instance, the faculty delivers the lecture via Zoom, changes its timing, or gives an alternative assignment.

In Singapore, it is nearly impossible to change sessions even if they overlap with important events, including family emergencies. Rescheduling sessions requires permission from the Dean. At one faculty meeting in Singapore, MD learned that several successful academics had been fired for missing sessions. So, while faculty members in Singapore have autonomy regarding topics and style, they have less autonomy for rescheduling than in Canada and the United States. For KM, there has also been variance. While Qatar, Australia, and Korea did not have Singapore-style strictness, in all three countries, faculty could conduct an online class (via pre-recorded lectures and activities) if a class was missed. However, in all three locations for KM, faculty should aim to not miss more than one class per course via Dean-approved travel.

In terms of classroom dynamics, there are differences. In Canada, like in the United States, teaching assistants (TAs) can grade assignments, and students respect TA authority. In Singapore, however, academic rankings matter. Even if a TA is an overachiever (e.g., published in top academic journals while studying for their PhD), none may grade written assignments, and many students may not respect TA knowledge. In Singapore, MD observed that in core courses, most students expect faculty to be the sole authority and to influence the final decision about a discussion point, even if a discussion question is normative.

Neither KM nor KS have experienced such Singaporean interactions. In Sweden and the Netherlands, classroom interaction tends to be more formal and to remind KS of Japanese universities. In Korea and Jamaica for KM, classes were lecture-driven (more formal in Korea than Jamaica) and TAs were rare. If the faculty employed a student in either country, it was as a research assistant. Since public sector management is an undergraduate degree and a graduate degree in Jamaica, this meant that for the undergraduates, a weekly lecture was followed by a tutorial in which group-based exercises were common. For the graduate degree, it was a longer single session, often lecture-dominant.

In Australia, faculty were strongly encouraged to flip their classrooms; while in Qatar, Sweden, and the Netherlands, faculty are free to choose their classroom style. In Australia and Qatar, TAs are infrequently hired within public policy programs.[7] Unique to KM's prior university in Australia, its 1000-point workload system meant that if faculty did not have enough teaching points, they would be required to serve as TA-equivalent in another faculty member's course and/or teach a university-wide course regardless of their faculty rank.

Context by Grading Expectations

Our final insight is that "students are students" no matter where in the world we have taught. They, like us, when we were students, want to know how to get from "A to Z" in their course, how we will grade, whether we will accept a late submission, and ask what *really* must be done in the course. We find this observation to be true regardless of the student's home country, gender, religion, socioeconomic class, and/or ethnicity.

But there are differences, too. For example, in the Netherlands, KS observed that most students do not ask him to reconsider grades, do not seek clarification for the grade given, and do not openly challenge him in class. This is also consistent with MD's observation in Canada and KM's observations in Jamaica, Qatar, and Korea. However, in Singapore, MD observed fierce competition among Singaporean students (e.g., not sharing notes or helping classmates), and some students were too concerned of grades (e.g., countless office hours to challenge grades). The reason may be Singapore's system, since the early years of education, for examination-focused evaluation along with a university policy that no more than one-third of students can earn an "A" level grade (A or A-).

In only Australia and Jamaica did KM face syllabus design restrictions. In Australia, this included whether an examination must be given (depending on other course grading assignments) and the allowable percentage of a student's final grade, which must arise from faculty-monitored assignments. In Jamaica, of an undergraduate's grade and of a graduate's grade must come from proctored final examinations. The frequent American preference within upper-level social science courses to assign a final paper with a value of up to 40% of a student's final grade was less available. Such detailed requirements were not found in Canada, Korea, the Netherlands, Qatar, Singapore, or Sweden.

Specific to the Netherlands, KS noted an expectation that publicly disclosed course outlines ("e-prospectus") should align with the content of the syllabi. Given that its MPA program lasts only one year and each class is completed in eight weeks, there is a desire to avoid overloading students and faculty with excessive assignments. Following university regulations, providing students with a re-sit opportunity is mandatory, allowing those who received a failing grade on their initial assignment to redo it.

When it comes to grading, many (if not most) countries do not have a U.S.-style A-F system. Or if they do, expectations of what an "A" is varies. In the

United States, if a student successfully achieves what is required, they will earn an "A." In Australia, the grade options are "High Distinction" (grade of 80–100), "Distinction" (70–79), "Acceptable Standard of Achievement" or "C" (60–69), and "Pass" (50–59). The above-average student would be thrilled with a grade point average (GPA) in the low 70s. The rare student, that is, the 1-in-200 student, may have a GPA in the low 80s.

For KM in Australia and MD in Singapore, faculty do not immediately enter a student's final course grade into the university system once the course has ended. Instead, faculty meet two to three weeks after the semester ends to discuss all final grades in a mandatory meeting in which grade summaries of prior years for that course are presented. If group discussion requires it, individual faculty will be asked to modify the grade of a student or group of students. Only after such discussions were concluded could faculty share the student's final grade with the university.

For MD in Singapore, the university rule was that no more than 10% of students in a course could receive an "A+," no more than 10% could receive an "A," and the cap for A-level grades (A+, A, and A-) must be 33%. A similar rule, but with different percentages, was also found by KM in Korea. This is particularly challenging for faculty who teach elective courses. For example, if only 10 students are in a class, only one person can earn an "A+," one can earn an "A," and one can earn an "A-" (or one "A" and two "A-"). For KS in the Netherlands, the system ranges from 1 to 10, with 1 being the lowest and 10 the highest grade. A passing score for an individual subject is 5.5. Despite the 1 to 10 scale, grades 1 to 3 and 9 to 10 are rarely assigned. The most frequently awarded grades are 6 and 7.

In Jamaica, the grades were A–F, but the cultural expectation was that only a tiny minority of students would earn an "A." This is not because the students did not have the skills – they did – but because the "A" was to be given rarely. To ensure equivalency across courses and given a requirement that 50–60% of a student's final grade must be determined via blue book final examinations, faculty would grade their own examinations and then be assigned the graded blue books of other departmental courses to review. This ensured that one faculty member's understanding of what an "A" or "A-" is was the same as another. This process was repeated at the college and university levels before a student's grade was posted to their transcript.

Such differences are not surprising to TCPs. Yildiz et al. (2011) observed content and delivery differences among American, European, Asian, and African public policy programs. For example, state universities in the United States rely less on government funding than state universities in Europe and Asia. While public policy and public management education in the United States and Canada may be more connected to practice, they have limited comparative research and theory foci (DeLeon, 2006; Geva-May & Maslove, 2006).

As such, internships are expected in the US and Canada. In Canada, almost all students do co-ops (internships) with government agencies due to the prestige and reputation of the school (oldest graduate school in public administration/policy school in Canada), location (Ottawa, the capital city), and the network (strong ties with the government's thanks to alumni who have become influential bureaucrats and politicians who previously studied at Carleton University). There are also several full-time employees working in the government who may enroll as full-time or part-time students. In the MPA program in the Netherlands that KS is involved in, most students are full-time since the program only lasts for one year. For MD, all students are full-time in Singapore. While some students serve as part-time TA or research assistant, none work full-time. However, many students also work part-time and participate in internships for their future careers. In contrast, for KM, internships were rare in Jamaica, a limited option in Australia, and in Qatar, they are an option. However, in all three countries, most students work full-time, and thus, internships are less prioritized.

Conclusion

Our chapter started by exploring the expatriate academic concept before suggesting the relevance of adding a third culture professor as a new concept and as a new subcategory of the expatriate academic concept. Neither EAs nor TCPs are researched subjects within the public administration and public policy disciplines. This oversight is a symptom of two disciplines that infrequently foray into, or have considerations of, non-American and non-Western canons, experiences, and contributions. If the disciplines are to operationalize their oft-stated but continually underrealized goal to internationalize, EAs and TCPs must be reframed as disciplinary assets. This includes an increased valuation, respect for, and understanding of who was not discussed in our chapter: the research academics in non-Western universities, the majority of whom are not EAs or TCPs.

By splitting our analysis into three sections (adjustment contexts, research contexts, and teaching context), we were able to continually re-emphasize the values of adaptability and understanding local and national contexts. Our combined nine subsections have highlighted our chapter's earlier observation: *active listening, patience, limited mountain-making when the issue is a molehill, and a deep well of curiosity-laced resilience are minimum requirements for being a successful TCP.*

The call arising from our chapter goes beyond more research on EAs, TCPs, and local academics in non-Western universities. It is a call for our disciplines to constantly question its inherent hegemonies, its canon, its knowledge directionalities, and its assumptions of the "other." Whether our disciplinary responses are more research, altered program designs (especially at the PhD level), reformed journal practices, new pedagogical considerations, and/or other avenues of improved discipline-specific theories, concepts, methods, and practices, what is clear is that the road ahead is broad, multi-faceted, and awaiting a truly global discussion of what is or is not administrative and policy practice around the world.

Notes

1 Borrowing from the TCK concept, we acknowledge that TCPs may also carry altered feelings of (non-)belonging when they return to their home country. However, due to chapter word limits, we removed this section from our chapter. It is a topic for future research.

2 Narratives methodologies are part of descriptive and hermeneutic phenomenology. This chapter leans toward the latter.

3 The third is process reflection: "procedures and processes of problem-solving, including connections to prior learning" (Kirpalani, 2017, p. 73). Process reflections occurred as we conceptualized the chapter but its locations within the chapter are more difficult to highlight than the other two self-reflection types.

4 There is an enormous amount of discussion about the last five to seven years of Australian higher education. This includes local and international coverage, blogs, and multiple locations of leaked university documents. For just a start, see Cassidy (2023) in *The Guardian* about tutors and separately, see Anonymous (2023) in *The Guardian* about faculty. An online search for any specific Australian university and faculty issues will often find even more articles including, in several instances, coverage of faculty walk-outs and street protests.

5 To simplify cross-national discussions, we use American terminology on what is a major, course, unit, and class. The major is the student's intended degree program, a course is semester-long content, a unit is a small multi-week portion of that course, and a class is the specified meeting date/time of the course. This is not the terminology of many other countries. In Australia, for example, the course was the student's degree program (e.g., B.Sc. in political science), the unit was the semester-long content, and the class is the meeting time of the unit.

6 The latter is often not directly observable in a CV but can become apparent in interviews.

7 This is likely specific to her university in Australia. Other Australian universities have more TAs (tutors) in the social sciences.

References

Akanwa, E. E. (2015). International students in Western developed countries: History, challenges, and prospects. *Journal of International Students, 5*(3), 271–284.

Anonymous (2023, May 26). Australia's universities are failing academics like me – and they're failing the country. *The Guardian.* https://www.theguardian.com/commentisfree/2023/may/26/australia-universities-failing-academics-and-country-uni-university

Asif, U., Bano, N., & Al Najjar, H. (2020). Experiences of expatriate university teachers in a health science university in Saudi Arabia-A qualitative study. *Pakistan Journal of Medical Sciences, 36*(4), 799–803. https://doi.org/10.12669/pjms.36.4.1896

Austin, A. E., Chapman, D. W., Farah, S., Wilson, E., & Ridge, N. (2014). Expatriate academic staff in the United Arab Emirates: The nature of their work experiences in higher education institutions. *Higher Education, 68,* 541–557. https://doi.org/10.1007/s10734-014-9727-z

Banks, J. A. (1993). Multicultural education: Development, dimensions, and challenges. *The Phi Delta Kappan, 75*(1), 22–28.

Banks, J. A. (2015). *Cultural diversity and education: Foundations, curriculum, and teaching.* Routledge.

Baracskay, D. (2021). Teaching diversity, cultural competency, and globalization to American public affairs students: Integrating comparative approaches to public administration and policy. *Teaching Public Administration, 39*(3), 287–317. https://doi.org/10.1177/0144739420921918

Baulderstone, J., & O'Toole, P. (2005). But it's different in my country: Teaching public administration using western materials. In Jak Jabes (Ed.), *The role of public administration in alleviating poverty and improving governance* (pp. 576–586). Asian Development Bank.

Bevir, M. (2011). Public administration as story-telling. *Public Administration, 89*(1), 183–195. https://doi.org/10.1111/j.1467-9299-2011.01908.x

Cai, L., & Hall, C. (2016). Motivations, expectations, and experiences of expatriate academic staff on an international branch campus in China. *Journal of Studies in International Education, 20*(3), 207–222. https://doi.org/10.1177/1028315315623055

Cassidy, C. (2023, April 10). 'Appallingly unethical': Why Australian universities are at breaking point. *The Guardian.* https://www.theguardian.com/australia-news/2023/apr/10/appallingly-unethical-why-australian-universities-are-at-breaking-point

Chan-Tiberghien, J. (2004). Towards a 'global educational justice' research paradigm: Cognitive justice, decolonizing methodologies and critical pedagogy. *Globalisation, Societies and Education, 2*(2), 191–213. https://doi.org/10.1080/14767720410001733647

Cinar, E., Demircioglu, M. A., Acik, A. C., & Simms, C. (2024). Public sector innovation in a city state: Exploring innovation types and national context in Singapore. *Research Policy, 53*(2), 104915. https://doi.org/10.1016/j.respol.2023.104915

Clandinin, D. J. (2006). Narrative inquiry: A methodology for studying lived experience. *Research Studies in Music Education, 27*(1), 44–54. https://doi.org/10.1177/1321103X060270010301

Cockburn, L. (2002). Children and young people living in changing worlds: The process of assessing and understanding the 'third culture kid'. *School Psychology International, 23*(4), 475–485. https://doi.org/10.1177/0143034302234008

Cronin-Furman, K., & Lake, M. (2018). Ethics abroad: Fieldwork in fragile and violent contexts. *PS: Political Science & Politics, 51*(3), 607–614. https://doi.org/10.1017/S1049096518000379

Dean, T. (1989). Multicultural classrooms, monocultural teachers. *College Composition and Communication, 40*(1), 23–37. https://doi.org/10.2307/358178

DeLeon, P. (2006). The historical roots of the field. In M. Moran, M. Rein, & R. E. Goodin (Eds.), *The Oxford handbook of public policy* (pp. 39–57). Oxford University Press.

Demir, C. E., Aksu, M., & Paykoç, F. (2000). Does Fulbright make a difference? The Turkish perspective. *Journal of Studies in International Education, 4*(1), 103–111. https://doi.org/10.1177/102831530000400107

Demircioglu, M. A., & Audretsch, D. B. (2024). *Public Sector Innovation.* Cambridge University Press.

Devereux, E. A., & Durning, D. (2001). Going global? International activities by US schools of public policy and management to transform public affairs education. *Journal of Public Affairs Education, 7*(4), 241–260. https://doi.org/10.1080/15236803.2001.12023521

Geva-May, I., & Maslove, A. (2006). Canadian public policy analysis and public policy programs: A comparative perspective. *Journal of Public Affairs Education, 12*(4), 413–438. https://doi.org/10.1080/15236803.2006.12001449

Haque, M. S. (2013). Public administration in a globalized Asia: Intellectual identities, challenges, and prospects. *Public Administration and Development, 33*(4), 262–274. https://doi.org/10.1002/pad.1658

Hendrix, K. G., Jackson, R. L., & Warren, J. R. (2003). Shifting academic landscapes: Exploring co-identities, identity negotiation, and critical progressive pedagogy. *Communication Education, 52*(3/4), 177–190. https://doi.org/10.1080/0363452032000156181

Herd, P., & Moynihan, D. P. (2019). *Administrative burden: Policymaking by other means.* Russell Sage Foundation.

Jennings, E. T., & White, H. (2005). Introduction: Symposium on globalization and international approaches to public affairs education. *Journal of Public Affairs Education, 11*(2), 69–72. https://doi.org/10.1080/15236803.2005.12001380

Kahn, S., & MacGarvie, M. (2016). Do return requirements increase international knowledge diffusion? Evidence from the Fulbright program. *Research Policy, 45*(6), 1304–1322. https://doi.org/10.1016/j.respol.2016.02.002

Kirpalani, N. (2017). Developing self-reflective practices to improve teaching effectiveness. *Journal of Higher Education Theory and Practice, 17*(8), 73–80.

Kwon, J. (2019). Third culture kids: Growing up with mobility and cross-cultural transitions. *Diaspora, Indigenous, and Minority Education, 13*(2), 113–122.

Langer, P. C. (2016). The research vignette: Reflexive writing as interpretative representation of qualitative inquiry – A methodological proposition. *Qualitative Inquiry, 22*(9), 735–744. https://doi.org/10.1177/1077800416658066

Llera, D. J., Saleem, R., Roffman, E., & Dass-Brailsford, P. (2009). Teaching to transform: Multicultural competence and classroom practice. *Asian Journal of Counselling, 16*(1), 51–66.

Makiva, M., Ile, I. U., & Fagbadebo, O. M. (2022). Decolonising public administration content curriculum in a post-colonial African university: Policy monitoring and evaluation perspective. *African Journal of Governance and Development, 11*(2), 479–497. https://doi.org/10.36369/2616-9045/2022/v11i2a6

Manoharan, A. P., & Rangarajan, N. (2023). Public administrators as storytellers: Nurturing narrative competence to enrich their professional identity. *Administrative Theory & Praxis, 45*(2), 158–169. https://doi.org/10.1080/10841806.2022.2086753

Marlina, R. (2009). "I don't talk or I decide not to talk? Is it my culture?" – International students' experiences of tutorial participation. *International Journal of Educational Research, 48*(4), 235–244. https://doi.org/10.1016/j.ijer.2009.11.001

Matsiliza, N. S. (2020). Decolonisation in the field of public administration: The responsiveness of the scholarship of teaching and learning. *Teaching Public Administration, 38*(3), 295–312. https://doi.org/10.1177/0144739420901743

Moloney, K., Chou, M. H., Osei, P., & Campbell, Y. (2023). Methodological Americanism: Disciplinary senility and intellectual hegemonies in (American) public administration. *Administrative Theory and Praxis*, 44(4), 261–276. https://doi.org/10.1080/10841806.2022.2140387

Moloney, K., & Chu, H. Y. (2016). Linking Jamaica's public service motivations and ethical climate. *American Review of Public Administration*, 46(4), 436–458. https://doi.org/10.1177/0275074014557022

Nistotskaya, M. (2020). Quality of government (QoG) as impartiality: Review of the literature on the causes and consequences of QoG. *KIPA Public Policy Review*, 1(1), 25–49.

Peeters, B. (2004). Tall poppies and egalitarianism in Australian discourse: From key word to cultural value. *English World-Wide*, 25(1), 1–25. https://doi.org/101075/eww.25.1.02pee

Pollock, D. C., Van Reken, R., & Pollock, M. V. (Eds.). (2017). *Third culture kids: Growing up among worlds* (3rd ed.). Nicholas Brealey Publishing.

Przytula, S. (2023). Expatriate academics: What have we known for four decades? A systematic literature review. *Journal of Global Mobility: The Home of Expatriate Management Research*, 21(1), 31–56. https://doi.org/10.1108/JGM-03-2023-0024

Rhodes, R. A. W. (2019). *Public administration, the interpretive turn and story-telling*. Edward Elgar.

Richardson, C., & Wong, H. W. (2018). Expatriate academics in Malaysia: Motivation, adjustment, and retention. *Journal of Management Development*, 37(3), 299–308.

Riessman, C. K. (2008). *Narrative methods for the human sciences*. Sage.

Romanowski, M. H., & Nasser, R. (2015). Identity issues: Expatriate professors teaching and researching in Qatar. *Higher Education*, 69(4), 653–671. https://doi.org/10.1007/s10734-014-9795-0

Rothstein, B., & Teorell, J. (2008). What is quality of government? A theory of impartial government institutions. *Governance*, 21(2), 165–190. https://doi.org/10.1111/j.1468-0491.2008.00391.x

Sabharwal, M., & Varma, R. (2015). Transnational research collaboration: Expatriate Indian faculty in the United States connecting with peers in India. *East Asian Science, Technology and Society: An International Journal*, 9(3), 275–293. https://doi.org/10.1215/18752160-3141241

Shin, J. C., & Gress, D. R. (2018). Expatriate academics and managing diversity: A Korean host university's perspective. *Asia Pacific Education Review*, 19(2), 297–306. https://doi.org/10.1007/s12564-018-9539-4

Stillman, R. J. (1990). The peculiar 'stateless' origins of American public administration and the consequences for government today. *Public Administration Review*, 50(2), 156–167. https://doi.org/10.12307/976863

Straussman, J. D., & Guinn, D. E. (2023). Teaching international comparative public management through a development lens. *Teaching Public Administration*, 41(2), 257–265. https://doi.org/10.1177/01447394211042853

Sultana, F. (2007). Reflexivity, positionality and participatory ethics: Negotiating fieldwork dilemmas in international research. *ACME: An International Journal for Critical Geographies*, 6(3), 374–385.

Suzuki, K. (2017). Government expenditure cuts and voluntary activities of citizens: The experience of Japanese municipalities. *Asia Pacific Journal of Public Administration*, 39(4), 258–275. https://doi.org/10.1080/23276665.2017.1403179

Suzuki, K., & Demircioglu, M. A. (2021). Is impartiality enough? Government impartiality and citizens' perceptions of public service quality. *Governance*, *34*(3), 727–764. https://doi.org/10.1111/gove.12527

Suzuki, K., Dollery, B. E., & Kortt, M. A. (2021). Addressing loneliness and social isolation amongst elderly people through local co-production in Japan. *Social Policy & Administration*, *55*(4), 674–686. https://doi.org/10.1111/spol.12650

Suzuki, K., & Sakuwa, K. (2016). Impact of municipal mergers on local population growth: An assessment of the merger of Japanese municipalities. *Asia Pacific Journal of Public Administration*, *38*(4), 223–238. https://doi.org/10.1080/232 76665.2016.1258887

Tan, E. C., Wang, K. T., & Cottrell, A. B. (2021). A systematic review of third culture kids empirical research. *International Journal of Intercultural Relations*, *82*, 81–98. https://doi.org/10.1016/j.ijntrel.2021.03.002

Trembath, J. L. (2016). The professional lives of expatriate academics: Construct clarity and implications for expatriate management in higher education. *Journal of Global Mobility*, *4*(2), 112–130.

van der Wal, Z., & Demircioglu, M. A. (2020). Public sector innovation in the Asia-pacific trends, challenges, and opportunities. *Australian Journal of Public Administration*, *79*(3), 271–278. https://doi.org/10.1111/1467-8500.12435

van Jaarsveldt, L. C., de Vries, M. S., & Kroukamp, H. J. (2019). South African students call to decolonize science: Implications for international standards, curriculum development, and Public Administration. *Teaching Public Administration*, *37*(1), 12–30. https://doi.org/10.1177/0144739418790779

Van Renken, R. E. (2009, November 13). Third culture kids: Expat children experience the world in a different way to most people. With the election of Barack Obama perhaps their time has come. *The Telegraph*. https://www.telegraph.co.uk/education/expateducation/6545869/Third-culture-kids.html

Yildiz, M., Babaoğlu, C., & Demircioglu, M. A. (2016). E-government education in Turkish public administration graduate programs: Past, present, and future. *Journal of Public Affairs Education*, *22*(2), 287–302. https://doi.org/10.1080/1 5236803.2016.12002246

Yildiz, M., Demircioğlu, M. A., & Babaoğlu, C. (2011). Teaching public policy to undergraduate students: Issues, experiences, and lessons in Turkey. *Journal of Public Affairs Education*, *17*(3), 343–365. https://doi.org/10.1080/15236803.2 011.12001649

SECTION II

Becoming Experts in the Craft

9

BECOMING AN EXPERT IN THE CRAFT

Norma M. Riccucci

Rutgers University, Newark, Newark, NJ

Teaching for me has always been an integral part of being an academic. Imparting knowledge and mentoring is very high on my value scale of being a professor. While academic tenure standards, particularly at R1 institutions, putatively rely on teaching evaluations, research, and service, scholarly publications tend to dominate the decisions to grant or deny tenure to assistant professors. In effect, teaching can fall by the wayside for those prioritizing research over teaching and service. For me, being an effective teacher has never been motivated by a carrot or stick. Still, rather it has always been intrinsic: the rewards of engaging in meaningful discussions, reading outstanding papers and examinations – which reflect student learning – helping my students craft their dissertations, and overall, assisting my students as best as possible to achieve their educational goals.

My approach to teaching depends on whether I am working with MPA or PhD students. My classes' focus, format, and goals differ, as do the requirements. My adage for teaching (as well as research) has always been that there is *no one best way*. What will be gleaned below is a reflection of my teaching philosophy.

Teaching for MPA Students

Engaging students in classroom learning has always been a priority for me. But the format depends on the size of my classes and the topic. Both theory and practice are covered. A few examples follow.

DOI: 10.4324/9781032671291-11

Teaching HRM

When I first started teaching human resources management (HRM) classes – previously called public personnel administration – these classes were required for MPA students and, hence, were very large, comprising anywhere between 25 and 35 students. With a class this size, the best approach for me was to begin by writing the material on a chalkboard (that's all we had back then!). So, for the first half of the class, I would begin presenting my notes on that day's topic and elicit comments and questions. Students responded very favorably to this, as the discussions were always very lively and meaningful. The second half of the class was devoted to experiential learning. I would break the students into small groups to work on exercises or cases related to practical HRM issues and problems related to the day's topics. I still maintain that this type of hands-on learning is invaluable for students who were going into practice; the exercises would simulate issues or challenges that future HR managers would encounter; the goal was for students to demonstrate the competencies needed to manage and lead in public sector workforces.

Thus, the exercises did not focus on functional or nuts-and-bolts aspects of HR such as writing a job description or developing classification and compensation databases, but on managing or executing the systems. As such an exercise would focus on, for example, hiring someone for an entry-level management position. Any exercises around recruitment, hiring, promotion, or retention always centered on ensuring diversity in the workplace.

Social equity is and has historically been an essential feature of HRM. Moreover, it has been the centerpiece of my research since graduate school. Therefore, I devote several classes during the semester to topics that include, for instance, addressing the legal status of affirmative action (e.g., its contours as set forth by the courts), illustrating the importance of promoting diversity, equity, inclusion, and accessibility (DEIA); acknowledging individual differences and recognizing these differences as invaluable to the organization; and measures for eradicating colorism, discrimination, microaggressions, and harassment – race, sex, gender identity, or sexual orientation – in the workplace. Other topics that traverse the issues surrounding DEIA were also addressed.

Early on, when the class focused on polemical issues such as affirmative action, challenges were inevitably raised by questions posed by certain students – mainly men who were white. How does a "teacher" address these encounters in a classroom, especially when there was little to no ethnic or racial diversity among the study body (as was the case for me in the early years of teaching)? In some cases, women would step up to the plate to challenge the regressive philosophies of those challenging the importance of affirmative action. In this case, a stimulating, enriching discussion ensued. This is significant for educational development. But, what if students were too intimidated by the vociferousness of those challenging the importance of the goal of affirmative action as well as diversity? The professor is responsible for making this a teachable, learning moment. It was always important for me to step up to the plate and provide responses to those who might equate, for example, affirmative action with "reverse discrimination." I relied on the Hegelian dialectic: I challenged every dismissive, abrogating proposition that relied on experiences and practical knowledge – and my opposing, antithetical propositions helped to quell or at least overwhelm the detractors. This may not have assuaged the visceral convictions of those opposing the significance of affirmative action and diversity, but it did provide some resolution at a higher level of truth. Nonetheless, I am certain that some of this resulted in poor teaching evaluations. But if you as a teacher emphasize receiving stellar teaching evaluations, especially at the expense of "speaking truth to power," then you may be in the wrong profession.

Teaching Public Sector Labor Relations

A critical skill for HR managers is navigating and operating within a government organization that is unionized. Governments at almost every level have collective bargaining contracts that guide, for example, working conditions and dispute resolution techniques affecting public employees. Indeed, depending on the jurisdiction, some HR managers or supervisors are protected by those contracts. In public administration, which promotes values such as equality and equity, I have always maintained that unions are essential for workers' needs, interests, and satisfaction. These courses are typically not required, so the class size ranged from 10 to 15 students. Thus, I ran seminar-style sessions where we sat around a large conference table and engaged in a colloquy of relevant topics.

There is no national law for public sector labor relations. Thus, it was important to focus on the state where I was teaching. So, for example, when I taught at SUNY Albany, I paid particular attention to the law and public policies governing labor relations in New York State. Because MPA students in Albany were planning to enter into state government employment, I felt it was important for them to learn about the experiences of those on the "other" side – the unions. Thus, I brought in guest speakers from the AFL-CIO, which is affiliated with most of the public employee unions in New York State. This provided a level of balance for the students.

Experiential learning is also important for a labor relations course, so I required the students to form labor and management teams to renegotiate a collective bargaining contract. This was extraordinarily effective, and students entered the roles easily and enthusiastically. If an impasse occurred, students were then required to intervene as third-party mediators or arbitrators. I had some experience as a negotiator as well as a mediator when bargaining reached an impasse and, therefore, was able to provide feasible advice to both sides.

Teaching Online MPA Courses

In 2008, Massive Open Online Courses (MOOCs) were introduced; these are free online courses available for anyone to enroll. In addition, "edX," an online learning platform founded by Harvard and MIT to ensure anyone across the globe could receive the best education, began as an experiment to offer MOOCs to anyone. Some of these MOOCs can be transferred into academic programs with credit. The tradition of eLearning burgeoned. Following this wave, my school began to offer online MPA courses, especially core courses, around 2009.

At the time, the majority of our faculty (including myself) were opposed to offering online courses, but our dean at the time made a persuasive argument for us to think more about the prospects of admitting students from all over the globe to enroll in our MPA program. He made this proclamation: the train is on the platform, and we either refuse to get on or get on and move with the goal of providing students with new skills and assisting them in advancing their careers in public service for the 21st century. I reluctantly signed on and developed my HRM class as an online, asynchronous course for the MPA program. It was still a requirement so it was sure to attract a plethora of students.

I continue to teach the HRM class every semester. Pedagogically I would grade asynchronous online courses with a D. For students who seek expediency in earning a master's degree, I would grade these courses with an A. To be sure, synchronous online courses may provide greater opportunities for communication and interaction between and among students and their professors, but I have not had any experience with synchronous online teaching. Key to effective pedagogy, in my opinion, is face-to-face contact and the ability to engage in meaningful discussions with the entire classroom. This is sacrificed with asynchronous online teaching. Moreover, it diminishes any type of social interaction and can easily lead to isolation. Indeed, some studies show that online courses may lead to isolation and depression among young students. The most popular classes in our program are the asynchronous online courses and students can attain their MPA in this format.

However, I had an epiphany shortly after I began teaching in this format. I discovered that at least one-half of my students each semester in HRM are single mothers raising children. I recognized that they deserve a chance to develop skills and competencies in HRM and this can assist them in building their careers. It provides them with an opportunity they would otherwise not have in pursuing a master's degree. This has altered my evaluation of asynchronous online teaching. The moral of the story here? Always be aware of your student population – this matters greatly!

Teaching for PhD Students

I have taught several PhD courses over the years, but the two I have taught regularly include the Intellectual History of Public Administration and Leadership and Equity and Diversity. Both are taught as seminars as this is the most effective approach for doctoral training as it ensures students will think analytically about the theoretical and epistemic traditions of public administration as a disciplinary field within the social sciences. I emphasize "field," as public administration has evolved from its early conception as a practice to a field of study.

Teaching Intellectual History of Public Administration

This course has been one of my favorite courses as it helps students understand the historical and philosophical contexts of the origins of public administration. The field has a rich intellectual heritage that illustrates its emergence: how early contributors sought to conceptualize and articulate what exactly public administration is. And in addressing the history of the field, its interdisciplinary nature manifests. In simple terms, consider Dwight Waldo's interpretation of public administration as political theory with Herbert Simon's view as administrative theory. Borrowing theories and methodologies from disciplines of the social and natural sciences provides another example.

I also address the historical context of public administration in terms of *when* public administration was studied and practiced. Stivers and McDonald (2023) have written an incisive essay on this issue. They pose this question: "What responsibility must "public administration" – theory and practice – take for the decisions and trends over the decades that have played a part in today's institutional racism and nativism?" (Stivers & McDonald, 2023, p. 276). They provide this astute response:

> The groundwork was laid in the early years of the first White people's arrival on the North American continent. What role did administrative governance play in keeping these structures in place over hundreds of years?

138 Norma M. Riccucci

Acknowledging America's injustices of the past is necessary to frame the development of the field. It provides insight into how the field could address and respond to our imperialist, colonialist, racist, and misogynistic past. We cannot continue to refer to the works of Woodrow Wilson, for example, without acknowledging his racist legacy. Wilson segregated the offices of the federal government; he threw a civil rights leader, Willima Monroe Trotter, out of the Oval Office, and he premiered in the White House one of the most racist films in the history of cinema, "The Birth of a Nation" (see, Lehr, 2015; Patler, 2004). The Ku Klux Klan is featured as heroes and Blacks – white actors in blackface – were portrayed as inferior, ignorant savages. Black men were seen as sexual predators and Black women were characterized as mammies (Lehr, 2014). The film depicted the KKK as a protector of white women, but predominantly of "American values." This seems to have a resounding resemblance to white supremacy in America today!

Although I also stress the public administration is an applied field; it seeks to apply scientific knowledge to identifying and solving real-world problems. The focus is *not* to train students for practice, but on improving the operations of public and nonprofit sectors for the standpoint of efficiency, economy, and equity.[1]

In addressing the various intellectual periods of public administration, there are two topics that are among my favorites. One is New Public Administration (NPA), which emerged from the Minnowbrook I conference, spearheaded by Dwight Waldo to address the social and political turmoil of the 1960s.[2] Reflecting the zeitgeist of the late 1960s, the NPA was an explicit challenge to and movement away from administrative behavior and theory, and its emphasis on promoting social equity was significant for me. It emphasized the relevancy of social and political problems to public administration and that the field was indeed value-laden and was responsible for addressing and responding to these problems. Government agencies were expected to be client-focused, and public servants were expected to act politically and civically, serving as advocates for the disenfranchised, disadvantaged, and marginalized populations. Postpositivism and normative research were valued, and it was perfectly natural for researchers to adopt social agendas that supported such issues as racial justice, equality in voting rights, support for equal employment and educational opportunities and economic equality for Blacks, Latinx, white Women, and other persons of color. This drew me in.

The NPA greatly influenced me as an undergraduate student. I appreciated that the NPA was a normative theory and philosophy that called for activism. The NPA had an underlying moral tone that resonated with me.

As an undergraduate student in public administration, I instinctively knew that I wanted to go on for a PhD in the field and focus on social change issues. I was particularly interested in race and gender relations, and these issues have suffused my life in every way, and they continue to do so.

The other topic I enjoy teaching in this class is the logic of inquiry, where I address the field's ontological, existential, metaphysical, phenomenological, and methodological aspects. As I write on these topics in my book, *Public Administration: Traditions of Inquiry and Philosophies of Knowledge*:

> The field of public administration today supports and promotes a variety of research traditions. Some are wholly quantitative, whereas others are qualitative. And some are mixed, relying on both qualitative and quantitative methods. In addition, some research is empirically based, whereas other studies are strictly normative. . . . To be sure, there continues to be conflict and dissonance among scholars as well as practitioners over the relevancy and applicability of the various research or epistemic approaches. . . . The field would be more consonant with the recognition that knowledge is derived from impressions on both the intellect and the senses.
>
> *(Riccucci, 2010, pp. 1–3)*

I strongly believe in the importance of qualitative research in public administration. When I spearheaded revisions to the PhD program at my school, I insisted that we require qualitative methods courses to balance out the requirement for quantitative courses. There are extremely few departments or schools nationwide that require qualitative methods courses in their PhD programs. If we support such methods in the field of public administration, it is imperative that we teach our PhD students how to apply them.

For this class, I require students to write a weekly essay or synthesis paper interpreting and analyzing the readings for each week in the context of what substantiates the theory and methods of public administration. This helps facilitate the discussion and allows me to provide copious feedback to first-semester PhD students on their writing skills.

Teaching Leadership, Equity, and Diversity

As I discussed earlier, I have a great passion for studying and teaching in areas aimed at improving the lives of women and people of color. I developed this course with the full support of my School, whose mission is to pursue the values of diversity and social equity. As with the field of public administration, this course has evolved over the years. That is to say, I have moved the needle forward in terms of the manner in which such topics as race, gender, and ethnicity have been addressed in the field. I have been very progressive about how I have addressed these topics throughout my entire career; for example, when the field engaged in the topic of racial discrimination, I directed attention to racism. As this is a doctoral-level class, it is aimed more at theory and research than practice. But certainly, as noted earlier, I encourage my students to think about the linkages between theory and practice as we are an applied field.

The class begins with a historical focus on racism, sexism, and homophobia in the United Sates, examining the role of government here, especially around the evolution of structural inequities. One of the required books, Gooden's (2014) *Race and Social Equity: A Nervous Area of Government*, provides an important overview of the role of government. As she has argued, "Issues of equity and justice are fundamental concerns of public administrators, who constantly struggle to evaluate the country's social climate and ensure equity in governance. . . . Such evaluation is unlikely to occur in a serious way if organizations are fundamentally too uncomfortable to directly engage with the topic. The result is an important, taken for granted but unacknowledged, context of nervousness, which is debilitating to our public sector organizations and thwarting our progress toward achieving racial equity in governance" (Gooden, 2014, p. 4).

Through lived experiences, I have always understood the value and importance of social equity and social justice. Indeed, my lifetime commitment to the broad areas of social equity and social justice has been an asset and advantage to my teaching this course, which covers topics such as diversity, equity, inclusion, and accessibility (DEIA); representative bureaucracy; how race, ethnicity, and gender matter for leadership and management; statutory and constitutional law surrounding the unequal treatment of women, Blacks, Latinx, indigenous Americans, and disabled persons; feminist theory (and the insightful work of Camilla Stivers[3]); and critical race theory (CRT) and queer theory.

When I first introduced CRT to my class, some students seemed confounded about its applicability to public administration. I point out that CRT, as with any form of critical theory, is a theoretical approach that seeks to confront the social, historical, and ideological forces and structures that produce and constrain them. I note that early studies in CRT were derived from law and examined the intersection of race with gender in antidiscrimination laws with a focus on white supremacy and structural racism in legal progresses. Other social sciences, such as sociology and social work, apply this framework, I say, so why should not public administration?

Among a number of relevant journal articles, I also require my book, *Critical Race Theory Exploring Its Application to Public Administration* (Riccucci, 2022), which addresses CRT in the context of public administration research and proposes areas within the field that could benefit from its application. This moves the field forward, which is desirable given the high priority the field places on social equity, the third pillar of public administration (Frederickson, 1990; Gooden, 2014). If there is a desire to achieve social equity and justice, racism needs to be addressed and confronted directly. The Black Lives Matter (BLM) movement is one example of the urgency and significance of applying theories from various disciplines to studying racism in public administration.

I stress to my students that the CRT framework is critical for dismantling structural and institutional racism in our society. In addition, I point out that while many critical race theorists argue that qualitative approaches are more suitable for studies on race and ethnicity, others have pointed to the need for quantitative studies. Reflecting my views on the logic of inquiry in public administration, I urge that a pluralistic approach seems suitable for CRT studies, particularly in the social sciences. I then illustrate how scholars apply CRT to studies that rely on qualitative and quantitative methods.

Postscript

Many scholars in public administration have stressed the importance of mentorship for graduate students (see, Meier, 2023; Rinfret et al., 2023). For example, Rinfret et al. (2023, p. 398) point out that "for graduate students, mentorship offers valuable emotional support during the highly stressful phases of their academic journey, with long-lasting effects on their careers." They go on to say that mentoring is particularly important for traditionally underrepresented students in public affairs and administration. Mentorship of graduate students has been a high priority for me throughout my career.

Also, there is no best way to teach, mentor, practice, or study (i.e., to conduct research) in public administration. Thus, each individual will develop their own unique approach and identity. Years from now, students and scholars may return to this essential book to glean some insights into various teaching philosophies. And I certainly hope that the field of public administration continues to move forward in a progressive manner, leading, reforming, and innovating to ensure our persistent relevancy in teaching and research.

142 Norma M. Riccucci

Notes

1 Frederickson (1990) referred to these three e's as the pillars of the field of public administration.
2 The Minnowbrook Center is a conference center of Syracuse University. It is located in the central Adirondack Mountains, overlooking the pristine Blue Mountain Lake.
3 See, among a few of her works, Stivers (1991, 2000, 2002, 2005).

References

Frederickson, H. G. (1990). Public administration and social equity. *Public Administration Review, 50*(2), 228–237. https://doi.org/10.2307/976870

Gooden, S. T. (2014). *Race and social equity: A nervous area of government.* Routledge.

Lehr, D. (2014). *The birth of a nation: How a legendary filmmaker and a crusading editor reignited America's civil war.* Public Affairs.

Lehr, D. (2015, November 27). The racist legacy of Woodrow Wilson. *The Atlantic.* https://www.theatlantic.com/politics/archive/2015/11/wilson-legacy-racism/417549/

Meier, K. J. (2023). It all depends: Reflections on the art of mentoring PhD students in public affairs. *Journal of Public Affairs Education, 29*(3), 313–326. https://doi.org/10.1080/15236803.2022.2157191

Patler, N. (2004). *Jim Crow and the Wilson administration: Protesting federal segregation in the early twentieth century.* University Press of Colorado.

Riccucci, N. M. (2010). *Public administration: Traditions of inquiry and philosophies of knowledge.* Georgetown University Press.

Riccucci, N. M. (2022). *Critical race theory: Exploring its application to public administration.* Cambridge University Press.

Rinfret, S. R., Young, S. L., & McDonald, B. D. (2023). The importance of mentorship in higher education: An introduction to the symposium. *Journal of Public Affairs Education, 29*(4), 398–403. https://doi.org/10.1080/15236803.2023.2260947

Stivers, C. (1991). Toward a feminist perspective in public administration theory. *Women & Politics, 10*(4), 49–65. https://doi.org/10.1300/J014v10n04_03

Stivers, C. (2000). *Bureau men, settlement women: Constructing public administration in the progressive era.* University of Kansas Press.

Stivers, C. (2002). *Gender images in public administration: Legitimacy and the administrative state.* Sage.

Stivers, C. (2005). Dreaming the world: Feminisms in public administration. *Administrative Theory & Praxis, 27*(2), 364–369.

Stivers, C., & McDonald, B. D. (2023). Teaching public administration historically. *Journal of Public Affairs Education, 29*(3), 275–279. https://doi.org/10.1080/15236803.2023.2205805

10

BECOMING AN EXPERT TEACHER

Turn It Inside Out

Rosemary O'Leary

University of Kansas, Lawrence, KS

While I have won 11 teaching awards – two of them national – the idea that I am an expert teacher seems as curious today as it did when I started teaching 35 years ago. Teaching, for me, will always be a challenge – a wonderfully rewarding challenge. However, I feel comfortable sharing the "secret" of my success as a teacher. My advice to new teachers is to turn it inside out. Focus on the students as great learners, not yourself as a great teacher (O'Leary, 2002).

I am happy to share the evolution of my philosophy of teaching and learning. To do so, I must take you back three decades. Consider the following scenario from my PhD years at the Maxwell School of Citizenship and Public Affairs at Syracuse University in the mid-1980s:

> When public administration professor Richard Goldsmith (not his real name) entered the classroom, the students quivered. "There he is!" exclaimed a student in the back of the room. Goldsmith walked confidently toward the blackboard and began to scribble furiously. Within five minutes, diagrams and formulas covered the board. In only minutes, he had solved a problem that had taken the best students in the class three hours the night before to solve. One student could not maintain her decorum. "Professor," she exclaimed, "I never could have solved that problem!" Goldsmith regarded her with amusement. "Ha! Young woman," he replied, "if you could have solved it, you would be the professor and I the student."

There is nothing wrong with this view of the ideal teacher at one level. I remember, for example, calling John Nalbandian, one of my favorite

DOI: 10.4324/9781032671291-12

professors in the MPA program at the University of Kansas, "Gandhi" because he was so wise.

On another level, however, this view of the ideal teacher is troublesome. It conveyed to me subtle and not-so-subtle messages, including:

- A focus on the teacher, as opposed to a focus on the learner;
- The male teacher as the omniscient sage;
- The view that to be a great teacher one needs to prepare a perfect lecture that keeps the students entertained; and
- A view of the student as a passive knowledge sponge.

This was the model I had been presented in more than one hundred courses in higher education. To paint an even bleaker picture, out of those one hundred professors of higher education, only two were women. Even sadder is that not one of those one hundred teachers was a person of color. I call this phenomenon "the great man theory of teaching" (O'Leary, 1997).

I have been asked to address the issue of my development as a teacher, and the title of this essay reflects part of that evolution. If there is one idea I hope you will remember it is this: There has been a wonderful paradigm shift in higher education, *a movement away from a focus on teaching, toward a focus on learning.* That paradigmatic shift in thinking describes what saved me from disgrace and ruin in the classroom as I initially sought to implement "the great man theory of teaching."

Flashback to 1988. When I completed my PhD program at the Maxwell School that year and headed off to Indiana University to become an assistant professor, I had no teaching experience beyond teaching swimming lessons for 10 summers. The focus of the PhD experience in those days was primarily on memorizing theory and learning how to do quantitative empirical research. At a going away dinner for PhD graduates, another internationally known scholar advised me, "They will forgive poor teaching, but they will not forgive poor research. Funnel your energy into your research."

In my course evaluations after my first semester, there were numerous comments to the effect that "her hands were shaking so badly the first day of class she could barely hand out the syllabus." But it was halfway into the semester that true disaster struck. I had spent hours preparing a brilliant great man lecture on the impact of courts on public administration (the subject of my award-winning dissertation) only to find most of the class asleep 15 minutes into my lecture. The crowning blow was when I realized that all the students in the front row were asleep.

I went home more depressed than I had ever been in my life. Clearly, teaching was not for me. Out of desperation, I stayed up several nights trying to figure out how to engage the students. Honestly, my intent at the time was not to become a great or even a good teacher, but merely to survive in the classroom. This was war. I was desperate. I would try anything.

That is when I became a "pedagogy guerrilla," quietly taking on the great man theory of teaching to forge my identity as a university professor. Instead of preparing a lecture, I returned to class the next week with 25 prepared Socratic questions for the students. I saw a glimmer of hope as a handful of students attempted to answer the questions. However, I found myself giving away the answers when the silence between the questions and the answers grew too loud. The number of questions I prepared for class dwindled from 25 to 20, then to 15, and then to 10. Some days, I came into the classroom ready to engage the students in a discussion of the three most important ideas of the day. As I experimented and tried new things, it finally hit me: *It is about the students as great learners! It is not about me as a great teacher, and it's not about being a great man.* Once I figured that out, teaching became a wonderfully fun challenge. Working with students became, hands down, the most rewarding part of my career.

Now, my class preparation goes something like this: After rereading all the assigned text for the day, I give myself, in the privacy of my office, quiet time where I ask myself, "What do these students really need to know from this material? What are the most important ideas for them to take from class today?" I try to focus on three to five key ideas for undergraduates for a one-hour class. For graduate students, I concentrate on 10 key concepts for a one-hour class. (Of course, this number ebbs and flows based on the subject matter.) Second, I ask myself, "What is the best way for these students to learn this material? Is it a lecture? Discussion? Debate? Research? Or is there some other way of learning that would best fit here?"

Looking back, I now realize I created my own version of a "flipped classroom" before the term existed. Some of the ways of engaging students in active learning, particularly problem-based learning, that have worked for me include the following: A moment of silence at the beginning of class where I ask the students to focus on the most important points of the reading or to think about a pressing public policy problem; workgroups; case studies; role-playing simulations; analyses of real-world public organizations and real-world public challenges; problem-solving essays; position papers; memos to themselves; and "elevator speeches."

My introduction to the elevator speech came from John White, a former Maxwell School professor who ran the presidential campaign of billionaire Ross Perot in the 1990s. Money seemingly was no object for Perot's campaign, so White had the luxury of hiring a staff of PhD student analysts from the top 20 ranked schools of public affairs, public policy, and public administration in the United States. After a failed campaign (Perot won

146 Rosemary O'Leary

nearly 20 million votes but no Electoral College votes), White lamented that even the best and brightest PhD students he hired from the best programs could write dissertations but could not condense their ideas into one- to two-page policy papers. Worse, they could not succinctly convey their ideas in short (1–3-minute) briefing sessions – approximately the time to ride an elevator in a tall building. My students' elevator speeches require them to pitch a new public policy or public management idea that they have thoroughly researched succinctly to an imaginary boss with tough questions following from the class.

I also put a warning label on the front of my syllabus that reads something like this:

> Warning! This is a course with a unique blend of traditional readings and lectures, mixed with nontraditional role-playing, student participation, and discussion groups. Class sessions will be interactive with high-quality, thoughtful, open-minded, and respectful class discussion expected. If you are interested in a safe lecture class where students are allowed to act as passive knowledge sponges, this class is not for you. I look forward to a great semester!

My classes are now approximately interactive and lecture, where I pull together the ideas that have emerged in class discussions, emphasizing the most important points. Contrary to the great man perspective, I believe that my job is not only to impart knowledge but, more importantly, to assist students in cultivating a critical thinking process that can be used throughout their lives. Because I teach students who will have careers in government and nonprofit organizations, other facets of my job include encouraging the students to think creatively about solutions to pressing public policy problems, instilling in them a belief that they can make a difference in today's society, and conveying to them an enthusiasm about public service.

After 35 years of teaching public affairs graduate students, I have concluded that it all boils down to four things: Knowledge, critical thinking, creative thinking, and an enthusiasm for public service. These are the things I try to impart and cultivate in every class session. These goals can be met in a wide variety of ways, leaving room for new approaches.

So what? Who cares? What are the implications of the paradigm shift in higher education away from the great man theory of teaching to a focus on student learning? First, it is a wonderful relief to realize that no one has to be a great man to be a facilitator of active learning. This view of teaching accommodates all of us – every size, shape, and color, embracing a wide variety of talents, backgrounds, perspectives, and lived experiences.

Second, no one gets it right the first time they teach a course. No one. It is an immense challenge to figure out the best way for students to learn, and it is wonderfully liberating to realize that you are allowed to think creatively and refine your approach as you gain experience. I will confess that there have been a few times when I have returned to the classroom the day after a learning experiment, apologized to the students, and started over, addressing the same material, yet using another learning approach. Happily, each semester is a clean slate and an opportunity to reconsider learning approaches.

Third, there is no excuse for poor teaching. With a focus on student learning and the shift away from the great man theory of teaching, it is okay to ask for help. It is okay to borrow ideas from others (and it is important to share your ideas and teaching materials with others). It is okay that you're not the perfect entertainer in the classroom. Beat poet Edward S. Burroughs once said, "A good poet borrows, a great poet steals." I would paraphrase that statement to read, "A good teacher borrows, a great teacher steals." We are all dedicated to ensuring "excellence in education and training for public service and to promote the ideal of public service" (the mission of the Network of Schools of Public Policy, Public Affairs, and Public Administration). I have benefited from ideas stolen (with permission) from dozens of colleagues throughout the years. And I've tried to give back by co-creating at E-PARCC at the Maxwell School of Syracuse University: Free online teaching and learning materials on civic engagement, collaboration, and conflict resolution used by hundreds of thousands around the world. E-PARCC thrives today.[1]

My advice to new teachers: Turn it inside out. Begin your movement away from a focus on teaching toward a focus on learning. The great man theory of teaching is dead, something that all of us who are mere mortals can celebrate. It is time to move the limelight off ourselves and onto our students.

Note

1 E-PARCC can be accessed at https://www.maxwell.syr.edu/research/program-for-the-advancement-research-on-conflict-collaboration/e-parcc.

References

O'Leary, R. (1997). The great man theory of teaching is dead. *Journal of Public Administration Education, 3*(2), 127–131. https://doi.org/10.1080/10877789.1997.12023422

O'Leary, R. (2002). Advice to new teachers: Turn it inside out. *PS: Political Science & Politics, 35*(1), 91–92. https://doi.org/10.1017/S1049096502000215

11

TEACHING WITH AN INFORMED MIND AND RELENTLESS CURIOSITY

Stephen Page

University of Washington, Seattle, WA

Teaching is an applied science, an art, and a craft (Johnson, 2017), as is management (Bardach, 1998; Lynn, 1996). So, as a scholar and teacher of public management, I regularly wrestle with how best to blend craft, science, and art in the classroom. This chapter explains these concepts and how they inspire me to teach public management with an informed mind and relentless curiosity.

The Science, Art, and Craft of Teaching Public Management

Good teaching applies the science of learning to instruction (see, e.g., Bloom, 1956); at the same time, good teaching is an art – the practice of creativity within constraints (Acar et al., 2019; Krulwich, 2016). Good teaching is also a craft in that craft workers cultivate a repertoire of skills and tools and then use judgment and creativity to apply them to individual projects or tasks in situationally appropriate ways (Bardach, 1998). Thus, we might consider the science of learning and the craft of instruction significant constraints that good teachers understand and keep in mind as they artfully develop and implement their lesson plans.

Public management similarly mixes science, art, and craftwork. Managers must identify and apply relevant concepts, frameworks, and tools derived from social science research to assess and strategize creatively to navigate the situational constraints and opportunities they encounter (Lynn, 1996).

Therefore, teaching public management entails building a crafty repertoire of teaching tools and skills through experience to harness and apply

DOI: 10.4324/9781032671291-13

Teaching with an Informed Mind and Relentless Curiosity **149**

science artfully in the classroom. Good teaching plans, analogously, help practitioners deepen their understanding of social science findings about management concepts to build their craft skills and apply them artfully to the managerial challenges they face. For example, I take care to mix clarity and ambiguity in different measures as a course progresses and students' analytic and strategic abilities increase along with their comfort levels in engaging issues and using frameworks amid uncertainty.

To make these principles concrete and actionable, I strive to design my lesson plans with the science of learning and the social science of management in mind. Evidence on teaching and learning informs my design of learning competencies for courses and learning objectives for individual classes (Bloom, 1956). While I recognize that management is a craft in that managers make decisions and take action based on practical training, observation of others, and their own experiences, social science provides important evidence about effective management systems and practices. Research findings offer managers' insights and guidance on network structures, stakeholder engagement, personnel policies and practices, organizational strategy, performance management, and human-centered design, to give just a few examples.

Through hard experience over years of teaching, I've learned that applying social scientific findings about learning and public management to design and deliver lesson plans is a craft – particularly when one teaches professional students in an interdisciplinary field like public management. Professional students need instruction that engages them and gives them repeated practice with a range of tools for management, policymaking, and professional development. Designing lessons, exercises, and assignments for practicing professionals requires recognizing that some may know more about how a particular concept or framework works in practice than I do. As practicing managers, they may have more experience or insights related to certain concepts or frameworks than I do as a faculty member, because job is devoted more to research and teaching than to the practice of management itself. Humility and an open mind are thus central to the craft of teaching public management.

Moreover, devising learning tools – assignments, online discussion prompts, classroom exercises, etc. – that actively engage professional students requires some familiarity with their work contexts and challenges. Ongoing engagement with the field is central to the craft, so I conduct primary, qualitative research that allows me to learn directly from practitioners. I regularly seek opportunities to train or consult managers in public service organizations.

Social science and craft knowledge offer a potent mix of instructional resources and insights. However, I have also learned that they can fall flat in the classroom without an artful approach to lesson planning. Active

150   Stephen Page

engagement and interactive learning are critically important for the retention and application of lessons (Moreno & Mayer, 2007), particularly for practicing professionals. Case teaching, role plays, simulations, and applied exercises focused on students' problems of practice enable students to learn from one another as much or more than from me. However, they require experimentation and continuous improvement to be used successfully. Hence, I try to plan my lessons with artistic creativity – bounded by the constraints offered by social science research on management – along with the craft worker's attention to developing and refining my teaching skills through experience (Johnson, 2017).

Experimentation and continuous improvement require taking risks and staying open-minded and humble – qualities that can be challenging to practice in classroom settings that typically frame instructors as experts. The remainder of this chapter draws on my professional development as a teacher to explain how a reflective, intentional practice of humility, open-mindedness, and ongoing engagement with practicing public leaders has enhanced my teaching.

Informed Mind

John Boehrer, one of my teaching mentors, regularly reminded me that planning a good class discussion requires answering the question, "What discussion do you want to have?" (Boehrer, 1999). I quickly learned in the classroom that we, as instructors, don't get to determine the focus of class discussion on our own. Another mentor, Jon Brock, reminded me that instructors can only control the first question they ask in class, and "after that, it's like riding a bucking bronco" (Brock, 1999). With this bracing guidance in mind, I strive to prepare and teach every class session with what Sue-Jean Sung (2020) calls an "informed mind" – a combination of preparation, contextual understanding, open-mindedness, and willingness to learn from others' voices.

Using the blend of science, art, and craft described earlier, I design interactive lesson plans that engage students in analytic and strategic exercises using managerial concepts and frameworks. I then try to keep an open mind as students react and respond to the concepts, frameworks, and exercises in class. For me, a "good" class session doesn't follow a strict lesson plan. Instead, it is one in which I stay attuned and recognize and respond nimbly to insights, questions, and dynamics that emerge in discussion. However unexpected or surprising they turn out to be. Students inevitably bring experiences, perspectives, and wisdom to the discussion that I don't anticipate and from which all of us in the room can learn. During class discussions, therefore, I seek to acknowledge and amplify examples and insights from students with the potential to enhance understanding of the frameworks, concepts, and issues under investigation.

At the same time, I remind myself that not everything will work well in every class; my questions and exercises may not resonate, students may misinterpret my prompts, or I may misunderstand or misinterpret important questions or comments. When class discussions fail to unfold as I hoped or anticipated – especially when students offer feedback or concerns – I aim to remain open and curious. Sometimes, I replay unexpected developments in my head or discuss them with students outside of class. A handful of times, I have devoted a portion of a subsequent class session to revisiting or debriefing issues from a prior session in which I failed to recognize or respond to an unfolding dynamic or concern among the students. In so doing, I hope to model reflective leadership and rebuild a positive learning environment. As a helpful byproduct, I often gain valuable insights about how to adapt my lesson plans and attune my instructional craft in the future.

In the spirit of continuous craft improvement, I review and revise my lesson plan each time I prepare to teach a particular topic based on how the class discussion unfolded the previous time I taught it. These revisions often borrow or adapt pedagogical techniques (types of questions and exercises for class discussion, online discussion topics, and assignment formats) from other courses and instructional colleagues.

After classes (or entire courses) that are particularly rich in surprises or unexpected moments, I take time to make sense of what happened, how the students and I responded, and how our responses shaped their learning about management and leadership. I then identify any changes to my instructional craft or art of lesson planning to hone them for future class sessions or courses.

Relentless Curiosity About Managerial Practice

As these tactics suggest, I maintain an informed mind by practicing relentless curiosity in my research and teaching activities, aiming to connect theory and research to practice. In addition to attending and responding to how my lesson plans and class discussions unfold, I try to remain curious about how the research-based concepts and frameworks I teach apply to the work our students do as public managers and leaders. I practice curiosity in three different aspects of my work as a faculty member:

- Qualitative primary field research;
- Developing teaching cases and other practice-based learning exercises; and
- Ongoing inquiry and dialogue with practitioners about management challenges.

152 Stephen Page

Below, I explain how I approach each of these aspects of my work with curiosity and an explicit intention to deepen my understanding of the craft of public management and how to teach it.

Primary Field Research

My research examines collaborative efforts among different public service organizations to address "wicked problems" (Rittel & Weber, 1973) of policy and service delivery that lack easy solutions and require significant changes in organizational thinking and behavior. Most of my data collection involves firsthand fieldwork – interviews with practitioners, participant observation of public events and meetings, and reviews of planning and evaluation documents – on complex challenges of public management and leadership. Gathering qualitative data myself can be time-consuming, but doing so puts me directly in touch with practicing managers and line staff, exposing me to the challenges and opportunities they face and the different ways they think about and address issues. Coding the qualitative data I collect gives me additional chances to analyze and make sense of my observations, which in turn help inspire and focus my lesson plans and classroom teaching.

While my academic contributions aim to build theory, my publications also seek to offer useful recommendations to inform practitioners' understanding, analysis, and strategizing. Pushing beyond theory to the practical implications of my findings forces me to think like a public manager, which in turn helps connect my thinking and teaching more concretely to the situations my students are likely to confront in their work.

Developing Teaching Cases and Practice-Based Learning Exercises

Since I began teaching, I have used the case method pioneered in business schools and later adopted by some public policy and management schools. The case method asks students to prepare by reading a stylized summary (or "case") about a real-life unsolved policy or management challenge. Instructors then pose a series of questions in class to guide the students to analyze the challenge in the case and develop a strategy to address it using specific concepts and frameworks drawn from the research literature.

Good cases enable rich, insightful, sometimes contentious class discussions. As such, they draw on pressing challenges of practice and require careful, intentional design and writing. Cases need to provide students with enough information and context to conduct informed analyses and design realistic strategies without overwhelming them with detail or closing off alternative lines of inquiry and strategy (Lundberg, 2015). Helping students design, develop, and write teaching cases has exposed me to numerous dilemmas of policy and management and forced me to think through the various analytical and strategic opportunities embedded in them with the case writers. (I've advised numerous MPA and Executive MPA students' capstone projects that produced teaching cases. For an example, see Rouse & Page [2016].)

The case method of teaching is part of a broader category of pedagogy, sometimes called practice-based (or experiential) learning (Kallio et al., 2017). Practice-based learning engages professional students in applying concepts and frameworks to issues and challenges they face (or may face in the future) in their work. It requires instructors to understand what those issues or challenges might be and which concepts and frameworks might benefit students to apply to them. Instructors then need to be able to design classroom exercises or homework assignments to give students practice using those concepts and frameworks. Like developing cases and teaching the case method, designing class discussions and homework assignments to enable practice-based learning engages me in an ongoing dialogue between research-based concepts and frameworks, on the one hand, and my students' practical work, on the other.

Conversations With Practitioners

In addition to my field research, I talk regularly with practicing public managers about the contexts in which they work, the challenges they face, and how they tackle them. I engage with them in several ways.

- I organize my class discussions and assignments around real-life examples of management challenges drawn from teaching cases or students' professional experiences and observations. I ask students to apply concepts and frameworks to analyze those challenges and design strategies to address them. Some assignments and class discussions go further and give students practice implementing the strategies they craft – for example, through capstone or other types of practicum courses or via role plays or simulations in class.
- When I invite practitioners into class to serve as guest speakers, I encourage them to do more than simply lecture or tell "war stories" from their work. I ask them to devote part of the time they spend in my class to giving students opportunities to strategize to address a specific challenge or dilemma the speakers have faced.
- I also talk with and listen carefully to students outside of class or in other school conversations (e.g., committee discussions and social gatherings) to learn more about aspects of their jobs and careers that relate to the concepts and frameworks that I teach.

154 Stephen Page

Cultivating an informed mind through relentless curiosity has deepened my understanding of public management and enhanced my craft skills as a teacher. Conducting field research, writing teaching cases, and listening to practitioners about their work have helped me sustain humility and openness about my understanding of management while deepening my familiarity with the daily, weekly, and long-run contexts and challenges my students face. For these reasons, they help me harness research and theory to design lesson plans and assignments that offer students relevant practice inside and outside the classroom. I always try to deliver on what another mentor of mine, Pat Dobel, would remind our mid-career and executive students during their weekend classes: "What you learn on Saturday, you can use at work on Monday" (2007).

The Humilities and Insights of Relentless Curiosity

Keeping abreast of professional students' challenges at work and crafting lesson plans that address them in useful, constructive ways is humbling. Periodically, I find that teaching techniques I've used successfully in the past fail to connect or resonate with students' understandings of issues or their approaches to learning. These moments expose the limits of my craft knowledge as new challenges of practice emerge. When craft knowledge fails us, the doubts and difficulties that accompany creativity get revealed even more starkly as part of the art of teaching.

In those moments, the insights I gain from my ongoing exchanges with practitioners – through research, case writing, and conversations – help me retool my craft and reinspire my approach to the art of teaching. I try (but too often fail) to keep in mind more advice from my mentor, Pat Dobel – to "take it seriously, but hold it lightly." More colloquial (if equally useful) words of wisdom come from an interview with the actor Bradley Whitford, in which he described his three stages of responding to feedback about his acting as, " 'F – you,' 'I suck,' and 'OK, what?'" (Whitford, 2020). Taken together, the advice of Dobel and Whitford reminds me that my students need me to attend to their reactions to my teaching, forget my ego, and make a good faith effort to learn and improve – over and over again.

References

Acar, O., Tarakci, M., & van Knippenberg, D. (2019). Creativity and innovation under constraints: A cross-disciplinary integrative review. *Journal of Management*, 45(1), 96–121. https://doi.org/10.1177/0149206318805832

Bardach, E. (1998). *Getting agencies to work together: The practice and theory of managerial craftsmanship*. The Brookings Institution.

Bloom, B. S. (1956). *Taxonomy of educational objectives. Handbook I: The cognitive domain.* David McKay Co Inc.

Boehrer, J. (1999, June). *Lesson planning.* Lecture during training, Case Teaching, University of Washington, Evans School of Public Affairs.

Brock, J. (1999, June). Personal communication.

Dobel, J. P. (2007, September). *Why are we here?* Lecture during Executive MPA course, Strategic Leadership, University of Washington, Evans School of Public Affairs.

Johnson, A. (2017). *Teaching strategies for all teachers.* Rowman and Littlefield.

Kallio, K., Russo-Spena, T., Lappalainen, I., & Mele, C. (2017). Practice-based approaches to learning and innovating. In T. Russo-Spena, C. Mele, & M. Nuutinen (Eds.), *Innovating in practice: Perspectives and experiences* (pp. 83–109). SpringerLink.

Krulwich, R. (2016). Stravinsky's secret and the art of saying no. *National Geographic.* https://www.nationalgeographic.com/science/article/stravinskys-secret-the-art-of-saying-no-krulwich

Lundberg, K. (2015). *Writing a teaching case study: 10 easy steps.* The Lundberg Case Consortium. https://caseresources.hsph.harvard.edu/publications/writing-teaching-case-study-10-easy-steps

Lynn, L. (1996). *Public management as art, science, and profession.* Chatham House.

Moreno, R., & Mayer, R. (2007). Interactive multimodal learning environments. *Educational Psychology Review, 19*(3), 309–326. https://doi.org/10.1007/s10648-007-9047-2

Rittel, H. W. J., & Weber, M. M. (1973). Dilemmas in a general theory of planning. *Policy Sciences, 4*(2), 155–169. https://doi.org/10.1007/bf01405730

Rouse, A., & Page, S. (2016). *Community engagement for organizational change: Planning for a sustainable future for the City of Seattle's Langston Hughes Performing Arts Institute.* E-PARCC, Maxwell School of Citizenship & Public Affairs, Syracuse University. https://www.maxwell.syr.edu/research/program-for-the-advancement-research-on-conflict-collaboration/e-parcc/cases-simulations-syllabi/cases/community-engagement-for-organizational-change

Sung, S. J. (2020, June 29). What the deep south taught me about the pitfalls and potential of design. *Medium.* https://medium.com/ideo-stories/what-the-deep-south-taught-me-about-the-pitfalls-and-potential-of-design-823bf15695f0

Whitford, B. (2020, June 8). *Interview, Armchair Expert with Dax Shepard podcast episode 213.* https://armchairexpertpod.com/pods/bradley-whitford.

12

LEARNING HOW TO TEACH, TEACHING HOW TO LEARN

Camilla Stivers
Cleveland State University, Cleveland, OH

When I got my first teaching job at The Evergreen State College (TESC), I was 49 years old and had worked for almost 20 years in nonprofit organizations, most community-based and grant-supported. My total previous experience as an instructor consisted of teaching small-boat sailing at a camp one summer in college. Thus, as far as knowing how to teach, I started as pretty much a blank slate.

It was my great fortune to land at TESC, which has to be an exemplar among learning institutions that take teaching seriously; Evergreen puts it first ahead of scholarship and service. This value-ordering is not without drawbacks, but if what you need is to learn how to learn or how to teach, there is (I'm ready to bet) no better place to do so. Evergreen was founded in the late 1960s in reaction to higher education's perceived irrelevance and authoritarianism.

It's worth giving some details about how Evergreen was organized at the time because the structure was intended to support collaborative learning – what was known as the "learning community." When I was there, classes were team-taught around interdisciplinary topics (e.g., "Rags and Riches" and "The Listening Self"), and there were no departments as such (faculty were semiorganized in clusters around humanities, science, art, etc.). Students signed up for one course (referred to as a "program") at a time – a full load for that term, typically amounting to 15–18 contact hours per week. The centerpiece of every program was the "seminar," or small-group discussion, which met two or three times a week to discuss the assigned reading (supplemented by a lecture or two and some kind of hands-on activity, laboratory, studio, or workshop). Each faculty member facilitated

DOI: 10.4324/9781032671291-14

their seminar group and was responsible for writing those students' evaluations (rather than giving grades). In return, students were responsible for evaluating the faculty. Faculty team members were obligated to meet once a week in their own "faculty seminar" to discuss the week's readings and adjust planned activities. They also evaluated themselves and one another. All evaluations were exchanged and discussed in face-to-face conferences.

One upshot of this arrangement was that a novice faculty member like me (as well as the old hands) not only got constant feedback from other faculty and students but also had a chance to observe how others "did it." Student and faculty evaluations went into one's portfolio, which was reviewed by one of several deans (all but one were faculty rotating into the deanery) and was the basis for making decisions about whether to renew one's contract – first for three more years, and then for eight years if all went well. There was no faculty rank and no tenure. The intense collaboration with colleagues required to plan and deliver the program resulted in a lot of learning about teaching along the way. A lot.

As a degree program for practicing professionals, the MPA was somewhat different. Because Evergreen is located in Olympia, the capital of Washington State, the MPA has had a built-in market of career civil servants since its inception. In contrast to the undergrad "whatever floats your boat" approach, the curriculum featured a required set of programs (plus electives) that began with "The Political and Economic Context of Public Administration" and concluded with a final project, done in student teams and usually involving some sort of empirical investigation culminating in a written report. Still, like the undergraduate curriculum, it strived to be as interdisciplinary as possible, and indeed, quite a few faculty who taught in the MPA program had degrees in organization sociology, economics, business management, and political science rather than public administration per se. Though this variety seemed a distinct advantage to me, it resulted in a shared view of public administration as a practice embedded in a complex context; it prevented the degree from qualifying for NASPAA certification, which required a stable set of faculty. Indeed, MPA faculty, similar to those in the undergraduate curriculum, had to rotate out of their primary subject area to teach something else every third year.

I've described the unusual structure at Evergreen as I realized when I left after 10 years to teach at the Levin College of Cleveland State University that structure matters. Evergreen's philosophy centers on the notion of a "learning community" in which everyone is both a learner and a teacher, and the teaching challenge is to facilitate students' ability to take charge of their learning. No structure is perfect, and Evergreen had (and probably still does) its distinctive problems. These included difficulty defining

158 Camilla Stivers

advanced work (since nobody majored in anything) and a pretty unorganized faculty that often found it hard to agree on anything, including the merits or demerits of various administrative bright ideas. It turns out that it often helps in teaching something if you've studied it deeply. Still, as a place to learn to teach, I'm pretty sure it was peerless.

When I went to the Levin College, I found myself in a much more conventional (though first-rate) institution, so I had to adjust my teaching approach in various ways. The worst was having to give grades because grades are such empty feedback, and I found myself trying to compensate by writing extensive comments on student papers. Turning classes into discussion groups like the Evergreen seminar was also challenging. Students' expectations about the amount of structure were already set. Still, Cleveland State classes were filled with many students who were the first in their families to go to college, and a lot of them wanted to get the most out of the opportunity and welcomed having a voice in the classroom once they believed I meant it. I did give up on trying to get them to call me "Cam" instead of "Dr. Stivers" when I realized I was just making them uncomfortable. Otherwise, I absorbed the learning community as an ideal and did my best to continue to follow it. I retired in 2008, which meant I escaped having to teach online and deal with smartphones in the classroom. In what follows, I try to offer what I know about teaching with all this in mind. Different strategies work better or worse depending on the setting, rules, and expectations.

The Learning Community

The notion of learning as a collaborative enterprise appealed to me right from the start, probably because I had worked in grassroots communities in Washington, D.C. I came away from that previous experience with the belief, as I neared the dissertation stage of my formal education, that political arguments against democracy as a nice idea but one that doesn't work were not persuasive. I had seen, first-hand, ordinary folk overseeing the running of a community health center, acting as stewards of grant funds, and interpreting federal regulations and policies so that services were both consistent with the law and met community needs as they understood them. This was real, if limited, governing power. Board members didn't just give input to funding agencies. They had actual discretionary authority. In Aristotelian terms, they both "ruled and were ruled in turn" (Aristotle, 1981, p. 1277b13–6). Their work inspired me to develop the notion of "active citizenship in the administrative state" in my dissertation.

Based on my Evergreen experience, it seems to me that a learning community is one in which members are much like Aristotle's citizens: they teach and learn in turn. John Dewey (1916), who was notably interested in education, argued that experts can control knowledge acquisition or it can be democratic. He viewed democracy not as narrowly political but as a mode of associated living. Democratic knowledge, he maintained, is created in collaborative processes in which citizens, experts, and officials participate on as equal a footing as possible. Mary Parker Follett (1924) said much the same thing: The views of experts, officials, and the people at large all affect the situation. The expert must find a place within the social process.

Democratic knowledge emerges from debate, deliberation, and collaboration. In a learning community, students can contribute to and benefit from the learning process and learn to debate and judge the merits of ideas gathered from course content and discussions. When public administration classes are structured so that plenty of time is devoted to conversation and debate, students are more likely to develop the "public" side of their professional personas and the "administrative," or rule-governed, efficiency-driven side. As a result, they may be more likely to see themselves as servants rather than as masters in public spaces.

The notion of the learning community builds on the familiar but neglected idea that one can't learn to be democratic in a hierarchical setting (e.g., Snyder, 1971). Should professional education be about disciplining people according to approved content, or should it be about getting them to think, reflect, and ponder the deeper dimensions of their work? (I would almost say their calling.) What do mid-career students take from a curriculum that dismisses their work experience as "anecdotal"? How many of our classes are structured like the bureaucratic pyramid, with us instructors at the point, dispensing wisdom to the assembled ranks below? The way we teach constitutes a political commitment. Is it one we want to continue making?

If we believe in democracy, we need to help students learn how to foster it on the job: how to involve citizens in the investigation and analysis of public problems, how to facilitate deliberative input rather than "likes" on a website, how to handle conflict, how to organize public meetings to encourage attention to the less-obvious aspects of what's at stake, and how to establish and maintain a web of relationships with people and organizations in the relevant communities. We need to prepare (or upgrade) public servants not to "manage" collaboration but to work collaboratively with citizens. Not every tactic works in every setting, but a commitment to democratic learning can temper even the most technical agency mission or the most traditional learning institution.

When I helped out with public executive seminars at Cleveland State, I was often the one who would handle the "citizen rap." Participants (mostly from local governments) were often skeptical, if not hostile, to the

160 Camilla Stivers

notion of involving citizens in agency activities. So, I'd ask them to do a cost–benefit sketch. What are the costs and benefits of citizen involvement? They were asked to volunteer ideas. Costs: it takes time and money, they'll be opposed, they won't understand, etc. Benefits: we will find out stuff we didn't know about the situation, we will get to know people we can call on later, maybe if they know more, they won't be so opposed, and so on. They began to realize that the benefits temper the costs.

Participation in public space isn't a quick fix. It's a long game. I would say the same about democracy in the classroom. As Jane Addams (1905) put it, the role of public servants is not to supervise the civic machinery but to become a part of it and help it to flourish. The same can be said about the learning community. The role of instructors is not, or not only to supervise the learning process but also to become a part of it and help it to flourish. The significance of a learning community of ordinary people becoming experts in governing is profound. As Foucault (1984, p. 47) once asked: "How can the growth of capabilities be disconnected from the intensification of power relations?" The *way* we teach makes a difference.

What We Teach

My sense of teaching as a practice within public administration is shaped by the "hows" of teaching, as above, and the "whats." As it happens, the two PA programs I have first-hand familiarity with are both noticeably interdisciplinary. I've already touched on Evergreen. Cleveland State was, in its way, also structurally interdisciplinary. The Levin College of Urban Affairs consisted of one big department of urban studies, made up of tracks not only in urban studies itself but also in public administration, economic development, and urban planning. An "urban center" also engaged faculty in research contracted by local governments and foundations. This arrangement made possible a great deal of disciplinary interchange, both intellectually and practically. The faculty associated with each track were likely to view that track as situated in a broader and more complex urban context. Although there was not as much interchange among faculty teaching assignments as at Evergreen, Levin students all took courses outside their principal interest area, and the result was a shared sense among students and faculty of their disciplinary focus as situated in broader political, economic, intellectual and practical contexts, such as the modern city.

During my 20+ years teaching public administration, I perceived a noticeable narrowing of the field's focus, both intellectually and methodologically. As a doctoral student at Virginia Tech's Center for Public Administration and Policy, I acquired a sense of both the field and the practice of public administration, organized around a constitutive tension between politics (publicness) and administration (effective management). My central source for this view was Dwight Waldo's *The Administrative State* (1948), which produced an epiphany that transformed my sense of the enterprise and greatly increased my interest in being a part of it. Waldo declared in his opening paragraph: "Despite occasional claims that public administration is a science with principles of universal validity, American public administration has evolved political theories unmistakably related to unique economic, social, governmental, and ideological facts (1948, p. 3)." Waldo's larger point, still valid, is that American public administration has never quite come to terms with the fact that the government's administrative and managerial activities take place not in a controlled laboratory setting or the university ivory tower but in a material and ideological context that these activities participate in shaping and are in turn shaped by.

Today, the field is arguably even farther from acknowledging this fact than it was in Waldo's day. Like Woodrow Wilson (1887), who claimed that "administration lies outside the proper sphere of politics," the task of public administration as an intellectual – and pedagogical – enterprise is now said to be to "straighten the paths of government, make its business less unbusinesslike . . . strengthen and purify its organization, and . . . crown its dutifulness" (p. 201). The central issue underneath this definitional thrust is whether the practice of public administration, because it is public, is different from business management in being permeated with issues of political legitimacy and public accountability. How can it be politically legitimate to turn the running of government over to people who insist that what they do and the decisions they make, even though permeated with broader legal and policy implications, are scientific rather than political? Yet career civil servants can become tenured, and no one has elected them. What makes their authority legitimate?

The contemporary answer from the intellectual field of public administration, "public management" for preference today, is the same as that Alexander Hamilton once gave in Federalist Paper 68: "The true test of a good government is its aptitude and tendency to produce good administration" (see also Koritansky, 1979). That is, what ordinary citizens want (or what they are likely to be satisfied with) is not a say in how agencies operate but efficient and effective government: results specified in policies and programs approved by the legislature. How, why, and whether this approach still makes sense or is itself politically legitimate were once debated issues in the field. Today the debate has largely gone silent. Like legendary New York mayor Fiorello LaGuardia, we have decided that "there's no Democratic or Republican way to pick up the garbage," and the rest is calculation (Renn, 2020).

162 Camilla Stivers

Today's orthodoxy is that public administration tasks are complex, requiring a scientific-analytical approach. Most citizens won't understand the science and don't particularly care about the process, but only the results. They will be reassured by the idea that expert administration is scientific rather than political. And, as Wilson (1887) declared, it's hard to draw a firm boundary between the administrative and the political, so it's best to leave it up to the administrator-expert to draw it. In any situation, argued Wilson, the administrator has the power to decide where administration (instrumental tactics, scientifically determined) leaves off and politics (substantive policy decisions) takes over. The complacency of this kind of thinking lies behind the administrator's vision as a referee among interests, an overseer of the game rather than a player, at least at that moment when the decision about what's at stake is up to them.

My argument is that the widely successful effort to redefine PA education in scientific-analytical terms has worrisome political implications. Today's students become familiar with the scientific method and the varieties of quantitative empiricism in social science. There is probably no MPA program in the United States that does not require a statistics course. There are few that offer, let alone require, a course in political philosophy or what used to be known as "PA theory," particularly one that acquaints students with the *method* of political theorizing, let alone the interpretive or process methodology that enables exploration of interactions that make up the public sphere and the bureaucratic organization.

According to Wolin (1969), political theorizing reflects on political practices within various contexts – political, economic, and social – exploring their implications and offering alternative "visions" of how things might be done differently, thus enlightening people's self-understandings. Neglecting this body of theoretical and philosophical work in our pedagogy has destabilized, perhaps even obliterated, our once shared understanding of what public administration is: administrative and constitutively public. The publicness of public administration still matters. Public authority must be debated and justified rather than taken for granted. Neglecting it is turning our academic programs into scientific-expert factories, even as the exercise of administrative discretionary judgment remains at the center of the practice, struggling for wisdom in the face of growing public tension, unrest, and loss of belief in government as a positive force.

Today more than ever, our pedagogy needs the right answers to empirical questions, the collaborative debate over public issues, practice in toning up the judgment muscles, and a deeper exploration of where administration fits in governance overall. The lure of being right leads the field and the country it serves down a risky path. The tension between our political foundations and the quest for scientific legitimacy must be maintained, not resolved. Otherwise, the publicness of public administration is in peril. The challenge starts in the classroom, both in what we study and how.

References

Addams, J. (1905). Problems of municipal administration. *American Journal of Sociology, 10*(4), 425–444. https://doi/10.1086/211316

Aristotle. (1981). *The politics*. Penguin.

Dewey, J. (1916). *Democracy and education*. Free Press.

Follett, M. P. (1924). *Creative experience*. Longmans, Green.

Foucault, M. (1984). What is enlightenment? In P. Rabinow (Ed.), *The Foucault reader* (pp. 32–50). Pantheon.

Koritansky, J. C. (1979). Alexander Hamilton's philosophy of government and administration. *Publius, 9*(2), 99–122. https://doi.org/10.1093/oxfordjournals.pubjof.a038547

Renn, A. M. (2020, April 7). The pandemic and the strengths of our networked governance. *Governing*. https://www.governing.com/now/the-pandemic-and-the-strengths-of-our-networked-governance.html

Snyder, G. H. (1971). "Prisoner's Dilemma" and "Chicken" models in international politics. *International Studies Quarterly, 15*(1), 66–103.

Waldo, D. (1948). *The administrative state*. Ronald Press.

Wilson, W. (1887). The study of administration. *Political Science Quarterly, 2*(2), 197–222. https://doi.org/10.2307/2139277

Wolin, S. (1969). Political theory as a vocation. *American Political Science Review, 63*(4), 1062–1082. https://doi.org/10.2307/1955072

13

PRACTICING CURIOSITY AS AN INSTRUCTOR, A SCHOLAR, AND AN INDIVIDUAL

William Hatcher

Augusta University, Augusta, GA

My first college-level course was a disaster, at least in my mind. After teaching my first class, I decided to explore other career opportunities. Maybe I should be more directed. I wanted to run far away from the classroom. I made a silent pact to take a different route for my career. Luckily, this pact did not last, and my aversion to teaching did not hold. Now, I find myself in my perfect job: a professor of public administration and academic leader, helping students and faculty learn how to advance our political system and public administration. Over 15 years after my silent pact to not teach, I reflect that a little curiosity about what may be down the road as an instructor helped me stick with it long enough to appreciate and love the craft of teaching.

Before I discuss my approach to college teaching, though, we need to go back to my undergraduate career, which at first was a struggle and not a career. I started college completely lost. I went to a high school that did a poor job helping students plan for their academic futures. My first year of college was such a disaster that I almost did not return. However, thankfully, some excellent professors at Georgia College took the time to mentor me in the classroom.

Moreover, their curiosity about me as a student saved me academically, and I found the path toward where I am today – a path that has led me to a rewarding academic career and the opportunity to help train and educate current and future public servants. Through practicing curiosity in response to my early failures as an undergraduate, I learned to love learning (I know it is a cliché but true for me), and simply put, I realized that I love the university and never want to leave.

DOI: 10.4324/9781032671291-15

Practicing Curiosity as an Instructor, a Scholar, and an Individual **165**

How did this happen during my undergraduate years? I took a seemingly normal class on state and local government that turned out to be abnormal for my career. Through this class, I learned more about how important state and local governments were for our nation and the health and well-being of our communities. The instructor in the course sparked in me a curiosity in public administration that has not stopped since then. This curiosity led me to do an MPA and later earn a PhD in public policy and administration. The curiosity to know how "the doing side of government" works to improve theory and practice was sparked inside me and has not stopped burning since. I credit this curiosity with opening many doors for me – including a professional and personal life that has been very rewarding. Additionally, this seemingly ordinary course made me curious about whether I could also have such a positive effect as an instructor on the careers and academic lives of others.

Over time, though, this curiosity has faced challenges along with periods of growth. I want to discuss a few of them. Given that my high school education did not prepare me for college-level work, I faced struggles at each new step in my education – when I started college, the first semester of my MPA, and the first semester of my PhD program. The first semester of my PhD program was especially challenging. While I had a strong foundation in public administration, government, and social sciences, I had to work on improving the quality of my writing and practice better time management. Living away from home for the first time also made things even more difficult. Honestly, this was the hardest challenge for me to overcome. Luckily, I overcame these challenges and started to succeed. Curiosity made this possible. I was curious to learn what my PhD program's professors could teach me. I was curious to learn how to conduct independent research, and I had the broader curiosity to discover a career path that would allow me to stay at the university.

While I am coming to understand how curiosity has driven so much of my life and career decisions, I still struggle with change. When I started my first tenure-track job, this difficulty with change almost stopped my career development. I started my first job being ABD, and moving hundreds of miles to a new city with a new job and multiple course preparations made it difficult, to say the least, to finish the dissertation. However, again, I met the challenge and defended my dissertation during the first year of my new job. Nevertheless, this was only possible through curiosity. In particular, I was curious to teach students from Eastern Kentucky who share socioeconomic backgrounds and challenges similar to mine. The curiosity to study topics beyond what I focused on in my graduate studies, such as community development and issues at the intersections of health policy and public administration.

This essay is about how curiosity has driven my academic career and how I approach teaching. But what do I mean by curiosity? It is being motivated to objectively learn how the world works for the joy of knowing (Hatcher, 2023). Researchers have identified various aspects of curiosity, such as a joyous exploration of learning, realizing when we have deficits in knowledge, dealing with the stress of not knowing, and enjoying the social aspect of learning (Kashdan et al., 2018). This drives individuals to gather knowledge that can be useful in their professional, personal, and social lives.

Curiosity is the prescription for improvements to so many ills, from seeking to understand how people from different backgrounds experience the world to wanting to learn everything possible about a topic. In the classroom, instructors employing curiosity seek to be better at their craft. They seek to understand their students and practice compassion and empathy in doing so. Through understanding their students, they can do a better job of teaching them. On the other hand, students employing curiosity seek to be better at their craft. They seek to understand the material for the sake of knowing it, but this leads them to have knowledge that helps them succeed in the class and advance their career goals. Seeking to practice curiosity leads them to want to know more about their courses and instructors, leading to engagement in their classes. For both faculty and students, curiosity encourages them to be humble and recognize that they do not know everything. Admitting a lack of knowledge and being humble about it is the step toward knowing more about how the world works and then applying that knowledge in meaningful ways (Hatcher, 2019, 2023). Let us talk a little about curiosity in teachers and students.

Curious Teachers

Curious instructors practice empathy and caring in seeking evidence-based pedagogical methods to teach students as effectively as possible. This is especially important for public administration instructors, given the importance of educating public servants who work in high-pressure environments with high incidences of burnout (Hatcher, 2019, 2023). Being curious about the background of their students helps instructors in our field appreciate the importance of understanding emotional labor (Guy et al., 2014). From advising students to discuss their grades and giving career guidance, instructors do much emotional labor as part of their jobs. It takes a certain level of curiosity to engage in this work properly. Unfortunately, public administration, as a field, struggles to teach emotional labor, even though advances have been made in this area thanks to Mary Guy and her colleagues. Our field needs to discuss the importance of the emotional work being done by practicing public managers and faculty members, helping them in the classroom and beyond when these public servants are working in the frontlines of the government (Mastracci et al., 2010).

Curiosity can be used as a linkage to encourage faculty members to appreciate their students' emotional labor and teach it in the classroom. In a paper published in *Teaching Public Administration*, I suggested plans for how curiosity can be integrated into the public administration curriculum and our classrooms (Hatcher, 2019). This can be done by connecting program-wide student learning outcomes focusing on curiosity with classroom assignments that engage students in reflection and empathy and dispelling the frustration of not knowing how the world works in searching for knowledge.

Demonstrating kindness is essential to being a curious instructor who worries about their students and understands the emotive parts of their work. I had instructors practice kindness toward me. My first semester in my PhD program was successful because my instructors understood the challenges of starting such an endeavor. My professors at Georgia College practiced extraordinary kindness when they showed themselves to be curious about me and my career goals.

Lastly, curious teachers, to truly be concerned about emotive work, need to assist their students in being able to balance their work, lives, and families. This does not mean that standards need to be adjusted. But it does mean that instructors should be curious within professional boundaries about the lives of their students so that they can be the best learners they can be. And as with teachers, this learning starts with curiosity.

Curious Students

Just as instructors have responsibilities, students also have them in the classroom. They must take the material seriously, be prepared, and demonstrate kindness. Students in MPA also need to have a certain degree of respect for public service. If not, then why are you earning a public service-focused degree? In public administration, we need to do a better job of celebrating the public sector and the calling of being a public servant. We need to model this respect for our students. A life in public service changes the lives of others and the life of the public servant. I know it has positively affected my life.

A Teaching Philosophy Informed by Curiosity

Being driven by curiosity has led to the following personal philosophy on teaching and learning. My philosophy of teaching is comprised of three areas of focus for instructors. First, the instructor is driven by an underlying vision of education. This is based on how the instructor views education and what they think the students should take away from their classes. My vision of learning involves an appreciation of civic education's role in our society, an appreciation that I try to instill in my students. This vision pushed me to select teaching as a career and public administration as my area of expertise. As political science and public administration instructors, we are concerned with teaching students the importance of a functioning government. We are also concerned with students learning how to be effective, efficient, and fair administrators and, in doing so, better their public agencies and nonprofit organizations. Second, instructors attempt to convey their vision in the classroom by applying appropriate models of instruction. The material's nature and the students' educational level are the two factors that I consider when deciding on the appropriate models of instruction to implement in a class. Third, the instructor's commitment to preparation, accessibility, and evaluation ensures that students see how the vision and material are implemented, how the course's model of learning works, and how performance is measured in the course? My views on these vital parts are elaborated in the following paragraphs.

My vision of teaching is based on my experience as a liberal arts student and as a political science instructor in three varying types of institutions of higher education (a community college, a regional comprehensive university, and two research universities). My education at Georgia College & State University (GCSU), the state's designated public liberal arts institution, taught me the importance of gaining knowledge and using this knowledge to better my communities. Throughout my courses, there was a strong emphasis on public service and using the material learned in class to "make a difference" outside the classroom. As teachers, we often mimic the practices of our mentors, and as I have stressed, my professors at GCSU had a lasting impact on my overall approach to education. From their classes, I developed the following pedagogical views toward government instruction. In a representative government, the teaching of government should be based on the need to produce engaged citizens who will contribute to the nation's political discourse. The ability of citizens to formulate their ideologies and then have the ability to contribute is a necessary component of a functioning representative government. To a certain degree, the knowledge needed to achieve this comes from the material learned in political science classrooms. Given this, I believe political science instructors have a special responsibility to teach civic values and help students be well-equipped citizens. When I was given my first class at Georgia Military College, I continued this vision of education, which I learned from my liberal arts background that quality civic education should produce students who excel inside and outside of the classroom. This is my overall vision: to help students realize their civic responsibility and potential, with the caveat that I want to also encourage individual curiosity in them for the material.

In *The Art & Craft of College Teaching,* Robert Rotenberg (2016) reviews the major models of instruction found in the scholarly literature. In his section on models of thinking skills, Rotenberg traces the development of a transitional critical thinking model. In this model, students move from dualistic thinking, where they are not adequately analyzing the material, to more critical thinking, where they critically assess the subject matter. Throughout Rotenberg's discussion, the overall theme is that there is no ideal method of instruction. When I structure my courses, I believe in utilizing multiple methods. In my selection of the appropriate models, I am primarily guided by two factors: the students and the material.

First, let us discuss the nature of the student. Students in an American government survey course should be given a primer on participating in our nation's political system. It should be stressed here that my overall civic engagement vision does not cause me to emphasize one ideology at the expense of others or one party at the expense of others. In fact, I do the opposite by trying to be as neutral as possible or arguing the minority opinion in the class, especially within my lower-level courses. For example, I approach the teaching of a survey course in American government from the perspective that the students are not being trained to be political scientists but rather to be engaged and educated citizens. To accomplish this goal, I focus on the basics of our political system with these students, but I also want them to think critically about our government and current events. Students are required to complete weekly blogs on political, social, and economic events. Students must analyze these events in these blogs and discuss how they relate to the course material. I believe these exercises force students to refine their views about politics and our society's challenges.

Another example of how I attempt to guide students toward understanding their ideological preferences is my coverage of the ideological spectrum. I present the students with the four ideologies based on the two continuums of more or less government involvement in the market and more or less government involvement in the social order. After this, I have the students critically examine their ideological preferences. We discuss their results and how they relate to their perceived preferences and past voting records. In undergraduate research methods, I often divide the students into groups to answer questions regarding concepts illustrated earlier in my lectures. I believe this "hands-on" approach helps the students learn how to apply the material to conduct research. Accordingly, with my lower-level courses, I take an overall top-down approach to the material. However, I also try to infuse critical analysis exercises and discussions that help them understand their own opinions regarding the political world. For my upper-level and graduate courses, I view the role of the instructor as a facilitator of critical discussions of concepts in conjunction with prepared students.

Based on this viewpoint, my model of instruction for my upper-level and Master of Public Administration (MPA) courses is a more bottom-up approach than the traditional lecture style found in my lower-level courses. In both settings, lectures are supplemented with interactive exercises, useful media, critical essays, and student presentations. For example, in my public policy courses, the students must watch Frontline documentaries on current issues and analyze these films through in-class policy discussion. I try to simulate a "town hall" forum when discussing their opinions on these policy issues rather than lecturing them on my opinion or the opinions found in their textbooks. My upper-level and graduate courses engage the students in a more question-and-answer style. They must also participate in regular panel discussions, explaining and answering questions on a week's readings. To facilitate this, students have a diverse collection of readings and have to explain the readings in in-class discussions.

In my MPA courses, I train and educate current and future public managers so they must learn how to connect public administration theory with practice. This encourages learning that is experiential and multiple assessment methods, such as examinations but mostly applied assignments, reflective papers, case studies, memo writing assignments, etc. The assignments mimic the students' work as managers in public agencies and nonprofit organizations.

In addition to the nature of students, the material (i.e., the course content) should be considered when selecting the instruction model. Many of my courses, such as research methods and public finance, require much experiential learning. Students must participate in applied projects to learn the habits of mind necessary for systematic research. In my undergraduate research methods course, I have such an applied project. Students have to construct a typical research design and explain the meaning of each section in the design. The project is done in stages over the semester. At each step, I give the students detailed feedback regarding their progress so they learn systematic research processes by actually doing them. In my MPA courses, the nature of the material certainly influences my focus on the importance of linking theory with practice.

Assignments from my MPA courses illustrate how vital this linkage is to me. As I detailed in a *Journal of Public Affairs Education* (Hatcher, 2015) paper I wrote years ago, an assignment that I get genuinely excited about is using the community development simulation SimCity in my planning and community development courses. In this assignment, students use *SimCity* to simulate the role of a community developer and then the mayor of their city. The project calls for students to construct a vision of their community and implement this plan through the simulation. In my intergovernmental relations and urban government courses, I require my students to identify problems with a chosen municipality, prepare plans to address these challenges, and secure the funds to pay for the programs. To do this, students play the role of a city manager or mayor to prepare a program and find a grant to fund it. In my public budgeting course, students selected a municipality and evaluated the city's budget based on industrial standards of what constitutes a quality budget document.

Another meaningful way I link theory and practice in my courses is by maintaining an active research agenda and using the results from my research to illustrate concepts in my courses. I use my research findings on the viewpoints of local government planners, municipal budgeting officers, economic developers, and city managers in all of my MPA courses. For example, in my courses on public budgeting, I use findings from a research paper that surveyed municipal budget directors' viewpoints on the efficacy of public participation in the budgeting process.

In assessing student knowledge of the material after implementing these methods of instruction, I like to utilize multiple methods of assessment. My examinations seek to be challenging but also fair. They incorporate various types of questions. I have examinations ranging from multiple-choice formats to essay-based ones. I attempt to create an interactive learning environment in all my courses. In Introduction to American Government, I often engage the students in a question-and-answer style, including several stimulation-based exercises. For example, I group the students into teams (presidents and their security advisors) to illustrate presidential decision-making to solve different national security scenarios. I have discussed some of the interactive exercises in my MPA classes already. Interactive learning in my classes is one of the most critical factors driving the content and design of my courses, and I try to develop examinations, assignments, and exercises based on this.

Lastly, we come to the crucial final step in my philosophy of teaching, the importance of being dedicated to the day-to-day work of the job. Again, curiosity is the driving force behind this dedication. The instructor could have the most idealistic vision of education and the best-constructed models of instruction. However, without dedication to the day-to-day work, they will fail in the classroom. This last link involves the instructor's commitment to preparation for each class, accessibility, and evaluation, ensuring that students understand the vision and material of the course and the measures by which their work is evaluated. For preparation, the teacher should come to each class ready with a detailed plan and a command of the material. If not, the instructor wastes valuable educational resources and can hamper the future progress of their students. I feel as though being unprepared as an instructor is malpractice in education. In preparing for a class, I will spend about two to three hours for each hour in the classroom. If I have taught the course multiple times, the preparation time is much less, but I still plan out each day's lecture the night before. Our political system is constantly changing and being influenced by current events in the world. Yes, the fundamental aspects of most political science courses change in increments, but the events influencing our political system often cause rapid change. Therefore, preparation for courses, even ones taught many times, must be an ongoing process to incorporate new ideas. For example, I have taught Introduction to American Government and Survey of Public Administration numerous times, but I am consistently refining the courses. I often add new material, new graphs, and new simulations.

Accessibility and evaluation are necessary components that lead the students to be prepared for course assignments and then to know how they performed on them to improve their command of the information. I take these tasks very seriously as well. Students should know what is expected of them, so I often give them pointers regarding assignments and examinations. I serve more than the expected office hours per week. Regarding evaluation, I try to return assignments and examinations by the next class meeting. Also, being collegial with others in my field, my college, and my department and working together on teaching-related issues is crucial to this last step. Throughout this process, it is essential to rely on colleagues for advice and assistance in teaching. The management of the class is the last crucial step to this philosophy of teaching that calls for a vision, the material, an appropriate model of learning, and then simply hard work on the instructor's part.

The Craft of Curious Teaching

As an instructor for nearly 20 years in multiple college environments, from a community college to a teaching regional university to a research- oriented university, I have learned specific lessons from implementing my teaching philosophy rooted in curiosity. My time as a program director and now chair of a large multidisciplinary department has also informed these lessons. Learning needs to be fun, but instructors need to make the case for how their fields affect the everyday lives of their students. In American government survey courses, instructors must make the case that the material advances our democracy. In MPA courses, the instructor needs to link the material to how it will improve the work being done by current and future public servants.

Teaching is not being the sage in front of the class. As discussed, multiple active methods need to be used in classrooms. The need for multiple teaching methods also comes with the need for multiple assessment methods. The grade given is essential, but learning material is a vital component of classes. This is obvious, but it often does not happen, so we must repeatedly stress it.

Some Concluding Thoughts

Often, students seem to forget that their professors live everyday lives and face similar struggles. Over the years, students have often been surprised when I see them at the grocery store, the mall, and other places out in the world. To be effective in the classroom, students need to understand that there is a separation between the instructor and them. However, humanity needs to be shared, and curiosity on both sides helps accomplish this. In public administration classrooms, as Mary Guy and colleagues have so effectively demonstrated (see Mastracci et al., 2010), there is an added need for instructors and students to discuss and appreciate the emotional labor of public service. Curiosity can help spread the need to talk about emotion in the public administration classroom.

I have dealt throughout my life with anxiety, and at times, anxiety has caused me to struggle with the professional and personal parts of my life. Living with such anxiety has helped me be more empathetic to others and, in doing so, practice curiosity. It has also helped me appreciate the importance of effective and efficient public administration and the need for supportive and caring public administration that understands how public administrators are not cogs in bureaucracy but humans doing complex work. Having a career in academia that has evolved due to curiosity (and some anxiety) has helped me craft a practical teaching philosophy and practice that seeks to spread curiosity and the importance of being practical but also fair public servants.

Education can transform communities and individuals. It only takes some curiosity. I know this because education and curiosity have changed my life.

References

Guy, M. E., Newman, M. A., & Mastracci, S. H. (2014). *Emotional labor: Putting the service in public service*. Routledge.

Hatcher, W. (2015). Teaching the importance of community betterment to public managers: Community development in NASPAA member programs. *Journal of Public Affairs Education, 21*(2), 165–178.

Hatcher, W. (2019). Teaching curiosity in public affairs programs. *Teaching Public Administration*, 37(3), 365–375. https://doi.org/10.1177/0144739419858702

Hatcher, W. (2023). *The curious public administrator.* Routledge.

Kashdan, T. B., Disabato, D. J., Goodman, F. R., & Naughton, C. (2018). The five dimensions of curiosity. *Harvard Business Review*, 96(5), 58–60.

Mastracci, S. H., Newman, M. A., & Guy, M. E. (2010). Emotional labor: Why and how to teach it. *Journal of Public Affairs Education*, 16(2), 123–141. https://doi.org/10.1080/15236803.2010.12001590

Rotenberg, R. (2016). *The art and craft of college teaching: A guide for new professors and graduate students.* Routledge.

14

BECOMING AN ENGAGED INSTRUCTOR IN THE MPA CLASSROOM

Beth M. Rauhaus

University of Louisiana at Lafayette, Lafayette, LA

When I first began my tenure-track position 11 years ago, I was 27 years old and younger than many of my MPA students. I had just completed my PhD with little teaching experience, minimal professional work experience beyond graduate assistantships and internships, and no formal training in pedagogy. Prior to completing my PhD in Public Policy and Adminis-tration, I had earned my MA in Political Science. This degree helped me understand political affairs and political theory. Graduate courses in Politi-cal Science were theory-based and lacked practical focus, which is very different from MPA courses. I had never been in an MPA classroom until I was on the job market doing teaching demonstrations, and then a few months later, I was instructing MPA courses as a tenure-track professor in Georgia. I quickly realized that in order to master effective teaching in an MPA program, I would need to rely on the knowledge I obtained through-out my graduate training and use my research experience from completing my dissertation to add legitimacy to my role as an educator and practice my teaching philosophy that I am a lifelong learner.

I certainly received lots of advice from mentors on how to be an effective instructor. My graduate training emphasized linking theory to practice and mastering the appropriate core content of public affairs and administra-tion. Much of the advice I received varied widely regarding the appropriate degree of rigor, how to be firm but also approachable, confident but not arrogant, and serious but not too serious. Many mentors cautioned me of being too friendly with students and to set a strictly professional tone early on in the classroom, which was a bit unnatural. I was not even aware of the term "imposter syndrome" at this time but being the smartest one in the

DOI: 10.4324/9781032671291-16

176   Beth M. Rauhaus

room and having authority over others felt uncomfortable to me. Being a naturally shy individual, I was horrified of standing in front of a group of students and leading a discussion. I had serious doubts of my ability to be an effective instructor, getting tenure, and learning how to manage my time.

All of the varying and often contrary advice on how to present myself professionally left me to quickly realize that I would need to find a balance between being in the classroom and being with the students. Once I found this balance and what worked for me, I relaxed and focused on getting to know my students and their needs. There were two main components that helped to discover an effective teaching style. The first was teaching subject matter in my areas of expertise, which is nested in public administration theory. The second approach was abandoning the imposter syndrome and becoming an engaged learner and instructor.

As I gained experience as an instructor and found my own stride in the classroom, I discovered that I was a stronger teacher when I taught subject matter that I was well-versed in. While it was not always possible to teach courses that I preferred, I learned to incorporate content that I knew well into courses I was assigned to teach. I became an engaged instructor almost by accident, when discovering that MPA students do not always understand or appreciate theory, leading me to think creatively about how to make theory more useful to students with and without practical experience in public service. Nearly every semester, I taught the introductory public administration course in the MPA program, which is rooted in classical theories and quickly realized that students were overwhelmed with the amount of information and content of the course in addition to the complexities of theory. In courses that were not theory driven, I relied on my theoretical training to present course content and concepts of public affairs to the students.

Linking Theory to Practice

Linking theory to practice in public affairs and administration is essential. To prepare students to be leaders in public service, nearly all academics will introduce theoretical underpinnings in MPA courses. Textbooks in the discipline, such as *Public Administration: Traditions of Inquiry and Philosophies of Knowledge* by Riccucci (2010) and *The Public Administration Theory Primer* by Frederickson et al. (2016), emphasize the theoretical frameworks widely used to understand, describe, and prescribe best practices of governing. These textbooks, among others, introduce students to the core principles of public administration and highlight how each approach adds value to governing and public service. Academic journals devoted to public affairs pedagogy, such as the *Journal of Public Administration*

Education, the *Journal of Public Affairs Education*, and *Teaching Public Administration*, offer instructors endless ideas of how to incorporate theory into the MPA classroom, highlight the importance of teaching theory, and extend theory building into methodological approaches throughout the social sciences. In fact, in 1997, the *Journal of Public Administration Education* published a special edition spotlighting theory in the MPA classroom. Articles focused on educating future public servants by using theories that link to practice and questioned the usefulness of using theory in the classroom to prepare students to address real-world problems (Broadnax, 1997; Hummel, 1997; Miller, 1997).

Recognizing the fundamentals of theory in the field, I taught each lesson with at least one theoretical framework included, applied it to a case study from course materials, and discussed the course readings with the students. The discussions in class felt generic, and when evaluating the students' understanding of the theory, it was clear that the approach was not the most effective. I learned that I would need to adapt my approach if I really wanted students to understand the theoretical fundamentals of public affairs and administration. To do so, I had to overcome the imposter syndrome and become more engaged in both the classroom and community. This is how I became an engaged instructor.

Engaged Learning and Listening as an Engaged Instructor

To become an engaged instructor in the MPA classroom, I immersed myself in personalizing class prep to fit student needs and the environment in which I was preparing them to lead. Like most faculty teaching at universities, I was not a native to the area, so it was important to familiarize myself with the culture, expectations, and norms of the community. After all, preparing students to serve in diverse communities requires understanding the uniqueness of the community. To do so, I watched the local news daily to understand which wicked problems the community faced. I occasionally saw my students and program alumni being interviewed as expert public servants. In the classroom, I would incorporate examples of the wicked problems that appeared on the local news to help students understand the public affairs content and to create critical thinking skills that would allow them to develop solutions to combat these wicked problems that plagued the community. Each example that I used from the local community applied to a theory in the lesson. Regardless of the students' understanding of the theory in the lesson, they were eager to discuss the local issue and add their experiences and ideas to classroom discussion. This became a jumping off point for them to really understand theoretical foundations of public affairs and administration.

178 Beth M. Rauhaus

Another technique of preparing for the classroom was creating an activity for the first day of class that allowed me to get to know my students. At the beginning of each semester, I would assess students' needs, goals, and abilities by having a discussion of how they see "public service" and get to know more about their professional journey and goals. I simply asked them to fill in an index card detailing information about themselves, their career aspirations, and why they were interested in public affairs. Knowing this information helped me find appropriate cases and readings that would be of interest to students.

In class, I would listen to their stories, lecture less, and learn more about their experiences. By listening to their stories, I learned more about the actual practices of "public service" than I ever had. As I introduced theories, such as incrementalism or public service motivation, and applied them to cases in the classroom, students were quick to offer examples of how those theories may or may not work in practice in their agency, department, or station. I realized that I needed to tap into the student's experience, as I had a classroom full of street-level bureaucrats and public leaders with a wealth of professional experiences from across many fields to share. A mutual respect was developed and continued to thrive.

Often times, even after students would graduate and go on to lead local government and nonprofit agencies, they would call or email me for advice about how to solve organizational problems or human resource issues they were encountering. In some instances, I could quickly provide recommendations on how to help achieve more citizen engagement in city planning initiatives or how to effectively communicate with multiple fire stations throughout a large city with varying schedules. In other instances, the phone calls from alumni were not easily solved with a quick conversation and many of those turned into service-learning projects. Each of these calls provided me with an opportunity to become an engaged learner and truly immerse myself in public service practices in the real world.

Instructors have a large burden of teaching, service, and scholarship and face challenges juggling all responsibilities. It is not uncommon that instructors are unwilling to update courses, begin new projects, or decline service opportunities due to burnout and the harsh reality of work–life balance being unattainable. I, too, had all of these concerns, especially during my tenure-track years. Over time, I learned that when I combined the three responsibilities of teaching, service, and scholarship, I became more confident and effective as an instructor. I discovered this through community engagement.

One day, a former student who holds a leadership role in the fire department called and asked me if I would serve on the Civil Service Board and Commission for the city. He had taken a Human Resources course with me a few semesters prior and was looking for a community member to serve in this role for a three-year term. I was very hesitant at first due to my busy schedule, prior commitments, and the fact that I am an academic with little knowledge of public service in practice. I thought about this opportunity and accepted it a few days later as part of my quest to be a lifelong learner and to help others. During my three-year term, I served as chair for both the Civil Service Board and Commission and mastered how theory links to practice. From my experience in hearing civil servants' experiences in the workplace and having to make a decision regarding the city's decision on their individual employment status, I clearly saw how practices, behaviors, and actions are rooted in theory. Using my experience there, I would adapt and modify the cases I heard at city hall to share with students in the classroom. I would never share names or the agency involved in the cases I heard, but I would modify the case for my classroom discussion. After this, my examples in the MPA classroom were so much more realistic and the link between theory and practice became much more apparent for students. Discussions were lively, and I gained even more respect from my students when they learned I served the community in this capacity.

From this point on, I began to think of service opportunities through community engagement as an excellent opportunity rather than as an additional service burden. A few months later, I received another call from an alumna of the MPA Program asking for assistance with a large undertaking. She was serving as a city planner of Rockport, Texas, tasked with creating a 10-year strategic plan during the aftermath of Hurricane Harvey. The city she worked for was a small neighboring town of the university and had been devastated by the hurricane. The tasks of rebuilding and resilience were demanding enough before adding in additional goals of creating a strategic plan for the locality. She was focused on creating a strong strategic plan and wanted my advice on how to achieve representative input from citizens during a challenging time. We discussed how to engage citizens, many of whom were displaced, struggling to rebuild and return to a sense of normalcy after the hurricane. After brainstorming a few options and discussing various approaches, she asked if this could become a service-learning project.

At this time in my career, I felt like I was ready to do something different with my classes. I was not familiar with service-learning projects and had no idea how to begin incorporating a real-life project into a semester-long course. Just as the previous call from a former student left me with reservations and doubts about whether or not I could do this and do it well, this call did, too. I was well-versed in community engagement in democratic settings and theories of representation; however, I never had a class in community planning, strategic planning, emergency management, or disaster recovery. I learned how to adapt the qualitative methodological training

180 Beth M. Rauhaus

I had received in my PhD program to teach my students the skills necessary to conduct focus groups and surveys to assist local government agencies throughout the region. Rather than resort back to the imposter syndrome, I began to think of this as an opportunity to learn more about the surrounding community, city planning, and disaster recovery and resilience.

I also reflected back to my experience as an undergraduate student in South Louisiana during the aftermath of Hurricane Katrina. I drew parallels to the aftermath of Hurricane Harvey in South Texas. Both regions were filled with social inequities in hurricane recovery and had very limited resources. During the aftermath of Hurricane Katrina, I was graduating from college with a degree in Government. At the same time, many residents were displaced across the country, including those being housed in the college gymnasium. Job opportunities were very limited, which led me to consider going to graduate school. After thinking back to this time, I felt like my experience in the aftermath of Hurricane Katrina could be useful to the city of Rockport's strategic planning project during the aftermath of Hurricane Harvey as well as offer insight into linking theory to practice for my MPA students.

My philosophy of being a lifelong learner was in practice, and I accepted this challenge. I knew it would take extensive planning to be successful, and I also knew I had high standards for my class performance, as they were responsible for portions of a city plan that the public would see and live by for the next 10 years. I wanted my pre-service students to have more hands-on experience and to work collaboratively with those in professional positions in local government. I also wanted students to be able to build research skills to make them more marketable professionals in public service and, of course, connect theory to practice by examining real-world problems and creating solutions. By taking on this project, I became an engaged learner and a more engaged faculty member. My MPA Capstone students and I were able to facilitate conversations and create spaces for under-represented voices during the aftermath of Hurricane Harvey in South Texas (Rauhaus, 2022). From this experience, my MPA Capstone students learned how to conduct focus groups, collect data, and, most importantly, listen to citizen's concerns. As an instructor, I felt a sense of pride that not only was I educating MPA students, but also I was providing them with essential tools to help them become leaders in the public sector and in their communities.

Service-Learning Projects as Engaged Learning

Service-learning is defined as experiential education, where students engage in activities that solve social and community needs through the means of structured educational opportunities designed to enhance the students' learning experience (Velotti et al., 2022). Prior to the phone call I received from the city planner, I had never heard of the formal term "service-learning" and certainly could not define it. I knew I wanted to provide my students with more hands-on experiences beyond the classroom. Students, the university, and the community can all benefit from service-learning projects (Mitchell & Buckingham, 2020).

My goals of adding value to students' experiences and the opportunity really aligned, and it turns out that public administration faculty were using service-learning all along. The MPA program at the University of Central Florida has offered a strategic planning service-learning course for the last 20 years (Mitchell & Buckingham, 2020). Service-learning opportunities engage future public administrators and public administration faculty in their communities and provide an excellent opportunity to really make a difference. Rather than lecturing on theories such as public service motivation and representative bureaucracy, the service-learning opportunity allowed me to really illustrate to my students how public servants can make a difference throughout communities.

According to Barth (2018), engagement is important in transmitting the craft knowledge of the profession of public administration to students through case studies, internships, applied projects, and community-based projects. Both pre-service students and in-service students benefit from service-learning projects. All students can use practical experience in data collection and data analysis as well as learn how to communicate with clients, manage time, and present information to varied audiences. Through the use of service-learning projects incorporated into my class, I learned that it is acceptable for students to excel in certain areas while working diligently to master other content. There is no best way for teaching and learning. I discovered this when I really got to know my students, their goals, and their abilities.

While I had hesitations in incorporating service-learning projects in the MPA classroom, as students had varying degrees of abilities, skill sets, and time availability, I realized everyone would benefit from the project in some way. In-service students excelled at networking with others throughout the local government, learned data collection and analysis techniques, and practiced mentoring pre-service classmates. Pre-service students were exposed to real problems local governments face, learned how to solve problems in a timely manner with limited resources, and practiced data collection and analysis techniques that are instrumental in preparing for a career in public service. Students interested in furthering their education and pursuing an academic degree also benefitted from service-learning projects. With my mentorship, these students were able to highlight the results of the data collected

182 Beth M. Rauhaus

at open houses for the community, participate in academic conferences, and write peer-reviewed publications. For this particular service-learning project, I was able to work with an MPA student to publish findings and provide him insight into academic expectations for scholarship in public affairs (Rauhaus & Guajardo, 2021). Through this process, the student learned about writing literature review drafts, presenting a research design and findings of a project, and had first-hand insight into the submission and revision process of academic publishing, which will prepare him for a PhD program in the future. Introducing students to the publication process and mentoring them throughout the various stages of research has proven to be beneficial in so many ways. By equipping my students with these tools and skills developed in the service-learning project, they can achieve their respective goals in public service and in furthering their education.

By using service-learning projects in my MPA courses, I was able to accomplish more than I originally thought. First, I was able to provide my MPA students with invaluable opportunities to solve real-life problems in their communities. Second, I was able to highlight the connection between the university and the surrounding communities. Next, through the use of service-learning projects, my students and I were able to assist program alumni with professional services and development. Finally, I learned more about the teaching and learning aspects of public administration and became a more effective instructor. While service-learning projects take immense planning in advance and flexibility in the class schedule, they open doors for community engagement, active learning, and scholarship enhancement.

Concluding Thoughts

As I reflect on my growth and development as an MPA faculty member, I realize that I have learned a great deal in the last 11 years and still have much to learn. Learning alongside students is not a sign of weakness. Being a lifelong learner is important for both students and instructors. I am glad that I leaned into these opportunities to become more engaged in the community and in the learning process and truly learned more about public service in practice. Learning more about practical elements of public service from my students, alumni, and community has truly enhanced my teaching and research skills. When I think about the success of my students with much pride, I am also grateful that they trusted me with these opportunities to listen and learn.

References

Barth, T. J. (2018). Escaping the vines of the ivory tower: Reflections of an engaged professor. *Journal of Community Engagement and Scholarship, 10*(2), 9–19.

Broadnax, W. (1997). Educating tomorrow's public administrators: Embracing theory and practice. *Journal of Public Administration Education, 3*(3), 391–396. https://doi.org/10.1080/10877789.1997.12023454

Frederickson, H. G., Smith, K. B., Larimer, C. W., & Licari, M. J. (2016). *The public administration theory primer* (3rd ed.). Westview Press.

Hummel, R. P. (1997). On the usefulness of theory to practitioners. *Journal of Public Administration Education, 3*(3), 375–382. https://doi.org/10.1080/1087 7789.1997.12023452

Miller, H. T. (1997). Why teaching theory matters. *Journal of Public Administration Education. 3*(3), 363–373. https://doi.org/10.1080/10877789.1997.12023451

Mitchell, D., & Buckingham, G. (2020). Transforming plans into community impact: Strategic planning as service-learning in public and nonprofit administration graduate programs. *Teaching Public Administration, 39*(1), 9–25. https://doi.org/10.1177/0144739420929380

Rauhaus, B. M. (2022). Developing a service-learning capstone to assist in local government resilience and strategic planning efforts. In L. Velotti, R. M. Brenner, & E. A. Dunn (Eds.), *Service-learning for disaster resilience: Partnerships for social good* (pp. 138–148). Routledge.

Rauhaus, B. M., & Guajardo, J. M. (2021). The practice of youth inclusion in community planning and resiliency: The case of post-Hurricane Harvey. *Journal of Health and Human Services Administration, 44*(1), 67–85. https://doi.org/10.37808/jhhsa.44.1.4

Riccucci, N. M. (2010). *Public administration: Traditions of inquiry and philosophies of knowledge*. Georgetown University Press.

Velotti, L., Brenner, R. M., & Dunn, E. A. (2022). *Service-learning for disaster resilience: Partnerships for social good*. Routledge.

15

LEARNING TO BE A TEACHER

Bruce D. McDonald III
Old Dominion University, Norfolk, VA

It never occurred to me until I walked into my first classroom that I would have to teach. I chose an academic career because I have always loved to write, and academia was a great way of ensuring a steady income that other writing-oriented careers did not have. An added benefit was that it would also allow me to make a significant contribution to the communities around me. Writing was to be my career, not teaching. As a deep-rooted introvert, the idea of standing in front of any audience where all the attention is placed on me is paralyzing. It was not until I walked into my first class that I realized I would actually have to teach as part of the career I had chosen. And I was petrified.

That first class was, perhaps, my greatest learning experience during my PhD program. I had been given orders from the department and the Dean's office to kill the class's reputation as the go-to class for an easy A. I was told that at least half the class needed to earn a C or lower and that I should ensure that grade distribution by any means necessary. Scared out of my mind and fully aware that the students would hate me because of the marching orders, I quickly learned what kind of teacher I did not want to be. But I did not know what kind of teacher I wanted to become.

Having come from a PhD program that spent no time preparing us to teach and manage our classrooms, my first few teaching experiences were bound to be rough. However, I knew that it had to be possible to create a classroom environment that was a positive experience for everyone and supportive of all the students while ensuring that the required course material was imparted. I just needed to learn how to accomplish that goal.

DOI: 10.4324/9781032671291-17

Learning to Be a Teacher **185**

In writing this essay, I am reflecting on my journey to becoming the teacher I am today. It was a slow undertaking as I also had to learn to balance the teaching, service, and research expectations of my department. When I could, I attended pedagogy workshops and read research on the scholarship of teaching and learning. When students struggled in class, I would talk with them about their experience to learn how the class could be adjusted to best suit their needs. And when students succeeded, I asked them what aspects worked best. Eventually, I even began taking classes from the College of Education to supplement or advance what I had learned on my own. Day by day, and little by little, I began to understand how to teach and engage with my students in the classroom. For me, being a good teacher is about understanding how my students best learn and how I can meet those learning styles.

How We Learn

One of the first big challenges I experienced in the classroom was learning to understand who my students were and what worked best for them. It was easy to think of students as "being like me." If something I experienced as a student helped me, surely it would help them. In many ways, the field of education even pushes for this kind of thinking through the prominence it gives to best practices. What I quickly learned, however, is that this approach does not work.

I have always preferred classes with heavy reading loads. Even if that meant there was not enough time in class to discuss all of the readings, I would gleefully work my way through them. And, while I despised any class assignment that involved group work or public speaking, the opportunity to write a paper or complete a project on my own was perfection. The greatest enemy of my success was an in-class test. It is no surprise that, given all of this, the first classes that I taught reflected my preferences. The problem was that while I found the structure of the classes appealing, my traditional students preferred tests over papers, and my nontraditional students hated the heavy reading load and missed group projects.

By default, I am not representative of my typical student. Only about 1.4% of people in the United States are estimated to have a PhD (U.S. Census, 2021). In comparison, 23.5% of people in the United States have a bachelor's degree. It is inevitable that what works for me is not likely to work for the vast majority of students in my classroom. The problem was that the only experience I had in how to teach during my doctoral studies taught me to force students into a particular mold of learning. Whether it was the most effective learning style or not, students were expected to adhere to the style I imposed.

My path to understanding how people learn was a long and windy one. I took many of the typical first steps that you might imagine. I talked with my colleagues from my department about how they taught. But, we were a small department where faculty specialized, and it was not always clear to me how some of the ideas proposed by my colleagues would transfer from a class such as political philosophy into one on financial management and governmental accounting. I even attended many of the pedagogy-related workshops offered by the university. Ultimately, I approached learning more about classroom pedagogy and student learning the same way I did traditional research – through hours of reading every book and article I could find on the topic.

There is a large and incredibly helpful literature on how people learn.[1] Research into the development of educational theory as it applies to adults has been conducted for more than 70 years (Walker, 1999). During this time, researchers have taken a variety of viewpoints on how they view and understand the characteristics of adult learners. Knowles (1973), for example, suggested that learners are characterized as either propounders or interpreters. Propounders are those who create a comprehensive system of ideas, whereas interpreters bring order to material by identifying categories or domains of understanding. An easy way of thinking about the difference is that the propounder is a visionary leader looking to understand where they are headed. Conversely, the interpreter is a more pragmatic manager who wants to understand how they can get there.

Traditional students are more likely to be propounders, whereas adult learners are more likely to be interpreters. This division is based on how learners experience the environment around them. While traditional students are accustomed to the classroom environment, adult learners have to pick up information as they go about their daily lives, forcing them to understand the material and subjects through interpretation.

There are a number of factors that come into play when considering the different ways that people can learn (Merriam & Bierema, 2014). The first consideration we must give is what style of learning students have most recently experienced. Traditional students, for example, who have remained in the classroom consistently since elementary school through their high school graduation and on into college, are more experienced with traditional pedagogical approaches of long lectures and classroom tests. Nontraditional students enrolled in a higher education program are less prepared for that environment, choosing instead to seek out classes with more engagement in the classroom and alternative assignments such as group projects. The more experience with an approach a student has, the more likely they are to succeed in a classroom that utilizes it.

This is, of course, a simplification. There are a number of factors that influence a student's learning style besides just whether they are traditional or nontraditional. Troves could be, and have been, filled with everything we need to know about how best to meet a student's learning needs in the classroom, and there is not enough space here to repeat it. But there are two areas that I would like to give particular note given their prominence in the public administration classroom. These are the impact of age and culture.

MPA programs are filled with nontraditional students, the majority of whom are returning to pursue their graduate education after several years of experience in the workforce. We know, for example, that mental cognition changes with age. As many older adults participate in MPA programs, understanding how learning capabilities and styles change as we age is incredibly important for the field.

Age does not mean our students cannot learn, but it might have an impact on how they *best* learn. Walker (1999) believed that the learning styles applicable to adults incorporate the knowledge, skills, and problem-solving base necessary for the material. She argued that adult education can be either formal or informal. It is only within the context of classifying how we learn that Walker argued that adult learners are characterized by their age, gender, ethnicity and culture, literacy level, autonomy, and social support. Age, gender, ethnicity, and culture are characteristics that are outside the learner's control but can still influence their capacity. As adult learners age, for example, their ability to recall information becomes challenging, and the time needed to commit information to long-term memory increases. Not all mature learners align with the active, hands-on learning profile emphasized in adult education literature. Instead, it is argued that with age, there is a proclivity to adopt a more reflective and observational approach within the learning environment (Truluck & Courtenay, 1999). On the other hand, the adult learner can more easily control characteristics such as literacy level, autonomy, and social support. When taken back into the context of formal or informal education, the balance of characteristics for adult learners can vary significantly, with some characteristics influencing one context more than the other.

MPA programs have also seen a significant increase in the diversity of our students. This diversity comes from increasing the number of international students enrolling in our programs and better recruiting students from different races, ethnicities, and cultural backgrounds (Jensen & Butz, 2018). Each community has its own way of learning that appeals to them, and having a mismatch between their preferred learning style and the style of learning that you incorporate into the classroom can create an avoidable barrier to education (Wilkes & Burnham, 1991).

In their study on the impact of culture on the way individuals learn, Joy and Kolb (2009) found that individuals exhibit a tendency toward a more abstract learning style in countries characterized by high levels of in-group collectivism, institutional collectivism, uncertainty avoidance, future orientation, and gender egalitarianism. Conversely, individuals in countries with high levels of in-group collectivism, uncertainty avoidance, and assertiveness may lean toward a more reflective learning style. There is also a measure of self-directed learning that takes place. In the United States, we have removed much of the personal responsibility for learning and thrown that responsibility to the teacher (see Brockett & Hiemstra, 1991). Evidence of this can be seen when policies that hold teachers fully responsible for student outcomes are implemented. In many other countries and cultures, the responsibility for learning is placed at the feet of students or their families. Understanding how the students view their responsibility might shift how assignments are structured or how you engage with that student.

If you are like me, you probably started teaching before you ever considered the learning style of your students. A good first step would be to find out what your preferred learning style is. After all, you probably never put much thought into it but have done what feels natural to you. The Educational Planner (2022) website has an online assessment tool that can help determine your best approach. It is a quick, 20-question quiz, and while it might not provide much detail, it does at least point you in a direction on how to learn more about what works best for you and why.

Understanding my preferred learning style helped me understand the learning bias I bring when I walk into the classroom. I have, upon occasion, used the tool in the classroom itself, either at the start of the semester or at the midway point, so I can tailor class to the students enrolled that semester. My experience doing this, however, has always come back mixed as it adds significant work to revamp a course in the first few weeks if there is a large mismatch, and large changes can leave the students uncertain of where the class is going. (In the next section, I discuss using the Universal Design for Learning (UDL) as a framework to address all learning styles in the classroom.)

What I have found successful, however, is providing the link to students on the first day of class with a recommendation that they take the quiz to learn more about themselves. As someone who teaches budgeting, financial management, and statistics, I am used to students walking into my classroom nervous about how hard the content will be. Having students understand their preferred learning style has allowed me to engage with them when they need help because they understand how they best learn and can help me speak to them in that style.

Universal Design for Learning

While I came to understand that everyone learns differently, the question I then faced was how I could teach in a way that addresses the unique learning modalities of my students. To help with this, I used my faculty tuition benefits and enrolled in the Master of Education program at NC State University, focusing on instructional design. From 2017 to 2020, I enrolled in one to two classes a semester, and it was through that coursework that I learned about the Universal Design for Learning (UDL) and began incorporating it into my classes.[2]

UDL is an educational framework that improves and optimizes teaching and learning for all people based on scientific insights into how humans learn (CAST, 2018; Hall et al., 2012). This approach revolutionizes the traditional methods of designing course instruction, materials, and content by prioritizing flexibility and choice to accommodate diverse learning styles and abilities (Izzo et al., 2008). The fundamental intent behind UDL is to create a learning environment that caters to the needs of all students from the outset of a class, thereby minimizing the necessity for retrofitting the course or having to make accommodations later in the semester. By utilizing UDL, an instructor can teach their courses while also addressing the learning styles of all students in the classroom simultaneously.

One of the fundamental principles underpinning UDL is the rejection of a one-size-fits-all educational model. Recognizing the inherent diversity in students' learning preferences, strengths, and challenges, UDL advocates for the incorporation of flexibility and choice from the outset. Instructors embracing UDL principles seek to provide a learning environment that addresses the needs of all students, fostering a culture of equity, diversity, and inclusion. The three core principles of UDL – representation, engagement, and expression – serve as a guiding framework for educators. Representation emphasizes the need for offering content in diverse formats, ensuring that information is presented in various ways to accommodate different learning styles. This may include incorporating visual aids, auditory materials, and tactile elements to enhance comprehension for a broad spectrum of learners.

Engagement, the second principle, encourages instructors to provide multiple avenues for students to become engaged with the learning process. Recognizing that students have varied interests and motivations, UDL prompts educators to design courses that capture attention through different mediums and approaches. This can involve interactive activities, multimedia resources, and diverse instructional methods to keep students actively involved in their learning journey. The third principle, expression, focuses on providing students with various means to demonstrate their

190 Bruce D. McDonald III

understanding of the content. Traditional assessments may not capture the full range of students' capabilities, so UDL encourages educators to diversify assessment methods. This could involve offering choices in how students present their knowledge, such as through written assignments, oral presentations, or multimedia projects, accommodating different communication and expression preferences.

In adopting UDL, educators become catalysts for positive change in education, fostering a culture of inclusion and breaking down traditional barriers that may hinder some students' academic success. UDL aligns with legal requirements for accommodation and goes beyond compliance by promoting a philosophy of equity and accessibility for all.

When I first learned about UDL, I wondered how I could apply its principles to my classes. Little has been written within the public administration literature on teaching pedagogy, and the literature on the UDL framework that has emerged out of education is often challenging to follow and apply. Ultimately, however, I found six key points on how to incorporate UDL into my teaching. These are as follows:

- Distribute slides before each class via email or your learning management system (i.e., Blackboard, Canvas, Moodle). This enables students to concentrate on the spoken content during class rather than scrambling to transcribe information from slides.
- Adjust the pace of lessons to maintain engagement, allowing time for both individual and group interaction with the material.
- Utilize diverse methods to convey information. In traditional lectures, incorporate slides or other visual aids together with verbal instruction. When employing visual diagrams, supplement them with written or audio explanations.
- Record your lectures and post them to your learning management system. This provides students the opportunity to revisit lectures for clarification or to catch up on missed content.
- Provide concrete examples and applications specific to the field. Do not assume that your students can generalize the course material. Rather, provide real-life examples from the field that demonstrate the material in action. This will help students with their understanding of the material and with their ability to transfer course material.[3]
- Foster collaborative learning by sharing notes. Encourage students to share their notes with the class or collaborate on a shared platform like Google Docs. This allows students to address misunderstandings in real time while helping them learn collaboratively.

While trying to adopt all six in any single course can be overwhelming, it became manageable for me to think of them as being progressively

Learning to Be a Teacher **191**

implemented. For example, in the first semester of applying the principles, I began to incorporate UDL into my MPA budgeting course by focusing on just one point: posting course slides before the start of class. The next time I taught the course, I also began to vary the pacing of lessons. In each of the semesters that followed, I added one or two of the ideas until they were all incorporated. The result was a significant change in the classroom environment and a noticeable increase in student learning.

In addition to changing how a class is taught, UDL can also be applied to course assessments. My temptation is to rely heavily on tests, an assessment tool I am very familiar with, having spent most of my life in an educational environment. But, when looking at how people learn, tests are not the most effective assessment tool for the typical MPA student. Instead, I look to UDL for four key points when designing my assessment tools. These are as follows:

- Provide frequent, individualized feedback. This allows students to assess their comprehension of the material and guide their learning more effectively.
- Eliminate timed assessments. Time limits can present obstacles for students, including those with disabilities, those for whom English is not their primary language, and those who are nontraditional students.
- Present assessment choices to students. This might be giving students the option between writing a paper and a presentation or between an examination and a project. This approach helps eliminate barriers associated with specific assessment formats.
- Diversify the question formats in examinations. If examinations remain the preferred assessment method, incorporate a range of question types to address potential barriers that students may encounter with certain formats (e.g., multiple choice or true/false). This variety facilitates a more accurate assessment of students' grasp of the content, distinguishing between content comprehension and challenges with specific question formats.

Concluding Thoughts

Research is important for the discipline's development and our impact on the science of public administration, but it is not all of what we do. I would even go so far as to suggest that it is not the most impactful thing that we do in our careers. One of the criticisms of the academy is that we are too focused on the production of scientific research when the true impact that we can have in our careers is in the classroom (see Hall & McDonald, 2023; McDonald, 2023). If we are exceedingly lucky, then the research we produce will be read by thousands and shape the discourse of government

192 Bruce D. McDonald III

action. Most of our research will only be read by a few scholars, producing, at best, a barely noticeable ripple of impact. It is in the classroom that we help shape and guide the leaders of the future. It is through our teaching of these leaders that we are able to make significant impacts with lasting effects.

In this essay, I have talked about my journey and approach to being a good teacher in the classroom. Too often, we pay little attention to the act of teaching within public administration (see Farrell et al., 2022; McDonald et al., 2022), but teaching can be a noble endeavor. I certainly do not have answers on how to be great in the classroom, but I hope this chapter has helped spark a curiosity about who your students are and how they best learn. If nothing else, while more attention to research on the scholarship of teaching and learning is needed within public administration (see McDonald et al., 2024), perhaps this essay has opened your eyes to exploring the literature of other fields to fill our gaps.

I am certainly not the best teacher in the world, though I am definitely better than I once was. Thinking back to that first teaching experience, I am still filled with anxiety. I do not remember all of the students' names or faces, but I have regretted that experience for both the students and myself ever since. I know the likelihood that any of them will ever read this chapter is small, but I do hope that one day they might know that the experience we went through together set me on a path to be the best that I can be for the students that followed.

Notes

1 For those who are looking for more information on how students, particularly nontraditional students, learn, I recommend starting with either Merriam et al. (2007) or Merriam and Bierema (2014).
2 Those interested in learning more about the Universal Design for Learning are encouraged to read Meyer et al. (2013) and Merry (2023).
3 The incorporation of practitioners as guest speakers is a great approach to accomplishing this. An excellent resource to help with this is Schafer and McDonald's (2025) book on engaged learning. I would also encourage you to read Schwoerer et al.'s (2022) work on incorporating practice.

References

Brockett, R. G., & Hiemstra, R. (1991). A conceptual framework for understanding self-direction in adult learning. In R. G. Brockett, & R. Hiemstra (Eds.), *Self-direction in adult learning: Perspectives on theory, research, and practice* (pp. 18–33). Routledge.
CAST Incorporated. (2018). *Universal design for learning guidelines version 2.2.* http://udlguidelines.cast.org

Educational_Planner. (2022). *What is your learning style? 20 questions.* http:// www.educationplanner.org/students/self-assessments/learning-styles-quiz.shtml

Farrell, C., Hatcher, W., & Diamond, J. (2022). Reflecting on over 100 years of public administration education. *Public Administration, 100*(1), 116–128. https://doi.org/10.1111/padm.12808

Hall, J. L., & McDonald, B. D. (2023). Scholarly hypocrisy or apostasy in public administration: Preaching to the choir, or to an empty room? *Public Administration Review, 83*(4), 725–733. https://doi.org/10.1111/puar.13686

Hall, T. E., Meyer, A., & Rose, D. H. (2012). An introduction to universal design for learning: Questions and answers. In T. E. Hall, A. Meyer, & D. H. Rose (Eds.), *Universal design for learning in the classroom: Practical applications* (pp. 1–8). The Guilford Press.

Izzo, M. V., Murray, A., & Novak, J. (2008). The faculty perspective on universal design for learning. *Journal of Postsecondary Education and Disability, 21*(2), 60–72.

Jensen, J. L., & Butz, N. T. (2018). The impact of enhanced student diversity on diversity opinions. *Journal of Public Affairs Education, 24*(4), 430–448. https:// doi.org/10.1080/15236803.2018.1429809

Joy, S., & Kolb, D. A. (2009). Are there cultural differences in learning style? *International Journal of Intercultural Relations, 33*(1), 69–85. https://doi. org/10.1016/j.ijintrel.2008.11.002

Knowles, M. (1973). *The adult learner: A neglected species.* Gulf Publishing Company.

McDonald, B. D. (2023). The dark horse of public administration: The challenge of pedagogical research. *Teaching Public Administration, 41*(1), 3–10. https://doi. org/10.1177/01447394231159983

McDonald, B. D., Hatcher, W., & Abbott, M. E. (2022). History of public administration education in the United States. In K. A. Bottom, P. Dunning, I. Elliot, & J. Diamond (Eds.), *Handbook on the teaching of public administration* (pp. 57–64). Edward Elgar Publishing.

McDonald, B. D., Hatcher, W., Bacot, H., Evans, M. D., McCandless, S. A., McDougle, L. M., Young, S. L., Elliott, I. C. Emas, R., Lu, E. Y., Abbott, M. E., Bearfield, D. A., Berry-James, R. M., Blessett, B., Borry, E. L., Diamond, J., Franklin, A. L., Gaynor, T. S., Gong, T., . . . Zhang, Y. (2024). The scholarship of teaching and learning in public administration: An agenda for future research. *Journal of Public Affairs Education, 30*(1), 11–27. https://doi.org/10.1 080/15236803.2023.2294654

Merriam, S. B., & Bierema, L. L. (2014). *Adult learning: Linking theory and practice.* Jossey-Bass.

Merriam, S. B., Caffarella, R. S., & Baumgardner, L. M. (2007). *Learning in adulthood: A comprehensive guide* (3rd ed.). John Wiley & Sons.

Merry, K. L. (2023). *Delivering inclusive and impactful instruction: Universal design for learning in higher education.* Cast Incorporated.

Meyer, A., Rose, D. H., & Gordon, D. (2013). *Universal design for learning: Theory and practice.* Cast Incorporated.

Schafer, J. G., & McDonald, B. D. (2025). *Engaged learning in the public service classroom.* Routledge.

Schwoerer, K., Keppeler, F., Mussagulova, A., & Puello, S. (2022). CO-DESIGN-ing a more context-based, pluralistic, and participatory future for public administration. *Public Administration, 100*(1), 72–97. https://doi.org/10.1111/padm. 12828

Truluck, J. E., & Courtenay, B. C. (1999). Learning style preferences among older adults. *Educational Gerontology*, 25(3), 221–236. https://doi.org/10.1080/036012799267846

U.S. Census. (2021). About 13.1 percent have a master's, professional degree or doctorate. *America Counts: Stories*. https://www.census.gov/library/stories/2019/02/number-of-people-with-masters-and-phd-degrees-double-since-2000.html

Walker, E. A. (1999). Characteristics of the adult learner. *The Diabetes Educator*, 25(6s), 16–24. https://doi.org/10.1177/014572179902500619

Wilkes, C. W., & Burnham, B. R. (1991). Adult learner motivations and electronic distance education. *American Journal of Distance Education*, 5(1), 43–50. https://doi.org/10.1080/08923649109526731

16

CONCLUDING THOUGHTS ON THE CRAFT OF TEACHING

William Hatcher[1], Beth M. Rauhaus[2], and Bruce D. McDonald III[3]

[1]*Augusta University, Augusta, GA,* [2]*University of Louisiana at Lafayette, Lafayette, LA, and* [3]*Old Dominion University, Norfolk, VA*

The idea for this book came from a discussion among us about how our field struggles to train our graduate students to teach and PhD programs often fail to teach students the fundamentals of pedagogy. We started talking about our experiences, and while two of us taught a good bit during our PhD programs, all three of us did receive formal education and mentoring in teaching. As we argue in this book, some of this may be due to how our field historically has had little respect for the scholarship of teaching and learning (SoTL), which is counterintuitive because public administration is a scholarly discipline that educates practitioners/professionals and needs to connect theory with practice in our classrooms. Still, in recent decades, the tide has turned, and the field has started to realize the importance of SoTL, with the emergence of the *Journal of Public Affairs Education* as a key outlet. However, as discussed in Chapter 2, even the field's SoTL journals (*Journal of Public Affairs Education* and *Teaching Public Administration*) fail to dedicate most of their pages to studies specifically on teacher quality in public affairs (see also McDonald et al., 2024).

We hope this book is a turning point for the discipline of public affairs to emphasize and discuss teacher quality. In this text, we seek to fill the gap in the literature by examining fundamental aspects of teaching today, such as teaching graduate students, teaching undergraduate students, teaching online, and other issues of classroom design. We supplement these chapters on fundamental issues with essays from faculty who have been successful in the classroom. These testimonials build rich descriptive information on what practices have worked and what has not worked for teachers in public affairs. The information in these pages offers insight to aspiring public

DOI: 10.4324/9781032671291-18

affairs educators and those searching for approaches and techniques to improve their teaching. One common theme we identified throughout these expert essays is how many faculty, with a wealth of experience, were on a journey of growth and development as educators. Over time, these experts crafted a teaching approach that others can use in public affairs.

As graduate students, two of us started teaching over 80 students in Introduction to American Government courses without any experience in the classroom, and it was an ordeal by fire that almost caused them to forgo earning a PhD. But it was a learning process requiring patience, curiosity, and innovation in teaching, professional development, and learning to love being in the classroom. However, it was a challenging learning process, and having more instruction on teaching and pedagogy would have made the road easier for us and our students. One thing we all three have learned, and supported throughout this book, is that so much of teaching is learned by doing. Practice is the key theme that reappears again and again in the book.

What Are the Other Themes?

Faculty discussed how they were not originally focused on teaching when starting in academia but, through experience, learned how to be effective instructors in our field. As McDonald wrote, "It never occurred to me until I walked into my first classroom that I would have to teach. . . . Day by day, and little by little, I began to understand how to teach and engage with my students in the classroom. For me, being a good teacher is about understanding how my students best learn and how I can meet those learning styles."

Faculty experts also highlighted the importance of formal and informal mentorships in their development as public affairs educators. At the core of this text, we share experts' advice for teaching and their journey in crafting a strong model for teaching public affairs. O'Leary offers secrets of successful teaching and shares advice for new educators. Her chapter can easily be used as a tool to mentor those new to the public affairs classroom. Sabharwal's chapter offers valuable information on mentorship as a continual process that can assist public affairs educators' growth and development and enhance their ability to incorporate current trends and analyses in the classroom. Sabharwal shared the "importance of adapting mentoring practices to meet the unique needs of individual students and celebrate the increasing diversity within public administration."

Faculty stressed the importance of being curious and caring about students. As Hatcher wrote in his essay on teaching, "Curious instructors practice empathy and caring in seeking evidence-based pedagogical methods to teach students as effectively as possible." Stephen Page stressed the importance of having "an informed mind and restless curiosity" as an instructor. This "restless curiosity" is applied to learning about the material and being informed about the material.

Faculty emphasized the need for innovative assignments and exercises to teach their students and to learn about their students. One of us (Rauhaus) talked about the importance of engaged learning in classes and how implementing engaged learning assignments helped become an engaged instructor. Being an engaged instructor means knowing the material, students, and where the students live and work. As Rauhaus described her approach, "In order to become an engaged instructor in the MPA classroom, I immersed myself in personalizing class prep to fit student needs and the environment in which I was preparing them to lead." As Rosemary O'Leary wrote in her essay, "My advice to new teachers is to turn it inside out. Focus on the students as great learners, not yourself as a great teacher."

And teaching should be adapted based on the type of student in the classroom. For instance, Norma Riccucci described how she differs in her instructional approaches based on whether the class is for undergraduate, postgraduate, or PhD students. As she wrote, "My approach to teaching depends on whether I am working with MPA or PhD students. My classes' focus, format, and goals differ, as do the requirements. My adage for teaching (as well as research) has always been that there is *no one best way.*" Hatcher also agrees with this need to know your students and design learning around them by writing, "Based on this viewpoint, my model of instruction for my upper-level and Master of Public Administration (MPA) courses is a more bottom-up approach than the traditional lecture style found in my lower-level courses." McDonald also stresses the need to know our students in his essay by emphasizing the importance of understanding how students learn.

Faculty argued for experiential learning, especially for pre-service students. For example, in her chapter on teaching undergraduates in public affairs, Madinah Hamidullah details innovative assignments that she could offer her students, including an experiential philanthropy project that allowed her and her students to award over $7,500 to local nonprofits in the Greater Newark area.

Lastly, and of course, it is of little surprise that all our authors discussed the importance of lifelong learning. Lifelong learning is indispensable, particularly for us as educators, because it fosters professional growth, adaptability, and innovation within the dynamic landscape of public affairs and the universities where we work. In an ever-evolving world where technological advancements and societal changes constantly reshape the learning environment, we must remain abreast of the latest pedagogical techniques, curriculum developments, and educational research. Continual learning equips teachers in public affairs with the knowledge and skills needed to effectively meet our students' diverse needs. By embracing lifelong learning, we can enhance our teaching methodologies, incorporate emerging technologies into their classrooms, and cultivate inclusive learning environments catering to each student's strengths and challenges. Moreover, ongoing professional development encourages us to reflect critically on our practices, fostering a culture of self-improvement and dedication to excellence in our teaching.

Lifelong learning also empowers educators to stay relevant and responsive to the needs of a rapidly changing society. As educators engage in continuous education, they develop an adaptive mindset that encourages experimentation, risk-taking, and resilience in facing challenges. By seeking out new knowledge and experiences, educators model the value of lifelong learning to their students, inspiring them to become lifelong learners. Moreover, lifelong learning enables educators to embrace diversity, equity, and inclusion in their teaching practices, fostering a more equitable and accessible educational experience for all students. Ultimately, by prioritizing lifelong learning, we enrich our professional lives and contribute to creating a more informed, innovative, and equitable society.

Based on these themes in the book's chapters/essays, we can build a framework that helps us describe quality teaching in public affairs. The framework is based on the following:

1. The need for experiential learning.
2. The importance of mentorship.
3. The need for faculty to be curious and to care about students.
4. The need for faculty to learn how to teach by doing it.
5. The importance of lifelong learning as it constantly improves the craft of teaching.

Improving the State of Teaching

Given these factors, what actions can faculty and program leaders take to improve the state of teaching in public affairs? First, as we stressed when arguing why this book is needed, PhD programs should include experiential opportunities in their curricula that provide students with opportunities to learn and practice their craft of teaching. These opportunities need to include more than assigning PhD students as teaching assistants and instructors of records. These experiences are part of the process, but these students need courses and training that help them learn how to teach. Having a community of practice for graduate students to learn how to teach in

Concluding Thoughts on the Craft of Teaching **199**

various classroom situations and environments, create appropriate measures of assessment, and more would be beneficial in developing a craft of teaching.

Second, PhD programs in the field need to model quality mentorship and provide training and educational opportunities that help their students seek solid mentors and be effective mentors themselves (Alshayhan et al., 2023; Evans et al., 2023; Rinfret et al., 2023). Mentorship of women and minorities will remain an important element of crafting strong educators in public affairs as the field becomes more diverse. Public affairs faculty often have varying experiences that they bring to the classroom and as faculty members, highlighting the importance and need for both formal and informal mentors. Adequate mentorship for women and minorities is key to academic productivity as these faculty members have unique professional experiences, which often include greater service burdens and mentorship of others (Scutelnicu Todoran, 2023; Rauhaus & Carr, 2019).

Third, our programs and faculty need to be concerned with the overall health of their students, modeling appropriate well-being activities for their students. Such activities will demonstrate to students that their faculty and programs care about them. Through these caring activities, students will hopefully be able to model that behavior when they become faculty and program leaders. This approach has the promise to leave our students who are emerging public leaders with a sense of the importance of practicing a work–life balance in their professional careers and having empathy for others.

Lastly, schools and departments in public affairs need to build the infrastructure to teach their students how to teach and encourage their faculty to be lifelong learners seeking to improve their teaching. Such infrastructure may include robust teaching-related professional development opportunities. Additionally, academic leaders can consider incorporating professional development requirements in teaching as part of their annual evaluation processes, especially for faculty with significant teaching loads.

References

Alshayhan, N., Yusuf, J., Saitgalina, M., & Corbett, M. E. (2023). Career mentorship of graduate students in public administration and the intersection of the relationship between students and faculty. *Journal of Public Affairs Education*, 29(4), 497–521. https://doi.org/10.1080/15236803.2023.2234796

Evans, M. D., Knepper, H. J., & Henley, T. J. (2023). An intersectional consideration of mentoring in public administration. *Journal of Public Affairs Education*, 29(4), 421–440. https://doi.org/10.1080/15236803.2023.2247472

McDonald, B. D., Hatcher, W., Bacot, H., Evans, M. D., McCandless, S. A., McDougle, L. M., Young, S. L., Elliott, I. C. Emas, R., Lu, E. Y., Abbott, M. E., Bearfield, D. A., Berry-James, R. M., Blessett, B., Borry, E. L., Diamond, J., Franklin, A. L., Gaynor, T. S., Gong, T., . . . Zhang, Y. (2024). The scholarship of teaching and learning in public administration: An agenda for future research. *Journal of Public Affairs Education, 30*(1), 11–27. https://doi.org/10.1080/1523 6803.2023.2294654

Rauhaus, B. M., & Carr, I. A. S. (2019). The invisible challenges: Gender differences among public administration faculty. *Journal of Public Affairs Education.* 26(1), 31–50. https://doi.org/10.1080/15236803.2018.1565040

Rinfret, S. R., Young, S. L., & McDonald, B. D. (2023). The importance of mentorship in higher education: An introduction to the symposium. *Journal of Public Affairs Education, 29*(4), 398–403. https://doi.org/10.1080/15236803.2023. 2260947

Scutelnicu Todoran, G. (2023). The contribution of formal and informal mentorship to faculty productivity: Views of faculty in public affairs programs. *Journal of Public Affairs Education, 29*(4), 404–420. https://doi.org/10.1080/1523680 3.2023.2220096

INDEX

Note: Page numbers in *italic* indicate a figure and page numbers in **bold** indicate a table on the corresponding page.

Abel, C. F. 13
academic integrity 77
active learning 20, 22–23, 145, 146
activities *see* classroom activities
Addams, J. 94, 160
administrative lessons: public affairs
  majors 29–30; recruitment 31–33;
  student ambassadors 33–34;
  transfer students 30–31
The Administrative State (Waldo) 161
adult learners 186–187
age, learners' 187
Ahuja, K. 52
Allen, T. D. 58
American Society for Public
  Administration (ASPA) 90, 95
analytical methods, teaching of 14–15
Aristigueta, M. P. 14
The Art & Craft of College Teaching
  (Rotenberg) 169
artificial intelligence (AI) 77
assessment: curriculum/program 15,
  21; online learning 20; multiple
  170–171; student, holistic 13–14;
  traditional 190
assessment tools 191; online 188
assignments, analytical 153, 170–171,
  172, 197; for DEIA 99–103

asynchronous online courses 136; vs.
  synchronous 78–82
Australia: grading system 122–123;
  pedagogical context 118; TAs
  in 121–121; teaching load 118;
  university environment 115; ways of
  addressing faculty 117
authenticity in teaching 40–41

Barth, T. J. 181
Baulderstone, J. 118
blended learning *see* hybrid
  learning
Blended Learning Distance Mediation
  Framework (BLDM) 16
Blessett, B. 48, 93
Boehrer, J. 150
Bohórquez, E. B. 79
Bolman, L. G. 101, 102
Bottom, K. A. 4
Brock, J. 150
Brown, B. W. 78, 80
Bryan, T. K. 80
Burroughs, E. S. 147

Campbell, H. E. 17
Canada 59; asynchronous vs.
  synchronous online learning 79–80;

grading system 122–124; lecture style 120–121; pedagogical context 119; university environment 114
capstone learning experiences 21
Careaga, M. 15
caring approach 49, 196–197, 199
case method 15, 152–153
Center for Applied Special Technology (CAST) 85
ChatGPT 19, 20
cheating, online classes 77
citizen involvement 158–160
Clarke, R. J. 15
class preparation *see* lesson plans
classroom activities 13–14, 69–70, 79, 84–85; group 83, 14; service learning 180–181; well-being 199
classroom engagement 14–16
classroom management 19–20
collaborative learning 13–14, 16, 20, 156, 190
communication with students 47, 178–179
community analysis 15
community-engaged learning 23
community engagement and service 28–29, 38–39, 179–180
competency-based evaluation 50–52, **51**
content, public affairs teaching 160–163
content reflection 111
Conyers, A. 93
Cooper, T. 93
Corley, E. 57
country research environment 115–116
county colleges 37
course: content/material for teaching 170; design 84–85
COVID-19 pandemic 18; and effects on students 46; and online education 23, 74
craft of teaching 5–6, 12, 69, 166; curiosity and 151–152, 154, 172–173; informed mind 150–151; of teaching public management 148–150
critical localism 119
critical race theory (CRT) 95, 140–141
Critical Race Theory Exploring Its Application to Public Administration (Riccucci) 141

Cropf, R. A. 35
cultural sensitivity 70
culture: of inclusion 189, 190; impact on learning 188; local, familiarizing with 177; *see also* third culture professors (TCP)
Cunningham, R. 4
curiosity: among students 167; among teachers 166–167; aspects of 166; benefits to students and faculty 166; career in academia and 173; craft of teaching and 151–152, 154, 172–173; driving life and career decisions 165–166; lesson plans and 172; practicing 164–173; teaching philosophy informed by 167–172
curiosity about managerial practice 151–154; case method 152–153; conversations with practitioners 153–154; practice-based learning exercises 152–153; primary field research 152
curious teaching, craft of 151–152, 154, 172–173
curriculum: adaptation 17–18; approaches to 43–44, 48–52; care for students 49; design 48–52; and program development 37; variety in 30–31

Dahlstrom-Hakki, I. 82
Deal, T. E. 101, 102
DEIA *see* diversity, equity, inclusion and accessibility (DEIA)
democracy in classroom 159–160
democratic governance 21–22, 23
Dewey, J. L. 53, 159
Dickson, E. L. 14
discussion boards 79, 83
diversity 13; in public organizations 22; of students 36–37, 187, 188
diversity, equity, inclusion and accessibility (DEIA)103: analytical assignments to teach 99–103; audience to be taught 91–92; embodying respect 93; expanding definition of "We the People" 94; frameworks 96–99; law, role of 93–94; neutrality 93; questions about past and present 94–95; teaching HRM 134; as a state of mind 89–90; usability 92

diversity, equity and inclusion (DEI) 5, 22, 69–70
Diversity in Academia Initiative 66
Dobel, P. 154
doctoral students/PhD students *see* PhD students/doctoral students
Dunn, T. P. 75

EA *see* expatriate academics (EA)
Educational Planner website188
edX (online learning platform)136
elevator speech 145–146
Emerson, K. 16
Emotional Labor: Putting Service in Public Service 50
engaged learning 177–180
E-PARCC 147
ethics and democracy in the classroom 21–22
evaluation, student 172; *see also* competency-based evaluation
The Evergreen State College (TESC) 156–158; faculty evaluating faculty 157; problems at 157–158; seminar groups 156–157; students evaluating faculty 157
evidence-based framework 19
expatriate academics (EA) 108; defined 108
experiential learning 15, 23, 134, 136
experiential philanthropy in courses 37
experimentation 150
expert teacher, becoming 143–147; class preparation 145; key ideas and concepts to be taught 145; ways of engaging students 145

feedback, students to teachers: continuous 70–71, 151, 154; to improve course design 17
feedback, teachers to students 50–52, 51, 170, 191
feedback to faculty members 66–67, 157
Fenwick, J. 17
Figlio, D. 78
flexibility for students 75–76, 77
flipped classrooms 20, 69, 145
Follett, Mary Parker 94, 159
Foucault, M. 160
frameworks 96–99; access, process, quality, and outcomes 97;

applying 98–99; law, politics, and management 96–97; naming, identifying causation, and accountability 97; pursuing accountability 98
Frederickson, H. G. 13, 94

Gannon, K. 53
general education students *vs.* public affairs majors 29–30
Gerlak, A. K. 16
Gibbs, L. 50
goals/expectations 83–84
Gooden, S. T. 92, 94, 97, 98, 103
Goodsell, C. T. 50
grading expectations 122–124
grading system 50
graduate program 39–40
grants 114, 118
great man theory of teaching 144
group activities 14, 70, 83
group discussions 14, 123, 156–157

Hamilton, Alexander 161
Handbook of Teaching Public Administration 4
Hart, C. M. 78
Heifetz's theory of adaptive leadership 102
Holzer, M. 13
human resources management (HRM), teaching 134–135
humility in mentors 59–60
hybrid learning 77–78, 79
HyFlex 79

improving teaching 198–199
in-class test 185
inclusive language 70
inclusive teaching 56–71; platform for shared experiences 65; role of mentors 64–65
informed mind 150–151; continuous craft improvement 151
infrastructure, schools/departments 199
in-service students 13, 181
instructors: authenticity 40–41; bottom-up approach 170; classroom management 19–20; curiosity 166–167; demonstrating kindness 167; evaluation of students 172; lessons for 22–24; motivation for

53; need for self-improvement 23; need to understand students 45–48; in online classrooms 16; planning classes 171–172; responsibility to teach civic values 168; as role models 70–71; role of 160; student assessment 171; teaching political systems 169–170; theory and practice, linking 171; tips for 24; vision of education 168–169
Intellectual History of Public Administration, teaching 137–139; logic of inquiry 139; New Public Administration (NPA) 138; qualitative research 139
interactive teaching 13, 146, 150, 171
international students: challenges faced by 62; cultural and social support 63–64, 64; enriching academic landscape 62; mentoring 61–64; racism against 66–67; transition to new academic and cultural environment 63
Internet equal access to education 74
internships 15, 21, 124
interpreters vs. propounders concept 186
introspection 150–151

Jamaica 113; grading system 122, 123, 124; internships 124; lecture style 121; pedagogical system 119; research environment 116; syllabus design restrictions 122; university environment 114; visas and paperwork 112
Japan: lecture style 121; research environment 116; visas and paperwork 112
Jelier, R. W. 15
Johnson, N. J. 97, 98, 101
Journal of Public Administration Education 176–177
Journal of Public Affairs Education (JPAE) 4, 11, 12, 117, 177, 195; teaching literature in 12–17
Joy, S. 188

Khalil, R. 81
Knowles, M. 186
Kohler, J. M. 35
Kolb, D. A. 188

LaGuardia, F. 161
Larson, S. J. 98
law, role of 93–94
leadership, equity, and diversity, teaching 139–141
learner-centric model 48
learning community 156, 157, 158–160; conversation and debate 159; democracy in classrooms 159–160
learning how to teach 156–163
learning styles 185–189
lecture styles 120–122
Lee, A. 59
lessons 22–24; see also administrative lessons
lesson plans 148–150; class discussion 150–151; curiosity and 172; managerial practice 151–152; practitioners consultation and 153–154; public field research 152
lessons pace 190–191
Levin College of Urban Affairs 160
Liedholm, C. E. 78, 80
lifelong learners 180, 182
lifelong learning 197–198
listening to students 178
Love, J. M. 93

Massive Open Online Courses (MOOCs) 136
Master of Public Administration (MPA) 1, 43–44; curriculum design 48–52; focus of 43; future of 52–53; reasons for teaching 44–45
master's programs 91
McIntosh, P. 50
Meier, K. J. 59
Meine, M. F. 75
Menifield, C. 93
mental health support 60–61
mentoring 13; defined 57; of graduate students 141; importance for women and minority students 66; international students 61–64; as key to inclusion 64–65; monitoring 67–68; positive impact of 58; qualities of 58–61; research self-efficacy and 61; significance of 57; toxic 59; women and minorities 199
mentor–mentee relationship 58–61

mentors: authentic 59; caring about mentee's well-being 60–61; commitment to mentee's growth 58–59; as counselors 60–61; humility in 59–60; providing cultural and social support to international students 63–64, 64; role in inclusive teaching 64–65; as role models 70–71; toxic 59

Miller, A. C. 49

Mills, B. 49

MPA level students 43–53; curriculum design for 48–52

MPA instructor 175–182; engaged-learning 177–180; familiarizing with local culture 177; linking theory to practice 176–177; maintaining communication with students 178–179; service-learning projects 180–182

MPA programs 39–40; diversity in students 187, 188; exciting ways of teaching 39–40; teaching online 136–137

multi-modal instruction 70

NASPAA 31, 46, 75; PhD Pathways Initiative 65; study on inclusion 65–67

Netherlands: grading system 122, 123, 124; lecture style 121; pedagogical context 118–119; research environment 116; teaching load 117–118; visas and paperwork 112

Network of Schools of Public Policy, Affairs, and Administration (NASPAA) see NASPAA

neutrality 93

New Public Administration (NPA) 138–139

Nguyen, T. 76

Ni, A. Y. 16

Nollenberger, K. 79

nontraditional students 186–187

online education 5, 15, 20, 23, 34–35; academic integrity 77; advantages 75–76; asynchronous vs. synchronous classes 78–82; challenges in 76–77; cost-effective 76, 77; effectiveness of programs 77–78; flexibility for students

75–76, 77; modalities 34–35; opportunities in 76–77; in public affairs, evolution of 75–76; and students of color 77

online engagement and interaction 82–85; course design 84–85; discussion boards 83; goals and expectations 83–84; group activities 83; productive struggle 84; progress monitoring 84; student accountability 84

online program management companies (OPMs) 77

online teaching 74–85, 136–137

opportunities for students, online education 76–77

Otani, K. 17

O'Toole, P. 118

Oztok, M. 79, 80

paradigm shift in higher education 144, 146

pedagogical contexts, international 118–120

pedagogy: of care 49, 52; critical 119; effective 136; evidence-based 12; practice-based 153; public administration 12–17, 162, 176–177; restrictive 119; traditional 119; workshops 185, 186

peer mentoring 66

Perot, R. 145–146

PhD students/doctoral students 91–92; depression and anxiety among 61; international 67; mentoring 57–58, 59–60, 61; teaching 69–71, 137

pipeline development 35–36

planning classes 171–172

political theorizing 162

portfolios 15

Portillo, S. 66, 93

positionalities 95–96

power dynamics, in mentoring 67

practice-based learning exercises, developing 152–153

practitioners consulting 153–154

preferred learning style 81, 187, 188

premise reflection 111

pre-service students 13, 181

primary field research 152

problem-based learning 145

206 Index

problems and solutions: description, explanation, prediction, and prescription 101–102
productive struggle 84
professional development activities 15
professional organizations 37–38
professional students 149, 150
program management 20–21
progress monitoring 84
promotion practices 114–115
public administration: and business management 161collaborative learning 13–14; effective 173; historical context of 137–138; scientific-analytical approach 162; teaching content 160–163; uncertainty in practice of 13
The Public Administration Theory Primer (Frederickson) 176
Public Administration: Traditions of Inquiry and Philosophies of Knowledge (Riccucci) 139, 176
public affairs majors *vs.* general education students 29–30
public management, teaching 148–150
public sector labor relations, teaching 135–136
public servants, role of 160
public service: hope for the future of 52–53; professions 44

Qatar 113; grading system 122; internships 124; lecture style 121; pedagogical context 118–120; visa and paperwork 112; way of addressing faculty 117
queer theory 95

Raadschelders, J. 12
racism: against international students 66–67
Raffel, J. A. 14
Rampal, R. 80
recording lectures 190
recruitment: alumni network 33; student ambassadors 33–34; of undergraduate students to public affairs education 31–33
reflective learning style 188
Reframing Organizations (Bolman and Deal) 101
research environment, international 115–116
research self-efficacy 61

Rhodes, R. A. W. 110
Riffell, S. 78
Roblyer, M. D. 81
Rosenbaum, A. 18
Rosenbloom, D. 96, 102
Rotenberg, R. 169
Russell, T. L. 82
Rutledge, P. 94

Saldivar, K. M. 14
scholarship of teaching and learning (SoTL) 2–4, 11–12, 21–22, 185, 192, 195; future of research in 24
seminars 156–157
service learning 39
service-learning projects 180–182
sexual misconduct, mentoring 67, **68**
Shahabadi, M. M. 80–81
Shea, J. 16
Sibley, D. 78
Simon, H. 137
Singapore: grading system 122–124; lecture style 120–121; pedagogical context 118–120; research environment 116; university environments 114; way of addressing faculty 117
slides 190
social equity 90, 140
social justice 140
South Korea: grading system 122–123; pedagogical context 119; visa and paperwork 112–113; way of addressing faculty 117
stories 110–111
student accountability 84
student ambassadors 33–34
student-driven engagement 82–85; *see also* online engagement and interaction
student evaluation of teaching (SET) 16–17, 21
students, getting to know 45–48
Sue-Jean Sung 150
Svara, J. H. 98
Sweden 113; grading system 122; lecture style 121; pedagogical context 119; research environment 116; teaching load 117–118; university environments 115; visa and paperwork 112; way of addressing faculty 117
synchronous online courses 136; vs. asynchronous 78–82

Tabak, F. 80
teachers in public affairs 11–24
teaching: cultural sensitivity practiced
    70; effective 69; human resources
    management (HRM) 134–135;
    improving 198–199; Intellectual
    History of Public Administration
    137–139; leadership, equity and
    diversity 139–141; and learning as
    mutual processes 69; moving focus
    towards learning 144, 146, 147;
    online 74–85; public sector labor
    relations 135–136
teaching assistants (TAs) 121–122
teaching cases, developing 152–153
teaching effectiveness 17
teaching how to learn 156–163
teaching load, international variance
    117–118
Teaching Public Administration (TPA)
    11, 12, 117, 167, 177; objective of
    18; teaching literature in 17–19;
    teaching with technology 18–19;
    works featured in 18
teaching with informed mind 148–154;
    craft of teaching public management
    148–150
humilities and insights of relentless
    curiosity 154; relentless curiosity
    about managerial practice 151–154;
    team-based learning 14, 20
Teams 76
technology: use in public affairs
    education 18–19, 20
TED talks 39
theory and practice, linking 171,
    176–177; academic journals
    176–177
third culture kids (TCK) 108, 109
third culture professors (TCP) 109;
    country research environment
    115–116; faculty, addressing 117;
    grading expectations 122–124;
    lecture style 120–122; non-work
    observations 113–114; pedagogical
    choice 118–120; teaching load
    117–118; university environments
    114–115; visas and paperwork
    112–113
toxic mentorship 59
traditional students 186

transfer students 30–31
transitional critical thinking
    model 169
Tschirhart, M. 13
Tullous, R. 69

Undergraduate Diversity Scholars
    Program 38
undergraduate programs: instruction
    39–40
undergraduate public affairs students:
    diversity of 36–37; experiences
    29; online education modalities
    for 34–35; pipeline development
    35–36; recruitment of 31–33;
    transfer students 30–31
ungrading 50
United States: bureaucracy 50; grading
    system 123; internships 124; lecture
    style 121; pedagogical context
    118; teaching load 117; university
    environments 115; visa and
    paperwork 112; way of addressing
    faculty 117
Universal Design for Learning (UDL)
    85, 189–191; course assessments
    191; engagement 189; expression
    189–190; representation 189
university 114–115
Uplane, M. 80–81
Utecht, R. L. 69

van der Wal, Zeger 116
Vogel, M. D. 53

Waldo, D. 13, 137, 138
Walker, E. A. 187
Weschler, L. 4
White, John 145–146
White Jr, R. D. 13
Whitford, B. 154
Whittington, L. A. 13
Williams, H. F. 94
Williams, S. A. S. 93
Wilson, W. 137, 161, 162
Wise, L. R. 13
Wolin, S. 162

Yildiz, M. 123

Zoom 76, 79, 121

Printed in the United States
by Baker & Taylor Publisher Services

"This meticulously organized A-Z guide arrives at a crucial moment in our global pursuit of sustainable development. It strikes an excellent balance between theoretical depth and practical application. What sets this book apart is its accessibility and clear focus on governance and implementation challenges, making it an invaluable resource for students, policymakers, and sustainability practitioners alike"

–**Måns Nilsson**, *Executive Director of Stockholm Environment Institute*

"This book is an essential resource for anyone seeking to understand and accelerate progress toward the Sustainable Development Goals. Its accessible format, A-Z structure, and practical examples make complex concepts easy to navigate. Offering valuable insights from global experts with a focus on transformative change, the book will equip policymakers, practitioners, and advocates with tools to drive real impact. To address the halting pace of change, we must redouble efforts to build inclusive societies and a livable planet. This guide is indispensable for shaping a more just, peaceful, and sustainable future."

–**Anita Bhatia**, *Assistant Secretary-General of the United Nations and Deputy Executive Director of UN Women*

"Sharing knowledge and research to support coordinated and informed decision-making is crucial to accelerating progress on the interlinked Sustainable Development Goals. This timely publication delivers much needed practical solutions and shows how everyone can contribute to transformative change."

–**Astra Bonini**, *Senior Sustainable Development Officer at the Division for the Sustainable Development Goals, United Nations Department of Economic and Social Affairs*

"As a youth representative having participated in the processes of the 2030 Agenda, I believe that this book can be very useful to any person willing to understand the problems and challenges related to the implementation of the SDGs. It presents key concepts in an easy-to-navigate fashion. I hope it will help structure the thinking of people who wish to fight for a better world."

–**Jean Servais**, *Belgian UN Youth Delegate for Sustainable Development 2022–24*

"This book is an invaluable resource for anyone working to advance the Sustainable Development Goals. With contributions from experts worldwide—including researchers from Southern Voice—it offers a clear, accessible, and practical guide to the essential concepts shaping the global effort to implement the 2030 Agenda. At a time of uneven SDG progress and growing urgency, this A–Z guide is a timely tool to help those in academia, policy, and practice navigate complexity and sharpen their contribution to sustainable development."

–**Margarita Gómez**, *Executive Director at Southern Voice and Visiting Fellow at the Blavatnik School of Government, Oxford University*

Essential Concepts for Implementing the Sustainable Development Goals

This book provides a highly accessible and user-friendly overview of the essential concepts and terms related to the current global endeavour to implement the Sustainable Development Goals.

With the first decade of the 15-year timespan of the 2030 Agenda now past, the SDGs show limited progress and several goals are even regressing. It is imperative that SDG implementation is accelerated until 2030 and beyond to foster transformations and set the world onto a sustainable and resilient path. The book starts with a thematic introduction to contextualize the topic and set the stage for the individual entries. It then follows an A-Z format, with over 100 entries which describe an important concept or term, using practical examples to illustrate how it connects to the overall debate about sustainable development. It offers swift introductions to key concepts and terms that are discussed and explained by scholarly and policy experts from around the world in a concise and user-friendly way.

The guide is comprehensive in scope, practically oriented and focused on political and societal processes to drive change on a larger scale. With cross-references to related terms in the entries, this book will be a highly valuable resource for students and practitioners engaged with the SDGs and sustainable development more broadly.

Frank Biermann is Professor of Global Sustainability Governance at the Copernicus Institute of Sustainable Development, Utrecht University, the Netherlands, and the 2025 Zennström Visiting Professor in Climate Change Leadership at Uppsala University, Sweden.

Thomas Hickmann is Associate Professor in the Department of Political Science at Lund University in Sweden. He is highly committed to interdisciplinary collaborations, research-based education and engagements with civil society to identify pathways towards sustainability transformations.

Yi hyun Kang is Postdoctoral Researcher in the Department of Political Science at Lund University in Sweden. Her research explores the role of civil society and technology in environmental politics and governance. Her research interests have been shaped by professional experiences in journalism, international development, and applied research.

Carole-Anne Sénit is Assistant Professor of Inclusive Sustainability Governance with the Copernicus Institute of Sustainable Development at Utrecht University, the Netherlands. The corpus of her research assesses the democratic legitimacy of sustainability governance, with a particular attention to whether and how citizens can take part in and influence the decisions that affect their lives.

Yixian Sun is Associate Professor in International Development and a UKRI Future Leaders Fellow at the University of Bath, United Kingdom. He studies transnational governance, environmental politics and sustainable development with a focus on emerging economies.

A-Z Guides for Environment and Sustainability

This series provides accessible, easy-to-navigate overviews of a range of different topics related to environment and sustainability. Following an A-Z format, each book contains entries which map out an important concept or term and illustrates how it connects more broadly to other ideas and disciplines. With related terms and further reading included alongside the entries, these innovative volumes will be of great interest to students and scholars learning, teaching and researching in this field.

Essential Concepts of Sustainable Finance
An A-Z Guide
Edited by Elisa Aracil and Ibrahim Sancak

Essential Concepts of Land Politics
An A–Z Guide
Saturnino M. Borras Jr. and Jennifer C. Franco

Essential Concepts for Implementing the Sustainable Development Goals
An A-Z Guide
Edited by Frank Biermann, Thomas Hickmann, Yi hyun Kang,
Carole-Anne Sénit and Yixian Sun

For more information about this series, please visit: www.routledge.com/A-Z-Guides-for-Environment-and-Sustainability/book-series/AZES

Essential Concepts for Implementing the Sustainable Development Goals
An A-Z Guide

Edited by Frank Biermann, Thomas Hickmann,
Yi hyun Kang, Carole-Anne Sénit and Yixian Sun

Designed cover image: Shutterstock

First published 2025
by Routledge
4 Park Square, Milton Park, Abingdon, Oxon OX14 4RN

and by Routledge
605 Third Avenue, New York, NY 10158

Routledge is an imprint of the Taylor & Francis Group, an informa business

© 2025 selection and editorial matter, Frank Biermann, Thomas Hickmann, Yi hyun Kang, Carole-Anne Sénit and Yixian Sun; individual chapters, the contributors

The right of Frank Biermann, Thomas Hickmann, Yi hyun Kang, Carole-Anne Sénit and Yixian Sun to be identified as the authors of the editorial material, and of the authors for their individual chapters, has been asserted in accordance with sections 77 and 78 of the Copyright, Designs and Patents Act 1988.

The Open Access version of this book, available at www.taylorfrancis.com, has been made available under a Creative Commons Attribution-Non Commercial-No Derivatives (CC-BY-NC-ND) 4.0 license.

Any third party material in this book is not included in the OA Creative Commons license, unless indicated otherwise in a credit line to the material. Please direct any permissions enquiries to the original rightsholder.

Trademark notice: Product or corporate names may be trademarks or registered trademarks, and are used only for identification and explanation without intent to infringe.

British Library Cataloguing-in-Publication Data
A catalogue record for this book is available from the British Library

ISBN: 978-1-032-85725-1 (hbk)
ISBN: 978-1-032-84169-4 (pbk)
ISBN: 978-1-003-51956-0 (ebk)

DOI: 10.4324/9781003519560

Typeset in Sabon
SPi Technologies India Pvt Ltd (Straive)

Contents

About the editors xi
List of contributors xiii
Acknowledgements xviii

Essential concepts for implementing the Sustainable Development Goals: An introduction 1

2030 Agenda for Sustainable Development 9

A 11

Accountability 11
Anthropocene 12
Artificial intelligence 14

B 16

Brundtland Report 16
Budgeting for Sustainable Development 17
Business sector 19

C 21

Civil society 21
Climate change and sustainable development 22
Climate finance 24
Commission on Sustainable Development (CSD) 26
Coordination 27
Corporate Social Responsibility (CSR) 29
Custodians 31

D 33

Data gaps 33
Development banks 35
Discourse and discursive effects 36

viii   *Contents*

E   39

Education for Sustainable Development 39
Effectiveness 40

F   43

Finance mechanisms 43
Fragmentation 44

G   47

Gender mainstreaming 47
Global Sustainable Development Reports (GSDR) 49
Governance by global goal-setting 50

H   52

High-level Political Forum on Sustainable Development (HLPF) 52
Human rights 53

I   55

Implementation 55
Inclusiveness 57
Independent Group of Scientists (IGS) 58
Indicators 60
Indigenous views 61
Inequality (global and national) 63
Institutions and institutional effects 65
Integration 66
Integrity (ecological and planetary) 68
Interaction and interlinkages 70
International Environmental Agreements 71
International Monetary Fund (IMF) 73
International organizations 74

J   77

Justice perspectives 77

L   79

Leave No One Behind 79
Legitimacy 81
Living wages 82
Localization 84

M   86

Major Groups and other Stakeholders 86
Millennium Development Goals (MDGs) 88

Contents ix

Modelling 89
Multilevel governance 91

N 93

National sustainable development strategies 93
Negotiation of the Sustainable Development Goals 95
Network analysis 96
Nexus governance 98
Norms and normative effects 100
North-South relations 101

O 104

Official development assistance (ODA) 104
Orchestration 105

P 108

Paris Agreement 108
Participation 110
Partnerships 111
People, Planet, Prosperity, Peace, Partnerships (5 Ps) 113
Philanthropic foundations 116
Planetary boundaries 117
Policy coherence and integration (at domestic level) 119
Policy coherence for sustainable development (at global level) 121
Political impact and steering effects 122
Political will and leadership 124
Private finance 126
Private governance 128

R 130

Rainbow washing 130
Rankings and performance measurement 131
Regional organizations 133
Responsibility 135

S 137

Science, technology and innovation 137
Scientific community 138
SDG summits 140
Silo approach 142
Stockholm+50 143
Subnational initiatives 145
Summit of the Future (2024) 146

x Contents

Sustainable finance 148
Synergies and goal complementarity 150

T   152

Targets 152
Trade-offs and goals conflicts 154
Transdisciplinarity 155
Transformation 157

U   159

United Nations Conference on Environment and Development (1992) 159
United Nations Conference on Sustainable Development (2012) 161
United Nations Conference on the Human Environment (1972) 162
United Nations Department of Economic and Social Affairs (UN DESA) 164
United Nations Development Programme (UNDP) 166
United Nations Environment Programme (UNEP) 167
United Nations General Assembly (UNGA) 169
United Nations Secretary-General (UNSG) 170
United Nations Statistical Commission 172
Universality 173
UN Sustainable Development Solutions Network (SDSN) 175

V   177

Voluntary Local Reviews 177
Voluntary National Reviews 179
Vulnerability 181

W   183

World Bank 183
World Commission on Environment and Development (WCED) 184
World Health Organization (WHO) 186
World Summit on Sustainable Development (2002) 188
World Trade Organization (WTO) 189

Y   192

Youth 192

Annex: The 17 Sustainable Development Goals   194

About the editors

Frank Biermann is Professor of Global Sustainability Governance at the Copernicus Institute of Sustainable Development, Utrecht University, the Netherlands. He has authored or co-edited 20 books and published over 250 articles and book chapters. Among other functions, he founded and served as the first chair of the Earth System Governance Project, a global transdisciplinary research network. Until February 2025, he led a EUR 2.5 million project on the impacts of the Sustainable Development Goals, funded by an Advanced Grant from the European Research Council. In 2021, he received the Distinguished Scholar Award in Environmental Studies from the International Studies Association, and in 2024, he was honoured with the Volvo Environment Prize 'for defining new pathways for international environmental governance in a period of global change'.

Thomas Hickmann is Associate Professor in the Department of Political Science at Lund University in Sweden. He is highly committed to interdisciplinary collaborations, research-based education and engagements with civil society to identify pathways towards sustainability transformations. He is the principal investigator in the project 'Exploring institutional complexity in global biodiversity and climate governance', funded by the research platform Biodiversity and Ecosystem Services in a Changing Climate (BECC). He is moreover an associate editor of *International Environmental Agreements: Politics, Law and Economics* and a senior research fellow of the Earth System Governance Project, co-convening the taskforce on the Sustainable Development Goals. His research has been published in prestigious academic journals including *Ambio, International Studies Review* and *Nature Sustainability*.

Yi hyun Kang is Postdoctoral Researcher in the Department of Political Science at Lund University in Sweden. Her research focuses on the role of civil society and technology in environmental politics and governance. Her research interests have been shaped by professional experiences in journalism, international development, and applied research. She worked as a postdoctoral researcher at UCLouvain Saint-Louis Bruxelles in Belgium, where she focused on the role of youth actors in global environmental politics. She received her PhD from the Technical University of Munich, Germany, with a dissertation on climate change adaptation in river management, comparing discursive and institutional responses in Germany and South Korea.

Carole-Anne Sénit is Assistant Professor of Inclusive Sustainability Governance with the Copernicus Institute of Sustainable Development at Utrecht University, the Netherlands. She is a political scientist by training, with a career spanning both research on and xii *About the editors*

practice in the civil society sector. Her research explores the democratic legitimacy of sustainability governance with expertise across a broad range of disciplines, methods and topics, including knowledge production, philanthropic foundations, SDGs and civil society. She is a senior research fellow of the Earth System Governance Project, co-convenor of the project's taskforce on the Sustainable Development Goals and managing editor of the *Earth System Governance* journal. She obtained her PhD from Utrecht University, in joint supervision with the Paris-based thinktank IDDRI (Institut du développement durable et des relations internationales). Prior to her doctoral studies, she worked as a research fellow at CEVIPOF and IDDRI.

Yixian Sun is Associate Professor in International Development at the University of Bath, United Kingdom. He studies transnational governance, environmental politics and sustainable development with a focus on emerging economies. Currently, he leads a GBP 1.7 million project on sustainability governance of China's global infrastructure investments funded by the UKRI Future Leaders Fellowship. He is the author of *Certifying China* and has published over 30 peer-reviewed articles and chapters in high-impact journals and books. He is an associate editor of *Global Environmental Politics* and *World Development Perspectives*. Moreover, he is an adjunct senior research fellow at the Institute for Environment and Sustainability of the National University of Singapore and a member of the Earth System Governance Project's Scientific Steering Committee.

Contributors

Cameron Allen is Senior Research fellow at Monash Sustainable Development Institute, Australia.

Guísela Almeida de Pereira is Project and Research Associate at Southern Voice.

Liliana B. Andonova is Professor at the Department of International Relations/Political Science at the Geneva Graduate Institute, Switzerland.

Ginette Azcona is Practitioner Fellow at the University of British Columbia's School of Public Policy and Global Affairs, on sabbatical from the Research and Data Section of United Nations Women in New York.

Janis Bragan Balda is Lecturer at Vackar College of Business and Entrepreneurship, University of Texas Rio Grande Valley, United States.

Simon Beaudoin is PhD Researcher in the Department of Political Science, University of British Columbia, Canada.

Elizabeth A. Bennett is Joseph M. Ha Endowed Professor of International Affairs and Director of Political Economy at Lewis and Clark College, United States.

Steven Bernstein is Distinguished Professor of Global Environmental and Sustainability Governance in the Department of Political Science, University of Toronto, Canada.

Magdalena Bexell is Associate Professor in the Department of Political Science at Lund University, Sweden.

Antra Bhatt is Statistics Specialist with the Research and Data Section at United Nations Women.

Maya Bogers is Senior Advisor at the Netherlands Scientific Climate Council, the Netherlands.

Noémi Bontridder is Researcher at the Justice and AI Jean Monnet Centre of Excellence, University of Liège, Belgium.

Basil Bornemann is Senior Researcher and Lecturer at the University of Basel and the University of Zurich, Switzerland.

Valentina Brogna is Guest Lecturer of International Relations and EU Politics at the UCLouvain Saint-Louis Bruxelles, Belgium.

Maximilian Bruder is Research Fellow at the Stockholm Environment Institute, Sweden.

Chol Bunnag is Assistant Professor in the Faculty of Economics of Thammasat University, Thailand.

xiv *Contributors*

Aurelie Charles is Associate Professor in Global Sustainability at the University of Bath, United Kingdom.

Estefanía Charvet is an International Development Consultant and Director of Programmes and Research at Southern Voice, a network of Global South think tanks.

Pamela Chasek is Professor of Political Science at Manhattan University, United States.

Loïc Cobut is Associate Researcher at Centre de Recherche en Science Politique, UCLouvain Saint-Louis Bruxelles, Belgium.

Tara Patricia Cookson holds the Canada Research Chair in Gender, Development and Global Public Policy at the University of British Columbia, Canada.

Matteo De Donà is Postdoctoral Researcher at the Department of Political Science of Lund University, Sweden.

Fronika de Wit is Postdoctoral Researcher with the GlobalGoals Project at Utrecht University, the Netherlands.

Hristo Dokov is Senior Assistant Professor in the Department of Regional and Political Geography, Sofia University 'St. Kliment Ohridski', Bulgaria.

Elise Dufief is Senior Research Fellow at the Institute for Sustainable Development and International Relations (IDDRI), France.

Daniel Duma is Research Fellow at the Stockholm Environment Institute, Sweden.

Mark Elder is Director of Research and Publications at the Institute for Global Environmental Strategies, Japan.

Joshua Philipp Elsässer is Postdoctoral Researcher at the Faculty of Economics and Social Sciences of the University of Potsdam, Germany.

Okechukwu Enechi is PhD Researcher at Vrije Universiteit Amsterdam, The Netherlands.

Karmen Erjavec is Professor of Communication at the University of Novo mesto, Slovenia.

Moira V. Faul is Senior Lecturer of International and Development Studies at the Geneva Graduate Institute, Switzerland.

Denis Francesconi is Senior Scientist at the Department of Teacher Education, University of Vienna, Austria.

Rodrigo Führ is Coordinator at the Global Covenant of Mayors for Climate and Energy – Americas Helpdesk, Brazil.

Grayson Fuller is Senior Manager for the SDG Index, data and statistics at the UN Sustainable Development Solutions Network (SDSN), Paris Office, France.

Thiago Gehre Galvão is Professor at the Postgraduate Program of the Institute of International Relations, University of Brasília, Brazil.

Lisa-Maria Glass is Postdoctoral Fellow at the Copernicus Institute of Sustainable Development at Utrecht University, the Netherlands.

Crystal Green is Research Director at HundrED and an affiliated researcher at the University of Helsinki, Finland.

Leonie Grob is Urban Governance Professional at Cities Alliance/United Nations Office for Project Services.

Yuen Gu is PhD researcher in the Department of Social and Policy Sciences at the University of Bath, United Kingdom.

Ibrahima Hathie is Distinguished Fellow at Initiative Prospective Agricole et Rurale (IPAR), Senegal.

Elisabeth Hege is Senior Research Fellow at the Institute for Sustainable Development and International Relations, France.

Guilherme Iablonovski is Geospatial Data Scientist at the UN Sustainable Development Solutions Network, Paris Office, France.

Maria Ivanova is Professor and Director of School of Public Policy and Urban Affairs at Northeastern University, United States.

Sajid Amin Javed is Deputy Executive Director and founding head of the Policy Solutions Lab at the Sustainable Development Policy Institute, Pakistan.

Dhanasree Jayaram is Assistant Professor (Senior Scale) in the Department of Geopolitics and International Relations, Manipal Institute of Social Sciences, Humanities and Arts, Manipal Academy of Higher Education, Manipal, India.

Marie Stissing Jensen is PhD Researcher at the Department of Political Science at Lund University, Sweden.

Kristina Jönsson is Associate Professor in the Department of Political Science at Lund University, Sweden.

Norichika Kanie is Professor at the Graduate School of Media and Governance at Keio University, Japan.

Elke Kellner is Marie Curie Fellow at the School of Sustainability, Arizona State University, United States and at the University of Bern, Switzerland.

Utkarsh Khot is PhD Researcher in the Integrated Research on Energy, Environment, and Society (IREES) group at the University of Groningen, the Netherlands.

Rakhyun E. Kim is Associate Professor of Earth System Governance at the Copernicus Institute of Sustainable Development at Utrecht University, the Netherlands.

Teun Kluck is PhD Researcher in the Integrated Research on Energy, Environment, and Society (IREES) group at the University of Groningen, the Netherlands.

Florian Koch is Professor of Real Estate Management, Smart Cities and Urban Development at Hochschule für Technik und Wirtschaft (HTW) Berlin, Germany.

Montserrat Koloffon Rosas is PhD Researcher with the Transformative Partnerships 2030 Project at the Institute for Environmental Studies (IVM), Vrije Universiteit Amsterdam, the Netherlands.

Kerstin Krellenberg is Professor of Urban Studies at the Department of Geography and Regional Research at the University of Vienna, Austria.

Denise Kronemberger is Head of Institutional Relations at the Brazilian Institute of Geography and Statistics, Brazil.

xvi *Contributors*

Citra Kumala is Associate Social Affairs Officer at the United Nations Economic and Social Commission for Asia and the Pacific.

Noémie Laurens is Postdoctoral Researcher in the Department of International Relations/ Political Science at the Geneva Graduate Institute, Switzerland.

Chaohui Li is Researcher of Sustainability Science at Potsdam Institute for Climate Impact Research, Germany, and Peking University, China.

Jing Li is PhD Researcher in the Integrated Research on Energy, Environment, and Society (IREES) group at the University of Groningen, the Netherlands.

Li Li is Associate Professor at the College of Humanities and Development Studies and the College of International Development and Global Agriculture, China Agricultural University, China.

Ivonne Lobos Alva is Team Leader for Sustainable Transitions at the Stockholm Environment Institute (SEI) in its Latin America Centre.

Shirin Malekpour is Associate Professor and Director of Graduate Research at Monash Sustainable Development Institute, Australia.

Isabella Massa is Senior Manager at the UN Sustainable Development Solutions Network (SDSN), Paris Office, France.

Amandine Orsini is Professor of International Relations at the UCLouvain Saint-Louis Bruxelles, Belgium.

Félicien Pagnon is Postdoctoral Researcher on quantification, alternative indicators to GDP and ESG data at Kedge Business School, France.

Hyeyoon Park is Assistant Professor in International Politics at the University of Stirling, United Kingdom.

Susan Park is Professor of Global Governance at the University of Sydney, Australia.

Lena Partzsch is Professor of Comparative Politics with a focus on environmental and climate politics at Freie Universität Berlin, Germany.

Dario Piselli is Senior Manager, Biodiversity and Pollution at KPMG in Sweden.

Alex San Martim Portes is Visiting Fellow at the School of Regulation and Global Governance at the Australian National University, Australia.

Prajal Pradhan is Assistant Professor in the Integrated Research on Energy, Environment, and Society (IREES) group at the University of Groningen, the Netherlands.

Michele Joie Prawiromaruto is Research Fellow in the GlobalGoals Project at Utrecht University, the Netherlands.

Guilherme de Queiroz-Stein is Strategic Analyst at FINEP Innovation and Research, Brazil.

Ilona Rac is Researcher in the Department of Animal Science at the University of Ljubljana, Slovenia.

Laura Rahm is Jean Monnet Fellow at the European University Institute, Florence, Italy.

Rodrigo Correa Ramiro is PhD Researcher at the University of Brasília, Brazil.

Jano Richter is Research Assistant in the GlobalGoals Project at Utrecht University, the Netherlands.

Virgi Sari is Lecturer in the Department of Social and Policy Sciences at the University of Bath, United Kingdom.

Andrea Schapper is Professor of International Politics at the University of Stirling, United Kingdom.

Philip Schleifer is Associate Professor in Transnational Governance at the University of Amsterdam, the Netherlands.

Jakob Skovgaard is Associate Professor in the Department of Political Science at Lund University, Sweden.

Joanna Stanberry is Vice Chancellor's Sustainability Research Fellow in the Initiative for Leadership and Sustainability at the University of Cumbria, United Kingdom.

Sujoy Subroto is PhD Researcher in the Department of Geography at the University of Calgary, Canada.

Samory Toure is Economic Analyst at the UN Sustainable Development Solutions Network (SDSN), Paris Office, France.

Cornelia Ulbert is Executive Director of the Institute for Development and Peace (INEF) at the University of Duisburg-Essen, Germany.

Shrijana Vaidya is Guest Researcher at the Leibniz Centre for Agricultural Landscape Research, Germany.

Ha B. Vien is PhD Researcher in the Department of Public Administration at North Carolina State University, United States.

Maximilian S. T. Wanner is Postdoctoral Researcher at the Department of Political Science, Stockholm University and the Institute for Future Studies, Sweden.

Anne Warchold is PhD Researcher in the Integrated Research on Energy, Environment, and Society (IREES) group at the University of Groningen, the Netherlands.

Rosalind Warner is Continuing College Professor of Political Science at Okanagan College, Canada.

Amber Webb is Managing Director of the SDG Academy at the UN Sustainable Development Solutions Network (SDSN), New York Office, United States.

Sabine Weiland is Associate Professor of Political Science at the Université catholique de Lille, France.

Nina Weitz is Senior Research Fellow and Team Leader for the Global Goals and Systems team at the Stockholm Environment Institute, Sweden.

Mara Wendebourg is Postdoctoral Researcher with the GlobalGoals Project at Utrecht University, The Netherlands.

Julia Wesely is Postdoctoral Researcher at the Department of Geography and Regional Research at the University of Vienna, Austria.

Fariborz Zelli is Professor in the Department of Political Science at Lund University, Sweden.

Acknowledgements

This *A-Z Guide on Essential Concepts for Implementing the Sustainable Development Goals* is a collective endeavour by a large team of scholars, without whom this project would not have been feasible. We would thus like to express our gratitude, first of all, to our contributing authors for dedicating their time to write the 105 entries. Many contributing authors are members of the Earth System Governance Project's Taskforce on the Sustainable Development Goals, and the enthusiasm and energy within this taskforce gave us the confidence to develop and complete this project. We also thank the Earth System Governance Project's larger community and its International Project Office, which supported various activities of our initiative, including meetings during the 2023 Annual Conference on Earth System Governance in Nijmegen, the Netherlands, and the 2024 Virtual Forum on 'Re-imagining Earth System Governance in an Era of Polycrisis'.

Special thanks go also to the GlobalGoals Project at Utrecht University, which has been funded by a European Research Council's Advanced Grant (grant agreement No 788001) providing critical support to our work. In particular, the 2024 GlobalGoals conference in Utrecht was instrumental for this book. We moreover thank our own institutions – Utrecht University, Lund University and the University of Bath – for supporting our research on the governance and politics of the 2030 Agenda and the Sustainable Development Goals and the encouragement that we have received from our colleagues.

Last but not least, we are thankful to Grace Harrison, Rohita Divyanshu, Meghna Rodborne, Radhika Gupta, Matthew Shobbrook, and Govindaram Devaa S. for all their support and effective cooperation in the production process of this book and for comments from five anonymous reviewers for their constructive feedback on the original book proposal and detailed recommendations for realizing this publication project.

Frank Biermann, Thomas Hickmann, Yi hyun Kang,
Carole-Anne Sénit and Yixian Sun
Editors of this A-Z Guide

Essential concepts for implementing the Sustainable Development Goals

An introduction

Frank Biermann, Thomas Hickmann, Yi hyun Kang, Carole-Anne Sénit and Yixian Sun

Sustainable development has been a central concern of the United Nations since the term became popular following the 1987 Brundtland report of the World Commission on Environment and Development. Numerous meetings on sustainable development have been held, and thousands of documents, reports and press releases around this concept have been published. In September 2015, the United Nations General Assembly took a novel and, in their words, 'bold' step by adopting a '2030 Agenda for Sustainable Development' with 17 'Sustainable Development Goals' (SDGs), supported by 169 specific targets. With this new set of documents, the United Nations aims to provide clearer direction for public policies and inspire societal actors to drive sustainable development forward.

The launch of the SDGs was met with immense optimism, as officials at the United Nations and governments expressed strong confidence that this new programmatic framework would serve as a catalyst to 'transform our world for the better by 2030' (United Nations General Assembly 2015: 35). After a decade of policies to implement the SDGs, however, several scientific assessments concluded that 'the world is not on track to achieve the Goals by 2030' (Global Sustainable Development Report 2023: 1). According to the 2024 progress report of the United Nations, only 17% of targets with sufficient data are likely to be achieved by 2030. 83% show limited progress or are even regressing (United Nations 2024: 4). A growing number of studies on the SDGs all point in the same direction. While the 17 SDGs are presented by the United Nations and governments as the so far most comprehensive attempt of a universal policy framework for sustainability, the goals have failed to push political and societal processes to 'transform our world' (Biermann et al. 2022a, 2022b; Hickmann et al. 2024). In turbulent and uncertain times marked by geopolitical tensions, growing inequalities and rapid environmental degradation, the SDGs are facing strong headwinds – and many backlashes. Yet despite these enormous political challenges, there seems to be no alternative. In short, to foster political and societal transformations towards global sustainability and peace, societies must drastically accelerate their efforts to implement the SDGs (Fuso Nerini et al. 2024).

Against this backdrop, this *A-Z Guide* offers an accessible and user-friendly overview of the essential concepts and terms needed to understand the implementation of the SDGs. Crafted in the form of an encyclopaedia, the volume presents 105 entries on important concepts and terms and their links to academic and policy debates. Each entry offers basic definitions of the concept or term at issue, followed by a brief discussion with illustrative examples and forward-looking reflections on science or policy. Together, all entries serve as a key reference for a wide global audience, ranging from students and researchers to policymakers, activists, consultants and other practitioners engaged with sustainable development.

DOI: 10.4324/9781003519560-1

This chapter has been made available under a CC-BY-NC-ND license.

2   *Essential Concepts for Implementing the SDGs*

In the next sections we take stock of global efforts to implement the SDGs, point to governance areas where political changes due to the SDGs have been observed, and discuss calls for reforming the SDGs to make them more transformative. In the final paragraphs we present the main rationale of this A-Z Guide.

Taking stock of the global efforts to implement the SDGs

Owing to their universal reach, broad coverage and the deteriorating state of global sustainability efforts, the SDGs have become a topic for much research and debate in academia and policymaking. Given the centrality of the 17 SDGs within and beyond the United Nations, many programmes and initiatives have been launched to support their achievement. While it is broadly recognized that the SDGs have not led to large-scale transformations, they seem to still have had some influence on political and public discourses. In particular, studies suggest that the SDGs may have changed the framing and understanding of sustainability issues and may have prompted a rethinking of traditional approaches to economic growth, social equality and environmental protection (Biermann et al. 2022a). The goals have also catalyzed a global conversation about sustainability that influenced the language, policies and imaginations of sustainable futures. Other positive developments might be observed regarding some first institutional and normative effects of the SDGs, for example, when new administrative bodies or new policies in support of the SDGs are launched. And yet, research has also shown that these changes often replicate existing priorities and trajectories.

Overall, it remains questionable whether the SDGs could bring about deeper institutional and normative changes. Observable institutional and normative effects have not yet reached the scale that would make the SDGs truly transformative (Biermann et al. 2022b). Also, the SDGs have not generated the deep, systemic changes needed for lasting improvements in public-administrative systems. Many institutions are still insufficiently aligned with the SDGs. Funding, especially large-scale financial commitments, has not been redirected or sufficiently increased for SDG implementation. Moreover, policies are not becoming more stringent or comprehensive, and few new policies are introduced that impose stricter sustainability measures. In addition, binding regulations are lacking that would hold governments, businesses and other stakeholders accountable and responsible for their actions towards the SDGs. In short, the SDGs have not yet led to far-reaching structural, financial, policy or legal changes.

Drawing on the literature, four key governance challenges seem to hamper SDG implementation. First, the voluntary nature of the SDGs allows governments and other public and private actors to implement the goals in a way that benefits their self-interests. State and non-state actors tend to prioritize those goals and targets that are easy to reach, leaving more challenging ones behind. For instance, high-income countries often do not address goals that would require substantial efforts and disrupt business-as-usual processes, or they develop strategies of incremental change while neglecting more complex goals such as reducing unsustainable consumption (SDG 12), phasing out fossil fuels (SDGs 7 and 13), protecting biodiversity (SDGs 14 and 15), raising financial support for poorer countries and strengthening global partnerships for sustainable development (SDG 17) (Biermann et al. 2023). For example, some agri-food multinationals, specifically those exposed to international scrutiny, seem to strategically cherry-pick selected targets to claim their support for SDGs and gain legitimacy for their profit-maximizing practices.

Second, discrepancies are growing between the promises and the actions of governments and non-state actors. While the SDGs are increasingly integrated into strategies and operations of these actors, concerns about 'SDG washing' or 'rainbow washing' have been raised as well, that is, that governments and businesses would make vague or even false claims about their actual contributions to the SDGs. Some businesses may have reframed their practices and portfolios around corporate social responsibility and environmental, social and governance by adopting the new language of the SDGs while not changing their daily practices (Órdoñez Llanos et al. 2022). In fact, state and non-state actors often use the SDGs to legitimize their actions, but if they then fail to deliver on their promised commitments, they may jeopardize the credibility of the SDGs to achieve sustainability transformations. Furthermore, the widening gap between rhetoric and practice delays the implementation of urgently needed action for sustainable development, especially for environmental problems such as climate change, biodiversity loss and land degradation.

Third, many governments seem to fail to mobilize the political will that is needed to prioritize the SDGs in strategies and development plans. In many countries, the implementation of the SDGs has been stymied by a lack of political leadership and political volatility. For example, shortly after adoption of the SDGs in 2015, Sri Lanka established a new Ministry of Sustainable Development to implement the goals. In 2018, however, constitutional conflicts in the legislature led to changes in previously created institutional structures for SDG implementation, with presidential elections in 2019 changing these again (De Zoysa et al. 2020). Brazil, as a second example, was one of the few countries that created a robust institutional framework to coordinate the national targets and indicators for the SDGs and to articulate domestic uptake of the goals, with substantive participation from non-state actors through a new National Commission for the SDGs. However, this commission was dismantled after President Bolsonaro took office in 2019 (Siegel and Bastos Lima 2020) and only later reinstalled when President Lula was elected in 2023. Eventually, institutional instability had negative repercussions on SDG but paved the way for civil society organizations to become key actors in the complex governance of the 2030 Agenda in Brazil (Gehre and Ramiro 2023).

Fourth, the SDGs are not yet fully incorporated in domestic political systems and structures, nor do they foster institutional integration. Admittedly, a few governments, such as Germany, have begun to integrate the SDGs in national strategies and action plans in a comprehensive approach that is reflected in institutional arrangements within the federal government (Bornemann 2014). In many other high-income countries, however, the responsibility for SDG implementation often lies with the ministries of foreign affairs or environment, showing here a more sectoral and siloed approach. Overall, the SDGs have not taken root in most national political systems. Governments seem to be stuck to traditional divisions of tasks between line ministries without effective mechanisms to develop and formulate cross-sectoral policies and programmes that turn the holistic vision of the SDGs into coherent policies.

Governance areas where the SDGs had some political impact

In light of these challenges, a study by Hickmann et al. (2024) has investigated in more detail the actual political changes due to the SDGs. Drawing on an expert survey and a series of online workshops, the study identified five areas where some policies seem to have changed because of the SDGs: global governance, national policy integration, subnational initiatives, private governance and education and learning. Subsequently, five

4 *Essential Concepts for Implementing the SDGs*

research groups organized by the Taskforce on the Sustainable Development Goals under the Earth System Governance Project followed up by in-depth studies on each area, offering nuanced answers about a few small but incrementally growing effects of the SDGs and identifying many knowledge gaps.

First, as for global governance, the SDGs have been designed as a framework produced by, and partially for, the United Nations system to streamline sustainable development into global governance. A key mechanism is here the High-level Political Forum for Sustainable Development, which has been set up to track progress on SDG implementation. However, the High-level Political Forum is consistently assessed as being too weak to hold governments to account for their lack of action towards sustainable development. While some international organizations and partnerships have internalized the SDGs in their operations, it remains questionable whether this integration has fully advanced global sustainability governance. Although research has explored the impact of SDGs on diverse areas such as human mobility, governance and partnerships, most studies suggest only limited steering potential for global policy integration. Research also suggests many remaining challenges with partnerships, such as the exclusion of marginalized actors and weak accountability, monitoring and reporting (Bäckstrand et al. 2022). In short, more research is needed on the role of the SDGs in multilateralism and the effectiveness of SDG partnerships in global sustainability governance.

Second, the complexity of the SDGs presents significant challenges for national policy integration, policy interlinkages and implementation. SDG integration has been found to be multi-directional and shaped by domestic contexts and political priorities, with adaptation to national and subnational contexts being a crucial factor. Studies have shown that while some countries, particularly those with higher incomes, have made progress in aligning their political discourse and public administration systems with the SDGs, policy coherence for implementation remains limited. Moreover, the Voluntary National Reviews, which are a central part of SDG reporting, had little impact on changing dominant development paradigms and planning. While the deadline for SDG achievement by 2030 approaches, the first effects of the SDGs on national decision-making are just beginning to emerge. Future research needs to focus now on identifying good practices, better understanding capacity-building for SDG implementation and exploring how governments can better navigate synergies, trade-offs and stakeholder conflicts to promote successful integration of the 17 global goals in domestic policies.

Third, the SDGs must ultimately be implemented in local communities to impact people's lives. This situation has led to a burgeoning literature on 'SDG localization', that is, how local actors engage with the global goals. Much of this literature portrays case studies, particularly in pioneering cities with a long track record of sustainability initiatives. Such studies often explore the effects of Voluntary Local Reviews, which are not required but welcomed by the United Nations, on local policy integration and goal implementation. Other studies examine how to translate the SDGs into local targets, investigate synergies and trade-offs in local communities or develop frameworks to guide subnational implementation. Here, future research may focus on understanding the diverse forms and challenges of SDG localization, assessing the variant success of local initiatives, identifying factors that contribute to successful implementation and designing practical strategies to strengthen subnational governance and local accountability for SDG implementation.

Fourth, how public-private partnerships or private governance initiatives implement the SDGs has become the object of many studies. Reports like 'Better Business-Better World' and 'SDG Ambition' claim an important role in private sector engagement and

Essential Concepts for Implementing the SDGs 5

commercial opportunities linked to SDG implementation. Research on corporate involvement often focuses on sustainability reporting, revealing concerns about 'SDG washing' or 'rainbow washing' and the limited scope of engagement, especially from corporations in the Global North. While the role of private actors in SDG implementation may indeed seem critical, significant knowledge gaps remain, particularly regarding the interconnected nature of the SDGs and how this affects the private sector. Future research should explore the broader governance roles of private actors, investigating different types of steering effects, such as discursive, institutional or relational, and how businesses use the SDGs to shape strategies, create institutional change, form partnerships and reallocate resources. Ultimately, understanding the conditions for private sector engagement in transformative SDG governance across diverse contexts is crucial for developing effective strategies and policies.

Finally, education and learning are essential for driving behavioural and structural change towards sustainability. SDG 4, which focuses on education, was designed to support this transformation. However, the effectiveness of the SDGs in advancing sustainability through education remains unclear; research on this topic is still limited. Much of the literature explores the relationship between 'Education for Sustainable Development' and the SDGs in educational institutions, such as challenges of operationalization and integration. While the literature highlights the impact of the SDGs on curricula, teaching methods and pedagogical approaches, further research is needed on how to better integrate and operationalize the SDGs in education. Another key area of research looks into the integration of the SDGs in higher education institutions, where there is often a lack of awareness, critical understanding and resources. Many initiatives, particularly rankings and standardized measures, overlook local contexts and the Global North-South divide. Moving forward, research should address synergies between 'Education for Sustainable Development' and the SDGs, investigate the role of educational institutions as agents of change in SDG implementation, explore the complexity of education for sustainability and examine how decolonial and pluriversal approaches can challenge dominant global educational frameworks to foster more inclusive and sustainable practices.

In sum, the uptake of the SDGs remains patchy and often symbolic across governance levels. While there are pioneering SDG initiatives by some progressive governments, cities, local administrations and businesses, no clear pathway has emerged towards sustainable development. The success stories of policy changes due to the SDGs are inspiring, but how they can be scaled up remains unclear. Most actors and institutions continue with business-as-usual approaches despite some discursive shifts and the increasing prominence of rhetoric that uses the SDGs. While the SDGs have helped reframe the debate on sustainable development and led to new narratives, some new policies and even a few new institutions, overall, they had only limited political impact. A core problem is still that the SDGs are not yet strongly supported in political systems and that accountability mechanisms remain scattered and weak. If so, the question arises of whether governance by global goal-setting is effective and whether and how we could make it more effective. Much depends on how political and societal actors and institutions will hold governments accountable for their formal commitments to the SDGs.

Accelerating goal implementation and reforming the SDGs

Given the slow progress towards the SDGs, researchers as well as policymakers have suggested numerous reform proposals. Many have emerged in research and policy circles

6 Essential Concepts for Implementing the SDGs

as a result of disappointment and frustration with the lack of progress in SDG implementation. For example, the 2023 Global Sustainable Development Report, which had been written by 15 scientists appointed by the United Nations Secretary-General, suggested several specific interventions to accelerate progress on the SDGs. They emphasized levers such as governance, science and technology, business and finance, individual and collective action and capacity-building, all of which should be used for more transformative interventions in areas with potential for systemic effects, such as sustainable food systems, human well-being and energy decarbonization.

Similarly, another group of experts on SDG governance proposed four urgent reforms in this field, namely differentiation, dynamization, legalization and institutionalization (Biermann et al. 2023). They argued, first, that high-income countries should commit to more ambitious policies, also in complex areas such as unsustainable consumption and reductions in fossil fuel use. Second, the SDGs should be more dynamic, with regular revisions that would raise ambitions in a way similar to the Paris Agreement. Third, the researchers suggested stronger legal commitments, including binding agreements among like-minded countries on specific SDGs, such as plastic pollution or fossil fuel phaseout. Fourth, more institutional support was called for, especially for SDGs that focus on inequality, sustainable consumption and better governance. The researchers also argued for stronger global governance mechanisms, better support for local actions and a reduction of the financing gaps for sustainable development.

This reform call was further specified at the International Research Conference 'GlobalGoals2024 – The Future of the SDGs' held in Utrecht, the Netherlands, in August 2024. This event brought together over 150 researchers and practitioners from the Global North and South, who presented a roadmap for sustainability governance until 2030 and beyond, offering further strategies to revitalize progress towards the SDGs. The discussions were summarized in the Utrecht Roadmap, which highlights four concrete avenues for reform (Biermann et al. 2024). The first avenue calls for improving the global architecture of sustainability governance by developing stronger monitoring and accountability frameworks to ensure a more systematic, inclusive and transparent review of how governments and international institutions engage with the SDGs. Specifically suggested were reforms of the High-level Political Forum, a better science-policy interface for SDG monitoring and stronger mechanisms for the participation of civil society. Second, to curtail cherry-picking and 'siloization', researchers called for actions that facilitate national and subnational SDG coordination and governance, including the creation and appropriate funding of cross-sectoral SDG coordination units among governments and the development of national and subnational SDG acceleration plans. Third, it was recommended to consolidate goals by setting more specific, adaptive and ambitious targets and to strengthen data collection and monitoring systems. Finally, the researchers advocated for a shift towards more inclusive development strategies that would move away from the gross domestic product as the primary measure of progress, embrace the circular economy and human well-being as core principles of national policies and advance broader reforms in the global economic system to better support a just transition, particularly in low-income countries.

Similarly, and echoing previous calls for stronger accountability mechanisms, bolstered targets and a reform of the global financial architecture for sustainable development, Fuso Nerini et al. (2024) recommended mission-based approaches for SDG implementation that would have the potential to foster collaboration across sectors, technologies and types of firms to achieve ambitious goals. Still others have looked at how to reform the SDGs towards realizing their ambition of leaving no one behind. Members of the so-called Earth Commission, a group of scientists who seek to define safe and just planetary boundaries, have called for systemic transformations, resource redistribution and transferable and accessible sustainable technologies for the SDGs to reach justice in access to minimum resources and support socioeconomic human rights without breaching environmental thresholds (Gupta et al. 2024).

At the time of writing, merely five years are left to implement the SDGs by 2030. In September 2024, governments convened for the Summit of the Future and reaffirmed their commitment to advance the SDGs. The outcome document of this summit, the 'Pact for the Future', recognizes the need to plan for the long term, and invites the High-level Political Forum to consider in 2027 how the international community advances sustainable development by 2030 and beyond. While the 'Pact for the Future' aimed on achieving the greatest possible gains on SDG implementation and accelerating efforts, the future of the SDGs beyond 2030, and global sustainability governance more broadly, remains still undefined.

Main rationale of this A-Z Guide

Given the complexities of debates around SDG implementation, this A-Z Guide has been designed to offer the reader succinct elaborations of the 105 most central concepts and terms that are widely used in the debate on the SDGs. All entries are related to goal implementation and circle around the topic of governing transformations towards sustainable development. Written by a diverse group of academic and policy experts from all over the world, the 105 entries offer up-to-date knowledge and concise insights into a wide range of themes around the SDGs. The volume follows an encyclopaedic format, that is, each entry provides first a definition or basic description of the respective concept or topic and then discusses relevant practical examples with critiques and caveats derived from the state of knowledge and policy practices. The volume has been designed for a broad audience and formulated in an accessible language to inform both academics and practitioners.

Different from other works, this A-Z Guide has a clear focus on SDG implementation, while discussing concepts and terms from a critical academic and policy perspective. Moreover, this A-Z Guide takes a global approach to serve as a key resource for students in a diverse set of study programmes and at the same time to function as a knowledge base for policy advice and practices on the broad field of sustainable development. The entries refer to key theoretical approaches and methods that are used in the research on global sustainability governance. Additionally, they deal with the historical background of the SDGs explaining key instruments and milestones of the pathway towards the 2030 Agenda and the SDGs.

The SDGs are one of the most prominent global policy frameworks of our time, aiming to redirect policies in United Nations agencies, national and local governments and among a wide range of non-state actors. And yet, despite some progress, the SDGs have fallen short of their intended impact. More transformative changes at all governance levels and societal scales are needed. Any meaningful and impactful discussion about the SDGs and their future requires a deep understanding of the core principles that underpin this agenda. This A-Z Guide provides exactly that, offering 105 authoritative short analyses of key concepts and terms to equip readers with a solid foundation for their work.

8   Essential Concepts for Implementing the SDGs

Ultimately, the SDGs can serve as a vital cornerstone in the global effort to advance human society and our planet towards sustainability. We hope that this A-Z Guide provides comprehensive grounds for discussions on accelerating global sustainability goals and shaping reform debates in the years ahead.

References

Bäckstrand, K., Koliev, F., and Mert, A. (2022). Governing SDG partnerships: The role of institutional capacity, inclusion, and transparency. In E. Murphy, A. Banerjee, and P. P. Walsh (Eds.), *Partnerships and the Sustainable Development Goals* (pp. 41–58). Cham: Springer Nature.

Biermann, F., de Queiroz Stein, G., Wendebourg, M., de Wit, F., Banik, D., Beisheim, M., ... and Sun, Y. (2024). *Reinvigorating the sustainable development goals: The Utrecht roadmap.* Statement of the International Research Conference 'GlobalGoals2024'. Utrecht, The Netherlands. 30 August 2024. www.globalgoalsproject.eu

Biermann, F., Hickmann, T., and Sénit, C.-A. (Eds.). (2022a). *The Political Impact of the Sustainable Development Goals: Transforming Governance through Global Goals?* Cambridge University Press. https://doi.org/10.1038/s41893-022-00909-5

Biermann, F., Hickmann, T., Sénit, C. A., Beisheim, M., Bernstein, S., Chasek, P., ... and Wicke, B. (2022b). Scientific evidence on the political impact of the Sustainable Development Goals. *Nature Sustainability*, 5(9), 795–800.

Biermann, F., Sun, Y., Banik, D., Beisheim, M., Bloomfield, M. J., Charles, A., ... and Sénit, C. A. (2023). Four governance reforms to strengthen the SDGs. *Science*, 381(6663), 1159–1160.

Bornemann, B. (2014). *Policy-Integration und Nachhaltigkeit: Integrative Politik in der Nachhaltigkeitsstrategie der deutschen Bundesregierung.* Wiesbaden: Springer.

De Zoysa, U., Gunawardena, A., and Gunawardena, P. (2020). *Localising the Transformation in the New Normal: A Domestic Resource Mobilization Framework for Sustainable Development Goals in Sri Lanka.* Janathakhan (GTE) Ltd. and Centre for Environment and Development.

Fuso Nerini, F., Mazzucato, M., Rockström, J., van Asselt, H., Hall, J. W., Matos, S., ... and Sachs, J. (2024). Extending the sustainable development goals to 2050 – A road map. *Nature*, 630(8017), 555–558.

Gehre, T., & Ramiro, R. (2023). The complex governance of the 2030 Agenda and the steering effects of implementing the SDGs in Brazil (2015-2022). *Carta Internacional*, 18(1), e1306. https://doi.org/10.21530/ci.v18n1.2023.1306

Global Sustainable Development Report. (2023). *Times of Crisis, Times of Change: Science for Accelerating Transformations to Sustainable Development.* New York: United Nations.

Gupta, J., Fezzigna, P., Gentile, G., Rammelt, C., and Scholtens, J. (2024). Reinforcing the SDGs to live within safe and just thresholds. *Science-Policy Brief for the Multistakeholder Forum on Science, Technology and Innovation for the SDGs*, May 2024. https://sdgs.un.org/sites/default/files/2024-05/Gupta%2C%20et%20al._Reinforcing%20the%20SDGs%20to%20live%20within%20safe%20and%20just%20thresholds.pdf

Hickmann, T., Biermann, F., Sénit, C. A., Sun, Y., Bexell, M., Bolton, M., ... and Weiland, S. (2024). Scoping article: Research frontiers on the governance of the Sustainable Development Goals. *Global Sustainability*, 7, e7. https://doi.org/10.1017/sus.2024.4

Órdoñez Llanos, A., Raven, R., Bexell, M., Botchwey, B., Bornemann, B., Censoro, J., ... and Yunita, A. (2022). Implementation at multiple levels. In F. Biermann, T. Hickmann, and C.-A. Sénit (Eds.), *The Political Impact of the Sustainable Development Goals: Transforming Governance through Global Goals?* (pp. 59–91). Cambridge: Cambridge University Press.

Siegel, K. M., and Bastos Lima, M. G. (2020). When international sustainability frameworks encounter domestic politics: The Sustainable Development Goals and agri-food governance in South America. *World Development*, 135, 105053. https://doi.org/10.1016/j.worlddev.2020.105053

United Nations. (2024). *Sustainable Development Goals Report 2024.* United Nations. https://unstats.un.org/sdgs/report/2024/

United Nations General Assembly. (2015). Transforming our world: The 2030 agenda for sustainable development. A/RES/70/1. https://www.un.org/en/development/desa/population/migration/generalassembly/docs/globalcompact/A_RES_70_1_E.pdf

2030 Agenda for Sustainable Development

Steven Bernstein

The 2030 Agenda for Sustainable Development (United Nations General Assembly 2015), which contains the 17 Sustainable Development Goals (SDGs) and 169 targets, provides the UN's framework to implement the SDGs and the broader sustainable development agenda until 2030. Its preamble presents a vision based on five 'P's': people, planet, prosperity, peace and partnerships, while recognizing that 'eradicating poverty in all its forms and dimensions…is the greatest global challenge'. It also articulates several normative aspirations, including 'leaving no one behind', human rights and gender equality. The SDGs, it states, are 'indivisible' and 'integrated', ought to 'balance' economic, social and environmental dimensions, and apply universally to all countries, while taking account of national circumstances.

The 2030 Agenda's last third is devoted to implementation. It builds on the idea of 'global partnership' (SDG 17), which includes macroeconomic, finance, technology and multi-stakeholder partnerships components. It also emphasizes civil society and private sector mobilization, along with states and international institutions, to realize the 2030 Agenda. The need for 'policy and institutional coherence' (SDG 17 and paras 63, 70, 82 and 87) among international institutions and governance arrangements, and within different countries, is another prominent theme.

The 2030 Agenda also lays the groundwork for follow-up and review at national, regional and global levels, identifying the High-level Political Forum on Sustainable Development (HLPF) as the lead institution. Whereas participation in the HLPF's Voluntary National Reviews has been high, calls persist for more systemic, comprehensive, accountable and compulsory review mechanisms and increased involvement of civil society (Biermann et al. 2023). The 2030 Agenda also proposed a Technology Facilitation Mechanism comprised of a United Nations inter-agency task team on science, technology and innovation, supported by a multi-stakeholder forum and an online platform of initiatives and programmes (United Nations Technology Facilitation Mechanism n.d.). While the 2030 Agenda mentions finance, negotiators left details to a parallel process that produced the Addis Ababa Action Agenda of the Third International Conference on Financing for Development, adopted in July 2015.

The 2030 Agenda's framing under the rubric of sustainable development was not a foregone conclusion. It evolved from 'post-2015' development agenda discussions, in reference to the deadline to achieve the 2000 Millennium Development Goals (MDGs). By 2011, when the United Nations officially began considering the next agenda, shifting development discourse and material conditions of developing countries resulted in discussions more explicitly addressing the multidimensional nature of poverty, with

DOI: 10.4324/9781003519560-2

This chapter has been made available under a CC-BY-NC-ND license.

10 *Essential Concepts for Implementing the SDGs*

particular attention to inequality, growth and employment, and integration of environmental sustainability, as well as governance, justice and peaceful societies (Hulme and Wilkinson 2014). When the United Nations General Assembly adopted the Open Working Group's report containing the SDGs in September 2014, that cemented the new 'sustainable development' framing of the 2030 Agenda's formal negotiations, starting in January 2015 (Chasek et al. 2016). While formally negotiated by governments, stakeholder consultations and several international, stakeholder and regional reports fed into negotiations.

Implementing the 2030 Agenda has faced several challenges, including the effects of the COVID-19 pandemic, geopolitical dynamics including the Ukraine war and climate change. Scholarly critiques push in several, and not always consistent, directions. Some call for improved performance measures and modelling and a more systems-based approach, while others propose viewing indicators as tools for conversation across geographies rather than endpoints (Arora-Jonsson 2023). Partially in response, the UN's Global Sustainable Development Reports have focused on synergies, trade-offs and 'coherence' (Independent Group of Scientists 2023). Others call for greater integration of the SDGs into international agreements and law (Biermann et al. 2023). Still others argue that the 2030 Agenda fails to address tensions or contradictions among and within goals, between 'integration' and 'balance', or between 'global partnership' and 'partnerships', which can undermine inclusive development or fail to address structural and institutional drivers of unsustainability, poverty or inequality (Fukuda-Parr and Smaavik Hegstad, 2018; Bernstein et al. 2025).

References

Arora-Jonsson, S. (2023). The Sustainable Development Goals: A Universalist Promise for the Future. *Futures* 146, 103087. https://doi.org/10.1016/j.futures.2022.103087

Bernstein, S., Glas, A., and Laurence, M. (2025). *Norms, Practices, and Social Change in Global Politics*. Cambridge: Cambridge University Press. https://doi.org/10.1017/9781009560986

Biermann, F., et al. (2023). Four Governance Reforms to Strengthen the SDGs. *Science* 381(6663): 1159–1160. https://www.science.org/doi/10.1126/science.adj5434

Chasek, P.S., Wagner, L.M., Leone, F., Lebada, A.-M. and Risse, N. (2016). Getting to 2030: Negotiating the Post-2015 Sustainable Development Agenda. *RECIEL* 25(1): 5–14. https://doi.org/10.1111/reel.12149

Fukuda-Parr, S., and Smaavik Hegstad, T. (2018). 'Leaving No One Behind' as a Site of Contestation and Reinterpretation. *Journal of Globalization and Development* 9(2): 20180037. https://doi.org/10.1515/jgd-2018-0037

Hulme, D., and Wilkinson, R. (2014). The UN and the Post-2015 Development Agenda. In *Post-2015 UN Development*, pp. 181–194. Routledge.

Independent Group of Scientists. (2023). Global Sustainable Development Report: Science for Accelerating Transformations to Sustainable Development. https://sdgs.un.org/gsdr/gsdr2023

United Nations General Assembly. (2015). Transforming Our World: The 2030 Agenda for Sustainable Development. A/RES/70/1. https://sdgs.un.org/publications/transforming-our-world-2030-agenda-sustainable-development-17981

United Nations Technology Facilitation Mechanism. (n.d.). United Nations Technology Facilitation Mechanism. https://sdgs.un.org/tfm

A

Accountability

Magdalena Bexell

Accountability refers to an actor having to answer for the way in which the actor has carried out its obligations and exercised its power. It involves an assumption of monitoring and sanctioning and can therefore drive the implementation of agreements forward. Accountability is important for accelerating progress towards the Sustainable Development Goals (SDGs) because goal implementation is uneven. While each individual can support SDG implementation through sustainable practices, actors with great institutional and other resources are at the focus of accountability debates due to their greater power. Key questions for accountability are: Who is accountable? For what actions (or lack of action) are they accountable? How is accountability demanded? And towards whom is a power-holder accountable? In theory, elected politicians are accountable to their electorates. Similarly, chief executive officers are accountable to their company boards and civil society organizations are accountable to their members and constituencies. In practice, however, accountability relations are complex, often weak and dependent on transparency and credible threats of sanctions. Moreover, many stakeholders may be affected by the actions of decision-makers without having the means to hold them accountable.

Accountability is a great challenge for sustainable development politics, including for the SDGs (Ocampo and Gómez-Arteaga 2016; Partzsch 2023). For global political agreements of a non-binding nature such as the 2030 Agenda, there is no enforcement mechanism like police or courts. Governments, who hold the main responsibility for SDG implementation, can be held accountable domestically by voters and civil society for how they address the SDGs, at least in democratic countries. Such political accountability is dependent on voter interest and on the extent to which the SDGs become part of national political debate, including in parliaments (Bexell and Jönsson 2022). Elections and parliamentary oversight over governmental action are forms of *vertical* accountability. This includes institutionalized mechanisms that allow citizens to hold political executives to account for their performance. Yet, opinion polls show that sustainable development is rarely at the top of voters' election issues.

Horizontal accountability is a more diverse category than vertical accountability. It can be found in both domestic and international domains. It appears when national institutions hold each other to account, for example, national supreme audit institutions in

DOI: 10.4324/9781003519560-3

This chapter has been made available under a CC-BY-NC-ND license.

12 *Essential Concepts for Implementing the SDGs*

relation to governments (Breuer and Leiniger 2021). More often, horizontal accountability is less institutionalized. It can take market-based forms, public reputational forms or peer-based forms (Grant and Keohane 2005). Market accountability relies on decisions made by investors and consumers on where to invest and which companies to buy from. This is manifested for instance when investors make decisions to divest from fossil fuels companies. Public reputational accountability can be effective if power holders care about their reputation and therefore change their behaviour. For instance, annual SDG country rankings such as the SDG Index rely on 'naming and shaming' strategies. Peer accountability comes about through mutual evaluations of organizations and experts by their counterparts. The High-level Political Forum, which is a global arena for follow-up of the SDGs, is based on such 'soft' accountability measures of peer review. Civil society and the media also have important horizontal accountability functions. Their reporting exposes the actions of power-holders to public scrutiny (Karlsson-Vinkhuyzen et al. 2018).

Several kinds of powerful actors impact the realization of the SDGs. Therefore, a variety of accountability forms is needed to accelerate goal implementation. The forms mentioned here are complementary. In the ideal case, they can reinforce each other and create a multilayered web of answerability for sustainable development. In practice, this web is weak or even missing in many contexts. Broader challenges to transparency, free media, civil society and democratic institutions across the world need to be addressed for SDG accountability to become stronger.

References

Bexell, M., and Jönsson, K. (2022). Realizing the 2030 Agenda for Sustainable Development – Engaging National Parliaments? *Policy Studies*, 43(4), 621–639. https://doi.org/10.1080/01442 872.2020.1803255

Breuer, A., and Leiniger, J. (2021). Horizontal Accountability for SDG Implementation: A Comparative Cross-National Analysis of Emerging National Accountability Regimes. *Sustainability*, 13, 7002. https://doi.org/10.3390/su13137002

Grant, R.W., and Keohane, R.O. (2005). Accountability and Abuses of Power in World Politics. *American Political Science Review*, 99(1), 29–43.

Karlsson-Vinkhuyzen, S., Dahl, A., and Persson, Å. (2018). The Emerging Accountability Regimes for the Sustainable Development Goals and Policy Integration: Friend or Foe?. *Environment and Planning C*, 36(8), 1371–1390. https://doi.org/10.1177/2399654418779995

Ocampo, J., and Gómez-Arteaga, N. (2016). Accountability in International Governance and the 2030 Development Agenda. *Global Policy*, 7(3), 305–314. https://doi.org/10.1111/1758-5899. 12322

Partzsch, L. (2023). Missing the SDGs. Political accountability for insufficient environmental action. *Global Policy*, 14, 438–450. https://doi.org/10.1111/1758-5899.13213

Anthropocene

Denis Francesconi

The term 'Anthropocene' was introduced in 2000 by chemist and Nobel Laureate Paul Crutzen and later elaborated in an article co-authored by Crutzen and biologit Eugene F. Stoermer (Crutzen and Stoermer 2000). The term is meant to signify the 'epoch of humans', a new geological period dominated by human activity (Lövbrand et al. 2015), and to explain how humans have become the leading geological force on the planet (Steffen et al. 2007).

The debate about the starting point of the Anthropocene has sparked intense discussion within geology and has extended to the social sciences and humanities. Scholars have proposed various starting points, such as the mastery of fire around 400,000 years ago, the development of agriculture between 8,000 and 5,000 years ago, the Industrial Revolution and the Atomic Age (Wallenhorst 2024). In 2023, an Anthropocene Working Group proposed Crawford Lake in Canada and the Atomic Age as the candidate site and time to mark the onset of the Anthropocene series. This proposal was rejected, however, in 2024 by the International Subcommission on Quaternary Stratigraphy in a decision that was later confirmed by the International Union of Geological Sciences. Nonetheless, many in the scientific community agree that we live in the Anthropocene, even though some suggest that the Anthropocene should be seen as an unfolding event rather than a distinct epoch or time interval with clear temporal limits (Edgeworth et al. 2024).

The idea that humans have profoundly impacted the planet, however, predates Crutzen and Stoermer's work and their notion of the Anthropocene. In the 19th century, for instance, Italian geologist Antonio Stoppani referred to the 'Anthropozoic' era to acknowledge humanity's geological influence as a 'new telluric force which in power and universality may be compared to the greater forces of earth' (Crutzen and Stoermer 2000, 17). In the 1920s and 1930s, Soviet geologist Vladimir Vernadsky developed the theory of three interconnected stages, which he labelled as the geosphere (Earth), the biosphere (life) and the noosphere (knowledge). Later, also French Jesuit Pierre Teilhard de Chardin contributed to the idea of noosphere.

The concept of a noosphere offers a different perspective on the Anthropocene and necessitates the involvement of social scientists and humanity scholars (Ellis et al. 2016). Indeed, the notion of the Anthropocene fundamentally depends on human cognition and culture, collective learning and the accumulation and distribution of knowledge, as these are primary drivers of geological, environmental and biological changes on earth. Social sciences and humanities can help reframe and decolonize the term Anthropocene, promote a new human self-awareness of our unprecedented power and usher in an era of planetary stewardship, aligning closely with the Sustainable Development Goals. Education, as expressed in SDG 4, can play a crucial role in increasing collective awareness and agency around the concept of the Anthropocene through new school curricula, educational policies and activities (White et al. 2023).

In conclusion, the Anthropocene is not only a geological or environmental phenomenon, but also a cognitive, educational and socio-political one. As suggested by SDG 17, collective actions and partnerships between academics, institutions, economy and citizens should be implemented to assure the way to planetary health, sustainable development and quality of life for all. As Crutzen and Stoermer stated,

> To develop a worldwide accepted strategy leading to the sustainability of ecosystems against human-induced stresses will be one of the great future tasks of mankind, requiring intensive research efforts and wise application of the knowledge thus acquired in the noosphere, better known as the knowledge or information society.
>
> (Crutzen and Stoermer 2000, 18)

14 *Essential Concepts for Implementing the SDGs*

References

Crutzen, P. J. and Stoermer, E. F. (2000). The 'Anthropocene', *Global Change Newsletter*, 41, 17–18.

Edgeworth, M., Bauer, A. M., Ellis, E. C., Finney, S. C., Gill, J. L., Gibbard, P. L., et al. (2024). The Anthropocene is more than a time interval. *Earth's Future*, 12, e2024EF004831. https://doi.org/10.1029/2024EF004831

Ellis, E., Maslin, M., Boivin, N., and Bauer, A. (2016). Involve social scientists in defining the Anthropocene. *Nature*, 540(7632), 192–193.

Lövbrand, E., Beck, S., Chilvers, J., Forsyth, T., Hedrén, J., Hulme, M., ... and Vasileiadou, E. (2015). Who speaks for the future of Earth? How critical social science can extend the conversation on the Anthropocene. *Global Environmental Change*, 32, 211–218.

Steffen, W, Crutzen, P.J., and McNeill, J. R. (2007). The Anthropocene: Are humans now overwhelming the great forces of nature? *AMBIO: A Journal of the Human Environment*, 36(8), 614–621. https://doi.org/10.1579/0044-7447(2007)36[614:TAAHNO]2.0.CO;2

Wallenhorst, N. (2024). Dating the dawn of the Anthropocene. *Paragrana*, 33(1), 177–190. https://doi.org/10.1515/para-2024-0014

White, P. J., Ardoin, N. M., Eames, C., and Monroe, M. C. (2023). Agency in the Anthropocene: Supporting document to the PISA 2025 Science Framework. *OECD Education Working Papers*, No. 297, OECD Publishing. https://doi.org/10.1787/8d3b6cfa-en

Artificial intelligence

Noémi Bontridder and Yi hyun Kang

There is no universally agreed definition of artificial intelligence (AI) in the United Nations. AI was originally described as a field in computer science that investigates methods to make machines simulate intelligent behaviour (McCarthy et al. 2006). Current discussions on AI in international and regional organizations (for example, Organisation for Economic Cooperation and Development 2024; Regulation [EU] 2024/1689 2024) refer more specifically to machine-based systems that are configured to compute, based on data they receive, how to generate outputs such as predictions, content or recommendations.

While discussions on AI in the United Nations system have raised ethical concerns, they have tended to highlight its potential to contribute positively to achieving the Sustainable Development Goals (SDGs). Since 2017, the International Telecommunication Union has run a digital platform with information on AI solutions for the SDGs, called 'AI for Good'. Key United Nations documents have emphasized the importance of 'safe, secure and trustworthy' AI that can contribute to humanity, as well as cooperation towards benefit-sharing. For example, the United Nations General Assembly adopted in 2024 a resolution on seizing the opportunities of AI systems to achieve all 17 SDGs (United Nations 2024a). Likewise, the Global Digital Compact, adopted at the 2024 Summit of the Future, pays attention to AI by setting the strengthening of international governance of AI 'for the benefit of humanity' as its fifth objective (United Nations 2024b).

International institutions mandated to govern AI technologies are still at an early stage as of 2024. The United Nations Secretary-General's High-level Advisory Body on AI was formed in 2023. Based on its report, the Summit of the Future agreed to establish a multidisciplinary Independent International Scientific Panel on AI in the United Nations to promote scientific assessments of the impacts, risks and opportunities of AI. They also agreed to launch a Global Dialogue on AI Governance that will involve governments and stakeholders (United Nations 2024b). The development of these institutions, however, remains to be seen.

The impact of AI on sustainable development is multifaceted, and deliberative approaches are needed when discussing the potential of AI to help achieve SDGs. While AI may be used to achieve some SDG targets, negative impacts are also predicted. For example, AI may facilitate the eradication of extreme poverty (SDG target 1.1) if satellite data is used to track areas of poverty and foster international cooperation. At the same time, AI may exacerbate poverty by increasing inequalities (Vinuesa et al. 2020). Furthermore, the potential benefits of using AI to achieve SDG targets may come at the cost of inhibiting the overall achievement of the 2030 Agenda, not least due to the high consumption of natural resources and energy associated with the development and use of AI (Crawford 2021). In this context, it is important to note that AI is often linked to economic interests by industry and political actors. The apparent high profitability of the technology may hinder balanced discussions among stakeholders, making it essential to encourage the assessment of the legal and ethical implications of AI technologies, including societal and environmental ones. Indeed, policymakers need a good understanding of the challenges posed by AI to formulate sound and effective policies (Vinuesa et al. 2020).

In conclusion, AI has rapidly become a significant topic in sustainable development discussions, and the United Nations has begun to take the first steps to ensure the governance of AI 'for the benefit of humanity' (United Nations 2024b). Yet given the apparent high profitability of AI and the debate's focus on its positive impact on SDG achievement, policymakers must also not overlook to assess the negative impacts of its development and use on sustainable development.

References

Crawford, K. (2021). *Atlas of AI: Power, Politics and the Planetary Costs of Artificial Intelligence*. Yale University Press.

McCarthy, J., Minsky, M. L., Rochester, N., and Shannon, C. E. (2006). A proposal for the Dartmouth Summer Research Project on Artificial Intelligence, August 31, 1955. *AI Magazine*, 27(4), 12. https://doi.org/10.1609/aimag.v27i4.1904

Organisation for Economic Cooperation and Development. (2024). Recommendation of the Council on Artificial Intelligence (Adopted 22/05/2019, Amended 03/05/2024). https://legalinstruments.oecd.org/en/instruments/OECD-LEGAL-0449

Regulation (EU) 2024/1689. (2024). Regulation (EU) 2024/1689 of the European Parliament and of the Council of 13 June 2024 laying down harmonized rules on artificial intelligence and amending Regulations (EC) No 300/2008, (EU) No 167/2013, (EU) No 168/2013, (EU) 2018/858, (EU) 2018/1139 and (EU) 2019/2144 and Directives 2014/90/EU, (EU) 2016/797 and (EU) 2020/1828 (Artificial Intelligence Act). European Parliament and Council. http://data.europa.eu/eli/reg/2024/1689/oj

United Nations. (2024a). Seizing the opportunities of safe, secure and trustworthy artificial intelligence systems for sustainable development [Resolution A/RES/78/265]. https://digitallibrary.un.org/record/4043244?ln=fr&v=pdf

United Nations. (2024b). Summit of the Future outcome documents: Pact for the Future, Global Digital Compact and Declaration on Future Generations. United Nations. https://www.un.org/sites/un2.un.org/files/sotf-pact_for_the_future_adopted.pdf

Vinuesa, R., Azizpour, H., Leite, I., Balaam, M., Dignum, V., Domisch, S., Felländer, A., Langhans, S. D., Tegmark, M., and Fuso Nerini, F. (2020). The role of artificial intelligence in achieving the Sustainable Development Goals. *Nature Communications*, 11(1), 233. https://doi.org/10.1038/s41467-019-14108-y

B

Brundtland Report

Rosalind Warner

The Brundtland Report, officially titled 'Our Common Future', is one of the most cited documents in the burgeoning sustainable development literature and sparked debate on issues that continue to this day. The report was the outcome of a four-year deliberation by the United Nations' World Commission on Environment and Development, an international group of environmental experts, politicians and civil servants. Named after Gro Harlem Brundtland, a former Prime Minister of Norway, the Commission was established to identify an international agenda for cooperation on environment and development, and its final report was published in 1987.

The decades following the post-World War II economic boom had brought a growing awareness that economic growth could breach the capacity of natural systems to sustain it (Meadows & Club of Rome 1972). It was increasingly recognized that environmental scarcity could threaten progress on poverty reduction that might be realized through global development efforts. The task of the commission, therefore, was to find ways of balancing concerns over economic development with increasingly severe environmental challenges like deforestation, desertification and climate change while taking the social dimension into account. Such a development would be sustainable, the report argued, with the vision to 'meet the needs of the present without compromising the ability of future generations to meet their own needs' (World Commission on Environment and Development 1987, 16).

The report highlighted the importance of public participation, called for reformed government policies and set a renewed focus on multilateralism and global governance. The report placed emphasis on the need for social equity to reduce poverty, both for moral reasons and to prevent poverty-driven environmental degradation. These insights helped develop the concept of sustainable development as a framework for balancing economic growth, social equity and environmental protection, later institutionalized as the three 'pillars' of economy, society and environment (Purvis et al. 2019; Daly 1996). The report made several policy recommendations to achieve sustainable development. It recommended assistance for developing countries in the form of aid, debt relief and fair trade. It advocated for industry to transition to clean energy sources to produce more with less of an environmental impact. It noted how environmental degradation

DOI: 10.4324/9781003519560-4

This chapter has been made available under a CC-BY-NC-ND license.

contributes to conflict and instability and recommended reallocating resources for sustainable development to reduce the need for military spending.

The influence of the report was evident in the formulation of Agenda 21, adopted at the 1992 United Nations Conference on Environment and Development, also known as the Earth Summit, in Rio de Janeiro and later in the Sustainable Development Goals (SDGs) adopted as part of the 2030 Agenda. Its publication inspired a wave of interest in a wide variety of fields, including but not limited to international development, environmental and ecological sciences, sustainability, finance, management, technology and urban studies (Schubert and Láng 2005). Over the 1990s, contestation over the concepts defined in the Brundtland Report resulted in the term 'sustainability' gaining traction over 'sustainable development', leading some critics to decry the tendency for an overly flexible definition to provide cover for a lack of credible action.

Critics also noted the contradictions between renewed calls for economic growth with enhanced levels of ecological conservation and the inattention to the actors and institutions supporting unsustainable development (Sneddon et al. 2006). Other scholars claimed that the notion of sustainable development was little more than a new means to impose a colonial structure upon developing nations (Redclift 1987), reinforcing efforts to prevent poor nations from getting themselves out of poverty using natural resources.

References

Daly, H. E. (1996). *Beyond Growth: The Economics of Sustainable Development*. Beacon Press, Boston.

Meadows, D. H., and Club of Rome. (1972). *The Limits to Growth; A Report for the Club of Rome's Project on the Predicament of Mankind*. Universe Books, New York.

Purvis, B., Mao, Y., and Robinson, D. (2019). Three pillars of sustainability: In search of conceptual origins. *Sustainability Science*, 14(3), 681–695. https://doi.org/10.1007/s11625-018-0627-5

Redclift, M. R. (1987). *Sustainable Development: Exploring the Contradictions*. Routledge, London.

Schubert, A., and Láng, I. (2005). The literature aftermath of the Brundtland report 'Our Common Future'. A scientometric study based on citations in science and social science journals. *Environment, Development and Sustainability*, 7(1), 1–8. https://doi.org/10.1007/s10668-003-0177-5

Sneddon, C., Howarth, R. B., and Norgaard, R. B. (2006). Sustainable development in a post-Brundtland world. *Ecological Economics*, 57(2), 253–268. https://doi.org/10.1016/j.ecolecon.2005.04.013

World Commission on Environment and Development. (1987). *Report of the World Commission on Environment and Development: Our Common Future*. United Nations.

Budgeting for Sustainable Development

Elisabeth Hege

As the primary political and economic expression of governmental policy, the budgeting process is highly relevant for national SDG implementation. Several countries mention efforts to align their national budgets with the SDGs in their Voluntary National Reviews (Hege et al. 2019; Okitasari and Kandpal 2022). Budgeting for the SDGs includes practices that use SDG goals or indicators in budget planning, formulation and debate, or

18 *Essential Concepts for Implementing the SDGs*

monitoring and evaluation. SDG budgeting is expected to improve policy coherence, transparency, accountability and international comparability (Hege et al. 2019).

Since 2015, different SDG budgeting practices have emerged, intervening at different steps of the budgetary cycle (Poghosyan et al. 2022). Ex ante, SDGs can be integrated into budget strategic planning when countries translate goals and indicators into national priorities. A gap analysis or an SDG costing exercise to identify SDG funding and implementation gaps can feed into strategy. Furthermore, SDGs can also be used in budget formulation, when, for instance, ministries signal links between their budget proposal and the achievement of sustainable development priorities. In Finland, for example, the Ministry of Finance requested that each ministry include a short paragraph under each of the main titles in their budget proposal explaining how it will contribute to sustainable development (Hege et al. 2019; Montero 2024). Little evidence exists on the systematic consideration of SDGs during budget hearings (Hege et al. 2019).

Most empirical examples use SDGs ex post, meaning after strategic planning and decision-making. The most common practice is the so-called SDG Budget Tagging (Poghosyan et al. 2022). This means mapping or tracking expenditures against SDGs at either goal or indicator level, sometimes using automatic text analysis tools (Guariso et al. 2023). SDGs can also be used in budget performance evaluations, as initiated by Mexico or can be the basis of a spending review, as in Germany (Hege et al. 2019).

Finally, looking at budget oversight, several Supreme Audit Institutions have provided analyses based on the SDGs, such as in Austria, the Netherlands and Germany. For instance, the German Federal Court of Audit has recommended anchoring the principle of sustainability in all steps of the budgetary cycle and using SDGs in prior impact assessments of subsidies. In practice, however, countries rarely use the SDGs in budget-making to ensure that the proposed budget seeks the best outcome for the goals. They rather use the SDGs as a tool to provide an ex-post overview of contributions to sustainable development.

Globally, budgeting for SDGs is not widespread and rarely mainstreamed into the whole budget cycle (Poghosyan et al. 2022). A review of 74 countries in 2023 showed that 13 out of them had integrated the SDGs into national budgets (Sachs et al. 2023). SDG budgeting methods exist across countries of different income levels. They are not limited to developing countries where SDG budgeting is often part of efforts to establish an Integrated National Financing Framework – a tool to finance national sustainable development strategies, as it is the case in Ghana (Barchiche et al. 2023). Empirical examples also exist at local levels, for instance in the cities of Strasbourg, Malmö and Castilla y Léon (Okitasari and Kandpal 2022).

SDG budgeting methods can be administratively heavy and costly to put in place given the complexity of the SDG indicator framework and the need for coordination across ministries (Guariso et al. 2023). Most of the empirical examples seem to improve transparency with regard to budget allocations and expenditures in relation to sustainable development priorities. However, whether this information increases accountability, or even strategic budgetary decision-making, depends on how this information is used by actors seeking accountability, such as parliamentarians or civil society and by decision-makers. Further research is needed to more systematically assess the impact of budgeting practices on accelerating progress in SDG implementation, also drawing on lessons learnt from similar efforts to integrate social and environmental priorities within budgetary processes (for example, gender budgeting and green budgeting).

References

Barchiche, D., Dufief, E., Lobos, I., Keijzer, N., and Marbuah, G. (2023). *Financing Sustainable Development: Insights from Ghana, Indonesia, Mexico and Senegal*. IDDRI.

Guariso, D., Guerrero, O. A., and Castañeda, G. (2023). Automatic SDG budget tagging: Building public financial management capacity through natural language processing. *Data and Policy*, 5, e31.

Hege, E., Brimont, L., and Pagnon, F. (2019). Sustainable development goals and indicators: can they be tools to make national budgets more sustainable?. *Public Sector Economics*, 43(4), 423–444.

Montero, A. G. (2024). *UN DESA Policy Brief No. 164: The Integrated Nature of the Sustainable Development Goals as a Lever for Trust, Institutional Resilience and Innovation*. UN DESA.

Okitasari, M., and Kandpal, R. (2022). *Budgeting for the SDGs: Lessons from the 2021 Voluntary National Reviews*. United Nations University.

Poghosyan, S., Wescott, C., Middlebrook, P., Ishtiaq, N., and Péteri, G. (2022). *Budgeting for the Sustainable Development Goals. A Modular UNDP Handbook*. United Nations Development Programme.

Sachs, J., et al. (2023). *Sustainable Development Report 2023: Implementing the SDG Stimulus*. SDSN/Dublin University Press.

Business sector

Janis Bragan Balda

The United Nations in its guidelines on cooperation with the business sector describes the sector as 'either for-profit and commercial enterprises or businesses; or business associations and coalitions (cross-industry, multi-issue groups; cross industry, issue-specific initiatives; industry-focused initiative)' and includes corporate philanthropic foundations (United Nations 2015, 3). The two guiding documents for business are the United Nations Global Compact and the United Nations Guiding Principles on Business and Human Rights, known as the Ruggie Principles.

The Ten Principles of the Global Compact ask companies to embrace, support and enact a set of core values addressing human rights, labour standards, the environment and anti-corruption. Within the Guiding Principles, corporate responsibility to respect human rights refers to having in place policies and processes appropriate to the size and circumstances of each enterprise, in addition to carrying out human rights due diligence. Though often used interchangeably, the term 'private sector' is a broader concept consisting of organizations, not under direct government control and ownership, including businesses of various sizes and scopes, as well as civil society, which includes not-for-profits such as advocacy groups, charities, philanthropists, social enterprise, endowments and impact investors (Hickmann et al. 2024).

Business-led multi-stakeholder collaborations, including partnerships, existed before the adoption of the 2030 Agenda, but since the launch of the SDGs, the role of business has become larger. The strengths the sector brings include knowledge, financial resources and innovation capabilities. In particular, the business sector is considered essential to bridging the SDG (finance) implementation gap (Hickmann et al. 2024). As noted in the 2030 Agenda, private business activity, investment and innovation are major drivers of productivity, inclusive economic growth and job creation (Article 67).

20 *Essential Concepts for Implementing the SDGs*

While expected to bring creativity and innovation to solving sustainable development challenges, there has not been a rapid and broad adoption of the SDGs by businesses. Not surprisingly, businesses have tended to address those SDGs most in line with their business purpose and strategy. The result is that the Agenda's core principle of 'leave no one behind' is frequently neglected (Stanberry and Balda 2023). While various frameworks have been developed to align business activity with the SDGs, clarity and consistency on what SDG alignment looks like is often missing (Sachs and Sachs 2021). A major weakness is the inability of the business sector to scale up and broaden possible solutions to the grand challenges represented by the SDGs.

There is increasing consensus that 'a much deeper, faster and more ambitious response [is needed] to unleash the social and economic transformation needed to achieve our 2030 goals' (United Nations Department of Economic and Social Affairs 2019, 2). The business sector itself must engage more extensively and effectively to increase coherence and collaboration and seek transformative change in terms of business models to bring them into alignment with natural and social realities (Waddock 2020). Going beyond business-as-usual involves interdisciplinary work, which incorporates knowledge and learning from the social-ecological systems approach to corporate sustainability (van Zanten and van Tulder 2021).

At the same time, transformation of the context within which business operates, including the public policy environment and private governance structures and processes, need to enable more effective and collaborative arrangements within which business can align itself. To do so requires a different core purpose beyond economic growth and higher GDP and conceptualizing sustainability differently (Dahlmann 2024). Use of other indices, such as the Human Development Index and the measurement of contributing factors from business, would initiate new practices and processes, serve the SDGs better and at the same time limit 'SDG washing' by the business sector.

References

Dahlmann, F. (2024). Conceptualising sustainability as the pursuit of life. *Journal of Business Ethics*. https://doi.org/10.1007/s10551-024-05617-y

Hickmann, T., Biermann, F., Sénit, C.-A., Sun, Y., Bexell, M., Bolton, M., ... Weiland, S. (2024). Scoping article: Research frontiers on the governance of the Sustainable Development Goals. *Global Sustainability*, 7, e7. https://doi.org/10.1017/sus.2024.4

Sachs, J. D., and Sachs, L. E. (2021). Business alignment for the 'decade of action'. *Journal of International Business Policy*, 4(1), 22–27.

Stanberry, J., and Balda, J.B. (2023). A conceptual review of SDG 17: Picturing politics, proximity and progress. *Journal of Tropical Futures: Sustainable Business, Governance and Development*, 1(1). https://doi.org/10.1177/27538931231170509

United Nations. (2015). *Guidelines on a principle-based approach to the cooperation between the United Nations and the business sector*. https://www.un.org/en/ethics/assets/pdfs/Guidelines-on-Cooperation-with-the-Business-Sector.pdf

United Nations Department of Economic and Social Affairs. (2019). *Global reporting initiative/United Nations global compact – Integrating the SDGs into corporate reporting: A practical guide*.https://sdgs.un.org/documents/griun-global-compact-integrating-sdgs-corporate-reporting-practical-guide-34073

van Zanten, J. A., and van Tulder, R. (2021). Improving companies' impacts on sustainable development: A nexus approach to the SDGS. *Business Strategy and the Environment*, 30(8), 3703–3720. https://doi.org/10.1002/bse.2835

Waddock, S. (2020). Achieving sustainability requires systemic business transformation. *Global Sustainability*, 3(e12), 1–12. https://doi.org/10.1017/sus.2020.9

C

Civil society

Carole-Anne Sénit

Civil society was integral to the development of the 2030 Agenda (Sénit 2017) and has been actively involved in efforts to achieve the Sustainable Development Goals (SDGs) at all governance levels since their adoption in 2015. As progress reports highlight that most goals and targets will be missed by far (for example, United Nations 2023), civil society is increasingly perceived as a crucial actor able to turn the tide of SDG implementation.

Civil society generally consists of a political space separate from both state and economy, where voluntary associations explicitly seek to shape the rules – including specific policies, wider norms and deeper social structures – that govern one or the other aspect of social life (Scholte 2002). Far from being a homogeneous whole, civil society constitutes a diverse array of actors with contending visions and interests about which strategies and development pathways should be pursued. In this entry, civil society is understood as progressive non-profit and voluntary groups representing specific causes or constituencies that organize themselves at local, national or global levels in the field of sustainable development. Those groups include actors such as NGOs operating within the developmental and environmental fields, social movements, civic associations and citizens who voice their political preferences through their demonstrations, votes and donations.

Civil society actors participate in the implementation of the 2030 Agenda and the SDGs in several ways (Órdoñez Llanos et al. 2022). First, they play a role in influencing agenda-setting and policy processes on sustainable development at national and subnational levels. By raising awareness, sharing information and providing their expertise on a specific issue or cause related to one or the other SDGs, civil society seeks to influence public and private actors in defining their strategy for sustainable development and in setting priorities for SDG realization. Second, civil society actors contribute to localizing the SDGs and mobilizing people's participation in their implementation. Here, civil society collaborates with public and private actors within projects that steer progression towards goals and targets. Third, civil society plays a key role in monitoring progress, by using the SDG indicator framework, to ensure the accountability of public and corporate actors in achieving the SDGs. Civil society also demands accountability by organizing campaigns or protests that condemn the lack of progress on SDGs and by producing their own evaluations of SDG implementation, so-called shadow reports.

DOI: 10.4324/9781003519560-5

This chapter has been made available under a CC-BY-NC-ND license.

22 *Essential Concepts for Implementing the SDGs*

However, civil society's capacity to act as a powerful game changer in SDG implementation is constrained by several factors. First, civil society engaging in SDG implementation lacks diversity. As important information on the goals does not seem to trickle down to civil society organizations in remote areas (for example, Al Sabbagh and Copeland 2019), country-level goal implementation and monitoring often leave out local or grassroot organizations that could be powerful change agents, such as cooperatives or village associations. Second, civil society often lacks human and financial resources, with uncertainty over funding sources further affecting the roles of civil society actors in SDG implementation (for example, Arhin 2016). Finally, in many countries, trends of autocratization shrink civic space and shift priorities away from sustainable development to security, thus limiting the transformative potential of civil society in SDG implementation (Hossain et al. 2019).

Civil society increasingly participates in SDG implementation, taking on different roles in agenda-setting, implementation and monitoring of the goals and targets. However, civil society's capacity to act as a game changer for SDG implementation is limited by a series of internal and external factors. This calls for future research that systematically analyses those factors and identifies key conditions of transformative civil society impact for SDG implementation.

References

Al Sabbagh, S., and Copeland, E. (2019). Partnering for sustainable development: Case study of a 10-year donor–recipient partnership. *Development in Practice*, 29(5), 651–661. https://doi.org/10.1080/09614524.2019.1601161

Arhin, A. (2016). Advancing post-2015 SDGs in a changing development landscape: Challenges of NGOs in Ghana. *Development in Practice*, 26(5), 555–568.

Hossain, N., Khurana, N., Nazneen, S., Oosterom, M., Schröder, P., and Shankland, A. (2019). *Development Needs Civil Society – The Implications of Civic Space for the Sustainable Development Goals*. Institute of Development Studies and ACT Alliance. https://hdl.handle.net/20.500.12413/14541

Órdoñez Llanos, A., Raven, R., Bexell, M., Botchwey, B., Bornemann, B., Censoro, J., ... Yunita, A. (2022). Implementation at multiple levels. In F. Biermann, T. Hickmann, and C. A. Sénit (Eds.), *The Political Impact of the Sustainable Development Goals: Transforming Governance Through Global Goals?* (pp. 59–91). Cambridge University Press.

Scholte, J. A. (2002). Civil society and democracy in global governance. *Global Governance*, 8(3), 281–304. https://doi.org/10.1163/19426720-00803004

Sénit, C. A. (2017). *Taking Democracy to the Next Level? Global Civil Society Participation in the Shaping of the Sustainable Development Goals from Rio to New York (2012–2015)*. Utrecht University. https://dspace.library.uu.nl/bitstream/handle/1874/358322/S_nit.pdf?sequence=1

United Nations. (2023). *The Sustainable Development Goals Report 2023: Special Edition. Towards a Rescue Plan for People and Planet*. United Nations. https://unstats.un.org/sdgs/report/2023/

Climate change and sustainable development

Shrijana Vaidya, Jing Li and Prajal Pradhan

In 2015, the Paris Agreement to the United Nations Framework Convention on Climate Change was signed to combat climate change, adapt to its adverse effects and provide greater support to developing countries. In the same year, the United Nations adopted the

2030 Agenda for Sustainable Development with 17 Sustainable Development Goals (SDGs), including a goal of climate action (SDG 13). The Sixth Assessment Report of the Intergovernmental Panel on Climate Change (2022) recognizes the set of 17 SDGs as valuable in moving beyond a narrow focus on separate climate mitigation and adaptation options, emphasizing instead the need to act on the climate and sustainable development agendas together.

However, both agendas were developed and implemented independently, leading often to fragmented policy outcomes and limited opportunities to explore linkages (Dzebo et al. 2019). Reconciling the climate and sustainable development agendas is crucial to overcoming their challenges, offering win-win solutions while minimizing trade-offs and supporting transitioning to zero-emissions and climate-resilient sustainable development (Pradhan et al. 2024).

The links between climate impacts, climate actions and sustainable development are manifold. There is substantial research on how the actions of the Paris Agreement and the 2030 Agenda are interconnected. For instance, research shows that progress on SDG 7 (on affordable and clean energy) and SDG 13 (on climate action) could catalyze synergies with other goals. The evidence indicates that while climate change threatens most SDGs, climate change mitigation and adaptation can also undermine the achievement of some SDGs (Fuso Nerini et al. 2019). For example, the negative impacts of climate change on agricultural production have a major implication that can undermine efforts to reduce poverty and hunger (Intergovernmental Panel on Climate Change 2022).

Researchers also indicate that stringent climate change mitigation policies might slow down efforts to reduce poverty in developing countries (Campagnolo and Davide 2019). Many policies on climate change adaptation, however, positively affect the implementation of the SDGs. However, maladaptation and unintended negative consequences of adaptation negatively affect some SDGs, for example, increased land, water and biomass competition (Intergovernmental Panel on Climate Change 2022). The SDGs provide an opportunity to revisit the climate impacts and climate actions and to identify strategies to leverage their synergies and tackle trade-offs in a wider sustainability context.

It is widely recognized that creating synergies and reducing fragmentation between climate action and sustainable development is urgently needed. Still, challenges remain in achieving this coherence effectively. While mitigation and adaptation activities in the Nationally Determined Contributions of countries are linked to all 17 SDGs, most are not harmonized with other domestic policies (Hermwille et al. 2023). Addressing these critical agendas requires therefore to break down silos, fostering synergistic approaches that maximize benefits while minimizing trade-offs. To this end, deep transformations are needed across various sectors, including energy, buildings, transportation, agriculture, forestry and other land-use areas (United Nations 2024).

Challenges persist due to insufficient and ineffective investment in aligning climate action with sustainable development, as the international financial system is not structured to support this alignment. Countries in the Global South, particularly those particularly vulnerable to climate impacts, continue to face inadequate funding for climate-related challenges and sustainable development. While international agencies have tried to align climate finance with SDGs, such as the Integrated National Financing Frameworks, the implementation of the Paris Agreement and the SDGs still progresses in a fragmented manner. More systematic approaches are thus urgently needed to address the gaps across sectors, policy frameworks and future investments.

References

Campagnolo, L., and Davide, M. (2019). Can the Paris deal boost SDGs achievement? An assessment of climate mitigation co-benefits or side-effects on poverty and inequality. *World Development*, 122, 96–109. https://doi.org/10.1016/j.worlddev.2019.05.015

Dzebo, A., Janetschek, H., Brandi, C., and Iacobuta, G. (2019). Connections between the Paris Agreement and the 2030 Agenda: The case for policy coherence. *SEI Working Paper*, Stockholm Environment Institute, Stockholm.

Fuso Nerini, F., Sovacool, B., Hughes, N., Cozzi, L., Cosgrave, E., Howells, M., Tavoni, M., Tomei, J., Zerriffi, H., and Milligan, B. (2019). Connecting climate action with other Sustainable Development Goals. *Nature Sustainability*, 2(8), 674–680.

Hermwille, L., Dzebo, A., Iacobuță, G. I., and Obergassel, W. (2023). Global stocktake and the SDG midterm review as opportunities for integration. *Nature Climate Change*, 13(10), 1002–1004.

Intergovernmental Panel on Climate Change. (2022). Summary for policymakers. In H.-O. Pörtner, D.C. Roberts, M. Tignor, E.S. Poloczanska, K. Mintenbeck, A. Alegría, M. Craig, S. Langsdorf, S. Löschke, V. Möller, A. Okem, and B. Rama (Eds.), *Climate Change 2022: Impacts, Adaptation and Vulnerability. Contribution of Working Group II to the Sixth Assessment Report of the Intergovernmental Panel on Climate Change* (pp. 3–34). Cambridge University Press.

Pradhan, P., Weitz, N., Daioglou, V., et al. (2024). Three foci at the science-policy interface for systemic Sustainable Development Goal acceleration. *Nature Communications*, 15, 8600. https://doi.org/10.1038/s41467-024-52926-x

United Nations. (2024). Synergy solutions for climate and SDG action: Bridging the ambition gap for the future we want. United Nations. https://sdgs.un.org/basic-page/synergy-solutions-climate-and-sdg-action-bridging-ambition-gap-future-we-want-56115

Climate finance

Yuen Gu and Yixian Sun

The establishment of the United Nations Framework Convention on Climate Change in 1992 laid the foundation for climate finance. A broad definition of climate finance includes 'local, national or transnational financing, drawn from public, private and alternative sources of financing, that seeks to support mitigation and adaptation actions to address climate change' (UNFCCC 2022). But in practice, different actors and organizations have used their own definitions to classify climate finance. As a result, debates remain on the boundary between narrow official climate finance and broad climate investments and whether climate finance should be considered new and additional funds rather than finance from existing official development assistance.

Climate finance has been widely considered as an important tool for achieving the SDGs. From a mitigation perspective, by supporting low-carbon technologies (for example, renewable energy), climate finance can drive progress in reducing carbon emissions, contributing to SDG 7 (affordable and clean energy) and SDG 13 (climate action), but also other goals such as SDGs 8 (decent work and economic growth), 9 (industry, innovation and infrastructure), 14 (life below water) and 15 (life on land). For example, the Lake Turkana wind farm in Kenya, supported by the African Development Bank, provides 310 megawatts of clean energy (Michaelowa et al. 2020). In addition, from an adaptation perspective, climate finance can provide national and local governments with resources to cope with growing climate impacts. Examples include a range of projects across the globe such as the development of climate-resilient crops, natural flood control systems, water conservation and mangrove protection. In addition to SDG 13, these projects can make a positive impact on multiple other SDGs, including SDG 2 on food security, SDG 3 on health and SDG 11 on cities and communities (UNDRR 2024).

While climate finance has the potential to significantly achieve synergies among the SDGs, improper use of funds can hinder the realization of such co-benefits. According to Savvidou et al. (2021), between 2014 and 2018, approximately 65% of climate finance (USD 30.6 billion) was allocated to mitigation in Africa, while only 35% (USD 16.5 billion) was directed towards adaptation. This is mainly because developed countries are more interested in funding mitigation projects worldwide for reducing global emissions but less inclined to support adaptation projects that would bring more benefits to host countries in the Global South (Khan et al. 2019). This imbalance in climate finance allocation has prevented developing countries vulnerable to climate change from taking necessary actions to implement the 2030 Agenda and subsequently further exacerbated global inequality (Khan et al. 2019). Ultimately, developing countries having limited resources are likely to suffer more from the impacts of climate change and further off track from the achievement of the SDGs.

Transparency and accountability are key issues that affect the effectiveness of climate finance. For example, corruption in the forestry sector can prevent the appropriate allocation of international funds provided to a certain country for forest protection. Information disclosure alone cannot solve the complex challenges in the allocation and implementation of many climate finance projects. Hence, stronger governance and accountability mechanisms are needed to ensure appropriate use of funds for the benefit of the public and people who are impacted by relevant projects (Tirpak et al. 2014). More efforts are also needed to achieve a fair distribution of mitigation and adaptation finance to better pursue co-benefits among the SDGs. Stronger monitoring mechanisms of capital flows and evaluate them against the Paris goals will help developing countries better access and use climate finance for sustainability transition (Weikmans and Roberts 2017). Finally, the private sector's contributions should be encouraged to attract more capital for climate action and harnessing its synergies with other SDGs.

In conclusion, ensuring the effective use of climate finance is important for achieving the SDGs. By improving transparency and addressing imbalances in financial allocation, climate finance can better promote sustainable development and strengthen resilience to climate impacts.

References

Khan, M., Robinson, S., Weikmans, R., Ciplet, D., and Roberts, J. T. (2019). Twenty-five years of adaptation finance through a climate justice lens. *Climatic Change, 161*, 251–269. https://doi.org/10.1007/s10584-019-02563-x

Michaelowa, A., Hoch, S., Weber, A.-K., Kassaye, R., and Hailu, T. (2020). Mobilising private climate finance for sustainable energy access and climate change mitigation in Sub-Saharan Africa. *Climate Policy*, 1–16. https://doi.org/10.1080/14693062.2020.1796568

Savvidou, G., Atteridge, A., Omari-Motsumi, K., and Trisos, C. H. (2021). Quantifying international public finance for climate change adaptation in Africa. *Climate Policy, 21*(8), 1020–1036. https://doi.org/10.1080/14693062.2021.1978053

Tirpak, D., Brown, L. H., and Ballesteros, A. (2014). *Monitoring climate finance in developing countries: Challenges and next steps*. World Resources Institute. https://www.wri.org/publication/monitoring-climate-finance-developing-countries-challenges-and-next-steps

UNDRR. (2024). *Guide for adaptation and resilience finance*. Undrr.org. https://www.undrr.org/publication/guide-adaptation-and-resilience-finance

UNFCCC. (2022). *Introduction to climate finance.* Unfccc.int. https://unfccc.int/topics/introduction-to-climate-finance. Last accessed 15 November 2024.

Weikmans, R., and Roberts, J. T. (2017). The international climate finance accounting muddle: is there hope on the horizon? *Climate and Development, 11*(2), 97–111. https://doi.org/10.1080/17565529.2017.1410087

Commission on Sustainable Development (CSD)

Pamela Chasek

The Commission on Sustainable Development (CSD) was the first United Nations body to institutionally link environment and development. Agenda 21, the outcome document of the 1992 United Nations Conference on Environment and Development, also known as the Earth Summit, called for the creation of the CSD, as a subsidiary body of the United Nations Economic and Social Council to ensure effective follow-up of the Earth Summit, enhance international cooperation and examine progress in the implementation of Agenda 21 at the local, national, regional and global levels. In 1992, the United Nations established the CSD's terms of reference and composition, organization of work, relationship with other United Nations bodies, Secretariat arrangements and guidelines for the participation of Major Groups (United Nations General Assembly 1992). Fifty-three countries were elected to the CSD. Other United Nations Member States, intergovernmental organizations and Major Groups could attend as observers. The CSD held its first substantive session in June 1993 and convened annually at the United Nations Headquarters for 20 years.

During its first five years, the CSD systematically reviewed the implementation of all chapters of Agenda 21. The second five-year programme of work was organized around sectoral, cross-sectoral and economic thematic issues: industry, strategic approaches to freshwater management and technology transfer, capacity-building, education, science and awareness raising; tourism, oceans and seas and consumption and production patterns; sustainable agriculture and land management, integrated planning and management of land resources and financial resources, trade and investment and economic growth; and energy and transport, atmosphere and energy and information for decision-making and participation and international cooperation for an enabling environment (Chasek et al. 2013).

Following the 1994 United Nations Conference on the Sustainable Development of Small Island Developing States, the CSD was given the responsibility to follow-up on the implementation of the Barbados Programme of Action for the Sustainable Development of Small Island Developing States and review progress in the context of the CSD's Multi-Year Thematic Programme of Work (Chasek et al. 2013).

After the World Summit on Sustainable Development in 2002, the CSD was given the responsibility of providing policy guidance to follow-up on the Johannesburg Plan of Implementation. This plan reaffirmed that the CSD was the high-level forum for sustainable development within the United Nations system. Thus, the CSD's mandate was to coordinate the activities of other United Nations bodies as they relate to issues of sustainable development, analyse progress at the national, regional and international levels towards realizing Agenda 21 and the Johannesburg Plan of Implementation (United Nations General Assembly 2003). In response, in 2003 the Commission adopted a new multi-year programme of work to be organized as a series of two-year implementation cycles. Each cycle consisted of a Review Session and a Policy Session and considered both a thematic cluster of issues and cross-cutting ones. The CSD 12 and 13 cycle adopted recommendations to address water, sanitation and human settlements. CSD 14 and 15 considered energy, industrial development, air pollution/atmosphere and climate change but did not reach agreement on any recommendations. The CSD 16 and 17 cycle adopted recommendations related to drought, desertification, agriculture, land, rural development and Africa. The CSD 18 and 19 cycle focused on the thematic cluster of transport, chemicals, waste management, mining and sustainable consumption and production, but was also unable to adopt any recommendations (Chasek et al. 2013).

By the time of the 2012 United Nations Conference on Sustainable Development (Rio+20), the CSD was seen as a largely ineffective body (Chasek 2000; Kaasa 2007). Rio+20 called for the United Nations General Assembly to create a High-level Political Forum on Sustainable Development to replace the CSD as the main forum for sustainable development issues within the United Nations (United Nations General Assembly 2013). The High-level Political Forum was created to overcome the CSD's perceived institutional weaknesses. The CSD never carried much political weight as a 53-member body under the United Nations Economic and Social Council. The High-level Political Forum, instead, has universal membership and meets every four years at the heads of state level at the United Nations General Assembly.

References

Chasek, P. (2000). The United Nations Commission on Sustainable Development: The First Five Years. In *The Global Environment in the 21st Century: Prospects for International Cooperation* (editor). Tokyo: UNU Press.

Chasek, P., Leone, F., and Offerdahl, K. (2013). Summary of the First Meeting of the High-level Political Forum on Sustainable Development: 24 September 2013. *Earth Negotiations Bulletin*, 33(1). https://enb.iisd.org/events/final-session-un-csd-and-hlpf-inaugural-session/summary-report-24-september-2013

Kaasa, S. M. (2007). The UN Commission on Sustainable Development: Which Mechanisms Explain Its Accomplishments? *Global Environmental Politics*, 7(3): 107–129. https://doi.org/10.1162/glep.2007.7.3.107

United Nations General Assembly. (1992). *Institutional Arrangements to Follow Up the United Nations Conference on Environment and Development*. Resolution 47/191. https://undocs.org/A/RES/47/191

United Nations General Assembly. (2003). World Summit on Sustainable Development. Resolution 57/253. https://undocs.org/A/RES/57/253

United Nations General Assembly. (2013). Format and Organizational Aspects of the High-Level Political Forum on Sustainable Development. Resolution 67/290. https://undocs.org/A/RES/67/290

Coordination

Maya Bogers

Coordination refers to the collaboration among various actors – including national and local governments, international organizations, civil society, non-governmental organizations and the private sector – to align their efforts towards the SDGs, so that

28 Essential Concepts for Implementing the SDGs

implementation of the goals is effective and efficient (Biermann and Kanie 2017; Breuer et al. 2023). While coordination may take place between any combination of these actors, here we focus on coordination by national governments, given that they are ultimately responsible for implementing the SDGs.

Coordination is of high importance in achieving the SDGs. The SDGs are interconnected, meaning that the issues embedded in the goals are interdependent (Biermann and Kanie 2017). Progress on one goal or target may have positive or negative effects on achieving other goals or targets (see *Interaction and Interlinkages*). For example, efforts to increase food security (SDG2) by expanding agricultural land may lead to co-benefits for employment (SDG8) but may have trade-offs with conservation efforts (SDG15). As a result, one actor's efforts to advance a goal may be synergistic or conflictive with other actors' efforts to advance other goals. Coordination is needed to ensure *policy coherence* and prevent conflicting efforts, inefficiencies and missed opportunities for synergy (Breuer et al. 2023).

SDG coordination by governments commonly takes place across three dimensions. First, governments coordinate between different policy domains, which is often referred to as horizontal coordination (Breuer et al. 2023). For this purpose, many countries have inter-ministerial committees or working groups. In Finland, the *Inter-ministerial Coordination Network* consists of focal points in each ministry to coordinate policies for the SDGs at the national level (Organisation for Economic Cooperation and Development 2018). In Estonia, representatives from all ministries and the statistics office collaborate in the *Inter-ministerial Working Group on Sustainable Development* to compile indicators, data and SDG monitoring reports (Mulholland et al. 2018).

Second, central governments coordinate with other levels of government, often referred to as vertical coordination (Breuer et al. 2023). To do so, countries can set up platforms or make use of *Voluntary Local Reviews*. In Mexico, the *National Council for the 2030 Agenda* was established as a platform for aligning efforts at the federal, state and municipal levels (Organisation for Economic Cooperation and Development 2018). In Argentina, the *National Council for Social Policy Coordination* has explicitly focused on local SDG implementation, using the Voluntary Local Review of the capital Buenos Aires to align local and regional efforts (Narang Suri et al. 2021).

Third, governments coordinate with non-state actors, which is often referred to as *multi-stakeholder engagement* (Breuer et al. 2023). In Georgia, the *SDG Council* provides a platform for state and non-state actors to come together to share and debate experiences on SDG implementation (Cázarez-Grageda 2019).

While coordination is an essential part of achieving the SDGs and much effort has been made to increase coordination, it remains a key challenge for SDG implementation. Ample national coordination bodies for the goals exist, many of which predate the adoption of the SDGs. These coordination bodies are often hampered by path dependencies and are not always able to overcome silo-structures (Nilsson et al. 2022). Studies show that the SDGs are not yet perceived holistically throughout governments (Breuer et al. 2023).

In sum, coordination is of the utmost importance to ensure coherence and efficiency in efforts to achieve the SDGs. This is especially necessary due to the interconnected nature of the SDGs and the collaborative effort of many stakeholders that is required to achieve the goals. Many countries have designated bodies to coordinate policies, implementation and data sharing for the SDGs. Such bodies coordinate across different levels of government, across different policy domains and among a diverse range of stakeholders. Despite efforts, coordination remains one of the key challenges in achieving the SDGs.

References

Biermann, F., and Kanie, N. (2017). Conclusion: Key challenges for global governance through goals. In N. Kanie, and F. Biermann (Eds.), *Governing through goals: Sustainable development goals as governance innovation* (pp. 295–309). Cambridge, MA: The MIT Press.

Breuer, A., Leininger, J., Malerba, D., and Tosun, J. (2023). Integrated policymaking: Institutional designs for implementing the sustainable development goals (SDGs). *World Development*, 170, 106317.

Cázarez-Grageda, K. (2019). The whole of government approach: Initial lessons concerning national coordinating structures for the 2030 Agenda and how review can improve their operation.

Mulholland, E., Dimitrova, A., and Hametner, M. (2018). *SDG indicators and monitoring: Systems and processes at the global, European and national level*, ESDN Quarterly Report 48, April 2018. Vienna: ESDN Office.

Narang Suri, S., Miraglia, M., and Ferrannini, A. (2021). Voluntary local reviews as drivers for SDG localization and sustainable human development. *Journal of Human Development and Capabilities*, 22(4), 725–736.

Nilsson, M., Vijge, M. J., Alva, I. L., Bornemann, B., Fernando, K., Hickmann, T., ... Weiland, S. (2022). Interlinkages, integration and coherence. In F. Biermann, T. Hickmann, and C.-A. Sénit (Eds.), *The political impact of the Sustainable Development Goals: Transforming governance through global goals?* (pp. 92–115). Cambridge: Cambridge University Press.

Organisation for Economic Cooperation and Development. (2018). *Policy coherence for sustainable development 2018: Towards sustainable and resilient societies*. Paris: OECD Publishing.

Corporate Social Responsibility (CSR)

Philip Schleifer

The United Nations Industrial Development Organization defines corporate social responsibility as a management concept that seeks to integrate social and environmental concerns into business operations and companies' interactions with their various stakeholders (United Nations Industrial Development Organization 2024). On the global stage, driven by transnational corporations and their business associations, corporate social responsibility is closely intertwined with the United Nations' sustainable development agenda and the Sustainable Development Goals (SDGs).

Transnational corporations and their supply chains form the backbone of the global economy. These powerful actors have played a key role in the United Nations' sustainable development agenda since the 1992 Conference on Environment and Development in Rio de Janeiro and the formulation of Agenda 21. Ahead of the summit, international business leaders established the World Business Council for Sustainable Development, an important platform for agenda-setting, networking and policy advocacy on matters of corporate sustainability. The United Nations has also proactively sought business sector support for its sustainable development initiatives; in the early 2000s, former United Nations Secretary-General Kofi Annan launched the United Nations Global Compact, which outlined 10 global principles for sustainable corporate conduct. His successor, Ban Ki-moon, further emphasized the importance of United Nations-business partnerships, stating that 'partnerships with the private sector are crucial to achieving sustainable development' (United Nations 2013). Today, over 500 private-sector-led partnerships supporting the implementation of the SDGs are registered with the United Nations (United Nations n.d.).

30 Essential Concepts for Implementing the SDGs

The 2030 Agenda for Sustainable Development has been increasingly integrated into private governance initiatives, with research showing significant overlaps between the SDGs and the expanding landscape of voluntary sustainability standards, including organizations like the Forest Stewardship Council and Fairtrade International (Schleifer et al. 2022). To stimulate further private sector investment in SDG implementation, the United Nations-led Business and Sustainable Development Commission estimates that achieving the SDGs could create USD 12 trillion in market opportunities by 2030 (Business and Sustainable Development Commission 2017). This, among other calls to action, has prompted a surge in SDG-themed business initiatives. Today, most major companies worldwide provide detailed information about their SDG-related activities in their annual reports.

While these developments indicate that business actors have played an active role in advancing the United Nations' sustainable development agenda and implementing the SDGs, criticisms remain. One major critique is that many business engagements with the SDGs are superficial, limited to symbolic or discursive actions. Despite the growing centrality of sustainable development in corporate discourse, many unsustainable business models that degrade the environment and exploit workers in global supply chains have remained largely unchanged. In this context, companies have been accused of 'SDG washing' – presenting a façade of commitment to the SDGs without enacting substantive changes (Heras-Saizarbitoria et al. 2022).

Furthermore, the aggregate impact of corporate sustainability activities is often limited. Research on leading consumer goods companies, for instance, suggests that their sustainability strategies fail to address the root causes of environmental degradation, such as overconsumption. While major brands like Coca-Cola, McDonald's and Walmart are making efforts to reduce the resource intensity and pollution of their products, their business models still prioritize profit maximization through high sales volumes. Consequently, despite increased eco-efficiency per unit sold, the overall environmental impact may remain negative (Dauvergne and Lister 2012).

Transnational corporations wield significant influence over issues like climate change, biodiversity loss, workers' rights and livelihoods globally, making them critical actors in achieving the SDGs. However, to date, their corporate social responsibility activities and engagement with the SDGs has often been too shallow to be transformative. Voluntary, private corporate social responsibility measures alone have proven insufficient. Moving forward, a shift towards robust public regulation is needed to ensure that corporate activities meaningfully contribute to sustainable development and address the pressing challenges facing our world today.

References

Business and Sustainable Development Commission. (2017). Better Business Better World, report, January 2017. https://unglobalcompact.org/docs/news_events/9.3/better-business-better-world.pdf

Dauvergne, P., and Lister, J. (2012). Big Brand Sustainability: Governance Prospects and Environmental Limits. *Global Environmental Change*, 22(1), 36–45. https://doi.org/10.1016/j.gloenvcha.2011.10.007

Heras-Saizarbitoria, I., Urbieta, L., and Boiral, O. (2022). Organizations' Engagement with Sustainable Development Goals: From Cherry-picking to SDG-washing? *Corporate Social Responsibility and Environmental Management*, 29(2), 316–328. https://doi.org/10.1002/csr.2202

Schleifer, P., Brandi, C., Verma, R., Bissinger, K., and Fiorini, M. (2022). Voluntary Standards and the SDGs: Mapping Public-Private Complementarities for Sustainable Development. *Earth System Governance*, 14, 100153. https://doi.org/10.1016/j.esg.2022.100153

United Nations. (2013). Partnerships with Private Sector Crucial for Sustainable Development, Secretary-General Tells Hong Kong-United States Business Council, Press Release, 12 June 2013. https://press.un.org/en/2013/sgsm15102.doc.htm

United Nations. (n.d.). SDG Actions Platform. https://sdgs.un.org/partnerships/browse

United Nations Industrial Development Organization. (2024). Corporate Social Responsibility. https://www.unido.org/our-focus-advancing-economic-competitiveness-competitive-trade-capacities-and-corporate-responsibility-corporate-social-responsibility-market-integration/what-csr

Custodians

Thiago Gehre Galvão, Denise Kronemberger and Rodrigo Correa Ramiro

Custodian agencies are primarily international organizations responsible for developing new methodologies, collecting data, allowing data aggregation and harmonization, improving national statistical capacity and providing data on the 232 indicators for annual Sustainable Development Goals (SDGs) reports (United Nations Statistical Commission 2017). The metadata generated by the custodians (United Nations Department of Economic and Social Affairs 2024) is a guide for countries to produce data on their indicators, ensuring data standardization and allowing comparisons among them. More than half of the SDG indicators have more than one organization responsible for them. The ten custodian agencies with most indicators are the World Health Organization (32 indicators), United Nations Environment Programme (26), the World Bank (23), Food and Agricultural Organization (21), United Nations Educational, Scientific and Cultural Organization (18), United Nations Office on Drugs and Crime (17), United Nations Children's Fund (13), International Labour Organization (13), United Nations Office for Disaster Risk Reduction (11) and United Nations Habitat (9) as of 2024.

Custodians are collaborating in their specific area of expertise with national governments, local governments and civil society organizations on diverse issues related to SDG implementation. They provide capacity-building and technical assistance to countries and contribute to improving their statistics about the SDGs. For instance, custodians cooperate by implementing monitoring and evaluation mechanisms on development and poverty eradication; strengthening data production capabilities on health and education; disseminating data-related initiatives on human rights of vulnerable population groups, as well as indicators on employment and labour rights. Custodian agencies work together with National Statistical Offices (United Nations General Assembly 2017) and have focal points for each SDG indicator; countries have national focal points who receive requests for sending or validating data and filling out questionnaires that result in the production of indicators. This focal point system aims to facilitate the dialogue between countries and custodian agencies in producing aggregated data on global SDG indicators.

The work of custodian agencies is connected to the implementation of the Cape Town Global Action Plan for Sustainable Development Data (Cape Town Global Action Plan for Sustainable Development Data 2017). This Action Plan is a framework aiming to organize global data and to inform sustainable development policymaking in six strategic areas: the coordination and strategic leadership on data for sustainable development; the innovation and modernization of national statistical systems; the strengthening of basic

32 *Essential Concepts for Implementing the SDGs*

statistical activities and programmes, addressing the needs of the 2030 Agenda; the dissemination and use of sustainable development data; multi-stakeholder partnerships for sustainable development data; and resources mobilization and coordination efforts for statistical capacity-building.

The main challenges faced by custodians relate to that global governance system that is highly fragmented, oscillating between ad-hoc coordination efforts and the dominance of one agency. This creates inefficient data collection and capacity-building regarding the monitoring of progress of SDG implementation, especially on complex issue areas such as health, environment and climate. Institutional fragmentation also undermines custodians' power on the global architecture of SDG progress evaluation (van Driel et al. 2022). In addition, the lack of clearer institutional leadership weakens the orchestration ability of custodian agencies in the monitoring of SDG targets and indicators.

In sum, custodian agencies are relevant agents of the SDG framework at national and international levels. They have the potential to accelerate SDG implementation by inducing the transposition of global indicators into national and local indicators, a strategic step towards localizing the 2030 Agenda and fighting inequalities in local contexts (Galvao and de Menezes 2024).

References

Cape Town Global Action Plan for Sustainable Development Data. (2017). Cape Town Global Action Plan for Sustainable Development Data.

Galvao, T. G., and de Menezes, H. Z. (Eds.). (2024). *The Quest for the Sustainable Development Goals. Sustainable Development Goals Series*. Springer, Cham. https://doi.org/10.1007/978-3-031-59279-9_5

United Nations Department of Economic and Social Affairs. (2024). SDG Indicators Database. https://unstats.un.org/sdgs/dataportal

United Nations General Assembly. (2017). Work of the Statistical Commission pertaining to the 2030 Agenda for Sustainable Development. A/RES/71/313. https://documents.un.org/doc/undoc/gen/n17/207/63/pdf/n1720763.pdf

United Nations Statistical Commission. (2017). Report of the High-level Group for Partnership, Coordination and Capacity-Building for Statistics for the 2030 Agenda for Sustainable Development. 7. E/CN.3/2017/3

van Driel, M., Biermann, F., Kim, R. E., and Vijge, M. J. (2022). International Organizations as 'Custodians' of the Sustainable Development Goals? Fragmentation and Coordination in Sustainability Governance. *Global Policy*, 13, 669–682.

D

Data gaps

Guilherme Iablonovski, Isabella Massa and Samory Toure

Progress towards achieving the Sustainable Development Goals (SDGs) has been slower than anticipated (Sachs et al. 2024). One serious problem, among others, are data gaps (Espey 2019). Without timely, relevant and disaggregated data, policymakers are unable to identify challenges, allocate resources and gauge the effectiveness of sustainable development initiatives. The United Nations global indicator framework encompasses 232 indicators. Official datasets, endorsed by the United Nations Statistical Commission, are collected and submitted by custodian agencies and member states. Nonetheless, numerous institutions and researchers calculate indicators independently (Sachs et al. 2024).

Despite improvements, only 54 out of 193 United Nations member states have data availability for at least 50% of SDG indicators. Data on goals like SDGs 5 (Gender Equality), 13 (Climate Action) and 16 (Peace, Justice and Strong Institutions) is particularly scarce (Goessmann et al. 2023). Statistical capacity gaps, lack of political leadership and inadequate financing are some of the key factors leading to data challenges and differences in data availability across countries (Sustainable Development Solutions Network TReNDS 2019). Moreover, the adoption of the United Nations global indicator framework is voluntary and countries prioritize indicators based on their specific needs and data-collection capabilities, thus leading to inconsistencies in data quality and availability as well as to issues of data comparability across countries.

To address data gaps and improve SDG tracking, crucial actions can be leveraged. Firstly, more investment in national statistical systems is needed to enhance data collection and overall development. A global commitment to increase the share of Official Development Assistance allocated to data would be beneficial (Goessmann et al. 2023).

Secondly, tailored capacity-building, training and support for national statistical offices, as seen in programmes of international organizations, can significantly improve data collection, analysis and reporting (United Nations 2023). For instance, the United Nations Population Fund supports population and housing censuses – a key source of socioeconomic and development data – across multiple countries.

Thirdly, expanding beyond countries and custodian agencies-led efforts can enhance data availability. Partnerships between non-governmental organizations, public and

DOI: 10.4324/9781003519560-6

This chapter has been made available under a CC-BY-NC-ND license.

34   Essential Concepts for Implementing the SDGs

private sectors can leverage diverse data sources and improve data collection. Civil society organizations, such as the UN Sustainable Development Solutions Network, Oxfam, the Tax Justice Network and Reporters Without Borders, as well as peer-reviewed journals, produce valuable data for SDG indicators following rigorous data validation processes (Sachs et al. 2024). For example, in the latest edition of the UN Sustainable Development Solutions Network's Sustainable Development Report (Sachs et al. 2024), official and extra-official data sources providing global coverage informed 42% of all SDG indicators.

The use of global geospatial data, such as satellite data (for example, Sentinel, Landsat) and citizen-generated data (for example, OpenStreetMap), may also facilitate data collection – approximately 20% of SDG indicators can be measured using geospatial data – while offering high accuracy, consistency across space and global comparability (IAEG-SDG WGGI 2018). International agencies may use remote sensing datasets to calculate globally comparable indicators (for example, Iablonovski et al. 2024) and provide subnational results to official authorities for review.

Finally, enhancing data transparency and accessibility can lead to better decision-making. Aggregating data on online platforms and ensuring they are up-to-date and comparable can empower stakeholders and foster accountability (United Nations 2023). The development of common principles and standards for data gathering may also contribute to enhancing data comparability across countries and the capacity to integrate data from different sources (Sustainable Development Solutions Network TReNDS 2019).

Bridging the data gap is essential for realizing the SDGs and ensuring effective and equitable efforts towards sustainable development. By investing in national statistical systems, adopting innovative data-collection methods, building capacity and improving transparency, we can address data deficiencies and make meaningful progress towards the SDGs.

References

Espey, J. (2019). Sustainable development will falter without data. *Nature*, 571(7765), 299. https://doi.org/10.1038/d41586-019-02139-w

Goessmann, C., Idele, P., Jauer, K., Loinig, M., Melamed, C., and Zak, T. (2023). *Pulse of Progress: Mapping the State of Global SDG Data in 2023*. Zurich: United Nations.

Iablonovski, G., Drumm, E., Fuller, G., and Lafortune, G. (2024). A global implementation of the rural access index. *Frontiers in Remote Sensing*, 5, 1375476. https://doi.org/10.3389/frsen.2024.1375476

IAEG-SDG WGGI. (2018). *Global and Complementary (Non-authoritative) Spatial Data for SDG Indicators Reporting: Role and Utilization*. A discussion paper prepared by IAEG-SDGs WGGI Task Team. https://ggim.un.org/documents/Report_Global_and_Complementary_Geospatial_Data_for_SDGs.pdf

Sachs, J. D., Lafortune, G., and Fuller, G. (2024). *The SDGs and the UN Summit of the Future. Sustainable Development Report 2024*. Dublin: Dublin University Press. https://doi.org/10.25546/108572

Sustainable Development Solutions Network TReNDS. (2019). *Counting on the World to Act: A Roadmap for Governments to Achieve Modern data Systems for Sustainable Development*. Sustainable Development Solutions Network TRends: Sustainable Development Solutions Network's Thematic Research Network on Data and Statistics. https://countingontheworld.sdsntrends.org/

United Nations. (2023). *Power of Data: Unlocking the Data Dividend for the SDGs*. https://www.data4sdgs.org/initiatives/power-of-data-unlocking-data-dividend-sdgs

Development banks

Elise Dufief

The 2030 Agenda calls to 'pursue policy coherence and an enabling environment for sustainable development at all levels and by all actors' (United Nations General Assembly 2015). In Article 2.1 (c), the Paris Agreement calls for 'making finance flows consistent with a pathway towards low greenhouse gas emissions and climate-resilient development' (United Nations 2015). With now more than 500 institutions worldwide, owning around USD 23 trillion in assets and providing more than 10% of the world's annual investment, public development banks matter for the financing of Sustainable Development Goals (SDGs) (Mazzucato 2023). In 2020, at the first Finance in Common Summit, a group of public development banks committed to aligning their activities with the SDGs (Finance in Common 2020).

In practice there is no common definition of SDG alignment for public development banks, but a number of guidelines exist. The Organisation for Economic Cooperation and Development has put forward two dimensions to guide alignment efforts: equality (that is, resources should be mobilized to leave no one behind) and sustainability (that is, resources should accelerate progress on the long term while doing no other significant harm to other dimensions) (Organisation for Economic Cooperation and Development 2020).

At a more operational level, Riaño et al. (2022) have developed four principles to guide the actions by public development banks: lead internally; develop a holistic vision true to the integrated nature of the 2030 Agenda; mobilize transformative investments; and better integrate SDGs in policies. These have been further developed by the International Development Finance Club (a global network of selected development banks) and the sustainable development unit of Natixis (a French commercial bank) around a methodological guidance to support its members towards SDG alignment at the three levels: entity, activity and external partners (International Development Finance Club and Natixis 2022). These efforts are attempts to structure an approach of alignment for public development banks. They also created their own working group within the Finance in Common Summit. However, practices remain scattered. The challenge is now for public development banks to move from being SDG alignment takers (for their own business model) to being SDG alignment enablers (supporting country priorities and needs).

Most public development banks now embed SDGs and the 2030 Agenda in their long-term plans and adopt an institution-focused perspective to include climate-compatible and equitable socioeconomic dimensions in their financing decisions and project cycles (Riaño et al., 2022). For example, the Asian Development Bank launched an institution-wide reform, informed by an evaluation, which led to the development of a theory of change for the bank and its partners to align on the SDGs. It included a staff reorganization and new ways of working with countries of operations (Dufief and Barchiche 2022).

But these commitments tend to remain discursive. Only a few manage to apply them in their decision-making at the project level, with a view to maximizing co-benefits, redirecting harmful finances and avoiding trade-offs. Reducing alignment to an SDG mapping exercise, for internal and reporting purposes only, misses the point of creating impact for sustainable development. As a good practice, the Agence Française de Développement (French Development Agency) has developed a sustainable development analysis tool to

36 *Essential Concepts for Implementing the SDGs*

assess ex-ante the proposed contribution of a project to the SDGs, an assessment that weighs on the allocation (Dufief and Barchiche 2022).

Fewer public development banks manage to fully reach the last mile in their alignment efforts to support sustainable transformations in countries of operation. Since the SDGs are collective objectives, they come with shared responsibilities. Hence, public development banks also have a role to play in supporting national efforts towards alignment of national plans and policies with the SDGs. Enhancing this kind of support by public development banks at the country level would go a long way in current efforts to mobilize funds more efficiently while advancing the 2030 Agenda.

References

Dufief, E., and Barchiche, D. (2022). Operationalising multilateral development banks' alignment with the 2030 Agenda. https://www.iddri.org/en/publications-and-events/study/operationalising-multilateral-development-banks-alignment-2030-agenda

Finance in Common. (2020). Joint declaration of all public development banks in the world. https://financeincommon.org/sites/default/files/2021-06/FiCs%20-%20Joint%20declaration%20of%20Public%20Development%20Banks.pdf

International Development Finance Club and Natixis. (2022). Report PDBs catalytic role in achieving the SDGs https://www.idfc.org/wp-content/uploads/2022/12/cib-etude-green-hub-web-15dec-144dpi-compressed.pdf

Mazzucato, M. (2023). *Financing the Sustainable Development Goals through mission-oriented development banks*. UN DESA Policy Brief Special issue. New York: UN Department of Economic and Social Affairs; UN High-level Advisory Board on Economic and Social Affairs; University College London Institute for Innovation and Public Purpose.

Organisation for Economic Cooperation and Development. (2020). Global Outlook on financing sustainable development 2021.

Riaño, M.-A., Boutaybi, J., Barchiche, D., and Treyer, S. (2022). Scaling up public development banks' transformative alignment with the 2030 agenda for sustainable development. *Review of Political Economy*, 34(2), 286–317. https://doi.org/10.1080/09538259.2021.1977544

United Nations. (2015). Paris agreement. https://unfccc.int/sites/default/files/resource/parisagreement_publication.pdf

United Nations General Assembly. (2015). *Transforming our world: The 2030 agenda for sustainable development*. A/RES/70/1. https://sdgs.un.org/publications/transforming-our-world-2030-agenda-sustainable-development-17981

Discourse and discursive effects

Ilona Rac and Karmen Erjavec

Discourse analysis, which has been developed by theorists like Ferdinand de Saussure, Michel Foucault and Norman Fairclough, studies how language shapes social realities and reinforces power relations – a phenomenon recognized as the *discursive effect*. Foucault for instance has argued that powerholders use language to define what is accepted as 'truth', systematically excluding alternative perspectives, thus shaping societal norms and legitimizing dominant ideologies. Fairclough explores how language use in institutions and policies reinforces power structures (Fairclough 2013). Discourses shape how problems are understood and addressed, legitimizing certain actions and playing a central role in power dynamics.

In the context of the Sustainable Development Goals (SDGs), discourse analysis reveals how different discourses around the concept of sustainable development shape the understanding, prioritization and implementation of these global goals. Sustainable development can thus be seen as a discursive construct that constructs power relations and knowledge systems, positioning actors and practices in particular ways (Schojan et al. 2024). The SDGs, while intended to be a universal framework for sustainable development, are inherently shaped by competing discourses, which affect their governance and prioritization of outcomes. This discursive plurality has important implications for the SDGs' aspirations towards universality.

Sustainable development, although promoted as a forward-looking development paradigm, has also been seen as highly problematic and contested (Stough 2023). Firstly, the concept is ambiguous, facilitating adaptation to different contexts and stakeholders; secondly, it is criticized for aligning with neoliberal agendas by framing sustainability within a market-centric and growth-oriented paradigm (Redclift 2005; Weber 2017). In this discourse, sustainability is framed as compatible with and even reliant upon continued economic growth, technological progress and market-based solutions. Such framing appeals to political elites and allows countries to prioritize socioeconomic SDGs over environmental ones or addressing social equity issues (Biermann et al. 2022).

For example, multinational corporations and financial institutions can dominate the policy space and SDG implementation, which can marginalize local communities and vulnerable populations (Southern Voice 2020; Weber 2017). Biermann et al.'s (2022) analysis of the political impact of the SDGs concludes that the SDGs influence global conversations and values by framing development issues with terms like 'leaving no one behind'. However, they argue this shift is mostly symbolic; the discourse has changed, but it has not led to substantial policy or institutional reform. This reflects the fact that language alone does not necessarily challenge underlying power structures, but can reinforce them instead.

Discourse analysis also highlights the ideological disputes underpinning the implementation of the SDGs. Different actors – governments, international organizations, civil society groups and the private sector – advance competing visions of sustainable development with different implications for governance (Stough 2023). While some discourses advocate deep structural reforms, others align with established economic and political interests and promote more conservative, incremental approaches (Hopwood et al. 2005; Stough 2023). The discourse of 'shared responsibility', as promoted by SDG 17 (Partnership for the goals), for example, suggests that all social actors – states, businesses and individuals – must contribute to sustainable development. However, this narrative often obscures underlying power imbalances, blurs accountability and gives dominant actors disproportionate influence over SDG implementation while minimizing their responsibility for adverse outcomes. Simultaneously, alternative frameworks for sustainability, particularly those that challenge prevailing economic paradigms, tend to be marginalized, as the status quo and prevailing political and power structures are mutually reinforcing (Hopwood et al. 2005).

Discourse analysis indicates that the implementation of SDGs is significantly influenced by the power structures embedded in the discourses that define and perpetuate prevailing interpretations of sustainable development. These discourses shape which goals are prioritized and how they are pursued, reflecting the decision-making authority in SDG governance. Recognizing these dynamics is essential for revealing the underlying ideological and power shaping SDG implementation, providing a foundation for promoting changes that are not only effective but also equitable and genuinely transformative.

38 *Essential Concepts for Implementing the SDGs*

References

Biermann, F., Hickmann, T., Sénit, C. A., Beisheim, M., Bernstein, S., Chasek, P., ... and Wicke, B. (2022). Scientific evidence on the political impact of the Sustainable Development Goals. *Nature Sustainability*, 5(9), 795–800.

Fairclough, N. (2013). Critical discourse analysis and critical policy studies. *Critical Policy Studies*, 7(2), 177–197. https://doi.org/10.1080/19460171.2013.798239

Hopwood, B., Mellor, M., and O'Brien, G. (2005). Sustainable development: Mapping different approaches. *Sustainable Development*, 13(1), 38–52. https://doi.org/10.1002/sd.244

Redclift, M. (2005). Sustainable development (1987–2005): An oxymoron comes of age. *Sustainable Development*, 13(4), 212–227. https://doi.org/10.1002/sd.281

Schojan, F., Machin, A., and Silberberger, M. (2024). Sustainable development discourse and development aid in Germany: Tracking the changes from environmental protectionism towards private sector opportunities. *Critical Policy Studies*, 18(3), 446–469. https://doi.org/10.1080/1946 0171.2023.2265988

Southern Voice. (2020). *Global State of the SDGs – Three Layers of Critical Action*. http://southernvoice.org/wp-content/uploads/2020/08/State-of-the-SDGs-Global-Report-2019-Southern-Voice.pdf

Stough, T. (2023). Critical reflection on discourses of sustainable development. In R. Brinkmann (Ed.), *The Palgrave Handbook of Global Sustainability* (pp. 2137–2151). Springer. https://doi.org/10.1007/978-3-031-01949-4_139

Weber, H. (2017). Politics of 'leaving no one behind': Contesting the 2030 sustainable development goals agenda. *Globalizations*, 14(3), 399–414. https://doi.org/10.1080/14747731.2016.1275404

E

Education for Sustainable Development

Thiago Gehre Galvão and Crystal Green

Education and learning are at the heart of the implementation of the Sustainable Development Goals (SDGs). Multiple channels of formal and informal education create a system of learning by example, circulating ideas and practices on how to implement the 2030 Agenda worldwide. Education is a structural transformative force that can influence the accomplishment of all 17 SDGs, encourage an interdisciplinary and transversal approach, enlighten critical thinking and trigger a synergetic interpretation of the SDGs (Ferrer-Estévez and Chalmeta 2021).

SDG 4 targets education. It aims to improve the quality of education, which is expected to positively influence income generation, job growth, reduction of inequalities and life change opportunities. SDG 4 indicators serve to bring political coherence and accountability among governments and stakeholders by allowing the measurement of educational policies, their quality and the degree of collaboration through partnerships and international cooperation. In addition, SDG 4 contains elements that could forge a new cultural frame of social relations that prioritize inclusiveness, equality and opportunities more than meritocracy. Therefore, SDG 4 could impact both SDG politics (the system of formulation, decision and implementation of policies related to the SDGs into societies) and SDG culture (the integration of ideas, beliefs, habitus and practices related to the SDGs into systems, institutions and territories) (Cabral and Galvão 2022).

One substantial concept for implementing SDG 4 is Education for Sustainable Development, which seeks to integrate and make sense of complex environmental, economic and social phenomena. It is embraced in Target 4.7, which focuses on the acquisition of knowledge and skills needed to promote a broader concept of sustainable development, include human rights, gender equality and the promotion of a culture of peace, non-violence and diversity (Sarabhai 2015). Through education and learning, it is possible to focus on implementing integrated innovative SDG-led solutions. In addition, it is in the field of education where we can access intellectual tools (concepts, theories and traditional knowledge) on how to localize SDG implementation in different contexts, particularly along the Global North/South divide (Galvão et al. 2024).

The adoption of the SDGs impacted education and learning by creating opportunities and allowing agents to challenge entrenched inequalities. First, methods and strategies

DOI: 10.4324/9781003519560-7

This chapter has been made available under a CC-BY-NC-ND license.

40 Essential Concepts for Implementing the SDGs

for SDG integration within undergraduate and graduate courses are influencing curriculum, teaching methods and pedagogical approaches (Serafini et al. 2022). These include, for instance, concept maps and case-based learning to identify synergies and solve problems from an SDG perspective. Moreover, SDG territorialization is driven by outreach activities that connect pedagogical tools of Education for Sustainable Development with practical knowledge. Second, institutional adaptations are created because of the SDGs, such as specialized centres and administrative units inside universities, schools and other bureaucracies to follow SDG implementation, as well as specific funds and public notices for the development of SDG-oriented actions (Hickmann et al. 2024).

Some persistent challenges are the lack of awareness of the SDGs and the lack of financial, human and material resources. There is also a competition of education models in the processes of standardization and privatization of education. Moreover, global education is marked by a dynamic of knowledge production and practices that do not consider synergies and local contexts, power relations and asymmetries between the Global North and South (Galvão et al. 2024).

Educators use the SDG as a sort of language to communicate ideas, values and solutions linked to sustainability transformation; to share living experiences related to sustainability and social inclusion; and to address decolonial and pluriversal perspectives of development (Hickmann et al. 2024). In sum, education and learning for the SDGs encompass a language that connects people, institutions, countries and regions, paving the way for an inclusive, just and sustainable society in the 21st century.

References

Cabral, R., and Galvão, T. G. (2022). Reimagining the UN 2030 agenda by connecting the SDG to culture, art and communication. *Revista Latinoamericana de Ciencias de la Comunicación* 21(41): 44–59.

Ferrer-Estévez, M. and Chalmeta, R. (2021). 'Integrating Sustainable Development Goals in educational institutions'. *The International Journal of Management Education* 19(2): 100494. https://doi.org/10.1016/j.ijme.2021.100494

Galvão, T. G., et al. (2024). Challenges and opportunities of a Brazilian network of universities for the SDG implementation. In T. G. Galvao, and H. Z. de Menezes (Eds.), *The Quest for the Sustainable Development Goals. Sustainable Development Goals Series.* Springer, Cham. https://doi.org/10.1007/978-3-031-59279-9_5

Hickmann, T. et al. (2024). Scoping article: Research frontiers on the governance of the Sustainable Development Goals. *Global Sustainability* 7(e7): 1–12. https://doi.org/10.1017/sus.2024.4

Sarabhai, Kartikeya V. (2015). ESD for Sustainable Development Goals (SDGs). *Journal of Education for Sustainable Development* 9: 121–123.

Serafini, P. G., Moura, J. M. D., Almeida, M. R. D., and Rezende, J. F. D. D. (2022). Sustainable Development Goals in higher education institutions: A systematic literature review. *Journal of Cleaner Production* 370: 133473. https://doi.org/10.1016/j.jclepro.2022.133473

Effectiveness

Moira V. Faul, Liliana B. Andonova and Dario Piselli

The notion of effectiveness is central to discussions of the Sustainable Development Goals (SDGs) and to their implementation. Ever since their adoption, the SDGs have served as a normative framework for benchmarking progress towards sustainability. And yet, as the world continues to be off track to achieve the 2030 Agenda (United Nations 2024), critical questions on more effective implementation remain. To address continuing challenges in conceptualizing, measuring and operationalizing effectiveness for sustainability, we define effectiveness as the contribution to implementing the SDGs through a set of pathways and institutional factors that affect actors and their collective capacity to advance relevant objectives and public purpose (Andonova et al. 2022).

Multiple approaches exist to assess the effectiveness of the SDGs. So far, the formal attainment of targets and indicators, including variation across and within SDGs and polities, has been the main approach to understanding effectiveness. In this way, statistical knowledge is codified into authoritative practice in SDG monitoring. The elaboration of quantitative indicators provides opportunities to monitor certain aspects of SDG implementation and for comparability across institutions and SDGs. However, quantification narrows the scope of the SDGs to what can be measured only and elides other forms of knowledge (Mbembe 2019). Furthermore, even if the adopted indicators show goal attainment, effectiveness could be endogenous to their level of ambition and/or external factors (Andonova et al. 2022; Widerberg et al. 2023).

Effectiveness also goes beyond a single SDG. Detecting the many cross-cutting and interconnecting aspects of the SDGs is needed to facilitate theoretical and methodological advances in research and also inform more systemic and effective solutions for sustainability. Since SDG interlinkages vary across world regions, effectiveness depends on detecting those nexuses that are relevant to different localities rather than assuming global homogeneity (Faul and Laumann 2024).

In practice, however, concerns abound about the effectiveness of governance by goal-setting and the SDGs. While the SDGs have been effective in framing discourses around sustainable development, they show otherwise limited political impact (Biermann et al. 2022). The integration of SDG objectives into national policies and agency capacities is unclear and highly variable. Subnational governments and coalitions appear to be more proactively integrating the SDGs into their work, and while international organizations have orchestrated interlinkages across SDGs, they appear to lack sufficient capacity for their effective implementation.

Therefore, another prominent line of inquiry focuses on the effectiveness of multi-stakeholder partnerships as the 'means of implementation' (SDG 17.16 and 17.17) towards achieving sustainable development and legitimating global governance (Andonova 2017). However, many partnerships are inactive, and many lack resources for achieving their objectives (Widerberg et al. 2023). While a partnership may be successfully established, causal analysis is needed to link a partnership with problem-solving for sustainability (Andonova et al. 2022).

Research suggests several criteria that need to be fulfilled for more effective implementation. For instance, the effectiveness of multi-stakeholder partnerships for the SDGs should depend on five different conditions, including goal attainment, effective collaboration, value created for partners and impacts on other institutions and on affected constituencies (Andonova et al. 2022). Other factors shaping effectiveness of SDG implementation have also been identified, such as examining contractual arrangements, credible commitment of resources, adaptability and innovation. This theoretical approach can be applied across different areas, disciplines and levels of governance, using complementary methodologies to fully assess potential contributions to SDG effectiveness. Working with an expanded conceptualization of effectiveness – such as that we offer here – will be crucial to realizing the SDGs and developing the next global sustainability agenda.

References

Andonova, L. B. (2017). *Governance Entrepreneurs: International Organizations and the Rise of Global Public-Private Partnerships*. Cambridge University Press.

Andonova, L. B., Faul, M. V., and Piselli, D. (Eds.). (2022). *Partnerships for Sustainability in Contemporary Global Governance: Pathways to Effectiveness*. Routledge. https://doi.org/10.4324/9781003148371

Biermann, F., Hickmann, T., and Sénit, C.-A. (Eds.). (2022). *The Political Impact of the Sustainable Development Goals: Transforming Governance Through Global Goals?* Cambridge University Press. https://doi.org/10.1038/s41893-022-00909-5

Faul, M. V., and Laumann, F. (2024). Complex interlinkages between the SDGs and their importance to African development. *African Journal of Sustainable Development*, 14(1), 269–285.

Mbembe, Achille. (2019). Future knowledges and their implications for the decolonization project. In J. Jansen (Ed.), *Decolonization in Universities: The Politics of Knowledge* (pp. 239–254). Wits University Press.

United Nations. (2024). *Progress towards the Sustainable Development Goals: Report of the Secretary-General*. A/79/79-E/2024/54. United Nations General Assembly, United Nations Economic and Social Council.

Widerberg, O., Fast, C., Rosas, M. K., and Pattberg, P. (2023). Multi-stakeholder partnerships for the SDGs: Is the 'next generation' fit for purpose? *International Environmental Agreements: Politics, Law and Economics*, 23(2), 165–171. https://doi.org/10.1007/s10784-023-09606-w

F

Finance mechanisms

Aurelie Charles

Accelerating the implementation of the Sustainable Development Goals (SDGs) after the setback from the COVID-19 crisis demands that SDG financing be upscaled, from billions to trillions annually, in order to close the so-called financing gap (Mazzucato 2023). Such a challenge requires a variety of financing mechanisms, each playing a pivotal role in addressing the multi-levelled governance challenges posed by SDG implementation. Current finance mechanisms include public financing (taxation, for example), private sector investment, blended finance (public and private), development finance (from microfinance to Official Development Assistance) and new financing tools such as payment for ecosystem services and debt-for-nature swaps. These are channelled through diverse stakeholders seeking to achieve financial performance and/or developmental goals to various degrees. They range from financial speculators in financial markets, philanthropes giving to foundations and non-governmental organizations, to governments with multilateral development banks and development finance institutions for Official Development Assistance, impact investment or debt-for-nature swaps.

Since 2015, the landscape of SDG financing has evolved from looking at the source of financing, that is, private or public, to financing by purpose, that is, development or commercial finance flows (Organisation for Economic Cooperation and Development 2018). This reconciles the trade-off between short-term financial returns and long-term goals while also allowing a focus on the context-based impact of investments. Over the last 40 years of financialization, while global finance has been increasingly in private hands, public financing has remained a cornerstone for SDG implementation. Governments allocate budgetary resources to critical SDG areas such as healthcare, education and infrastructure with an ideal United Nations target of 0.7% of gross national income going towards Official Development Assistance. Development aid and grants from international organizations and developed countries also form a significant part of public financing. These funds are often channelled through multilateral development banks and development finance institutions or initiatives like the Green Climate Fund, which supports projects aimed at mitigating climate change impacts in developing countries, which are most in need of support for SDG financing (Kharas and McArthur 2019; Mawdsley 2021).

Given the scale of investment required, private sector investment is increasingly recognized as essential for SDG implementation as long as financial motives are not tapping

DOI: 10.4324/9781003519560-8

This chapter has been made available under a CC-BY-NC-ND license.

44 Essential Concepts for Implementing the SDGs

into groupthink to create unsustainable patterns of speculative investments and resource use (Charles 2024). As argued by Mazzucato (2023), channelling finance towards mission-oriented goals and public-private investments through multilateral development banks is reducing the risk and uncertainty linked to the volatile nature of financial flows on SDG targets, while maximizing the social impact of development finance. Blended finance has therefore emerged as a mechanism that combines public and private resources to leverage greater total investment for SDG-related projects. This approach aims to de-risk investments for private financiers by using public funds as a buffer, thereby attracting private capital into sectors and areas that are otherwise deemed too risky.

The current finance mechanisms for the SDGs are based on purpose or mission with blended finance, which alleviates the speculative threat and volatility of private finance. Assessing and monitoring the contextual impact of investment decisions has also become central to ensuring the stability of long-term goals. To accelerate and close the financing gap, however, there is an urgent need for restructuring the global governance of finance to account for the voice of developing countries (Griffiths 2018) and to channel finance locally for a more resilient economic system. What makes an economic system resilient? It is one that first recognizes the role of group behaviour in financial accumulation and manages to redirect its excesses where needed (Charles 2024).

References

Charles, A. (2024). 'Sustainable Earnings in a Resilient Economic System: The Power of Groupthink in Channelling Finance Towards Sustainable Goals', in *SpringerBrief in Economics*. https://link.springer.com/book/9783031675720

Griffiths, J. (2018). 'Financing the Sustainable Development Goals (SDGs)', *Development* 61, 62–67. https://doi.org/10.1057/s41301-018-0178-1

Kharas, H., and McArthur, J. (2019). 'Building the SDG Economy: Needs, Spending and Financing for Universal Achievement of the Sustainable Development Goals', Global Economy and Development at Brookings, Working Paper 131, October 2019.

Mawdsley, E. (2021). 'Development Finance and the 2030 Goals,' in Chaturvedi, S., Janus, H., Klingebiel, S., Li, X., de Mello e Souza, A., Sidiropoulos, E., and Wehrmann, D. (Eds.), *The Palgrave Handbook of Development Cooperation for Achieving the 2030 Agenda* (pp. 51–57). Cham: Palgrave Macmillan.

Mazzucato, M. (2023). Financing the Sustainable Development Goals through Mission-oriented Development Banks, UN DESA Policy Brief Special issue. New York: UN Department of Economic and Social Affairs; UN High-level Advisory Board on Economic and Social Affairs; University College London Institute for Innovation and Public Purpose. https://desapublications.un.org/file/18480/download

Organisation for Economic Cooperation and Development. (2018). *Making Blended Finance Work for the Sustainable Development Goals*. Paris: OECD Publishing. https://doi.org/10.1787/9789264288768-en

Fragmentation

Joshua Philipp Elsässer and Fariborz Zelli

Fragmentation has emerged as a concept to capture the rapid growth and differentiation of international institutions in the past decades. It captures the decentralized and evolving nature of the contemporary international system, where a diverse set of institutions

– both intergovernmental and transnational – coexist, overlap and interact (Elsässer et al. 2022). The concept has been defined as a 'patchwork' of international institutions – organizations, regimes and norms – that vary in type, scope (from local to global) and focus areas (Biermann et al. 2009, 16). Often used interchangeably with related terms like institutional complexity, fragmentation itself carries no inherent positive or negative connotations and does not imply a normative preference for a centralized authority. Fragmentation primarily describes an empirical phenomenon, which may produce complementary, synergetic or even conflicting relationships among institutions. At the level of actors, high degrees of fragmentation may render difficulties in navigating and developing adequate responses to transboundary problems.

Global sustainability governance is a policy domain characterized by a particularly high degree of fragmentation. The regulatory scope of the Sustainable Development Goals (SDGs), for instance, ranges from transboundary environmental problems to human development, global health, trade and even security. Given the absence of an overarching institutional framework, governing sustainable development has come to involve multiple, interdependent regimes, each with its own varying degrees of fragmentation and different institutional centres (Zelli 2011). This decentralized structure presents both opportunities and challenges. On the one hand, the presence of diverse institutions creates more opportunities for alliances aimed at addressing transboundary environmental issues (Hickmann and Elsässer 2020). On the other, there has been frequent competition among international institutions for regulatory primacy, as illustrated by emissions trading, a key issue in both the United Nations climate regime and the World Trade Organization (Zelli and van Asselt 2010). Moreover, powerful governments frequently engage in 'forum-shopping' behaviour to achieve their policy goals within preferred forums, thereby juxtaposing economic growth with environmental concerns (Kellow 2012).

There are still key knowledge gaps with regard to fragmentation in global sustainable development governance despite significant progress in mapping and analyzing the phenomenon. First, we need to know more about how fragmentation interacts with new forms of power, accountability and legitimacy within complex institutional systems, particularly regarding issues of equity and justice. This is particularly relevant to understand fragmentation amid the rise of transnational governance or the crisis of multilateralism (Sommerer et al. 2022). Second, fragmentation studies have predominantly drawn on institutionalist perspectives in international relations research and thus leave room for a more interdisciplinary research agenda going forward. Such new research could complement existing approaches beyond international relations scholarship on interplay management and the role of agents in coping with fragmentation (e.g., Elsässer 2024). Third, we also need a deeper understanding of the means and mechanisms driving fragmentation, while also taking into account new societal developments. For example, incorporating perspectives from science and technology studies, research on fragmentation may investigate how human-technology interfaces and data use contribute to governance complexities.

For practitioners, understanding fragmentation is essential to navigate both its challenges and opportunities, especially in global sustainability governance. Fragmented governance structures can complicate coordination efforts due to overlapping mandates and the diversity of actors and institutions involved. This often results in inefficiencies or sometimes even conflicts. At the same time, fragmentation offers flexibility, allowing policymakers to utilize multiple institutions to address specific needs that may exceed the capacity of any single forum. To manage fragmentation effectively, practitioners should harness the potential of institutional integration and, for instance, strengthen skills in network coordination, cross-sector learning and interplay management.

46 *Essential Concepts for Implementing the SDGs*

In relation to the SDGs, considerations of fragmentation should already be embedded in early stages of policy development and implementation, rather than dealing with fragmentation after policy goals have already been established. A proactive approach to fragmentation may thus foster more coherent and adaptable governance for sustainable development.

References

Biermann, F., Pattberg, P., van Asselt, H., and Zelli, F. (2009). The fragmentation of global governance architectures: A framework for analysis. *Global Environmental Politics, 9*(4), 14–40. https://doi.org/10.1162/glep.2009.9.4.14

Elsässer, J. P. (2024). Managers of complex change? How United Nations treaty secretariats jointly govern institutional interplay in global environmental governance. *Environmental Policy and Governance,* 1–13. https://doi.org/10.1002/eet.2105

Elsässer, J. P., Hickmann, T., Jinnah, S., Oberthür, S., and Van de Graaf, T. (2022). Institutional interplay in global environmental governance: Lessons learned and future research. *International Environmental Agreements: Politics, Law and Economics, 22*(2), 373–391. https://doi.org/10.1007/s10784-022-09569-4

Hickmann, T., and Elsässer, J. P. (2020). New alliances in global environmental governance: How intergovernmental treaty secretariats interact with non-state actors to address transboundary environmental problems. *International Environmental Agreements, 20,* 459–481. https://doi.org/10.1007/s10784-020-09493-5

Kellow, A. (2012). Multi-level and multi-arena governance: The limits of integration and the possibilities of forum shopping. *International Environmental Agreements, 12*(4), 327–342. https://doi.org/10.1007/s10784-012-9172-3

Sommerer, T., Agné, H., Zelli, F., and Bes, B. (2022). *Global Legitimacy Crises: Decline and Revival in Multilateral Governance.* Oxford University Press. https://doi.org/10.1093/oso/9780192856326.001.0001

Zelli, F. (2011). The fragmentation of the global climate governance architecture. *Wiley Interdisciplinary Reviews: Climate Change, 2*(2), 255–270. https://doi.org/10.1002/Wcc.104

Zelli, F., and van Asselt, H. (2010). The overlap between the UN climate regime and the World Trade Organization: Lessons for post-2012 climate governance. In F. Biermann, P. Pattberg, and F. Zelli (Eds.), *Global Climate Governance Beyond 2012: Architecture, Agency and Adaptation* (pp. 79–96). Cambridge University Press.

G

Gender mainstreaming

Antra Bhatt, Laura Rahm and Tara Patricia Cookson

Gender mainstreaming was first introduced as a global strategy to promote gender equality in the 1995 Beijing Platform for Action. It was defined as 'the process of assessing the implications for women and men of any planned action, including legislation, policies or programmes, in all areas and at all levels' (United Nations Economic and Social Council 1997, 3). Gender mainstreaming is thus a means to achieve gender equality, rather than an end in itself.

The gender mainstreaming approach of the Millennium Development Goals was criticized for being technocratic and donor-driven (Palmary and Nunez 2009). By contrast, the Sustainable Development Goals (SDGs) opened pathways for greater local expertise and national ownership, pointing towards a *Gender Mainstreaming 2.0* approach (Novovic 2023). In practice, however, gender mainstreaming remains an unachieved agenda.

The 2030 Agenda for Sustainable Development emphasizes the ambition to realize human rights for all, including achieving gender equality and empowerment of all women and girls (United Nations General Assembly 2015). The adopted resolution explicitly states that 'the achievement of full human potential and of sustainable development is not possible if one half of humanity continues to be denied its full human rights and opportunities' and that 'the systematic mainstreaming of a gender perspective in the implementation of the Agenda is crucial' (United Nations General Assembly 2015, 6). Thus, the monitoring of the SDGs is expected to consider progress on a stand-alone goal (SDG 5) as well as gender as a cross-cutting issue influencing all other SDGs.

Gender mainstreaming has been particularly impactful in areas like education and maternal health. In education, efforts have focused on ensuring equal access for girls and boys. Global gender parity in primary and lower secondary education was achieved in 2009 and in upper secondary education in 2013, even if specific countries have followed various trajectories towards or away from parity. In maternal health, gender mainstreaming has been instrumental in addressing maternal mortality and reproductive health services as critical components of SDG 3. In countries like Rwanda, gender-sensitive health

DOI: 10.4324/9781003519560-9

This chapter has been made available under a CC-BY-NC-ND license.

48   *Essential Concepts for Implementing the SDGs*

interventions have improved maternal survival rates by expanding access to prenatal and postnatal care.

Despite these wins, barriers to mainstreaming gender across all the SDGs remain. Data gaps are part of this story: 4 of the 18 indicators and sub-indicators under SDG 5 cannot be fully assessed globally. Out of 232 indicators selected for global monitoring of the SDGs, only 52 are gender-specific (Bhatt et al. 2024). Structural power imbalances, especially in resource sharing, are missing from the SDGs (MacGregor and Ursula Mäki 2023). For instance, climate-related goals such as SDG 13 (Climate Action), SDG 14 (Life Below Water) and SDG 15 (Life on Land) overlook gendered dimensions of access to natural resources and the vulnerabilities of women farmers. A major challenge has been data disaggregation to identify and monitor progress for groups that face multiple inequalities and deprivations and deliver on the promise to 'leave no one behind' (United Nations Women 2018).

Gender mainstreaming is a powerful tool for SDG implementation that can ensure that gender perspectives are incorporated into all aspects of policy and programme development. Its implementation, however, faces challenges. Tokenistic approaches, data gaps and political resistance continue to undermine efforts towards gender equality. To fully realize its transformative potential, a more comprehensive and intersectional approach is needed, supported by robust data and accountability mechanisms such as the Gender Equality Marker, Voluntary National Reviews and a stocktaking of gender mainstreaming efforts by policymakers during the annual Commission on the Status of Women (United Nations Women 2018). Only then can the SDGs be inclusive and effective in addressing the gendered dimensions of sustainable development.

References

Bhatt, A., Fortuny, G., Frick, F., Min, Y., Page, H., Tosi, N., and You, S. (2024). *Progress on the Sustainable Development Goals: The Gender Snapshot 2024*. United Nations Women. https://unstats.un.org/sdgs/gender-snapshot/2024/GenderSnapshot2024.pdf

MacGregor, S., and Ursula Mäki, A. (2023). 'We do not want to be mainstreamed into a polluted stream': An ecofeminist critique of SDG 5. In L. Partzsch (Ed.), *The Environment in Global Sustainability Governance* (pp. 220–242). Bristol University Press. https://doi.org/10.51952/9781529228021.ch018

Novovic, G. (2023). Gender mainstreaming 2.0: Emergent gender equality agendas under Sustainable Development Goals. *Third World Quarterly*, 44(5), 1058–1076. https://doi.org/10.1080/01436597.2023.2174848

Palmary, I., and Nunez, L. (2009). The orthodoxy of gender mainstreaming: reflecting on gender mainstreaming as a strategy for accomplishing the millennium development goals. *Journal of Health Management*, 11(1), 65–78. https://doi.org/10.1177/097206340901100105

United Nations Economic and Social Council. (1997). *Mainstreaming the Gender Perspective Into All Policies and Programmes in the United Nations System* (A/52/3). United Nations. https://www.un.org/womenwatch/osagi/pdf/ECOSOCAC1997.2.PDF

United Nations General Assembly. (2015). *Transforming Our World: The 2030 Agenda for Sustainable Development*. A/RES/70/1. https://sustainabledevelopment.un.org/content/documents/21252030%20Agenda%20for%20Sustainable%20Development%20web.pdf

United Nations Women. (2018). *Turning Promises into Action. Gender Equality in the 2030 Agenda*. United Nations Women. https://www.unwomen.org/en/digital-library/publications/2018/2/gender-equality-in-the-2030-agenda-for-sustainable-development-2018

Global Sustainable Development Reports (GSDR)

Shirin Malekpour and Cameron Allen

The Global Sustainable Development Report (GSDR) is a science-policy report prepared every four years by an Independent Group of Scientists appointed by the United Nations Secretary-General to synthesize available evidence on how transformational change to achieve the Sustainable Development Goals (SDGs) could be facilitated. The GSDR was mandated in 2016 by the United Nations (UN) member states as an important component of the review and follow-up process for the 2030 Agenda. The Ministerial Declaration (E/HLS/2016/1) of the High-level Political Forum on Sustainable Development asked for the report to provide strong evidence-based instruments and recommendations to support policymakers in advancing sustainable development. It also requested the formation of the Independent Group of Scientists for each quadrennial report, comprising 15 independent experts from diverse scientific disciplines, ensuring geographical and gender balance. This was a shift away from prototype editions of the GSDR prior to the adoption of the SDGs that were written within the United Nations system.

The GSDR differs from and complements the Sustainable Development Goals progress report prepared annually by the United Nations. The Sustainable Development Goals progress report uses the global indicator framework and data from national or regional statistical systems to quantitatively report on SDG progress. The GSDR, on the other hand, is more qualitative and analytical in nature, with a focus on providing frameworks, tools and policy recommendations for SDG transformations. Government officials and policymakers in United Nations member states are the main audience of the GSDR. Countries, such as Germany, have adopted the frameworks offered by the GSDR in their national sustainable development planning and strategy making (German Federal Government 2021). The report has also been used by other societal actors and in different sectors (for example, Allen et al. 2024; United Cities and Local Governments 2024).

While the GSDR relies on scientific evidence, extensive consultation is undertaken in different regions and input is sought from different sectors at all levels, including governments, the private sector, scientific bodies and expert groups. The report also draws on other major assessments and substantive reports prepared by the United Nations system or other global and regional policy organizations. The draft is peer-reviewed by a large international group of experts from various fields.

The first GSDR was launched in 2019 and the second in 2023 (Independent Group of Scientists 2019, 2023). Both reports identified six 'entry points' that offer the most promise for transformations at scale and support a systemic approach considering SDG interconnections. The entry points are: human well-being and capabilities, sustainable and just economies, sustainable food systems and healthy nutrition, energy decarbonization with universal access, urban and peri-urban development, and global environmental commons. Both reports also suggested 'levers' of change, highlighting the means of implementation and the multiple and complementary roles different societal actors can play in SDG transformations. The levers include governance, economy and finance, individual and collective action, science and technology, and capacity-building.

With the COVID-19 pandemic between the two reports, the 2023 GSDR emphasizes the need for accelerated and strategic action to turn the dial on SDG progress. It

50 *Essential Concepts for Implementing the SDGs*

synthesizes evidence from global scenario modelling to highlight that business-as-usual action will not achieve the SDGs by 2030 or even 2050. However, working through the six entry points and setting deliberate policies could unleash rapid progress. The report lists key transformative shifts and interventions that can accelerate progress across different entry points. The 2023 report also provides a framework for understanding the different phases of transformation as they unfold over time, highlighting impediments and enablers in each phase. The framework emphasizes that transformation processes need to be strategically driven from emergence to acceleration to stabilization, while unsustainable systems need to simultaneously go through phases of decline. The next GSDR is expected to be published in 2027 and lay the scientific foundation for the post-2030 global agenda.

References

Allen, C., Biddulph, A., Wiedmann, T., Pedercini, M., and Malekpour, S. (2024). Modelling six sustainable development transformations in Australia and their accelerators, impediments, enablers and interlinkages. *Nature Communications*, 15(594). https://doi.org/10.1038/s41467-023-44655-4

German Federal Government. (2021). *German Sustainable Development Strategy*. http://www.sustainable-development.gov.uk/publications/pdf/strategy/SecFut_complete.pdf

Independent Group of Scientists. (2019). *Global Sustainable Development Report 2019: The Future is Now: Science for Achieving Sustainable Development*. United Nations.

Independent Group of Scientists. (2023). *Global Sustainable Development Report 2023: Times of Crisis, Times of Change: Science for Accelerating Transformations to Sustainable Development*. United Nations.

United Cities and Local Governments. (2024). *Towards the Localization of the SDGs*. https://www.uclg.org/sites/default/files/towards_the_localization_of_the_sdgs.pdf

Governance by global goal-setting

Norichika Kanie

Governance by global goal-setting is an emerging concept which was conceptualized during the formulation of the 2030 Agenda and the Sustainable Development Goals (SDGs). It can be regarded as a strategy of global governance that is based on the idea of setting a wide range of goals around a particular issue. In the case of the SDGs, goals and associated targets, which describe further details of the goals, do not include explicit means of implementation. Rather, a variety of implementation pathways can emerge so long as they are heading towards the goals. Such a process provides an opportunity for partnerships and collaboration as well as social and technical innovations.

Goal-setting is not an entirely new phenomenon or a novel practice in international relations and global governance (Kanie and Biermann 2017). In fact, most international institutions, United Nations programmes or multilateral agreements are rooted in broad goals and objectives, such as peace and justice or protecting the global climate. The United Nations Framework Convention on Climate Change, for example, states as its objective in Article 2: 'to achieve, in accordance with the relevant provisions of the Convention, stabilization of greenhouse gas concentrations in the atmosphere at a level that would prevent dangerous anthropogenic interference with the climate system' (United Nations 2015).

The SDGs, however, differ from those cases of goals and objectives by both quantity and quality: quantity in terms of their wide range of coverage, involving basically all issues related to sustainable development, and quality in terms of detailed description of targets and target years associated with the goals (Kamau et al. 2018).

The characteristics of governance by goal-setting can be further clarified by comparing them with governance by rule-setting, which is represented by international regimes as a set of rules (Young 2017). Governance by goal-setting is future-oriented; therefore, its governance forms are back-casting in nature, whereas governance by rule-setting is based upon the legal framework and forecasting in nature. International negotiations for governance by goal-setting is a consensus-making process for sharing goals and visions, whereas governance by rule-setting is marked by changes within legal frameworks. There is thus no fixed implementation mechanism associated with governance by goal-setting, and it is also not legally binding.

This nature could be regarded as weaknesses of governance by goal-setting, but at the same time it leaves space for innovation in ways of implementation, which could be a strength and potentially an integrative force for many stakeholders involved in the global endeavour to achieve global goals.

References

Kamau, M., Chasek, P., and O'Connor, D. (2018) *Transforming Multilpateral Diplomacy: The Inside Story of the Sustainable Development Goals*. New York: Routledge.

Kanie, N., and Biermann, F. (Eds.). (2017) *Governing through Goals: Sustainable Development Goals as Governance Innovation*. Cambridge: MIT Press.

United Nations. (2015) *Paris Agreement*. https://unfccc.int/sites/default/files/resource/parisagreement_publication.pdf

Young, O. R. (2017) Conceptualization: Goal Setting as Strategy for Earth System Governance, in Kanie, N., and Biermann, F. (Eds.), *Governing through Goals: Sustainable Development Goals as Governance Innovation* (pp. 31–51). Cambridge: MIT Press.

H

High-level Political Forum on Sustainable Development (HLPF)

Thomas Hickmann

The High-level Political Forum on Sustainable Development (HLPF) was formally established in July 2013 through a resolution of the United Nations General Assembly (United Nations 2013). It is a key outcome of the 2012 United Nations Conference on Sustainable Development held in Rio de Janeiro, Brazil. The HLPF replaced the earlier Commission on Sustainable Development that was widely seen as being incapable of attracting the attention of high-level policymakers and of fostering concrete actions and policy impact on sustainable development (Abbott and Bernstein 2015). Therefore, the HLPF was endowed with a stronger mandate to provide political leadership for sustainable development, and it was designed as the central platform for the review and follow-up of the 2030 Agenda and the Sustainable Development Goals (SDGs). In the annual events of the HLPF at the headquarters of the United Nations in New York, heads of state, ministers and societal stakeholders assess the progress of SDG implementation, and countries submit and present their respective Voluntary National Reviews.

While the HLPF takes a central position in the global governance system to promote SDG implementation in domestic settings, researchers have pointed out that it lacks clear means to hold governments accountable for advancing the SDGs (Beisheim and Fritzsche 2022; Partzsch 2023). First and foremost, the reporting system is essentially a soft governance instrument based on the idea to foster peer-to-peer learning about best or good practices of SDG implementation in national jurisdictions (Bernstein 2017). Governments are free to decide whether they submit Voluntary National Reviews or not and how they formulate their individual reports. While a large number of countries have submitted reports, most reports fail to critically engage with the problems of goal implementation and instead rather showcase single success stories. Civil society actors do not have a strong role in the review and thus cannot act as watchdogs drawing attention to deficiencies and delays in SDG implementation. Growing political conflicts in multilateral settings and limited resources are additional reasons that impede the effectiveness of the HLPF.

Looking ahead, the HLPF could become more impactful if it would evolve into a forum with stronger mechanisms for accountability, potentially incorporating binding commitments or clearer enforcement measures. The forum's inclusivity could be expanded

DOI: 10.4324/9781003519560-10

This chapter has been made available under a CC-BY-NC-ND license.

through larger participation of civil society, local governments and the private sector to ensure that diverse perspectives are reflected in discussions. Finally, integration of digital tools and platforms could help improve transparency and accessibility of the HLPF, making it more responsive to global and regional challenges as they arise. Such ideas to upgrade the HLPF, however, are highly unlikely to materialize, because conflict lines from other areas of global cooperation and fears of governments to be publicly shamed for underperformance continue to block the further development of the HLPF (Beisheim 2021).

References

Abbott, K. W., and Bernstein, S. (2015). The high-level political forum on sustainable development: Orchestration by default and design. *Global Policy, 6*(3), 222–233.

Beisheim, M. (2021). *Conflicts in UN reform negotiations: Insights into and from the review of the High-level Political Forum on Sustainable Development.* SWP Research Paper 9.

Beisheim, M., and Fritzsche, F. (2022). The UN high-level political forum on sustainable development: An orchestrator, more or less? *Global Policy, 13*(5), 683–693.

Bernstein, S. (2017). The United Nations and the governance of sustainable development goals. In Kanie, N., and Biermann, F. (eds.), *Governing through Goals: Sustainable Development Goals as Governance Innovation.* Cambridge: MIT Press, 213–240.

Partzsch, L. (2023). Missing the SDGs: Political accountability for insufficient environmental action. *Global Policy, 14*(3), 438–450.

United Nations. (2013). *Format and Organizational Aspects of the High-Level Political Forum on Sustainable Development.* A/RES/67/290. New York: United Nations General Assembly.

Human rights

Andrea Schapper

Human rights are intersubjectively shared norms and principles to which everyone is entitled by virtue of being human (Schmitz and Sikkink 2013). According to social contract theory, human rights define the relationship between a state government and its citizens. However, we increasingly see other actors governed by human rights and engaged in human rights governance, such as non-governmental actors or multinational corporations (Schmitz and Sikkink 2013). Most human rights are anchored in international or regional legal frameworks and institutions. Within the United Nations (UN) human rights system, there are nine core international human rights instruments and their respective monitoring bodies (OHCHR 2024).

Human rights play a key role in all three dimensions of sustainable development, including economic, social and environmental concerns. The preamble of the 2030 Agenda for Sustainable Development highlights that one objective of the Sustainable Development Goals (SDGs) is '[...] to realize human rights for all' (United Nations General Assembly 2015). The Agenda is based on important human rights principles, like non-discrimination and equality. Some SDGs have strong overlaps and synergies with concrete human rights. Examples are zero hunger (SDG 2) and the right to food; good health, well-being (SDG 3) and the right to health; or quality education (SDG 4) and the right to education. Whereas these are mainly economic, social and cultural rights, goals like gender inequality (SDG 5) and reduced inequalities (SDG 10) embrace civil and political rights as well. In addition to

54 Essential Concepts for Implementing the SDGs

individual rights, the SDGs correspond with collective rights, including the right to development (for example, 'no poverty' SDG 1) and the right to a healthy environment (for example, 'climate action' SDG 13, 'life below water' SDG 14, 'life of land' SDG 15).

Despite these strong overlaps between human rights and the SDGs, concrete policy programmes and projects implemented under the framework of the 2030 Agenda can also conflict with rights. A prime example is large-scale renewable energy projects, like hydroelectric dam projects or solar power plants. These are often planned and funded by development banks, governments or private investors, who use the SDGs, especially 'affordable and clean energy' (SDG 7), 'industry, innovation and infrastructure' (SDG 9) or 'climate action' (SDG 13) to justify and seek co-funding for their activities. There is ample evidence that, in the implementation process, large-scale renewable energy projects can infringe on individual human rights and the rights of Indigenous Peoples (Schapper 2021; Schapper et al. 2020). These can be direct rights violations via forceful relocations of local community groups that can endanger their rights to life, personal integrity, security or health, or indirect rights infringements when communities lose access to their traditional lands or water and their rights to self-determination, food, water, health or education are at risk (Bartmann et al. 2023; Schapper 2021). In addition to these substantive rights, procedural rights, such as Indigenous Peoples' right to free, prior and informed consent, are also often neglected in the context of projects justified under the SDG Agenda (Schapper 2021).

One way forward could, therefore, be a better integration of human rights in the 2030 Agenda for Sustainable Development. This could be done by making use of the established human rights monitoring mechanisms and bodies for SDG reporting, or by using human rights impact assessments when implementing UN-funded projects under the framework of the SDGs. Moreover, including procedural rights, such as the right to information, transparency, participation in decision-making and access to remedies in SDG implementation projects, can prevent adverse human rights effects on the ground and enable just transitions (Bexell et al. 2023).

References

Bartmann, M., Halsband, A., and Schapper, A. (2023). *Climate Justice: Ethical Aspects and Policy Aspects* (Vol. 26). Baden-Baden: Verlag Karl Alber.

Bexell, M., Hickmann, T., and Schapper, A. (2023). Strengthening the Sustainable Development Goals through integration with human rights. *International Environmental Agreements: Politics, Law and Economics*, 23, 133–139. https://doi.org/10.1007/s10784-023-09605-x

OHCHR. (2024). The Core International Human Rights Instruments and their monitoring bodies. https://www.ohchr.org/en/core-international-human-rights-instruments-and-their-monitoring-bodies

Schapper, A. (2021). Climate justice concerns and human rights trade-offs in Ethiopia's green economy transition: The case of Gibe III. *European Journal of Development Research*, 33, 1952–1972.

Schapper, A., Unrau, C., and Killoh, S. (2020). Social mobilization against large hydroelectric dams: A comparison of Ethiopia, Brazil and Panama. *Sustainable Development*, 28(2), 413–423. https://doi.org/10.1002/sd.1995

Schmitz, H. P., and Sikkink, K. (2013). International human rights. In W. Carlsnaes, T. Risse, and B. A. Simmons (Eds.), *Handbook of International Relations* (pp. 827–852). London: SAGE.

United Nations General Assembly. (2015). Transforming our world: The 2030 agenda for sustainable development. A/RES/70/1. https://sdgs.un.org/publications/transforming-our-world-2030-agenda-sustainable-development-17981

I

Implementation

Kristina Jönsson and Marie Stissing Jensen

Implementation can be defined as the process of turning a policy, or a decision, into action. One could also define it as what happens between policy expectations and policy results (Buse et al. 2023). Here, implementation specifically refers to the implementation of the Sustainable Development Goals (SDGs) and their targets and to the 2030 Agenda as a global policy framework. This implies both governance through ranking and reporting on the SDG indicators and implementation through policy steering at multiple levels (Órdoñez Llanos et al. 2022). The overall aim is to govern transformations towards sustainable development.

The 2030 Agenda includes a specific goal – SDG 17 – dedicated to the means of implementation. Both the preamble of the 2030 Agenda and SDG 17 state that its implementation requires a 'revitalized global partnership', which mainly refers to a call for high-income countries to support lower income countries by emphasizing two main pathways to implementing the goals: 1) through financial redistribution between countries and strengthening of domestic resource mobilization and 2) through multi-stakeholder partnerships – not the least by focusing on underrepresented and cross-cutting goals (Glass et al. 2023). This approach involves integration across sectors, societal actors and countries.

The responsibility for realizing the SDGs lies primarily with national and local governments. This means that there are no sanctions at the global level for *not* implementing the SDGs other than 'naming and shaming' through reporting and pointing fingers. Governments can implement the SDGs through legislation, strategies and policies. They can do this through existing institutions or by creating new ones (Bexell and Jönsson 2021). Subnational governments are supposed to align with these initiatives, but so far, the impact of SDG implementation has been limited at this level (Hickmann et al. 2024). Other actors, such as business, academia, civil society and citizens are expected to contribute to the implementation in their different capacities, for example, through partnership brokering, facilitating knowledge sharing and technology transfer.

DOI: 10.4324/9781003519560-11

This chapter has been made available under a CC-BY-NC-ND license.

56 Essential Concepts for Implementing the SDGs

In practice, SDG implementation faces many hurdles. According to the 2030 Agenda, each country should implement the SDGs based on its own context and circumstances, leaving plenty of room for interpretations of what to implement. As a result, cherry-picking occurs in implementation, whereby governments implement only those goals on which they are able to achieve progress (Forestier and Kim 2020). In some cases, the implementation of the SDGs reflects 'business as usual' as it largely overlaps with existing policies. In other words, some actors merely use the SDGs as a communication tool to relabel existing policies, while others use the SDGs to strive for transformative change by breaking down organizational silos and building new institutions to cater for the implementation of the SDGs (Órdoñez Llanos et al. 2022).

Halfway through the 2030 Agenda, the implementation of the SDGs is seriously off track (Sachs et al. 2024). Some countries face larger challenges than others because of limited resources or political obstacles, but even the wealthiest countries will fail to implement all the SDGs by 2030. As current societal challenges are worsening, the implementation of the SDGs will face increasing competition from other political initiatives to tackle multiple crises, such as conflicts in several regions, a cost-of-living and debt crisis and climate-related disasters.

In sum, the implementation of the SDGs is a complex process of transforming policies into action, which requires collaboration at multiple levels. Some countries focus on individual SDGs while others take a more holistic approach by working with the whole 2030 Agenda. Progress is uneven with many challenges, including limited resources and multiple crises impeding success by the year 2030.

References

Bexell, M., and Jönsson, K. (2021). *The Politics of the Sustainable Development Goals – Legitimacy, Responsibility and Accountability.* London and New York: Routledge. https://doi.org/10.4324/9781003043614

Buse, K., Mays, N., Colombini, M., Fraser, A., Khan, M., and Walls, H. (2023). *Making Health Policy.* Open University Press.

Forestier, O and Kim, R. E. (2020). Cherry-picking the Sustainable Development Goals: Goal prioritization by national governments and implications for global governance. *Sustainable Development*, 28, 1269–1278. https://doi.org/10.1002/sd.2082

Glass, L. M., Newig, J., and Ruf, S. (2023). MSPs for the SDGs – Assessing the collaborative governance architecture of multi-stakeholder partnerships for implementing the Sustainable Development Goals. *Earth System Governance*, 17, 100182. https://doi.org/10.1016/j.esg.2023.100182

Hickmann, T., Biermann, F., Sénit, C. A., Sun, Y., ... and Weiland, S. (2024). Scoping article: Research frontiers on the governance of the Sustainable Development Goals. *Global Sustainability*, 7, e7. https://doi.org/10.1017/sus.2024.4

Órdoñez Llanos, A., Raven, R., Bexell, M., Botchwey, B., Bornemann, B., Censoro, J., Christen, M., Diaz, L., Hickmann, T., Jönsson, K., Scholz, I., Scobie, M., Sun, Y., Thompson, J., Thwaites, J., and Yunita, A. (2022) Implementation at multiple levels. In Biermann, F., Hickmann, T., and Sénit, C. A. (Eds.), *The Political Impact of the Sustainable Development Goals. Transforming Governance through Global Goals?* (pp 59–91). Cambridge: Cambridge University Press. https://www.cambridge.org/core/books/the-political-impact-of-the-sustainable-development-goals/3EA0D6589094B68A527FCB05C895F73E

Sachs, J. D., Lafortune, G., and Fuller, G. (2024). *The SDGs and the UN Summit of the Future. Sustainable Development Report 2024.* Dublin: Dublin University Press. https://doi.org/10.25546/108572

Inclusiveness

Guilherme de Queiroz-Stein

The concept of inclusiveness brings to the sustainable development discussion principles linked to the defence of human rights, redistributive and procedural justice and capacity-building. This idea has gained political appeal under the motto 'Leaving no one behind', which calls for a sustainable, equitable and fair development, both nationally and internationally. It is, therefore, a conception with a strong normative component, necessarily intersectional, involving criteria of age, race, gender, social class and ethnicity to overcome the mechanisms that generate exclusion and inequalities (Sénit et al. 2022). Translating it to SDG implementation, actions encompass reducing the vulnerability of these populations to economic, environmental and health crises and increasing their chances of enjoying the value generated and accumulated collectively (Gupta and Vegelin 2016; Sen 1999). Analytically, it can be understood in socioeconomic, political and ecological dimensions.

Socioeconomic inclusiveness refers to providing solutions to material needs and fighting recognition faults to make the full participation of historically marginalized populations in the socioeconomic systems effective (Gupta and Vegelin 2016). All the SDGs between 1 and 11 contribute to this dimension, especially 1 – No Poverty, 2 – Zero Hunger, 5 – Gender Equality and 10 – Reduced Inequalities. Also, international cooperation is crucial here (SDG 17). The political dimension is intrinsically connected to democratic principles. Higher levels of freedom, fairness, participation, representativeness and accountability enhance political inclusiveness (Sénit et al. 2022). This dimension is closely related to SDG 16, which strives for maintaining peace and confronting all forms of violence, guaranteeing access to justice for all. Finally, ecological inclusiveness means guaranteeing the right of all countries, peoples and individuals to an ecologically healthy environment, reducing vulnerability to natural disasters and the climate crisis. Some SDGs explicitly deal with this dimension, regarding global warming issues (SDGs 7, 11, 12 and 13) and biodiversity protection (SDGs 14 and 15).

Operationalizing the SDGs in an inclusive way may face significant challenges. It is not enough to solve problems of material well-being. It is also necessary to tackle obstacles linked to the recognition and legitimate participation of minorities in social and institutional life (Fraser 2001). Furthermore, democratic arrangements must go beyond consolidating formal rules; the power relations that permeate concrete political dynamics must allow space for multiple voices and innovative forms of social organization to emerge (Fischer 2017). Finally, actions for environmental protection often need to better equate to the socioeconomic dimension, considering the decisive role of the traditional knowledge of Indigenous peoples and local communities and the need for combating urban poverty and inequalities (Queiroz-Stein and Siegel 2023).

Programmes and policies for SDG implementation must follow some specific directions to avoid these flaws. Actions for sustainability must bring together socioeconomic and ecological dimensions through a fair and equitable (re)distribution of available resources and capacities. Governments, judiciary institutions and civil society actors must protect access to natural resources and local ownership and promote the sustainable uses

58 *Essential Concepts for Implementing the SDGs*

of biodiversity for a healthy environment. Fighting stigmas and prejudices against minorities is also crucial. The knowledge and interests of these populations are decisive for building new sustainable development pathways. They must be included by truly participatory arrangements, in direct dialogue with excluded groups' claims, demands and ideas. Therefore, participation is the foundation for developing the adaptive capacity of cities and communities to face climate change and environmental degradation, building paths for restoring ecosystems and creating innovative green economic activities and jobs. Consequently, SDGs can only be achieved in an environment of high political inclusiveness and reinforcing democratic institutions and values. Above all, inclusiveness is about building more symmetrical relationships within societies and between humanity and nature.

References

Fischer, F. (2017). *Climate crisis and the democratic prospect: Participatory governance in sustainable communities.* Oxford: Oxford University Press.

Fraser, N. (2001). Recognition without ethics? *Theory, Culture and Society, 18*(2–3), 21–42.

Gupta, J., and Vegelin, C. (2016). Sustainable development goals and inclusive development. *International Environmental Agreements: Politics, Law and Economics, 16*, 433–448.

Queiroz-Stein, G., and Siegel, K. M. (2023). Possibilities for mainstreaming biodiversity? Two perspectives on the concept of bioeconomy. *Earth System Governance, 17*, 100181.

Sen, A. (1999). *Development as freedom.* Oxford: Oxford University Press.

Sénit, C.-A., Okereke, C., Alcázar, L., Banik, D., Lima, M. B., Biermann, F., Fambasayi, R., Hathie, I., Kronsell, A., Leonardsson, H., Niles, N., and Siegel, K. M. (2022). Inclusiveness. In F. Biermann, T. Hickmann, and C.-A. Sénit (Eds.), *The political impact of the Sustainable Development Goals: transforming governance through global goals?* (pp. 116–139). Cambridge University Press.

Independent Group of Scientists (IGS)

Ibrahima Hathie

The Independent Group of Scientists (IGS) comprises 15 experts appointed by the United Nations Secretary-General to draft the Global Sustainable Development Report, published every four years. Members of the IGS are selected through a structured and transparent process overseen by the United Nations Secretary-General. This process involves nominations from member states, compliance with diversity and expertise criteria and final appointments made by the Secretary-General. In the end, the 15 experts selected come from different scientific disciplines and geographical origins, with a gender balance, thus ensuring a diverse representation of perspectives. The aim of this approach is to create a well-balanced and effective group capable of meeting the complex challenges of sustainable development.

The IGS was first established following the 2016 High-level Political Forum on Sustainable Development, where member states mandated the creation of IGS to strengthen the science-policy interface in discussions on sustainable development (United Nations 2016). The group plays a crucial role in informing the High-level

Political Forum by providing evidence-based guidance on the state of global sustainable development and progress towards the SDGs. It is thus an essential component of the United Nations' efforts to integrate scientific knowledge into sustainable development policymaking.

The IGS is responsible for synthesizing information and assessments from a wide range of sources, including scientific literature, to produce a comprehensive report that addresses pressing global issues related to sustainable development. The United Nations Task Force supports IGS in its work to ensure that the report is comprehensive, well-informed and reflects diverse perspectives on sustainable development. The Task Force supports IGS by coordinating the contributions of a diverse network of stakeholders, providing technical assistance, facilitating collaboration and ensuring alignment with global goals. This multifaceted support is essential to the successful preparation and impact of the Global Sustainable Development Report.

In carrying out its mission, however, the IGS faces a number of challenges (IGS 2023). First, global inequalities are complex and, as a result, require context-specific research and solutions that take account of local realities, which make it difficult to implement the SDGs uniformly in different regions. Second, there is a lack of political will to implement the necessary transformations described in the Global Sustainable Development Report. Hence, the need to strengthen political leadership in order to overcome entrenched interests and resistance to change and mobilize resources effectively. Third, the siloed nature of the scientific community hinders the development of global solutions when a more transdisciplinary approach would enable complex global problems to be tackled with a greater chance of success. Finally, the under-funded scientific systems and the lack of local expertise in low- and middle-income countries are another challenge. Added to this is the importance of increasing scientific literacy and confidence in scientific data among policymakers and the public, to promote informed decision-making.

By producing the Global Sustainable Development Report, the IGS helps to shape international discourse and action on sustainability, ensuring that decisions are based on sound scientific evidence and diverse perspectives. The work of the IGS reflects a commitment to tackling global challenges collaboratively and effectively as the world strives to achieve the ambitious goals set out in the 2030 Agenda for Sustainable Development. It has received a very favourable response from the scientific community and is being listened to carefully by decision-makers, even though the challenges of putting the recommendations into practice remain (Malekpour et al. 2023).

References

Independent Group of Scientists. (2023). *Global Sustainable Development Report 2023: Times of Crisis, Times of Change: Science for Accelerating Transformations to Sustainable Development.* United Nations. https://doi.org/10.18356/9789213585115

Malekpour, S., Allen, C., Sagar, A., Scholz, I., Persson, Å., Miranda, J. J., Bennich, T., Dube, O.P., Kanie, N., Madise, N., Shackell, N., Montoya, J. C., Pan, J., Hathie, I., Bobylev, S. N., Agard, J., and Al-Ghanim, K. (2023). What scientists need to do to accelerate progress on the SDGs. *Nature*, 621, 250–254.

United Nations. (2016). Ministerial declaration of the 2016 high-level political forum on sustainable development, convened under the auspices of the Economic and Social Council, on the theme 'Ensuring that no one is left behind'. E/HLS/2016/1. Annex. https://sdgs.un.org/sites/default/files/documents/11654Annex_Min_declaration_HLPF2016.pdf

Indicators

Félicien Pagnon and Grayson Fuller

Indicators are one of the main vehicles for implementing the Sustainable Development Goals (SDGs). They allow tracking progress on the different dimensions of the SDGs. With the 2030 Agenda, adopted by the United Nations General Assembly, the 17 goals come to define the horizon for action on sustainable development, which break down into 169 targets and 244 indicators (232 without double counting).

The large number of indicators owes much to the diplomatic negotiations between states within the framework of the United Nations General Assembly (Caron and Châtaigner 2017): multiplying the number of dimensions covered by numbers had the advantage of producing an international consensus around the SDGs and bringing together a very large number of sovereign actors to validate their relevance.

Indicators can be defined as synthetic summaries of information in numerical form. They make it possible to grasp complex natural, social and economic phenomena simply by looking at the evolution of a figure. Most importantly, they enable us to objectify a phenomenon beyond words. For instance, Saudi Arabia's 2023 Voluntary National Review on SDGs claimed 'Saudi Arabia has taken major steps to address climate change and reduce its greenhouse gas emissions' (Government of Saudi Arabia 2023: 153). However, figures on greenhouse gas emissions per capita (SDG 13) do not appear, as it belies this claim. Indicators thus confer a form of transparency on information when they are produced and/or verified by an independent authority. They therefore offer citizens and civil society a means of holding political authorities accountable for public action (Porter 1995).

Scholars have questioned the role of quantified goals in policy implementation (Bruno et al. 2016), especially the use of indicators in global governance and international organizations (Davis et al. 2012). Indicators do not fully reflect the state of the world; instead, they are social constructs. They *indicate* something, show a direction to follow and set a horizon – which is why they are used as valuable governance tools. Once set, they depoliticize public policy and serve as a monitoring tool. Choosing indicators is therefore highly political.

SDG indicators have various functions in global and national governance: they can be used to describe a state, set quantified objectives (Ward 2004), but also to evaluate public policies, allocate budgets and direct aid and subsidies (Hege et al. 2019). Most importantly, the performance or perceived progress of a country depends on the indicators chosen. For instance, composite indices looking at economic criteria such as the Gross Domestic Product and the Gross National Income tell a different story than indicators that look at socioeconomic progress more systematically, such as the Human Development Index, which themselves give very different pictures than indicators focused primarily on the environment or sustainable development (Pagnon 2022).

The use of indicators to govern sustainable development also has significant limitations. First, United Nations member states' ability to produce data is highly uneven, creating technical dependency on the United Nations Statistics Division for countries without adequate statistical services. Secondly, the profusion of indicators allows for 'cherry-picking' among the most convenient indicators to demonstrate progress towards sustainable development. This is especially true for high-income countries, which have already largely achieved their targets and for whom many indicators are of little relevance. Finally, SDGs may risk encouraging states to focus on the performance of individual indicators, at the risk of losing a holistic and integrated view of sustainable development. This calls for caution when using and interpreting SDG indicators and all indicators more broadly, to guide public policy.

References

Bruno, I., Jany-Catrice, F., and Touchelay, B. (2016). *The social sciences of quantification: From politics of large numbers to target-driven policies.* Springer Cham.

Caron, P., and Châtaigner, J.-M. (eds.). (2017). *Un défi pour la planète: les objectifs de développement durable en débat.* IRD Éditions.

Davis, K. E., Fisher, A., Kingsbury, B., and Engle, Merry S. (eds.). (2012). *Governance by indicators: Global power through quantification and rankings.* Oxford University Press and Institute for International Law and Justice.

Government of Saudi Arabia. (2023). Accelerating to achieve a sustainable future: Saudi Arabia's Voluntary National Review, 1444–2023.

Hege, E., Brimont, L., and Pagnon, F. (2019). Sustainable Development Goals and indicators: Can they be tools to make national budgets more sustainable?. *Public Sector Economics*, 43(4), 423–444. https://doi.org/10.3326/pse.43.4.5

Pagnon, F. (2022). *Après la croissance. Controverses autour de la production et de l'usage des indicateurs alternatifs au PIB.* Doctoral thesis in Sociology, Paris-Dauphine-PSL University.

Porter, T. M. (1995). *Trust in numbers: The pursuit of objectivity in science and public life.* Princeton University Press.

Ward, M. (2004). *Quantifying the world. UN ideas and statistics.* Indiana University Press.

Indigenous views

Rosalind Warner

The United Nations Declaration on the Rights of Indigenous Peoples, adopted in 2007 by the General Assembly, enjoins all member states to 'respect, protect and fulfil' the rights of Indigenous peoples through the United Nations, including the 2030 Agenda and the Sustainable Development Goals (SDGs). Indigenous perspectives play a significant role in the SDGs adopted in 2015, reflecting a more inclusive approach compared to previous global normative frameworks on sustainable development. Indigenous peoples were one of the nine 'major groups' that were involved in consultations and discussions in the lead-up to the adoption of the 2030 Agenda. In addition, the 2030 Agenda includes six direct references to Indigenous peoples, in the political declaration, specific targets (Goal 2 on Zero Hunger and Goal 4 on Education) and in the section on follow-up and review (United Nations Division for Inclusive Social Development 2022).

As a result of the United Nations Declaration on the Rights of Indigenous Peoples and the participation of Indigenous peoples in the negotiations of the SDGs, the SDGs' broader view of development as 'a plan of action for people, planet and prosperity' aligns with Indigenous worldviews more closely than previous perspectives, in that it recognizes the interconnectedness of human well-being and environmental sustainability.

62   *Essential Concepts for Implementing the SDGs*

Indigenous peoples play an outsized role in advancing the SDGs in their territories and regions under their control through their traditional knowledge and practices, particularly in promoting food systems that provide healthy nutrition (SDGs 2 and 3), climate resilience (SDG 13) and sustainable natural resource management (SDGs 14 and 15). For example, Indigenous territories cover approximately 28.1% of Earth's terrestrial surface. Globally, tree cover loss in such areas is lower on Indigenous lands (Simkins et al. 2024), contributing to one of the key targets of SDG 15.2, which is to reduce deforestation and restore and sustainably manage forests. In another example, one study has shown that maintaining Indigenous healing practices and intergenerational transmission of Indigenous culture are associated with better health, advancing SDG 3, which aims to promote health and well-being (Gallardo-Peralta et al. 2019).

Despite their contribution to SDG implementation, Indigenous peoples are also some of the most vulnerable groups and among those most likely to be 'left behind' when it comes to eliminating poverty (SDG 1) and protecting their land rights. The 2030 Agenda has been criticized by Indigenous peoples for its anthropocentric focus, lack of integration of cultural goals and the potential conflict between economic growth targets and Indigenous rights, particularly land rights and ownership of knowledge systems (van Norren 2020: 444). In addition, concerns exist around the invisibility of Indigenous Peoples in the SDG indicators, since they are often being clustered together under the broader category of vulnerable groups (Indigenous Peoples' Major Group on the SDGs 2024). SDG implementation can also hinder the rights of Indigenous peoples, especially when governments utilize colonial practices and policies. During the COVID-19 pandemic in Canada, public health mandates requiring Indigenous people to travel to urban centres for birth clashed with Indigenous peoples' interest in continuing their community birthing practices and reducing their own risk of exposure to the coronavirus (Murdock et al. 2024).

While the SDGs represent a significant step forward in incorporating Indigenous perspectives into global development goals, there is still room for improvement in fully recognizing and integrating Indigenous views and rights in sustainable development efforts. Indigenous peoples have identified a series of key priorities for the SDGs to further take indigenous perspectives into consideration, including, inter alia, the recognition of collective rights to land, territories and natural resources; culturally sensitive policies for education and health; a focus on Indigenous women, children, youth and persons with disabilities; the recognition of culture as the fourth pillar of sustainable development; the implementation of free, prior and informed consent for economic development projects that impact indigenous livelihoods (in alignment with the United Nations Declaration on the Rights of Indigenous Peoples); and the establishment of partnerships on Indigenous development issues.

References

Gallardo-Peralta, L. P., Sánchez-Moreno, E., and Rodríguez-Rodríguez, V. (2019). Strangers in their own world: Exploring the relation between cultural practices and the health of older adults in native communities in Chile. *British Journal of Social Work*, 49(4), 920–942. CINAHL Complete. https://doi.org/10.1093/bjsw/bcz045

Indigenous Peoples' Major Group on the SDGs. (2024, March 26). The indigenous world 2024: Sustainable Development Goals (SDGs) and Indigenous Peoples. *International Work Group for Indigenous Affairs*. https://iwgia.org/en/the-sustainable-development-goals-sdgs-and-Indigenous-peoples/5413-iw-2024-sdg.html

Murdock, M., Campbell, E., Durant, S., Couchie, C., Meekis, C., Rae, C., Kenequanash, J., Jeyamohan, A. E., Barry, J., Boivin, L., and Lawford, K. (2024). Indigenous Peoples' evaluation of health risks when facing mandatory evacuation for birth during the COVID-19 pandemic: An Indigenous feminist analysis. *BMC Health Services Research*, 24(1). Springer Nature Journals. https://doi.org/10.1186/s12913-024-11489-9

Simkins, A. T., Donald, P. F., Beresford, A. E., Butchart, S. H. M., Fa, J. E., Fernández-Llamazares, A. O., Garnett, S. T., and Buchanan, G. M. (2024). Rates of tree cover loss in key biodiversity areas on Indigenous Peoples' lands. *Conservation Biology*, 38(3), e14195. https://doi.org/10.1111/cobi.14195

United Nations Division for Inclusive Social Development. (2022). 2030 Agenda and Indigenous Peoples. https://social.desa.un.org/issues/Indigenous-peoples/2030-agenda-and-Indigenous-peoples/2030-agenda-and-Indigenous-peoples

van Norren, D. E. (2020). The Sustainable Development Goals viewed through Gross National Happiness, Ubuntu and Buen Vivir. *International Environmental Agreements: Politics, Law and Economics*, 20(3), 431–458. https://doi.org/10.1007/s10784-020-09487-3

Inequality (global and national)

Hristo Dokov

Inequality, both on a global and national scale, is one of the most pressing challenges of our time, often associated with overarching moral values such as justice, fairness and solidarity. Stark disparities in income, wealth and access to opportunities threaten the social fabric, undermine economic stability and hinder efforts to combat poverty and environmental degradation. The inclusion of 'leaving no one behind' as a central theme of the entire 2030 Agenda and the addition of inequality as a stand-alone goal – Sustainable Development Goal (SDG) 10 – reflect the urgency of addressing this issue. Moreover, the inequality goal represents the indivisibility that guided the design of the 2030 Agenda, with direct links to targets across most of the SDGs (Sénit 2020).

For decades, development studies have focused on exploring inequalities, often distinguishing between constructive/destructive inequality and inequality of outcome/opportunity (van Niekerk 2020). While it is difficult to define an 'acceptable' degree of inequality, empirical evidence suggests that, in general, more equal societies experience higher levels of well-being. Over time, the growing understanding of development as a multidimensional construct – extending beyond income and wealth to encompass social, political and environmental factors – has shifted the paradigm for measuring inequalities, moving from assessing single (economic) indicators to employing more complex methodologies. The process of 'moving beyond GDP' has led to the creation of numerous composite indices and indicator sets that assess overall development or specific aspects of it. While this is unquestionably a step forward, no irrefutable or universally accepted measures exist yet. The challenge of finding the right approaches and tools for measurement is critical, as responses to rising inequality must be built around effective institutions and people-centred policies (Chancel et al. 2018).

Research confirms that inequalities are steadily growing, both across and within nations (van Niekerk 2020; Biermann et al. 2022a). The staggering extent of global inequality is well illustrated by Oxfam's calculation that, in 2024, the world's richest 1% own more wealth than 95% of humanity. Such extreme economic inequality fuels other

64 *Essential Concepts for Implementing the SDGs*

forms of inequality, including gender and environmental injustice. The wealthiest individuals and nations continue to invest heavily in carbon-based economies, contributing to climate change, while the poorest populations disproportionately bear the brunt of its impacts.

Against this backdrop, the inclusion of inequality as SDG 10 was highly contentious, as countries varied significantly in their positions and proposed strategies (Sénit 2020). Consequently, SDG 10 has often been poorly supported and marginalized, with an unclear roadmap and weak targets that focus more on social inclusion than on directly reducing inequalities (Fukuda-Parr 2019). Furthermore, the limited academic research on the relationship between the SDGs and national and global inequality (Biermann et al. 2022a) highlights knowledge gaps that hinder more effective policy development and critique.

While SDG 10 establishes a strong normative framework for reducing inequality, the operationalization of these objectives remains weak, with a significant gap between rhetorical commitments and the institutional and normative changes needed to achieve substantial progress (Biermann et al. 2022b). A major challenge in advancing SDG 10 is the fragmented custodianship, which has resulted in a lack of clear leadership and coordination. Without a dedicated agency to streamline efforts, inequality reduction initiatives remain disjointed, limiting their visibility and impact. Institutions like the World Bank have been criticized for using 'organizational jiu-jitsu' techniques to exploit the SDGs for advancing their own agendas without real policy shifts (van Driel et al. 2023).

Addressing inequality, both globally and nationally, is a crucial yet complex endeavour. While the inclusion of inequality in the SDGs represents a significant step forward, the progress remains uneven, and the frameworks to measure and achieve this goal are still underdeveloped. For meaningful change, a more transformative approach is needed – one that prioritizes equality as a core aspect of sustainable development rather than an afterthought. Only then can we create a more just, sustainable future where no one is left behind.

References

Biermann, F., Hickmann, T., Sénit, C. A., and Grob, L. (2022a). The Sustainable Development Goals as a Transformative Force?: Key Insights. In: Biermann, F., Hickmann, T., and Sénit, C. A. (eds.). *The Political Impact of the Sustainable Development Goals: Transforming Governance Through Global Goals?*. Cambridge University Press, 204–226.

Biermann, F., Hickmann, T., Sénit, C. A., et al. (2022b). Scientific Evidence on the Political Impact of the Sustainable Development Goals. *Nature Sustainability*, 5, 795–800. https://doi.org/10.1038/s41893-022-00909-5

Chancel, L., Hough, A., and Voituriez, T. (2018). Reducing Inequalities Within Countries: Assessing the Potential of the Sustainable Development Goals. *Global Policy*, 9(1), 5–16. https://doi.org/10.1111/1758-5899.12511

Fukuda-Parr, S. (2019). Keeping Out Extreme Inequality from the SDG Agenda – The Politics of Indicators. *Global Policy*, 10(1), 61–69. https://doi.org/10.1111/1758-5899.12602

Sénit, C. A. (2020). Leaving No One Behind? The Influence of Civil Society Participation on the Sustainable Development Goals. *Environment and Planning C: Politics and Space*, 38(4), 693–712. https://doi.org/10.1177/2399654419884330

van Driel, M., Biermann, F., Vijge, M. J., and Kim, R. E. (2023). How the World Bank Engages with the Sustainable Development Goal on Reducing Inequalities: A Case of Organizational Jiu-Jitsu. *Global Studies Quarterly*, 3(3), 1–13. https://doi.org/10.1093/isagsq/ksad035

van Niekerk, A. J. (2020). Inclusive Economic Sustainability: SDGs and Global Inequality. *Sustainability*, 12, 5427. https://doi.org/10.3390/su12135427

Institutions and institutional effects

Ha B. Vien

Institutions play a crucial role in implementing the Sustainable Development Goals (SDGs) by helping policymakers understand the path dependencies that contribute to the persistence of specific policies, technologies or objectives over time. These institutional effects can also influence how readily certain goals are achieved. While the term 'institutions' has diverse definitions across disciplines, in political science institutions are often seen as formal and informal rules, norms and structures that shape political behaviour and governance (North 1990). The Institutional Analysis and Development framework further describes institutions as 'human-constructed constraints or opportunities' that shape choices and their outcomes (McGinnis 2011, 170), driven by 'rules, norms and shared strategies' that organize structured interactions – or the absence of them (Ostrom 2009, 3–5).

Institutions go beyond the physical boundaries of organizations, encompassing visible and invisible institutional arrangements that link individuals in organizations to the broader society. For instance, the United Nations is an organization, not an institution. However, the frameworks and principles it establishes – such as the United Nations Charter and the SDGs – are institutions. These institutions set norms, rules and shared strategies that guide the actions of the United Nations and its member states in areas such as peacekeeping or sustainable development.

Scholars in the field of Institutional Analysis and Development distinguish between rules-in-use and rules-in-form, where the former refers to the rules used in practice, while the latter denotes formalized, documented rules. Due to the voluntary nature of SDG implementation, policymakers should prioritize rules-in-use, as these informal practices and norms can be more influential in achieving real-world outcomes than formal regulations, leading to more effective and sustainable progress in advancing the SDGs.

The concept of institutions spans multiple scales, aligning with a polycentric governance system. Vertically, institutions exist on multiple levels, ranging from international, regional, national, state, to local scales. Each governance level has its own set of rules, norms and shared strategies. The implementation of SDGs as global goals involves international and national institutions originating from actors such as the United Nations and governments. If scholars analyse these actors solely as organizations without considering their institutional arrangements, that is, the relevant political and economic institutions, political power along with their rules and shared strategies, their analysis will be incomplete.

Furthermore, scholars have asked for SDG localization that leads to the attention to multiple smaller scales of local resources and communities. The questions of how communities' rules and norms influence SDG implementation have formed different scale properties of SDG implementation. Horizontally, in a polycentric governance system, each level includes a range of governmental and non-governmental decision-making centres. Formal governmental entities at the local level include state and local governments, while non-governmental actors include the private sector, non-profits, interest groups and communities. Importantly, SDG researchers should consider the institutions governing these actors to understand how they shape each sector's role in advancing the SDGs.

66 Essential Concepts for Implementing the SDGs

Understanding the concept of institutions enables policymakers to assess the institutional effects on implementing SDGs. Institutions can serve as either opportunities or barriers; policymakers need to consider this when aiming to enhance or mitigate their effects on organizational behaviour. Beyond focusing on standardized external measurement methods, attention should be given to informal socialization processes and internal oversight to gain deeper insights into inter-organizational structuration and institutional effects (Lawrence et al. 2002).

Assessing institutional effects seems to be more complex, decentralized and less clearly defined than in the case of markets and hierarchies. Achieving SDGs may be more attainable if policymakers consider the isomorphic processes of institutions – namely coercive, mimetic and normative mechanisms (DiMaggio and Powell 1983), for example, the case of universities (Vien and Galik 2024). The application of these mechanisms varies based on organizational characteristics and contexts, resulting in different types of institutional pressures.

References

DiMaggio, P. J., and Powell, W. W. (1983). The iron cage revisited: Institutional isomorphism and collective rationality in organizational fields. *American Sociological Review*, 147–160.

Lawrence, T. B., Hardy, C., and Phillips, N. (2002). Institutional effects of interorganizational collaboration: The emergence of proto institutions. *Academy of Management Journal*, 45(1), 281–290. https://doi.org/10.2307/3069297

McGinnis, M. D. (2011). An introduction to IAD and the language of the Ostrom workshop: A simple guide to a complex framework. *Policy Studies Journal*, 39(1), Article 1. https://doi.org/10.1111/j.1541-0072.2010.00401.x

North, D. C. (1990). *Institutions, institutional change and economic performance*. Cambridge University Press.

Ostrom, E. (2009). *Understanding institutional diversity*. Princeton University Press.

Vien, H., and Galik, C. S. (2024). Individual and interlinked SDGs: Higher education institutions and metro area sustainability performance. *International Journal of Sustainability in Higher Education*, 25(5), 962–987. https://doi.org/10.1108/IJSHE-06-2023-0231

Integration

Basil Bornemann

The concept of integration, broadly understood as the linking of diverse elements into an integrated whole, has shaped sustainability thinking and governance from its inception. Historically, the emergence of sustainable development can be understood as a process of discourse integration, in the course of which several formerly separate discourses – 'environment' and 'development' – intertwine to form a new, integrated discourse. Embarking on changes in these discourses from the mid-1970s onwards, the Brundtland Report became the decisive contribution that turned the two into a single discourse. Sustainable development offered a way out of the prevailing 'growth versus environment' polarity, suggesting that it is possible to realize economic and social development compatible with sound environmental stewardship. By promoting an integrated set of goals, an integrated worldview and an integrated strategy for change, sustainable development has set out to transform the political arena in an integrative sense, bringing together actors from different sectors and levels and catalyzing the formation of new coalitions across traditional lines of conflict. In particular, the widespread belief in win-win relationships between environmental and development goals fostered new cooperation between previously opposing interests (Meadowcroft 2000).

As a central discourse motif, integration runs through important programmatic documents on sustainable development. The Brundtland Report of 1987 presents sustainable development as a framework for integrating environmental policies and development strategies to overcome the fragmentation of national and international institutions. Agenda 21 of 1992 emphasized the need to integrate environment and development concerns to satisfy basic needs, a higher standard of living for all, better protected and managed ecosystems and a more secure and prosperous future. Apart from specific commitments to integrated programmes, plans and strategies in various thematic chapters, Agenda 21's entire Chapter 8 is devoted to concretizing an integrative approach to governance (United Nations Conference on Environment and Development 1992).

Standing in this tradition, the 2030 Agenda of 2015 makes integration a central feature (Le Blanc 2015). The Sustainable Development Goals (SDGs) are 'integrated and indivisible and balance the three dimensions of sustainable development: the economic, social and environmental', according to a description in the preamble repeated throughout the Agenda (United Nations General Assembly 2015: Preamble). Achieving such an integrated set of goals requires not only integrated policy strategies for specific SDGs but also a more fundamental overcoming of institutional silos and new forms of cooperation between levels and societal actors (Stafford-Smith et al. 2017).

In terms of the meaning of integration, the 2030 Agenda shows notable shifts. While earlier views were based on overly optimistic notions of synergistic relationships, that is, different goals reinforcing each other, the integrated quality of the SDGs has been assessed more ambivalently. It was argued early on that the SDGs form a complex network of goals with positive (synergistic) and negative (conflicting) relationships (Le Blanc 2015), which led to the development of a research field on SDG integration (Bennich et al. 2020). In addition to overarching and context-specific analyses of the interactions between the SDGs, this debate has generated a number of governance approaches to harness the differentiated integrative character of the SDGs during implementation. They aim to identify neuralgic SDGs that could be targeted to lever systemic change, thus opening new perspectives for overcoming institutional fragmentation, forming new actor coalitions and creating spaces for joint action (Bornemann and Weiland 2021). Integration is likely to remain at the heart of sustainable development in the future. Especially in a world in which transformations towards sustainability are increasingly controversial and the world is becoming more and more divided, integration seems to be the concept of our time. Integration is relevant not only in the sense of an evidence-based alignment of policy goals and measures, but also in a more fundamental political sense, such as the recognition of diversity and a serious commitment to bringing actors together across lines of conflict.

References

Bennich, T., Weitz, N., and Carlsen, H. (2020). Deciphering the scientific literature on SDG interactions: A review and reading guide. *Science of the Total Environment*, 728. https://doi.org/10.1016/j.scitotenv.2020.138405

68 *Essential Concepts for Implementing the SDGs*

Bornemann, B., and Weiland, S. (2021). The UN 2030 Agenda and the quest for policy integration: A literature review. *Politics and Governance*, 9(1). https://doi.org/10.17645/pag.v9i1.3654

Le Blanc, D. (2015). Towards integration at last? The sustainable development goals as a network of targets. *Sustainable Development*, 23(3), 176–187. https://doi.org/10.1002/sd.1582

Meadowcroft, J. (2000). Sustainable development: A new(ish) idea for a new century? *Political Studies*, 48(2), 370–387. https://doi.org/10.1111/1467-9248.00265

Stafford-Smith, M., Griggs, D., Gaffney, O., Ullah, F., Reyers, B., Kanie, N., Stigson, B., Shrivastava, P., Leach, M., and O'Connell, D. (2017). Integration: The key to implementing the Sustainable Development Goals. *Sustainability Science*, 12(6), 911–919. https://doi.org/10.1007/s11625-016-0383-3

United Nations Conference on Environment and Development. (1992). *Agenda 21*. New York: United Nations.

United Nations General Assembly. (2015). *Transforming Our World: The 2030 Agenda for Sustainable Development*. A/RES/70/1. https://sdgs.un.org/publications/transforming-our-world-2030-agenda-sustainable-development-17981

Integrity (ecological and planetary)

Rosalind Warner

The term 'ecological integrity' refers to the full functioning of a suite of natural processes. In other words, integrity is said to exist when native living and non-living components are intact and interact through processes without human interference (Mackey 2004). The term is widely used in international domestic laws and policies, including by the International Union for the Conservation of Nature, the United States Environmental Protection Agency and national park legislation in Canada. The term originated in the work of Aldo Leopold (1949), who argued that actions are right when they preserve the 'integrity, stability and beauty of the biotic community' and wrong when they do otherwise. Over time, ecological integrity has evolved into a central theme in environmental science and policy, used to assess and guide the management of natural resources and ecosystems across various contexts. As discussed by Kotzé et al. (2022), the term 'planetary integrity' is derived from the concept of ecological integrity but extends it to the global scale to refer to the overall health and stability of Earth's interconnected systems and processes that support life and maintain the planet's habitability.

While it is difficult to identify one single founding moment, it could be argued that interest in the idea of ecological and planetary integrity began with the widespread publication of the 'Earthrise Photo' taken in December 1968, by the crew of the Apollo 8 mission. The photo pictured the planet for the first time as a fragile, interconnected whole, isolated in the vastness of space. The 'Earthrise Photo' inspired environmental movements across the globe to focus on the importance of maintaining Earth's overall health and stability to ensure a habitable planet for all life forms. In particular, the idea of Earth as a self-organizing complex system (termed Gaia) became central to the work of James Lovelock and Lynn Margulis in the 1970s. It also inspired the work of the Club of Rome, most widely known by the 1972 report, *The Limits to Growth* (Meadows et al. 1972), and has been central to the work of the Planetary Boundaries project led by Johan Rockström et al. (2009).

Maintaining planetary integrity is crucial for long-term sustainability and the well-being of both human societies and ecosystems. However, human activities are increasingly threatening planetary integrity, for example, through climate change, biodiversity loss and pollution. While the Sustainable Development Goals (SDGs) could potentially serve as steering mechanisms to address the loss of planetary integrity (particularly through SDGs 6, 13, 14 and 15), their effectiveness in this regard is debated (Biermann et al. 2022).

One of the chief complaints about the term ecological or planetary integrity is the lack of a consensual definition or agreed benchmark indicators to measure it. Originally referring to 'nature' in its pristine and wild state, using the term today risks overlooking the extensive manipulation of the natural world that has gone on for millennia by humans. In turn, this complicates the integration of ecological and planetary integrity principles into laws, policies and treaties for implementation. Another set of controversies surrounds the ethical basis for ecological and planetary integrity. The recognition of the ethical holism of the planet and the intrinsic value of nature suggests a reformulation of the human-nature relationship in more radical ways than the SDGs and 2030 Agenda currently appear to address.

While there is a clear implicit connection between the SDGs and the necessity of ensuring ecological and planetary integrity, the SDGs are relatively silent on the issue. For instance, SDG 14 (Life Below Water) and SDG 15 (Life on Land) relate to preserving ecological integrity of marine and terrestrial ecosystems, but much of the attention around ecological and planetary integrity has emerged from other United Nations tracks, particularly the Convention on Biological Diversity and the United Nations Framework Convention on Climate Change. As a result, while the concept of ecological integrity has roots in mid-20th-century ecological thought, its formal adoption and application in SDG implementation remains somewhat uneven and unrealized.

References

Biermann, F., Hickmann, T., Sénit, C., Beisheim, M., Bernstein, S., Chasek, P., Grob, L., Kim, R., Kotzé, L., Nilsson, M., Órdoñez Llanos, A., Okereke, C., Pradhan, P., Raven, R., Sun, Y., Vijge, M. J., van Vuuren, D., and Wicke, B. (2022). Scientific evidence on the political impact of the sustainable development goals. *Nature Sustainability*, 5(9), 795–800. https://doi.org/10.1038/s41893-022-00909-5

Kotzé, L. J., Kim, R. E., Burdon, P., du Toit, L., Glass, L.-M., Kashwan, P., Liverman, D., Montesano, F. S., Rantala, S., Sénit, C.-A., Treyer, S., & Calzadilla, P. V. (2022). Planetary integrity. In C.-A. Sénit, F. Biermann, and T. Hickmann (Eds.), *The Political Impact of the Sustainable Development Goals: Transforming Governance Through Global Goals?* (pp. 140–171). Cambridge University Press. https://doi.org/10.1017/9781009082945.007

Leopold, A. (1949). *A Sand County Almanac*. Oxford University.

Lovelock, J. E. (1972). Gaia as seen through the atmosphere. *Atmospheric Environment (1967)*, 6(8), 579–580. https://doi.org/10.1016/0004-6981(72)90076-5

Mackey, B. G. (2004). The earth charter and ecological integrity – Some policy implications. *Worldviews*, 8(1), 76.

Meadows, D. H., Randers, J. and D. L. Meadows for the Club of Rome. (1972). *The Limits to Growth: A Report for the Club of Rome's Project on the Predicament of Mankind*. Universe Books.

Rockström, J., Steffen, W., Noone, K., Persson, Å., Chapin, F. S. I., Lambin, E., Lenton, T. M., Scheffer, M., Folke, C., Schellnhuber, H. J., Nykvist, B., de Wit, C. A., Hughes, T., van der Leeuw, S., Rodhe, H., Sörlin, S., Snyder, P. K., Costanza, R., Svedin, U., ... Foley, J. (2009). Planetary boundaries: Exploring the safe operating space for humanity. *Ecology and Society*, 14(2), art32. https://doi.org/10.5751/ES-03180-140232

Interaction and interlinkages

Ivonne Lobos Alva

The 2030 Agenda and the Sustainable Development Goals (SDGs) were designed as an 'integrated and indivisible' set and every goal must be met equally to attain sustainable development. This means assessing interactions and interlinkages between the SDGs is a central element of the 2030 Agenda, including the need for strategies that maximize synergies and mitigate trade-offs and conflicts among the goals (Bennich et al. 2023). The integrated nature of the SDGs increases the complexity of their achievement because making progress on one goal might hinder progress in others, due to the interlinkages between them. In practices, SDG implementation requires systems thinking, searching for synergies and identifying potential conflicts. This is often not the way policies are formulated and implemented. The primary challenge facing those working towards achieving the SDGs concerns making decisions today that properly orient development trajectories towards realizing this integration aspiration.

There is a wide understanding among governments, the scientific community and international organizations of the need to identify interactions between goals and targets. The basic concept implies that advances or changes in one goal or target can have positive or negative effects in the achievement of others through systemic interactions (Hernández-Orozco et al. 2022).

The scientific community and international institutions have dedicated significant efforts to develop a wide array of methodologies and methods to assess these interlinkages and to support decision-makers in their efforts to achieve more integration of the SDGs (for an overview, see Bennich et al. 2020). While many governments have tried to include interlinkages in their policy planning, the call to increase the consideration of interlinkages remains relevant. There is no generally agreed-upon methodology to decipher the synergies and trade-offs that arise in SDG implementation, so that decision-makers can take their pick, in terms of the approach that best suits their interests. In this sense, there is a debate regarding the methods that should be used in identifying these connections, including the advantages and disadvantages of qualitative approaches, quantitative methodologies or a combination of both (Bennich et al. 2020).

Additionally, a limited number of online decision-support tools are being developed by research groups to display SDG connections. For example, the Institute for Global Environmental Strategies' 'SDG Interlinkages Analysis and Visualization tool' (Institute for Global Environmental Strategies 2019) shows synergies and trade-offs between SDG targets for various Asian countries, based on correlations between national development indicators. The United Nations Environment Management Group's 'Nexus Dialogues Visualization Tool' (Environment Management Group 2019), where a group of experts discussed and assessed interactions between SDGs in the context of global environmental issues. The SDG Synergies tool (Stockholm Environment Institute 2020) is based on a decision-support approach designed to guide priority setting and policy coherence amongst key stakeholders. The aim of SDG Synergies is to support decision-makers in dealing with multiple interlinked targets. The methodology uses cross-impact analysis and a 7-point scale to score interactions. The SDG Synergies tool, developed by the Stockholm Environment Institute, provides an accessible interface and allows the scoring of interactions in an online matrix – the web platform then creates graphics that enable a quick visualization of results.

As these methodologies and tools are incrementally applied across different countries, it will become feasible to conduct comparative studies and examine the specific effects they are having at the national and, hopefully, also at the subnational level. It is important to mention that all these methodologies and tools solve specific policy problems. This means decision-makers are advised to seek the accompaniment and counselling of experts and the United Nations System, in order to identify the best one for their particular needs.

References

Bennich, T., Persson, Å., Beaussart, R., Allen, C., and Malekpour, S. (2023). Recurring patterns of SDG interlinkages and how they can advance the 2030 Agenda. *One Earth*, 6(11), 1465–1476. https://doi.org/10.1016/j.oneear.2023.10.008

Bennich, T., Weitz, N., and Carlsen, H. (2020). Deciphering the scientific literature on SDG interactions: A review and reading guide. *Science of the Total Environment*, 728, 1–13. https://doi.org/10.1016/j.scitotenv.2020.138405

Environment Management Group. (2019). United Nations environment management group nexus dialogues visualization tool. https://embed.kumu.io/f29ef5c11bd23aa4bb17d5adec370161#overview/

Hernández-Orozco, E., Lobos-Alva, I., Cardenas-Vélez, M. et al. (2022). The application of soft systems thinking in SDG interaction studies: A comparison between SDG interactions at national and subnational levels in Colombia. *Environment, Development and Sustainability*, 24, 8930–8964. https://doi.org/10.1007/s10668-021-01808-z

Institute for Global Environmental Strategies. (2019). *SDG Interlinkages Analysis and Visualization Tool (V3.0)*. https://sdginterlinkages.iges.jp

Stockholm Environment Institute (SEI). (2020). *SDG Synergies Tool*. https://www.sdgsynergies.org/

International Environmental Agreements

Rakhyun E. Kim

International environmental agreements (IEAs) are legally binding treaties between nations aimed at addressing environmental challenges that transcend national borders. In addition to customary practices, general principles and judicial decisions, IEAs serve as a significant source of international environmental law. The institutions they create, such as conferences of the parties and scientific advisory bodies, play a critical role in shaping global environmental governance. Despite their importance, IEAs have often fallen short of their objectives, with compliance and implementation remaining significant challenges. Moreover, the proliferation of IEAs, now numbering over 3,000, has led to conflicts and inconsistencies among agreements (Mitchell et al. 2020). The Sustainable Development Goals (SDGs) aim, in part, to address this fragmentation and promote greater synergy between IEAs. In turn, IEAs are vital tools for achieving the SDGs, as many treaties promote sustainable development. Thus, the nexus between IEAs and the SDGs is complex and requires a nuanced understanding to maximize synergies.

72 Essential Concepts for Implementing the SDGs

The SDGs are derived, in part, from existing international legal frameworks, including IEAs. This ensures that environmental sustainability is integrated into the broader sustainable development agenda. Specific SDG targets reflect commitments made under various IEAs, such as Target 15.7, which aims to end poaching and trafficking of protected species, aligning with the objectives of the Convention on International Trade in Endangered Species of Wild Fauna and Flora. IEAs thus provide legal frameworks, guidelines and monitoring mechanisms that countries can leverage to achieve the SDGs. However, because the SDGs are based on existing IEAs, they mirror the fragmented and compartmentalized structure of international environmental law, which undermines the SDGs' claim of being indivisible and integrated (Kim 2016). The SDGs represent a non-hierarchical list of equally important global priorities in the absence of an internal mechanism to address conflicts. It remains unclear when environmental concerns should take precedence over social or economic goals and to what extent (Underdal and Kim 2017).

While the environment was relatively weak in the Millennium Development Goals (MDGs), it is central to the SDG framework (Elder and Olsen 2019). It was hoped that this emphasis on environmental sustainability as a core pillar of sustainable development would enhance the effectiveness of IEAs, especially in comparison to powerful international institutions like those governing trade. For example, the SDGs' focus on sustainable consumption and production (SDG 12) could support the objectives of multiple IEAs by reducing pressure on natural resources and ecosystems. However, the political impact of the SDGs on improving environmental protection remains limited (Kotzé et al. 2022). The SDGs could have served as a unifying framework to align the objectives and actions of the many IEAs, helping to avoid conflicts and enhance synergies. However, this potential has not been fully realized due to inherent design limitations. While the SDGs aim to be comprehensive, they often create trade-offs and conflicts between goals. For instance, the pursuit of economic growth (SDG 8) can conflict with environmental sustainability goals (SDGs 13, 14 and 15), complicating the orchestration of IEAs. In fact, the SDGs have sometimes exacerbated the fragmentation and siloing of international institutions (Bogers et al. 2022).

To improve the relationship between IEAs and the SDGs, or any future global goals, it is essential to agree on overarching, long-term objectives for both frameworks. A potential goal for IEAs could be an overarching environmental SDG that guides the coordination of IEAs. The potential conflicts and synergies between this environmental goal and other SDGs could be addressed by establishing an overarching goal for the SDGs as well (Costanza et al. 2014). Currently, a clear, long-term vision for sustainable development beyond 2030 is lacking.

References

Bogers, M., Biermann, F., Kalfagianni, A., Kim, R. E., Treep, J., and de Vos, M. G. (2022). The impact of the Sustainable Development Goals on a network of 276 international organizations. *Global Environmental Change*, 76, 102567. https://doi.org/10.1016/j.gloenvcha.2022.102567

Costanza, R., McGlade, J., Lovins, H., and Kubiszewski, I. (2014). An overarching goal for the UN Sustainable Development Goals. *Solutions*, 5(4), 13–16.

Elder, M., and Olsen, S. H. (2019). The design of environmental priorities in the SDGs. *Global Policy*, 10, 70–82. https://doi.org/10.1111/1758-5899.12596

Kim, R. E. (2016). The nexus between international law and the Sustainable Development Goals. *Review of European, Comparative and International Environmental Law*, 25(1), 15–26. https://doi.org/10.1111/reel.12148

Kotzé, L. J., Kim, R. E., Burdon, P., Du Toit, L., Glass, L. M., Kashwan, P., Liverman, D., Montesano, F. S., Rantala, S., Sénit, C. A., Treyer, S., and Calzadilla, P. V. (2022). Planetary integrity. In F. Biermann, T. Hickmann, and C. A. Sénit (Eds.), *The political impact of the Sustainable Development Goals: Transforming governance through global goals?* (pp. 140–171). Cambridge University Press. https://doi.org/10.1017/9781009082945.007

Mitchell, R. B., Andonova, L. B., Axelrod, M., Balsiger, J., Bernauer, T., Green, J. F., Hollway, J., Kim, R. E., and Morin, J. F. (2020). What we know (and could know) about international environmental agreements. *Global Environmental Politics*, 20(1), 103–121. https://doi.org/10.1162/glep_a_00544

Underdal, A., and Kim, R. E. (2017). The sustainable development goals and multilateral agreements. In N. Kanie, and F. Biermann (Eds.), *Governing through goals: Sustainable Development Goals as governance innovation* (pp. 241–258). The MIT Press. https://doi.org/10.7551/mitpress/10894.003.0017

International Monetary Fund (IMF)

Jakob Skovgaard

The International Monetary Fund (IMF) is an international organization founded in 1944 in Bretton Woods to ensure the stability of the international monetary system. Together with the World Bank, it is commonly referred to as a 'Bretton Woods institution'. The IMF's core activities are (1) lending to countries that cannot pay for essential imports or their debts, (2) capacity development within countries and (3) surveillance of member states' economies. These activities grant it considerable power over countries, especially its borrowers, which will have to accept the IMF's conditions to borrow money. The impact of what the IMF does, both through its direct efforts to address the Sustainable Development Goals (SDGs) and its day-to-day operations promoting economic growth and stability, will be vital for implementing the SDGs.

The IMF's approach has been described as part of the 'Washington Consensus', a policy paradigm shared with the World Bank, which emphasizes structural reform such as privatization and liberalization, the protection of private property rights and cutting public deficits. The emphasis on liberalization and cutting public expenditure was criticized for its impact on sustainable development, particularly inequality and the environment. Regarding inequality, the IMF policies have been criticized for inducing countries to reduce social spending and adopt policies that increase inequality (Stieglitz 2002). Regarding the environment, the IMF's advice and conditionalities have been criticized for inducing countries to exploit natural resources, including rainforests and minerals, stimulate carbon-intensive growth and cut expenditure on environmental protection (Soener 2024).

Yet, since the 1997–1998 Asian debt crisis, there has been gradual change at the IMF to address these criticisms, with the IMF's attention to inequality and climate change increasing (Clark and Zucker 2023). This is particularly pertinent in relation to the SDGs, which have a closer involvement of the IMF than the Millennium Development Goals (Roy 2019).

The IMF structures its SDG efforts along the following five pillars (see *5 Ps*). First, *people*: The IMF particularly focuses on how fiscal policy can be 'deployed to reduce inequality – through spending on health, education and social protection and ensuring the progressivity of tax systems' (IMF 2024a). Second, *prosperity*: 'The IMF sees growth,

74 *Essential Concepts for Implementing the SDGs*

especially in low-income countries, is a precondition for the SDGs, especially through 'growth-enhancing and inequality-reducing investments in health, education, infrastructure and agricultural productivity...' (IMF 2024a). Third, *planet*: The IMF focuses particularly on climate change and promotes carbon pricing and fossil fuel subsidy reform as means of mitigating climate change, as well as helping vulnerable countries with improving their resilience to climate impacts (Skovgaard 2021). Fourth, *peace*: The IMF's work in this pillar concerns strengthening governance and reducing corruption within countries, which are seen as preconditions for meeting SDGs. Fifth, *partnerships*: The IMF's arguably most important role concerns the financing necessary for achieving the SDGs. This role concerns how to increase public spending on selected areas and raise finance through strengthening tax capacity and increasing aid and private finance.

While the IMF's efforts to implement the SDGs are notable, they remain circumscribed by two fundamental characteristics of the organization, which have been the subject of criticism from civil society and the Global South. The first is the emphasis on economic growth, which downplays discussions of limits to growth. The second is the governance structure of the IMF, which grants industrialized countries a majority of the votes and ensures the Managing Director is from Europe and the first Deputy Managing Director from the United States (IMF 2024b). Of these two characteristics, it is arguably easier to change the governance structure. If countries with low income and high vulnerability to environmental change become more influential within the IMF, it can become a stronger force for meeting the SDGs.

References

Clark, R., and Zucker, N. (2023). Climate Cascades: IOs and the Prioritization of Climate Action. *American Journal of Political Science, Early View*. https://doi.org/10.1111/ajps.12793
IMF. (2024a). *Sustainable Development Goals*. https://www.imf.org/en/Topics/SDG#overview
IMF. (2024b). *IMF Members' Quotas And Voting Power and IMF Board of Governors*. https://www.imf.org/external/np/sec/memdir/members.aspx
Roy, P. (2019). *The IMF, World Bank and SDGs*. https://eprints.soas.ac.uk/id/eprint/31285
Skovgaard, J. (2021). *The Economisation of Climate Change: How the G20, the OECD and the IMF Address Fossil Fuel Subsidies and Climate Finance*. Cambridge: Cambridge University Press.
Soener, M. (2024). Are IMF programs raising greenhouse gas emissions in the Global South? *Socio-Economic Review*, 22(4), 1637–1662. https://doi.org/10.1093/ser/mwae006
Stieglitz, J. E. (2002). *Globalization and Its Discontents*. New York: WW Norton and Company.

International organizations

Thomas Hickmann

The Sustainable Development Goals (SDGs) are the result of intense negotiations between governments and, as such, a product of the United Nations system (Chasek et al. 2016). While the main responsibility for implementing the SDGs lies with national governments, international organizations within and outside the United Nations system seek to advance the various goals and targets by providing platforms for multilateral cooperation and giving impulses for national policymaking.

International organizations adopt a range of roles and functions in the global endeavour to advance the SDGs. They set agendas and frameworks for policy initiatives, engage in coordination efforts across regions and countries, offer technical assistance and expertise to countries with a lack of adequate resources, compile data and monitor progress of goal implementation and raise awareness about sustainable development among the general public, policymakers and other stakeholders. In this context, numerous international organizations have incorporated the SDGs into their portfolios while scholars have criticized the strong 'siloization' around the 17 goals in the work of international organizations (Bogers et al. 2022).

Studies have moreover shown that the efforts of international organizations in fostering multilateral cooperation and driving domestic policies for SDG implementation have been seriously hampered by a number of factors. They include, but are not limited to, growing institutional fragmentation and problem shifting, lack of political will among many governments, inadequate funding and resources for sustainable development, the non-binding nature of the goals and targets and the all-encompassing scope of the SDGs (Biermann et al. 2022; van Driel et al. 2022).

At the same time, authors have pointed to some positive developments and institutional changes in the United Nations system, indicating that the SDGs, to an increasing extent, get incorporated into the strategic work of international organizations (Montesano et al. 2023). By this means, international organizations shape national SDG agendas and influence discourses on sustainable development at different governance levels. Yet, there is evidence that the efforts of international organizations have not led to large-scale goal implementation in national public-administrative systems due to lacking national ownership, prioritization and resources for the SDGs (Hickmann et al. 2024).

In this regard, an emerging body of research focuses on the concept of orchestration. In the area of the SDGs, this concept is based on the premise that international organizations adopt coordination and facilitation functions to foster the advancement of the SDGs (Haas and Ivanovskis 2022). As a case in point, international organizations may collaborate and interact with non-state actors to induce governments to take more ambitious steps for implementing goals and targets. Such orchestration strategies require that international organizations have adequate resources and mandates which allow them to reach out to non-state actors and pool their resources to launch initiatives aimed at advancing the SDGs. While researchers have pointed to the potential of international organizations to act as orchestrators, especially those within the United Nations system, we do not have sufficient knowledge about the effectiveness of such orchestration strategies.

Overall, despite the growing number of studies in this area, there is still a great need for further research on international organizations in relation to the SDGs. In particular, studies are warranted on the future of multilateralism and global cooperation in light of the changing geopolitical environment. Key areas of investigation include power struggles, diverging interests and conflicting norms within international organizations operating in the field of sustainable development. This requires deeper exploration of the political dynamics within international organizations and enhanced cross-disciplinary collaboration.

References

Biermann, F., Hickmann, T., and Sénit, C.-A. (Eds.). (2022). *The Political Impact of the Sustainable Development Goals: Transforming Governance Through Global Goals?* Cambridge University Press. https://doi.org/10.1038/s41893-022-00909-5

76 *Essential Concepts for Implementing the SDGs*

Bogers, M., Biermann, F., Kalfagianni, A., Kim, R. E., Treep, J., and de Vos, M. G. (2022). The impact of the Sustainable Development Goals on a network of 276 international organizations. *Global Environmental Change*, 76, 102567. https://doi.org/10.1016/j.gloenvcha.2022.102567

Chasek, P., Wagner, L. M., Leone, F., Lebada, A. M., and Risse, N. (2016). Getting to 2030: Negotiating the post-2015 sustainable development agenda. *Review of European, Comparative and International Environmental Law*, 25(1), 5–14. https://doi.org/10.1111/reel.12149

Haas, P. M., and Ivanovskis, N. (2022). Prospects for implementing the SDGs. *Current Opinion in Environmental Sustainability*, 56, 101176. https://doi.org/10.1016/j.cosust.2022.101176

Hickmann, T., Biermann, F., Sénit, C. A., Sun, Y., Bexell, M., Bolton, M., … and Weiland, S. (2024). Scoping article: Research frontiers on the governance of the Sustainable Development Goals. *Global Sustainability*, 7, e7. https://doi.org/10.1017/sus.2024.4

Montesano, F. S., Biermann, F., Kalfagianni, A., and Vijge, M. J. (2023). Can the Sustainable Development Goals green international organisations? Sustainability integration in the International Labour Organisation. *Journal of Environmental Policy and Planning*, 25(1), 1–15.

van Driel, M., Biermann, F., Kim, R. E., and Vijge, M. J. (2022). International organisations as 'custodians' of the sustainable development goals? Fragmentation and coordination in sustainability governance. *Global Policy*, 13(5), 669–682. https://doi.org/10.1111/1758-5899.13114

J

Justice perspectives

Elke Kellner

The concept of justice plays a critical role in the implementation of the Sustainable Development Goals (SDGs). The 2030 Agenda adopts a universal approach to justice, emphasizing equality, dignity and inclusion, with a focus on addressing the needs of the poorest and most vulnerable people. Its conceptualization of justice aligns with concepts of cosmopolitanism construing a global society that supports its poorest members living in poverty on a 'needs-based minimum floor principle' but less on a 'global difference principle' (Biermann and Kalfagianni 2020). The cosmopolitan approach is combined with 'liberal egalitarianism and libertarianism in its focus on cooperation among states combined with free trade' (Biermann and Kalfagianni 2020, 8). It remains open whether this approach will lead to a realignment of global policies supporting justice.

Over the years, various types of justice have emerged, each with diverse definitions. For decades, *environmental justice* has been central, focusing on the fair distribution of environmental benefits and burdens (Schlosberg 2013). The concept also integrated concerns regarding endangered species or landscapes, which was later framed as *ecological justice*, focusing on the rights of non-human entities and ecosystems. After years of debates, ecological entities like rivers have gained the legal status of a living entity, for example, the Whanganui River in New Zealand.

Branches of environmental justice include *climate justice*, which focuses on the fair distribution of burdens and benefits related to climate action and inaction, and *energy justice*, which examines the energy lifecycle, from extraction to production to consumption to waste (Carley and Konisky 2020). SDG 7, for instance, aims to ensure access to clean and affordable energy. Place-based and resource-centric types of justice emerged, such as *food justice* or *water justice*, which focus on fair distribution and access to clean water, aligning with SDG 6. *Planetary justice* has emerged as a response to human impacts on planetary systems and flows, focusing on the intertwined relation between social and ecological entities and impacts on material flows (Biermann and Kalfagianni 2020; Winter and Schlosberg 2023).

Planetary justice scholars call for a profound shift in how justice is understood in the Anthropocene, critique anthropocentrism and urge deeper engagement with the non-human world. Gupta et al. (2023) propose *earth system justice*, which minimizes the risks

DOI: 10.4324/9781003519560-12

This chapter has been made available under a CC-BY-NC-ND license.

78   *Essential Concepts for Implementing the SDGs*

of global environmental change to maintain safety while promoting well-being through fair and equitable sharing of nature's benefits, risks and responsibilities among all people, within safe and just earth system boundaries.

Justice in these contexts goes beyond the equitable distribution of benefits and burdens (*distributive justice*). *Procedural justice* addresses inclusiveness through transparent and fair processes, including access to information and how decisions are made and by whom. *Recognitional justice* emphasizes acknowledging and respecting the diverse rights, needs and values of individuals and communities, considering cultural, social and historical identities of particular groups. *Epistemic justice* is closely related but focuses on different sources and types of knowledge. It seeks to address valuing and fairly integrating knowledge and perspectives, as well as access to different types of knowledge (Fricker 2007).

Another dimension of justice includes relationships between humans: *Intragenerational justice* focuses on relationships between present humans, and *intergenerational justice* examines relationships between present and future generations.

Despite the growing body of work on justice, the literature still lacks clear and precise definitions, and different forms and dimensions of justice often overlap. Many definitions also stem from Global North perspectives with underlying colonial, utilitarian, majoritarian, liberalist or masculinist assumptions, overlooking gender, race, Indigeneity and other intersecting inequalities (Sovacool et al. 2023). Scholars need to critically evaluate these biases and engage more directly with affected communities to develop more inclusive approaches to justice. Although complete justice may be unattainable, the world can undoubtedly become less unjust.

References

Biermann, F., and Kalfagianni, A. (2020). Planetary justice: A research framework. *Earth System Governance*, 6, 100049. https://doi.org/10.1016/j.esg.2020.100049

Carley, S., and Konisky, D. M. (2020). The justice and equity implications of the clean energy transition. *Nature Energy*, 5(8), 569–577. https://doi.org/10.1038/s41560-020-0641-6

Fricker, M. (2007). *Epistemic Injustice: Power and the Ethics of Knowing*. Oxford University Press. https://doi.org/10.1093/acprof:oso/9780198237907.001.0001

Gupta, J., Liverman, D., Prodani, K., Aldunce, P., Bai, X., Broadgate, W., Ciobanu, D., Gifford, L., Gordon, C., Hurlbert, M., Inoue, C. Y. A., Jacobson, L., Kanie, N., Lade, S. J., Lenton, T. M., Obura, D., Okereke, C., Otto, I. M., Pereira, L., … Verburg, P. H. (2023). Earth system justice needed to identify and live within Earth system boundaries. *Nature Sustainability*, 6(6), 630–638. https://doi.org/10.1038/s41893-023-01064-1

Schlosberg, D. (2013). Theorising environmental justice: The expanding sphere of a discourse. *Environmental Politics*, 22(1), 37–55. https://doi.org/10.1080/09644016.2013.755387

Sovacool, B. K., Bell, S. E., Daggett, C., Labuski, C., Lennon, M., Naylor, L., Klinger, J., Leonard, K., and Firestone, J. (2023). Pluralizing energy justice: Incorporating feminist, anti-racist, Indigenous and postcolonial perspectives. *Energy Research and Social Science*, 97, 102996. https://doi.org/10.1016/j.erss.2023.102996

Winter, C. J., & Schlosberg, D. (2023). What matter matters as a matter of justice? *Environmental Politics*, 33(7), 1205–1224. https://doi.org/10.1080/09644016.2023.2220640

L

Leave No One Behind

Rodrigo Correa Ramiro

The principle of 'Leave No One Behind' is a cornerstone of the 2030 Agenda for Sustainable Development. Paragraph 4 of resolution 70 adopted by the United Nations General Assembly underscores this commitment:

> …we pledge that no one will be left behind. Recognizing that the dignity of the human person is fundamental, we wish to see the Goals and Targets met for all nations and peoples and for all segments of society. And we will endeavour to reach the furthest behind first.
>
> (United Nations 2015)

The principle of 'Leave No One Behind' embodies a commitment to eradicating poverty, ending discrimination and exclusion and addressing inequalities and vulnerabilities that marginalize people (United Nations 2019). It focuses on inclusiveness through three dimensions: recognition, ensuring respect for rights, safety and cultural identities; representation, enabling participation in decision-making; and distribution, ensuring equitable access to resources and opportunities (Sénit et al. 2022). The principle of 'Leave No One Behind' also shapes the implementation of the Sustainable Development Goals (SDGs) by structuring participation – empowering individuals, groups and nations to influence decisions – and outcomes, prioritizing vulnerable populations and least developed countries (Vijge et al. 2020).

The 2030 Agenda marks a significant step forward compared to earlier development frameworks, expanding its focus to include human rights, equality and non-discrimination. It mandates non-discrimination based on race, ethnicity, migration status, indigeneity or 'other status' while promoting human rights and fundamental freedoms (Achiume 2022). The principle of 'Leave No One Behind' also strengthens civil society's ability to hold governments and other actors accountable for addressing social inequities. Leveraging this framework, civil society can drive systemic change, prioritize marginalized populations and foster inclusion and accountability to achieve sustainable development goals.

However, the impact of the principle of 'Leave No One Behind' in fostering inclusiveness remains limited. While the SDGs have heightened awareness of disadvantaged and

DOI: 10.4324/9781003519560-13

This chapter has been made available under a CC-BY-NC-ND license.

80   *Essential Concepts for Implementing the SDGs*

vulnerable groups – especially women, children, adolescents and persons with disabilities – the progress has been uneven. LGBTQ+ population, racialized groups, Indigenous peoples and migrants often remain marginalized in both policy and practice (Sénit et al. 2022). Incorporating intersectionality and strengthening the rights of marginalized groups are essential to fully realizing the potential of the principle of 'Leave No One Behind'. Without dismantling structural inequalities, the vision of leaving no one behind will remain unrealized (Achiume 2022).

The principle of 'Leave No One Behind' emphasizes addressing inequalities both between and within countries and regions, requiring the transformation of systemic barriers at all levels. It acknowledges the significant global disparities faced by marginalized populations, who often endure compounded disadvantages due to geography, economic status and intersecting vulnerabilities. Operationalizing the principle of 'Leave No One Behind' demands tackling the root causes of inequality through inclusive governance, equitable resource distribution and targeted interventions. This process involves not only bridging gaps but also fostering accountability, collecting disaggregated data and establishing mechanisms that prioritize the most vulnerable populations and regions. Without these systemic changes, disparities will persist, jeopardizing progress towards achieving the SDGs (United Nations 2019).

Limited progress suggests that the discourse on 'Leave No One Behind' has been more performative than transformative (Sénit et al. 2022). While central to the SDG framework, the principle of 'Leave No One Behind' faces significant political and technical challenges. It requires cross-cutting, whole-of-government approaches that integrate equality across sectoral policies, moving beyond isolated social protection measures. Operating within the SDGs' 'governance through global goals' approach, the principle of 'Leave No One Behind' relies on national discretion and global institutional frameworks to steer countries towards shared objectives without enforcement mechanisms. This ambiguity and flexibility raise concerns about the degree to which the principle of 'Leave No One Behind' is effectively institutionalized at the national level (De Jong and Vijge 2024).

In sum, the principle of 'Leave No One Behind' highlights the need to address systemic inequalities and global disparities. Its effective implementation requires inclusive governance, equitable resource distribution, targeted interventions, robust accountability and disaggregated data to prioritize the most vulnerable. Without these efforts, achieving the SDGs will remain a challenge.

References

Achiume, E. T. (2022). *2030 Agenda for Sustainable Development, the Sustainable Development Goals and the fight against racial discrimination*. UNGA, Human Rights Council Fiftieth session 13 June–8 July 2022 – Racism, racial discrimination, xenophobia and related forms of intolerance: Follow-up to and implementation of the Durban Declaration and Programme of Action.

de Jong, E., and Vijge, M. J. (2024). Institutionalizing leaving no one behind: Operationalizing and analyzing worldwide national efforts. *Globalizations*, 1–19. https://doi.org/10.1080/14747731.2024.2401702

Sénit, C.-A., Okereke, C., Alcázar, L., Banik, D., Lima, M. B., Biermann, F., Fambasayi, R., Hathie, I., Kronsell, A., Leonardsson, H., Niles, N., and Siegel, K. (2022). Inclusiveness. In F. Biermann, T. Hickmann, and C.-A. Sénit (Eds.), *The Political Impact of the Sustainable Development Goals* (1st ed., pp. 116–139). Cambridge University Press. https://doi.org/10.1017/9781009082945.006

United Nations. (2019). Leaving No One Behind: An UNSDG operational guide for UN country teams. Retrieved November 25 2021, from https://unsdg.un.org/sites/default/files/Interim-Draft-Operational-Guide-onLNOB-for-UNCTs.pdf

United Nations General Assembly. (2015). Transforming our world: The 2030 agenda for sustainable development. A/RES/70/1. https://www.un.org/en/development/desa/population/migration/generalassembly/docs/globalcompact/A_RES_70_1_E.pdf

Vijge, M. J., Biermann, F. Kim, R. E., Bogers, M., van Driel, M., Montesano, F. S., Yunita, A., and Kanie, N. (2020). Governance through global goals. In F. Biermann, and R. E. Kim (Eds.), *Architectures of Earth System Governance: Institutional Complexity and Structural Transformation* (pp. 254–274). Cambridge University Press.

Legitimacy

Matteo De Donà

Legitimacy is one of the key ingredients for the exercise of political power. It is also fundamental for policy implementation at different levels of governance. As a major multiscale policy process, the implementation of the 2030 Agenda and the Sustainable Development Goals (SDGs) is no exception. Although legitimacy is a multifaceted concept that can be interpreted differently across contexts and scholarly literatures, it is often understood as 'a generalized perception or assumption that the actions of an entity are desirable, proper, appropriate within some socially-constructed system of norms, values, beliefs and definitions' (Suchman 1995: 574). In a more political acceptation, legitimacy can refer to 'the acceptance and justification of shared rule by a community' (Bernstein 2004: 142) or to 'the normative belief by an actor that a rule or institution ought to be obeyed' (Hurd 1999: 381).

Political scientists conceive of legitimacy in either *normative* or *sociological* terms: in its normative meaning, legitimacy refers to the right of an institution to rule based on a set of predefined standards, principles and values; in a sociological (or empirical) sense, legitimacy denotes the widely held belief that an institution has the right to rule (Buchanan and Keohane 2006). In other words, while the normative perspective is concerned with universal ethical criteria for assessing legitimacy, the sociological approach focuses on actors' and audiences' perceptions of legitimacy. At the same time, when assessing legitimacy in practice, the normative and sociological aspects of legitimacy are often intertwined.

Regardless of whether understood normatively or sociologically, legitimacy can derive (or, in the case of *legitimation*, can be claimed) on the basis of different *sources*. In particular, it is common to distinguish between *input* and *output* legitimacy: the former refers to procedural aspects of decision-making (such as participation, inclusiveness and transparency), while the latter pertains to performance and effectiveness, including the capacity to solve a problem (Scharpf 1999). To attain legitimacy, policy actors should strive to enjoy satisfactory levels of both input and output legitimacy. For example, a government may be able to effectively and fully implement policy in accordance with the 2030 Agenda by realizing universal health coverage (SDG Target 3.8) at the national level: this would amount to achieving output legitimacy. However, in order to have input legitimacy as well, such a government would have to pursue that health policy goal through an inclusive and participatory process, in accordance with the expectations of the government's constituencies. Input-oriented and output-oriented sources of legitimacy are not the only possible lenses to make sense of legitimacy in the framework of SDG implementation. Other sources of legitimacy may include, but are not limited to, *substantive legitimacy*,

82 *Essential Concepts for Implementing the SDGs*

focusing on the congruence between policies and the broader societal values and purposes prevailing in a given period and *expert-based legitimacy*, putting the emphasis on decision-making rooted in expertise and specialized knowledge (Bexell 2014).

Finally, legitimacy is considered one of the three key criteria (together with 'credibility' and 'salience') for effectively linking knowledge to action in the framework of sustainable development. In this context, legitimacy 'reflects the perception that the production of information and technology has been respectful of stakeholders' divergent values and beliefs, unbiased in its conduct and fair in its treatment of opposing views and interests' (Cash et al. 2003: 8086). Hence, echoing ideals of input legitimacy, scientific advisory processes for sustainable development are to be considered legitimate only if they meet appropriate standards of inclusiveness, transparency and procedural fairness.

In sum, legitimacy is an important relational and intersubjective concept that indicates whether power and authority are exercised in a way that is considered proper and acceptable. With a view to a successful implementation of the SDGs, it is crucial that relevant decision-making actors enjoy legitimacy in the eyes of policy recipients.

References

Bernstein, S. (2004). Legitimacy in global environmental governance. *Journal of International Law & International Relations*, 1, 139–166.

Bexell, M. (2014). Global governance, legitimacy and (de)legitimation. *Globalizations*, 11(3), 289–299. https://doi.org/10.1080/14747731.2014.919744

Buchanan, A., and Keohane, R. O. (2006). The legitimacy of global governance institutions. *Ethics and International Affairs*, 20(4), 405–437.

Cash, D. W., Clark, W. C., Alcock, F., Dickson, N. M., Eckley, N., Guston, D. H., Jäger, J., and Mitchell, R. B. (2003). Knowledge systems for sustainable development. *Proceedings of the National Academy of Sciences of the United States of America*, 100(14), 8086–8091. https://doi.org/10.1073/pnas.1231332100

Hurd, I. (1999). Legitimacy and authority in international politics. *International Organization*, 53(2), 379–408.

Scharpf, F. (1999). *Governing in Europe: Effective and democratic?* Oxford University Press.

Suchman, M. (1995). Managing legitimacy: Strategic and institutional approaches. *Academy of Management Review*, 20(3), 571–610.

Living wages

Elizabeth A. Bennett

A living wage is

> the remuneration received for a standard workweek by a worker in a particular place sufficient to afford a decent standard of living for the worker and her or his family. Elements of a decent standard of living include food, water, housing, education, health care, transportation, clothing and other essential needs, including provision for unexpected events.
>
> (Global Living Wage Coalition 2024)

Simply put, a living wage aims to ensure that if someone works full time, they will have the income they need to take care of themselves and their families, at the most basic level.

The international community has long committed to promoting living wages. Article 23 of the 1948 United Nations (UN) Declaration of Human Rights reads: 'Everyone who works has the right to just and favourable remuneration ensuring for himself and his family an existence worthy of human dignity'. The constitution of the International Labour Organization (ILO), adopted in 1919, similarly commits to 'the provision of an adequate living wage' and 'a minimum living wage to all employed'. In recent years, both organizations have reaffirmed this commitment. In 2019, the ILO's Global Commission on the Future of Work identified living wages as a central component to decent work. And in 2023, the UN Global Compact's Forward Faster programme selected living wages to be one of five key strategies for businesses to promote human rights.

Living wages are closely related to several of the Sustainable Development Goals (SDGs). They can address poverty (SDG 1) and hunger (SDG 2) by increasing incomes, reducing vulnerabilities and decreasing the number of working poor (Saxena 2023). They can also promote decent work and economic growth (SDG 8) by reducing turnover, increasing productivity and growing markets for consumer goods (Barford et al. 2022). Finally, living wages can reduce inequalities (SDG 10) by raising wages for low-wage workers and reducing material depravation and poor quality of life (Marshall 2019).

Although most countries have adopted a legal minimum wage – a minimum hourly amount that businesses are required to pay employees – it often falls below what workers require to meet their basic needs. Furthermore, some workers are paid informally or participate in special labour programmes exempt from labour protections. Today, the estimated gap between actual and living wages for workers worldwide is USD 674 billion annually (Hall and Suh 2020). One way to increase the number of people receiving a living wage is to increase the legal minimum wage, improve enforcement and expand coverage. Another approach is to convince companies to voluntarily pay a living wage and commit to only transacting with other companies that do the same. Challenges to voluntary living wage payments include agreeing on how to calculate a living wage and the cost of estimating and updating living wages for every city, county or region of the world (Anker and Anker 2017).

Not everyone agrees that living wages are an efficient strategy for promoting the SDGs. Some argue that higher wages will increase pressure on workers to increase productivity, reduce levels of employment, inflate consumer prices, disadvantage small enterprises and drive more workers into informal employment (Brennan 2019). Others are sceptical that laws will improve, or voluntary initiatives will realize their ambitions (Bennett 2018).

Although living wages are generally recognized as a key strategy for advancing the SDGs, technical, financial and political barriers have thus far prevented governments from mandating them and companies from voluntarily implementing them. Whether these dynamics will shift remains to be seen.

References

Anker, M., and Anker, R. (2017). Living wages around the world: Overview of the Anker living wage methodology, in *Living wages around the world: Manual for measurement*. Edward Elgar Edward. https://doi.org/10.4337/9781786431462

Barford, A., Gilbert, R., Beales, A., Zorila, M., and Nelson, J. (2022). The case for living wages: How paying living wages improves business performance and tackles poverty. Report for business fights poverty, University of Cambridge Institute for Sustainability Leadership and Shift. https://doi.org/10.17863/CAM.80370

84 *Essential Concepts for Implementing the SDGs*

Bennett, E. A. (2018). Voluntary sustainability standards: A squandered opportunity to improve workers' wages. *Sustainable Development*, 26, 65–82. https://doi.org/10.1002/sd.1691

Brennan, J. (2019). Should employers pay a living wage? *Journal of Business Ethics*, 157, 15–26. https://doi.org/10.1007/s10551-017-3724-y

Global Living Wage Coalition. (2024). https://www.globallivingwage.org/about/what-is-a-living-wage

Hall, M. R., and Suh, S. (2020). How large is the global living wage gap and the price increase needed to close it? *Socio-Economic Review*, 18(2), 555–574. https://doi.org/10.1093/ser/mwy040

Marshall, S. (2019). *Living wage: Regulatory solutions to informal and precarious work in global.* Oxford, UK: Oxford University Press.

Saxena, S. (2023). *Achieving a living wage for garment workers needs price-squeezing to stop.* Institute for Human Rights and Business. https://www.ihrb.org/latest/achieving-a-living-wage-for-garment-workers-needs-price-squeezing-to-stop

Localization

Rodrigo Führ

Localization refers to the local implementation of the Sustainable Development Goals (SDGs). It can involve how local authors define, plan, implement, monitor, evaluate and report their local strategies aimed at achieving the 2030 Agenda (United Cities and Local Governments 2024; United Nations 2024). Whereas local governments are included in the SDGs in a specific goal (SDG 11), subnational actors are related to at least 65% of the goals and targets of the 2030 Agenda (United Nations 2023, 48–49). Therefore, while national governments are mainly responsible for implementing the SDGs, there is growing recognition of the need to include, or even centre, subnational actors in implementation processes (United Cities and Local Governments 2024).

Localization is not exclusive to the 2030 Agenda but rather a process expected to all international norms, especially those with top-down approaches. Four decades of scholarship and practice on 'norm diffusion' have sought to understand why some norms are internalized by local authors while others are rejected or, most commonly, contested by regional and local orders. The localization of international norms hinges on, for example, the cultural match between the global and local contexts; the pre-existence of norms and institutions, either formal or informal, which may impact the implementation of the new norm; and processes of 'norm subsidiarity', meaning the intention of local actors to preserve their autonomy from power relations inherent to the norm diffusion (Acharya 2004).

Other variables specific to SDGs localization have also been identified. One of the key themes that affect localization in different contexts is the institutional and constitutional design of each country. Localization efforts might vary due to the multilevel governance arrangement in each nation, which changes the level of independence, autonomy, legitimacy and power delegated to local governments. Another variable is the capabilities of local authorities to comprehend, plan, implement and report strategies related to the 2030 Agenda. For instance, large metropoles with high technical expertise, counting on the support of their national government and funding from international organizations, are best equipped to localize the SDGs, while small rural towns with no support and limited budgets might find it difficult to implement local actions related to the 2030 Agenda.

In domestic settings with strong regional authorities such as provinces, departments or states, these intermediate actors might also play a role in either accelerating local action or hampering localization efforts. The degree of national convergence with the 2030 Agenda and national governments' leadership (or lack thereof) also impact the effectiveness of localization and the role that local governments play in the 2030 Agenda implementation. Since the start of the agenda, less than half of the countries that have reported Voluntary National Reviews have informed the presence of local authorities in SDGs coordination processes (United Cities and Local Governments 2024, 15). Finally, another identified variable is the prioritization of actions. While conceptually the SDGs were designed with the intent of having an indivisible nature, local actors are 'cherry-picking' goals and targets while rejecting others, either by interest, limitation of capabilities or pre-existent priorities at the local level (Forestier and Kim 2020).

While there is evidence that the 2030 Agenda has impacted local politics, the degree and ways in which it has been occurring are still being assessed. Most research linking local policies to the 2030 Agenda has shown that local authorities have shifted discourse practices, while there is evidence of institutional and normative effects as well (Órdoñez Llanos et al. 2022). However, localization varies significantly between local governments in different national settings, with observed differences between local governments in the Global North and South. Disparities in technical and financial capacities also have been shown to affect localization at all levels. This scenario suggests that the localization of SDGs is not universal and that implementation policies should be consistent with local contexts to be effective.

References

Acharya, A. (2004). How Ideas Spread: Whose Norms Matter? Norm Localization and Institutional Change in Asian Regionalism. *International Organization*, 58(2), 239–275. https://doi.org/10.1017/S0020818304582024

Forestier, O., and Kim, R. E. (2020). Cherry-picking the Sustainable Development Goals: Goal Prioritization by National Governments and Implications for Global Governance. *Sustainable Development*, 28(5), 1269–1278. https://doi.org/10.1002/sd.2082

Órdoñez Llanos, A., Raven, R., Bexell, M., Botchwey, B., Bornemann, B., Censoro, J., ... Yunita, A. (2022). Implementation at Multiple Levels. In F. Biermann, T. Hickmann, and C.-A. Sénit (Eds.), *The Political Impact of the Sustainable Development Goals: Transforming Governance Through Global Goals?* (pp. 59–91). Cambridge University Press.

United Cities and Local Governments. (2024). Towards the Localization of the SDGs: Local and Regional Governments Driving Equality, Climate Action and a New Agenda for Peace. Local and Regional Governments' Report to the 2024 HLPF. https://gold.uclg.org/sites/default/files/uploaded/HLPF2024.pdf

United Nations. (2023). *The Sustainable Development Goals Report 2023: Special Edition. Towards a Rescue Plan for People and Planet*. United Nations. https://unstats.un.org/sdgs/report/2023/

United Nations. (2024). *Inter-agency Policy Brief: Accelerating SDG Localization to Deliver on the Promise of the 2030 Agenda for Sustainable Development*. https://sdglocalaction.org/wp-content/uploads/2024/06/Policy-Brief-FINAL-May-29-5-24.pdf

M

Major Groups and other Stakeholders

Jano Richter and Carole-Anne Sénit

The Major Groups and other Stakeholders (MGoS) system is the central mechanism for non-state actors to participate in the High-level Political Forum on Sustainable Development, which is tasked with the follow-up and review of progress on the 2030 Agenda at the global level. MGoS are independent umbrella advocacy networks representing different societal constituencies. Each MGoS has a distinct membership and governing structure with elected Organising Partners. Members can range from individual activists to large humanitarian non-governmental organizations or business associations with the United Nations continuously recognizing new stakeholder groups that can form independently.

MGoS were created in response to the increasing number of stakeholders wanting to engage with the global governance of sustainable development (Corson et al. 2015). At the 1992 United Nations Conference on Environment and Development, also known as Earth Summit, the United Nations recognized nine societal constituencies central to sustainable development. These were Women, Children and Youth, Indigenous People and their Communities, Non-governmental Organizations, Local Authorities, Workers and their Trade Unions, Business and Industry, Scientific and Technological Communities and Farmers. Following the Earth Summit, the United Nations granted the MGoS formalized access to the Commission of Sustainable Development, which featured multi-stakeholder dialogues (Dodds 2019).

More recently, representatives of MGoS advocated for the interests of their constituencies during the negotiations on the SDGs. With the creation of the High-level Political Forum, the United Nations reinforced non-state actors' participatory rights in the global governance of sustainable development. Within this Forum, MGoS attend and intervene in official meetings, have access to official information and documents, submit position papers and present oral contributions, make recommendations and organize side events and roundtables, in cooperation with Member States and the United Nations (United Nations General Assembly 2013). Throughout the years, the MGoS system has evolved in an experimental manner into an intricate stakeholder engagement mechanism with today 21 groups and an overarching coordination mechanism for collective advocacy and coordination with the United Nations Secretariat and member states.

DOI: 10.4324/9781003519560-14

This chapter has been made available under a CC-BY-NC-ND license.

There is mixed evidence on the effectiveness of MGoS advocacy to date. In SDGs negotiations, civil society was overall more successful in its advocacy in informal and exclusive participatory spaces and early in the negotiations (Sénit 2020). While youth demands were hardly incorporated into the text of the 2030 Agenda (Orsini 2022), the Women's Major Group saw some of its demands integrated into the gender equality goal (Gabizon 2016). As for the monitoring and review of SDG implementation at the High-level Political Forum, it is questionable whether MGoS representatives can influence at all the core outcomes of the Forum, as the intergovernmental negotiations on the political and ministerial declarations are finalized prior to the annual sessions of the High-level Political Forum.

While MGoS have presented shadow reports as accountability supplements to the National Voluntary Reviews, this practice has not been officially recognized, and the High-level Political Forum is thus missing out on non-state actors' implementation capabilities and independent policy monitoring. Funding and visa restrictions are other main concerns that limit the participation of a broad range of stakeholders. MGoS representatives, especially from the Global South, face financial constraints in attending the High-level Political Forum and travel funding from the United Nations is sparse. This can lead to sensitive imbalances in the representativeness of the system, thus undermining its legitimacy (Sénit and Biermann 2021).

The MGoS unite voices and capabilities from all societal sectors and are vital to the achievement of the SDGs. In the follow-up of SDG implementation at the global level, the High-level Political Forum provides a valuable platform for those societal sectors to exchange with policymakers from all levels of governance. However, while MGoS participation in United Nations policy processes on sustainable development has been extensive, there is much room for improvement to make the MGoS system more inclusive and effective, so as to increase accountability within the High-level Political Forum and the SDG follow-up and review process.

References

Corson, C., Brady, B., Zuber, A., Lord, J., and Kim, A. (2015). The right to resist: disciplining civil society at Rio+20. *Journal of Peasant Studies*, 42(3–4), 859–878. https://doi.org/10.1080/03066 150.2014.992884

Dodds, F. (2019). The emergence of stakeholder democracy. In F. Dodds (Ed.), *Stakeholder Democracy Represented Democracy in a Time of Fear* (pp. 41–98). Routledge. https://doi.org/10.4324/9781351174428

Gabizon, S. (2016). Women's movements' engagement in the SDGs: Lessons learned from the Women's Major Group. *Gender and Development*, 24(1), 99–110. https://doi.org/10.1080/135 52074.2016.1145962

Orsini, A. (2022). Youth goals? Youth agency and the sustainable development goals. *Youth and Globalization*, 4(1), 108–139. https://doi.org/10.1163/25895745-04010001

Sénit, C. (2020). Leaving no one behind? The influence of civil society participation on the Sustainable Development Goals. *Environment and Planning C: Politics and Space*, 38(4), 693–712. https://doi.org/10.1177/2399654419884330

Sénit, C., and Biermann, F. (2021). In whose name are you speaking? The marginalization of the poor in global civil society. *Global Policy*, 12(5), 581–591. https://doi.org/10.1111/1758-5899.12997

United Nations General Assembly. (2013, August 23). *Format and Organizational Aspects of the High-Level Political Forum on Sustainable Development* (A/RES/67/290). Resolution adopted by the General Assembly on July 9 2013. https://documents.un.org/doc/un.oc/gen/n12/496/00/pdf/n1249600.pdf?token=UxQHEfr0ZwKgBFIgo&fe=true

Millennium Development Goals (MDGs)

Estefanía Charvet

The Millennium Development Goals (MDGs) were a group of eight measurable objectives globally established to address essential social and economic aspects of human development (United Nations 2000). The MDGs were expected to be achieved by 2015 and consisted of 48 indicators and 18 targets that subsequently expanded to 21 (United Nations, n.d.). They laid the groundwork for the Sustainable Development Goals (SDGs) launched in 2015.

The origins of the MDGs date back to September 2000 when 189 countries at the United Nations General Assembly adopted the Millennium Declaration. This was a powerful yet non-binding commitment to face some of the world's most pressing and long-standing challenges, especially focused on overcoming poverty (United Nations 2000). The set of eight goals that emerged from the Declaration included eradicating extreme poverty and hunger; achieving universal primary education; promoting gender equality and empowering women; reducing child mortality; improving maternal health; combating HIV/AIDS, malaria and other major diseases; ensuring environmental sustainability; and fostering a global partnership for development. Progress of the MDGs was measured using 1990 as the baseline year.

By 2015, the global community had achieved noticeable progress, including poverty reduction, decreasing child mortality and increasing primary education enrolment (United Nations 2015). One of the most remarkable accomplishments was reducing the proportion of people living in extreme poverty by approximately half (United Nations 2015). The MDGs mobilized the global community towards a common aim, although it is difficult to attribute these gains solely to the goals as other contextual factors likely played a role.

Progress in achieving the MDGs varied across regions. Sub-Saharan Africa in particular lagged behind (United Nations 2015). This regional imbalance underscores one of the main critiques of the MDGs. Establishing global targets in relative terms, such as reducing maternal mortality by three-quarters, obscures the substantial effort some countries or regions make to attain the same relative value (Vandemoortele 2009). In other words, the lower the countries' initial human development conditions, the greater the resources and effort needed. There were also concerns about the implications of setting quantitative targets that leave qualitative aspects on the side (Greig and Turner 2024). For instance, achieving MDG2 (universal primary education) might occur without investing in educational infrastructure, thus risking a decline in quality education despite increasing enrolment.

Another common criticism goes back to the formulation of the MDGs: the lack of an inclusive initial consultation undermined the sense of ownership in the Global South. Furthermore, there was a perception that the design and development of the MDGs were donor-driven (United Nations 2012). The involvement of a task force of multilateral organizations crafting MDG's targets and indicators might have reinforced this view (Greig and Turner 2024). Similarly, environmental concerns were not sufficiently addressed in the MDGs. This limitation reflects a broader oversight of how the goals interacted with one another. For instance, ensuring access to water and sanitation may be challenging without a primary commitment to environmental sustainability (Fehling et al. 2013).

Overall, the MDGs received many positive and negative feedback. Some argue that they were unrealistic, while others believe that their limited scope fails to capture the complexity of development issues (Fehling et al. 2013). Most importantly, the MDGs managed to unite efforts and created global momentum for human development as never seen before. As Greig and Turner (2024) argue, the MDGs created an institution of hope. And what is the world without hope? In the aftermath of the MDGs, a set of far more inclusive, comprehensive and ambitious goals emerged, the SDGs. These new goals and targets, galvanized by the United Nations Conference on Sustainable Development (Rio+20) in 2012, built upon its predecessor's momentum and legacy of hope. The SDGs cover a greater range of global challenges than the MDGs and surfaced to respond to new international development priorities from 2015 onward.

References

Fehling, M., Nelson, B. D., and Venkatapuram, S. (2013). Limitations of the Millennium Development Goals: A literature review. *Global Public Health*, 8(10), 1109–1122. https://doi.org/10.1080/17441692.2013.845676

Greig, A., and Turner, M. (2024). Policy and hope: The millennium development goals. *Global Policy*, 15(1), 66–77.

United Nations. (2000). *United Nations Millennium Declaration*. https://www.ohchr.org/en/instruments-mechanisms/instruments/united-nations-millennium-declaration

United Nations. (2012). *Review of the Contributions of the MDG Agenda to Foster Development: Lessons for the Post-2015 UN Development Agenda*. https://www.un.org/millenniumgoals/pdf/mdg_assessment_Aug.pdf

United Nations. (2015). *The Millennium Development Goals Report 2015*. https://www.un.org/millenniumgoals/2015_MDG_Report/pdf/MDG%202015%20rev%20(July%201).pdf

United Nations. (n.d.). *United Nations Millennium Development Goals*. https://www.un.org/millenniumgoals/bkgd.shtml

Vandemoortele, J. (2009). The MDG conundrum: Meeting the targets without missing the point. *Development Policy Review*, 27(4), 355–371. https://doi.org/10.1111/j.1467-7679.2009.00451.x

Modelling

Chaohui Li, Teun Kluck and Prajal Pradhan

Models provide a simplified version of reality. Mathematical, statistical or computational models are used to analyze and project the impact of policies and actions related to Sustainable Development Goals (SDGs) (Pradhan et al. 2024). They can be used to analyse scenarios, identify optimal pathways and inform strategies to address complex issues. Many types of models have been developed, adopted and used to support SDG policymaking at global, national and local levels (Anderson et al. 2022). These models cover a wide range of methodologies, such as system dynamics, social simulations, network analysis, economic input-output and computational general equilibrium models (Aly et al. 2022). Models within the SDG framework can promote systems thinking in understanding SDG interactions, guide the design of holistic and effective strategies and offer plausible future pathways that encourage forward-thinking policies.

90   *Essential Concepts for Implementing the SDGs*

Models facilitate systems thinking in SDG analysis by revealing the interconnectedness of different subsystems and establishing connections. They can illuminate a complex system's hidden, distinct and seemingly irrelevant influence pathways. For example, econometric models have detected that climate change (SDG 13) can undermine women's welfare (SDG 5) by increasing the burden of water withdrawal (Carr et al. 2024). They have also unravelled that urban expansion (SDG 11) can result in increased segregation and inequalities of individuals and communities (SDG 10) (Nilforoshan et al. 2023).

Models also provide valuable insights into understanding the long chain of ripple effects of a single SDG policy across various subsystems. For example, input-output models have provided insights into how the implementation of additional tariffs can ripple across the economic-social-environment systems, leading to the reduction of global export volume (SDG 8), increase of carbon dioxide (SDG 13), increase of pollution-induced health burdens (SDG 3) and exacerbate inequality across developed and developing regions (SDG 10) (Lin et al. 2019). By understanding the complexities and systems dynamics of the real world through systems modelling, policymakers can design more holistic policies that minimize negative externalities.

Models also enable policymakers to evaluate the impacts of different SDG policies before implementation by providing projections and scenario-based analysis. For example, integrated assessment models have been widely used to project different sustainable development pathways. They can measure climate and socioeconomic outcomes and evaluate the effectiveness of intervention strategies, such as carbon pricing, migration, energy transition and changes in diet (Soergel et al. 2021). This will provide us with a roadmap of what to expect in the future under these different scenarios. The foresight these models provide is crucial for designing effective, forward-looking policies that align with SDG targets.

While SDG models are powerful tools, their capabilities are not without limitations. One challenge is the need for models to be more policy-oriented at local levels and to recognize regional specificity. Moreover, the real-world complexity presents a considerable challenge for SDG modelling. While models can effectively simulate specific systems, such as climate or economic markets, they struggle to capture the long-term and full range of socio-political factors influencing sustainable development, such as geopolitical dynamics, political conflicts and governance structures. The exclusion of these factors can lead to oversimplified models that do not fully reflect the complexities of global systems. Nevertheless, the current models provide sufficient insights to accelerate SDG progress (Pradhan et al. 2024).

In sum, models represent a powerful means of envisioning and planning for sustainable futures. The key to maximizing their impact lies in further refinement and expansion to address model limitations. Through advancements, models will be able to provide actionable intelligence and empower decision-makers to navigate the complexities of sustainable development with greater precision and confidence and to foster policies that are inclusive, forward-thinking and resilient.

References

Aly, E., Sondoss, E., and Ryan, M. J. (2022). A review and catalogue to the use of models in enabling the achievement of Sustainable Development Goals (SDG). *Journal of Cleaner Production* 340, 130803.

Anderson, C. C., Denich, M., Warchold, A., et al. (2022). A systems model of SDG target influence on the 2030 Agenda for Sustainable Development. *Sustainability Science* 17, 1459–1472. https://doi.org/10.1007/s11625-021-01040-8

Carr, R., Kotz, M., Pichler, P., Weisz, H., Belmin, C., and Wenz, L. (2024). Climate change to exacerbate the burden of water collection on women's welfare globally. *Nature Climate Change* 14, 700–706.

Lin, J., Du, M., Chen, L., Feng, K., Liu, Y., Wang, J., Ni, R., Zhao, Y., Kong, H., Weng, H., Liu, M., Van Donkelaar, A., Liu, Q., and Hubacek, K. (2019). Carbon and health implications of trade restrictions. *Nature Communications* 10(1), 1–12. https://doi.org/10.1038/s41467-019-12890-3

Nilforoshan, H., Looi, W., Pierson, E., Villanueva, B., Fishman, N., Chen, Y., Sholar, J., Redbird, B., Grusky, D., and Leskovec, J. (2023). Human mobility networks reveal increased segregation in large cities. *Nature* 624(7992), 586–592. https://doi.org/10.1038/s41586-023-06757-3

Pradhan, P., Weitz, N., Daioglou, V., Abrahão, G. M., Allen, C., Ambrósio, G., Arp, F., Asif, F., Bennich, T., Benton, T. G., Biermann, F., Cao, M., Carlsen, H., Chen, F., Chen, M., Daams, M. N., Dawes, J. H., Dhakal, S., Gilmore, E., ... Zimm, C. (2024). Three foci at the science-policy interface for systemic Sustainable Development Goal acceleration. *Nature Communications* 15(1), 1–4. https://doi.org/10.1038/s41467-024-52926-x

Soergel, B., Kriegler, E., Weindl, I. et al. (2021). A sustainable development pathway for climate action within the UN 2030 Agenda. *Nature Climate Change* 11, 656–664.

Multilevel governance

Aurelie Charles

There are different understandings of the term 'multilevel governance', and this entry builds upon the framing of the United Nations Habitat. According to this understanding, multilevel governance relates to the vertical and horizontal integration of governance systems to enable efficient policymaking, service delivery and cohesive leadership by and among all spheres of governance (United Nations Habitat 2024). This definition is used by the United Nations Habitat and its partners who launched a global initiative towards the enhancement of multilevel governance for effective local action to achieve the 2030 Agenda. While 'vertical integration' refers to the spatial scale from global to national, regional and local levels, 'horizontal integration' is concerned with the potential synergies and trade-offs between and across the Sustainable Development Goals (SDGs). Merging both perspectives leads to a complex system of scales, actors and levels of implementation. For example, Allen et al. (2023) identified six different governance approaches to the SDGs, namely, polycentric governance, meta-governance, transition management, adaptive and reflexive governance, anticipatory governance and transformative governance.

Top-down multilevel governance from global to local means that effective SDG implementation must come through collaborative and coherent strategies across different layers of governance. At the global level, the 2030 Agenda offers a comprehensive framework that all member states are encouraged to follow on a voluntary basis, but this is the main weakness for widespread implementation. Biermann et al. (2022) have shown that there has been a limited political impact on institutions and policies apart from discursive change and that legislative, normative and institutional impact remains rare. For example, the European Union integrates the SDGs into its policy frameworks, such as the European Green Deal, which aligns with SDG targets on climate action and sustainability. However, there is a lack of meta-analyses between countries to understand the extent to which the impact goes beyond the discursive implementation of the SDG framework

92 Essential Concepts for Implementing the SDGs

(Biermann et al. 2022). In that sense, institutionalizing and legalizing the SDGs in national frameworks would accelerate SDG implementation (Biermann et al. 2023).

At the national level, some countries have established national strategies seeking to integrate SDGs into policymaking. For example, the German Sustainable Development Strategy aligns national policies with the SDGs and includes specific SDG indicators to measure progress. Voluntary National Reviews for governments and Voluntary Subnational Reviews for regional and civil society organizations, such as Oxfam, also help monitor progress on SDG implementation. It is, however, down to political and institutional will to do so and to be transparent about the shortcomings in the progress. For example, the United Kingdom government did a Voluntary National Review in 2019, but no other Voluntary National Review has been published since, which makes it difficult to monitor progress.

At the local level, including cities and municipalities, local governments are at the forefront of implementing SDG-related projects and engaging directly with communities. An example is the city of New York, which has aligned its local development plans with the SDGs through its initiative OneNYC 2050. Many progressive cities and regions also use Voluntary Local Reviews as a useful tool to showcase local progress and map the dynamics of local action and partnerships (Matthews et al. 2023). Local authorities, however, face budgetary and institutional capacity constraints that require stronger support from stakeholders at other governmental levels and societal scale (Hickmann 2021). As a way forward and to enhance the principle of subsidiarity, community-level initiatives such as local Doughnuts (Raworth 2017) have started to emerge for local SDG governance actors.

The success of the SDGs ultimately depends on local action and contextual adaptation (see *Localization*), which the United Nations Habitat initiative is carrying forward. However, major challenges such as policy fragmentation, varying capacities and resource disparities among different governance levels remain and create bottlenecks to go in that direction.

References

Allen, C., Malekpour, S., and Mintrom, M. (2023). Cross-scale, cross-level and multi-actor governance of transformations toward the Sustainable Development Goals: A review of common challenges and solutions. *Sustainable Development*, 31(3), 1250–1267, https://doi.org/10.1002/sd.2495

Biermann, F., Hickmann, T., Sénit, C., Beisheim, M., Bernstein, S., Chasek, P., Grob, L., Kim, R., Kotzé, L., Nilsson, M., Órdoñez Llanos, A., Okereke, C., Pradhan, P., Raven, R., Sun, Y., Vijge, M. J., van Vuuren, D., and Wicke, B. (2022). Scientific evidence on the political impact of the sustainable development goals. *Nature Sustainability*, 5(9), 795–800. https://doi.org/10.1038/s41893-022-00909-5

Biermann, F., Sun, Y., Banik, D., Beisheim, M., Bloomfield, M. J., Charles, A., ... Sénit, C. A. (2023). Four governance reforms to strengthen the SDGs. *Science*, 381, 1159–1160. https://doi.org/10.1126/science.adj5434

Hickmann, T. (2021). Locating cities and their governments in multi-level sustainability governance. *Politics and Governance*, 9, 211–220.

Matthews, C., Airey, W., Remnant, F., Charles, A., and Copestake, J. (2023). The dynamics of the UN Voluntary Local Review using Causal Mapping within and across the Sustainable Development Goals: A case study of Bath and North East Somerset. Centre for Development Studies Report. September 2023.

Raworth, K. (2017). *Doughnut Economics: Seven Ways to Think Like a 21st-Century Economist*. White River Junction: Chelsea Green Publishing.

United Nations Habitat. (2024). https://www.multilevelgovernance.org/

N

National sustainable development strategies

Basil Bornemann

National sustainable development strategies date back to the early days of international sustainability governance (Steurer 2008). Agenda 21 stressed the need to integrate sustainable development into national policymaking and, in Chapter 8, identified national sustainable development strategies as key instruments in this regard. Defined as a coordinated, participatory and iterative process of thoughts and actions to achieve economic, environmental and social objectives in a balanced and integrated manner (Bass and Dalal-Clayton 2002), a national sustainable development strategy aims to harmonize a country's economic, social and environmental policies in the spirit of socially responsible economic development that protects the environmental resources for future generations.

In 1997, the United Nations General Assembly committed all countries to having such a strategy by 2002, and the 2002 Johannesburg Plan of Implementation urged member states to take immediate steps to advance implementation (Steurer 2008). The 2030 Agenda is, however, more ambiguous regarding national sustainable development strategies. While stressing that their role in linking the SDGs to relevant economic, social and environmental processes cannot be overemphasized, it calls on governments to decide for themselves how exactly to integrate the SDGs into national policymaking.

Governments began publishing national sustainable development strategies, particularly in the run-up to the 2002 World Summit on Sustainable Development. By 2003, about one-third of all countries had such a strategy. Actual implementation varies between regions and countries. Some European countries started early to develop comprehensive and detailed strategies with clear objectives, targets and monitoring frameworks (Steurer 2008). Other strategies remained in the tradition of the sectoral environmental policy plans that national sustainable development strategies aimed to overcome. It was only gradual, supported by guidelines (Bass and Dalal-Clayton 2002), that countries launched strategic processes that combine formal planning and incremental learning in a cross-sectoral approach. While this development was supported by a general surge of policy strategies (Bornemann 2016), there are exceptions and counter-movements. The United States never developed a sustainable development strategy, and

DOI: 10.4324/9781003519560-15

This chapter has been made available under a CC-BY-NC-ND license.

94   *Essential Concepts for Implementing the SDGs*

the European Union's strategy was abandoned in the 2010s as political attention shifted to the economic crisis.

National sustainable development strategies are usually formulated and implemented by the government and administration, supported by governance arrangements involving inter-ministerial coordination committees, parliamentary groups and social sustainability councils. In terms of content, such strategies combine assessments of current states and challenges, overarching government commitments and presentations of activities in different policy areas. Since the 2030 Agenda, many strategies have been aligned with the SDGs and linked to Voluntary National Reviews (Persson et al. 2016).

There is little generalizable evidence on the success of national sustainable development strategies. A dominant perception is that national sustainable development strategies serve to communicate sustainability rather than engender substantive policy change (Casado-Asensio and Steurer 2014). As administrative and often highly conceptual documents, they remain disconnected from day-to-day policymaking. Yet some see this as precisely their function: By providing overarching conceptual reference points for policy problems and solutions, they perform a meta-governance function that promotes sustainability-oriented integration, reflection and learning. As such, these strategies develop substantive effects rather indirectly but are more than just symbolic exercises (Meadowcroft 2007; Steurer 2008; Bornemann 2016).

With their institutionalization and initial experience, national strategies for sustainable development have lost some of their original appeal. Earlier attempts to promote a particular strategy model have given way to recognition of a diversity of strategic policy approaches – a pluralization that echoes the shift towards goal-oriented governance under the 2030 Agenda (Biermann et al. 2017). National sustainable development strategies are likely to remain relevant in countries where they exist, increasingly addressing the SDGs and linked to Voluntary National Reviews. However, there is no sign of a push for new strategies. Many countries will continue to go their own way, which may deviate from the once-established concept, and it remains to be seen which types of national policies or strategies will be most effective in implementing the SDGs.

References

Bass, S., and Dalal-Clayton, B. (2002). *Sustainable development strategies: A resource book.* Routledge. https://doi.org/10.4324/9781849772761

Biermann, F., Kanie, N., and Kim, R. E. (2017). Global governance by goal-setting: The novel approach of the UN Sustainable Development Goals. *Current Opinion in Environmental Sustainability*, 26–27, 26–31. https://doi.org/10.1016/j.cosust.2017.01.010

Bornemann, B. (2016). Integrative political strategies – Conceptualizing and analyzing a new type of policy field. *European Policy Analysis*, 2(1). https://doi.org/10.18278/epa.2.1.10

Casado-Asensio, J., and Steurer, R. (2014). Integrated strategies on sustainable development, climate change mitigation and adaptation in Western Europe: Communication rather than coordination. *Journal of Public Policy*, 34(03), 437–473. https://doi.org/10.1017/S0143814X13000287

Meadowcroft, J. (2007). national sustainable development strategies: Features, challenges and reflexivity. *European Environment*, 17, 152–163.

Persson, Å., Weitz, N., and Nilsson, M. (2016). Follow-up and review of the sustainable development goals: Alignment vs. Internalization. *Review of European, Comparative and International Environmental Law*, 25(1), 59–68. https://doi.org/10.1111/reel.12150

Steurer, R. (2008). Sustainable development strategies. In A. Jordan, and A. Lenschow (Eds.), *Innovation in environmental policy?* (pp. 93–113). Edward Elgar.

Negotiation of the Sustainable Development Goals

Pamela Chasek

The United Nations Conference on Sustainable Development (Rio+20) in June 2012 launched a process to develop a set of Sustainable Development Goals (SDGs) to build upon the Millennium Development Goals (Doran et al. 2012). Paragraph 248 in the outcome document, *The Future We Want*, reads:

> We resolve to establish an inclusive and transparent intergovernmental process on sustainable development goals that is open to all stakeholders, with a view to developing global sustainable development goals to be agreed by the General Assembly. An open working group...shall comprise thirty representatives, nominated by Member States from the five United Nations regional groups, with the aim of achieving fair, equitable and balanced geographical representation.
>
> (United Nations 2012)

It took seven months for Member States to reach an agreement on how to distribute the 30 seats among the five United Nations regional groups. When they asked for expressions of interest, 70 countries responded. Rather than holding elections, which could disenfranchise the losers, they found an innovative way to accommodate all 70 countries by sharing the 30 seats (Kamau et al. 2018). For example, Nauru, Palau and Papua New Guinea shared a Pacific island seat and usually spoke with one voice. Another group, Iran, Japan and Nepal, however, never coordinated and took turns speaking on behalf of their own country. In the end, all United Nations member states could participate in the Open Working Group, but priority was given to the 70 members who shared the 30 seats.

The Open Working Group held eight stocktaking sessions between March 2013 and February 2014, with each session focused on different clusters of sustainable development issues. Each stocktaking session included early-morning meetings with representatives of civil society, panel presentations by experts, question and answer periods and formal statements. By the time the Open Working Group began actual negotiations in 2014, there was a high level of cohesion, a common sense of purpose and a shared understanding of the issues (Kamau et al. 2018).

Once the negotiations began in March 2014, the Open Working Group had five sessions to reach agreement on the goals and targets. The co-chairs took an iterative approach in the negotiations by first releasing a series of 'focus areas' documents, which initially outlined 19 focus areas as the basis for discussions. As discussions of the focus areas continued, the Open Working Group added possible targets to accompany each focus area, with over 300 targets initially proposed (Chasek and Wagner 2016). The last two sessions in June and July 2014 narrowed down and determined the wording of the goals and targets and reduced the number by combining some goals and targets. There was a lot of disagreement on including targets on peaceful and inclusive societies (Goal 16), transboundary water management and goals on equality, energy, oceans-related issues and the Law of the Sea and women's reproductive rights and health, to name a few. Even at the very end, some countries did not want to adopt the goals because of one or more of these issues.

96   *Essential Concepts for Implementing the SDGs*

On 19 July 2014, the Open Working Group adopted the 'Proposal of the Open Working Group for Sustainable Development Goals', containing 17 goals and 169 targets covering a broad range of sustainable development issues, including ending poverty and hunger, improving health and education, making cities more sustainable, combating climate change, protecting oceans and forests and peace, justice and strong institutions (Chasek and Wagner 2016). In a shift from the Millennium Development Goals, the SDGs were intended to be universal – in other words, an agenda that recognizes shared national and global challenges among all countries, not just developing countries. Governments also committed to leave no one behind in the implementation of the SDGs, since many countries had not been able to meet the targets under the Millennium Development Goals.

On 10 September 2014, the United Nations General Assembly adopted resolution 68/309 welcoming the Open Working Group's report (United Nations 2014). A new set of negotiations then convened over eight sessions between January and August 2015 to prepare the outcome document for the United Nations Sustainable Development Summit. The document, *Transforming Our World: The 2030 Agenda for Sustainable Development*, contained the SDGs and targets as well as a declaration and sections on means of implementation, follow-up and review (United Nations 2015). The 2030 Agenda was formally adopted by heads of state and government during the Summit at United Nations Headquarters in New York in September 2015.

References

Chasek, P. S., and Wagner, L. M. (2016). Breaking the mold: A new type of multilateral sustainable development negotiation. *International Environmental Agreements: Politics, Law and Economics, 16*(3), 397–413. https://doi.org/10.1007/s10784-016-9320-2

Doran, P., Paul, D., Ripley, K., Risse, N., Van Alstine, J., and Wagner, L. (2012). UNCSD informal consultations: Tuesday, 19 June 2012. *Earth Negotiations Bulletin, 27*(48). https://enb.iisd.org/events/uncsd-rio20/daily-report-19-june-2012

Kamau, M., Chasek, P., and O'Connor, D. (2018). *Transforming Multilateral Diplomacy: The Inside Story of the Sustainable Development Goals*. London: Routledge.

United Nations. (2012). The future we want. Resolution 66/288. https://www.un.org/en/development/desa/population/migration/generalassembly/docs/globalcompact/A_RES_66_288.pdf

United Nations. (2014). Report of the Open Working Group on Sustainable Development Goals established pursuant to General Assembly resolution 66/288. Resolution 68/309. https://undocs.org/A/RES/68/309

United Nations. (2015). Transforming our world: The 2030 agenda for sustainable development. A/RES/70/1. https://sdgs.un.org/publications/transforming-our-world-2030-agenda-sustainable-development-17981

Network analysis

Anne Warchold, Utkarsh Khot and Prajal Pradhan

Given the integrated and indivisible nature of the 2030 Agenda, the multidimensional Sustainable Development Goals (SDGs) and their 169 targets form complex networks of interactions. Network analysis offers a holistic approach to understanding, visualizing and evaluating these interactions. The networks' entities are conceptualized as nodes, for example, the SDGs and targets, and the interactions and interlinkages between them as edges. Nodes in a network can be characterized by centrality measures, helping prioritize central actors in the network and, through cluster analysis, identifying broader patterns that guide coordinated policy interventions. The nature of these connections can differ significantly. Edges represent positive (synergy), negative (trade-off) or neutral influences, which can be direct or indirect and be weighted or unweighted in terms of strength (Dawes 2022). SDG-focused networks can be constructed at various scales, encompassing all SDGs, targets or indicators, a subset, or interactions with externalities (Dawes 2022; Warchold et al. 2022; Weitz et al. 2018). These networks can be analysed at global, regional, income, national, subnational or local levels (Issa et al. 2024).

Two primary applications of SDG network analysis include assessing interactions among goals and targets and examining the social networks of actors involved in SDG governance. Qualitative, semi-quantitative or quantitative approaches can be used to construct these two applications of SDG networks (Issa et al. 2024). *Qualitative network analysis*, often involving expert assessments, literature reviews, case studies or observational data, is particularly valuable for exploring networks with limited or non-quantifiable data and understanding context-specific interactions. For example, Weitz et al. (2018) employed expert assessments in Sweden to evaluate the interactions between SDG targets using a cross-impact matrix. By applying network theory, those results were analysed and visualized. This allows ministries, like one responsible for climate mitigation (Target 13.2), to identify influences on other targets and assess their own impact, which in turn fosters collaboration or highlights necessary negotiations. *Quantitative network analysis* relies on statistical methods to measure and model interactions between nodes, such as centrality measures, correlation and causality analysis. Thus, directed, weighted networks, resulting from these approaches, reveal which goals exert a stronger positive or negative influence on others, aiding SDG prioritization and understanding cascading effects. Dörgő et al. (2018) were among the first to propose a framework for quantitatively inferring causal interactions within the SDG system. By employing node centrality metrics in a network of sustainability indicators, the authors identify the most critical indicators, such as sanitation and drinking water (SDG 6), based on their position within a global SDG system of causal interactions. *Social network analysis* for SDG governance examines the relations among actors involved in achieving the SDGs, revealing their roles, influence and collaboration patterns. To effectively implement SDGs, these actors, such as states, local governments, non-governmental organizations, international organizations and businesses, must coordinate and collaborate, forming extensive global governance networks. Pärli et al. (2021) studied information exchange networks among Swiss actors working on SDG 6, demonstrating how collaborations between actors can positively impact SDG governance.

Network analysis offers valuable insights into the structural properties of the SDG system, identifying leverage points and hurdles for goal-prioritizing, which in turn reduces complexity and allocates resources effectively. Understanding the centrality and influence of goals through network analysis can help prioritize actions that yield significant co-benefits across multiple goals. However, network analysis faces challenges, including the quality and completeness of data, which can lead to misleading conclusions (Warchold et al. 2022). Networks may also assume static relationships, failing to capture second-order interactions and the dynamic nature of real-world systems (Issa et al. 2024). This can result in networks that are overly simplistic and fail to represent the complexities of the systems they aim to analyse. Future applications of SDG network analysis should emphasize close collaboration among researchers, stakeholders and policymakers. By

98 *Essential Concepts for Implementing the SDGs*

combining quantitative and qualitative analyses with knowledge co-creation, network analysis can facilitate a deeper understanding of SDG interactions and enable the effective implementation of policies at various levels (Pradhan 2023).

References

Dawes, J. H. P. (2022). SDG interlinkage networks: Analysis, robustness, sensitivities and hierarchies. *World Development*, 149, 105693. https://doi.org/10.1016/j.worlddev.2021.105693

Dörgő, G, Sebestyén, V, and Abonyi, J. (2018). Evaluating the interconnectedness of the Sustainable Development Goals based on the causality analysis of sustainability indicators. *Sustainability*, 10(10), 3766. https://doi.org/10.3390/su10103766

Issa, L., Mezher, T., and El Fadel, M. (2024). Can network analysis ascertain SDGs interlinkages towards evidence-based policy planning? A systematic critical assessment. *Environmental Impact Assessment Review*, 104, 107295. https://doi.org/10.1016/j.eiar.2023.107295

Pärli, R., Fischer, M., and Lieberherr, E. (2021). Information exchange networks among actors for the implementation of SDGs. *Current Research in Environmental Sustainability*, 3, 100049. https://doi.org/10.1016/j.crsust.2021.100049

Pradhan, P. (2023). A threefold approach to rescue the 2030 Agenda from failing. *National Science Review*, 10(7), nwad015. https://doi.org/10.1093/nsr/nwad015

Warchold, A., Pradhan, P., Thapa, P., Putra, M. P. I. F., and Kropp, J. P. (2022). Building a unified sustainable development goal database: Why does sustainable development goal data selection matter? *Sustainable Development*, 1043(30), 1278–1293. https://doi.org/10.1002/sd.2316

Weitz, N., Carlsen, H., Nilsson, M., et al. (2018). Towards systemic and contextual priority setting for implementing the 2030 Agenda. *Sustainability Science*, 13, 531–548. https://doi.org/10.1007/s11625-017-0470-0

Nexus governance

Montserrat Koloffon Rosas

Nexus refers to a series of connections linking two or more things and is commonly used in relation to governance when several issue areas are intrinsically interlinked (Boas et al. 2016). The nexus concept originated in the field of natural resource management in 1983 through the Food-Energy Nexus Programme, which focused on finding combined solutions to challenges related to food and energy scarcity (Liu et al. 2018). Over time, the concept gained prominence at international conferences, including the World Economic Forum in 2008, which emphasized water's role in driving economic growth through its connections with a nexus of issues; the Bonn 2011 Nexus Conference with its focus on the Water-Energy-Food nexus in focus (Hoff 2011); and the United Nations Conference on Sustainable Development in Johannesburg 2012, where it was acknowledged that fragmentation of sectors could no longer be maintained (Boas et al. 2016). The 2030 Agenda was negotiated against this backdrop, resulting in the 17 Sustainable Development Goals (SDGs), which are explicitly declared to be 'integrated and indivisible and balance the three dimensions of sustainable development' (United Nations General Assembly 2015).

The rationale behind a nexus approach is that it can support a transition to sustainability by focusing on system efficiency rather than on the productivity of isolated sectors (Hoff 2011). This approach stems from *systems thinking*, which involves understanding the world as a complex, interconnected system, whose elements are intricately linked to one another. When adequately implemented, nexus governance examines interactions among multiple sectors, allowing to harness synergies and avoid trade-offs (Liu et al. 2018), for example, by ensuring that 'investments made to achieve a given goal influence the approach, resourcing, and effectiveness of the delivery of others' (United Nations Department of Economic and Social Affairs 2014). Successfully achieving this, however, requires the fulfilment of various conditions such as (1) an accurate understanding of the system of interest to identify shared root causes that produce undesired behaviour in different issue areas; (2) an effective interaction of strategic stakeholders within the nexus; and (3) a fitting intervention design, often in transboundary contexts.

Despite the increasing popularity of nexus governance in sustainable development, in practice, institutions from the international to the local level continue mirroring the historical fragmentation of sustainable development. In rare cases where a nexus approach has been implemented, such as by the German Inter-ministerial Working Group on Sustainable Development, maintaining efficiency in administrative processes has reportedly been a significant challenge. Another popular governance mechanism that occasionally takes a nexus approach is multi-stakeholder partnerships (Widerberg et al. 2023). However, even when partnerships seem to simultaneously target various SDGs, they often address each goal through separate projects. Lastly, similar to the case of policy integration (Bornemann and Weiland 2021), the assumption of nexus governance as an effective approach to accelerate SDG implementation is largely based on theory, as empirical research on the feasibility of this nexus governance to unlock sustainability transformations and accelerate the achievement of the SDGs remains scarce.

In sum, the concept of nexus governance has gained popularity throughout the years. In the context of global sustainability governance, a nexus approach is assumed to contribute to designing synergistic interventions that avoid trade-offs between issue areas. The concept is used both in research and practice with the purpose of accelerating sustainability transformations to advance the SDGs; however, the few nexus governance efforts result in a gap of empirical evidence on the feasibility of this approach. This gap should encourage actors to strengthen the science-policy exchange and to ensure that lessons learnt in nexus governance for sustainable development are recorded and disseminated.

References

Boas, I., Biermann, F., and Kanie, N. (2016). Cross-sectoral strategies in global sustainability governance: Towards a nexus approach. *International Environmental Agreements: Politics, Law and Economics*, 16(3), 449–464. https://doi.org/10.1007/s10784-016-9321-1

Bornemann, B., and Weiland, S. (2021). The UN 2030 agenda and the quest for policy integration: A literature review. *Politics and Governance*, 9(1), 96–107. https://doi.org/10.17645/pag.v9i1.3654

Hoff, H. (2011). Understanding the Nexus. https://www.sei.org/publications/understanding-the-nexus/

Liu, J., Hull, V., Godfray, H. C. J., Tilman, D., Gleick, P., Hoff, H., Pahl-Wostl, C., Xu, Z., Chung, M. G., Sun, J., and Li, S. (2018). Nexus approaches to global sustainable development. *Nature Sustainability*, 1(9), Article 9. https://doi.org/10.1038/s41893-018-0135-8

United Nations Department of Economic and Social Affairs. (2014). HLPF Issue Briefs 5: From silos to integrated policy making. https://sdgs.un.org/publications/hlpf-issue-briefs-5-silos-integrated-policy-making-17778

100　*Essential Concepts for Implementing the SDGs*

United Nations General Assembly. (2015). Transforming our world: The 2030 agenda for sustainable development. A/RES/70/1. https://sdgs.un.org/publications/transforming-our-world-2030-agenda-sustainable-development-17981

Widerberg, O., Fast, C., Koloffon Rosas, M., and Pattberg, P. (2023). Nexus governance for transformative change: Technical report of the Transform 2030 data set. https://owiderberg.github.io/T2030-technical-report-html/

Norms and normative effects

Aurelie Charles

Norms can be defined as implicit or explicit rules in resource allocation. As implicit rules, norms shape human behaviour through personal and collective ideals and beliefs, they are therefore engrained in people's decision-making (Charles 2024). As explicit rules, norms can be institutionalized into a national or international legal framework and used as rules of governance. In the context of the Sustainable Development Goals (SDGs), normative effects are then adjustments in legislative and regulatory frameworks and policies in line with and because of the SDGs (Biermann et al. 2022). Both explicit and implicit types of norms are at the heart of individual and policy decision-making for resource allocation, and they are therefore central for an effective implementation of the SDGs.

As implicit rules, the SDGs offer cognitive messages to establish the value of global norms to the domestic audience (Okitasari and Katramiz 2022). Schmieg et al. (2018), for example, show that understanding the normative features of the SDGs helps both scientific and non-scientific sustainability discourses and allows a diverse system of norms that interrelates at the macro, meso and micro levels of implementation. As explicit rules, studies have doubted whether the SDGs will ever be able to transform legal frameworks towards increased political participation of these countries in global governance (Biermann et al. 2022). A continued lack of compliance with long-standing norms indicates the limited steering effect of the SDGs on the ability of poorer countries to fully participate in and benefit from the global economy (Biermann et al. 2022).

One primary challenge with explicit norms is the normative hierarchies and conflicts that can occur at the national or local level (Charles 2024). Local norms can conflict with and be prioritized differently from the global norms established by the SDGs, leading to resistance or selective adherence in line with local prioritization of the SDGs. For example, economic growth norms may conflict with environmental sustainability norms, leading to policies that favour short-term economic benefits over long-term sustainability. Another example is gender equality norms promoted by SDG 5 that may face resistance in patriarchal societies with deeply ingrained implicit norms. In the context of the financing mechanisms of the SDGs, donor and international organizations can exert normative influence that shapes the priorities and strategies of recipient countries, sometimes leading to misalignment with local needs. Finally, Fukuda-Parr and McNeill (2019) discuss the tensions between global and local priorities and their implications for policymaking, notably in terms of the danger to be governed by indicators. Emphasis on quantitative indicators in effect can lead to 'indicator chasing', where efforts are directed more towards improving metrics than addressing underlying local challenges.

Norms and normative effects are critical to the implementation of the SDGs, influencing how goals are prioritized, interpreted and enacted across different governance levels, both explicitly and implicitly. The strongest impact of the SDGs has certainly been in the way they have changed people's cognitive mechanisms towards a universal ideal. However, in terms of explicit rules of governance, challenges remain to address their normative ambiguity, the conflicts between global and local norms and the impact of monitoring mechanisms.

References

Biermann, F., Hickmann, T., Sénit, C.-A., Beisheim, M., Bernstein, S., Chasek, P., ... Wicke, B. (2022). Scientific evidence on the political impact of the Sustainable Development Goals. *Nature Sustainability*, 5, 795–800. https://doi.org/10.1038/s41893-022-00938-0

Charles, A. (2024). Sustainable earnings in a resilient economic system: The power of groupthink in channelling Finance towards sustainable goals. In *SpringerBrief in Economics*. https://link.springer.com/book/9783031675720

Fukuda-Parr, S., and McNeill, D. (2019). Knowledge and politics in setting and measuring the SDGs: Introduction to special issue. *Global Policy*, 10(S1), 5–15. https://doi.org/10.1111/1758-5899.12604

Okitasari, M., and Katramiz, T. (2022). The national development plans after the SDGs: Steering implications of the global goals towards national development planning. *Earth System Governance*, 12, 100136. https://doi.org/10.1016/j.esg.2022.100136

Schmieg, G., Meyer, E., Schrickel, I., et al. (2018). Modeling normativity in sustainability: a comparison of the sustainable development goals, the Paris agreement and the papal encyclical. *Sustainability Science*, 13, 785–796. https://doi.org/10.1007/s11625-017-0504-7

North-South relations

Dhanasree Jayaram

North-South relations mainly involve power dynamics and structural inequalities between the Global North (industrialized/developed countries) and the Global South (developing and least developed countries). These power dynamics are shaped by historical, socioeconomic, political and colonial legacies. These terms emerged during the Cold War based on the distinction between the Global North and South, considering income, technological, macroeconomic, infrastructure and educational disparities (Kowalski 2021). While the world has changed significantly since then, these inequities persist between the richer North and poorer South, with implications for the implementation of the Sustainable Development Goals (SDGs).

Although the SDGs are a universal agenda that lays equal emphasis on transformations across the Global North and South, the Global South receives special attention with the inclusion within the framework of issues such as inequality, poverty, hunger, economic growth and affordable energy. The SDGs typically emphasize partnerships (for example, North-South or South-South) and win-win cooperation, yet they largely fail to address power imbalances in a geopolitically fragmented international order (Martins 2020). Conflicts in different parts of the world; trade and technological disputes; the functioning of international organizations; international responses to transnational crises

102 *Essential Concepts for Implementing the SDGs*

such as climate change and pandemics; and global developments in Science, Technology and Innovation, among others, have reinforced the North-South divide.

For example, Global South countries such as the Democratic Republic of Congo, Chile and Papua New Guinea are leading producers of critical minerals (such as cobalt, copper and lithium) for energy transitions. However, not only do these countries face severe energy poverty, but also the extractivist operations are known to exacerbate marginalization, human rights violations, conflicts and poverty among the affected communities (Matanzima and Loginova 2024). North-South initiatives such as the Just Energy Transition Partnerships launched by the International Partners Group of donor countries in several countries of the Global South have been criticized for power asymmetries, a lack of mutual respect and recognition of priorities of the Global South and unequal financing instruments (mainly loans) that perpetuate dependency (Banerjee 2024).

North-South relations are marred largely by exclusionary and non-pluralistic processes of decision-making and policy implementation, including in the case of the SDGs. These processes reflect the persisting gap between the Global South and North in areas such as knowledge production, resource access and capacity development. Although the SDG framework tries to reduce this gap, the Global North has failed to deliver on key issues such as sustainable finance and aid/assistance, urgently needed by the Global South to tackle socio-ecological and socioeconomic crises. For example, the COVID-19 pandemic was marked by a substantial disparity in vaccine access between the Global South and North. Similarly, even North-South knowledge partnerships on SDG implementation tend to include a unidirectional transfer of knowledge or capacity from North to South, guided by donor-recipient relationships (Penderis et al. 2018). This overlooks the agency, characteristics and needs of the Global South's diverse contexts. For instance, the COVID-19 pandemic shed light on indigenous knowledge and practices in the Global South that helped many countries overcome the pandemic. However, this has largely been overlooked in global sustainability governance.

Yet, the SDGs present an important platform for all countries to address the sustainability challenges they face through multilateral collaboration. The trust deficit between the Global South and North created by historical and contemporary injustices may be bridged through a transformation of the sustainability governance architecture(s) through participatory processes (to cater to the most vulnerable communities), co-creation of knowledge (challenging the geopolitics of knowledge that prioritizes Northern science) and a socio-ecologically just allocation of resources, responsibilities and risks (Gupta and Lebel 2020). North-South relations must recognize the diverse realities within the Global South and North and tailor solutions through equitable South-North and South-South partnerships.

References

Banerjee, A. (2024). Transforming the rhetoric of Just Energy Transition Partnerships into reality: The devil lies in the details. *PLOS Sustainability and Transformation*, 3(8), e0000121. https://doi.org/10.1371/journal.pstr.0000121

Gupta, J., and Lebel, L. (2020). Access and allocation in earth system governance: Lessons learnt in the context of the Sustainable Development Goals. *International Environmental Agreements: Politics, Law and Economics*, 20(2), 393–410. https://doi.org/10.1007/s10784-020-09486-4

Kowalski, A. M. (2021). Global south-global north differences. In *No Poverty* (pp. 389–400). Cham: Springer International Publishing.

Martins, A. (2020). Reimagining equity: Redressing power imbalances between the global North and the global South. *Gender and Development*, 28(1), 135–153. https://doi.org/10.1080/1355 2074.2020.1717172

Matanzima, J., and Loginova, J. (2024). Sociocultural risks of resource extraction for the low-carbon energy transition: Evidence from the Global South. *The Extractive Industries and Society*, 18, 101478. https://doi.org/10.1016/j.exis.2024.101478

Penderis, S. P., Evans, H.-C., Ibsen, H., and Halvorsen, T. (Eds.). (2018). *Knowledge for Justice: Critical Perspectives from Southern African-Nordic Research Partnerships*. Project Muse.

O

Official development assistance (ODA)

Li Li and Hyeyoon Park

Official development assistance (ODA) was first invented as a statistical concept in 1969 by the Development Assistance Committee of the Organization for Economic Cooperation and Development. It is regarded as the 'gold standard' of governmental foreign aid that promotes the economic development and welfare of developing countries and shapes the relations between developing and developed countries (Bracho et al. 2021: 1).

The international society started debating ODA as one of the core financial sources for achieving the Sustainable Development Goals (SDGs). SDG 10.b aims to encourage ODA and financial flows, including foreign direct investment, to states where the need is greatest. Notably, SDG 17.2 re-endorses developed countries' commitment to achieving the target of 0.7% of gross national income for ODA (a UN resolution in 1970) (United Nations General Assembly 2015: 21, 26). Since then, the SDGs have become the backbone of ODA policy. The interlinkage between ODA and the SDGs has shown some positive effects. For instance, the contribution of climate-relevant ODA contributes to achieving multiple sustainability policy targets simultaneously, such as agriculture and water (Iacobuță et al. 2022).

Nevertheless, the current global volume of ODA is far behind in fulfilling developing countries' needs to achieve the SDGs for several reasons. First, the number of eligible ODA providers is limited – that is, 32 members of the Development Assistance Committee of the Organisation for Economic Cooperation and Development. Second, even if all these countries were to satisfy their duty of paying 0.7% of their gross national income, it is insufficient to reach all the SDGs with 169 targets (Mawdsley 2021). The United Nations Conference on Trade and Development estimated that between 2023 and 2030, USD 5.4–7.6 trillion per year is needed to achieve all goals, which represents a personal cost of USD 1,179–1,383 per year. However, many donor countries often fail to reach the 0.7% threshold (United Nations 2023).

Against this backdrop, how to catalyze money to narrow the financial gap became a primary policy issue. It sheds light on multiple types of financing routes, such as philanthropy, remittances, foreign direct investment and South-South flows, in addition to traditional ODA – including both public and private, national and international financing. The debate now centres on 'blended finance', aiming at unlocking private finance by utilizing ODA to de-risk private capital flows (Organisation for Economic Cooperation and Development 2021).

DOI: 10.4324/9781003519560-16

This chapter has been made available under a CC-BY-NC-ND license.

The increasing role of private finance in modernizing ODA via blended finance has brought many concerns, such as the risks of 'SDG washing' (Biermann et al. 2022). First, ODA, closely integrated with private finance, could serve market interests through the SDG business model aligned with 'neoliberal development' (Mawdsley 2021: 54). Blended finance is likely to support projects benefiting private investors' interest. Regarding climate change-related ODA, it tends to support more mitigation projects than the ones for adaptation, due to a lack of profitability (Iacobuță et al. 2022). Second, transparency is another controversial issue regarding what ODA information should be made public. ODA blended with private finance can worsen the transparency problem because of the private sector's confidentiality obligation (Mawdsley 2021). Third, the privatization of ODA could weaken the norm of the 0.7% gross national income as donor countries' national obligation.

In sum, the above-mentioned emerging challenges show a huge governance gap in the current ODA-SDG finance structure that doesn't fulfil developing countries' needs. The gap includes a risk of the emerging 'blended finance' approach wherein the private sector's role increases, and their interests could be centred within ODA projects. It could weaken the legitimacy and accountability of the current ODA system. Building inclusive institutional settings reflecting the demands of the Global South would be significant to realizing just and transformative governance of the SDGs.

References

Biermann, F., Hickmann, T., and Sénit, C.-A. (Eds.). (2022). *The political impact of the sustainable development goals: Transforming governance through global goals?* Cambridge: Cambridge University Press.

Bracho, G., Carey, R., Hynes, W., Klingebiel, S., and Trzeciak-Duval, A. (2021). *Origins, evolution and future of global development cooperation: The role of the Development Assistance Committee (DAC)*. Bonn: Deutsches Institut für Entwicklungspolitik. https://doi.org/10.1017/9781009082945

Iacobuță, G., Brandi, C., Dzebo, A., and Duron, S. (2022). Aligning climate and sustainable development finance through an SDG lens: The role of development assistance in implementing the Paris Agreement. *Global Environmental Change*, 74: 102509. https://doi.org/10.1016/j.gloenvcha.2022.102509

Mawdsley, E. (2021). Development finance and the 2030 goals. In Sachin Chaturvedi, S., Janus, H., Klingebiel, S., Xiaoyun, L., Souza, A., Sidiropoulos, E., and Wehrmann, D. (Eds.), *The Palgrave handbook of development cooperation for achieving the 2030 agenda*, (pp. 51–57). Palgrave Macmillan.

Organisation for Economic Cooperation and Development. (2021). The OECD DAC Blended Finance Guidance, OECD Development Co-operation Directorate, Paris.

United Nations. (2023). Annual cost for reaching the SDGs? More than $5 trillion. Global perspective human stories. *UN News*. 13 December. https://news.un.org/en/story/2023/09/1140997

United Nations General Assembly. (2015). Transforming our world: The 2030 agenda for sustainable development. A/RES/70/1. https://www.un.org/en/development/desa/population/migration/generalassembly/docs/globalcompact/A_RES_70_1_E.pdf

Orchestration

Joshua Philipp Elsässer

Orchestration has emerged as a prominent conceptual approach in the global governance literature, which foregrounds the importance of agency and actor dynamics in addressing complex global challenges. In essence, orchestration involves a principal actor with

106 *Essential Concepts for Implementing the SDGs*

limited resources (orchestrator), often an international organization, that seeks to mobilize and facilitate the voluntary cooperation of third-party actors (intermediaries) to achieve shared objectives (target). Introduced by Abbott and Snidal (2009), orchestration reflects the limitations of traditional, state-centric governance and recognizes the emergence of new governance structures in which non-state actors and transnational governance initiatives play critical roles in creating innovative norms and rules to address collective action problems. These new structures are characterized by complementary – and sometimes alternative – approaches between transnational and intergovernmental governance in a system marked by heterogeneous authority (Elsässer et al. 2022; Green 2014).

Unlike collaboration, orchestration is a mode of governance that is 'indirect', as it relies on intermediation rather than direct interaction. Moreover, it is a 'soft' governance mode, meaning that orchestrators lack the capabilities to enforce rules hierarchically or issue orders through principal-agent relationships. Instead, orchestration relies on persuasion, incentives, nudging or capacity-building to foster voluntary cooperation among a diverse set of actors. While states and other governors can generally use orchestration, it is particularly valuable for international organizations, which often cannot engage in hard, direct regulation. Due to restricted resources or mandates, international organizations are typically granted limited authority to govern states or private actors, as this would require strong enforcement mechanisms or interventions in domestic affairs, potentially undermining national sovereignty (Abbott and Snidal 2009).

Scholars in global sustainability governance have frequently employed orchestration to analyse how international organizations influence and mobilize actors, highlighting two central strategies with significant practical implications for achieving the Sustainable Development Goals (SDGs). First, international organizations can *manage* states by engaging intermediaries to shape state preferences, beliefs and behaviours, aligning them with the orchestrator's objectives. For instance, various environmental treaty secretariats under the United Nations have mobilized various non-state initiatives to exert pressure and drive intergovernmental negotiations towards ambitious policymaking (Hickmann and Elsässer 2020). Second, international organizations can also *bypass* states by engaging intermediaries to influence the behaviour of private actors. For instance, the United Nations Environment Programme has successfully promoted responsible investment guidelines that encourage private investors to adopt sustainability criteria, fostering alignment with environmental and social goals (van der Lugt and Dingwerth 2015).

While orchestration has become a popular framework for understanding how international organizations navigate complex policy landscapes, its application in practice often reveals a more nuanced reality than the theory suggests. The clear distinction between the roles of orchestrators and intermediaries, central to the theory, can blur in real-world settings. For instance, under prolonged orchestration dynamics, where benefits accrue to all parties involved, collaborative dynamics often emerge (Hickmann and Elsässer 2020). Similar to the analogy of an orchestra, where musicians play subordinate roles under the direction of an orchestrator, the theory sometimes struggles to account for the varying degrees of influence and control exerted by different actors, potentially obscuring the hierarchical elements inherent in many governance arrangements.

This suggests that while orchestration is a valuable starting point, it requires further investigation to capture the nuances and intricacies of actor dynamics of contemporary global governance. Future research on orchestration should thus focus on its underlying mechanisms and make further headway in measuring its impacts (Elsässer 2024). This may include further consideration of normative implications, such as questions of legitimacy (Bäckstrand and Kuyper 2017), or connecting the agency-centred approach to potential structural effects on institutional environments to better understand the potential and limitations of orchestration.

References

Abbott, K. W., and Snidal, D. (2009). Strengthening International Regulation through Transnational New Governance: Overcoming the Orchestration Deficit. *Vanderbilt Journal of Transnational Law*, 42(2), 501–578.

Bäckstrand, K., and Kuyper, J. W. (2017). The Democratic Legitimacy of Orchestration: The UNFCCC, Non-State Actors and Transnational Climate Governance. *Environmental Politics*, 26(4), 764–788. https://doi.org/10.1080/09644016.2017.1323579

Elsässer, J. P. (2024). Managers of Complex Change? How United Nations Treaty Secretariats Jointly Govern Institutional Interplay in Global Environmental Governance. *Environmental Policy and Governance*, 1–13. https://doi.org/10.1002/eet.2105

Elsässer, J. P., Hickmann, T., Jinnah, S., Oberthür, S., and Van de Graaf, T. (2022). Institutional Interplay in Global Environmental Governance: Lessons Learned and Future Research. *International Environmental Agreements: Politics, Law and Economics*, 22(2), 373–391. https://doi.org/10.1007/s10784-022-09569-4

Green, J. F. (2014). *Rethinking Private Authority: Agents and Entrepreneurs in Global Environmental Governance*. Princeton University Press.

Hickmann, T., and Elsässer, J. P. (2020). New Alliances in Global Environmental Governance: How Intergovernmental Treaty Secretariats Interact with Non-state Actors to Address Transboundary Environmental Problems. *International Environmental Agreements: Politics, Law and Economics*, 20(3), 459–481. https://doi.org/10.1007/s10784-020-09493-5

van der Lugt, C., and Dingwerth, K. (2015). Governing Where Focality is Low: UNEP and the Principles for Responsible Investment. In K. W. Abbott, P. Genschel, D. Snidal, and B. Zangl (Eds.), *International Organizations as Orchestrators* (pp. 237–261). Cambridge University Press.

P

Paris Agreement

Joshua Philipp Elsässer

The Paris Agreement was adopted in 2015 by the conference of the parties to the United Nations Framework Convention on Climate Change. The agreement has revitalized global climate governance after years of negotiation deadlock; for the first time, major emitters and superpowers, including China and the United States, committed to a common pathway to limit emissions, which sparked optimism that governments could collectively address the climate crisis.

The Paris Agreement is a complex and evolving treaty. Its overall design is meant to limit global warming to well below 2°C, with efforts to cap the increase at 1.5°C above pre-industrial levels. Its complexity stems from its ambitious goal of transforming global economies into low-carbon societies. Acknowledging the critical role of domestic politics for international climate policy, the agreement works through an implementation and ambition cycle, which spans multiple governance levels (WRI 2024). This cycle of planning, reviewing and implementing involves a broad range of stakeholders, with public consultations, reviews and impact assessments at the national level combined with international mechanisms to support implementation, promote compliance and enhance transparency.

Central to the Paris Agreement are the so-called Nationally Determined Contributions, which involve a mandatory, iterative 'ratcheting-up' process that requires countries to progressively increase their climate ambition and update their contributions to reduce greenhouse gas emissions every five years (Falkner 2016). Alongside mitigation targets, countries also have to outline their actions for adapting to climate change and enhancing resilience. While the Paris Agreement is primarily an intergovernmental treaty, it also advances a novel 'all hands on deck' approach that views non-state actors such as corporations and civil society as essential contributors to the treaty's implementation alongside states. While non-state actors are hoped to close governance gaps or catalyze more intergovernmental ambition, treaty implementation has yet to fully deliver on its promises (Elsässer et al. 2022; Hale 2016).

The Agreement's design allows for the addition of new elements and agenda points, increasing its comprehensiveness. The low-carbon transformations it envisions are

DOI: 10.4324/9781003519560-17

This chapter has been made available under a CC-BY-NC-ND license.

tied to the dependency on fossil fuels that has underpinned global economic development over the past decades, particularly in industrialized countries. In reducing this reliance, the Paris Agreement intersects with broader development areas also targeted by the Sustainable Development Goals (SDGs), including poverty alleviation, energy access or sustainable industrialization (Moreno et al. 2023). Simultaneously, SDG 13 on climate action explicitly recognizes the connections between climate mitigation and other development goals. While this overlap suggests potential synergies, alignment across the two frameworks has often remained elusive in practice (Campagnolo and Davide 2019). Taking a more critical perspective, the expanding scope of the Paris Agreement could even render the SDGs redundant in the long run in a development that is possibly accelerated by the increasing severity of climate change impacts around the world, which could result in a heightened priority to address climate change for development.

Looking ahead, the Paris Agreement faces many challenges. Key issues include unequal responsibility for climate change, contested mitigation technologies such as carbon capture and storage, and the need for increasing funding. While the Paris Agreement has established a solid framework for mitigation, adaptation has been only gradually introduced, with loss and damage still emerging as a critical issue. This is particularly relevant due to the asymmetric vulnerability of developing countries, which are disproportionately affected by rising sea levels, flooding, droughts and wildfires. Major science networks have warned that the world might exceed 2°C of warming and that efforts under the Paris Agreement are still insufficient (IPCC 2023). The central challenge now is the speed of action, given the complexities of socio-technical-economic transformations, including issues of equity and justice closely related to several SDGs and the costs from delayed action for the broader objectives of sustainable development.

References

Campagnolo, L., and Davide, M. (2019). Can the Paris deal boost SDGs achievement? An assessment of climate mitigation co-benefits or side-effects on poverty and inequality. *World Development*, 122, 96–109. https://doi.org/10.1016/j.worlddev.2019.05.015

Elsässer, J. P., Hickmann, T., Jinnah, S., Oberthür, S., and Van de Graaf, T. (2022). Institutional interplay in global environmental governance: Lessons learned and future research. *International Environmental Agreements: Politics, Law and Economics*, 22(2), 373–391. https://doi.org/10.1007/s10784-022-09569-4

Falkner, R. (2016). The Paris Agreement and the new logic of international climate politics. *International Affairs*, 92(5), 1107–1125. https://doi.org/10.1111/1468-2346.12708

Hale, T. (2016). 'All Hands on Deck': The Paris Agreement and nonstate climate action. *Global Environmental Politics*, 16(3), 12–22. https://doi.org/10.1162/GLEP_a_00362

IPCC. (2023). Climate Change 2023: Synthesis Report (Contribution of Working Groups I, II and III to the Sixth Assessment Report of the Intergovernmental Panel on Climate Change).

Moreno, J., Van de Ven, D.-J., Sampedro, J., Gambhir, A., Woods, J., and Gonzalez-Eguino, M. (2023). Assessing synergies and trade-offs of diverging Paris-compliant mitigation strategies with long-term SDG objectives. *Global Environmental Change*, 78, 102624. https://doi.org/10.1016/j.gloenvcha.2022.102624

WRI. (2024). Explaining the Paris Rulebook. https://files.wri.org/d8/s3fs-public/2022-10/unpacking-paris-rulebook-english.pdf?gl=1*1*6rqpmv*gcl_au*NDAzNjk5MTIwLjE3MjM2Mjg0NDI

Participation

Okechukwu Enechi

Participation is a multifaceted concept that has been a subject of debate among philosophers, policymakers, practitioners and academics for centuries. Within sustainable development, although the role of participation has been extensively explored, there is limited consensus on its meaning and its capacity to drive transformative change, as well as a lack of a clear framework for organizing and implementing participation at different governance levels (Carpentier 2012; Glass and Newig 2019).

Participation has been a key focus in sustainable development research and policymaking, with evidence supporting its role in fostering sustainability through democratic practices (Pickering et al. 2022). It is a key component of the United Nations (UN) 2030 Agenda for Sustainable Development, which positions participation as central to achieving the SDGs and realizing the 'leave no one behind' principle. SDG 16 explicitly calls for stakeholder participation in decision-making at all levels, while SDG 17 offers partnership mechanisms as a means of implementation. At the national level, the Voluntary National Reviews encourage participation of stakeholders in the review in order to achieve inclusion, integrate domestic-local contexts and empower the most affected towards achieving the SDGs.

Despite its central role in the SDGs framework, enhancing participation in SDG implementation is complicated due to limited clarity in how participation is conceptualized and should be implemented. A primary challenge is the lack of specific, measurable targets and indicators related to participation, which impedes analytical processes and effective monitoring. Although the process around Voluntary National Reviews is intended to promote participation and inclusiveness in SDG implementation, many countries fail to meaningfully involve the most affected and marginalized groups in the review of the SDGs at national level. This exclusion can be attributed to factors such as shrinking civic space and the contested representative role of civil societies in global governance (Sénit and Biermann 2021).

Furthermore, even when countries explicitly state their intention of including diverse stakeholders in the Voluntary National Reviews, there is often a lack of clarity regarding how the participation of subnational and local level stakeholders should be organized and implemented (Figueroa and Harrison 2022). Additionally, resource constraints, inadequate expertise and sustainability knowledge gaps also pose significant challenges to participation in the review of SDG implementation at different levels. These challenges question the extent to which Voluntary National Reviews can effectively address the participation gap in SDG governance, with potential consequences that include a dearth of empirical data for evaluating SDG implementation, particularly in regions like Sub-Saharan Africa (Biermann et al. 2022). Additionally, there is also a risk that lack of clarity in how participation should be implemented leads to tokenism or marginalization of stakeholders, thus further exacerbating inequalities in SDG governance at the local level (Mosse 2001).

Participation, while widely acclaimed as key to the implementation of the SDGs, remains challenging to define and materialize in national and global contexts. Therefore, to realize the potential of participation for sustainability transformation as envisioned in the 2030 Agenda, a robust framework is required that provides an unambiguous definition of participation, including the identification of relevant stakeholders and specific, measurable targets and indicators to assess both the level and quality of participation. In addition, there is a need to establish clear thresholds for the participation of stakeholders in SDG monitoring and review at national, subnational and local levels.

References

Biermann, F., Hickmann, T., Sénit, C.-A., Beisheim, M., Bernstein, S., Chasek, P., ... Wicke, B. (2022). Scientific evidence on the political impact of the Sustainable Development Goals. *Nature Sustainability*, 5, 795–800. https://doi.org/10.1038/s41893-022-00938-0

Carpentier, N. (2012). The concept of participation. If they have access and interact, do they really participate? *Revista Fronteiras*, 14(2), 164–177. https://doi.org/10.4013/fem.2012.142.10

Figueroa, D. J.-P., and Harrison, T. (2022). *Pieces of a Puzzle: Further Steps on a Journey*. Berlin: German Council for Sustainable Development (RNE). Retrieved March 7 2024, from https://sdgglobalforum.org/members/detail/cscsd

Glass, L. M., and Newig, J. (2019). Governance for achieving the sustainable development goals: How important are participation, policy coherence, reflexivity, adaptation and democratic institutions? *Earth System Governance*, 2. https://doi.org/10.1016/j.esg.2019.100031

Mosse, D. (2001). 'People's knowledge', participation and patronage: Operations and representations in rural development. In B. Cooke, and K. Uma (Eds.), *Participation: The New Tyranny* (pp. 16–35). New York: Zed Books Ltd.

Pickering, J., Hickmann, T., Bäckstrand, K., Kalfagianni, A., Bloomfield, M., Mert, A., ... Lo, A. Y. (2022). Democratising sustainability transformations: Assessing the transformative potential of democratic practices in environmental governance. *Earth System Governance*, 11. https://doi.org/10.1016/j.esg.2021.100131

Sénit, C.-A., and Biermann, F. (2021). In whose name are you speaking? The marginalization of the poor in global civil society. *Global Policy*. https://doi.org/10.1111/1758-5899.12997

Partnerships

Maximilian S. T. Wanner

Partnerships have been described and studied under terms such as collaborations, networks, alliances, coalitions, cross-sectoral or cooperative initiatives and multi-stakeholder platforms. Originally understood as collaborations between the public and private sector, scholars now refer to partnerships more broadly as 'voluntary agreements between public actors (international organizations, states, or substate public authorities) and nonstate actors (non-governmental organizations, companies, or foundations) [...] across multiple jurisdictions and levels of governance' (Andonova 2017, p. 2). Partnerships can be formal or informal initiatives in which actors from different sectors come together in diverse constellations for specific purposes. As such, they vary substantially depending on the issue area, actors involved, institutional structures and goals.

The concept of partnerships as a form of governance for sustainable development has been around for decades. International and national agencies began promoting partnerships for development in the 1980s, and their popularity grew especially after the 2002 World Summit on Sustainable Development (Higham et al. 2024; Pattberg and Widerberg 2016). Partnerships have since become key components of global governance for

112 *Essential Concepts for Implementing the SDGs*

sustainable development. With the adoption of the Sustainable Development Goals (SDGs), multi-stakeholder partnerships were integrated into the global sustainability agenda to address the scope and interconnectedness of the SDGs, specifically under the targets 17.16 and 17.17 of SDG 17, which aims to 'strengthen the means of implementation and revitalize the Global Partnership for Sustainable Development'. The rise of partnerships is associated with globalization and decentralization trends, the retreat of the state and the collaborative efforts of international organizations (Andonova 2017). Partnerships complement state efforts by pooling knowledge, expertise, technology and financial resources from different sectors, which are crucial given the scope and complexity of today's sustainability challenges. These collaborative and cooperative initiatives are seen as essential means for global action and the local implementation of the SDGs, as they are expected to generate synergies, effects larger than the sum of individual efforts, both between actors and the SDGs.

In the context of the SDGs, partnerships have been increasingly studied by scholars of global governance and organizational studies as modes of governance and forms of collaboration. These literatures have assessed their emergence and formation (for example, Andonova 2017; Higham et al. 2024), participation and institutional design (for example, Glass et al. 2023), accountability and legitimacy (for example, Bäckstrand et al. 2022), performance and effectiveness (for example, Higham et al. 2024; Pattberg and Widerberg 2016), synergies, transformative potential and future prospects (for example, Leal Filho et al. 2024; Widerberg et al. 2023). Research has identified various conducive conditions, including committed resources and institutionalization, collected in partnership guidebooks, such as *Unite to Ignite* by the Partnering Initiative and the United Nations Department of Economic and Social Affairs (Benton and Stibbe 2023).

However, partnerships have faced criticism for reinforcing unequal power relations and failing to deliver effective action at scale and to create needed synergies. As challenges such as securing long-term funding and poor coordination on a global scale persist, there are calls to reform the governance landscape by improving the orchestration and 'meta-governance' and developing better frameworks for aligning partnerships (Bäckstrand et al. 2022; Widerberg et al. 2023). Ultimately, the success of partnerships often depends on the will of governments that keep shaping the increasingly complex funding system and priorities in the world.

In conclusion, partnerships are vital to achieve the SDGs but face many challenges. Unlocking their full potential requires creating an enabling environment that provides partnerships with the necessary resources and support to generate more synergies between actors and SDG action.

References

Andonova, L. B. (2017). *Governance Entrepreneurs: International Organizations and the Rise of Global Public-Private Partnerships* (1st ed.). Cambridge University Press. https://doi.org/10.1017/9781316694015

Bäckstrand, K., Koliev, F., and Mert, A. (2022). Governing SDG Partnerships: The Role of Institutional Capacity, Inclusion and Transparency. In E. Murphy, A. Banerjee, and P. P. Walsh (Eds.), *Partnerships and the Sustainable Development Goals* (pp. 41–58). Springer International Publishing. https://doi.org/10.1007/978-3-031-07461-5_4

Benton, L., and Stibbe, D. (2023). UNITE TO IGNITE: Accelerating the Transformational Power of Partnerships for the SDGs and Beyond. The Partnering Initiative and UN DESA.

Glass, L.-M., Newig, J., and Ruf, S. (2023). MSPs for the SDGs – Assessing the Collaborative Governance Architecture of Multi-stakeholder Partnerships for Implementing the Sustainable

Development Goals. *Earth System Governance*, 17, 100182. https://doi.org/10.1016/j.esg.2023.100182

Higham, I., Bäckstrand, K., Fritzsche, F., and Koliev, F. (2024). Multistakeholder Partnerships for Sustainable Development: Promises and Pitfalls. *Annual Review of Environment and Resources*. https://doi.org/10.1146/annurev-environ-051823-115857

Leal Filho, W., Dibbern, T., Pimenta Dinis, M. A., Coggo Cristofoletti, E., Mbah, M. F., Mishra, A., Clarke, A., Samuel, N., Castillo Apraiz, J., Rimi Abubakar, I., and Aina, Y. A. (2024). The Added Value of Partnerships in Implementing the UN Sustainable Development Goals. *Journal of Cleaner Production*, *438*, 140794. https://doi.org/10.1016/j.jclepro.2024.140794

Pattberg, P., and Widerberg, O. (2016). Transnational Multistakeholder Partnerships for Sustainable Development: Conditions for Success. *Ambio*, *45*(1), 42–51. https://doi.org/10.1007/s13280-015-0684-2

Widerberg, O., Fast, C., Koloffon Rosas, M., and Pattberg, P. (2023). Multi-stakeholder Partnerships for the SDGs: Is the 'Next Generation' Fit for Purpose? *International Environmental Agreements: Politics, Law and Economics*, *23*(2), 165–171. https://doi.org/10.1007/s10784-023-09606-w

People, Planet, Prosperity, Peace, Partnerships (5 Ps)

Laura Rahm, Tara Patricia Cookson and Ginette Azcona

People, Planet, Prosperity, Peace and Partnership – also known as the 5 Ps – are the core pillars of the 2030 Agenda for Sustainable Development. They originate from the preamble of the 2030 Agenda as 'a plan of action for people, planet and prosperity [that] also seeks to strengthen universal peace…acting in collaborative partnership' (United Nations General Assembly 2015, 5). The 5 Ps highlight the interconnected, indivisible nature of the Sustainable Development Goals (SDGs) and serve as a guiding framework for their implementation across social, economic and environmental dimensions (Tremblay et al. 2020).

The **People** pillar aims to end poverty and hunger, ensuring that all individuals live with dignity and equality in a healthy environment.

The **Planet** pillar focuses on protecting ecosystems, addressing climate change and promoting responsible use of natural resources while curbing overproduction and overconsumption.

The **Prosperity** pillar seeks to foster sustainable, equitable growth, where everyone benefits from economic, social and technological progress, in harmony with nature.

The **Peace** pillar emphasizes promoting peaceful, just and inclusive societies where people can live without fear of violence and conflict.

The **Partnership** pillar underscores the need for collaborative efforts among governments, private sector entities, civil society and other stakeholders to achieve the SDGs and support the poorest and most vulnerable.

The 5 Ps are frequently used in progress reporting to the United Nations, such as the Common Country Analysis, Voluntary National Reviews, policies, strategies and programmes to illustrate the holistic and interconnected nature of the SDGs. The absence of an official mapping that links specific SDGs to individual pillars has led to variations in how different countries and organizations interpret and apply the framework. This is based on an understanding that many goals fall under more than one pillar. One alignment of pillars to the SDGs, which also illustrates the framework's framing of gender equality as a cross-cutting priority, is illustrated in Figure 1.

114 Essential Concepts for Implementing the SDGs

5-Ps of Sustainable Development and Gender Mainstreaming

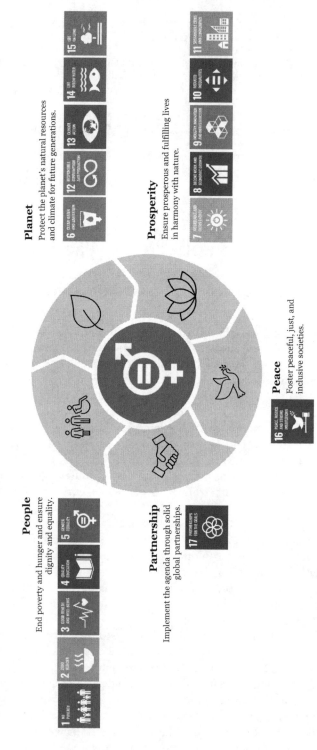

Figure 1 Five Pillars of the 2030 Agenda mapped by SDGs and Gender Equality (SDG 5) as a cross-cutting goal.
Author's own illustration.

The 5 Ps framework has been criticized as too vague, not distinguishing between primary and secondary goals (Holden et al. 2016). Moreover, despite the framework's intention to promote multi-sectoral approaches to SDG implementation, in practice, there is a tendency towards 'cherry-picking', where countries or sectors prioritize certain SDGs while neglecting others (Forestier and Kim 2020). This fragmented approach leads to siloed actions, ignoring the complex interconnections between goals (Bali Swain and Min 2023). For instance, prioritizing economic growth without considering its environmental or social consequences exacerbates inequalities and accelerates ecological degradation. Needed investments to promote accelerated progress and foster synergies across the 5 Ps have not materialized. Large funding gaps are evident in the areas of education, social protection, climate change, energy transition and gender equality. Additionally, a lack of coherence across government levels, policy sectors and societal actors further undermines the indivisibility of the SDGs (Breuer et al. 2023).

A systemic approach to implementing the SDGs would promote high synergy effects across the 5 Ps, mitigate trade-offs and spur accelerated progress across many goals. For example, SDG 5 (Gender Equality) has been identified as highly synergetic across the 5 Ps, as it both leverages progress towards other goals and targets and receives synergy effects from other SDGs (Xiao et al. 2023). By capitalizing on synergies, including through gender mainstreaming across goals, countries can accelerate progress towards the 2030 Agenda. To strengthen the 5 Ps framework, further research and data on synergistic approaches are needed, alongside a stronger commitment among decision-makers to effective coordination and policy coherence at all levels of policymaking.

References

Bali Swain, R., and Min, Y. (2023). Interlinkages and interactions among the Sustainable Development Goals. In R. Bali Swain, and Y. Min (Eds.), *Interlinkages between the Sustainable Development Goals* (pp. 1–15). Edward Elgar Publishing. https://doi.org/10.4337/9781803924946.00006

Breuer, A., Malerba, D., Srigiri, S., and Balasubramanian, P. (Eds.). (2023). *Governing the interlinkages between the SDGs: Approaches, opportunities and challenges.* Routledge, Taylor and Francis Group.

Forestier, O., and Kim, R. E. (2020). Cherry-picking the Sustainable Development Goals: Goal prioritization by national governments and implications for global governance. *Sustainable Development*, 28(5), 1269–1278. https://doi.org/10.1002/sd.2082

Holden, E., Linnerud, K., and Banister, D. (2016). The imperatives of sustainable development. *Sustainable Development*, 25(3), 213–226. https://doi.org/10.1002/sd.1647

Tremblay, D., Fortier, F., Boucher, J., Riffon, O., and Villeneuve, C. (2020). Sustainable development goal interactions: An analysis based on the five pillars of the 2030 agenda. *Sustainable Development*, 28(6), 1584–1596. https://doi.org/10.1002/sd.2107

United Nations General Assembly. (2015). Transforming our world: The 2030 agenda for sustainable development. A/RES/70/1. https://sdgs.un.org/publications/transforming-our-world-2030-agenda-sustainable-development-17981

Xiao, H., Liu, Y., and Ren, J. (2023). Synergies and trade-offs across sustainable development goals: A novel method incorporating indirect interactions analysis. *Sustainable Development*, 31(2), 1135–1148. https://doi.org/10.1002/sd.2446

Philanthropic foundations

Cornelia Ulbert

The landscape of actors in global governance has expanded considerably since the United Nations system opened up to non-state and business actors in the second half of the 1990s. The goal-oriented approach, which was introduced through the Millennium Development Goals, attracted more and more private foundations to engage in international development (Moran and Stone 2016). From the onset, the Sustainable Development Goals (SDGs) were promoted as 'converging interests' between governments and philanthropies (United Nations Development Programme 2016). The United Nations Development Programme, assisted by the Foundation Center and the Rockefeller Philanthropy Advisers, tried to engage philanthropies via an 'SDG Philanthropy Platform', which was later accompanied by an 'SDG Impact Fund' for pooling foundation funding among others.

Almost by definition – and legally required – private foundations are philanthropic and serve the public good. Within the spectrum of non-state actors, philanthropic foundations are situated between for-profit companies and nonprofit-making non-governmental organizations. The new type of philanthropists who have been actively involved in implementing the Millennium Development Goals and subsequently the SDGs adheres to a logic dubbed 'social entrepreneurship' or 'philanthrocapitalism'. Philanthrocapitalism is characterized as framing development issues as scientific problems, recipients as entrepreneurs and philanthropic funding as social investment (Haydon et al. 2021). From a more critical stance, philanthropic foundations belong to the 'new global governors' (Clarke 2019) who wield undue influence in global politics because of their financial means acquired through tax exemptions.

In fact, the funds that philanthropic foundations provide are needed to close the financial gap necessary to implement the SDGs. Over the last two decades philanthropic contributions have become a significant part of international development assistance: Based on data from 205 of the largest philanthropic organizations worldwide, the Organization for Economic Cooperation and Development reported the amount of USD 42.5 billion from private philanthropy for the period of 2016–2019, compared to USD 595.5 billion of official development assistance of the members of the Development Assistance Committee of the Organisation for Economic Cooperation and Development, which equals 7% of official development assistance (Organisation for Economic Cooperation and Development 2021, 32).

Funding projects, (international) organizations, policy initiatives and research activities, however, is just one means by which philanthropic foundations establish their power and influence. The decisive factor seems to be what kind of funds are made available and how they are used. With their material incentives, philanthropic foundations can act as agenda-setters. They also promote their agendas by advocacy often based on either campaigns or evaluations and monitoring reports. Besides education (SDG 4), philanthropies, first and foremost the Gates Foundation, as the largest private foundation, are especially engaged in the health sector (SDG 3).

Following a trend of state funding, foundations subsidize international organizations with earmarked funds. This enables them to better control the use of their contributions and thus pursue their own objectives through these organizations (Clinton and Sridhar

2017). Philanthropic foundations not only shape processes. They also develop structures and institutions by actively creating networks and by sponsoring and being partners in global public-private partnerships. One of the most prominent and successful examples of a global health partnership is GAVI, the Vaccine Alliance, founded in 2000 on the initiative of the Gates Foundation, which is still one of its most influential members.

Philanthropic foundations are agents of global governance and thus instrumental in implementing the SDGs. Their activities, however, usually happen outside the political and formalized procedures of representative decision-making and accountability, which poses a fundamental democratic problem of global governance. This is why their legitimacy is seen as critical, and there are repeated calls for better accountability, especially of the most influential private foundations (Harman 2016).

References

Clarke, G. (2019). The New Global Governors: Globalization, Civil Society and the Rise of Private Philanthropic Foundations. *Journal of Civil Society*, 15(3), 197–213. https://doi.org/10.1080/17 448689.2019.1622760

Clinton, C., and Sridhar, D. (2017). Who Pays for Cooperation in Global Health? A Comparative Analysis of WHO, the World Bank, the Global Fund to Fight HIV/AIDS, Tuberculosis and Malaria and Gavi, the Vaccine Alliance. *The Lancet*, 390(10091), 324–332. https://doi.org/10.1016/S0140-6736(16)32402-3

Harman, S. (2016). The Bill and Melinda Gates Foundation and Legitimacy in Global Health Governance. *Global Governance*, 22(3), 349–368. https://doi.org/10.1163/19426720-02203004

Haydon, S., Jung, T., and Russell, S. (2021). 'You've Been Framed': A Critical Review of Academic Discourse on Philanthrocapitalism. *International Journal of Management Reviews*, 23(3), 353–375. https://doi.org/10.1111/ijmr.12255

Moran, M., and Stone, D. (2016). The New Philanthropy: Private Power in International Development Policy? In J. Grugel and D. Hammett (Eds.), *The Palgrave Handbook of International Development* (pp. 297–313). Palgrave Macmillan UK. https://doi.org/10.1057/978-1-137-42724-3_17

Organisation for Economic Cooperation and Development. (2021). *Private Philanthropy for Development – Second Edition: Data for Action, The Development Dimension*. OECD Publishing. https://doi.org/10.1787/cdf37f1e-en

UNDP. (2016). *Converging Interests: Philanthropy-government Collaboration to Achieve the Sustainable Development Goals. Draft for Consultations at the High Level Political Forum, July 2016*. UNDP. https://www.undp.org/indonesia/publications/converging-interests-philanthropy-government-collaboration-achieve-sustainable-development-goals

Planetary boundaries

Lena Partzsch

The planetary boundaries framework informed the negotiations on the 2030 Agenda and the Sustainable Development Goals (SDGs). It identifies nine interrelated processes that are critical for maintaining the stability and resilience of the Earth system as a whole. Johan Rockström pioneered work on the framework, which was published in 2009, when he was director of the Stockholm Resilience Centre (Rockström et al. 2009). The framework was updated several times, in particular, by Steffen et al. (2015) and Richardson et al. (2023).

118 *Essential Concepts for Implementing the SDGs*

The boundaries establish a 'safe operating space' for human civilization on the Earth. Therefore, crossing these boundaries puts humanity into an unsafe space, endangering human well-being and human civilization. Six of the nine boundaries have now been transgressed: *Climate change, biosphere integrity (genetic diversity), biogeochemical flows (nitrogen and phosphorus), land system change, freshwater use* and *chemical pollution.* The transgression level has increased for all boundaries identified as overstepped since the first assessment. *Ocean acidification* is close to being breached, while *aerosol loading* regionally exceeds the boundary. *Stratospheric ozone levels* have recovered slightly (Richardson et al. 2023). These findings have been subject to considerable criticism. While the revisions have addressed issues of limited data availability and use, the framework continues to neglect historical and regional heterogeneity (Biermann and Kim 2020).

Almost all authors of the original framework have a background in the natural sciences. By design, their assessment effort is science-driven, neglecting human dimensions, including equity. The more recent concept of Earth system boundaries has evolved from the concept of planetary boundaries, identifying not only safe but also just boundaries at both global and sub-global scales. Seven of these eight global earth system boundaries have already been exceeded (Rockström et al. 2023). They have been further refined to 'planetary commons' in an effort to more persuasively argue for comprehensive stewardship obligations through earth system governance (Rockström et al. 2024). However, the conclusion remains that environmental sustainability needs to be prioritized in the implementation of the 2030 Agenda. Otherwise, planetary health and human civilization are at risk.

Arguments that developing countries cannot afford environmental sustainability, or that they should develop first and clean up later, are invalid if environmental damage from crossing planetary boundaries makes economic development impossible. This conclusion is shared by similar concepts such as just transition, nature-based solutions and nature's contribution to people, demonstrating a growing recognition of an integrated approach as seen in the SDGs. United Nations Environment Programme's *Sixth Global Environment Outlook* makes explicit reference to the planetary boundaries framework. The framework has raised alarm bells in scientific and political debates about the postponement and non-implementation of environmental targets under the SDGs. However, the prioritization of the environment in global sustainability governance has not been achieved, and environmental targets continue to be postponed during implementation (Partzsch 2023).

References

Biermann, F., and Kim, R. E. (2020). The boundaries of the planetary boundary framework: A critical appraisal of approaches to define a 'safe operating space' for humanity. *Annual Review of Environment and Resources*, 45(1), 497–521. https://doi.org/10.1146/annurev-environ-012320-080337

Partzsch, L. (Ed.). (2023). *The Environment in Global Sustainability Governance: Perceptions, Actors, Innovations.* Bristol University Press. https://doi.org/10.56687/9781529228021

Richardson, K., Steffen, W., Lucht, W., Bendtsen, J., Cornell, S. E., Donges, J. F., Drüke, M., Fetzer, I., Bala, G., Bloh, W. von, Feulner, G., Fiedler, S., Gerten, D., Gleeson, T., Hofmann, M., Huiskamp, W., Kummu, M., Mohan, C., Nogués-Bravo, D., … Rockström, J. (2023). Earth beyond six of nine planetary boundaries. *Science Advances*, 9(37), eadh2458. https://doi.org/10.1126/sciadv.adh2458

Rockström, J., Gupta, J., Qin, D., Lade, S. J., Abrams, J. F., Andersen, L. S., Armstrong McKay, D. I., Bai, X., Bala, G., Bunn, S. E., Ciobanu, D., DeClerck, F., Ebi, K., Gifford, L., Gordon, C.,

Hasan, S., Kanie, N., Lenton, T. M., Loriani, S., ... Zhang, X. (2023). Safe and just Earth system boundaries. *Nature*, 619(7968), 102–111. https://doi.org/10.1038/s41586-023-06083-8

Rockström, J., Kotzé, L., Milutinović, S., Biermann, F., Brovkin, V., Donges, J., Ebbesson, J., French, D., Gupta, J., Kim, R. E., Lenton, T., Lenzi, D., Nakicenovic, N., Neumann, B., Schuppert, F., Winkelmann, R., Bosselmann, K., Folke, C., Lucht, W., ... Steffen, W. (2024). The planetary commons: A new paradigm for safeguarding Earth-regulating systems in the Anthropocene. *Proceedings of the National Academy of Sciences*, 121(5), e2301531121. https://doi.org/10.1073/pnas.2301531121

Rockström, J., Steffen, W., Noone, K., Persson, A., Chapin, F. S., Lambin, E. F., Lenton, T. M., Scheffer, M., Folke, C., Schellnhuber, H. J., Nykvist, B., Wit, C. A. D., Hughes, T., van der Leeuw, S., Rodhe, H., Sörlin, S., Snyder, P. K., Costanza, R., Svedin, U., ... Foley, J. A. (2009). A safe operating space for humanity. *Nature*, 461(7263), 472–475. https://doi.org/10.1038/461472a

Steffen, W., Richardson, K., Rockström, J., Cornell, S. E., Fetzer, I., Bennett, E. M., Biggs, R., Carpenter, S. R., Vries, W. D., Wit, C. A. D., Folke, C., Gerten, D., Heinke, J., Mace, G. M., Persson, L. M., Ramanathan, V., Reyers, B., and Sörlin, S. (2015). Planetary boundaries: Guiding human development on a changing planet. *Science*, 347(6223). https://doi.org/10.1126/science.1259855

Policy coherence and integration (at domestic level)

Alex San Martim Portes

The domestic implementation of the Sustainable Development Goals (SDGs) is a challenging task that involves numerous actors and institutions working in various areas of domestic policymaking. Since the 17 SDGs span across economic, social and environmental dimensions, there are many points of possible conflict and trade-offs and policy integration and coherence are necessary to ensure that progress in one area supports, rather than undermines, progress in others.

Policy integration and policy coherence are similar and interrelated concepts commonly used in the global sustainability literature (Tosun and Lang 2017). Both concepts describe the breaking down of silos between government departments and sectors to enable coordinated action. Although many authors use these terms interchangeably (Glass and Newig 2019; Stafford-Smith et al. 2017), they are different concepts, both valuable in understanding the domestic implementation of the SDGs. Policy coherence suggests that different sectors should meet similar goals or not contradict and hamper each other's objectives (Organisation for Economic Cooperation and Development 2016). Policy integration goes further than coherence. It is understood as a political process that involves the coordination of actors, institutions and instruments from different policy sectors (Cejudo and Trein 2023). While policy coherence helps understand the implementation of different parts of the 2030 Agenda consistently, policy integration explains how this agenda is mainstreamed into national policies.

In the context of the SDGs, both policy integration and coherence are critical for addressing the complex and interrelated nature of sustainable development goals and targets. There are two main aspects of integration and coherence in the 2030 Agenda: within the agenda and with other policy instruments. Integration and coherence within the 2030 Agenda expect that the 17 SDGs 'are integrated and indivisible and balance the three dimensions of sustainable development: the economic, social and environmental' (United Nations 2015, 1). For example, environmental ministries must work closely with

120 *Essential Concepts for Implementing the SDGs*

economic and social ministries to ensure that environmental sustainability (SDGs 13, 14 and 15) is not sacrificed for short-term economic gains (SDG 8).

The implementation of the 2030 Agenda also requires countries to place it within existing policy structures in a way that creates synergies with 'national planning instruments, policies, strategies and financial frameworks' (United Nations 2019, 5). As such, countries must consider the best approach to ensure that the SDGs capitalize on existing efforts within ministries and institutions and do not create a burden or barrier in domestic policymaking.

Policy integration and coherence are often challenging because different sectors may have conflicting priorities, and political compromises are necessary to achieve outcomes. In addition, the success of policy integration and coherence often depends on a country's governance capacity. In many low- and middle-income countries, institutional weaknesses and resource constraints limit the ability to design and implement integrated policies effectively. For example, in Latin American countries like Brazil, integrating environmental and economic policies has been complicated by the competing demands of protecting the Amazon rainforest (SDG 15) and promoting agricultural exports (SDG 8). Here, policy integration is further complicated by the influence of agribusiness interests, which often dominate the policy agenda, making it difficult to reconcile economic development with environmental protection.

In conclusion, both policy integration and coherence are critical but complex processes necessary for achieving the SDGs. They require coordinated action across sectors and governance levels, involving both state and non-state actors. Such coordination can be challenging to achieve, particularly in contexts where political and economic interests clash. Ultimately, the success of policy integration will depend on the ability of governments to navigate these challenges, align policies with the overarching goal of sustainable development and ensure that progress in one area supports, rather than undermines, progress in others.

References

Cejudo, G. M., and Trein, P. (2023). Policy integration as a political process. *Policy Sciences*, 56(1), 3–8. https://doi.org/10.1007/s11077-023-09494-6

Glass, L.-M., and Newig, J. (2019). Governance for achieving the Sustainable Development Goals: How important are participation, policy coherence, reflexivity, adaptation and democratic institutions? *Earth System Governance*, 2. https://doi.org/10.1016/j.esg.2019.100031

Organisation for Economic Cooperation and Development. (2016). Better policies for sustainable development 2016: A new framework for policy coherence. OECD. https://doi.org/10.1787/978 9264256996-en

Stafford-Smith, M., Griggs, D., Gaffney, O., Ullah, F., Reyers, B., Kanie, N., Stigson, B., Shrivastava, P., Leach, M., and O'Connell, D. (2017). Integration: The key to implementing the Sustainable Development Goals. *Sustainability Science*, 12(6), 911–919. https://doi.org/10.1007/s11625-016-0383-3

Tosun, J., and Lang, A. (2017). Policy integration: Mapping the different concepts. *Policy Studies*, 38(6), 553–570. https://doi.org/10.1080/01442872.2017.1339239

United Nations. (2015). Transforming our world: The 2030 agenda for sustainable development. A/RES/70/1. https://sdgs.un.org/publications/transforming-our-world-2030-agenda-sustainable-development-17981

United Nations. (2019). Political declaration of the high-level political forum on sustainable development convened under the auspices of the General Assembly. A/RES/74/4. https://documents.un.org/doc/un.oc/gen/n19/318/21/pdf/n1931821.pdf

Policy coherence for sustainable development (at global level)

Amandine Orsini

Since the beginning of the 2000s, scholars of global politics have recognized that international problems could not be studied in isolation from one another anymore, contrary to what the international regime approach of the 1990s was supposing. Rather, concepts such as 'institutional interactions', 'regime complexes', 'global governance architectures' and more recently 'complex systems' and 'adaptive systems' have been coined to describe the cross-cutting institutional arrangements that form the structures that manage (or at least try to) global governance (Day 2024). These arrangements are made of many different international institutions such as international organizations, international treaties and international partnerships across several international regimes on a wide diversity of problems. Since these structures are formed by many different elements, the issue of their coherence has been at the centre of attention in global politics since the 2010s (Morin and Orsini 2013).

Adopted in this context, the 17 Sustainable Development Goals (SDGs) were meant to enhance policy coherence at the global level. Firstly, by including more topics compared to the Millennium Development Goals, they took a much more comprehensive approach to sustainable development. Their key overarching principles of people, prosperity, planet, partnership and peace (5 Ps) were already integrating the different goals into a coherent agenda of integral development (de Jong and Vijge 2021). Secondly, the SDGs not only detailed several targets within each goal, but the precise analysis of such targets reveals the existence of a network of targets across the goals, with specific targets being in practice related to several goals (Le Blanc 2015). Finally, to be sure that the goals would be understood in a coherent manner, policy coherence has been explicitly mentioned three times in the adopted text, with one specific target, Target 17.14, precisely entitled 'Enhance policy coherence for sustainable development'. These targets are key to avoiding the cherry-picking of objectives within the goals and are meant to consider them as *Nexus Governance*.

Actual coherence of the goals at the global level is confirmed by discourse analyses: compared to the Millennium Development Goals, the SDGs produce a much more coherent discourse with inclusion, human rights and action beyond economic priorities as important moves forward (de Jong and Vijge 2021). Coherence of the goals has also been confirmed by scholars using *Network Analysis* as a research tool, despite a few gaps (Le Blanc 2015). To the contrary, researchers who looked at their practical implementation with the measurement of targets' progression with relevant data are less convinced by their coherence as trade-offs have appeared across the goals (Coscieme et al. 2021, 1). In particular, environmental goals are found to be less coherent than social and economic goals as their targets are less clear and interrelated. Orchestration seems like an important strategy to correct these drawbacks.

More importantly, scholars recognize that 'policy coherence for development is not merely a technical tool, but rather a normative and political construct' (de Jong and Vijge 2021, 2). The Policy Coherence for Development agenda dating back to the

122 *Essential Concepts for Implementing the SDGs*

1990s and embraced by many countries which negotiated the goals, including member countries of the Organization for Economic Cooperation and Development and the European Union, is not free from power relations and tends to reiterate a domination of the North on the South (Zeigermann 2018). Rather, a variety of perspectives about policy coherence for development should be used when implementing the goals (Tosun and Leininger 2017). Studies of the normative coherence of the goals at the global level are also lacking, while there is a risk that the SDGs still correspond to the global norm of neoliberalism, giving upfront importance to economic development at the detriment of alternative models of human rights or gender equality (De Jong and Vijge 2021).

While they were precisely designed to improve policy coherence at the global level, the promise of the SDGs for such coherence should therefore stay at the centre of attention for academic and civil society.

References

Coscieme, L., Mortensen, L. F., and Donohue, I. (2021). Enhance environmental policy coherence to meet the Sustainable Development Goals. *Journal of Cleaner Production*, 296, 126502. https://doi.org/10.1016/j.jclepro.2021.126502

Day, A. (2024). *The Forever Crisis. Adaptive Global Governance for an Era of Accelerating Complexity*. Routledge.

de Jong, E., and Vijge, M. J. (2021). From millennium to sustainable development goals: Evolving discourses and their reflection in policy coherence for development. *Earth System Governance*, 7. https://doi.org/10.1016/j.esg.2020.100087

Le Blanc, D. (2015). Towards integration at last? The sustainable development goals as a network of targets. DESA Working Paper No. 141. https://www.un.org/esa/desa/papers/2015/wp141_2015.pdf

Morin, J.-F., and Orsini, A. (2013). Regime complexity and policy coherency: Introducing a co-adjustments model. *Global Governance*, 19(1), 41–51.

Tosun, J., and Leininger, J. (2017). Governing the interlinkages between the sustainable development goals: Approaches to attain policy integration. *Global Challenges*, 2017, 1. https://doi.org/10.1002/gch2.201700036

Zeigermann, U. (2018). Governing Sustainable Development through 'Policy Coherence'? The production and circulation of knowledge in the EU and the OECD. *European Journal of Sustainable Development*, 7(1), 133–149. https://doi.org/10.14207/ejsd.2018.v7n1p133

Political impact and steering effects

Frank Biermann

Ever since the United Nations General Assembly adopted the 17 Sustainable Development Goals (SDGs), there have been questions about their political impact on national and global governance, especially in addressing critical issues such as poverty, social justice and environmental protection. A 2022 meta-analysis of over 3,000 studies aimed to assess the SDGs' political impact and identified three types of possible effects: discursive, normative and institutional (Biermann et al. 2022a, 2022b). Discursive effects involve shifts in global and national debates, while normative effects reflect the adoption of policies inspired by the SDGs. Institutional effects involve the creation or restructuring of institutions to support the SDGs. When all three occur, they signal a transformative impact, a key goal of the 2030 Agenda.

The meta-assessment found that the SDGs have led to some discursive effects, such as the adoption of SDG-related language in global policy. However, their actual impact on global governance has been modest. Institutions have increasingly referenced the SDGs, but reforms have been limited. For example, the High-level Political Forum on Sustainable Development, meant to review SDG progress and promote global cooperation, has facilitated peer-learning but failed to catalyze the transformational changes needed to meet the SDGs by 2030.

At the domestic level, the SDGs' impact has been similarly restrained. While some countries have integrated the SDGs into national policies, implementation often mirrors existing agendas, without significant changes in resource allocation or policy reform. The SDGs have been selectively adopted, with governments prioritizing goals that align with their political interests. Subnational actors, such as cities and civil society organizations, have shown greater support, but the lack of national funding and commitment has hindered deeper transformations. Meanwhile, some private corporations have embraced sustainability rhetoric linked to the SDGs, raising important concerns about 'SDG washing' or 'rainbow washing'. Concerning institutional integration, some countries have set up coordination bodies to align their structures with the SDGs. However, policy coherence remains inconsistent across nations. The SDGs have rarely resulted in comprehensive cross-sectoral policies, and bureaucratic inefficiency and short-term agendas continue to impede progress.

The SDGs have been widely embraced for their focus on inclusivity, particularly the pledge to 'leave no one behind' (Sénit et al. 2022). This call for inclusivity has been a prominent narrative in development strategies. However, while the SDGs are used to justify existing policies, they have not led to significant institutional or normative shifts aimed at reducing inequality. Political elites often use the SDG discourse to legitimize the status quo, which may entrench power imbalances and marginalization. Internationally, the SDGs have not substantially changed global power dynamics or improved the position of the most vulnerable countries, and they have not steered global governance towards greater inclusiveness, particularly for least developed countries. Long-standing commitments to aid and trade privileges for poorer countries remain largely unmet, suggesting the SDGs' limited impact on global inequalities. However, emerging economies in the Global South have increasingly framed their aid and investment efforts in the context of the SDGs. Civil society organizations have also leveraged the SDGs to hold governments accountable, pushing for more inclusive policies. These efforts, though incremental, may help counterbalance powerful actors and push for more inclusive governance.

The SDGs aim to support environmental protection, but their impact on ecological integrity at the planetary scale has been limited. While the goals have influenced discussions on climate and biodiversity, many of these changes were already underway before their adoption in 2015. Despite some alignment with SDGs in environmental governance, national governments and regional bodies have shown little evidence of stronger environmental policies. Some scholars argue that the SDGs lack the ambition and coherence needed to drive meaningful change, as they often prioritize global economic growth (SDG 8), which conflicts with the environmental protection goals in the SDGs. Critics contend that the SDGs' focus on neoliberal sustainable development undermines planetary integrity and justice. As a result, while the SDGs raise awareness about environmental issues, they have not pushed for the transformative changes needed for ecological integrity.

124 *Essential Concepts for Implementing the SDGs*

In conclusion, while the SDGs may have raised awareness about sustainability issues, their political impact remains limited. The agenda has primarily functioned as a discursive tool rather than a transformative force. To realize the SDGs' full potential, more fundamental changes are needed in governance, funding and policy enforcement. Without these changes, the promise of a world free from poverty, inequality and planetary destruction remains distant.

References

Biermann, F., Hickmann, T., and Sénit, C. A. (Eds.). (2022a). *The political impact of the sustainable development goals: Transforming governance through global goals?* Cambridge University Press.

Biermann, F., Hickmann, T., Sénit, C. A., Beisheim, M., Bernstein, S., Chasek, P., ... Wicke, B. (2022b). Scientific evidence on the political impact of the Sustainable Development Goals. *Nature Sustainability*, 5(9), 795–800.

Sénit, C.-A., Okereke, C., Alcázar, L., Banik, D., Lima, M. B., Biermann, F., Fambasayi, R., Hathie, I., Kronsell, A., Leonardsson, H., Niles, N., and Siegel, K. M. (2022). Inclusiveness. In F. Biermann, T. Hickmann, and C.-A. Sénit (Eds.), *The political impact of the Sustainable Development Goals: transforming governance through global goals?* (pp. 116–139). Cambridge University Press.

Political will and leadership

Joanna Stanberry

Working definitions of political will invoke 'the commitment of actors to undertake actions to achieve a set of objectives and to sustain the cost of those actions over time' (Beisheim et al. 2025). It is thus conceived as a form of collective leadership not solely tied to *leaders* per se or individualistic leader-follower influence relationships. Drath et al.'s (2008) framing of leadership as direction, alignment and commitment can be applied to *processes* of leadership. In this way, networks of actors collaborate to determine a direction, align their goals and strategies and secure commitments in tangible ways.

While political leaders have responsibility for policy, formative agents are individuals or collectives who guide political will regardless of apparent or prescribed political power. They are 'so called because they give form to what justice, sustainability and related concepts should mean in practice...[and] shape the principles that ought to be adopted in particular contexts', thus enabling willingness as 'discourse entrepreneurs' (Dryzek and Pickering 2018, 105). Implementing the Sustainable Development Goals (SDGs) requires that formative agents, whether individuals, organizations, partnerships or social movements, harness three processes to shift norms, policy and behaviours: reframing the direction of policy pathways towards the transformative agenda, orchestrating alignment either through targeted coalitions or mobilizing majorities and securing the commitment of scarce resources such as time, attention and funding (Clark and Harley 2020).

Reforming the global financial architecture, negotiating end producer responsibilities for plastics and mitigating loss and damage from climate change are just a few of the leadership challenges that must be addressed at every level, from the local to the global,

Political will and leadership   125

across inequitable systems. The SDGs represent a voluntary, broad and coherent agenda for tackling these challenges in concert, but governments apply the SDGs towards their incumbent priorities, maintaining and legitimizing elite interests (Beisheim et al. 2025). Political will is often invoked as an ambiguous panacea and the absence of it as the critical element in policy failures.

Where political will has been harnessed towards change, it often emerges from multistakeholder and collaborative governance arrangements that advance informal learning (Stanberry et al. 2024). Within these arrangements, however, powerful actors outside traditional political institutions such as the private sector can represent both a problem to be overcome and a necessity for transformations (Stanberry and Balda 2023). For example, in Indonesia, multinational enterprises are demonstrating the ability to leverage their SDG initiatives into political influence through building constituencies, managing conflict and cross-sector partnerships (Röell et al. 2024).

In collaborative contexts, formative agents can contest assumptions and highlight diverse perspectives, thus heightening awareness of unpredictable human environment systems and aligning actors (Stanberry et al. 2024). The kind of leading from behind needed for the SDGs requires that initiatives at every level can make sense of their direction, alignment and commitment through the lenses of 1) politics, especially the distribution of resources and other forms of power; 2) proximity to the poor, including vulnerable people and places wherever they exist; and 3) progress, representing the myriad of qualitative improvements measured as SDG implementation, thus also embedding Indigenous and local ecological knowledges (Stanberry and Balda 2023). It may well be that political will to transform development trajectories will emerge more from bottom-up initiatives of local autonomy than in the spotlight on powerful actors.

While formative agency can result in positive change, it can simultaneously be 'disastrous' if it fails to respond to signals from the Earth System (Dryzek and Pickering 2018, 106). Examining the role of political actors at the global, national and subnational level reveals dominant arrangements that continue 'business-as-usual' development pathways that prevent progress (Clark and Harley 2020; Beisheim et al. 2025). It is precisely this willingness towards self-preservation that absorbs the direction, alignment and commitment needed to 'transform our world' as stipulated in the 2030 Agenda. Advancing new norms that support reflexive governance frameworks can help mitigate this resistance, activating and sustaining political will.

References

Beisheim, M., Asseburg, M., Ballbach, E. J., Eickhoff, K., Fischera, S., Godehardt, N., Kurtz, G., Meyer, M., Müllera, M., Rolla, S., Sahm, A., Wagner, C., and Zilla, C. (2025). Politics matters! Political will as a critical condition for implementing the sustainable development goals. *Earth System Governance*, 24, 100244. https://doi.org/10.1016/j.esg.2025.100244

Clark, W. C., and Harley, A. G. (2020). Sustainability science: Toward a synthesis. *Annual Review of Environment and Resources*, 45(1), 331–386. https://doi.org/10.1146/annurev-environ-012420-043621

Drath, W. H., McCauley, C. D., Palus, C. J., Van Velsor, E., O'Connor, P. M. G., and McGuire, J. B. (2008). Direction, alignment, commitment: Toward a more integrative ontology of leadership. *The Leadership Quarterly*, 19(6), 635–653. https://doi.org/10.1016/j.leaqua.2008.09.003

Dryzek, J. S., and Pickering, J. (2018). *The Politics of the Anthropocene*. Oxford University Press.

Röell, C., Arndt, F., Benischke, M. H., and Piekkari, R. (2024). Doing good for political gain: The instrumental use of the SDGs as nonmarket strategies. *Journal of International Business Studies*. https://doi.org/10.1057/s41267-024-00723-5

Stanberry, J., and Balda, J. B. (2023). A conceptual review of SDG 17: Picturing politics, proximity and progress. *Journal of Tropical Futures: Sustainable Business, Governance and Development,* 1(1). https://doi.org/10.1177/27538931231170509

Stanberry, J., Murphy, D. F., and Balda, J. B. (2024). Recognising ecological reflexivity: An alternative approach to partnership capabilities for collaborative governance. *Sustainability: Science, Practice, and Policy.* https://doi.org/10.3390/su16166829

Private finance

Lisa-Maria Glass

Private finance refers to financial resource allocation by individuals, organizations, companies and non-public financial institutions and investors, including private banks, insurances, pension funds and other asset owners and managers. Private finance has received growing attention as a critical mechanism for addressing the substantial investment gap for implementing the Sustainable Development Goals (SDGs). With an annual funding need estimated at over USD 4 trillion in developing countries alone and official development assistance amounting to USD 223.7 billion in 2023 (United Nations 2024), mobilizing private capital is seen as essential for scaling up efforts to meet global development objectives.

In corporate governance, the term private finance is frequently employed to highlight the potential contribution of companies to sustainable development. Corporate investments and operations can be aligned with sustainability objectives through the adoption of corporate social responsibility strategies, as well as the implementation of sustainable business models and practices both domestically and internationally (Pérez-Pineda and Wehrmann 2021). Moreover, foreign direct investment has become a key pillar of international development cooperation. These capital flows in the form of cross-border mergers and acquisitions, greenfield investments and project finance can potentially contribute to infrastructure improvements and technology transfer and generate employment and productive capacities, enabling the integration of developing countries into global value chains.

However, only 2.4% of the USD 1.33 trillion in global flows of foreign direct investment in 2023 targeted least developed countries, which remain heavily dependent on official development assistance and remittances (United Nations Conference on Trade and Development 2024). Financial investors, including institutional investors like pension funds and insurance companies, also play an important role in allocating private capital. Investment portfolios are increasingly aligned with environmental, social and governance principles, driven by growing pressure from investors and consumers and tightened regulation. The role of impact investing, seeking to generate positive non-financial impacts alongside financial returns, is further explicitly promoted in the Addis Ababa Action Agenda on Financing for Development.

Mobilizing private finance faces challenges, as private investors typically prioritize high-return, low-risk investments, which may not align with the long-term and often high-risk nature of sustainable development, particularly in least developed countries. To address this, governments and international financial institutions use mechanisms like blended finance, which pools public and private capital to improve the risk-reward profile of investments in sustainable development (Smith et al. 2022). For example, the public sector may provide guarantees or first-loss capital to de-risk investments for private investors. This approach has increasingly been employed in financing large infrastructure projects (Georgeson and Maslin 2018).

However, the growing involvement of private capital in sustainable development financing is not without controversy. Concerns have been raised about the accountability and transparency of private finance and public-private partnerships due to commercial privacy barriers, alongside warnings that systemic risks to recipients of these funds are often downplayed (Mawdsley 2018). The risk of 'greenwashing' or 'SDG washing (rainbow washing)' is also prevalent, where investments are marketed as sustainable without delivering meaningful environmental or social benefits. Others question the 'financialization' and emphasis on 'bankability' of development interventions per se, cautioning against power dynamics that can grant private finance undue influence over development priorities, potentially marginalizing the public interest and perpetuating inequalities (Yunita et al. 2023).

In summary, private finance plays an important role in the implementation of the SDGs, offering both opportunities and challenges. While it can provide essential resources to support sustainability transformations, its effectiveness depends on ensuring that investments align with long-term public interests and are held to high standards of accountability and transparency. A balanced approach that integrates private finance with robust governance mechanisms is crucial for achieving sustainable and equitable development.

References

Georgeson, L., and Maslin, M. (2018). Putting the United Nations Sustainable Development Goals into practice: A review of implementation, monitoring and finance. *Geo: Geography and Environment*, 5(1), e00049. https://doi.org/10.1002/geo2.49

Mawdsley, E. (2018). 'From billions to trillions': Financing the SDGs in a world 'beyond aid'. *Dialogues in Human Geography*, 8(2), 191–195. https://doi.org/10.1177/2043820618780789

Pérez-Pineda, J. A., and Wehrmann, D. (2021). Partnerships with the private sector: Success factors and levels of engagement in development cooperation. In S. Chaturvedi, H. Janus, S. Klingebiel, X. Li, A. de Mello e Souza, E. Sidiropoulos, and D. Wehrmann (Eds.), *The Palgrave Handbook of Development Cooperation for Achieving the 2030 Agenda* (pp. 649–670). Palgrave Macmillan. https://doi.org/10.1007/978-3-030-57938-8

Smith, J., Samuelson, M., Libanda, B. M., Roe, D., and Alhassan, L. (2022). Getting blended finance to where it's needed: The case of CBNRM enterprises in Southern Africa. *Land*, 11(5), 637. https://doi.org/10.3390/land11050637

United Nations. (2024). *Sustainable Development Goals Report 2024*. United Nations. https://unstats.un.org/sdgs/report/2024/

United Nations Conference on Trade and Development. (2024). *World Investment Report 2024: Investment facilitation and digital government*. United Nations. https://unctad.org/publication/world-investment-report-2024

Yunita, A., Biermann, F., Kim, R. E., and Vijge, M. J. (2023). Making development legible to capital: The promise and limits of 'innovative' debt financing for the Sustainable Development Goals in Indonesia. *Environment and Planning E: Nature and Space*, 6(4), 2271–2294. https://doi.org/10.1177/25148486231159301

Private governance

Yixian Sun

Private governance is broadly defined as the processes in which non-state actors adopt rules that seek to move behaviour towards shared, public goals. A central characteristic of this governance model is the provision of public goods without the state's enforcement (Andonova and Sun 2017). Concrete examples range from businesses' self-regulations through corporate social responsibility to multi-stakeholder partnerships that develop sustainability standards or governance initiatives led by non-governmental organizations. The rapid rise of private governance initiatives is a key feature of global sustainability governance since the 1990s, which has been jointly shaped by the expansion of global supply chains, erosion of state capacity and empowerment of global civil society (Falkner 2003).

Despite varying features and priorities across different initiatives, the work of most private governance initiatives is related to some Sustainable Development Goals (SDGs). Therefore, in the context of the 2030 Agenda, an important question in this respect is the extent to which private governance supports SDG implementation. While many private governance initiatives were developed far before the adoption of the 2030 Agenda in 2015, the 17 SDGs closely align with these initiatives' missions and work. From this perspective, the SDGs were expected to provide private governance initiatives with new opportunities to increase support from a wider audience and introduce transformative changes.

However, research shows mixed evidence on the impact of the SDGs on private governance. A mapping of policy linkages between 232 voluntary sustainability standards and the 17 SDGs conducted by Schleifer et al. (2022) show significant overlaps between the objectives of these standards and those of the SDGs, especially for people-centred and development-focused SDGs (for example, SDGs 1, 2, 5 and 8). The study, however, finds that these standards have no linkages for 70 out of 125 core SDG targets. These findings suggest that synergies between the SDGs and private governance have yet to be fully explored, and private governance initiatives may cherry-pick the goals that align with their ongoing work without making new efforts. In fact, a study on the Fortune Global 500 corporations finds that, despite the majority of these corporations refer to the SDGs on their website, 32.6% of them match their usual business, and only 22.8% have developed specific actions and strategies for specific SDGs (Song et al. 2022). This strategy of claiming SDG efforts without changing practices can be seen as a type of 'rainbow washing'. All in all, one can conclude that the SDGs have not yet been fully integrated into the work of private governance, and the contributions of relevant initiatives to SDG implementation remain limited.

As society-wide support is critical to the achievement of the SDGs, private governance should be a useful channel for SDG implementation. As the effectiveness of private governance has been increasingly put into question (for example, Grabs 2020), better alignment with the SDGs may help relevant initiatives introduce necessary reforms to enhance their impact. A key challenge lies in incentivizing private actors to recentre their actions towards the SDGs as research suggests that the motivation of private governance's engagement with the SDGs remains largely instrumental with the central aim to appeal to a wider group of stakeholders and attract more resources (for example, Sun 2022). At the same time, many SDG targets were designed with state actors as their primary audience. While this may increase the difficulty for private governance to engage with SDGs, it can also lead researchers and practitioners to identify synergetic interactions between public and private governance for SDG implementation (Cashore et al. 2021).

In conclusion, better integration of the SDGs into private governance is urgently needed to achieve the 2030 Agenda. Doing so would be a win-win for both state and non-state actors committed to sustainable development. For public regulators, cooperation with private governance can mobilize more stakeholders and resources for SDG implementation. For non-state actors championing private governance, connecting their work to a set of goals set by the international community can enhance the legitimacy of their governance initiatives.

References

Andonova, L. B., and Sun, Y. (2017). *Private Governance* [Dataset]. Oxford University Press. https://doi.org/10.1093/obo/9780199756223-0216

Cashore, B., Knudsen, J. S., Moon, J., and van der Ven, H. (2021). Private authority and public policy interactions in global context: Governance spheres for problem solving. *Regulation and Governance*, 15(4), 1166–1182. https://doi.org/10.1111/rego.12395

Falkner, R. (2003). Private environmental governance and international relations: Exploring the links. *Global Environmental Politics*, 3(2), 72–87. https://doi.org/10.1162/152638003322068227

Grabs, J. (2020). *Selling Sustainability Short: The Effectiveness and Limits of Private Governance in the Coffee Sector*. Cambridge University Press.

Schleifer, P., Brandi, C., Verma, R., Bissinger, K., and Fiorini, M. (2022). Voluntary standards and the SDGs: Mapping public-private complementarities for sustainable development. *Earth System Governance*, 14, 100153. https://doi.org/10.1016/j.esg.2022.100153

Song, L., Zhan, X., Zhang, H., Xu, M., Liu, J., and Zheng, C. (2022). How much is global business sectors contributing to sustainable development goals? *Sustainable Horizons*, 1, 100012. https://doi.org/10.1016/j.horiz.2022.100012

Sun, Y. (2022). *Certifying China: The Rise and Limits of Transnational Sustainability Governance in Emerging Economies*. MIT Press. https://doi.org/10.7551/mitpress/14192.001.0001

R

Rainbow washing

Elizabeth A. Bennett

The term 'washing', in the context of implementing the Sustainable Development Goals (SDGs), refers to the practice of making an institution, programme, practice or strategy *appear* more supportive of the SDGs than it actually is. Put another way, 'to wash' is to overstate commitments to implementing the SDGs. Washing may also be described as a 'performative gesture', 'empty promise', 'symbolic commitment' or 'virtue signalling'. Those who engage in washing are at times said to be 'talking the talk' without 'walking the walk'. Washing is often issue-specific. 'Greenwashing' overstates environmentalism, for example, while 'fair washing' suggests a trade relationship is more just or equitable than it actually is (Bennett 2020). 'Blue washing' – named for the colour of the United Nations flag – overstates alignment with United Nations programmes, such as the United Nations Global Compact for Business and Human Rights (Berliner and Prakash 2015), while 'CSR washing' refers to corporate social responsibility claims that overestimate potential outcomes. Finally, the term 'brown washing' refers to *down*-playing or *under*-reporting efforts to promote sustainable development. Institutions may do this to avoid being held accountable or identified as a target for activists (Kim and Lyon 2015).

The term 'rainbow washing' has several meanings. First, since the rainbow symbol is often associated with the LGBTQ+ (lesbian, gay, bisexual, trans, queer and questioning) movement, it commonly refers to overstating contributions to the LGBTQ+ movement. Second, since washing is sometimes linked to specific colours, 'rainbow washing' can refer to washing multiple issues at the same time. Finally, because the SDGs are often visually represented with many colours, 'rainbow washing' may refer to misleading claims about promoting the SDGs (Heras-Saizarbitoria et al. 2022).

Anyone can engage in 'rainbow washing', and there are many ways to 'rainbow wash' the SDGs. A company, for example, may claim to promote *all* of the SDGs, while in reality it only focuses on those that are most affordable. An NGO may claim to be deeply oriented around the SDGs, but only be marginally or superficially engaged. A government agency may highlight its positive contributions to the SDGs, while ignoring or obscuring how they cause harm (de Freitas Netto et al. 2020; Gutierrez et al. 2022).

On the one hand, rainbow washing presents a significant challenge to implementing the SDGs. Incomplete and inaccurate information about whether, how, when and to what

DOI: 10.4324/9781003519560-18

This chapter has been made available under a CC-BY-NC-ND license.

extent the SDGs are being implemented incumbers efficient resource allocation and effective policymaking (Lashitew 2021). At the same time, however, 'aspirational commitments' may also facilitate progress. Unsubstantiated claims may reinforce that SDGs are a priority, keep sustainable development on the agenda, invite pressure from external stakeholders or help attract the resources required for action.

Despite the potential benefits of aspirational commitments, rainbow washing is generally understood to impede – not support – global governance for sustainable development. Thus, several initiatives have emerged to encourage more accurate and credible claims. In global supply chains, for example, several non-governmental organizations have created standards for social, environmental, labour and governance business practices that align more closely with sustainable development than do legal regulations. Suppliers (for example, factories or farms) can voluntarily adopt these standards, hire an auditor to verify compliance and pay a licensing fee to have the non-governmental organization 'certify' that the product is sustainable. Although sustainability certifications and other credibility-oriented initiatives can, in some contexts, offer resistance to rainbow washing, they may also, at times, overestimate their potential or overstate their claims.

References

Bennett, E. A. (2020). The global fair-trade movement: For whom, by whom, how and what next. In M. Bell, M. Carolan, J. Keller, and K. Legun (Eds.), *The Cambridge handbook of environmental sociology* (pp. 459–477). Cambridge University Press. https://doi.org/10.1017/9781108554558.029

Berliner, D., and Prakash, A. (2015). 'Bluewashing' the firm? Voluntary regulations, program design and member compliance with the United Nations Global Compact. *Policy Studies Journal*, 43(1), 115–138. https://doi.org/10.1111/psj.12085

de Freitas Netto, S. V., Sobral, M. F. F., Ribeiro, A. R. B., and Soares, G. R. da L. (2020). Concepts and forms of greenwashing: A systematic review. *Environmental Sciences Europe*, 32(1). https://doi.org/10.1186/s12302-020-0300-3

Gutierrez, L., Montiel, I., Surroca, J. A., and Tribo, J. A. (2022). Rainbow wash or rainbow revolution? Dynamic stakeholder engagement for SDG-driven responsible innovation. *Journal of Business Ethics*, 180(4), 1113–1136. https://doi.org/10.1007/s10551-022-05190-2

Heras-Saizarbitoria, I., Urbieta, L., and Boiral, O. (2022). Organizations' engagement with sustainable development goals: From cherry-picking to SDG-washing? *Corporate Social Responsibility and Environmental Management*, 29(2), 316–328. https://doi.org/10.1002/csr.2202

Kim, E.-H., and Lyon, T. P. (2015). Greenwash vs. brownwash: Exaggeration and undue modesty in corporate sustainability disclosure. *Organization Science*, 26(3), 705–723. https://doi.org/10.1287/orsc.2014.0949

Lashitew, A. A. (2021). Corporate uptake of the Sustainable Development Goals: Mere greenwashing or an advent of institutional change? *Journal of International Business Policy*, 4(1), 184–200. https://doi.org/10.1057/s42214-020-00092-4

Rankings and performance measurement

Grayson Fuller and Félicien Pagnon

Composite indices and rankings are performance measurement tools that aggregate data to provide a panoramic view of performance on the concepts they aim to measure. Rankings and the composite indices that underlie them can encourage better performance when they are well-crafted, clear and transparent. The most widely used ranking tool to measure

132 *Essential Concepts for Implementing the SDGs*

performance on the Sustainable Development Goals (SDGs) is the SDG Index, published as part of the *Sustainable Development Report* (Sachs et al. 2024). The SDG Index aims to help render the SDGs actionable by translating the goals into easy-to-understand metrics, to raise awareness among policymakers and to hold countries accountable.

The official monitoring framework of the SDGs contains 232 indicators. For policymakers, 232 numbers may be too much information, making it difficult to grasp where a country's priorities lie. The SDG Index, in benchmarking countries using internationally harmonized data and targets, transforms a multitude of disparate numbers into easy-to-understand and comparable evaluations of countries' SDG progress. Many governments, as well as the European Union, use the SDG Index to guide SDG policies domestically (Pichon et al. 2021).

Rankings are newsworthy and draw attention to the concepts they measure (Saisana et al. 2011). Increasing awareness, not only among policymakers but also among academics, non-governmental organizations and the public, is key to promoting SDG policies. For example, *Sustainable Development Reports* include rankings of countries' performance on international spillovers, defined as transboundary impacts of one country on others (for example, imported deforestation or consumption-based CO_2 emissions). The International Spill-over Index has been carefully monitored by many governments and has helped raise awareness of the issue (Fuller and Bermont-Diaz 2024).

By providing an independent measure of country progress, the SDG Index shows which countries are fulfilling their SDG commitments. Rankings also create a 'race-to-the-top', whereby countries seek to improve their position and therefore take action to meet the SDGs. Many governments keep track of their position in the SDG Index rankings and report their position in their Voluntary National Reviews. The reputational risk of losing ranks in the SDG Index, often with regard to regional peers, also incentivizes countries not to neglect their SDG performance.

However, critics argue that rankings can be harmful because they create perverse incentives, encouraging countries to cheat or 'game the system' instead of improving performance. The case of the World Bank's *Doing Business* report, which had to be discontinued after the authors were caught distorting data on behalf of certain countries, is exemplary (Nicola 2021). This is why rankings must have certain safeguards in place, including autonomy and transparency. For instance, the SDG Index is calculated by an independent team of experts, while the methodology, an independent statistical audit and all underlying data are made publicly available online.

In addition, the SDG Index rankings have been critiqued for their correlation with gross domestic product per capita, with high-income countries tending to perform better on the SDG index overall and for their correlation with some measures of environmental harm. However, rankings ultimately reflect only the scope of the concepts they measure. The SDGs aim by design to capture not only environmental degradation but also socio-economic development more generally (SDGs 1–9). High-income countries have more fiscal resources to invest in these dimensions of the SDGs, and this is reflected in their performance on socioeconomic SDGs.

Composite indices summarize information and allow users to quickly understand how their country is performing in SDG implementation. Yet, for the SDG index rankings, it is important to go beyond their face value (Nardo et al. 2008). Composite indices and rankings should thus be seen broadly as invitations to dive into the data and indicators, to identify what specific issues are driving a given position in a ranking and to stimulate discussion.

References

Fuller, G., and Bermont-Diaz, L. (2024). *International Spillover Effects and Germany: An Analysis of Germany's Performance on Spillovers and the Policy Options to Manage Them*. Paris: SDSN, 2024. https://doi.org/10.13140/RG.2.2.17990.89922

Nardo, M., Saisana, M., Saltelli, A., Tarantola, S., Hoffman, A., and Giovannini, E. (2008). *Handbook on Constructing Composite Indicators*. OECD. https://doi.org/10.1787/9789264043466-en

Nicola, F. (2021). Scandal involving World Bank's 'Doing Business' index exposes problems in using sportslike rankings to guide development goals. *The Conversation*. https://theconversation.com/scandal-involving-world-banks-doing-business-index-exposes-problems-in-using-sportslike-rankings-to-guide-development-goals-169691

Pichon, E., Widuto, A., Dobreva, A., and Jensen, L. (2021). Ten composite indices for policy-making. EPRS (European Parliamentary Research Service). https://www.europarl.europa.eu/RegData/etudes/IDAN/2021/696203/EPRS_IDA(2021)696203_EN.pdf

Sachs, J. D., Lafortune, G., and Fuller, G. (2024). *The SDGs and the UN Summit of the Future. Sustainable Development Report 2024*. Dublin: Dublin University Press. https://doi.org/10.25546/108572

Saisana, M., d'Hombres, B., and Saltelli, A. (2011). Rickety numbers: Volatility of university rankings and policy implications. *Research Policy*, 40(1), 165177. https://doi.org/10.1016/j.respol.2010.09.003

Regional organizations

Chol Bunnag

A regional organization is defined as an international organization composed of three or more geographically proximate states having a continuous institutional framework (Haftel 2013). Generally, regional organizations are structured around an institutional framework designed to foster cooperation on specific issues shared by member states and support localizing initiatives and partnerships that promote regional goals and priorities. They are characterized by their capacity to establish and uphold membership norms, thereby influencing the regional community by setting criteria for membership that differentiate insiders from outsiders. These norms reflect the values and interests of the members, fostering a unified identity within the organization. Several regional organizations collaborate across sectors, that is, public, private, academia and civil society groups, to promote the region's agenda and address region-specific challenges (Flick et al. 2022). In addition, regional organizations frequently overlap in terms of mandates and memberships, which can lead to cooperative or conflicting interactions among member states (Nolte 2016).

The roles of regional organizations in the global effort to implement the Sustainable Development Goals (SDGs) are manifold. Several sustainability challenges are not limited to a nation's boundaries. There are transboundary environmental sustainability challenges, such as shared water resources, climate change mitigation and adaptation, marine resources and pollution management and biodiversity conservation. Some social sustainability issues are shared among the member states, such as poverty, climate disasters, economic development, migration and food security. Regional organizations provide a platform for countries to address shared regional issues, establish frameworks for shared

134 *Essential Concepts for Implementing the SDGs*

strategies, tackle problems that individual states cannot solve alone, create feedback mechanisms and amplify efforts to align with the related global agenda (Al-Sarihi and Luomi 2019; Hasanat and Karim 2018).

Regional organizations can enhance resource sharing, knowledge and capacity exchange and financial and technical support mobilizations (Muntschick and Plank 2024). They also help facilitate policy alignment across member states, create unified strategies and standards, develop region-specific action plans and monitor and assess the progress of the regional efforts to combat sustainability challenges. These organizations can also facilitate multilevel and multi-sectoral coordination as they foster local-level action and coordination, support collaboration between the public, private and academic sectors, build trust and accountability and facilitate communication between local, national and supranational bodies, which enhances regional relevance to the SDGs (Flick et al. 2022).

Regional organizations face several challenges in SDG implementation. Almost all regions of the world encounter slow SDG progress. In Asia and the Pacific, for example, the United Nations Economic and Social Commission for Asia and the Pacific (UNESCAP) reported in 2024 that no sub-region had sufficiently advanced to the expected level in 2023 (United Nations Economic and Social Commission for Asia and the Pacific 2024). Slow regional progress stems from low prioritization of the SDGs, slow adoption of SDG initiatives by member states and unclear targets and strategies, hindering the translation of agreements into policies (Al-Sarihi and Luomi 2019). Varying monitoring practices and limited long-term data impede the establishment of a shared knowledge base and progress tracking across member states, particularly in regional environmental issues (Hasanat and Karim 2018). Many regional organizations in the Global South lack the financial and personnel resources needed for effective SDG implementation, often relying on external support. This creates asymmetric dependence on powerful actors, reducing their regional autonomy (Muntschick and Plank 2024). Institutional weaknesses also hinder regional SDG progress, such as inadequate frameworks for transboundary issues, a lack of transparency and siloed approaches.

References

Al-Sarihi, A., and Luomi, M. (2019). *Climate Change Governance and Cooperation in the Arab Region*. Emirates Diplomatic Academy.

Flick, H. M., Braun, A., Örlygsdóttir, A., and Hauksdóttir, G. R. T. (2022). *The Implementation of the Sustainable Development Goals in the Nordic Arctic (ISDeGoNA)*. NORCE Norwegian Research Centre.

Haftel, Y. Z. (2013). Commerce and institutions: Trade, scope and the design of regional economic organizations. *The Review of International Organizations*, 8(3), 389–414. https://doi.org/10.1007/s11558-012-9162-9

Hasanat, A., and Karim, M. S. (2018). Ocean governance and marine environmental conservation. In *International Marine Environmental Law and Policy* (pp. 16–42). Routledge. https://doi.org/10.4324/9781315624921-2

Muntschick, J., and Plank, F. (Eds.). (2024). *The Performance of Regionalism in the Global South: A Multi-level Analysis*. Routledge. https://doi.org/10.4324/9781003318941

Nolte, D. (2016). Regional governance from a comparative perspective. In V. M. González-Sánchez (Ed.), *Economy, Politics and Governance Challenges* (pp. 1–15). Nova Science Publishers.

United Nations Economic and Social Commission for Asia and the Pacific. (2024). *Asia and the Pacific SDG Progress Report 2024: Showcasing Transformative Actions*. United Nations.

Responsibility

Magdalena Bexell

Responsibility refers to the obligations belonging to an actor in a forward-looking sense. In contrast, accountability refers to the backward-looking assessment of how these obligations have been fulfilled. Governments hold the main formal responsibility for the implementation of the Sustainable Development Goals (SDGs), having adopted the goals in the United Nations General Assembly in 2015. Beyond governments, other actors can also be argued to hold responsibility for advancing SDG implementation. Spheres of responsibility are not fixed but can be contested and subject to change over time.

On what grounds can responsibility for the SDGs be assigned to different actors, beyond formal government responsibility (Miller 2001)? According to the *connectedness principle*, responsibilities should be allocated based on closeness. This means that people with special ties have stronger obligations towards each other. It implies that governments first consider obligations to citizens before international obligations. In contrast, the *capacity principle* means that having the ability to act entails the obligation to do so. In other words, this means to have 'response-ability' (Fukuda-Parr and McNeill 2015).

The capacity principle is found in the 2030 Agenda outcome document, *Transforming Our World*, in the sense that high-income ('developed') states have greater responsibilities to ensure SDG implementation globally in certain respects. This is primarily through their commitments on development assistance and with regard to taking the lead on implementing SDG 12 on sustainable consumption and production. The principle also underpins demands that powerful actors of all kinds should assume responsibility for the SDGs. Examples are large companies, private foundations, multi-stakeholder partnerships and international organizations. Many companies across the world have taken on the SDGs as part of their corporate social responsibility schemes (Panda et al. 2024).

Yet another justification for why someone holds responsibility is offered by *the contribution principle*. This implies that an actor who caused a problem has a responsibility to address it. This would mean, for instance, that former colonial powers and large emitters have greater responsibilities to fulfil the SDGs (cf. Young 2006). The contribution principle is referenced in the notion of 'common but differentiated responsibilities', briefly mentioned in the 2030 Agenda. It means that state responsibilities vary due to differing contributions to environmental degradation – as first agreed on by governments in the Rio Declaration on Environment and Development of 1992. Accordingly, beyond formal government responsibilities, principles mirrored in the 2030 Agenda emphasize certain responsibilities of high-income countries.

Once responsibility has been allocated, many factors impact how it is realized in practice. Researchers often point out that implementation is a politically charged rather than a purely administrative or technical process. In practice, SDG responsibility is shaped by factors such as institutional mandates, financial resources, knowledge, goal conflicts and political will and priorities (Bexell and Jönsson 2021; Beisheim et al. 2025). In the broader political environment, the relative power of interest groups may also affect the realization of responsibility if these groups try to support or hinder implementation (May 2015). Furthermore, the presence of review processes and accountability mechanisms impacts the realization of responsibility (see *Accountability*).

136 *Essential Concepts for Implementing the SDGs*

The allocation of responsibilities for the SDGs taps into broad ideological debates on the obligations of the state, the market and civil society. It raises questions on international power and justice. At the same time, responsibility needs to be clearly distributed and supported by institutional resources and political will. Implementation of the SDGs will be more successful if a wide range of public and private actors assumes shared responsibility for the goals.

References

Beisheim, M., Asseburg, M., Ballbach, E. J., Eickhoff, K., Fischer, S., Godehardt, N., Kurtz, G., Meyer, M., Müller, M., Roll, S., Sahm, A., Wagner, C., and Zilla, C. (2025). Politics matters! Political will as a critical condition for implementing the sustainable development goals. *Earth System Governance*, 24, 100244. https://doi.org/10.1016/j.esg.2025.100244

Bexell, M., and Jönsson, K. (2021). *The Politics of the Sustainable Development Goals. Legitimacy, Responsibility and Accountability*. Abingdon: Routledge. https://doi.org/10.4324/9781003043614

Fukuda-Parr, S., and McNeill, D. (2015). Post 2015: A new era of accountability?. *Journal of Global Ethics*, 11(1), 10–17. https://doi.org/10.1080/17449626.2015.1004738

May, P. (2015). Implementation failures revisited: Policy regime perspectives. *Public Policy and Administration*, 30(3–4), 277–299. https://doi.org/10.1177/0952076714561505

Miller, D. (2001). Distributing responsibilities. *Journal of Political Philosophy*, 9(4), 453–471.

Panda, A. B., Ramegowda, A., Lakshmana, G., and Pawar, M. (2024). Corporate social responsibility and the Sustainable Development Goals. Insights from India. *International Journal of Community and Social Development*. https://doi.org//10.1177/25166026241261850

Young, I. M. (2006). Responsibility and global justice: A social connection model. *Social Philosophy and Policy*, 23(1), 102–130.

S

Science, technology and innovation

Yi hyun Kang

Science, technology and innovation (STI) are widely perceived as critical factors for economic growth and prosperity in modern societies. The positive connotation of STI is also applied to sustainable development. Sustainability science emerged here as a research field to facilitate a transition towards sustainability by understanding and improving the complex dynamics of nature-society interactions (Clark 2007, 1737). STI is also the central means of sustainable development defined by the 2030 Agenda. The Sustainable Development Goals (SDGs) have three targets on SDG 17 (that is, Targets 17.6, 17.7 and 17.8) that focus on international cooperation for technology transfer between industrialized and developing countries (Imaz and Sheinbaum 2017). In this context, the United Nations Technology Facilitation Mechanism was launched to promote multi-stakeholder collaboration on STI for the SDGs and to facilitate the sharing of information, experiences and best practices among governments, civil society, the private sector, the scientific community and international organizations.

Although the 2030 Agenda commenced with well-defined technology transfer institutions, the STI gap between states has been a persistent issue, especially between the Global North and South. Also, there has been limited participation of the Global South scientific community in decision-making on the SDGs (Adenle et al. 2023). Concerns about the technology gap have further increased with the rapid advancement of digital technology and innovation (United Nations 2023). Scientists in the Global South have pointed to a lack of cooperation in the global scientific community and poor infrastructure as the most important obstacles in applying STI for SDG implementation (Adenle et al. 2023).

STI solutions hold the potential to significantly accelerate the implementation of the SDGs. Evidence-based solutions that consider SDG synergies and trade-offs can drive substantial progress on the SDGs (Popovici et al. 2024). Moreover, environmentally sound technologies and innovation can play a crucial role in reducing pollution and resource use. Advanced technology and innovation can also contribute to poverty alleviation and human well-being. However, to harness the potential of STI solutions, a deeper understanding of their consequences for societies and planetary boundaries is required. Implementing STI solutions without a holistic analysis of their consequences may lead to a 'lock-in' effect, hindering transformative changes towards sustainability (Walsh et al.

DOI: 10.4324/9781003519560-19

This chapter has been made available under a CC-BY-NC-ND license.

138 *Essential Concepts for Implementing the SDGs*

2020). The ethical, fair and just use of technologies is another critical aspect to consider when applying STI solutions to the implementation of the SDGs.

To effectively leverage socially and environmentally sound and science-based approaches in sustainable development governance, it is crucial to foster mutual efforts between STI and policy actors. When research is perceived as credible, legitimate and salient to the needs of decision-makers, it is more likely to be used in decision-making. Therefore, it is encouraged to implement institutional measures such as increasing interaction between knowledge producers and users or involving stakeholders in research design to advance mutual understanding (Allen et al. 2021).

In conclusion, the need for STI to accelerate the implementation of the SDGs is widely acknowledged, and the field of sustainability science has expanded with the increasing call for problem-solving efforts (Clark 2007). To effectively use STI solutions for sustainable development, more attention is now required to the widening gap between the Global North and South, to the broad and long-term consequences of STI solutions, and to stronger mutual efforts of STI and policy actors.

References

Adenle, A. A., De Steur, H., Mwongera, C., Rola-Rubzen, F., De Barcellos, M. D., Vivanco, D. F., Timilsina, G. R., Possas, C., Alders, R., Chertow, M., Poons, S., and Scholes, B. (2023). Global UN 2030 agenda: How can science, technology and innovation accelerate the achievement of Sustainable Development Goals for all? *PLOS Sustainability and Transformation*, 2(10), e0000085. https://doi.org/10.1371/journal.pstr.0000085

Allen, C., Metternicht, G., and Wiedmann, T. (2021). Priorities for science to support national implementation of the sustainable development goals: A review of progress and gaps. *Sustainable Development*, 29(4), 635–652. https://doi.org/10.1002/sd.2164

Clark, W. C. (2007). Sustainability science: A room of its own. *Proceedings of the National Academy of Sciences*, 104(6), 1737–1738. https://doi.org/10.1073/pnas.0611291104

Imaz, M., and Sheinbaum, C. (2017). Science and technology in the framework of the sustainable development goals. *World Journal of Science, Technology and Sustainable Development*, 14(1), 2–17. https://doi.org/10.1108/WJSTSD-04-2016-0030

Popovici, A., Alam, M., Agurto Castillo, C. M., Dang, R., Eker, S., Fakoya, K., Falsarone, A., Ibeto, C., Kuhn, M., Liu, Q., Momanyi, S., Mycoo, M., Reiter, C., Shimpuku, Y., Van Kempen, L., Wagner, F., Salami, B., Stevance, A.-S., Kelly, W., and Gunalan, K. N. (2024). *From science to action: Leveraging scientific knowledge and solutions for advancing sustainable and resilient development*. International Science Council. https://doi.org/10.24948/2024.09

United Nations. (2023, 6 October). Widening digital gap between developed, developing states threatening to exclude world's poorest from next industrial revolution, speakers tell second committee. *Meetings coverage and press releases*. https://press.un.org/en/2023/gaef3587.doc.htm

Walsh, P. P., Murphy, E., and Horan, D. (2020). The role of science, technology and innovation in the UN 2030 agenda. *Technological Forecasting and Social Change*, 154, 119957. https://doi.org/10.1016/j.techfore.2020.119957

Scientific community

Mara Wendebourg

The scientific community refers to a network of scientists bound by a shared objective of fact-finding and a common understanding of the scientific method and of the values essential to adhere to the community, such as objectivity, transparency and accountability through peer review. The scientific community has played a valuable role in the development and implementation of the Sustainable Development Goals (SDGs). The contribution of the scientific community to the SDGs, and to global sustainability governance more broadly, indicates an underlying diversity of the scientific community.

The scientific community may produce science for research (or, scientific knowledge), but it can also be involved in the production of science for policy, which is also understood as regulatory science. Regulatory science builds on scientific knowledge and is co-produced by scientists and regulatory agencies with specific socio-political regulatory aims (Jasanoff 1998). The nuance between science as a fact-finding activity and as a regulatory science explains the plurality of the scientific community concerned with the development and implementation of the SDGs. Groups of scientists may be more or less organized, and they may be more or less discrete or integrated within the United Nations system. Like global groups of science, the scientific community at the regional and national levels is often fragmented.

Within the United Nations system, the science community is organized and institutionalized in numerous ways. For example, the Inter-agency and Expert Group on SDG Indicators brings together representatives of national statistical offices and is mandated to develop the indicator framework for the follow-up and review of the SDGs and their targets. The group also provides technical support for the implementation of the indicators and the monitoring framework. Such indicators are key tools to track progress towards the SDG targets; they have a decisive impact on SDG implementation but may have distorting effects since the reliance on indicators can harm the SDGs' ambition, integrity and legitimacy (Kim 2023).

A second organized science community regarding the implementation of the SDGs within the United Nations is the Independent Group of Scientists, appointed by the Secretary-General. It was instituted by the High-level Political Forum on Sustainable Development in 2016 to draft the Global Sustainable Development Report. This quadrennial report reviews the scientific knowledge to inform policymakers on how to best accelerate the sustainable development agenda by strengthening the science-policy interface at the High-level Political Forum.

Outside of the United Nations system, the Major Groups and other Stakeholders are formalized as autonomous and self-organized groups of civil society concerned with sustainable development. One of them is the Scientific and Technological Community Major Group, which aspires to integrate science into global sustainability governance. The group is co-organized by the International Science Council and the World Federation of Engineering Organizations. It uses its expert network to provide scientific knowledge for position papers and policy briefs, to organize side events and to participate in the High-level Political Forum.

This fragmentation of the scientific community into different groups results in the asymmetrical institutionalization of science, which in turn impacts their participation in policy processes. The Inter-agency and Expert Group on SDG Indicators, specifically, is mandated to define the indicators and set the standards by which the implementation of the SDGs is measured (Ordaz 2019). While the Inter-agency and Expert Group includes experts from the national statistical offices of some countries and international organizations, it does not include the Scientific and Technological Community Major Group or independent experts as observers. Participation of the broader scientific community, however, has been possible through the Expert Group Meetings that are facilitated by the United Nations Department of Economic and Social Affairs, such as the Global Expert Group Meeting in Support of the Mid-Point Review of SDG 7 at the 2023 High-level Political Forum.

140 *Essential Concepts for Implementing the SDGs*

In sum, the scientific community involved in global sustainability governance is diverse. This is reflected in the channels through which the community is working towards SDG implementation. Some institutions formulate regulatory science and have stricter membership requirements in comparison to those synthesizing and exchanging knowledge.

References

Jasanoff, S. (1998). *The Fifth Branch: Science Advisers as Policymakers*. Harvard University Press.

Kim, R. E. (2023). Augment the SDG indicator framework. *Environmental Science and Policy*, 142, 62–67. https://doi.org/10.1016/j.envsci.2023.02.004

Ordaz, E. (2019). The SDG s indicators: A challenging task for the international statistical community. *Global Policy*, 10, 141–143. https://doi.org/10.1111/1758-5899.12631

SDG summits

Chol Bunnag

The SDG summits are high-level events convened by the United Nations General Assembly every four years with the aim of assessing progress on the Sustainable Development Goals (SDGs). They are not to be confused with the annual sessions of the High-level Political Forum on Sustainable Development, a ministerial-level conference organized under the auspices of the United Nations Economic and Social Council usually taking place in July. In the sessions of the High-level Political Forum, progress on a specific set of goals is reviewed, while the SDG summits assess the overall performance of SDG implementation (Beisheim and Fritzsche 2022).

The SDG summits have become a crucial mechanism to support SDG implementation. First, the SDG summits are designed to be a robust high-level platform for a comprehensive review of the achievements and shortcomings of SDG implementation at the national, regional and global levels, setting priorities for action, marking key milestones in 2019, 2023 and 2027 and discussing course corrections (Desai 2023; Goodman 2023). Second, attended by heads of state and government, the SDG summits are intended to send a strong political signal urging all countries to reaffirm and hold themselves politically accountable for their commitments to the 2030 Agenda (Pattberg and Bäckstrand 2023). Third, the SDG summits aim to foster cooperation, enhance partnerships between United Nations member states and various stakeholders, mobilize global resources, maintain political momentum and catalyze new actions and commitments for sustainable development (Montéville and Kettunen 2019). Moreover, the SDG summits are an essential platform to galvanize financial support, implement systemic reforms and promote transformative changes (Goodman 2023).

The main challenge of the SDG summits that undermines its main function to support goal implementation is the current geopolitical environment, limited political will among governments and the lack of global solidarity (Beisheim and Fritzsche 2022). Tension and mistrust between nations hinder collective action in solving transboundary, regional and global issues related to sustainable development. Although the SDG summits provide opportunities for international dialogue, deep-rooted political differences cannot be resolved without strong global leadership. As a result, experts point to the ineffectiveness of the SDG summits in driving substantial progress towards the 2030 Agenda (Desai 2023; Goodman 2023; Pattberg and Bäckstrand 2023). Only 17% of the 169 SDG targets are on track, whereas nearly half show minimal progress and require acceleration, while one-third have stalled or regressed (United Nations 2024). Moreover, given that the SDGs are an inclusive agenda, the SDG summits are criticized for lacking specific and actionable support to address urgent needs in the world's poorest, most fragile and conflict-ridden states (Desai 2023). The ineffectiveness can be attributed to the insufficient translation of political declarations into action. Although solutions to SDG challenges have been discussed at SDG summits, the absence of political prioritization may lead to failures to implement and scale up transformative solutions (Goodman 2023).

Furthermore, the SDG summits operate within the framework of voluntary and non-binding commitments. They hence cannot function as a robust accountability mechanism for the member states (Beisheim and Fritzsche 2022; Pattberg and Bäckstrand 2023). Consequently, the SDG summit may not sufficiently address critical issues required for transformative actions. These issues include trade-offs between SDG goals and targets, the reform of the global and regional financial systems and emphasizing financial commitments for the least developed and developing countries, insufficient integration of governance and other structural issues and limited influence on global governance (Beisheim and Fritzsche 2022; Blind 2020). Finally, the SDG summits are not fully inclusive or reflective of the voices of those most heavily affected by sustainability challenges, such as women, indigenous peoples and youth (Pattberg and Bäckstrand 2023).

References

Beisheim, M., and Fritzsche, F. (2022). The UN high-level political forum on sustainable development: An orchestrator, more or less? *Global Policy*, 13(5), 683–693. https://doi.org/10.1111/1758-5899.13112

Blind, P. K. (2020). A post-SDG Summit governance primer: interlinking the institutional, peace and justice dimensions of SDG16 (2016-2019) [ST/ESA/2020/DWP/165]. United Nations.

Desai, B. H. (2023). The 2023 New York SDG summit outcome: Rescue plan for 2030 agenda as a wake-up call for the decision-makers. *Environmental Policy and Law*, 53, 221–231. https://doi.org/10.3233/EPL-239006

Goodman, D. (2023). Seven years to save nature and people: a proposed set of policies and actions for the SDG Summit. Gland, Switzerland, International Union for Conservation of Nature.

Montéville, M., and Kettunen, M. (2019). *Assessing and accelerating the EU progress on Sustainable Development Goals (SDGs) in 2019* [A briefing to inform the UN High Level Political Forum (HLPF) and the SDG Summit in New York (9–18 July and 24–25 September 2019)]. Institute for European Environmental Policy.

Pattberg, P., and Bäckstrand, K. (2023). Enhancing the achievement of the SDGs: Lessons learned at the half-way point of the 2030 Agenda. *International Environmental Agreements Politics Law and Economics*, 23(2), 107–114. https://doi.org/10.1007/s10784-023-09615-9

United Nations. (2024). *Progress towards the Sustainable Development Goals: Report of the Secretary-General*. A/79/79-E/2024/54. New York: United Nations General Assembly, United Nations Economic and Social Council.

Silo approach

Maya Bogers

A silo approach refers to the tendency of actors or organizations operating in one policy domain to work in relative isolation from actors and organizations operating in other policy domains (Bogers et al. 2022; Kim 2020). As a result, the structure of the global governance system as a whole is shaped in clusters of actors and organizations around different policy domains: the silos. With regard to the Sustainable Development Goals (SDGs), such a silo approach may cause actors to operate in myopic ways, focusing only on 'their' SDG or target. Silos can occur at all levels of governance, including at the global, national and local level.

A silo approach may hinder overall progress on the SDGs. Most importantly, the myopic tendencies of actors and organizations may lead to isolated efforts that advance progress in single-issue areas and goals, but do not consider possible synergies or trade-offs with other goals and targets, resulting in policy incoherence (Griggs et al. 2014). For example, actors seeking to increase agricultural productivity to address hunger (SDG 2) may not consider possible negative effects on biodiversity (SDG 15) or on water availability for other uses (SDG 6). Similarly, efforts aimed at fostering economic growth (SDG 8) that do not consider environmental sustainability (SDG 13) might result in short-term economic gains but long-term environmental degradation (Griggs et al. 2014). A silo approach may also lead to duplicate efforts, as actors and organizations operating in different SDG issue areas may face similar challenges, for example, in the use of data that is relevant to multiple SDG issue areas but is not shared (Okembo et al. 2024).

To overcome silo approaches, deliberate political strategies are required to facilitate actors and organizations to work across policy domains or SDG issue areas. Several initiatives have been proposed in this regard. They include facilitating coordination, policy integration and mainstreaming and orchestration (Bogers et al. 2023). With the adoption of the SDGs, many had hoped that the SDGs themselves, as a set of explicitly interrelated goals, could spur more collaboration across policy domains and the breakdown of silos (see *Synergies and goal complementarity*). Yet so far, the SDGs have not facilitated this effect (Órdoñez Llanos et al. 2022).

However, some scholars contend that silo approaches may not be so problematic. Silos are there for a reason: As societal issues have become more complex, actors or organizations working on those issues have proliferated and have increasingly specialized. There is clear value in organizations having deep, specialized knowledge on the issues they aim to address and in having a variety of organizational structures and processes in place to address societal issues (Niestroy and Meuleman 2016). Thus, while 'too strong' silos are considered problematic both in science and in policy practice, there is no clear evidence or consensus on when silos are indeed 'too strong'. There is little scientific evidence on how the structure of governance systems affects policy outcomes, or what ideal-type structures for governance systems are (Kim 2020).

To conclude, a silo approach refers to actors or organizations working in policy-domain based silos. Such silos may lead actors to work in myopic ways, neglecting the inherent and complex interdependencies between the SDGs. In the overall governance system, this can result in fragmented strategies that fail to address the root causes of the issues embedded in the SDGs, do not take advantage of potential synergies between different SDGs and lead to duplicate efforts. A silo approach may thus hamper overall progress on advancing the SDGs.

References

Bogers, M., Biermann, F., Kalfagianni, A., and Kim, R. E. (2023). The SDGs as integrating force in global governance? Challenges and opportunities. *International Environmental Agreements: Politics, Law and Economics*, 23(2), 157–164.

Bogers, M., Biermann, F., Kalfagianni, A., Kim, R. E., Treep, J., and de Vos, M. G. (2022). The impact of the Sustainable Development Goals on a network of 276 international organizations. *Global Environmental Change*, 76, 102567.

Griggs, D., Stafford-Smith, M., Gaffney, O., Rockström, J., Öhman, M. C., Shyamsundar, P., ... Noble, I. (2014). An integrated framework for sustainable development goals. *Ecology and Society*, 19(4), 49.

Kim, R. E. (2020). Is global governance fragmented, polycentric, or complex? The state of the art of the network approach. *International Studies Review*, 22(4), 903–931.

Niestroy, I., and Meuleman, L. (2016). Teaching silos to dance: A condition to implement the SDGs. IISD SD Policy and Practice. Guest Article.

Okembo, C., Morales, J., Lemmen, C., Zevenbergen, J., and Kuria, D. (2024). A land administration data exchange and interoperability framework for Kenya and its significance to the Sustainable Development Goals. *Land*, 13(4), 435.

Órdoñez Llanos, A., Raven, R., Bexell, M., Botchwey, B., Bornemann, B., Censoro, J., ... Yunita, A. (2022). Implementation at multiple levels. In F. Biermann, T. Hickmann, and C.-A. Sénit (Eds.), *The Political Impact of the Sustainable Development Goals: Transforming Governance Through Global Goals?* (pp. 59–91). Cambridge: Cambridge University Press.

Stockholm+50

Nina Weitz

Fifty years after the 1972 United Nations Conference on the Human Environment, the 2022 international meeting, *Stockholm+50: A Healthy Planet for the Prosperity of All – Our Responsibility Our Opportunity*, brought together the United Nations system, some 150 member states and numerous other stakeholders. The 1972 Stockholm conference marked the start of international environmental governance and diplomacy. It was also the first to link environment and human development and to agree on a global set of principles in the field of the human environment (United Nations 2022a). The 2022 Stockholm+50 meeting presented an opportunity to generate action on these foundational principles and commitments for environmental diplomacy, many of which had not made much progress since 1972.

At the time of Stockholm+50, it was widely agreed that humans cause unprecedented change to the global environment, with the risk of major and irreversible changes. Also, it was apparent that the multilateral system had not effectively delivered concrete measures (Stockholm Environment Institute and Council on Energy, Environment and Water 2022). Commemorating five decades of global cooperation for sustainable development, the Stockholm+50 meeting reflected on how the global context was drastically different from 1972, as well as on the state-of-affairs, lacking progress, continued gaps and possible ways forward. A negotiated outcome was not within the meeting's mandate (United Nations 2021).

144 *Essential Concepts for Implementing the SDGs*

Instead, the two co-hosts, Sweden and Kenya, and the United Nations Environment Programme aimed at actions that governments and others could take to deliver on the 2030 Agenda and at a mobilization of the global community behind strengthened cooperation on the SDGs (United Nations Environment Programme 2021). With these objectives and mandate, the meeting focused on reinforcing international and multi-stakeholder collaboration, addressing challenges such as unmet earlier commitments, declining trust in governance, increasing concerns about the future among youth and distrust between the Global South and North. Just like the 1972 Stockholm conference had initiated dialogues on links between economic growth, environmental pollution and well-being for all, Stockholm+50 emphasized the global interconnectedness of current challenges and the need to collectively address them through bold and deliberate actions, strengthened political will and solidarity.

The mandate of the meeting allowed for an open format with broad stakeholder involvement (United Nations 2022b), bolder dialogues, stronger focus on ideation and more demanding calls for system-wide change, rather than consensus-seeking. Discussion within three Leadership Dialogues contributed to the outcome document, *Stockholm+50 Agenda for Action, Renewal and Trust*, with ten recommendations for accelerating implementation. These recommendations focus on placing human well-being at the centre of a healthy planet for all, the right to a healthy and sustainable environment and need to restoring our relationship with nature; changing our economic system to address economic and financial drivers of environmental degradation and making fundamental changes in attitudes, habits and behaviour; strengthening intergenerational responsibility in policymaking and rebuilding trust, solidarity and multilateralism (United Nations 2022a).

The meeting format was also used to build support amongst stakeholders for progress in ongoing negotiations. For example, just after the Stockholm+50 meeting, a resolution on the human right to a clean, healthy and sustainable environment was adopted. This closed five decades of advocacy and collaboration since the first principle of the 1972 Stockholm Declaration had been agreed, which stated 'the fundamental right to freedom, equality and adequate conditions of life, in an environment of a quality that permits a life of dignity and well-being' (United Nations 1973, 2022c)

The Stockholm+50 meeting offered an opportunity to reflect on international cooperation for sustainable development over the past 50 years since the first United Nations Conference on the Human Environment in 1972. Its format highlighted a shift towards more networked and inclusive multilateralism and resulted in a set of recommended actions aimed at accelerating progress towards a healthy planet for the prosperity of all. These recommendations, however, now need to be taken forward in international processes and future policies.

References

Stockholm Environment Institute and Council on Energy, Environment and Water. (2022). Stockholm+50: Unlocking a better future. Stockholm Environment Institute. https://doi.org/10.51414/sei2022.011

United Nations. (1973). *Report of the United Nations Conference on the Human Environment*, Stockholm, 5–16 June 1972. A/CONF/48/14/Rev1. https://documents.un.org/doc/un.oc/gen/nl7/300/05/pdf/nl730005.pdf

United Nations. (2021). International meeting entitled 'Stockholm+50: A healthy planet for the prosperity of all – Our responsibility, our opportunity'. A/RES/75/280. https://www.un.org/pga/76/wp-content/uploads/sites/101/2022/03/A_RES_75_280_E-1.pdf

United Nations. (2022a). Stockholm+50: A healthy planet for the prosperity of all – Our responsibility, our opportunity Stockholm, 2 and 3 June 2022 report. A/CONF.238/9. https://documents. un.org/doc/undoc/gen/k22/117/97/pdf/k2211797.pdf

United Nations. (2022b). Summary of stakeholder contributions to Stockholm+50. A/CONF.238/ INF/3. https://documents.un.org/doc/undoc/gen/k22/118/22/pdf/k2211822.pdf

United Nations. (2022c). The human right to a clean, healthy and sustainable environment. A/ RES/76/300. https://documents.un.org/doc/undoc/gen/n22/442/77/pdf/n2244277.pdf

United Nations Environment Programme. (2021). Stockholm+50 overview: A healthy planet for the prosperity of all – Our responsibility, our opportunity. *An International Meeting Hosted by Sweden and Kenya Stockholm*, Sweden, 2–3 June 2022. https://wedocs.unep.org/bitstream/ handle/20.500.11822/37743/SAP.pdf?sequence=3&isAllowed=y

Subnational initiatives

Rodrigo Führ

The current architecture of global sustainability governance is characterized by a shift from a top-down approach to a more bottom-up design. This shift involves the increasing participation of local authorities in international decision-making (Global Taskforce of Local and Regional Governments 2013), which in turn leads to a greater focus on subnational initiatives – the actions and programmes taken by local actors to implement the Sustainable Development Goals (SDGs) locally. As a result, subnational initiatives have gained traction, also complexifying the extent and ways in which local governments are implementing actions for advancing the SDGs (Hickmann 2021). Two analytical points to consider here are the varying degrees of autonomy and capacity of local entities in implementing sustainable development policies and practices and the concrete challenges subnational actors face.

First, the implementation of subnational initiatives reveals stark disparities between local governments in different contexts. Local actors in high-income countries often have greater autonomy and capacity to implement the SDGs, as well as more resources and established governance structures. In contrast, many subnational authorities in the Global South lack capacities and resources even when they develop innovative approaches to sustainable development. This disparity between the Global South and North extends to the size of governments as well, with large cities having more capacity to implement actions (even in the Global South) while small and medium-sized municipalities often struggle with translating the SDG framework into their local context. These differences are further influenced by non-governmental groups and international organizations, which often have the expertise and financial resources to implement actions at the local level, thus playing a crucial local role.

Second, subnational actors face various challenges when they try to implement the SDGs at the local level. While finance is often the primary obstacle, other factors are significant, too. In the Global South, technical expertise is often lacking in areas crucial for SDG implementation. Some regions struggle with lacking institutional capacity, as their governance structures are ill-equipped to handle complex, multi-sectoral sustainable development projects. In the Global North, where technical expertise is often available, one challenge is how to gain and maintain political support for SDG initiatives, especially when these compete with national politics that run counter to the 2030 Agenda (United Cities and Local Governments 2024).

146 *Essential Concepts for Implementing the SDGs*

The main sources of information to understand the scope and width of subnational initiatives are voluntary reviews. Some countries have established governance mechanisms that allow local governments to share their best practices and challenges to inform their countries' Voluntary National Reviews.

However, national governments tend to disregard local governments in their reviews, with some exceptions (United Cities and Local Governments 2024). Cities and states are encouraged, then, to report through their own instrument, so-called Voluntary Local Reviews. They vary widely: one can find such Voluntary Local Reviews with quantitative reporting on indicators for goals and targets and others with broad qualitative reporting that focus on narrating the influence of the SDGs in local planning. Despite these differences, Voluntary Local Reviews are seen as relevant instruments for local governments to share how they implement the SDGs. A third form of reporting are Voluntary Subnational Reviews, which is an informal form of reporting originated from a partnership between United Cities and Local Governments and United Nations Habitat. Through Voluntary Subnational Reviews, local and regional governments' associations are invited to analyse trends of SDG localization, helping to systematize subnational initiatives within a country or region.

In addition, numerous local actions could be seen as a best practice of SDG subnational implementation but may not be reported by local actors as being steered by the 2030 Agenda (see Órdoñez Llanos et al. 2022). Analysing formal reports alone might not completely show how the 2030 Agenda is accelerating or influencing subnational initiatives. In sum, this complex landscape underscores the need for the international community to increase their attention to how subnational actors are implementing sustainable development initiatives.

References

Global Taskforce of Local and Regional Governments (GTF). (2013). UCLG supports a stand-alone urban goal: Join the awareness-raising campaign. https://www.global-taskforce.org/uclg-supports-stand-alone-urban-goal-join-awareness-raising-campaign

Hickmann, T. (2021). Locating cities and their governments in multi-level sustainability governance. *Politics and Governance*, 9(1), 211–220. https://doi.org/10.17645/pag.v9i1.3616

Órdoñez Llanos, A., Raven, R., Bexell, M., Botchwey, B., Bornemann, B., Censoro, J., ... Yunita, A. (2022). Implementation at Multiple Levels. In F. Biermann, T. Hickmann, and C.-A. Sénit (Eds.), *The Political Impact of the Sustainable Development Goals: Transforming Governance Through Global Goals?* (pp. 59–91). Cambridge University Press.

United Cities and Local Governments. (2024). Towards the localization of the SDGs: Local and regional governments driving equality, climate action and a new agenda for peace. Local and Regional Governments' Report to the 2024 HLPF. https://gold.uclg.org/sites/default/files/uploaded/HLPF2024.pdf

Summit of the Future (2024)

Fronika de Wit

The United Nations Summit of the Future, held on 22–23 September 2024 in New York, was a high-level event where governments discussed how to transform global governance to make it better fit for current and future challenges. The summit built upon the outcome of the earlier 2023 SDG Summit and focused among others on how to create conditions to turbocharge the implementation of the 2030 Agenda for Sustainable Development and its 17 Sustainable Development Goals (SDGs).

The proposal for organizing a Summit of the Future originated in the United Nations Secretary-General's 2021 report *Our Common Agenda*, which urges a complete re-evaluation of political, economic and social systems to ensure they function more fairly and effectively for all (United Nations 2021). The report has the 2030 Agenda and the SDGs at its core and was meant to serve as an action agenda.

During the Summit, five main areas were on the agenda: sustainable development and financing for development; international peace and security; science, technology and innovation; youth and future generations; and transforming global governance. The outcome was presented in the internationally negotiated, action-oriented Pact for the Future, which presented 56 actions in these 5 areas. The outcome also includes two annexed documents: First, the Global Digital Compact, which seeks to foster a fair, inclusive and secure digital future by bridging digital divides, addressing risks and leveraging technology and artificial intelligence for sustainable development. Second, the Declaration on Future Generations, which advocates for decision-making that prioritizes the well-being of future generations at national and international levels.

Although the Pact for the Future intended to offer a blueprint for consensual global institutional reform, global governance scholars highlight that the Summit's outcome may fall short of what is needed (Fuso Nerini et al. 2024; Mathiasen 2024; Pham 2024). Negotiations leading up to the Pact were difficult, with the main conflicts being the international financial architecture and competing interests, systems and actors (Mathiasen 2024). Also, despite efforts to include diverse voices in the drafting process, questions remain about the inclusion of marginalized groups and how their priorities will be upheld in practice (Pham 2024). Although achieving the 2030 Agenda was discussed during the Summit, they were not placed at the centre of the global policy agenda. Instead of focusing on SDG implementation until 2030, however, the Summit could have adapted and extended the SDG framework to guide national action and global cooperation beyond 2030 (Fuso Nerini et al. 2024).

To reinvigorate the SDGs, SDG researchers have proposed a wide variety of measures and governance reforms until and beyond 2030. Biermann et al. (2023) propose four governance reforms focused on differentiation, dynamization, legalization and stronger institutionalization. Moreover, in an effort to complement the Pact for the Future, participants of the international research conference GlobalGoals 2024 designed a roadmap with additional strategies and actions to revitalize SDG implementation. This conference statement presents reform avenues in relation to adapting the architecture of global governance; facilitating national SDG coordination and governance; recalibrating targets and indicators; and working towards a paradigm shift in economic policy (GlobalGoals 2024).

In conclusion, the Summit of the Future marked an important moment for global sustainability governance, aiming to align immediate actions with long-term strategies for achieving the 2030 Agenda and its SDGs. While the Summit emphasized the need to address future challenges and opportunities, the Pact for the Future – the main outcome document – offers a framework for action but remains insufficient on its own. To deliver meaningful results, the Pact must confront systemic power imbalances, promote equitable participation and prioritize justice among diverse actors. Without addressing these foundational issues, the ambitions of the Summit risk falling short of their transformative potential.

References

Biermann, F., Sun, Y., Banik, D., Beisheim, M., Bloomfield, M. J., Charles, A., Chasek, P., Hickmann, T., Pradhan, P., and Sénit, C.A. (2023). Four governance reforms to strengthen the SDGs: A demanding policy vision can accelerate global sustainable development efforts. *Science*, 381(6663), 1159–1160. https://doi.org/10.1126/science.adj5434

Fuso Nerini, F., Mazzucato, M., Rockström, J., van Asselt, H., Hall, J. W., Matos, S., Persson, Å., Sovacool, B., Vinuesa, R., and Sachs, J. (2024). Extending the Sustainable Development Goals to 2050 – A road map. *Nature*, 630(8017), 555–558. https://doi.org/10.1038/d41586-024-01754-6

GlobalGoals. (2024). Conference statement: Reinvigorating the sustainable development goals: The Utrecht roadmap. GlobalGoals Project. https://globalgoalsproject.eu/conferencestatement/

Mathiasen, K. (2024, September 25). UN pact for the future: Mired in the past and hamstrung by the present. Center for Global Development. https://www.cgdev.org/blog/un-pact-future-mired-past-and-hamstrung-present

Pham, M. (2024). Commentary: Toward a multilateral system that delivers. *Global Governance A Review of Multilateralism and International Organizations*, 30(2), 313–321. https://doi.org/10.1163/19426720-03002011

United Nations. (2021). *Our Common Agenda: Report of the Secretary-General*. United Nations. https://www.un.org/en/content/common-agenda-report/

United Nations. (2024). Summit of the Future outcome documents: Pact for the future, global digital compact and declaration on future generations. United Nations. https://www.un.org/sites/un2.un.org/files/sotf-pact_for_the_future_adopted.pdf

Sustainable finance

Maximilian Bruder and Daniel Duma

Sustainable finance can be broadly conceptualized as a set of practices, standards, norms, regulations and products that pursue financial returns alongside sustainable development objectives (UNEP 2016). It is an umbrella term that subsumes other related classifications such as climate finance, green finance, SDG finance and others (Migliorelli 2021). Sustainable finance therefore encompasses not only the environmental dimension of sustainability but also considers social, economic and governance issues. The ultimate aim is to align finance flows with the pursuit of the Sustainable Development Goals (SDGs).

The lagging progress towards the SDGs has led to the realization that additional finance needs to be mobilized. Public finance has traditionally been the primary source of funding for sustainable development, and there are calls for public and multilateral finance to be scaled up rapidly to tackle the enormously costly global challenges. However, given the limited availability of public funds, the recent focus has been on leveraging private profit-seeking finance for sustainable economic activities. This objective has been fundamental to the Addis Ababa Action Agenda, which was the outcome of the 2015 Third International Conference on Financing for Development that provided a framework for financing sustainable development by aligning all financing flows and policies with economic, social and environmental priorities.

There are calls for the private financial sector to fundamentally realign – whether through voluntary initiatives or regulatory measures – and redirect capital towards sustainable development and away from unsustainable practices. Key mechanisms include voluntary pursuits such as investing in line with environmental, social and governance criteria, further driven by new disclosure requirements like the European Union's Corporate Sustainability Reporting Directive. This type of sustainable finance is now firmly part of mainstream capital markets, with global environmental, social and governance-related assets surpassing USD 30 trillion in 2022 (Bloomberg 2024). However, with the sector's rapid expansion and lack of standardized criteria come concerns about 'greenwashing', where projects are labelled as sustainable without achieving actual verifiable impact (Delmas and Burbano 2011). Further, the investment trend is particularly pronounced in high-income countries, where favourable risk-reward conditions are encouraging.

On the other hand, low- and lower-middle-income countries are being left behind, suffering from chronically low investments in all sectors, not just those relevant for sustainable development (Songwe et al. 2022). This is due in part to the greater investment risk, resulting in higher risk premia and, thus, a higher cost of capital compared to investments in high-income countries. At the same time, it has been implicitly assumed that low- and lower-middle-income countries can absorb large amounts of capital and turn them into power capacity, sustainable transport infrastructure, climate-smart agriculture, sustainable business models and other desirable outcomes – an assumption that is not a given.

To better meet the demand of low- and lower-middle-income countries for sustainable finance, innovative instruments have been introduced into the sustainable development context to mitigate the risk for private investors of financing sustainable economic activities, for instance by blending public and private funds and offering guarantee instruments, thereby making investments more appealing. This approach has led to greater investment in low- and lower-middle-income countries, particularly in renewable energy capacity. Still, progress is far from what is needed. For example, in 2021, the private finance mobilized for sustainable development through blended finance was USD 40 billion, around 1% of the amount needed (Convergence Blended Finance 2022).

While the challenges around achieving the SDGs go far beyond the field of finance, sustainable finance approaches have shown promise in accelerating investment. With ongoing commitment, alignment and innovation, sustainable finance can meaningfully accelerate progress in SDG implementation and maximize the transformative potential of the global goals.

References

Bloomberg. (2024, February 8). Global ESG assets predicted to hit $40 trillion by 2030, despite challenging environment, forecasts Bloomberg Intelligence. *Bloomberg*. https://www.bloomberg.com/company/press/global-esg-assets-predicted-to-hit-40-trillion-by-2030-despite-challenging-environment-forecasts-bloomberg-intelligence/

Convergence Blended Finance. (2022). *The State of Blended Finance 2022: Climate Edition.* Convergence Report.

Delmas, M. A., and Burbano, V. C. (2011). The drivers of greenwashing. *California Management Review*, 54(1), 64–87. https://doi.org/10.1525/cmr.2011.54.1.64

Migliorelli, M. (2021). What do we mean by sustainable finance? Assessing existing frameworks and policy risks. *Sustainability*, 13(2), 975. https://doi.org/10.3390/su13020975

Songwe, V., Stern, N., and Bhattacharya, A. (2022). *Finance for climate action: Scaling up investment for climate and development.* London: Grantham Research Institute on Climate Change and the Environment, London School of Economics and Political Science.

UNEP. (2016). *Design of a sustainable financial system.* United Nations Environment Programme. https://wedocs.unep.org/bitstream/handle/20.500.11822/10603/definitions_concept.pdf

Synergies and goal complementarity

Simon Beaudoin

According to the Oxford English Dictionary, the notion of synergy refers to 'any interaction or cooperation which is mutually reinforcing; a dynamic, productive or profitable affinity, association, or link' (Oxford English Dictionary 2024). The notion stands out as a key concept to unite research on fundamentally interconnected socio-ecological issues (Beaudoin 2023, 15). In the context of the Sustainable Development Goals (SDGs), the notion is of great interest, given the reinforcing interactions, both positive and negative, between economic, social and environmental goals. Synergy is also a particularly relevant notion, as one of the main problems that cripples the quest for answering socio-ecological issues is that 'institutions, governance and research funders are commonly fragmented or siloed' (Scharlemann et al. 2020, 2). To reform these, attention should be paid to synergies in order to bring light to the connections across sectors, governance structures and funders' objectives.

The notion of goal complementarity is rooted in the idea that goals exhibit mutually complementing characteristics. These can be observed at multiple levels of governance, from the inherent structure of the goals and the targets and indicators associated with them to the very aims of the goals. In some cases, multiple goals are adopted with their connections in mind. In other cases, complementarity between goals is only recognized downstream, once goals are established. In the context of the SDGs, attempts were made to craft the goals and the encompassing 2030 Agenda in terms of complementarities between social, environmental and economic goals as a comprehensive and holistic governance framework (Caballero and Londoño 2022) (see *Policy coherence for sustainable development*).

Although the 2030 Agenda aimed to foster synergies between goals, the design of the SDGs taps only shallowly into the complementarity between economic, social and environmental goals. Indeed, the adoption of the SDGs saw early efforts to integrate these three categories of concerns being replaced by a progressively segmented and goal-specific stream of negotiation. As a result, the complementarity between the SDGs, rather than being explicitly integrated in the design of the goals, now needs to be exposed by researchers and goal advocates. Crafting the environmental, social and economic goals through the lens of their synergies and complementarity from the get-go would have greatly facilitated implementation. Nonetheless, promising research is currently exposing the synergies and trade-offs between goals and will certainly serve to implement coherent action plans and policies (Kim et al. 2023).

The study of interactions across multiples temporal, spatial and socio-ecological goals is of great importance for students of social and natural sciences interested in providing insights to socio-ecological issues that span beyond silos. Indeed, the contemporary context of deep interlinkages across sectors and scales calls for seizing synergies through integrated approaches (Hickmann et al. 2024). Whereas policies and implementation plans based on synergies can help bring together the environmental, social and economic dimensions, such approaches are often lacking or poorly integrated in decision-making. The design of the SDGs in separate goals rather than a coherent whole resulted in a difficult agenda to implement, hindering actors' ability to tap into existing connections between goals. This is challenging, I argue, as global environmental governance can no longer work in silos. It might remain true in the foreseeable future, as 'new problems have emerged, long-standing problems remain inadequately addressed and many diverse problems are becoming ever more tightly intertwined' (Burch et al. 2019, 2). In sum, the notions of synergies and goal complementarity are useful to think about socio-ecological systems in systemic, integrated and synergistic ways.

References

Beaudoin, S. (2023). Revue historique de la gouvernance mondiale de l'environnement (1945–2022). *Canadian Journal of Political Science/Revue Canadienne de Science Politique*, 56(4), 790–810. https://doi.org/10.1017/S0008423923000483

Burch, S., Gupta, A., Inoue, C. Y. A., Kalfagianni, A., Persson, Å., Gerlak, A. K., Ishii, A., Patterson, J., Pickering, J., Scobie, M., Van der Heijden, J., Vervoort, J., Adler, C., Bloomfield, M., Djalante, R., Dryzek, J., Galaz, V., Gordon, C., Harmon, R., ... Zondervan, R. (2019). New directions in earth system governance research. *Earth System Governance*, 1, 100006. https://doi.org/10.1016/j.esg.2019.100006

Caballero, P., and Londoño, P. (2022). *Redefining development: The extraordinary genesis of the sustainable development goals*. Lynne Rienner Publishers.

Hickmann, T., Biermann, F., Sénit, C.-A., Sun, Y., Bexell, M., Bolton, M., Bornemann, B., Censoro, J., Charles, A., Coy, D., Dahlmann, F., Elder, M., Fritzsche, F., Galvão, T. G., Grainger-Brown, J., Inoue, C., Jönsson, K., Rosas, M. K., Krellenberg, K., ... Weiland, S. (2024). Scoping article: Research frontiers on the governance of the Sustainable Development Goals. *Global Sustainability*, 7, e7. https://doi.org/10.1017/sus.2024.4

Kim, R. E., Girgiç, I., Adipudi, A. V., Raidma, H. M., Oelschläger, L., Scheibenreif, M., De Bruijne, R., Costa Macedo de Arruda, G., and Kozhanova, N. (2023). Problem shifts database. https://www.problemshifting.directory

Oxford English Dictionary. (2024). *Synergy*. https://www.oed.com/search/dictionary/?scope=Entries&q=synergy

Scharlemann, J. P. W., Brock, R. C., Balfour, N., Brown, C., Burgess, N. D., Guth, M. K., Ingram, D. J., Lane, R., Martin, J. G. C., Wicander, S., and Kapos, V. (2020). Towards understanding interactions between Sustainable Development Goals: The role of environment–human linkages. *Sustainability Science*. https://doi.org/10.1007/s11625-020-00799-6

T

Targets

Mark Elder

The 17 Sustainable Development Goals (SDGs) have 169 targets specifying more specific objectives or actions. Each SDG has at least three targets and includes both thematic targets and targets on means of implementation. For instance, SDG 12 on responsible consumption and production aims to substantially reduce waste generation through prevention, reduction, recycling and reuse (Target 12.5) by rationalizing inefficient fossil fuel subsidies that encourage wasteful consumption (Target 12.c). Targets are qualitative in nature, except for Target 8.1 on economic growth, which calls for an annual increase of at least 7% per year for least developed countries. The indicators, in contrast, are intended to quantify the targets to facilitate monitoring their progress.

The SDGs' targets, more than the headline goals or indicators, contain the SDGs' main substance. Many targets are broad, ambitious and wide ranging. For example, Target 1.1 aims to end extreme poverty for all people everywhere, while Target 8.4 seeks to decouple economic growth from environmental degradation. However, some targets are narrow, such as Target 8.9 on sustainable tourism. Targets also differ on whether they call for full or partial achievement. For example, some only aim to 'improve' or 'encourage' progress rather than 'ensure' or 'achieve' targets, and some targets have specific deadlines while others do not (Mustajoki et al. 2022).

The targets reflect the SDGs' integrated approach. Indeed, all SDGs have targets addressing at least two of the three dimensions of sustainable development – economic, social and environmental (Elder 2024). All SDGs, including especially the socioeconomic-oriented SDGs, can be interpreted as having at least one target related to the environment (Elder and Olsen 2019). Similarly, many 'economic' targets also promote environmental sustainability, such as Target 9.4 on sustainably upgrading infrastructure and retrofitting industry (Elder 2022).

SDG 6 (water) has the clearest integrated approach: Target 6.1 focuses on water access as a basic need (social), Target 6.3 focuses on water-use efficiency (economic), while Targets 6.5 and 6.6 concentrate on integrated water resources management and protection and restoration of water-related ecosystems, respectively (environmental). The targets are also synergistic, for example, the economic dimension – water-use efficiency – contributes

DOI: 10.4324/9781003519560-20

This chapter has been made available under a CC-BY-NC-ND license.

to both social and environmental dimensions by promoting water access and sustainable consumption.

Moreover, some targets reflect sustainability's holistic nature. For instance, while Target 9.1 on infrastructure may seem primarily 'economic', it specifies that infrastructure should be 'sustainable' and support 'human well-being' and 'equitable access', so it is also 'environmental' and 'social'. Similarly, Target 15.1 is not just about the conservation and restoration of terrestrial and freshwater ecosystems, but also their 'services' (ecosystem services), so the target contributes to all three dimensions of sustainable development.

Therefore, many studies of interlinkages among SDGs are based on targets (Allen et al. 2019; Anderson et al. 2022). These have generally concluded that there are more synergies than trade-offs among the targets (Independent Group of Scientists 2023).

The SDGs' quantitative indicators are intended to reflect the targets, although they are generally much narrower and do not fully align with the targets' breadth, scope and integrated nature. For example, Target 11.6 calls for reducing the overall environmental impact of cities, but the indicator only addresses municipal solid waste, excluding other environmental impacts. Also, indicators often do not reflect the environmental dimensions of the targets. For example, while Target 9.2 calls for industrialization to be 'inclusive' and 'sustainable', the indicators only address overall 'manufacturing' and not inclusiveness or sustainability.

Overall, the targets of the SDGs do not conform to the commonly recommended SMART (Specific, Measurable, Achievable, Realistic and Time Bound) framework, but were intended to be quantified by the indicators. However, it has been difficult to reconcile the quantitative SMART approach with broad holistic ambition and multidimensional integrated approaches pursued by the 2030 Agenda.

References

Allen, C., Metternicht, G., and Wiedmann, T. (2019). Prioritising SDG targets: Assessing baselines, gaps and interlinkages. *Sustainability Science, 14*(2). https://doi.org/10.1007/s11625-018-0596-8

Anderson, C. C., Denich, M., Warchold, A., Kropp, J. P., and Pradhan, P. (2022). A systems model of SDG target influence on the 2030 Agenda for Sustainable Development. *Sustainability Science, 17*(4), 1459–1472. https://doi.org/10.1007/s11625-021-01040-8

Elder, M. (2022, April 26). Using the SDGs to realize the G7's 'green revolution that creates jobs'. *T7 Task Force Climate and Environment Policy Brief.* https://www.iges.or.jp/en/pub/g7-green-revolution-creates-jobs/en

Elder, M. (2024). Integration versus prioritization in the Sustainable Development Goals: An argument to prioritize environmental sustainability and a just transition. *Sustainable Development.* https://doi.org/10.1002/sd.3130

Elder, M., and Olsen, S. H. (2019). The design of environmental priorities in the SDGs. *Global Policy, 10*(S1), 70–82. https://doi.org/10.1111/1758-5899.12596

Independent Group of Scientists. (2023). *Global Sustainable Development Report 2023: Times of Crisis, Times of Change: Science for Accelerating Transformations to Sustainable Development.* United Nations. https://doi.org/10.18356/9789213585115

Mustajoki, J., Borchardt, S., Büttner, L., Köhler, B., Lepenies, R., Lyytimäki, J., Mille, R., Pedersen, A. B., Reis, S., and Richard, D. (2022). Ambitiousness of Sustainable Development Goal (SDG) targets: Classification and implications for policy making. *Discover Sustainability, 3*(1), 36. https://doi.org/10.1007/s43621-022-00104-8

Trade-offs and goals conflicts

Alex San Martim Portes

The Sustainable Development Goals (SDGs) are a comprehensive policy framework aimed at achieving economic, social and environmental objectives. Despite the integrated vision of the SDGs, implementing the various goals and targets inevitably involves significant trade-offs and conflicts (Breuer et al. 2019; Kroll et al. 2019). These tensions emerge because progress in one area may create obstacles for others, making the implementation of the 2030 Agenda highly complex. The United Nations compares this process to solving a Rubik's cube, where 'all sides must be considered in relation to each other if the puzzle is to be solved' (United Nations Sustainable Development Group 2023, 1).

The conflicts and trade-offs within the 2030 Agenda are well recognized in the broad literature on sustainable development. Scholars have argued that overcoming these conflicts is a significant challenge in the domestic implementation of the 2030 Agenda (Stafford-Smith et al. 2017). The literature highlights the importance of considering how to deal with trade-offs and not avoid those conflicts, since avoiding conflicts in policymaking is a significant cause of the lack of transformational changes (Wong and van der Heijden 2019). In contrast, successful policymaking involves transforming these conflicts into synergies (Kroll et al. 2019).

A notable example is the tension between economic growth (SDG 8) and environmental sustainability (SDG 13). Most industrialized and emerging economies rely on industrial activities and natural resource exploitation to drive economic progress, which can result in significant environmental degradation. Xing et al. (2024), for example, describe the challenging trade-offs China must address when balancing environmental and climate action and economic development at national and local levels. Such cases exemplify the difficulties of integrating all SDGs and the importance of finding points of synergy that support a comprehensive implementation of the 2030 Agenda, avoiding silo approaches.

Another example is the promotion of clean energy (SDG 7) versus responsible consumption and production (SDG 12). While renewable energy sources like solar panels and wind turbines are vital for reducing reliance on fossil fuels, their production requires significant resources, such as rare earth metals. The extraction of these materials can cause environmental harm and social inequities, especially in the absence of regulatory frameworks. As Ramasubramanian and Ramakrishna (2023) argue, there is no one-size-fits-all approach to achieving SDG7, and each country should assess the trade-offs and synergies that apply to its domestic context.

Some policy areas, like agricultural production, involve various SDGs, and policymakers should carefully navigate potential trade-offs and synergies. For example, policies to increase agricultural production can be positive for ending hunger (SDG 2) but negative for protecting biodiversity (SDG 15) and people's health (SDG 3) if they involve reducing biodiversity and using pesticides.

Critically, these trade-offs and conflicts are not just technical but political. Different interest groups, including governments, private sector actors and civil society, will prioritize goals that align with their interests. Corporations, particularly in industries such as fossil fuels, may lobby for policies prioritizing their economic interests over environmental or social objectives, complicating efforts to achieve balanced outcomes. Addressing the political nature of trade-offs requires robust governance structures capable of balancing competing interests and fostering cross-sectoral collaboration.

In conclusion, trade-offs and goal conflicts are unavoidable in the pursuit of the SDGs, reflecting the diverse and sometimes competing objectives within the 2030 Agenda. While certain trade-offs can be mitigated through innovative policies and international cooperation, others require difficult political choices. Policymakers must be aware of these conflicts and develop strategies that minimize negative impacts while promoting integrated solutions.

References

Breuer, A., Janetschek, H., and Malerba, D. (2019). Translating sustainable development goal (SDG) interdependencies into policy advice. *Sustainability*, *11*(7), 2092.

Kroll, C., Warchold, A., and Pradhan, P. (2019). Sustainable Development Goals (SDGs): Are we successful in turning trade-offs into synergies? *Palgrave Communications*, *5*(1). https://doi.org/10.1057/s41599-019-0335-5

Ramasubramanian, B., and Ramakrishna, S. (2023). What's next for the Sustainable Development Goals? Synergy and trade-offs in affordable and clean energy (SDG 7). *Sustainable Earth Reviews*, *6*(1), 17.

Stafford-Smith, M., Griggs, D., Gaffney, O., Ullah, F., Reyers, B., Kanie, N., Stigson, B., Shrivastava, P., Leach, M., and O'Connell, D. (2017). Integration: The key to implementing the sustainable development goals. *Sustainability Science*, *12*(6), 911–919. https://doi.org/10.1007/s11625-016-0383-3

United Nations Sustainable Development Group. (2023). *Six Transitions: Investment Pathways to Deliver the SDGs*. https://unsdg.un.org/sites/default/files/2023-09/Six%20Transitions%20English.pdf

Wong, R., and van der Heijden, J. (2019). Avoidance of conflicts and trade-offs: A challenge for the policy integration of the United Nations Sustainable Development Goals. *Sustainable Development*, *27*(5), 838–845.

Xing, Q., Wu, C., Chen, F., Liu, J., Pradhan, P., Bryan, B. A., ... Xu, Z. (2024). Intranational synergies and trade-offs reveal common and differentiated priorities of sustainable development goals in China. *Nature Communications*, *15*(1), 2251.

Transdisciplinarity

Kerstin Krellenberg, Florian Koch and Julia Wesely

Transdisciplinarity often refers to the joint production of knowledge and decision-making of academic and non-academic actors. In the context of sustainability science and the 2030 Agenda, transdisciplinary research is frequently understood as knowledge co-production, which aims to localize the Sustainable Development Goals (SDGs) through collaborations between diverse actors (Krellenberg and Koch 2021), such as public and private sectors, civil society, social movements, non-governmental organizations, academia and other institutions.

Many approaches emphasize that transdisciplinarity is not an acupuncture tactic, but rather a long-term strategy and a relational practice to be deployed along the entire research process (Lawrence et al. 2022), which would start from the shared identification and framing of a complex societal problem and continue to the collaborative design and

156 *Essential Concepts for Implementing the SDGs*

implementation of a research methodology and the development of actionable knowledge on the SDGs, covering as well transversal processes such as communication and co-learning. Transdisciplinary research thus aims to achieve a delicate balance between producing relevant and reliable knowledge for addressing the SDGs based on sound methodologies, while creating impact for a range of stakeholders as part of the process and afterwards. While the former challenges ontologies and epistemologies, the latter provides an important critique and alternative to simplistic linear science-to-policy approaches.

Transdisciplinary collaborations between academic disciplines as well as scientific and other knowledge and practices open possibilities for new knowledge, partnerships and visions of sustainable futures to emerge. Drawing on experiences from nine African research projects as part of the Leading Integrated Research for Agenda 2030 in Africa initiative, for example, an assessment of transdisciplinarity contributions to contexts, processes and products highlighted their potential to overcome policy and institutional silos, foster transformative learning and agency, as well as produce concrete outputs such as tools, maps and handbooks to address interconnected SDGs (Thiam et al. 2021). The International Science Council and other global actors further recognize the potential of transdisciplinary research to target not only individual SDGs but also their interlinkages in terms of creating synergies and addressing trade-offs (International Science Council 2020). A study by Bandari et al. (2024), for instance, used transdisciplinary methodologies and scenario modelling to forecast the impacts of 11 local actions in an Australian region on global targets articulated through SDGs 2, 6, 8 and 15. It revealed strong synergies between actions to increase water-use efficiency on farms, increased total crop and dairy production (SDG2) and reduced agricultural land use (SDG 15), among many others.

Given the complexity and diversity of transdisciplinary research, its barriers and enablers are well known (McClure 2024). These include theoretical inconsistencies and disagreements in terms of transdisciplinary frameworks, practical aspects such as the commitment, competencies and skills of all participating actors and the availability of short- and long-term resources, especially time and money. Moreover, transdisciplinary research is often marked by different experiences and ownership of the problem and unequal decision-making powers, which demand an enabling environment for building relationships between institutions and people amidst deep structural inequalities.

In conclusion, transdisciplinary research can contribute to place-based and pluralist actions and strategies to accelerate the implementation of the SDGs through locally relevant and actionable knowledge (co-)production between non-academic actors and academic actors from various disciplines by contributing to the knowledge of institutional arrangements needed for SDG implementation at all governance levels. The scale and scope of impact for addressing the SDGs and their interlinkages, however, depend on a contextually specific enabling environment that frames all research stages from design to communication and co-learning.

References

Bandari, R., Moallemi, E.A., Kharrazi, A., Šakić Trogrlić, R., and Bryan, B.A. (2024). Transdisciplinary approaches to local sustainability: Aligning local governance and navigating spillovers with global action towards the Sustainable Development Goals. *Sustainability Science*, 19, 1293–1312. https://doi.org/10.1007/s11625-024-01494-6

International Science Council. (2020). *Advancing the 2030 agenda in African cities through knowledge co-production: Urban experiments led by early-career African scientists*. International Science Council. https://doi.org/10.24948/2020.01

Krellenberg, K., and Koch, F. (2021). How to support German cities in implementing the SDGs: Learning from and about co-design. *Global Sustainability*, 4, e18. https://doi.org/10.1017/sus.2021.16

Lawrence, M. G., Williams, S., Nanz, P., and Renn, O. (2022). Characteristics, potentials and challenges of transdisciplinary research. *One Earth*, 5(1), 44–61.

McClure, A. (2024). Enablers of transdisciplinary collaboration for researchers working on climate risks in African cities. *Sustainability Science*, 19, 259–273. https://doi.org/10.1007/s11625-023-01426-w

Thiam, S., Aziz, F., Kushitor, S. B., Amaka-Otchere, A. B. K., Onyima, B. N., and Odume, O. N. (2021). Analyzing the contributions of transdisciplinary research to the global sustainability agenda in African cities. *Sustainability Science*, 16, 1923–1944. https://doi.org/10.1007/s11625-021-01042-6

Transformation

Sabine Weiland

The 2030 Agenda and its 17 Sustainable Development Goals provide a normative framework and vision for a sustainable society. They call for deep transformations of our societies and economies from the current unsustainable state to more sustainable courses of development. Sustainability transformation refers to fundamental changes in the structural, functional, relational and cognitive aspects of how societies operate that lead to new patterns of interactions and outcomes (Patterson et al. 2017). This transformation is aimed at addressing the interconnected global challenges of poverty, inequality, environmental degradation and climate change.

The notion of transformation is increasingly relevant in sustainability discourse, as it reflects a shift from merely describing problems and identifying solutions to understanding pathways for sustainable change. However, although the term is omnipresent, it is often unclear what exactly is to be transformed and by which process. In an overview article, Scoones et al. (2020) systematize from the literature three strands of transformation concepts: (1) *structural approaches* that focus on fundamental changes in the foundations of politics, economy and society and an overhaul of the ideological underpinnings of social systems. One example of this approach can be seen in decarbonization paths and the transformation of global markets, both of which are aimed at radically changing production and consumption patterns (for example, Bulkeley et al. 2012); (2) *systemic approaches* that target the interdependencies of institutions, technologies and social practices, with the aim of steering complex systems towards sustainability objectives (Voulvoulis et al. 2022). An example is the introduction of new low-carbon innovations (for example, wind and solar power) that emerge in niches and trigger changes in the energy system with the backing of policies aimed at targeted change; (3) *enabling approaches* that emphasize fostering human agency and capacities to identify and enact pathways to desired futures. These approaches are often driven by grassroots movements, for example, community-owned wind power initiatives and ecological agricultural practices, where transformation directions are deliberated politically (Smith and Stirling 2018).

While these approaches are distinct and reflect different understandings of what transformation entails and how it can be achieved, they are also complementary in that each

158 *Essential Concepts for Implementing the SDGs*

addresses different aspects of transformation. The approaches can influence and enhance one another; for instance, structural changes in policies and institutions can create an environment that supports enabling approaches, such as grassroots movements and social alliances, which in turn can advocate for and implement systemic changes (Scoones et al. 2020).

Apart from these conceptual questions, the empirical question arises as to what extent the SDGs set transformative processes in motion. The Global Sustainable Development Report (Independent Group of Scientists 2023) finds that the progress towards the SDGs has been severely disrupted in the context of various economic, social, health and environmental crises. A scientific study on the transformative impact of the SDGs (Biermann et al. 2022) identifies some political impact on institutions and policies, even though this impact has mostly been detected in the area of discourses, that is, the way how actors understand sustainable development. More substantive impacts on institutions and regulations remain rare, which is interpreted as a limited transformative effect of the SDGs.

Sustainability transformations are complex and multifaceted processes that must be based on different approaches, plural pathways and political commitment. The slow and sometimes disappointing progress in implementing the SDGs is due to the complexity of the challenge.

References

Biermann, F., Hickmann, T., and Sénit, C. A. (Eds.). (2022). *The Political Impact of the Sustainable Development Goals: Transforming Governance Through Global Goals?* Cambridge University Press. https://doi.org/10.1038/s41893-022-00909-5

Bulkeley, H., Andonova, L., Bäckstrand, K., Betsill, M., Compagnon, D., Duffy, R., Kolk, A., Hoffmann, M., Levy, D., Newell, P., Milledge, T., Paterson, M., Pattberg, P., and VanDeveer, S. (2012). Governing Climate Change Transnationally: Assessing the Evidence from a Database of Sixty Initiatives. *Environment and Planning C: Government and Policy* 30(4), 591–612. https://doi.org/10.1068/c11126

Independent Group of Scientists. (2023). *Global Sustainable Development Report 2023: Times of Crisis, Times of Change: Science for Accelerating Transformations to Sustainable Development.* United Nations. https://doi.org/10.18356/9789213585115

Patterson, J., Schulz, K., Vervoort, J., Van Der Hel, S., Sethi, M., and Barau, A. (2017). Exploring the governance and politics of transformations towards sustainability. *Environmental Innovation and Societal Transitions*, 24, 1–16. https://doi.org/10.1016/j.eist.2016.09.001

Scoones, I., Stirling, A., Abrol, D., Atela, J., Charli-Joseph, L., Eakin, H., Ely, A., Olsson, P., Pereira, L., Priya, R., van Zwanenberg, P., Yang, L. (2020). Transformations to sustainability: Combining structural, systemic and enabling approaches, *Current Opinion in Environmental Sustainability*, 42, 65–75. https://doi.org/10.1016/j.cosust.2019.12.004

Smith, A., and Stirling, A. (2018). Innovation, sustainability and democracy: An analysis of grassroots contributions. *Journal of Self-Governance and Management Economics*, 6(1), 64–97. https://doi.org/10.22381/jsme6120183

Voulvoulis, N., Giakoumis, T., Hunt, C., Kioupi, V., Petrou, N., Souliotis, I., Vaghela, C., Wan Rosely, and Binti, W. I. H. (2022). Systems thinking as a paradigm shift for sustainability transformation. *Global Environmental Change*, 75, 102544. https://doi.org/10.1016/j.gloenvcha.2022.102544

U

United Nations Conference on Environment and Development (1992)

Pamela Chasek

In December 1989, the United Nations General Assembly adopted resolution 44/228, which called for convening the United Nations Conference on Environment and Development (UNCED), which has also become known as the Earth Summit. The conference was to examine the state of the environment and changes that have occurred since the 1972 United Nations Conference on the Human Environment in Stockholm, Sweden. The resolution said the conference should recommend measures to be taken at the national and international levels to protect and enhance the environment, taking into account the specific needs of developing countries, through the development and implementation of policies for sustainable and environmentally sound development, as well as to promote the further development of international environmental law (United Nations General Assembly 1989).

Canadian Maurice Strong, who had been the Secretary-General of the 1972 Stockholm Conference, was named UNCED Secretary-General. Strong believed that the complex General Assembly resolution needed to be translated into a clear set of final outputs from the UNCED, including an Earth Charter, building on the Stockholm Declaration, Agenda 21, an action programme, financial considerations, technology transfer, institutional follow-up and treaties on climate and biodiversity. There was supposed to be a treaty on forests, but this proved unrealistic due to major North-South divisions (Engfeldt 2009, 144–145).

The preparatory committee, which was established to negotiate the conference outcomes, held 4 substantive sessions for a total of 12 weeks between August 1990 and April 1992. There were significant disagreements between the developed and the developing world. Consequently, each group provided different inputs to the agenda-setting process: developed countries wanted to focus on ozone depletion, global warming, acid rain and deforestation, while developing countries wanted to explore the relationship between their sluggish economic growth and the economic policies of the developed countries. The concern was that an 'environmentally healthy planet was impossible in a world that contained significant inequities' (Miller 1995, 9).

DOI: 10.4324/9781003519560-21

This chapter has been made available under a CC-BY-NC-ND license.

160   *Essential Concepts for Implementing the SDGs*

UNCED convened in Rio de Janeiro, Brazil, in June 1992. It was one of the largest United Nations Conferences, with more than 30,000 participants from 176 countries, including 103 heads of state or government and nearly 10,000 members of the media (Sand 1994). The major output was Agenda 21 (referring to the 21st century), which set out a global plan of action for sustainable development. In 294 pages, comprising 40 chapters covering 115 separate topics, Agenda 21 reflected the emergence of an international consensus on the issues affecting the long-term sustainability of human society, including domestic social and economic policies, international economic relations and cooperation on issues concerning the global commons – the oceans, the atmosphere and space.

When negotiations on the 'Earth Charter' began, it was clear that governments did not support Strong's vision for a brief inspirational document intended for the general public. After difficult negotiations, delegates adopted the Rio Declaration on Environment and Development, which consisted of 27 principles, including the right to development, common but differentiated responsibilities and the precautionary approach. The Earth Summit also adopted the Statement of Forest Principles instead of a forest treaty, aimed at creating norms and expectations for sustainable forest management. Two legally binding treaties, the United Nations Framework Convention on Climate Change and the Convention on Biological Diversity, which were negotiated independently of the UNCED process, were opened for signature at the Earth Summit.

The Earth Summit concluded that sustainable development was an attainable goal for all people, regardless of whether they were at the local, national, regional or international level. It also recognized that integrating and balancing economic, social and environmental concerns is vital for sustaining human life on the planet and that such an integrated approach is possible (United Nations 1997).

At the same time, Agenda 21 is non-binding action plan. While the United Nations system did push forward on a number of recommendations, including negotiation of the United Nations Convention to Combat Desertification, the Fish Stocks Agreement and chemicals treaties, many member states did not implement Agenda 21. The Rio Declaration, however, continues to be cited in United Nations resolutions, including the 2030 Agenda and the Sustainable Development Goals (SDGs).

References

Engfeldt, L.-G. (2009). *From Stockholm to Johannesburg and Beyond*. Stockholm: Swedish Ministry for Foreign Affairs.

Miller, M. A. L. (1995). *The Third World in Global Environmental Politics*. Boulder: Lynne Rienner.

Sand, P. (1994). UNCED and the Development of International Environmental Law. *Journal of Natural Resources and Environmental Law*, 8(2). https://uknowledge.uky.edu/jnrel/vol8/iss2/4

United Nations. (1997). *United Nations Conference on Environment and Development*, Rio de Janeiro, Brazil, 3–14 June 1992. https://www.un.org/en/conferences/environment/rio1992

United Nations General Assembly. (1989). *United Nations Conference on Environment and Development*, Resolution 44/228. https://documents.un.org/doc/resolution/gen/nr0/549/87/pdf/nr054987.pdf

United Nations Conference on Sustainable Development (2012)

Frank Biermann

The United Nations Conference on Sustainable Development was held in Rio de Janeiro, Brazil, in June 2012. It was one of many mega-summits on global environmental and sustainability governance that began with the 1972 United Nations Conference on the Human Environment held in Stockholm, Sweden. Because the 2012 conference followed the 1992 Earth Summit, it has often been called Rio+20. This conference attracted 44,000 participants, including 79 heads of state, and it had 500 side events in the programme. Brazilian president Dilma Rousseff called it the most participatory conference in history.

The conference produced several declarations and financial pledges from richer countries, such as the United States committing USD 20 million to a partnership with African nations and the European Union pledging EUR 400 million for sustainable energy projects. The official outcome was a non-binding document, *The Future We Want*, accepted by all member states (United Nations 2012). It covered various areas of sustainable development, including energy, health, climate change and gender equality, with two main themes: the 'green economy' and the 'institutional framework for sustainable development'. These were where hopes for reform were focused but also where the most disappointment occurred.

Despite the strong participation, the conference fell short of expectations. The final document was a watered-down compromise, focusing on the lowest common denominator that all countries could support. Some contentious issues, like trade and environment, were removed to ensure consensus, which helped avoid a breakdown in negotiations but resulted in a document that largely reaffirmed the status quo (Biermann 2013).

The conference's primary institutional debates centred on three areas: strengthening the environmental pillar of the United Nations system, integrating sustainable development into global governance and agreeing on sustainable development goals. One of the most contentious discussions was the creation of a world environment organization to replace or 'upgrade' the United Nations Environment Programme, which had often been criticized for its limited mandate and effectiveness (Biermann et al. 2012). The idea of a world environment organization received support from the European Union, the African Union and some developing nations, but faced strong resistance from the United States, Japan, Russia and Brazil. Ultimately, the final document merely called for strengthening the role of the United Nations Environment Programme without offering concrete reforms or additional financial resources.

Another key issue was the integration of economic, social and environmental policies. The Commission on Sustainable Development, created in 1992, was intended to oversee this integration but has largely failed to generate substantial effects. Proposals for a more authoritative body, such as a United Nations Sustainable Development Council (Biermann et al. 2012), were discussed but addressed in a weakened form: a 'high-level political forum' was called for as a new body to replace the Commission on Sustainable Development without a clear mandate and authority to drive comprehensive reform (see *High-level Political Forum on Sustainable Development*).

162 *Essential Concepts for Implementing the SDGs*

Lastly, a proposal for a United Nations High Commissioner for Future Generations, designed to protect the interests of future generations, was discussed but rejected. Many developing countries feared that it would disproportionately impact their current development needs. Instead, governments agreed to consider the need for intergenerational solidarity but without concrete institutional reforms.

A key outcome of Rio+20 was the agreement to develop new *Sustainable Development Goals* (SDGs). Initially proposed by Colombia and Guatemala, these goals were envisioned to continue and expand the trajectory of the Millennium Development Goals and cover environmental, economic and social dimensions in a balanced way. Negotiations following Rio+20 eventually delivered these global goals, agreed upon by the United Nations General Assembly in September 2015.

In conclusion, while Rio+20 made some progress, it failed to produce the major reforms many had hoped for. However, the extensive preparations and dialogues may have laid the groundwork for more substantial changes, including the launch of the SDGs three years later (Kanie and Biermann 2017). Yet the challenge remains to achieve meaningful reforms in global governance that truly integrate sustainability across economic, social and environmental dimensions.

References

Biermann, F. (2013). Curtain down and nothing settled: Global sustainability governance after the 'Rio+20' Earth Summit. *Environment and Planning C: Government and Policy*, 31(6), 1099–1114.

Biermann, F., K. Abbott, S. Andresen, K. Bäckstrand, S. Bernstein, M. M. Betsill, H. Bulkeley, B. Cashore, J. Clapp, C. Folke, A. Gupta, J. Gupta, P. M. Haas, A. Jordan, N. Kanie, T. Kluvánková-Oravská, L. Lebel, D. Liverman, J. Meadowcroft, R. B. Mitchell, P. Newell, S. Oberthür, L. Olsson, P. Pattberg, R. Sánchez-Rodríguez, H. Schroeder, A. Underdal, S. Camargo Vieira, C. Vogel, O. R. Young, A. Brock, and R. Zondervan (2012). Navigating the Anthropocene. Improving earth system governance. *Science* 335(6074), 1306–1307.

Kanie, N., and F. Biermann (Eds.). (2017). *Governing through Goals: Sustainable Development Goals as Governance Innovation*. MIT Press.

United Nations. (2012). The future we want. Resolution 66/288. https://www.un.org/en/development/desa/population/migration/generalassembly/docs/globalcompact/A_RES_66_288.pdf

United Nations Conference on the Human Environment (1972)

Simon Beaudoin

The United Nations Conference on the Human Environment (UNCHE), which took place in Stockholm in June 1972, is a landmark moment in the history of global environmental politics. It spurred interest in environmental questions across governments and civil society and launched a series of initiatives that shaped the future of environmental diplomacy and cooperation (Beaudoin 2023; Morin and Orsini 2015). Not only did the conference bring to light the need for stronger integration of environmental concerns in national policies, but it also explicitly recognized the environmental damage of human activities (United Nations 1973). UNCHE also fostered the involvement of a plethora of actors in international environmental negotiations. It encouraged the creation of national ministries for environmental matters and facilitated the adoption of national and international policies and laws on these questions. The conference also promoted research on environmental challenges and encouraged citizens, non-governmental organizations, scientists, industry actors and governmental agencies to address environmental issues.

UNCHE was the result of years of advocacy stemming from political, social and academic arenas, pushing for strengthened collaboration on environmental issues, both nationally and internationally. Many preparatory discussions and meetings preceded the conference. Some were specifically designed to inform the agenda of UNCHE and led to the establishment of working groups and committees that proved key in the outcome of the conference (Johnson 1972). Reports and perspective pieces were produced ahead of the conference by international organizations, civil society members and scientists (United Nations Economic and Social Council 1968). Two reports were particularly influential. First, the 1971 Founex report was key in shaping the content of the conference by tying environmental concerns with development priorities (Manulak 2022). Second, the 1972 *Limits to Growth* report to the Club of Rome helped emphasize the environmental impacts of economic growth (Meadows and Club of Rome 1972).

The main outcomes of the conference include a Declaration of Principles and an Action Plan for the environment. Whereas the former highlights principles and responsibilities around environmental issues, the latter defined three avenues to address such issues, namely (1) an environmental assessment plan based on monitoring, information exchange and research, (2) an environmental management frame aiming to increase collaboration and planning, and (3) support measures, including information-sharing, professional training and education (United Nations 1973). In addition, UNCHE led to the creation of the United Nations Environment Programme, which plays a central role in coordinating and supporting environmental policies (Ivanova 2021).

UNCHE proved key for shaping and fostering the emergence of global environmental governance, which rippled over the years to ultimately influence the adoption of the Sustainable Development Goals (SDGs). The conference, however, entrenched an approach that tries to address environmental issues while prioritizing economic development. The approach consolidated at UNCHE, closely following the suggestions of the Founex report, placed environmental issues in an inferior, at best equal, position to economic priorities. This approach still pervades global environmental governance, motivating multiple attempts to integrate environmental considerations into the development agenda. The SDGs are one of the most recent iterations of this approach. It is particularly problematic as economic development depends on a healthy environment, not the other way around. Indeed, the focus on economic development remains a priority to many decision-makers, to the detriment of environmental concerns, such as climate change, biodiversity loss, ecosystem degradation and marine pollution.

In sum, UNCHE spurred a series of institutional developments at national and international levels. It will remain a major milestone worth revisiting when studying global environmental politics. However, it is still uncertain if its legacy of agenda-setting in sustainability governance will help bring about the social transformations needed to address contemporary socio-ecological issues.

References

Beaudoin, S. (2023). Revue Historique de La Gouvernance Mondiale de l'environnement (1945–2022). *Canadian Journal of Political Science*, 56(4), 790–810. https://doi.org/10.1017/S0008423923000483

Ivanova, M. (2021). *The untold story of the world's leading environmental institution: UNEP at fifty*. The MIT Press.

Johnson, B. (1972). The United Nations' institutional response to Stockholm: A case study in the international politics of institutional change. *International Organization*, 26(2), 255–301.

Manulak, M. W. (2022). *Change in global environmental politics: Temporal focal points and the reform of international institutions*. Cambridge University Press.

Meadows, D. H., and Club of Rome (Eds.). (1972). *The limits to growth: A report for the Club of Rome's project on the predicament of mankind*. Universe Books.

Morin, J.-F., and Orsini, A. (2015). *Politique internationale de l'environnement*. Presses de Sciences Po; Cairn.info. https://www.cairn.info/politique-internationale-de-l-environnement--9782724617450.htm

United Nations. (1973). *Report of the United Nations Conference on the Human Environment*, Stockholm, 5–16 June 1972. A/CONF.48/14/Rev.1. https://documents.un.org/doc/undoc/gen/nl7/300/05/pdf/nl730005.pdf

United Nations Economic and Social Council. (1968). *Activities of United Nations Organizations and programmes relevant to the human environment: Report of the Secretary-General* (E/4553). Economic and Social Council.

United Nations Department of Economic and Social Affairs (UN DESA)

Guísela Almeida de Pereira and Estefanía Charvet

Created in 1945, the United Nations Department of Economic and Social Affairs (UN DESA) supports United Nations member states in bridging global commitments and national development policies. UN DESA provides governments and United Nations bodies with information, policy analysis and advice, capacity-building opportunities and intergovernmental support (UN DESA 2024a). Led by the Under-Secretary-General for Economic and Social Affairs, appointed by the United Nations Secretary-General, UN DESA is based in New York.

With the consolidation of the 2030 Agenda, UN DESA was gradually reformed since 2016 to better engage in the monitoring and review of the Sustainable Development Goals (SDGs). The Division for SDGs, one of the department's nine subunits, coordinated meetings that allowed civil society to contribute to the formulation of the SDGs. It was, however, criticized for not formally reporting back to these contributors on the impact of their inputs, hindering accountability (Sénit et al. 2017). The division acts as the secretariat for the SDGs and is key to the evaluation of the implementation, advocacy and outreach activities around the 2030 Agenda (UN DESA 2024a).

UN DESA generates, compiles and disseminates critical information about the progress of SDG implementation. The department's Sustainable Development Goals Report is the only official UN report that monitors global progress on the 2030 Agenda. UN DESA's reports provide analyses and policy advice, identifying challenges and areas with high potential for SDG acceleration (UN DESA 2024b). UN DESA also helps gather input for the Global Sustainable Development Report, another resource on SDGs, with a research-policy focus. However, a critical issue remains: most countries lack the capacity to effectively collect and report data on SDG indicators, leading to data gaps in these reports (Bexell 2024). UN DESA's thematic reports and policy briefs inform bodies like the United Nations Economic and Social Council and the High-level Political Forum on Sustainable Development – the latter is mandated to oversee the follow-up and review of the SDGs.

As the secretariat of the High-level Political Forum for Sustainable Development, UN DESA coordinates the preparation and organization of the forum's events. By convening preparatory events and sharing background notes, reports and other inputs to inform discussions, UN DESA aims to shape the High-level Political Forum's agenda and to mobilize member states, United Nations bodies, stakeholders and experts for the implementation of the SDGs (Beisheim and Fritzsche 2022). However, some stakeholders have claimed these materials are not well known nor effectively used (Beisheim and Fritzsche 2022). Through the years, UN DESA convened over 300 side events at the High-level Political Forum, contributing to enriching global dialogues. However, despite UN DESA's efforts, the High-level Political Forum has yet to meet its full potential in providing strategic, actionable and concrete guidance to drive the global sustainability agenda forward (see *High-level Political Forum on Sustainable Development*).

Through advisory services, training, direct assistance and longer-term projects and programmes, UN DESA contributes to capacity development of member states on resource mobilization, inclusive social policies, evidence-based policy and strengthening their institutions, data collection and more. For instance, UN DESA convenes several programmes, regional workshops and events to foster peer-learning and reflection to strengthen Voluntary National Reviews. It also publishes an annual handbook and database with key lessons on Voluntary National Reviews. Nevertheless, while experts have identified improvements in the quality of national reporting about the SDGs, ensuring that countries act on feedback remains a huge challenge (Beisheim and Fritzsche 2022). Recognizing the importance of monitoring SDGs and integrating them into local planning, UN DESA launched in 2022 a demand-driven programme to support local governments in preparing Voluntary Local Reviews.

In conclusion, UN DESA provides the United Nations system and member states with crucial analysis, advice and information to guide policy implementation related to the SDGs. Although its ability to foster concrete recommendations by the High-level Political Forum and address information gaps is constrained by limited data availability and depends on the political will of member states, UN DESA's reports, briefings and capacity-enhancing initiatives have had a pivotal role in shaping the 2030 Agenda. These efforts will continue to be instrumental in driving progress towards achieving the SDGs in the years ahead.

References

Beisheim, M., and Fritzsche, F. (2022). The UN high-level political forum on sustainable development: An orchestrator, more or less? *Global Policy*, 13. https://doi.org/10.1111/1758-5899.13112

Bexell, M. (2024) Indicator accountability or policy shrinking? Multistakeholder partnerships in reviews of the sustainable development goals. *Global Policy*, 15. https://doi.org/10.1111/1758-5899.13348

Sénit, C.-A., Biermann, F., and Kalfagianni, A. (2017). The representativeness of global deliberation: A critical assessment of civil society consultations for sustainable development. *Global Policy*, 8, 62–72. https://doi.org/10.1111/1758-5899.12371

UN DESA. (2024a). *What We Do*. https://www.un.org/en/desa/what-we-do

UN DESA. (2024b). *The 17 Goals*. https://sdgs.un.org/goals

United Nations Development Programme (UNDP)

Sajid Amin Javed and Michele Joie Prawiromaruto

The United Nations Development Programme (UNDP) was formed in 1965 by the United Nations General Assembly through a merger of two prior entities: the United Nations Expanded Programme of Technical Assistance, established in 1949 and the United Nations Special Fund, founded in 1958 (UNDP n.d.). UNDP reports to the United Nations General Assembly, which approves its budget and policies. UNDP's mandate focuses on eradicating poverty, fostering democratic governance, upholding the rule of law and creating inclusive institutions. Since the adoption of the Sustainable Development Goals (SDGs) in 2015, UNDP has also played a critical role in assisting countries in their pursuit of the SDGs.

UNDP's strategic plan for 2022–2025 encapsulates its mandate within the '3x6x3 framework', consisting of three core directions, six signature solutions and three enablers (UNDP 2021). The first component includes three directions for change: structural transformation, leaving no one behind and building resilience, all driven by the SDGs as the guiding target for country progress. The second part lists six priority areas – poverty and inequality, governance, resilience, environment, energy and gender equality – where UNDP focuses to maximize development impact. The final segment includes three enablers: strategic innovation, digitalization and development financing, which are the operational strategies UNDP uses to assist countries in reaching the SDGs.

The enablers particularly show how UNDP works to support SDG implementation. UNDP provides institutional and governance support to enhance government performance on SDG-related policy issues through strategic innovation. This is especially crucial for developing countries where system transformations are necessary (UNDP 2021). To support digitalization, UNDP aids in building inclusive and ethical digital societies by embedding digital tools across its programmes and fostering inclusive digital policies (UNDP 2021). Development financing relies on voluntary contributions from United Nations member states, multilateral organizations, the private sector and other sources, with unrestricted core resources and earmarked funds for specific initiatives (UNDP 2024). In 2023, UNDP received USD 5 billion in contributions, with 89% from other resources and 11% from core funds, directing USD 1.525 billion to country-specific programmes and USD 359.8 million to development activities, with low-income countries receiving the largest share (UNDP 2024).

Despite its frameworks and strategic plans, UNDP faces several challenges. These include data gaps, unmet financing needs and deeper criticisms of reinforcing the neoliberal world order. The lack of relevant SDG data has been challenging, particularly in the Global South, limiting the capacity development role of the UNDP. In multiple countries, the unavailability of micro-level data has obstructed effective decision- and policymaking, as the stakeholders are unable to measure, track and trace progress (UNDP 2023). Financially, UNDP has struggled to attract and direct private sector investments towards SDG-related initiatives, especially as funding needs have surged following the COVID-19 pandemic and the war in Ukraine. Core funding for UNDP fell by 4% from 2022 to 2023, marking a second consecutive annual decline (UNDP 2024). Additionally, UNDP's depoliticized approach to development, which often emphasizes technical solutions, has been critiqued for overlooking the complex social, economic and political power structures that perpetuate poverty and inequality (Telleria 2017).

In response, there are calls for UNDP to focus on SDG acceleration that is more inclusive and nuanced, strengthen partnerships, restructure public and private financing around the SDGs and adopt a more politically aware approach that acknowledges development as deeply interconnected with power dynamics (Southern Voice 2023; Telleria 2017).

References

Southern Voice. (2023). *Global state of the SDGs 2: Leveraging abilities to navigate inequalities (report 2023)*. https://southernvoice.org/wp-content/uploads/2023/10/SV_Reporte-Global-2023-Final-V1.0.pdf

Telleria, J. (2017). Power relations? What power relations? The de-politicising conceptualisation of development of the UNDP. *Third World Quarterly*, 38(9), 2143–2158. https://doi.org/10.1080/01436597.2017.1298437

UNDP. (2021). *Strategic Plan 2022–2025*. https://strategicplan.undp.org/

UNDP. (2023). *UNDP: Mitigating data challenges is imperative for human development and getting the SDGs back on track*. https://www.undp.org/news/undp-mitigating-data-challenges-imperative-human-development-and-getting-sdgs-back-track

UNDP. (2024). Funding compendium 2023. In *UNDP*. https://www.undp.org/sites/g/files/zskgke326/files/2024-10/funding_compendium_2023-web_version.pdf

UNDP. (n.d.). *About us*. https://www.undp.org/about-us

United Nations Environment Programme (UNEP)

Maria Ivanova

Established in 1972 following the first United Nations Conference on the Human Environment, the United Nations Environment Programme (UNEP) is the 'anchor institution' for the global environment, designed to catalyze environmental action and foster collaboration across the United Nations system (Ivanova 2021). Today, UNEP plays a critical role in advancing the environmental dimensions of the Sustainable Development Goals (SDGs), focusing on SDGs 6 (Clean Water and Sanitation), 12 (Responsible Consumption and Production), 13 (Climate Action), 14 (Life Below Water) and 15 (Life on Land).

UNEP's role in supporting the SDGs builds on its core functions of environmental assessment, policy development and fostering international cooperation. One of its most significant contributions to the SDGs has been through scientific assessments, which inform global environmental policy. As the custodian of 25 SDG indicators, UNEP provides essential data for tracking progress on environmental targets. Initiatives like the World Environment Situation Room, which integrates geo-referenced data, remote sensing and earth observation with environmental statistics, have provided policymakers, scientists, businesses and citizens with real-time access to critical information. This has enhanced the ability of countries to monitor progress on sustainable development (Ivanova and Skaredina 2024). UNEP has also developed various scorecards to illustrate how countries and regions are progressing in meeting the environmental targets of the SDGs.

168 *Essential Concepts for Implementing the SDGs*

UNEP has promoted an integrated approach that links environmental sustainability with economic and social development, which can be a particularly challenging task in areas where development priorities may conflict with environmental sustainability. UNEP's work on tackling plastic pollution demonstrates how it has integrated environmental goals into broader global development agendas. The *Clean Seas Campaign* and the *Global Partnership on Marine Litter* are two of UNEP's leading initiatives to achieve SDG 12 and address marine ecosystem degradation (UNEP n.d.). They highlight UNEP's capacity to foster international collaboration and promote a circular economy – an essential step in advancing sustainable production and reducing environmental harm.

UNEP's convening power is key to aligning global actions towards shared environmental objectives. The capacity to bring together governments, international organizations, civil society and the private sector is particularly important in addressing cross-cutting issues like climate change, biodiversity loss and pollution, which require coordinated action across multiple sectors. Despite its successes, UNEP's efforts have been hampered by limited financial resources and political constraints. The Environment Fund, once UNEP's major source of financial support, has diminished over time, leading to a reliance on earmarked contributions that limit the organization's flexibility and ability to innovate (Ivanova 2021). Nevertheless, UNEP remains a critical convener of international environmental efforts. Its ability to mobilize partnerships – whether through the Finance Initiative, the Partnership for Environment and Disaster Risk Reduction, or the Partnership for Clean Fuels and Vehicles – demonstrates its ability to foster collective action on pressing environmental problems.

Challenges remain, however. The *Sustainable Development Goals Report 2023* reveals that more than 50% of the SDG targets related to environmental sustainability are showing weak progress or are reversing (United Nations 2023). Armed conflicts and economic disruptions have exacerbated environmental degradation. UNEP's limited capacity and funding further complicate its efforts to lead on global environmental governance (Independent Group of Scientists 2023). Yet, UNEP must build on and continue to strengthen its role as the leading global environmental authority.

In conclusion, UNEP's contributions to the SDGs have been indispensable in maintaining environmental sustainability as a global priority. Through data collection, partnerships and policy advocacy, UNEP continues to guide the international community towards achieving the environmental goals of the 2030 Agenda. Its success will depend on its capacity to be the convener and the scientific authority that guides global decision-making.

References

Independent Group of Scientists. (2023). *Global Sustainable Development Report 2023: Times of crisis, times of change: Science for accelerating transformations to sustainable development.* United Nations. https://doi.org/10.18356/9789213585115

Ivanova, M. (2021). *The untold story of the world's leading environmental institution: UNEP at fifty.* MIT Press.

Ivanova, M., and Skaredina, O. (2024). Evolving role of the United Nations Environment Programme in Advancing Global Environmental Governance and Sustainable Development Goals [Manuscript submitted for publication]. In P. Chasek (Ed.), *The Elgar companion to global governance and the sustainable development goals* (forthcoming). Edward Elgar Publishing.

UNEP. (n.d.). *Clean seas campaign.* https://www.cleanseas.org/

United Nations. (2023). *The sustainable development goals report: Special edition.*

United Nations General Assembly (UNGA)

Leonie Grob

The United Nations General Assembly (UNGA) serves as the principal deliberative and policymaking organ of the United Nations, comprised of all 193 United Nations member states. Since the creation of the United Nations in 1945, the UNGA convenes annually over the course of several months in what are known as 'sessions' to take key decisions for the overall United Nations system, such as the appointment of the non-permanent members of the United Nations Security Council and to adopt resolutions on various issue-specific matters (United Nations 2024a). Following negotiations lasting for two-and-a-half years, the UNGA formally adopted the 2030 Agenda as resolution A/RES/70/1 'Transforming Our World' in September 2015 in New York. Although adopted by all member states, resolutions adopted in the UNGA, including the 2030 Agenda, are non-binding, and the institution does not have enforcement mechanisms to compel implementation. This remains a key critique of both the UNGA and the 2030 Agenda framework (Biermann et al. 2017).

In 2010, the UNGA tasked then-Secretary-General Ban Ki-moon with launching post-2015 discussions as the Millennium Development Goals neared their conclusion. By 2012, the Rio+20 outcome document, *The Future We Want*, laid the foundation for the creation of action-oriented, concise and universally applicable Sustainable Development Goals (SDGs). Subsequently, in January 2013, the SDG negotiations began, aiming to incorporate economic growth, environmental sustainability and social justice into a unified goal-based framework. These negotiations followed a two-track process: the Open Working Groups established and defined the set of 17 goals. In 2015, it transitioned into intergovernmental negotiations, or *post-2015 negotiations*, focused on SDG implementation and monitoring mechanisms. While the post-2015 negotiations followed traditional coalitions and speaking structures within the UNGA, the Open Working Groups allowed for innovative, dynamic and collaborative arrangements (so-called *troikas*) between member states (see *Negotiation of the Sustainable Development Goals*). Therefore, the Open Working Groups are deemed to have democratized the process (Chasek et al. 2016). Additionally, side events to the negotiations, United Nations-led consultations in 88 Global South countries, or the *My World Survey*, involving over 9 million citizens, broadened participation (Sénit 2020).

To ensure effective implementation, the UNGA mandated the High-level Political Forum on Sustainable Development as the primary body for monitoring progress on the 2030 Agenda. Its effectiveness, however, remains contested (Beisheim and Fritzsche 2022). To reinforce the global endeavour to achieve the 2030 Agenda, the UNGA has passed several resolutions, influenced by global advocacy efforts and has hosted numerous conferences to discuss SDG progress. At the Summit of the Future in 2024, world leaders reconfirmed their commitment to the 2030 Agenda. After extensive negotiations, the *Pact for the Future* was adopted to strengthen multilateralism and international cooperation, with dedicated chapters underscoring sustainable development and climate finance as key to global progress (United Nations 2024b). The outcome documents also include the *Global Digital Compact* that commits to bridging global technology and digitalization gaps and the *Declaration on Future Generations* to safeguard long-term

170 *Essential Concepts for Implementing the SDGs*

global interests and sustainability. Although regarded as an actionable framework that may pave the way for necessary reforms, the Pact for the Future remains a non-binding, voluntary agreement.

References

Beisheim, M., and Fritzsche, F. (2022). The UN high-level political forum on sustainable development: An orchestrator, more or less? *Global Policy, 13*, 683–693. https://doi.org/10.1111/1758-5899.13112

Biermann, F., Kanie, N. and Kim, R. E. (2017). Global governance by goal-setting: The novel approach of the UN Sustainable Development Goals. *Current Opinion in Environmental Sustainability, 26*, 26–31. https://doi.org/10.1016/j.cosust.2017.01.010

Chasek, P. S., Wagner, L. M., Leone, F., Lebada, A. M., and Risse, N. (2016). Getting to 2030: Negotiating the post-2015 sustainable development agenda. *Review of European, Comparative and International Environmental Law, 25*(1), 5–14. https://doi.org/10.1111/reel.12149

Sénit, C.-A. (2020). Leaving no one behind? The influence of civil society participation on the Sustainable Development Goals. *Environment and Planning C: Politics and Space, 38*(4), 693–712. https://doi.org/10.1177/2399654419884330

United Nations. (2024a). *General Assembly of the United Nations.* https://www.un.org/en/ga/

United Nations. (2024b). *Pact for the future.* A/RES/79/1. https://docs.un.org/en/A/RES/79/1

United Nations Secretary-General (UNSG)

Michele Joie Prawiromaruto

In accordance with Article 97 of the Charter of the United Nations, the United Nations Secretary-General is appointed by the United Nations General Assembly upon the recommendation of the Security Council (United Nations 1945). Formally, the United Nations Secretary-General serves as the 'chief administrative officer of the Organization' and is entrusted with the responsibility to perform functions that have been entrusted by the United Nations Security Council, United Nations General Assembly, Economic and Social Council and other United Nations organs (United Nations n.d.). However, since the inception of the United Nations in 1945, the role has significantly extended beyond its original administrative and diplomatic functions to encompass broader responsibilities, reflecting the evolving global political landscape and the increasing complexity of international affairs (Haack 2018), which is also reflected in the activities of the current United Nations Secretary-General.

António Guterres, the ninth Secretary-General of the United Nations, assumed office on 1 January 2017 and has shaped the role within the context of contemporary global challenges during his time in office (United Nations n.d.). As each United Nations Secretary-General defines their tenure by addressing the most pressing issues of their time, in his 2021 vision statement, Guterres identified 'making peace with nature and climate action' as one of his key imperatives for the subsequent five years (Guterres 2021, 7). This vision explicitly referenced the Sustainable Development Goals (SDGs) as a negotiated blueprint to achieve these objectives (Guterres 2021, 8). In alignment with this focus, the 2023 annual report highlighted sustainable development as one of the eight key priorities established by the United Nations General Assembly, emphasizing the need to scale up support to countries' needs and priorities to realize the 2030 Agenda (United Nations 2023).

To fulfil these priorities, the United Nations Secretary-General has undertaken several initiatives, including scaling up financing for development, engaging with marginalized groups, maintaining momentum on climate action, supporting gender equality and enhancing regional collaborative platforms. For instance, one notable effort has been the active promotion of reforms to multilateral development banks and addressing sovereign debt distress to scale up financing for sustainable development (United Nations and Secretary-General 2024, 8). Additionally, the appointment of resident coordinators, who serve as the highest-ranking representatives of the United Nations development system in various countries, has been a critical step in providing the necessary resources and coordination to support the SDGs (United Nations and Secretary-General 2024, 11).

Furthermore, the role of the Cabinet of the United Nations Secretary-General – consisting of the Executive Office and the Senior Management Group – has similarly evolved in response to the growing complexity and scope of the United Nations work (Ramcharan 1990). The Cabinet, particularly through the efforts of key members such as the Under-Secretary-General for Economic and Social Affairs, who heads the United Nations Department of Economic and Social Affairs, plays a vital role in advancing the United Nations development agenda. The United Nations Department of Economic and Social Affairs specifically focuses on promoting sustainable development, advancing economic growth and addressing social issues. Despite initiatives and concerted efforts by the United Nations Secretary-General and his cabinet, their efforts have not yet proven to be highly effective in compelling governments to prioritize the SDGs. Therefore, while these initiatives underscore the commitment of the United Nations Secretary-General towards advancing the SDGs, considerable work is still needed to achieve the intended transformative impact.

References

Guterres, A. (2021). *Restoring trust and inspiring hope: The next five years for the United Nations. In the United Nations.* United Nations. https://www.un.org/sg/sites/www.un.org.sg/files/atoms/files/guterres_VisionStatement_2021.pdf

Haack, K. (2018). The UN Secretary-General, role expansion and narratives of representation in the 2016 campaign. *The British Journal of Politics and International Relations*, 20(4), 898–912. https://doi.org/10.1177/1369148118784706

Ramcharan, B. (1990). The history, role and organization of the 'Cabinet' of the United Nations Secretary-General. *Nordic Journal of International Law*, 59(1), 103–116. https://doi.org/10.1163/157181090x00251

United Nations. (1945). *Charter of the United Nations, Article 97.* https://www.un.org/en/about-us/un-charter/chapter-15

United Nations. (2023). Determined report of the Secretary-General on the work of the organization. In *United Nations.* https://www.un.org/sites/un2.un.org/files/sg_annual_report_2023_en_0.pdf

United Nations. (n.d.). *The role of the Secretary-General.* https://www.un.org/sg/en/content/the-role-of-the-secretary-general

United Nations and Secretary-General. (2024). *Report of the Secretary-General on the work of the Organization.* United Nations Digital Library. https://digitallibrary.un.org/record/4058745?ln=en&v=pdf

United Nations Statistical Commission

Citra Kumala and Virgi Sari

Founded in 1946, the United Nations Statistical Commission (UNSC) is a leading body in the global statistics system, bringing together Chief Statisticians from 24 member states worldwide. It oversees the United Nations Statistics Division and operates under the United Nations Economic and Social Council. The Commission plays a central role in driving international statistical endeavours by setting global standards, developing concepts and methodologies and supporting their implementation both internationally and nationally (United Nations Statistics Division 2024). Its core mandate is to coordinate global statistical efforts, improve data practices and standardize development indicators to ensure quality and comparability across member states.

Aligned with its mission, the UNSC plays a crucial role in the implementation, monitoring and evaluation of the Sustainable Development Goals (SDGs). It coordinates the development and production of SDG indicators. The commission coordinated efforts to develop a standardized framework for monitoring the SDGs, leading to the adoption of the global indicator framework for the SDGs and targets of the 2030 Agenda in 2017 (United Nations General Assembly 2017). This framework provides a standard for SDG global monitoring, guides policy and ensures accountability of member states (International Institute for Sustainable Development 2022). The Commission reviews the framework annually to ensure effective SDGs monitoring. For example, these efforts identified redundancies within SDGs indicators, revising the current list from 244 to 232 indicators (United Nations 2018). UNSC also supports member states to develop their own indicators to improve SDG monitoring at national level.

Building on its mandates, the UNSC focuses on strengthening member states' statistical capacity to support effective SDGs monitoring and implementation. Shortfall in statistical capacity at the global and national levels hinders the ability to assess the impact of SDGs (Georgeson and Maslin 2018; Dang and Serajuddin 2020), with some countries lack the capacity to measure progress across all SDGs indicators (World Bank 2016). To address these challenges, the Commission established the High-level Group for Partnership, Coordination and Capacity-Building for Statistics in 2015 to support the 2030 Agenda for Sustainable Development. This group consists of member states with regional and international agencies as observers and aims to build a global alliance for sustainable development data (United Nations Statistics Division 2024). Among its key contributions is the adoption of the Cape Town Global Action Plan for Sustainable Development Data to address critical gaps in national statistics and coordination identified for the 2030 Agenda. Addressing these gaps is vital to enhancing the use of country-generated statistics in calculating global SDG indicators (United Nations Statistics Division 2024). The Commission also facilitates knowledge exchange among member countries, enabling them to share best practices and address country-specific data concerns, contributing to a more unified strategy for monitoring the SDGs.

Despite continuous efforts to support member countries, the UNSC's role in ensuring quality monitoring of SDG progress remains challenged by uneven statistical capacities and limited country-specific data infrastructure. For instance, when SDG indicators require disaggregation by specific sub-groups (for example, gender or disability), existing data or survey often lack the necessary design to support this. Member countries also often face difficulties in operationalizing SDG indicators due to a lack of consensus on the definition of key concepts or the unavailability of necessary data.

Overall, the UNSC plays an important role in addressing data gaps in SDGs monitoring, particularly the lack of scientifically robust indicator definitions applicable across a wide range of national contexts (Schmidt-Traub et al. 2017). Through a collaborative approach, the Commission ensures that SDG indicator definitions and data collection align with international standards. Its support in strengthening member states' statistical capacities also enables countries to produce reliable data that informs policy, enhances accountability and accurately measures SDG progress.

References

Dang, Hai-Anh H., and Serajuddin, U. (2020). Tracking the sustainable development goals: Emerging measurement challenges and further reflections. *World Development*, 127, 104609. https://doi.org/10.1016/j.worlddev.2019.05.024

Georgeson, L. T., and Maslin, M. (2018). Putting the United Nations sustainable development goals into practice: A review of implementation, monitoring and finance. *Geo: Geography and Environment*, 5(1), e00049. https://doi.org/10.1002/geo2.49

International Institute for Sustainable Development. (2022). *UN Statistical Commission discusses new and updated SDG indicators*. Retrieved October 31 2024, from https://sdg.iisd.org/news/un-statistical-commission-discusses-new-and-updated-sdg-indicators/

Schmidt-Traub, G., Kroll, C., Teksoz, K., Durand-Delacre, D., and Sachs, J. D. (2017). National baselines for the Sustainable Development Goals assessed in the SDG Index and Dashboards. *Nature Geoscience*, 10(8), 547–555. https://doi.org/10.1038/ngeo2985

United Nations. (2018). *Global Indicator Framework for the Sustainable Development Goals and Targets of the 2030 Agenda for Sustainable Development*. New York: United Nations.

United Nations General Assembly. (2017). *Resolution adopted by the General Assembly on 6 July 2017 (A/RES/71/313): Work of the Statistical Commission pertaining to the 2030 Agenda for Sustainable Development*. Retrieved October 31 2024, from https://documents.un.org/doc/undoc/gen/n17/207/63/pdf/n1720763.pdf

United Nations Statistics Division. (2024). *United Nations Statistical Commission*. United Nations. Retrieved October 31 2024. https://unstats.un.org/UNSDWebsite/statcom/

World Bank. (2016). *Review and update of the World Bank safeguard policies*.

Universality

Carole-Anne Sénit

Along with integration, universality is one of the key principles of the 2030 Agenda for Sustainable Development and the Sustainable Development Goals (SDGs). It is extensively emphasized in the text of the 2030 Agenda, with 29 occurrences throughout the outcome document of the negotiations. Universality defines the scope for the implementation of the 2030 Agenda: globally, the SDGs are applicable to all countries across the Global North and Global South. This represents a major difference and upgrade compared to the predecessors of the SDGs, namely the Millennium Development Goals, which were to be implemented only by developing countries.

Within countries, universality also relates to the applicability of the goals to all groups and communities, with the ambition of 'leaving no one behind'. This applicability to all

174 *Essential Concepts for Implementing the SDGs*

is reflected in the ambition of some of the goals, which seek to achieve universal access to specific rights, public goods and services, such as health coverage (SDG 3), sexual and reproductive health and reproductive rights (SDG 5), safe and affordable drinking water (SDG 6), affordable and reliable energy (SDG 7), the internet (SDG 9) and safe, inclusive and accessible green and public spaces (SDG 12). Given its universal character both in terms of applicability and ambition, the 2030 Agenda and the SDGs are considered a major breakthrough in the global negotiations related to sustainable development.

However, research has shown that SDG implementation fails to uphold the promise of universality that the 2030 Agenda set out for the world in 2015. First, on the basis of ambition, implementation efforts show that there is insufficient progress to achieve most of the goals and targets that seek to ensure universal access to public goods and services (United Nations 2023). Second, in terms of universal applicability within countries, while the adoption of the SDGs has raised the saliency and uptake of the principle of 'leaving no one behind' in policy discourses and agendas, their national implementation has failed to advance the inclusiveness of vulnerable groups and communities (Sénit et al. 2022). This suggests that the universal reach of the SDGs within countries is far from realizing. Third, in terms of universal applicability between countries, SDG implementation is conditional on national circumstances and priorities. Recognizing this condition was key to ensuring the success of negotiations and the adoption of a global agreement. However, this resulted in countries tending to prioritize the goals and targets which can be easily achieved, leaving behind more challenging goals (Forestier and Kim 2020). For developed countries, for instance, this widespread cherry-picking is reflected in an insufficient focus on goals such as reducing unsustainable consumption (SDG 12) or phasing out fossil fuels (linked to SDGs 7 and 13), to name a few (Biermann et al. 2023). Finally, research has questioned the universality of the SDGs, which may have promoted a dominant Western narrative in global media, academia and civil society (Sénit and Biermann 2021). Scholars indeed show that by suggesting a unified 'humankind' embarking collectively in SDG implementation, the universal framing of the SDGs masks unequal consumption and emissions patterns among and within countries, perpetuating colonial injustices in global sustainability governance (Adelman 2018).

Overcoming these challenges to accelerate SDG implementation requires reforming the global goals by including a degree of differentiation, with developed countries committing to more ambitious targets (Biermann et al. 2023). It also requires that all state and non-state actors engaged in SDG implementation commit to reaching the furthest group and the furthest goal behind first.

References

Adelman, S. (2018). The sustainable development goals, Anthropocentrism and Neoliberalism. In D. French, and L. Kotzé (Eds.), *Sustainable Development Goals: Law, Theory and Implementation* (pp. 15–40). Edward Elgar.

Biermann, F., Sun, Y., Banik, D., Beisheim, M., Bloomfield, M. J., Charles, A., Chasek, P., Hickmann, T., Pradhan, P., and Sénit, C. A. (2023). Four governance reforms to strengthen the SDGs. *Science*, 381(6663), 1159–1160. https://doi.org/10.1126/science.adj5434

Forestier, O., and Kim, R. E. (2020). Cherry-picking the Sustainable Development Goals: Goal prioritization by national governments and implications for global governance. *Sustainable Development*, 28, 1269–1278. https://doi.org/10.1002/sd.2082

Sénit, C. A., and Biermann, F. (2021). In whose name are you speaking? The marginalization of the poor in global civil society. *Global Policy*, 12(5), 581–591. https://doi.org/10.1111/1758-5899.12997

Sénit, C. A., Okereke, C., Alcázar, L., Banik, D., Lima, M. B., Biermann, F., Fambasayi, R., Hathie, I., Kronsell, A., Leonardsson, H., Niles, N., and Siegel, K. (2022). Inclusiveness. In F. Biermann, T. Hickmann, and C. A. Sénit (Eds.), *The Political Impact of the Sustainable Development Goals: Transforming Governance Through Global Goals?* (pp. 116–139). Cambridge University Press. https://doi.org/10.1017/9781009082945.006

United Nations. (2023). *The Sustainable Development Goals Report 2023: Special Edition. Towards a Rescue Plan for People and Planet.* United Nations. https://unstats.un.org/sdgs/report/2023/

UN Sustainable Development Solutions Network (SDSN)

Amber Webb

Established in 2012, the UN Sustainable Development Solutions Network (SDSN) was formed to merge global expertise with policy action to advance progress towards sustainable development. Working under the auspices of the United Nations Secretary-General, the organization operates on a mandate to mobilize the world's leading knowledge institutions and leverage their strengths to promote and accelerate practical solutions for sustainable development. Guided by the Sustainable Development Goals (SDGs) and the Paris Agreement, SDSN centres its mission on the question of how to organize strategies to achieve the 17 SDGs (Sachs et al. 2019).

SDSN was founded by Jeffrey Sachs, economist and former Special Adviser to the United Nations Secretary-General (2001–2018) and Ban Ki-moon, United Nations Secretary-General (2007–2016). SDSN strives to advance major programmes of work at the intersection of science and policy. SDSN's efforts in three key areas – data and research, education for sustainable development and the mobilization of scholars and practitioners across national and regional networks – aim to advance the movement to achieve the SDGs. Through these pillars of work, SDSN seeks to develop and enrich a global knowledge commons, which is continually informed by evolving expertise and utilized by policymakers, practitioners and educators around the world.

Data and research are at the foundation of SDSN programmes. Since 2016, the SDSN has published the Sustainable Development Report to track and rank the performance of all UN member states on the SDGs (for example, Sachs et al. 2024). The report combines data and analyses produced by international organizations, national statistical commissions, civil society organizations and research centres. Furthermore, it assesses national progress towards SDG indicators, as well as the important spill-over effects that create impacts beyond national boundaries. The Sustainable Development Report offers an overview of annual development progress with key recommendations applicable to a wide array of stakeholders. Other SDSN reports, produced in partnership with renowned experts and institutions, contribute to the network's expertise. Notable works include such publications as the World Happiness Report, Global Commons Stewardship Index and Net Zero Pathways reports.

Building on its expertise in data and research, SDSN has developed several educational projects to disseminate knowledge on sustainable development. SDSN's SDG Academy is a notable example, which offers education and training initiatives. With a philosophy

176 *Essential Concepts for Implementing the SDGs*

that achieving the SDGs will require an intergenerational approach, the SDG Academy offers a robust open-access library of content, accredited graduate degree programmes and multiple communities of practice to enable sector-specific progress. As early adopters of digital innovations such as massive open online courses, the SDG Academy has reached over one million learners with its content and programmes.

The mobilization of national and regional networks of experts has been a core component of SDSN's mission since its foundation. SDSN Networks provide expertise that feeds into its data and research programmes. Over 1,900 institutions currently comprise more than 50 national and regional networks coordinated by the SDSN secretariat. The networks focus on distinct projects and priorities in line with their local contexts and challenges, while also coming together in forums aimed at global cooperation. The networks operate to translate the latest expertise in sustainable development into action.

SDSN has operated since the SDGs were first introduced into development discourse following the United Nations Conference on Sustainable Development (Rio+20). At the time, the details of the SDGs were very much up for debate and discussion, but it was clear that only a global movement could achieve the scope of what was envisioned (Sachs 2012). The establishment of SDSN aimed to address this need, and the network's efforts are continually focused on refining methods of progress through complex solutions and emerging innovations. Through a comprehensive approach, grounded in data and mobilizing a wide range of stakeholders, SDSN establishes pathways to achieve the 2030 Agenda and the SDGs.

References

Sachs, J. D. (2012). From millennium development goals to sustainable development goals. *The Lancet*, 379(9832), 2206–2211.

Sachs, J. D., Lafortune, G., and Fuller, G. (2024). *The SDGs and the UN Summit of the Future. Sustainable Development Report 2024*. Dublin: Dublin University Press. https://doi.org/10.25546/108572

Sachs, J. D., Schmidt-Traub, G., Mazzucato, M., Messner, D., Nakicenovic, N., and Rockström, J. (2019). Six transformations to achieve the sustainable development goals. *Nature Sustainability*, 2(9), 805–814.

V

Voluntary Local Reviews

Kerstin Krellenberg, Florian Koch and Julia Wesely

Voluntary Local Reviews are the local equivalent of Voluntary National Reviews and represent a flexible and voluntary form of SDG reporting at the local level. However, unlike Voluntary National Reviews, Voluntary Local Reviews are not officially integrated into the United Nations governance architecture for the 2030 Agenda. At present, there is no formal definition or mandated structure of what exactly constitutes a Voluntary Local Review or what it must include.

Nonetheless, organizations such as the United Nations, the European Commission, city networks and think tanks have published various guidelines to develop Voluntary Local Reviews. As of September 2024, around 245 municipalities and regional governments worldwide had published a Voluntary Local Review (Global Observatory on Local Democracy and Decentralization 2024), including cities such as Bonn (Germany), Cochabamba (Bolivia), Melaka (Malaysia) and Mwanza (Tanzania).

These Voluntary Local Reviews differ in their scope, structure, content and methodology, as there is no institutional peer-review system at a supra-local level or binding guidelines for cities. For example, some Voluntary Local Reviews report on all SDGs, others focus only on the SDGs that are particularly relevant to their municipality, while some provide in-depth reviews for the SDGs that are on the agenda of the annual High-level Political Forum on Sustainable Development.

However, all Voluntary Local Reviews share a common orientation towards the SDGs and have an international scope. The former implies that Voluntary Local Reviews assume a comprehensive lens on social, ecological and economic sustainability aspects, while the latter means that Voluntary Local Reviews are attuned to local-global dynamics rather than seeing the locality as an isolated entity.

One motivation for municipalities to develop a Voluntary Local Review is the opportunity to fulfil the city's commitments to sustainable development and systematically operationalize the SDGs at the local level (Ortiz-Moya and Reggiani 2023). Voluntary Local Reviews also offer cities the opportunity to internationalize by presenting the reviews at events such as the High-level Political Forum on Sustainable Development, thus fostering international dialogues and peer-learning. This reflects the growing role of local and regional governments in implementing the SDGs and their increasing desire to

DOI: 10.4324/9781003519560-22

This chapter has been made available under a CC-BY-NC-ND license.

178 *Essential Concepts for Implementing the SDGs*

become international actors. Voluntary Local Reviews are seen as drivers of SDG localization and can promote innovation in data and sustainability measurement, enhance transparency, serve strategic purposes and help overcome institutional fragmentation (Narang Suri et al. 2021). However, disparities in municipalities' capacities to produce Voluntary Local Reviews exist, even within the same national context (Croese and Parnell 2022).

Three features are central to the Voluntary Local Review process. The first one relates to the selection of indicators and data. Since there is no binding format for Voluntary Local Reviews, each local government can decide which SDGs, indicators and data to include. While this flexibility risks 'cherry-picking' SDGs (Ortiz-Moya and Kataoka 2024), it also allows municipalities to prioritize local needs and define relevant SDG indicators, while seeking appropriate data sources to monitor progress (Koch et al. 2023). Second, the lack of a common and predefined methodology for creating a Voluntary Local Review allows each locality to design its own process. Involving various actors from public administration and embedding sustainable development more holistically within municipal actors, as well as engaging with civil society, can strengthen local-level dialogue, even though it makes the process more complex. The third feature relates to the long-term perspective. Many municipalities have published not just one, but several Voluntary Local Reviews over the years, illustrating that a Voluntary Local Review is not a static document but part of ongoing sustainability management. Furthermore, the elaborated Voluntary Local Review indicators and data can be used continuously in online SDG monitoring platforms, such as Open SDG, to provide up-to-date information on local SDG implementation (Ortiz-Moya and Reggiani 2023).

Ultimately, the publication of a Voluntary Local Review is not an end in itself but a tool for fostering more sustainable local development. As such, the latest United Nations Habitat handbook outlines approaches for creating action-oriented Voluntary Local Reviews (United Nations Habitat 2024).

References

Croese, S., and Parnell, S. (Eds.). (2022). *Sustainable Development Goals Series. Localizing the SDGs in African Cities* (1st ed.). Springer International Publishing; Imprint Springer. https://doi.org/10.1007/978-3-030-95979-1

Global Observatory on Local Democracy and Decentralization. (2024). *Localizing the SDGs: A boost to monitoring and reporting.* https://www.gold.uclg.org/report/localizing-sdgs-boost-monitoring-reporting

Koch, F., Beyer, S., and Chen, C.-Y. (2023). Monitoring the Sustainable Development Goals in cities: Potentials and pitfalls of using smart city data. *GAIA – Ecological Perspectives for Science and Society*, 32(1), 47–53. https://doi.org/10.14512/gaia.32.S1.8

Narang Suri, S., Miraglia, M., and Ferrannini, A. (2021). Voluntary local reviews as drivers for SDG localization and sustainable human development. *Journal of Human Development and Capabilities*, 22(4), 725–736. https://doi.org/10.1080/19452829.2021.1986689

Ortiz-Moya, F., and Kataoka, Y. (2024). *State of the Voluntary Local Reviews 2024: Strengthening the local implementation of the 2030 Agenda.* https://doi.org/10.57405/iges-13753

Ortiz-Moya, F., and Reggiani, M. (2023). Contributions of the voluntary local review process to policy integration: Evidence from frontrunner cities. *Npj Urban Sustainability*, 3(1), 22. https://doi.org/10.1038/s42949-023-00101-4

United Nations Habitat. (2024). *Action-Oriented Voluntary Local Reviews.* United Nations Human Settlements Programme (UN-Habitat) and United Cities and Local Governments (UCLG).

Voluntary National Reviews

Mark Elder

Voluntary National Reviews are a core element of the follow-up and review process for the Sustainable Development Goals (SDGs), as mandated by the 2030 Agenda for Sustainable Development (para. 79). These reports are the basis for the annual review in the High-level Political Forum on Sustainable Development. Every year, about 30 to 40 countries submit reports and make short presentations to facilitate mutual learning. The contents are summarized in an annual synthesis report prepared by the United Nations Department of Economic and Social Affairs. As of 2023, 189 member states had submitted at least one Voluntary National Review and many countries submitted two or more. The United States and Myanmar were among the few countries which had not participated in this reporting exercise (United Nations Department of Economic and Social Affairs 2023).

The Voluntary National Reviews have no fixed format, although various guidelines and suggestions on preparing and organizing the reports have been recommended by the United Nations Secretary-General and others (Committee on Development Policy 2023). In practice, Voluntary National Reviews' formats and scope of coverage have varied widely, for example, their length and which SDGs and cross-cutting topics were covered (De Oliveira 2022; Elder and Newman 2023). The preparation process of a Voluntary National Review varies among countries, including stakeholder engagement procedures; multi-stakeholder participation is recommended and 83% of Voluntary National Reviews in 2021 included information on this (De Oliveira 2022).

Generally, countries report their progress on the SDGs and related topics. Common topics include efforts and challenges in implementing the SDGs, institutional processes for implementing the SDGs, implementation policies, integrated approaches to implementation, stakeholder engagement, the process for developing the review, involvement in international cooperation and themes such as 'leave no one behind' (De Oliveira 2022).

At the subnational level, many local governments have developed Voluntary Local Reviews (Ortiz-Moya and Reggiani 2023). These are generally not well-coordinated with national Voluntary National Reviews. While some have been presented at side events of the High-level Political Forum, national governments do not officially allow presentations of a Voluntary Local Review at the High-level Political Forum itself or recognize the contribution of Voluntary Local Reviews to the process.

The effectiveness of Voluntary National Reviews in promoting SDG implementation is mixed. The Committee on Development Policy, a subsidiary body of the United Nations Economic and Social Council advising it on SDG implementation, reviewed the Voluntary National Reviews from 2017–2021. It concluded that, on the one hand, Voluntary National Reviews are 'a valuable tool of review and follow-up [and] have contributed to the integration of the SDGs in national development plans, the broad embrace of the 2030 Agenda commitments and mobilized many initiatives' (Committee on Development Policy 2023, 9). On the other hand, despite steady improvement, currently the 'Voluntary National Reviews do not provide adequate substantive content [...] for mutual learning

180 *Essential Concepts for Implementing the SDGs*

and to foster transformative change' (Committee on Development Policy 2023, 9). Also, the Voluntary National Reviews

> are largely descriptive and lack analytical depth and policy focus, [...] do not match the ambition of the agenda or its integrated concept [and] are systematically under-reporting on the most transformative aspects of the agenda, including the means of implementation, inequality, environmental sustainability and structural constraints.
> (Committee on Development Policy 2023, 9)

The SDGs' sheer complexity could be one reason for this: with 169 targets and 232 indicators, many countries, especially from developing regions, may lack sufficient statistical and analytical capacity to comprehensively report their progress in implementing the SDGs. Fundamentally, Voluntary National Reviews are voluntary, limiting their ability to encourage more ambitious SDG implementation.

Recommended improvements to the process of Voluntary National Reviews include a clear focus on learning lessons; more attention to integrated approaches, human rights and respect for planetary limits; identification of key challenges; and more focus on transformation and means of implementation (Committee on Development Policy 2023). To make Voluntary National Reviews more effective, the scientific community and non-governmental organizations should also expand their monitoring. Currently, there is insufficient review of policies and implementation efforts even though Voluntary National Reviews discuss them extensively (Elder 2020; Elder and Newman 2023). Future assessments should examine policies and budgets more intensively, including assessing their effectiveness.

References

Committee on Development Policy. (2023). Implementing the SDGs: Strengthening the Voluntary National Reviews (VNRs). *CDP Background Paper No. 56, ST/ESA/2023/CDP/56.* https://www.un.org/development/desa/dpad/wp-content/uploads/sites/45/CDP-bp-2023-56.pdf

De Oliveira, A. (2022). *Progressing National SDGs Implementation: An Independent Assessment of the Voluntary National Review Reports Submitted to the United Nations High-level Political Forum on Sustainable Development in 2021.* Cooperation Canada.

Elder, M. (2020). *Assessment of ASEAN Countries' Concrete SDG Implementation Efforts: Policies and Budgets Reported in Their 2016–2020 Voluntary National Reviews (VNRs).* Institute for Global Environmental Strategies. https://www.iges.or.jp/en/pub/asean-sdg-vnrs/en

Elder, M., and Newman, E. (2023). Monitoring G20 countries' SDG implementation policies and budgets reported in their voluntary national reviews (VNRs). *Sustainability, 15*(22), Article 22. https://doi.org/10.3390/su152215733

Ortiz-Moya, F., and Reggiani, M. (2023). Contributions of the voluntary local review process to policy integration: Evidence from frontrunner cities. *NPJ Urban Sustainability, 3*(1), Article 1. https://doi.org/10.1038/s42949-023-00101-4

United Nations Department of Economic and Social Affairs. (2023). *2023 Voluntary National Reviews Synthesis Report.* United Nations Department of Economic and Social Affairs. https://hlpf.un.org/sites/default/files/2023-12/2023_VNR_Synthesis_Report.pdf

Vulnerability

Sujoy Subroto

The notion of 'vulnerability' has garnered widespread attention in global policy discussions, and reducing vulnerability has become central to achieving the 17 Sustainable Development Goals (SDGs), particularly in areas such as climate action (SDG 13), no poverty (SDG 1), reduced inequalities (SDG 10), good health and well-being (SDG 3), zero hunger (SDG 2) and clean water and sanitation (SDG 6), sustainable cities and communities (SDG 11) and global disaster risk reduction.

The concept of vulnerability is still evolving, and scholars draw on different epistemological traditions to approach it theoretically and empirically (Hufschmidt 2011). Generally, vulnerability is understood as a function of exposure, sensitivity and adaptive capacity (Engle 2011). The Sendai Framework for Disaster Risk Reduction 2015–2030, which defines vulnerability as '[t]he conditions determined by physical, social, economic and environmental factors or processes, which increase the susceptibility of a community to the impact of hazards' (United Nations Office for Disaster Risk Reduction n.d.).

Some scholars argue that vulnerability should be analysed as a coupled social-ecological system (Berrouet et al. 2018; Turner et al. 2003). Here, the biophysical dimension is characterized by the frequency and severity of specific hazards, their outcomes and exposure, while outcomes and impacts are shaped by social preconditions, especially social structures, power relations and other intersecting factors (such as caste, gender, race, religion or ethnicity) that determine access and entitlements and shape adaptive capacity (Clay 2022). Different human vulnerability to environmental hazards and climate change thus results from a combination of spatial, social, economic, historical and political factors (Barnett 2020).

In a similar vein, critical scholars warn that this dominant discursive framing of vulnerability should not be taken for granted and should rather be approached with caution. Considering the disjuncture between policy ideals and practice, Barnett (2020), for example, argued that vulnerability is fundamentally a matter of political economy. Powerful actors and institutions that create vulnerability often devise market-based solutions or create politicized agendas under the regime of climate adaptation (Paprocki 2018) to inject their own interest and maintain their legitimacy and authority over decision-making at the expense of marginalized actors, who are most at risk. This can ignore their agency, amplify inequalities, perpetuate systemic exclusion and obscure the root cause and drivers that create vulnerability in the first place.

In sum, vulnerability can be understood as a specific condition or perceived experience that arises from the interplay of biophysical and social, political and economic factors and actors across scales and levels. This dynamic process mediates exposure and sensitivity and determines adaptive capacity, leading to differentiated outcomes, for example, in the event of disaster or hazard.

Given the interconnected nature of the SDGs, evolving dynamics of risks and the challenges of implementing actions, it is imperative to identify the overarching issues and unique vulnerability contexts of countries, communities, sectors and ecosystems. This approach can help prevent crises, enhance risk response, build adaptive capacity to cope with shocks and strengthen overall resilience. Addressing the multifaceted dimensions,

182 *Essential Concepts for Implementing the SDGs*

differentiated exposure and disproportionate outcomes of vulnerability requires amplifying the voices and agencies of affected communities and devising solutions that are based on their traditional knowledge, lived experiences and practices, which are all crucial for ensuring just social and climate transitions and achieving the SDGs.

References

Barnett, J. (2020). Global environmental change II: Political economies of vulnerability to climate change. *Progress in Human Geography*, *44*(6), 1172–1184.

Berrouet, L. M., Machado, J., and Villegas-Palacio, C. (2018). Vulnerability of socio – ecological systems: A conceptual framework. *Ecological Indicators*, *84*, 632–647.

Clay, N. (2022). Vulnerability and resilience. In F. Nunan, C. Barnes, and S. Krishnamurthy (Eds.) *The Routledge Handbook on Livelihoods in the Global South* (pp. 44–55). Routledge.

Engle, N. L. (2011). Adaptive capacity and its assessment. *Global Environmental Change*, *21*(2), 647–656. https://doi.org/10.1016/j.gloenvcha.2011.01.019

Hufschmidt, G. (2011). A comparative analysis of several vulnerability concepts. *Natural Hazards*, *58*, 621–643. https://doi.org/10.1007/s11069-011-9823-7

Paprocki, K. (2018). Threatening dystopias: development and adaptation regimes in Bangladesh. *Annals of the American Association of Geographers*, *108*(4), 955–973. https://doi.org/10.1080/24694452.2017.1406330

Turner, B. L., Kasperson, R. E., Matson, P. A., McCarthy, J. J., Corell, R. W., Christensen, L., Eckley, N., Kasperson, J. X., Luers, A., Martello, M. L., Polsky, C., Pulsipher, A., and Schiller, A. (2003). A framework for vulnerability analysis in sustainability science. *Proceedings of the National Academy of Sciences*, *100*(14), 8074–8079. https://doi.org/10.1073/pnas.1231335100

United Nations Office for Disaster Risk Reduction. (n.d.). *Definition: Vulnerability*. https://www.undrr.org/terminology/vulnerability

World Bank

Susan Park

The World Bank is one of the largest multilateral development finance lenders (Park 2022). It is also a knowledge broker to developing states for economic growth and meeting the Sustainable Development Goals (SDGs). More recently, the World Bank has burnished its green credentials through its activities in climate finance, including hosting the new Loss and Damage Fund under the Paris Agreement. The International Bank for Reconstruction and Development (known as the World Bank) lends approximately USD 20 billion per annum for development through its loans, technical assistance and guarantees to developing countries at or near market rates for projects and programmes. It works with other parts of the World Bank Group that provide low-interest grants and loans, private sector investment and political risk. Perennial debates have been as to whether a bank, that requires loan repayments, can be a development institution.

The World Bank is relatively autonomous from its member states, who sit on its Executive Board and who make general policy decisions for the World Bank and the International Monetary Fund at the annual and spring meetings. Bank management can shape the lending activity of its borrowers, which is determined by internal policy debates (Cormier and Manger 2021). Nevertheless, there are correlations between its largest contributor, the United States and loans to United States allies (Vreeland and Dreher 2014).

The World Bank has been at the forefront of debates over how to green development. It began in the 1970s with guidelines for environmental impact assessments and piecemeal policies for mitigating the environmental and social impact of development. By the early 1980s it would be embroiled in transnational activist campaigns documenting how its loans were contributing to deforestation, biodiversity loss and pushing people off their lands. From the 1980s to the 2000s, environmentalists would continue to push the World Bank to have environmental and social 'safeguard' policies for their projects, backed by increased transparency and accountability mechanisms.

The Inspection Panel provides project-affected people the right to recourse should they be harmed because of the World Bank not following its policies pertaining to deforestation, biodiversity and involuntary resettlement, for example. Imbodied in its environmental and social framework, there are now comprehensive policies to ensure sustainable development, including Free Prior and Informed Consent. Nevertheless, the World Bank has been criticized

DOI: 10.4324/9781003519560-23
This chapter has been made available under a CC-BY-NC-ND license.

184 *Essential Concepts for Implementing the SDGs*

for its biodiversity public-private partnerships that struggle to meet their goals (Kramarz 2020). Campaigns by environmentalists and member states have also sought to ensure the World Bank does not lend for new fossil fuel projects, which have long been undertaken on the basis that energy is fundamental to poverty alleviation and economic growth.

The World Bank aims to achieve the SDGs mainly through its aspirations to end extreme poverty and boost shared prosperity. It seeks to do so through the provision of finance, data and helping borrowers implement the SDGs through country level uptake. In terms of SDG 13 on climate action, the World Bank only agreed to align its lending to the Paris Agreement in 2019 (Volcovici et al. 2021). As a financier, the World Bank is both a creator and governor of climate finance markets. By 2010, it was managing one-sixth of the carbon finance market (Alberola and Stephen 2010). Scholars have noted that climate finance tends to follow the same power dynamics as development finance in terms of being donor-driven, which complicates the World Bank's country-owned policy approach.

There is also scepticism as to whether carbon markets contribute to reducing emissions. There are mixed views on the World Bank becoming the interim host and secretariat for the impending UNFCCC Loss and Damage Fund. It will be a financial intermediary fund with an independent board housed in the World Bank. Yet, the World Bank was the interim secretariat for the Global Environment Facility and is now one of its executing agencies. Both the Loss and Damage Fund and the Global Environment Facility provide more financing for communities to tackle climate change, while the World Bank provides a range of support for implementing the SDGs.

References

Alberola, E. and Stephen, N. (2010). *Carbon Funds in 2010: Investment in Kyoto Credits and Emissions Reductions, Climate Report 23*. Paris: CDC Climate Research.
Cormier, B. and Manger, M. (2021). Power, Ideas and World Bank Conditionality. *Review of International Organization*. https://doi.org/10.1007/s11558-021-09427-z
Kramarz, T. (2020). *Forgotten Values: The World Bank and Environmental Partnerships*. Cambridge: MIT Press.
Park, S. (2022). *The Good Hegemon: United States Power, Accountability as Justice and the Multilateral Development Banks*. Oxford: Oxford University Press.
Volcovici, V., A. Shalal and Abnett, K. (2021, April 1). Exclusive: World Bank revises climate policy but stops short of halting fossil fuel funding. *Reuters*. https://www.reuters.com/article/climate-change-worldbank-exclusive-int-idUSKBN2BN3HE
Vreeland, J. and Dreher, A. (2014). *The Political Economy of the United Nations Security Council*. Cambridge: Cambridge University Press.

World Commission on Environment and Development (WCED)

Valentina Brogna

Sustainable development is known as 'development that meets the needs of the present without compromising the ability of future generations to meet their own needs'. We owe such a definition to the report Our Common Future, published by the World Commission on Environment and Development (WCED) in 1987. The WCED, also called 'Brundtland Commission' from the name of its chair Gro Harlem Brundtland (at the time Norwegian Prime Minister) (Brundtland 2005), was a catalyst for sustainable development to be subsequently transposed into policy commitments, agendas and objectives (Borowy 2014).

This special commission was established in December 1983 by the United Nations General Assembly, owing to disappointing results of the United Nations Environment Programme (UNEP). Indeed, UNEP had assessed the impact of its environmental policy activities and found that, particularly, state implementation had lagged (Nohl 2024). Therefore, the purpose of the WCED would be 'to propose long-term environmental strategies for achieving sustainable development by the year 2000 and beyond' (United Nations General Assembly 1983) as foundation for UNEP environmental perspective for 2000 (Reiser 2023).

The creation of the WCED saw opposing interests. The United States and the United Kingdom feared that the WCED would propose too strict recommendations against economic growth and the Soviet Union tried to stop its creation (Manulak 2022). UNEP also tried to control the process. At the same time, North-South politics played out in disagreements over the geographical composition, the role of the secretariat and the respective responsibilities of its chair and vice-chair (Manulak 2022). In the end, 23 independent commissioners composed the WCED – 12 from the Global South, 7 from the Global North and 4 from Communist states (Borowy 2021) – with a strong secretariat. Brundtland got political control, with support from financing countries (Manulak 2022).

The WCED aimed at a substantial agenda for change: an environmental agenda alternative to the standard one that focuses on pollution and resource management. Such an agenda would switch the focus from environment to development, allowing for a nexus between the two. The outcome report contained many social issues in a tripartite understanding of sustainable development (economic, social and environmental dimensions) (Borowy 2021). It balanced three main views about environment *and* development: systemic (natural resources are limited), liberal (economic growth can combat poverty and pollution) and structural (developing countries' economic growth can support environmental protection). In so doing, it showed a pro-growth bias (Borowy 2021). The WCED supported an increase of aid to developing countries, but it led to fears of 'green conditionalities' and adjustment of trade preferences in their favour (Manulak 2022, 146–150). It also foresaw sustainable development mainstreaming into the overall United Nations system.

From 1984 to 1987, the WCED held 9 meetings and 8 site visits in different countries, commissioned 75 studies and received hundreds of reports (Manulak 2022; Nohl 2024). Its working process was long – comprising discussion of studies and controversial topics during meetings, with experts and public hearings, text revision, further discussions – but it led to a dense report, 'Our Common Future'. The diversity of commissioners' worldviews (Borowy 2021) meant strong contrasts in negotiations around several considerations: balancing environment and economy; North and South interests; intergenerational justice; scientific evidence and political feasibility (Borowy 2014). Yet it also gave an example of global deliberation on potentially irreducible sustainability issues. The legacy of the Brundtland Report is perceivable today in global governance through the concept of sustainable development.

Despite significant challenges since its inception, which materialized a North-South divide around environmental protection and developmental concerns, the WCED had a foundational role in bridging the two concepts. It problematized their link and defined sustainable development, which today has its full place in global governance with the 2030 Agenda for Sustainable Development.

References

Borowy, I. (2014). *Defining Sustainable Development for Our Common Future: A History of the World's Commission on Environment and Development (Brundtland Commission).* Routledge.

Borowy, I. (2021). The social dimension of sustainable development at the UN: from Brundtland to the SDGs. In Ch. Deeming (ed.), *The Struggle for Social Sustainability. Moral Conflicts in Global Social Policy* (pp. 89–108). Bristol University Press.

Brundtland, G. H. (2005). *Madam Prime Minister: A Life in Power and Politics.* Farrar, Straus and Giroux.

Manulak, M. W. (2022). *Change in Global Environmental Politics: Temporal Focal Points and the Reform of International Institutions.* Cambridge University Press.

Nohl, A. M. (2024). Brundtland commission. In N. Wallenhorst and Ch. Wulf (eds.), *Handbook of the Anthropocene* (pp. 1593–1597). Springer.

Reiser, D. (2023). Brundtland report. In S. O. Idowu, R. Schmidpeter, N. Capaldi, L. Zu, M. Del Baldo and R. Abreu (eds.), *Encyclopedia of Sustainable Management* (pp. 378–381). Springer.

United Nations General Assembly. (1983). Process of preparation of the Environmental Perspective to the year 2000 and beyond. Res. 38/161. https://documents.un.org/doc/resolution/gen/nr0/445/53/pdf/nr044553.pdf

World Health Organization (WHO)

Cornelia Ulbert

The World Health Organization (WHO) was founded in 1948 as a specialized agency of the United Nations to achieve the 'enjoyment of the highest attainable standard of health' (WHO 2020, 1) worldwide. For about 50 years since its establishment, economic development was seen as a prerequisite for a better state of health (Dagron and Hasselgård-Rowe 2023). Only from the early 2000s onwards, WHO explicitly acknowledged that good health was a means to further economic development.

Health is one of the central goals of the 2030 Agenda, with Sustainable Development Goal (SDG) 3 focusing on ensuring healthy lives and promoting well-being for all at all ages. Thematically and normatively, achieving universal health coverage is the most prominent SDG 3 target (3.8), ensuring social justice and uniting health policies under a single framework. With its focus on the underlying determinants of health shaped by political, economic and social factors, SDG 3 is a good example of the complex interlinkages between the SDGs. This is also reflected by the concept of global health governance, which acknowledges that in a globalized world, coping with health risks and the capacity to influence health determinants, do not rest with states and international organizations alone, but depend on the collective efforts of governments, international organizations, civil society and private actors like businesses and philanthropic foundations (Frenk and Moon 2013).

Therefore, WHO has broadened its reach beyond its traditional constituency of member states. To ease civil society's concerns about the undue influence of corporate actors and private foundations on WHO's work, the organization adopted a 'Framework of Engagement with Non-State Actors' in 2016. Since then, it has continuously developed its regulatory framework for engaging with the various types of non-state actors seeking to influence and work with WHO (WHO 2018).

Already for implementing the Millennium Development Goals, WHO used the instrument of partnerships, which has developed into a norm for governing the implementation of the SDGs (Sondermann and Ulbert 2021). Over more than two decades, WHO has promoted and hosted many formal global health partnerships and has been managing many networks. One partnership explicitly dedicated to furthering the attainment of SDG 3 is the Global Action Plan for Healthy Lives and Well-Being for All, a collaborative platform of 13 agencies working in health, development and humanitarian response led by WHO. The Global Action Plan for Healthy Lives and Well-Being for All resumed its work in 2019 to accelerate country progress on the health-related SDG targets. However, due to the negative impact of the COVID-19 pandemic, after five years, the overall record of the partnership is still somewhat mixed (WHO 2023).

Consequently, in reaction to the outbreak of the COVID-19 pandemic, WHO started to promote the concept of 'One Health'. It is defined as an 'integrated, unifying approach that aims to sustainably balance and optimize the health of people, animals and ecosystems' (One Health High-Level Expert Panel 2023, 4). In 2021, WHO, the Food and Agriculture Organization, the World Organization for Animal Health and the United Nations Environment Programme (calling themselves 'Quadripartite') founded the One Health Initiative. This initiative is supported by a 'One Health High-level Expert Panel' and is based on a rapidly extending One Health community of researchers and practitioners. In contrast to the Global Action Plan for Healthy Lives and Well-Being for All, the One Health Initiative explicitly addresses 9 out of the 17 SDGs.

The One Health Initiative is the culmination point of the WHO's learning experience in implementing the SDGs. It reflects core insights of research on the SDGs: transforming Global Health Governance must be based on a coherent concept, respecting planetary integrity, acknowledging interlinkages and including different communities to be able to implement the goals on multiple levels. It remains to be seen if concepts like 'One Health' will contribute to breaking up the silos of thematically isolated problem-solving approaches. However, since a major part of WHO's funding depends on voluntary contributions, like with many international organizations, its impact on achieving the SDGs is considerably restrained by a lack of financial means, which has been aggravated by the withdrawal of the United States by the Trump Administration announced in January 2025.

References

Dagron, S., and Hasselgård-Rowe, J. (2023). Sustainable Development: The 2030 Agenda and Its Implications for Global Health Law. In L. O. Gostin, and B. M. Meier (Eds.), *Global Health Law and Policy: Ensuring Justice for a Healthier World* (pp. 259–283). Oxford University Press. https://doi.org/10.1093/law/9780197687710.003.0011

Frenk, J., and Moon, S. (2013). Governance Challenges in Global Health [Review]. *New England Journal of Medicine, 368*(10), 936–942. https://doi.org/10.1056/NEJMra1109339

One Health High-Level Expert Panel. (2023). *The One Health Definition and Principles Developed by OHHLEP*. World Health Organization. https://www.who.int/publications/m/item/one-health-definitions-and-principles

Sondermann, E., and Ulbert, C. (2021). Transformation through 'Meaningful' Partnership? SDG 17 as Metagovernance Norm and Its Global Health Implementation. *Politics and Governance, 9*(1), 152–163. https://doi.org/10.17645/pag.v9i1.3656

188 *Essential Concepts for Implementing the SDGs*

WHO. (2018). *Handbook for Non-State Actors on Engagement with the World Health Organization.* World Health Organization. https://www.who.int/publications/i/item/9789240089303

WHO. (2020). *Basic Documents, Forty-ninth Edition.* World Health Organization. https://apps.who.int/gb/bd/pdf_files/BD_49th-en.pdf

WHO. (2023). *What Worked? What Didn't? What's Next? 2023 Progress Report on the Global Action Plan for Healthy Lives and Well-being for All.* WHO. https://iris.who.int/bitstream/handle/10665/367422/9789240073371-eng.pdf?sequence=1

World Summit on Sustainable Development (2002)

Loïc Cobut

The World Summit on Sustainable Development (WSSD) was held in Johannesburg, South Africa, between 26 August and 4 September 2002. It took place ten years after the Earth Summit and aimed to reaffirm the will of states to commit to sustainable development (United Nations 2002). The decade preceding the WSSD was marked by particular attention to integrating development and environmental concerns, rather than addressing them separately (Morin et al. 2020). This has been concretized by the eight Millennium Development Goals (MDGs), adopted in 2000 at the United Nations General Assembly, which aimed to halve extreme poverty as well as to ensure environmental sustainability.

The main outcome from the WSSD is the promotion of public-private partnerships. These partnerships may be defined as 'institutionalized transboundary interactions between public and private actors, which aim at the provision of collective goods' (Schäferhoff et al. 2009, 455). In the United Nations system, these partnerships are referred to as Type II agreements to distinguish them from the politically negotiated agreements, regarded as the primary outcome of the summit (Hale and Mauzerall 2004). Type II agreements represent various activities such as advocacy, exchange of knowledge, research and development or the creation of markets.

On the one hand, these partnerships mark an evolution in global environmental governance as they embody a governance system where non-state actors create new types of collaboration in a system commonly seen as being under strict state control. On the other hand, it is notable that only a few of these partnerships concerned environmental protection, as most of them pertain to issues of social and economic development (Morin et al. 2020).

The outcome of the WSSD received some criticism. Critics questioned how public-private partnerships help reach the goal of sustainable development. Biermann et al. (2007) identified three governance deficits that had to be addressed at the time of the WSSD: participation, implementation and regulatory deficits. These partnerships were seen as a tool to enhance the participation of various actors, such as non-governmental organizations (NGOs), businesses and vulnerable groups, in implementing effective sustainable development policies. However, the two objectives, broad participation and effective policy implementation, did not evolve together as anticipated. Furthermore, the partnership system failed to address the regulatory gap, as it focused on voluntary collaborations that were not intended to close the participation or implementation gaps. These three objectives ultimately contradicted each other, resulting in governance deficits

(Biermann et al. 2007). A second criticism underlines that the promotion of public-private partnerships reflected the political strategy of the business sector to stabilize its hegemony and design a governance system inclusive of corporate interests (Schäferhoff et al. 2009). Another criticism of the WSSD outcomes points out that it failed to address the coloniality of sustainable development strategies as well as the associated development industry (Ndlovu-Gatsheni 2020; Brogna 2023).

In conclusion, the WSSD sought to combine development and environmental concerns through public-private partnerships. However, those partnerships failed to successfully combine those two subjects as much as they failed to increase participation, prevent corporate capture and address the coloniality of sustainable development strategies. Nevertheless, it is noteworthy that the WSSD contributed to broadening global sustainability governance by widening participation opportunities for ordinary people (Seyfang 2003), and such legacy was reflected in the negotiation process of the Sustainable Development Goals (SDGs) after a decade.

References

Biermann, F., Chan, M., Mert, A., and Pattberg, P. (2007). Multi-stakeholder Partnerships for Sustainable Development: Does the Promise Hold? In *Partnerships, Governance and Sustainable Development*. Edward Elgar Publishing. https://doi.org/10.4337/9781847208668.00023

Brogna, V. (2023). *From Sustainable Development to African Renaissance? Transnational Civil Society Organisations narrating development between Europe and Africa*. PhD dissertation, University of Louvain.

Hale, T. N., and Mauzerall, D. L. (2004). Thinking Globally and Acting Locally: Can the Johannesburg Partnerships Coordinate Action on Sustainable Development? *The Journal of Environment and Development*, 13(3), 220–239. https://doi.org/10.1177/1070496504268699

Morin, J.-F., Orsini, A., and Jinnah, S. (2020). *Global Environmental Politics*. Oxford University Press.

Ndlovu-Gatsheni, S. J. (2020). *Decolonization, Development and Knowledge in Africa*. Routledge. https://doi.org/10.4324/9781003030423

Schäferhoff, M., Campe, S., and Kaan, C. (2009). Transnational Public-Private Partnerships in International Relations: Making Sense of Concepts, Research Frameworks and Results. *International Studies Review*, 11(3), 451–474.

Seyfang, G. (2003). Environmental Mega-conferences—From Stockholm to Johannesburg and Beyond. *Global Environmental Change*, 13(3), 223–228. https://doi.org/10.1016/S0959-3780(03)00006-2

United Nations. (2002). *Report of the World Summit on Sustainable Development Johannesburg, South Africa, 26 August–4 September 2002*.

World Trade Organization (WTO)

Noémie Laurens

International trade has the ambiguous potential to foster and hamper the achievement of the Sustainable Development Goals (SDGs). On the one hand, it allows countries to access larger markets, thus boosting production and creating jobs. The resulting economic growth may fund infrastructure projects, enhance education and healthcare services and improve living standards. It may also stimulate innovation and the diffusion of

190 *Essential Concepts for Implementing the SDGs*

environmentally friendly technologies. On the other hand, trade may lead to negative outcomes, such as environmental degradation, increased pollution and lower employment in some sectors. Additionally, free trade can exacerbate inequalities within and between countries, as its benefits are not always evenly distributed.

The World Trade Organization (WTO), established in 1995, plays a central role in global trade, facilitating negotiations, settling disputes and overseeing the implementation of trade agreements among its member countries. With the advent of the SDGs in 2015, there has been an increasing emphasis on aligning global trade practices with social, economic and environmental objectives.

One prominent example of the WTO's contribution to the SDGs is its efforts to curb harmful subsidies. In 2015, the Nairobi Decision eliminated export subsidies in agriculture (SDG Target 2.b). This decision prevents advanced economies from artificially boosting their agricultural exports through subsidies, thereby levelling the playing field for farmers in poor countries. Moreover, after 20 years of discussions, WTO members adopted the landmark 2022 Agreement on Fisheries Subsidies (SDG Target 14.6). The latter prohibits certain subsidies that encourage unsustainable and illegal fishing practices. Another notable area where the WTO contributes to the achievement of SDGs is its various development-friendly policies. For instance, the Aid-for-Trade programme supports developing countries, particularly least-developed countries, in integrating into the global economy. Aid-for-Trade projects support all SDGs, with SDGs 9, 7 and 2 attracting the most disbursements (World Trade Organization and Organisation for Economic Cooperation and Development 2024, 104). In line with SDG Target 8.a, which calls donors to increase Aid for Trade, disbursements reached an all-time high of USD 51.1 billion in 2022.

Despite these laudable accomplishments, the WTO's implementation of the SDGs shows important shortcomings. First, the WTO's primary focus on free trade may overshadow sustainability objectives. For instance, WTO rules may discourage countries from implementing stringent social and environmental regulations to avoid potential trade disputes (Eckersley 2004). Some scholars even argue that encouraging economic growth is incompatible with environmental SDGs (Hickel 2019). Second, despite Aid-for-Trade and so-called special and differential treatment (SDG Target 10.a), there are still significant gaps in addressing the needs of the most vulnerable countries. Contrary to SDG 17, between 2015 and 2019, there was no change in the level of tariffs faced by least-developed countries' products in developed regions, and the share of duty-free least-developed countries' products decreased by 1.4% (WTO 2021). Third, the WTO's consensus-based decision-making often results in lengthy negotiations and delays in launching crucial reforms (Hoekman and Mavroidis 2021). This may lead to prioritizing the interests of the most powerful countries and impede the timely achievement of the SDGs, particularly those requiring immediate action, such as SDG 13 (climate action). This is most notable in the difficult talks around the Doha negotiations: the fossil fuel subsidy reform and the liberalization of environmental goods have been on the WTO's and its Trade and Environment Committee's agendas for years (Deere Birbeck 2019).

In summary, through its various initiatives and agreements, the WTO holds the potential to support multiple SDGs. However, the organization faces numerous challenges, including criticisms of prioritizing trade liberalization at the expense of sustainability, a cumbersome decision-making process, an overall lack of binding sustainability commitments and a significantly weakened dispute settlement mechanism. Addressing these issues is essential for the WTO to ensure that trade acts as a catalyst for achieving the SDGs.

References

Deere Birbeck, C. (2019). WTO reform: A forward-looking agenda on environmental sustainability. In T. Soobramanien, B. Vickers, and H. Enos-Edu (Eds.), *WTO Reform: Reshaping Global Trade Governance for 21st Century Challenges* (pp. 33–59). Commonwealth Secretariat. https://doi.org/10.14217/544517c5-en

Eckersley, R. (2004). The big chill: The WTO and multilateral environmental agreements. *Global Environmental Politics*, 4(2), 24–50. https://doi.org/10.1162/152638004323074183

Hickel, J. (2019). The contradiction of the sustainable development goals: growth versus ecology on a finite planet. *Sustainable Development*, 27(5), 873–884. https://doi.org/10.1002/sd.1947

Hoekman, B., and Mavroidis, P. C. (2021). WTO reform: Back to the past to build for the future. *Global Policy*, 12, 5–12. https://doi.org/10.1111/1758-5899.12924

World Trade Organization and Organisation for Economic Co-operation and Development. (2024). Aid for trade at a glance. https://www.oecd.org/en/publications/aid-for-trade-at-a-glance-2024_7a4e356a-en.html

WTO. (2021). WTO contribution to the 2021 High-Level Political Forum. https://sustainabledevelopment.un.org/content/documents/27479WTO_2021_HLPF_Input.pdf

Y

Youth

Yi hyun Kang

Youth is a flexible term with varying definitions by country and organization. The United Nations (UN) defines youth as persons between 15 and 24, but many global youth platforms have different membership criteria, up to 30 or 35 years of age.

Youth have been considered vital actors for sustainable development since the United Nations Conference on the Human Environment in 1972. More formal recognition of the importance of youth was realized at the 1992 Earth Summit when Agenda 21 listed children and youth as one of the nine major groups, acknowledging the need to mobilize the creativity, ideals and courage of youth for sustainable development (United Nations 1992). Subsequently, the Major Group of Children and Youth was established as an independent mechanism for youth participation in sustainable development. With more than 8,000 members worldwide that consist of youth-focused organizations and individuals under 30, the Major Group of Children and Youth seeks to foster participation in the United Nations processes beyond sustainable development.

As the world faces climate change, biodiversity loss and pollution, young people are becoming more vocal, urging everybody to act for environmental protection. While youth-led climate movements have received heightened attention since the late 2010s, youth have already been active in international environmental negotiations, and the number of youth participants has steadily increased over the last three decades since the Earth Summit (Orsini and Kang 2023). The forms of youth participation in international negotiations vary. While most youth attend as non-governmental observers, more and more countries send national youth delegates. Additionally, the United Nations General Assembly agreed to establish the United Nations Youth Office in 2022, aiming to facilitate the integration of youth voices in the United Nations system.

The growing number of youth participants in global sustainability politics and the institutionalization of their engagement by states and UN agencies are widely seen as a positive experience of participatory governance. However, whether such phenomena are leading to meaningful youth participation remains questionable. For example, although youth representatives were active during the negotiations on the 2030 Agenda for Sustainable Development, the final text hardly incorporated youth claims (Orsini 2022). Youth participants in climate and biodiversity negotiations also point out that they are

DOI: 10.4324/9781003519560-24

This chapter has been made available under a CC-BY-NC-ND license.

increasingly invited to participate on many occasions, but they doubt that their voices are reflected in the outcomes of decision-making processes. Such behaviour of non-youth actors has been criticized as 'youth-washing' or tokenism (Sloan Morgan et al. 2023).

Financial constraints are another critical factor that challenges the more meaningful participation of young people in sustainable development governance. Global youth platforms such as the Major Group of Children and Youth are run by volunteers who do not receive remuneration (Marquardt et al. 2023). Most UN youth delegate programmes continuously experience budgetary limitations (Future Agents NOW 2023). The lack of resources can make youth participation dependent on a few resourceful individuals, undermine the legitimacy of youth participation or even make youth vulnerable to co-optation. Furthermore, it causes high turnover and fatigue among active members of youth platforms.

Although many conditions are unfavourable, youth have made efforts to engage in and contribute to sustainable development. Youth representatives actively form alliances with other actors, such as women and indigenous groups. All global youth platforms have promoted capacity-building by organizing their own events and facilitating youth-led action at multiple governance levels. Such efforts have strengthened the effectiveness of youth participation in global sustainability governance over time.

In addition, youth can help accelerate the implementation of the Sustainable Development Goals. For example, youth-led environmental movements have changed the political landscape, as we saw in the results of the 2019 European elections held after the Fridays for Future movement emerged. Also, youth-led initiatives at national and subnational levels have contributed to implementing the SDGs such as gender equality (for example, Choonara et al. 2018). To maximize the potential of youth's contribution, it would be necessary to recognize youth as agents of change and promote their meaningful participation at all levels of sustainable development governance.

References

Choonara, S., Banda, R., Chitimira, R., Ditsele, G., Hwengwere, M., Magwenzi, T., ... Masikati, I. (2018). Sustainable Development Girls: Mapping Youth Advocacy and Action to Achieve Sexual and Reproductive Health Rights in Africa. *Agenda*, 32(1), 97–106. https://doi.org/10.1080/10130950.2018.1427812

Future Agents NOW. (2023). *Global Youth Voices: A Mapping Report of Youth Delegate Programmes to the UN*. Future Agents NOW.

Marquardt, J., Lövbrand, E., and Buhre, F. (2023). The Politics of Youth Representation at Climate Change Conferences: Who Speaks, Who Is Spoken of and Who Listens? *Global Environmental Politics*, 24 (2), 19–45. https://doi.org/10.1162/glep_a_00736

Orsini, A. (2022). Youth Goals? Youth Agency and the Sustainable Development Goals. *Youth and Globalization*, 4(1), 108–139. https://doi.org/10.1163/25895745-04010001

Orsini, A. J., and Kang, Y. H. (2023). European Leadership and European Youth in the Climate Change Regime Complex. *Politics and Governance*, 11(2), 84–96. https://doi.org/10.17645/pag.v11i2.6500

Sloan Morgan, O., Melchior, F., Thomas, K., and McNab-Coombs, L. (2023). Youth and Climate Justice: Representations of Young People in Action for Sustainable Futures. *The Geographical Journal*, 12547. https://doi.org/10.1111/geoj.12547

United Nations. (1992). 'Report of the United Nations Conference on Environment and Development'. A/CONF.151/26 (Vol. I).

Annex

The 17 Sustainable Development Goals

Goal 1. End poverty in all its forms everywhere

1.1   By 2030, eradicate extreme poverty for all people everywhere, currently measured as people living on less than $1.25 a day.

1.2   By 2030, reduce at least by half the proportion of men, women and children of all ages living in poverty in all its dimensions according to national definitions.

1.3   Implement nationally appropriate social protection systems and measures for all, including floors, and by 2030 achieve substantial coverage of the poor and the vulnerable.

1.4   By 2030, ensure that all men and women, in particular the poor and the vulnerable, have equal rights to economic resources, as well as access to basic services, ownership and control over land and other forms of property, inheritance, natural resources, appropriate new technology and financial services, including microfinance.

1.5   By 2030, build the resilience of the poor and those in vulnerable situations and reduce their exposure and vulnerability to climate-related extreme events and other economic, social and environmental shocks and disasters.

1.a   Ensure significant mobilization of resources from a variety of sources, including through enhanced development cooperation, in order to provide adequate and predictable means for developing countries, in particular least developed countries, to implement programmes and policies to end poverty in all its dimensions.

1.b   Create sound policy frameworks at the national, regional and international levels, based on pro-poor and gender-sensitive development strategies, to support accelerated investment in poverty eradication actions.

Goal 2. End hunger, achieve food security and improved nutrition and promote sustainable agriculture

2.1   By 2030, end hunger and ensure access by all people, in particular the poor and people in vulnerable situations, including infants, to safe, nutritious and sufficient food all year round.

2.2   By 2030, end all forms of malnutrition, including achieving, by 2025, the internationally agreed targets on stunting and wasting in children under five years of age and address the nutritional needs of adolescent girls, pregnant and lactating women and older persons.

2.3	By 2030, double the agricultural productivity and incomes of small-scale food producers, in particular women, indigenous peoples, family farmers, pastoralists and fishers, including through secure and equal access to land, other productive resources and inputs, knowledge, financial services, markets and opportunities for value addition and non-farm employment.
2.4	By 2030, ensure sustainable food production systems and implement resilient agricultural practices that increase productivity and production, that help maintain ecosystems, that strengthen capacity for adaptation to climate change, extreme weather, drought, flooding and other disasters and that progressively improve land and soil quality.
2.5	By 2020, maintain the genetic diversity of seeds, cultivated plants and farmed and domesticated animals and their related wild species, including through soundly managed and diversified seed and plant banks at the national, regional and international levels and promote access to and fair and equitable sharing of benefits arising from the utilization of genetic resources and associated traditional knowledge, as internationally agreed.
2.a	Increase investment, including through enhanced international cooperation, in rural infrastructure, agricultural research and extension services, technology development and plant and livestock gene banks in order to enhance agricultural productive capacity in developing countries, in particular least developed countries.
2.b	Correct and prevent trade restrictions and distortions in world agricultural markets, including through the parallel elimination of all forms of agricultural export subsidies and all export measures with equivalent effect, in accordance with the mandate of the Doha Development Round.
2.c	Adopt measures to ensure the proper functioning of food commodity markets and their derivatives and facilitate timely access to market information, including on food reserves, in order to help limit extreme food price volatility.

Goal 3. Ensure healthy lives and promote well-being for all at all ages

3.1	By 2030, reduce the global maternal mortality ratio to less than 70 per 100,000 live births.
3.2	By 2030, end preventable deaths of newborns and children under 5 years of age, with all countries aiming to reduce neonatal mortality to at least as low as 12 per 1,000 live births and under-5 mortality to at least as low as 25 per 1,000 live births.
3.3	By 2030, end the epidemics of AIDS, tuberculosis, malaria and neglected tropical diseases and combat hepatitis, water-borne diseases and other communicable diseases.
3.4	By 2030, reduce by one-third premature mortality from non-communicable diseases through prevention and treatment and promote mental health and well-being.
3.5	Strengthen the prevention and treatment of substance abuse, including narcotic drug abuse and harmful use of alcohol.
3.6	By 2020, halve the number of global deaths and injuries from road traffic accidents.

196 *Annex*

3.7 By 2030, ensure universal access to sexual and reproductive healthcare services, including for family planning, information and education and the integration of reproductive health into national strategies and programmes.

3.8 Achieve universal health coverage, including financial risk protection, access to quality essential healthcare services and access to safe, effective, quality and affordable essential medicines and vaccines for all.

3.9 By 2030, substantially reduce the number of deaths and illnesses from hazardous chemicals and air, water and soil pollution and contamination.

3.a Strengthen the implementation of the World Health Organization Framework Convention on Tobacco Control in all countries, as appropriate.

3.b Support the research and development of vaccines and medicines for the communicable and non-communicable diseases that primarily affect developing countries, provide access to affordable essential medicines and vaccines, in accordance with the Doha Declaration on the TRIPS Agreement and Public Health, which affirms the right of developing countries to use to the full the provisions in the Agreement on Trade-Related Aspects of Intellectual Property Rights regarding flexibilities to protect public health and, in particular, provide access to medicines for all.

3.c Substantially increase health financing and the recruitment, development, training and retention of the health workforce in developing countries, especially in least developed countries and small island developing States.

3.d Strengthen the capacity of all countries, in particular developing countries, for early warning, risk reduction and management of national and global health risks.

Goal 4. Ensure inclusive and equitable quality education and promote lifelong learning opportunities for all

4.1 By 2030, ensure that all girls and boys complete free, equitable and quality primary and secondary education leading to relevant and effective learning outcomes.

4.2 By 2030, ensure that all girls and boys have access to quality early childhood development, care and pre-primary education so that they are ready for primary education.

4.3 By 2030, ensure equal access for all women and men to affordable and quality technical, vocational and tertiary education, including university.

4.4 By 2030, substantially increase the number of youth and adults who have relevant skills, including technical and vocational skills, for employment, decent jobs and entrepreneurship.

4.5 By 2030, eliminate gender disparities in education and ensure equal access to all levels of education and vocational training for the vulnerable, including persons with disabilities, indigenous peoples and children in vulnerable situations.

4.6 By 2030, ensure that all youth and a substantial proportion of adults, both men and women, achieve literacy and numeracy.

4.7 By 2030, ensure that all learners acquire the knowledge and skills needed to promote sustainable development, including, among others, through education for sustainable development and sustainable lifestyles, human rights, gender equality, promotion of a culture of peace and non-violence, global citizenship and appreciation of cultural diversity and of culture's contribution to sustainable development.

Annex 197

4.a   Build and upgrade education facilities that are child, disability and gender sensitive and provide safe, non-violent, inclusive and effective learning environments for all.

4.b   By 2020, substantially expand globally the number of scholarships available to developing countries, in particular least developed countries, small island developing States and African countries, for enrolment in higher education, including vocational training and information and communications technology, technical, engineering and scientific programmes, in developed countries and other developing countries.

4.c   By 2030, substantially increase the supply of qualified teachers, including through international cooperation for teacher training in developing countries, especially least developed countries and small island developing States.

Goal 5.   Achieve gender equality and empower all women and girls

5.1   End all forms of discrimination against all women and girls everywhere.

5.2   Eliminate all forms of violence against all women and girls in the public and private spheres, including trafficking and sexual and other types of exploitation.

5.3   Eliminate all harmful practices, such as child, early and forced marriage and female genital mutilation.

5.4   Recognize and value unpaid care and domestic work through the provision of public services, infrastructure and social protection policies and the promotion of shared responsibility within the household and the family as nationally appropriate.

5.5   Ensure women's full and effective participation and equal opportunities for leadership at all levels of decision-making in political, economic and public life.

5.6   Ensure universal access to sexual and reproductive health and reproductive rights as agreed in accordance with the Programme of Action of the International Conference on Population and Development and the Beijing Platform for Action and the outcome documents of their review conferences.

5.a   Undertake reforms to give women equal rights to economic resources, as well as access to ownership and control over land and other forms of property, financial services, inheritance and natural resources, in accordance with national laws.

5.b   Enhance the use of enabling technology, in particular information and communications technology, to promote the empowerment of women.

5.c   Adopt and strengthen sound policies and enforceable legislation for the promotion of gender equality and the empowerment of all women and girls at all levels.

Goal 6.   Ensure availability and sustainable management of water and sanitation for all

6.1   By 2030, achieve universal and equitable access to safe and affordable drinking water for all.

6.2   By 2030, achieve access to adequate and equitable sanitation and hygiene for all and end open defecation, paying special attention to the needs of women and girls and those in vulnerable situations.

6.3   By 2030, improve water quality by reducing pollution, eliminating dumping and minimizing release of hazardous chemicals and materials, halving the proportion of untreated wastewater and substantially increasing recycling and safe reuse globally.

198　*Annex*

6.4　By 2030, substantially increase water-use efficiency across all sectors and ensure sustainable withdrawals and supply of freshwater to address water scarcity and substantially reduce the number of people suffering from water scarcity.

6.5　By 2030, implement integrated water resources management at all levels, including through transboundary cooperation as appropriate.

6.6　By 2020, protect and restore water-related ecosystems, including mountains, forests, wetlands, rivers, aquifers and lakes.

6.a　By 2030, expand international cooperation and capacity-building support to developing countries in water- and sanitation-related activities and programmes, including water harvesting, desalination, water efficiency, wastewater treatment, recycling and reuse technologies.

6.b　Support and strengthen the participation of local communities in improving water and sanitation management.

Goal 7.　Ensure access to affordable, reliable, sustainable and modern energy for all

7.1　By 2030, ensure universal access to affordable, reliable and modern energy services.

7.2　By 2030, increase substantially the share of renewable energy in the global energy mix.

7.3　By 2030, double the global rate of improvement in energy efficiency.

7.a　By 2030, enhance international cooperation to facilitate access to clean energy research and technology, including renewable energy, energy efficiency and advanced and cleaner fossil fuel technology and promote investment in energy infrastructure and clean energy technology.

7.b　By 2030, expand infrastructure and upgrade technology for supplying modern and sustainable energy services for all in developing countries, in particular least developed countries, small island developing States and landlocked developing countries, in accordance with their respective programmes of support.

Goal 8.　Promote sustained, inclusive and sustainable economic growth, full and productive employment and decent work for all

8.1　Sustain per capita economic growth in accordance with national circumstances and, in particular, at least 7% gross domestic product growth per annum in the least developed countries.

8.2　Achieve higher levels of economic productivity through diversification, technological upgrading and innovation, including through a focus on high-value-added and labour-intensive sectors.

8.3　Promote development-oriented policies that support productive activities, decent job creation, entrepreneurship, creativity and innovation and encourage the formalization and growth of micro-, small- and medium-sized enterprises, including through access to financial services.

8.4　Improve progressively, through 2030, global resource efficiency in consumption and production and endeavour to decouple economic growth from environmental degradation, in accordance with the ten-year framework of programmes on sustainable consumption and production, with developed countries taking the lead.

| 8.5 | By 2030, achieve full and productive employment and decent work for all women and men, including for young people and persons with disabilities and equal pay for work of equal value. |

8.5 By 2030, achieve full and productive employment and decent work for all women and men, including for young people and persons with disabilities and equal pay for work of equal value.

8.6 By 2020, substantially reduce the proportion of youth not in employment, education or training.

8.7 Take immediate and effective measures to eradicate forced labour, end modern slavery and human trafficking and secure the prohibition and elimination of the worst forms of child labour, including recruitment and use of child soldiers, and by 2025 end child labour in all its forms.

8.8 Protect labour rights and promote safe and secure working environments for all workers, including migrant workers, in particular women migrants and those in precarious employment.

8.9 By 2030, devise and implement policies to promote sustainable tourism that creates jobs and promotes local culture and products.

8.10 Strengthen the capacity of domestic financial institutions to encourage and expand access to banking, insurance and financial services for all.

8.a Increase Aid-for-Trade support for developing countries, in particular least developed countries, including through the Enhanced Integrated Framework for Trade-Related Technical Assistance to Least Developed Countries.

8.b By 2020, develop and operationalize a global strategy for youth employment and implement the Global Jobs Pact of the International Labour Organization.

Goal 9. Build resilient infrastructure, promote inclusive and sustainable industrialization and foster innovation

9.1 Develop quality, reliable, sustainable and resilient infrastructure, including regional and transborder infrastructure, to support economic development and human well-being, with a focus on affordable and equitable access for all.

9.2 Promote inclusive and sustainable industrialization, and by 2030, significantly raise industry's share of employment and gross domestic product, in line with national circumstances and double its share in least developed countries.

9.3 Increase the access of small-scale industrial and other enterprises, in particular in developing countries, to financial services, including affordable credit and their integration into value chains and markets.

9.4 By 2030, upgrade infrastructure and retrofit industries to make them sustainable, with increased resource-use efficiency and greater adoption of clean and environmentally sound technologies and industrial processes, with all countries taking action in accordance with their respective capabilities.

9.5 Enhance scientific research, upgrade the technological capabilities of industrial sectors in all countries, in particular developing countries, including, by 2030, encouraging innovation and substantially increasing the number of research and development workers per 1 million people and public and private research and development spending.

9.a Facilitate sustainable and resilient infrastructure development in developing countries through enhanced financial, technological and technical support to African countries, least developed countries, landlocked developing countries and small island developing States.

200   *Annex*

9.b   Support domestic technology development, research and innovation in developing countries, including by ensuring a conducive policy environment for, inter alia, industrial diversification and value addition to commodities.

9.c   Significantly increase access to information and communications technology and strive to provide universal and affordable access to the Internet in least developed countries by 2020.

Goal 10.   Reduce inequality within and among countries

10.1   By 2030, progressively achieve and sustain income growth of the bottom 40% of the population at a rate higher than the national average.

10.2   By 2030, empower and promote the social, economic and political inclusion of all, irrespective of age, sex, disability, race, ethnicity, origin, religion or economic or other status.

10.3   Ensure equal opportunity and reduce inequalities of outcome, including by eliminating discriminatory laws, policies and practices and promoting appropriate legislation, policies and action in this regard.

10.4   Adopt policies, especially fiscal, wage and social protection policies and progressively achieve greater equality.

10.5   Improve the regulation and monitoring of global financial markets and institutions and strengthen the implementation of such regulations.

10.6   Ensure enhanced representation and voice for developing countries in decision-making in global international economic and financial institutions in order to deliver more effective, credible, accountable and legitimate institutions.

10.7   Facilitate orderly, safe, regular and responsible migration and mobility of people, including through the implementation of planned and well-managed migration policies.

10.a   Implement the principle of special and differential treatment for developing countries, in particular least developed countries, in accordance with World Trade Organization agreements.

10.b   Encourage official development assistance and financial flows, including foreign direct investment, to States where the need is greatest, in particular least developed countries, African countries, small island developing States and landlocked developing countries, in accordance with their national plans and programmes.

10.c   By 2030, reduce to less than 3% the transaction costs of migrant remittances and eliminate remittance corridors with costs higher than 5%.

Goal 11.   Make cities and human settlements inclusive, safe, resilient and sustainable

11.1   By 2030, ensure access for all to adequate, safe and affordable housing and basic services and upgrade slums.

11.2   By 2030, provide access to safe, affordable, accessible and sustainable transport systems for all, improving road safety, notably by expanding public transport, with special attention to the needs of those in vulnerable situations, women, children, persons with disabilities and older persons.

11.3   By 2030, enhance inclusive and sustainable urbanization and capacity for participatory, integrated and sustainable human settlement planning and management in all countries.

Annex 201

11.4 Strengthen efforts to protect and safeguard the world's cultural and natural heritage.

11.5 By 2030, significantly reduce the number of deaths and the number of people affected and substantially decrease the direct economic losses relative to global gross domestic product caused by disasters, including water-related disasters, with a focus on protecting the poor and people in vulnerable situations.

11.6 By 2030, reduce the adverse per capita environmental impact of cities, including by paying special attention to air quality and municipal and other waste management.

11.7 By 2030, provide universal access to safe, inclusive and accessible, green and public spaces, in particular for women and children, older persons and persons with disabilities.

11.a Support positive economic, social and environmental links between urban, peri-urban and rural areas by strengthening national and regional development planning.

11.b By 2020, substantially increase the number of cities and human settlements adopting and implementing integrated policies and plans towards inclusion, resource efficiency, mitigation and adaptation to climate change, resilience to disasters and develop and implement, in line with the Sendai Framework for Disaster Risk Reduction 2015–2030, holistic disaster risk management at all levels.

11.c Support least developed countries, including through financial and technical assistance, in building sustainable and resilient buildings utilizing local materials.

Goal 12. Ensure sustainable consumption and production patterns

12.1 Implement the ten-year framework of programmes on sustainable consumption and production, all countries taking action, with developed countries taking the lead, taking into account the development and capabilities of developing countries.

12.2 By 2030, achieve the sustainable management and efficient use of natural resources.

12.3 By 2030, halve per capita global food waste at the retail and consumer levels and reduce food losses along production and supply chains, including post-harvest losses.

12.4 By 2020, achieve the environmentally sound management of chemicals and all wastes throughout their life cycle, in accordance with agreed international frameworks and significantly reduce their release to air, water and soil in order to minimize their adverse impacts on human health and the environment.

12.5 By 2030, substantially reduce waste generation through prevention, reduction, recycling and reuse.

12.6 Encourage companies, especially large and transnational companies, to adopt sustainable practices and to integrate sustainability information into their reporting cycle.

12.7 Promote public procurement practices that are sustainable, in accordance with national policies and priorities.

12.8 By 2030, ensure that people everywhere have the relevant information and awareness for sustainable development and lifestyles in harmony with nature.

12.a Support developing countries to strengthen their scientific and technological capacity to move towards more sustainable patterns of consumption and production.

202 *Annex*

12.b Develop and implement tools to monitor sustainable development impacts for sustainable tourism that creates jobs and promotes local culture and products.

12.c Rationalize inefficient fossil fuel subsidies that encourage wasteful consumption by removing market distortions, in accordance with national circumstances, including by restructuring taxation and phasing out those harmful subsidies, where they exist, to reflect their environmental impacts, taking fully into account the specific needs and conditions of developing countries and minimizing the possible adverse impacts on their development in a manner that protects the poor and the affected communities.

Goal 13. Take urgent action to combat climate change and its impacts*

13.1 Strengthen resilience and adaptive capacity to climate-related hazards and natural disasters in all countries.

13.2 Integrate climate change measures into national policies, strategies and planning.

13.3 Improve education, awareness-raising and human and institutional capacity on climate change mitigation, adaptation, impact reduction and early warning.

13.a Implement the commitment undertaken by developed-country parties to the United Nations Framework Convention on Climate Change to a goal of mobilizing jointly $100 billion annually by 2020 from all sources to address the needs of developing countries in the context of meaningful mitigation actions and transparency on implementation and fully operationalize the Green Climate Fund through its capitalization as soon as possible.

13.b Promote mechanisms for raising capacity for effective climate change-related planning and management in least developed countries and small island developing States, including focusing on women, youth and local and marginalized communities.

Goal 14. Conserve and sustainably use the oceans, seas and marine resources for sustainable development

14.1 By 2025, prevent and significantly reduce marine pollution of all kinds, in particular from land-based activities, including marine debris and nutrient pollution.

14.2 By 2020, sustainably manage and protect marine and coastal ecosystems to avoid significant adverse impacts, including by strengthening their resilience and taking action for their restoration in order to achieve healthy and productive oceans.

14.3 Minimize and address the impacts of ocean acidification, including through enhanced scientific cooperation at all levels.

14.4 By 2020, effectively regulate harvesting and end overfishing, illegal, unreported and unregulated fishing and destructive fishing practices and implement science-based management plans, in order to restore fish stocks in the shortest time feasible, at least to levels that can produce maximum sustainable yield as determined by their biological characteristics.

---

* Acknowledging that the United Nations Framework Convention on Climate Change is the primary international, intergovernmental forum for negotiating the global response to climate change.

Annex 203

14.5 By 2020, conserve at least 10% of coastal and marine areas, consistent with national and international law and based on the best available scientific information.

14.6 By 2020, prohibit certain forms of fisheries subsidies that contribute to overcapacity and overfishing, eliminate subsidies that contribute to illegal, unreported and unregulated fishing and refrain from introducing new such subsidies, recognizing that appropriate and effective special and differential treatment for developing and least developed countries should be an integral part of the World Trade Organization fisheries subsidies negotiation.

14.7 By 2030, increase the economic benefits to Small Island developing States and least developed countries from the sustainable use of marine resources, including through sustainable management of fisheries, aquaculture and tourism.

14.a Increase scientific knowledge, develop research capacity and transfer marine technology, taking into account the Intergovernmental Oceanographic Commission Criteria and Guidelines on the Transfer of Marine Technology, in order to improve ocean health and to enhance the contribution of marine biodiversity to the development of developing countries, in particular small island developing States and least developed countries.

14.b Provide access for small-scale artisanal fishers to marine resources and markets.

14.c Enhance the conservation and sustainable use of oceans and their resources by implementing international law as reflected in UNCLOS, which provides the legal framework for the conservation and sustainable use of oceans and their resources, as recalled in paragraph 158 of The Future We Want.

Goal 15. Protect, restore and promote sustainable use of terrestrial ecosystems, sustainably manage forests, combat desertification and halt and reverse land degradation and halt biodiversity loss

15.1 By 2020, ensure the conservation, restoration and sustainable use of terrestrial and inland freshwater ecosystems and their services, in particular forests, wetlands, mountains and drylands, in line with obligations under international agreements.

15.2 By 2020, promote the implementation of sustainable management of all types of forests, halt deforestation, restore degraded forests and substantially increase afforestation and reforestation globally.

15.3 By 2030, combat desertification, restore degraded land and soil, including land affected by desertification, drought and floods and strive to achieve a land degradation-neutral world.

15.4 By 2030, ensure the conservation of mountain ecosystems, including their biodiversity, in order to enhance their capacity to provide benefits that are essential for sustainable development.

15.5 Take urgent and significant action to reduce the degradation of natural habitats, halt the loss of biodiversity and, by 2020, protect and prevent the extinction of threatened species.

15.6 Promote fair and equitable sharing of the benefits arising from the utilization of genetic resources and promote appropriate access to such resources, as internationally agreed.

15.7 Take urgent action to end poaching and trafficking of protected species of flora and fauna and address both demand and supply of illegal wildlife products.

204 *Annex*

15.8   By 2020, introduce measures to prevent the introduction and significantly reduce the impact of invasive alien species on land and water ecosystems and control or eradicate the priority species.

15.9   By 2020, integrate ecosystem and biodiversity values into national and local planning, development processes, poverty reduction strategies and accounts.

15.a   Mobilize and significantly increase financial resources from all sources to conserve and sustainably use biodiversity and ecosystems.

15.b   Mobilize significant resources from all sources and at all levels to finance sustainable forest management and provide adequate incentives to developing countries to advance such management, including for conservation and reforestation.

15.c   Enhance global support for efforts to combat poaching and trafficking of protected species, including by increasing the capacity of local communities to pursue sustainable livelihood opportunities.

Goal 16.   Promote peaceful and inclusive societies for sustainable development, provide access to justice for all and build effective, accountable and inclusive institutions at all levels

16.1   Significantly reduce all forms of violence and related death rates everywhere.

16.2   End abuse, exploitation, trafficking and all forms of violence against and torture of children.

16.3   Promote the rule of law at the national and international levels and ensure equal access to justice for all.

16.4   By 2030, significantly reduce illicit financial and arms flows, strengthen the recovery and return of stolen assets and combat all forms of organized crime.

16.5   Substantially reduce corruption and bribery in all their forms.

16.6   Develop effective, accountable and transparent institutions at all levels.

16.7   Ensure responsive, inclusive, participatory and representative decision-making at all levels.

16.8   Broaden and strengthen the participation of developing countries in the institutions of global governance.

16.9   By 2030, provide legal identity for all, including birth registration.

16.10   Ensure public access to information and protect fundamental freedoms, in accordance with national legislation and international agreements.

16.a   Strengthen relevant national institutions, including through international cooperation, for building capacity at all levels, in particular in developing countries, to prevent violence and combat terrorism and crime.

16.b   Promote and enforce non-discriminatory laws and policies for sustainable development.

Goal 17.   Strengthen the means of implementation and revitalize the global partnership for sustainable development

Finance

17.1   Strengthen domestic resource mobilization, including through international support to developing countries, to improve domestic capacity for tax and other revenue collection.

Annex   205

17.2   Developed countries to implement fully their official development assistance commitments, including the commitment by many developed countries to achieve the target of 0.7% of ODA/GNI to developing countries and 0.15 to 0.20% of ODA/GNI to least developed countries; ODA providers are encouraged to consider setting a target to provide at least 0.20% of ODA/GNI to least developed countries.

17.3   Mobilize additional financial resources for developing countries from multiple sources.

17.4   Assist developing countries in attaining long-term debt sustainability through coordinated policies aimed at fostering debt financing, debt relief and debt restructuring, as appropriate and address the external debt of highly indebted poor countries to reduce debt distress.

17.5   Adopt and implement investment promotion regimes for least developed countries

Technology

17.6   Enhance North-South, South-South and triangular regional and international cooperation on and access to science, technology and innovation and enhance knowledge sharing on mutually agreed terms, including through improved coordination among existing mechanisms, in particular at the United Nations level and through a global technology facilitation mechanism.

17.7   Promote the development, transfer, dissemination and diffusion of environmentally sound technologies to developing countries on favourable terms, including on concessional and preferential terms, as mutually agreed.

17.8   Fully operationalize the technology bank and science, technology and innovation capacity-building mechanism for least developed countries by 2017 and enhance the use of enabling technology, in particular information and communications technology.

Capacity-building

17.9   Enhance international support for implementing effective and targeted capacity-building in developing countries to support national plans to implement all the sustainable development goals, including through North-South, South-South and triangular cooperation.

Trade

17.10   Promote a universal, rules-based, open, non-discriminatory and equitable multilateral trading system under the World Trade Organization, including through the conclusion of negotiations under its Doha Development Agenda.

17.11   Significantly increase the exports of developing countries, in particular with a view to doubling the least developed countries' share of global exports by 2020.

17.12   Realize timely implementation of duty-free and quota-free market access on a lasting basis for all least developed countries, consistent with World Trade Organization decisions, including by ensuring that preferential rules of origin applicable to imports from least developed countries are transparent and simple and contribute to facilitating market access.

206   Annex

Systemic issues

Policy and institutional coherence

17.13   Enhance global macroeconomic stability, including through policy coordination and policy coherence.

17.14   Enhance policy coherence for sustainable development.

17.15   Respect each country's policy space and leadership to establish and implement policies for poverty eradication and sustainable development.

Multi-stakeholder partnerships

17.16   Enhance the global partnership for sustainable development, complemented by multi-stakeholder partnerships that mobilize and share knowledge, expertise, technology and financial resources, to support the achievement of the sustainable development goals in all countries, in particular developing countries.

17.17   Encourage and promote effective public, public-private and civil society partnerships, building on the experience and resourcing strategies of partnerships.

Data, monitoring and accountability

17.18   By 2020, enhance capacity-building support to developing countries, including for least developed countries and small island developing States, to increase significantly the availability of high-quality, timely and reliable data disaggregated by income, gender, age, race, ethnicity, migratory status, disability, geographic location and other characteristics relevant in national contexts.

17.19   By 2030, build on existing initiatives to develop measurements of progress on sustainable development that complement gross domestic product and support statistical capacity-building in developing countries.

Printed in the United States
by Baker & Taylor Publisher Services